The Shaping of
MODERN FRANCE

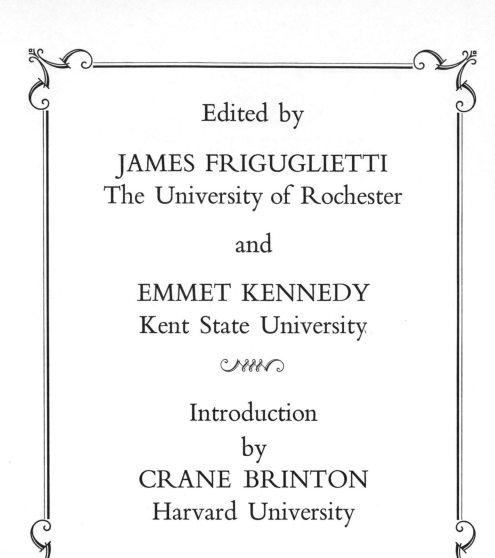

Edited by

JAMES FRIGUGLIETTI
The University of Rochester

and

EMMET KENNEDY
Kent State University

Introduction
by
CRANE BRINTON
Harvard University

The Macmillan Company

THE
SHAPING
OF
MODERN
FRANCE

WRITINGS
ON FRENCH HISTORY
SINCE
1715

Collier-Macmillan Limited, London

Library of Congress catalog card number: 69-10541

THE MACMILLAN COMPANY
COLLIER-MACMILLAN CANADA, LTD., TORONTO, ONTARIO

Printed in the United States of America

Preface

ᐊᕼᕼᕼᐅ

Numerous texts have been written to explain French history to Americans, but anyone who has studied or taught the subject at the college level realizes that the standard textbook approach is far from satisfactory. No single book can treat all aspects of modern French history in depth; no one author can be master of the many complex problems of interpretation involved.

The Shaping of Modern France is designed to remedy this shortcoming by offering the student a large collection of narrative and interpretive writings by specialists in their fields and taken from a variety of sources, many of which were previously unavailable to the general reader. Almost half of the material was edited from scholarly journals, and more than a third of the selections were translated from the French originals. Arranged chronologically and topically, the chapters may thus be used to supplement any text or even be read independently. The introduction to each chapter ties the selections together, interprets the character of the given period or movement, and indicates problems of interpretation. The "Suggestions for Further Reading" at the end of each chapter offers a guide to wider study. An index is included to facilitate reference.

For reasons of space, the editors have had to eliminate most of the original footnotes, but they have added explanatory notes when necessary and have translated all passages in French. All deletions in the text are indicated by ellipses. James Friguglietti is responsible for Chapters Four, Six, Eight, Nine, Ten, Fourteen, Fifteen, Sixteen, Seventeen, and Eighteen; Emmet Kennedy is responsible for Chapters One, Two, Three, Five, Seven, Eleven, Twelve, Thirteen, and Nineteen.

In preparing this volume, the editors have had the assistance of many individuals. They are especially grateful to Miss Louise Apfelbaum, Hans D. Kellner, Miss Nancy Marcolla, Miss Ann New, Charles L. Noyes, Robert Pawlowski, and John S. Whitehead for the translations which appear with their names in the footnote acknowledgments; to Mrs. Jane M. Kennedy and Hans D. Kellner for helping to prepare the manuscript; to James McMahon, Joseph Werne, and Claudia Schulte for their valuable proof-reading assistance; to M. Gérard Regnier of the Louvre Museum for suggestions incorporated into the introductions to Chapters Twelve and

Nineteen; to Mr. and Mrs. Robert E. Kennedy for their helpful editorial suggestions and proofreading; to Professor Norman F. Cantor, whose book *The English Tradition* supplied a model for this work; and to the late Professor Crane Brinton for his interest and encouragement in this project from the time of its inception.

J. F.
E. K.

Contents

❧

1   INTRODUCTION BY CRANE BRINTON

CHAPTER ONE: SOCIAL CLASSES UNDER THE OLD REGIME

6   *Introduction*

8   FRANKLIN L. FORD
Robe and Sword, the Regrouping of the French Aristocracy After Louis XIV

12   ALBERT GOODWIN
A Re-evaluation of the "Aristocratic Revolt"

18   GEORGE V. TAYLOR
Capitalist and Proprietary Wealth and the Definition of the Bourgeoisie

25   GEORGES LEFEBVRE
The Peasantry on the Eve of the French Revolution

30   MAURICE G. HUTT
Ideas of Reform Among the French Lower Clergy, 1787–1789

33   Suggestions for Further Reading

CHAPTER TWO: THE ENLIGHTENMENT

36   *Introduction*

38   CRANE BRINTON
Desertion of Intellectuals and Nobles as a Pre-Revolutionary Phenomenon

42   PETER GAY
The Philosophes and Their Environment

47   R. R. PALMER
The French Jesuits in the Age of Enlightenment

53   EVERETT C. LADD, JR.
The Political Philosophy of Helvétius and d'Holbach

58   HENRI PEYRE
The Influence of Eighteenth-Century Ideas on the French Revolution

63   DURAND ECHEVERRIA
      The Image and Influence of America in the French Enlightenment
67   Suggestions for Further Reading

CHAPTER THREE: THE DECLINE OF THE OLD REGIME AND
THE DEBACLE OF FRENCH FOREIGN POLICY

70   *Introduction*
71   G. P. GOOCH
      Louis XV: The Monarchy in Decline
74   ALBERT SOREL
      The Diplomatic Revolution and the Debacle of French Foreign
      Policy
78   ALPHONSE AULARD
      France and the Financing of the American Revolution
82   ALFRED COBBAN
      The Parlements of France in the Eighteenth Century
87   DOUGLAS DAKIN
      Turgot and the Fate of His Six Edicts
93   ERNEST LABROUSSE
      The Fiscal and Economic Crises at the End of the *Ancien Régime*
97   Suggestions for Further Reading

CHAPTER FOUR: FRANCE MAKES A REVOLUTION

100   *Introduction*
102   GEORGE RUDÉ
      Why Was There a Revolution in France?
110   ALBERT SOBOUL
      The "Mainspring of the Revolution": The Paris Sans-culottes
120   ALBERT GOODWIN
      The Directory — A Revaluation
130   Suggestions for Further Reading

CHAPTER FIVE: THE COUNTERREVOLUTION

134   *Introduction*
136   EMMANUEL VINGTRINIER
      Counterrevolutionary Politics: The Emigration and Intrigues of the
      Princes
141   ANDRÉ LATREILLE
      The Church and the Counterrevolution

146 CHARLES TILLY
A Sociological Analysis of Counterrevolution: The Vendée
152 HARVEY MITCHELL
Counter-revolutionary Espionage: Francis Drake and the Comte d'Antraigues
157 JACQUES GODECHOT
Counterrevolutionary Terror
161 PAUL H. BEIK
Counter-revolutionary Thought
165 Suggestions for Further Reading

CHAPTER SIX: NAPOLEONIC IMPERIALISM

168 Introduction
170 GEORGES LEFEBVRE
Napoleon Seizes Control of the Revolution
176 FELIX MARKHAM
Napoleonic Imperialism at Its Zenith: The Grand Empire and the Continental System
183 LOUIS MADELIN
The Spirit of the Napoleonic System
189 HANS KOHN
Napoleon and the Age of Nationalism
193 Suggestions for Further Reading

CHAPTER SEVEN: THE RESTORATION AND FALL OF THE BOURBONS

196 Introduction
197 GEORGES LACOUR-GAYET
Talleyrand at the Congress of Vienna
201 FREDERICK B. ARTZ
The Electoral System in France During the Bourbon Restoration, 1815–1830
207 GUILLAUME DE BERTIER DE SAUVIGNY
French Society Under the Restoration
212 VINCENT W. BEACH
Charles X, Polignac, and the Application of Article XIV of the Charter
217 DAVID H. PINKNEY
A New Look at the French Revolution of 1830
222 Suggestions for Further Reading

CHAPTER EIGHT: BOURGEOIS MONARCHY AND
DEMOCRATIC REPUBLIC

226   *Introduction*
228   JEAN LHOMME
       Bourgeois Supremacy During the July Monarchy
235   DOUGLAS JOHNSON
       A Reconsideration of Guizot
242   ALBERT J. GEORGE
       The Romantic Revolution and the Industrial Revolution in France
248   PETER AMANN
       The Changing Outlines of 1848
255   ANDRÉ-JEAN TUDESQ
       The Napoleonic Legend in France in 1848
262   Suggestions for Further Reading

CHAPTER NINE: "SOCIALISM" AND "CAESARISM":
THE DOMESTIC POLICIES OF THE SECOND EMPIRE

264   *Introduction*
265   GEORGES PRADALIÉ
       The Economic Transformation of France Under the Second
       Empire
273   HENDRIK BOON
       The Social and Economic Policies of the Emperor
282   MARCEL PRÉLOT
       The Constitutional Significance of the Second Empire
291   THEODORE ZELDIN
       The Myth of Napoleon III
296   Suggestions for Further Reading

CHAPTER TEN: "THE EMPIRE MEANS PEACE":
THE FOREIGN POLICY OF THE SECOND EMPIRE

300   *Introduction*
302   LOUIS GIRARD
       The Second Empire and Italian Unity
309   J. P. T. BURY
       "The Great Idea of the Reign": The Mexican Expedition
314   LYNN M. CASE
       Napoleon III and the Austro-Prussian War
323   MICHAEL E. HOWARD
       "Red Rag" and "Gallic Bull": The Hohenzollern Candidature
330   Suggestions for Further Reading

CHAPTER ELEVEN: SOCIALIST THOUGHT AND THE PARIS COMMUNE

334 *Introduction*

335 MAXIME LEROY
The Development of Socialist Doctrines from the Revolution to the Commune

340 EDWARD S. MASON
The Paris Commune: An Episode of the Socialist Movement

346 SAMUEL BERNSTEIN
The First International, Proudhonists, Blanquists, and the Paris Commune

353 EUGENE W. SCHULKIND
The Activity of Popular Organizations During the Paris Commune of 1871

360 Suggestions for Further Reading

CHAPTER TWELVE: REALISM, IMPRESSIONISM, AND SYMBOLISM

362 *Introduction*

363 PIERRE MARTINO
Flaubert and Naturalism

366 LIONELLO VENTURI
Impressionism, a Break with Tradition

372 A. G. LEHMANN
German Idealism and French Symbolism

379 Suggestions for Further Reading

CHAPTER THIRTEEN: CHALLENGES TO THE THIRD REPUBLIC

382 *Introduction*

384 FRESNETTE PISANI-FERRY
The Attempted *Coup d'Etat* of May 16, 1877

389 ADRIEN DANSETTE
The Significance of Boulangism

394 DAVID SHAPIRO
The Ralliement in the Politics of the 1890's

399 DOUGLAS JOHNSON
France and the Dreyfus Affair

407 EUGEN WEBER
The Nationalist Revival in France

412 Suggestions for Further Reading

CHAPTER FOURTEEN: IMPERIALISM, TRIPLE ENTENTE, AND WORLD WAR I

416 *Introduction*
418 FRESNETTE PISANI-FERRY
     Jules Ferry and the Growth of French Imperialism
426 D. W. BROGAN
     The Entente Cordiale and the First Moroccan Crisis
434 PIERRE RENOUVIN
     The War Aims of the French Government, 1914–1918
443 JACQUES CHASTENET
     The Costs of World War I
445 Suggestions for Further Reading

CHAPTER FIFTEEN: FRANCE BETWEEN TWO WARS (1919–1940)

448 *Introduction*
450 ARNOLD WOLFERS
     France's Search for "Security" After 1919
455 RENÉ RÉMOND
     The Resurgence of the Right After World War I
459 GEOFFREY WARNER
     The Stavisky Affair and the Riots of February 6th, 1934
466 GEORGES DUPEUX
     Léon Blum and the Failure of the Popular Front
472 JOHN C. CAIRNS
     Along the Road Back to France 1940
478 Suggestions for Further Reading

CHAPTER SIXTEEN: FRANCE AGAINST HERSELF: VICHY AND THE RESISTANCE

482 *Introduction*
484 ROBERT ARON
     Vichy's "National Revolution"
491 HENRI MICHEL
     The Vichy Regime and Collaboration
498 HENRI MICHEL
     Free France and Its Plans for the Future of France
606 STANLEY HOFFMANN
     The Effects of World War II on French Society and Politics
516 Suggestions for Further Reading

CHAPTER SEVENTEEN: THE "UNLOVED" FOURTH REPUBLIC

518   *Introduction*

520   JEAN LECERF
       The Transformation of the French Economy After World War II

527   RAYMOND ARON
       The Political "System" of the Fourth Republic

537   DOROTHY PICKLES
       Why the Fourth Republic Failed to Solve the Algerian Problem

543   PHILIP WILLIAMS
       How the Fourth Republic Died: The Revolution of May, 1958

554   Suggestions for Further Reading

CHAPTER EIGHTEEN: THE FIFTH REPUBLIC: THE FINAL SYNTHESIS?

558   *Introduction*

559   DOUGLAS JOHNSON
       The Political Principles of General de Gaulle

567   W. W. KULSKI
       De Gaulle and the Decolonization of Africa

575   ALFRED GROSSER
       The Foreign Policy Conceptions of General de Gaulle

582   LOUIS J. HALLE
       De Gaulle and the Future of Europe

589   Suggestions for Further Reading

CHAPTER NINETEEN: THE INTELLECTUAL CRISIS OF THE TWENTIETH CENTURY

592   *Introduction*

594   GEORGES LEMAITRE
       Dadaism

598   JOHN CRUICKSHANK
       The Novelist as Philosopher, 1930–1960

604   JEAN-PAUL SARTRE
       Existentialism

611   GABRIEL MARCEL
       The Philosophy of Existentialism

616   H. STUART HUGHES
       Claude Lévi-Strauss and the Changing Temper of the 1960's

623   Suggestions for Further Reading

625   INDEX

The Shaping of
MODERN FRANCE

Introduction
by Crane Brinton

The history of France since the Enlightenment of the eighteenth century can be an admirable case history to help in the understanding of our own Time of Troubles in this mid-twentieth century. More than that, and in spite of the recent American tendency to denigrate France and underestimate her importance in the world today, it is still true that for the foreseeable future we shall have to reckon with her as one of the key factors in our relations with the rest of the world, and in particular, with western Europe. On both counts, the modern—what the French call "contemporary"—history of France deserves much more careful study than it usually gets in this country.

The break with the past represented by the French Revolution—it was of course no total break—was one prepared for by decades of material growth, intellectual change, and accompanying strains and conflicts. R. R. Palmer has applied to the whole Western world in Europe and in the Americas in the second half of the eighteenth century the term *the Age of the Democratic Revolution*. And seen in the broadest general perspective, one can defend the thesis that in these decades the American Revolution, the French Revolution, other less well-known political revolutions, the so-called Industrial Revolution, and the intellectual revolution known as the Enlightenment, do indeed separate the beginnings of our contemporary world and the endings of an earlier one. No single label can be applied—or at least has not been so applied in ways acceptable to all historians, as readers of this book will note—to either of these worlds. Yet most of the terms in antithesis—*medieval-modern, aristocratic-democratic, agricultural-industrial, aristocracy-bourgeoisie, particularism-nationalism, privilege-equality, authority-liberty*, right on to the antithetical cosmologies of the book of Genesis, a universe created as it now is by Jehovah some six thousand years ago and that of modern geology, a universe not "created" at all, our planet earth some billions of years old—most of these antitheses at least help focus attention on the reality of the change the last two centuries have brought about.

In France the break between the old and the new was deep, clear-cut, and yet extraordinarily complex, with the millions of individual French men and women who after all *are* somehow the reality of France grouped in changing yet persistent parties, sects, classes, schools of thought, faiths. Here too there is an oversimple but still useful dualism: *les deux France*, the two Frances, one opposed to the work of the great Revolution, the other inspired to further that work, the first the France of "throne and altar" (note the throne comes first) and the second the France of the republic and—to put it mildly—anticlericalism. The French Revolution itself at its height in the Reign of Terror in 1793–1794 gave conservatives of the Western world a fright perhaps greater, because of its contrast with the comparative stability and orderliness of eighteenth-century states, than that produced in our century by the Bolshevik October Revolution. The actual bloodshed of the Reign of Terror in France—the generally accepted figure among historians is some 30,000 victims—was not remarkable in a century which had seen at its very beginning that many casualties on one side alone in the bloody battle of Malplaquet, and which was soon to witness the hecatombs of the world war of 1792–1815.

Such casualties, however, came in the course of that accepted institution, formal warfare among organized states. The casualties of the Reign of Terror were casualties of civil war—or if you prefer the "sterile" vocabulary suitable to the social sciences, internal warfare—a kind of conflict endemic enough in our West, but surely never accepted as a respectable institution. Moreover, the Reign of Terror saw the first systematic attempt in hundreds of years in the West to wipe out, not just a Christian heresy, but the whole of Christian worship. The attempt was a failure, and in 1801 Napoleon, himself no Christian, signed a Concordat with the Pope formally re-establishing the Roman Catholic faith as that of the majority of Frenchmen. It is significant of the long struggle since then between the two Frances that the anticlerical republican historian Aulard at the end of the nineteenth century could write wistfully that one more push in 1794 might well have finished off Christianity in France, in both senses of that phrase, for good.

To a degree the whole Western world, even that model of stability, law-abidingness, "evolution, not revolution," Great Britain, has in the last two centuries had to try to work out the problems set by these eighteenth-century democratic revolutions. Put in perfectly sound terms of symbolism, not by any means mere "ideologies," men everywhere in the West—and in the second half of the twentieth century everywhere in the world—have been seeking to realize, at least to bring into some rough consonance with the facts of life, those remarkable war cries, *Liberté, Egalité, Fraternité* and the self-evident truths "that all men are created equal, that they are endowed by their Creator with certain unalienable Rights, that among these are Life, Liberty, and the pursuit of Happiness."

In the United States and in Great Britain and her colonies of settlement, that effort was made easier, the conflicts aroused in its course less acute, by the fact that until only yesterday, when the Russians exploded their atomic bomb, these English-speaking lands enjoyed what the American historian Vann Woodward has aptly called "free security." The simple facts of geography, the protection afforded by saltwater, even though for England this was no more than the sea-moat of the Channel, and for the United States the additional fact that after France had been driven from North America in 1763 we had no neighboring power we could possibly fear as a menace to our safety—these, though they by no means kept us out of war, did save us from the real if ill-understood mass psychological pressures of national insecurity. Even so, we in this country had to undergo in the great abortive revolution in the South in 1861–1865 a crisis at least as serious as any the

French have undergone, and one we know cannot be said to have solved all the problems it set for us. And, now that American historians seem for the most part to have got beyond the naïveté of an economic, dollars-and-cents interpretation of the Civil War, it can be said simply that the great problem so left unsolved was that of reconciling Jefferson's preamble to the Declaration of Independence with the facts of Negro existence in this country.

France was the only major power among the European democracies that were direct heirs of the age of democratic revolutions of the eighteenth century; and France, unlike the English-speaking lands, has for many centuries been far from enjoying "free security." On the contrary, she has by her importance as a major power, and by her geographic situation, been involved in almost every war in Europe for hundreds of years. She has a long inheritance of defeat and invasion as well as of victory and expansion. It is this fact of her history that helps explain —no single "fact" can wholly explain any complex historical situation—French lapses from democratic regularity, her political instability in the last two centuries, her two Napoleons, her Boulanger, her *nous*, *Philippe Pétain* (such was the Marshal's royal style), her de Gaulle. Yet throughout all these troubles, the emotions, the ideas, the traditions summed up in many symbols, Marianne, the tricolor of the Revolution, the Marseillaise, *Liberté, Egalité, Fraternité*, have persisted, never really suppressed.

The editors of this admirable collection have put before the reader, not of course a connected historical narrative, but a most useful supplement to any such narrative. By drawing on a wide range of historians and great variety of historical approaches, political, economic, social, intellectual, they point up in a way no single historical narrative can the diversity and depth of the problems the French have wrestled with in the last two centuries. At the very least, they have assembled the materials from which a student can draw his own clinical diagnosis of the condition of France in the Fifth Republic of today. He can attempt to decide whether the French have made genuine progress in their wrestlings, whether the two Frances are in any real sense closer together than they were in the last century. More important, some readers may be moved by this book to reflect on the possible pertinence for nations as for individuals of the Horatian

Mutato nomine de te
Fabula narratur.

Change but the name, and it is of yourself this tale is told.

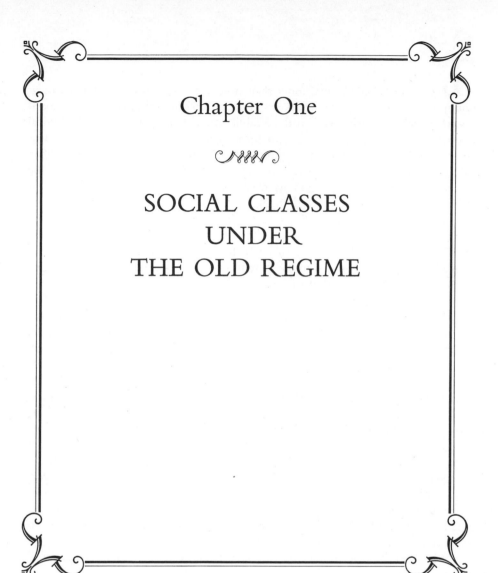

Chapter One

SOCIAL CLASSES
UNDER
THE OLD REGIME

THE OLD REGIME was more than simply the government of the Bourbon monarchs before the French Revolution of 1789. It embraced an entire social system which had originated in the Middle Ages. During a period of physical insecurity, pre-eminence belonged to those who prayed to God for what was beyond human power and to those whose arms and prowess guaranteed the maximum possible security. In an uncommercial age, land was the principal source of wealth, and its ownership fell to those who defended it rather than to those who tilled it. A hierarchy of functions was performed by a hierarchy of classes, or Estates—the First Estate (the clergy), the Second Estate (the nobility), the Third Estate (the peasantry).

The changes which took place in the medieval social structure by the eighteenth century are usually attributed to the growth of a merchant class within the Third Estate and the obsolescence of the privileged position of the aristocracy and the feudal burdens of the peasantry. Gradually the development of modern warfare and the introduction of gun powder, foot soldiers, and mercenaries limited the noble to the position of officer so that the military life ceased to absorb all the talents of the aristocracy. The latter became increasingly inactive and impoverished. Deprived of any useful function and prohibited by the code of his Estate from entering most commerce, he languished on his inherited land or depended on church positions or royal favors while still enjoying immunities from taxation and the services from the peasants he formerly protected with his arms. The growth of a merchant class whose wealth lay in personal property and whose productivity in an incipient capitalist economy exceeded that of an economically static noble class, accentuated the inequity of the medieval social structure. Although the peasant was no longer a serf or attached by law to a particular manor, vestiges of the seigneurial regime in the form of feudal dues and services continued to exist without their old justification. Although the Church witnessed the greatest survival of its medieval role, its wealth was considered out of proportion to its needs, and its exemption from taxation unjustified.

It is generally believed that a series of reactions to these social anomalies contributed to the causes of the French Revolution. The clash was initiated not by those whose grievances were most serious, but by the privileged class, whose position was most difficult to justify. The nobility tried to compensate for its decline by reasserting itself politically to control royal offices and favors under Louis XV; it asserted itself financially by exacting more stringently the feudal dues and services from the peasantry. The "aristocratic reaction" provoked the first disturbance in the social order and led to dissatisfaction and envy among both the bourgeoisie and the peasantry. The ensuing Revolution would restore "the harmony between fact and law."

Several American and British historians have recently attempted to revise this picture of the Old Regime in the light of new evidence. The composition and condition of each class and its role in causing the Revolution are being re-examined.

Professor Franklin Ford of Harvard University qualifies the distinction between the old nobility of the "sword"—or the nobility of medieval, military origin—and the nobility of the "robe," who had purchased a noble title or an office with a noble title attached or who had been ennobled by the king from among the bourgeois legal profession. Professor Ford notes that the aristocratic resurgence which followed the reign of Louis XIV (1661–1715), when the aristocracy was deprived of an active political role, was led by the nobility of the robe in the sovereign courts or *parlements*. The older nobility found its interests best defended by this new aristocracy who opposed abolition of noble privileges in matters of taxes and seigneurial dues. Thus the line between "robe" and "sword," bourgeoisie and aristocracy, was beginning to fade.

The British historian Albert Goodwin, in the second selection, re-examines the widely held account of the "aristocratic reaction" mentioned earlier. Noble exemption from taxation was more limited than usually imagined. Exemptions from direct taxation were also frequently enjoyed by the bourgeoisie, and in many areas these taxes actually fell on the aristocracy. The degree to which the *parlements* opposed abolition of tax exemptions is also found to be less than assumed. Similarly, the responsibility for collecting seigneurial dues from the peasantry often lay with bourgeois agents or landlords rather than with aristocrats. The revival of *terriers*, or land registers, recording feudal dues may have been motivated more by a desire to confirm existing dues than by a desire to increase them. Finally Professor Goodwin analyzes the nature of the alleged aristocratic control of offices in the army, Church, and court. Like Professor Ford, he finds that the new nobility led this resurgence rather than nobles of the "sword." Taking everything into account, the existence and nature of an "aristocratic reaction" may have to be seriously qualified.

In a similar vein, Professor George V. Taylor of the University of North Carolina has pointed out the difficulties of identifying the bourgeoisie with capitalist wealth and the aristocracy with traditional proprietary wealth. He notes a fusion of economic interests of the bourgeoisie and aristocracy, just as Professor Ford noted social fusion. Much of the bourgeoisie had its wealth in landed property, whereas much of the aristocracy possessed capital investments. Identification of either class with any form of economic wealth or production is found difficult; an explanation of the revolutionary role of either class in terms of its economic interests may well be impossible.

In the fourth selection, Georges Lefebvre, the late French historian of the Revolution, seeks to resolve the paradox noted by Tocqueville, that the French peasantry enjoyed conditions superior to those of any other European country in terms of personal freedom and landownership, yet it was the most dissatisfied and restless. Lefebvre points out that although the figures of peasant ownership of land appear high, these figures have meaning only when compared to the total number of heads of families and the amount of land necessary to obtain a decent living. He also shows the great variation of the peasant's status from that of landholder to farm tenant. The latter was subject to the intrusion of capitalism in two forms—the exclusion from use of communal lands due to the aggregation of large landholdings for "capitalist" farming purposes, and the collection of feudal dues by a class of "capitalist" agents. In summary, the position of the peasant was in many instances quite grievous because he suffered a peculiar combination of capitalist and feudal burdens.

The difficulties of identifying estate with class become most apparent in the clergy, for friction is found between the lower clergy, or curés, and the upper clergy or bishops. Professor Maurice G. Hutt of the University of Sussex, England, analyzes this class antagonism within the First Estate. Although the First Estate represented the most coherent "Order" in the eighteenth century in terms of unity of function, it cannot be identified with the propertied class. Although the upper clergy held large benefices, resisted radical reform, and opposed the Revolution, it was precisely members from the lower clergy who favored reform and became key defectors from the First Estate in June, 1789, when they joined the revolutionary Third Estate.

From the new evidence, an old conclusion seems certain. The medieval estates no longer corresponded to the social classes of the eighteenth century. The Third Estate had given rise to a bourgeoisie completely separated from the peasantry; within the First Estate two classes as distinct as nobility and peasantry had evolved.

It also seems that the distinction between bourgeois and noble was beginning to disappear. Bourgeois were becoming nobles and the nobles' most vociferous defenders. Nobles, in turn, were engaging in capitalist investments. The extent to which one can now speak of class conflict in terms of economic interest as a cause of the Revolution seems questionable. The "aristocratic reaction" understood as the last attempt of a privileged class to withhold power from a rising bourgeoisie also needs scrutinizing. The "aristocratic reaction" may well have been largely a bourgeois upsurge to capture for itself the social distinctions and privileges of the aristocracy. The conflict that ultimately does emerge may be more psychological than economic in origin. It was only the bourgeoisie excluded from noble privilege that demanded abolition of the old order; the ennobled bourgeoisie, however much capitalist, became its champion.

※

ROBE AND SWORD, THE REGROUPING
OF THE FRENCH ARISTOCRACY
AFTER LOUIS XIV

FRANKLIN L. FORD

On the morning of Sunday, September 1, 1715, in a fetid room at Versailles, the longest reign in modern history came to an end. Within the hour, couriers were pounding over the dusty road to Paris, while behind them in

Reprinted by permission of the publishers from Franklin L. Ford, *Robe and Sword* (Cambridge, Mass., Harvard University Press) 3, 5–6, 246–248, 250, 252. © 1953 by the President and Fellows of Harvard College.

the great palace the halls and reception rooms began to fill with courtiers, brought scurrying from their cramped but precious sleeping quarters by the whispered words of serving men. From Versailles to the capital and thence out across the provinces and the rest of Europe, even to the scattered colonies across the seas, the news spread as swiftly as hoof and sail could carry it. The king was dead. . . .

The arch of Ludovican society had first been reared with the approval of a population which had turned from the anarchy of the Fronde to seek order as an absolute good. Its principle of construction had been the king's determination to separate actual power from apparent grandeur in the population beneath him. Its aesthetic appeal lay in a vision of unity, of static symmetry, with every rank and every individual assigned a fixed place in relation to the crown. By 1715 the arch, at no time as perfect as its principle, was obviously crumbling in a number of places; but it had survived as an official concept as long as its original keystone had remained in place.

Now the keystone was gone. Therein lies the real significance of the deathbed at Versailles. Changes in actual power relationships, many of them of some years' standing, were translated into overt demands for recognition with an attendant clamor and confusion which contemporaries felt and which their accounts still transmit to the modern reader. When such demands had been voiced under Louis XIV, they had appeared piecemeal, with relative timidity, in a wholly different atmosphere; for the old king, by insisting at every point on the stability of each group's relationship to himself, had succeeded to a remarkable extent in maintaining the stability of its relationship to all the others. His skill, whether artful or instinctive, in containing the thrust of a variety of forces by keeping them convergent on a center he controlled, was a characteristic of his reign which the Duc d'Orléans, acting for the five-year-old Louis XV and lacking the public sanction with which his predecessor had emerged from the Fronde, could not hope to duplicate. For the great lords, for the nobility in general, for the parlements, for the Gallican enemies of the late ruler's Jesuit advisers, for the increasingly powerful business class, even for the peasantry, hopeful of a lightened tax load and fewer troops swarming over the countryside, long-suppressed ambitions were at last able to emerge onto the surface of public life. . . .

The feudal reaction in eighteenth-century France took the form of a resurgence of power to obstruct the crown—until the very moment when the explosion came from below, the nobility's face was to be turned suspiciously upward toward the king. To explain this resurgence I have had to call attention to a definite regrouping of politically significant elements at court, in the church, and in the army, around the high nobility of the robe. It follows from this interpretation that the term "feudal" is best employed in this connection to indicate not that the original feudal class regenerated itself from within, but that an infinitely more potent group had become in fact a new feudality, which under Louis XV lent its strength to the old. This process was well under way, though obscured, even before 1715, became apparent at the surface of political events in the first years after Louis XIV's death, and was essentially complete by the time Montesquieu published his *Spirit of the Laws* in 1748.

The discussion leading up to these conclusions concentrated successively on three main topics: the situation of the nobility and especially the noblesse de robe in 1715, the elements which underlay the magistracy's rise to power and prestige in the ensuing period, and finally, the overt indications of aristocratic regrouping in the politics, social relationships, and intellectual trends of the years between 1715 and 1748. In purely quantitative terms, the retrospective observations and the consideration of relatively stable conditions unquestionably have outweighed the analysis of identifiable alterations in noble tactics, attitudes, and theories. Yet the core of my presentation has remained the process of change within a privileged class. The statics have been introduced only to the end that the dynamics might become comprehensible.

Just what factors have emerged as the essential agents underlying these dynamics? First was the fluid situation arising out of the end of a long, personalized reign and the accession of a five-year-old child. An important element in this situation was the confusion bequeathed by a king who had stripped the nobility of political power during his lifetime but had not destroyed its ability to rebound after his death. From this in turn followed the need to examine the legal boundaries of a noble order composed of almost two hundred thousand soldiers, churchmen, magistrates, municipal officers, and country gentlemen; and to take note of the variations in wealth, prestige, and influence which further subdivided that class. In order to be prepared for the subsequent progress of events, it was necessary to pause for an institutional analysis of the thirty-one sovereign courts whose officers made up the high noblesse de robe, then concentrate . . . on the special legal and social position of the superior magistracy within a nobility of which it constituted scarcely more than one percent. The age-old line between robe and sword proved to be still sharp in 1715.

But the sovereign court officers possessed attributes destined to give them a place of honor within the Second Estate. Associated in the public mind with Jansenist Gallicanism, with opposition to new taxes, and with the defense of regional privileges, they added a growing body of popular support to their newly recovered weapon: the right to remonstrate while delaying the registration of new laws. They owned their public offices outright. They belonged to families many of which had by this time been noble for several generations and most of which were now adding military or ecclesiastical prestige, or both, to their judicial dignities. They were wealthy, for their fortunes included not only their offices, in themselves representing large investments, but also a formidable accumulation of securities, urban property, and rural seigneuries.

Under the Regency the peerage made an abortive bid for leadership within the nobility and lost that leadership to the high robe, which benefited from the violent reaction of all the other nobles against the hauteur of the peers. By their remonstrances and by their active participation in the surviving provincial estates the magistrates proceeded to uphold the aristocracy's opposition to undifferentiated taxation, encroachments on seigneurial autonomy, and ministerial assaults on the fortress of regional particularism. The passing years revealed the nobility coming to recognize more and more clearly the indispensable services of the courts and to accept the primacy of this one remaining institution still under noble control. The social concomitants of this tactical alliance produced, if not the total obliteration of the old robe-épée line, at least its virtual disappearance as a factor in French public life. And the aristocratic spokesmen of the mid-eighteenth century, most of all Montesquieu, represented the amalgamation of feudal and parlementary arguments. In institutional, political, social, or ideological terms, the pattern is the same.

Thus, in place of the seventeenth century's characteristic triangle of tension —the crown, the sword, and the still half-bourgeois robe—there had now appeared a triangle composed of the crown, the middle class reformers, and the noble defenders of existing privileges based on birth and office. The last-mentioned group, speaking through published tracts, through the resolutions of the First and Second Estates in provincial assemblies, through the pastoral letters of bishops and the whispered suggestions of great courtiers, above all, through the remonstrances of the sovereign courts, showed a solidarity which seems to me more important for subsequent history than was the residue of old differences. Not even the Fronde offered a precedent for what was happening under Louis XV; for in 1650 the high robe had still been a narrow professional fraternity with aims distinct from those of the feudal class. Now it emerged as the self-conscious, recognized standard bearer of a nobility which without its institutional strength would have lapsed into atomized, voiceless impotence. . . .

In the Marxian view the performance of the aristocracy after Louis XV can, of course, be fully explained by its material interests. This was an old possessing class, left over from an era when control of land had conferred control over the means of production, but now engaged in a losing battle against the new possessing class based on commerce and money power. The political reaction and the internal closing of ranks are nothing but the reflexive acts of just such an endangered class; and the whole intellectual development culminating in Montesquieu is portrayed as simply the ideological smoke screen for a position ultimately determined by economic considerations.

Marxian analysis had made an undeniable contribution to our understanding of the final spasms of the ancien régime. It does not, however, fit all aspects of the situation here examined. The noblesse de robe sprang from the bourgeoisie and never wholly lost its stake in the capitalist development; but over the last century of its existence it identified itself increasingly with the landed aristocracy, so that in the end it was leading the battle of the declining class against the forces of national monarchy and capitalist liberalism. Once it found itself in that situation it acted in a fashion quite in accordance with Marxian laws, but the process of its transformation in the seventeenth and early eighteenth centuries involved prestige values which did not correspond at all to its economic interests. . . .

By the mid-eighteenth century the government was faced with a situation in which high robe power had become the crux of the aristocratic problem. On the crown's response to this challenge would ultimately depend not only the settlement of the question of privilege but its own fate as well. History had a solution to recommend. The age-old technique of the Capetian house when defied by an entrenched class of officials had been to transfer the original delegation of authority to a new and more dependent stratum. But this time there was lacking the firmness which had neutralized provosts in the twelfth century, bailiffs and senechals in the thirteenth, and lordly governors general in the seventeenth. As late as 1771, when Chancellor Maupeou announced the suppression of the parlements and the substitution of appointive judicial boards, it appeared for a moment that the old expedient was being success-fully re-applied. Just three years later, however, the new King Louis XVI inaugurated his series of surrenders by reinstating the magistrates. Their return was greeted by joyous public demonstrations; and to many historians of the sovereign courts that fact has sufficed to make the events of 1774 appear as a popular victory over despotism. But the freedom which had conquered was the freedom of the medieval nobleman, clutching his special bundle of prerogatives, crying "Liberty" and meaning only "mon droit." It was to this doomed conception that the crown was henceforth hopelessly committed.

A RE-EVALUATION OF THE "ARISTOCRATIC REVOLT"

Albert Goodwin

The debate on the social origins of the revolution of 1789 has increasingly emphasized the tensions and economic misery which aristocratic privilege and exclusiveness are said to have provoked in the pre-revolutionary period.

Albert Goodwin, "The Social Origins and Privileged Status of the French Eighteenth-century Nobility," *The John Rylands Library Bulletin*, XLVII, no. 2 (March, 1965), 382–389, 391–394. © *The John Rylands Library Bulletin*. Used by permission.

At the root of those tensions lay three issues which have been re-examined by scholars whose conclusions point towards a revaluation, or at least a reconsideration, of the economic privileges and social attitudes of the French nobility on the eve of its eclipse. The first of these issues was raised by the nobility's fiscal immunities, the extinction of which seemed to contemporaries to provide the key to the solution of the monarchy's recurrent financial problems and to be in line with the growing demands for fiscal equality. The second issue which has received renewed attention from historians is the nature and scope of the so-called "seigneurial reaction," which was long supposed to have been an important contributory factor in the deepening economic distress of the French peasantry in the reign of Louis XVI. The third issue which has come under closer scrutiny is that presented by the alleged social inhibitions and political frustrations of important sections of the professional and commercial middle class in the face of the apparently increasing solidarity and social exclusiveness of the whole hierarchy of the judicial, clerical and lay aristocracy. In the view of at least one contemporary polemicist, in 1787 the Notables had defended their privileges against the Throne and in 1788 they had defended their privileges against the Nation. Looking back over the eighteenth century as a whole one could agree that the nobility had indeed stubbornly defended its privileges whenever and however those privileges had been threatened. Nevertheless there are sound reasons for supposing that the extent and reality of the fiscal and other privileges of the French nobility in the later stages of the *Ancien Régime* have been exaggerated and that the degree of social mobility within the hierarchical structure of French society in the pre-revolutionary period has been undervalued. In this lecture my main aim will be to clarify the economic, social and political attitudes of the various sections of the French nobility in the eighteenth century and against the background of social and economic change.

In terms of privilege no institution of the *Ancien Régime*, so we have been repeatedly assured, was more resented by the mass of the French population in the latter part of the eighteenth century than the continued legal exemption of the clergy and lay nobility from certain forms of direct taxation. It is still widely believed that even those direct taxes—the *capitation* [proportional head tax] and the *vingtièmes* [income taxes]—to which the lay nobility, as well as members of the Third Estate, had been subjected in the course of the eighteenth century were extensively evaded by the nobles with the open or tacit connivance of the fiscal authorities. The powers of self taxation still enjoyed at that period by the quinquennial assemblies of the Gallican church are also thought to have reduced the clergy's voluntary contributions to state revenue to a level much below what in equity—though not in canon law— it should have been. Above all the continued immunity of the clergy and lay nobility from the most productive source of revenue—the notorious *taille* [direct tax on income or land]—is considered to have restricted the incidence of this tax exclusively to the members of the Third Estate. Thus it is often assumed that the total sums paid to the Treasury by the French nobility in the eighteenth century must have been trivial in amount and completely out of relation to its taxable capacity. These conclusions and the assumptions and comparisons on which they are often based have recently been challenged by Miss Behrens.[1]

Her detailed arguments necessarily turn on technicalities, but her general conclusions are valuable for the new light thrown on the economic difficulties of the French nobility in the eighteenth century and on the motivation behind its consistent defence of its remaining fiscal privileges. She reminds us, incidentally, that those privileges which were confined to the nobility— such as the right to armorial bearings, the right to wear swords when not in uniform and the prerogative of being tried for certain criminal offences in special courts—were mainly honorific. Much more valuable, however, were the right to own *seigneuries* [noble manors] and thus to levy feudal dues and the right of exemption from the servile obligations of the *taille*, the *corvée* [compulsory road repair] and service in the militia. These latter privileges were not the exclusive monopoly of the nobility and were, in fact, often possessed by commoners—though in some cases only with special permission and in return for special dues paid to the crown. Similarly, as far as fiscal immunities recognized in law were concerned, the most numerous class of privileged persons and those with the most extensive privileges were not the nobles but the *bourgeois* of the *villes franches* [free towns] such as Paris and Lyons. The latter, whilst sharing the nobles' immunity from the *taille*, were, unlike the nobility, also largely immune from the other forms of direct taxation.

Miss Behrens also demonstrates convincingly that the nobility's legal exemption from the *taille* was much less substantial in practice than has often been assumed, because it was "broken through by the facts of economics." As the result of local custom, royal intervention or the familiar processes of economic friction the incidence of this tax, from which the nobility was technically exempt, came to rest, not exclusively on the shoulders of the unprivileged, but at least partially on the nobility itself. . . .

What emerges from all this is that the French nobility appears to have borne a relatively heavier burden of direct taxation than the British nobility at this period and that the abolition or voluntary surrender of the nobility's fiscal immunities would not have solved the French government's chronic financial problems. This conclusion, in itself, should lead one to take a less censorious view of the resistance offered by the nobility both in the Assembly of Notables of 1787 and in the *Parlement* of Paris to Calonne's proposal for

---

[1] "Nobles, Privileges and Taxes in France at the end of the Ancien Régime," *Economic History Review*, 2nd ser., XV (1963), 451–475.

the imposition of a graduated land tax in place of the tripled *vingtièmes*. It should be remembered that, despite their ministerial contacts, neither the "administrative" bishops, who led the opposition to the government's fiscal reforms inside the Assembly of Notables, nor the judicial aristocracy of the *Parlement* of Paris were, at that stage, fully aware of the financial impact of France's participation in the war of American Independence or of the real origins of the annual deficit. As public finance had until 1787 been a closely guarded state secret it was hardly surprising that the first Assembly of Notables should have sought an explanation of the government's difficulties in Calonne's own prodigality as Controller-General of Finance. Radical pamphleteers such as Carra and Gorsas did their best to embroider this theme and to rally public indignation in the capital against the minister who was generally regarded as a charlatan. Professor Egret has also noted that the Notables put forward suggestions, not for the outright rejection, but for the modification of the proposed land tax, which were in themselves reasonable and constructive. In place of a tax whose yield would have been indeterminate, both as regards its amount and duration, the Notables pressed for a repartitional tax of which the product would be fixed in relation to the proved needs of the budgetary situation and which would be assessed locally by provincial assemblies with executive and not merely consultative powers. However insincere the Notables' offers to forego their fiscal immunities may have been on this occasion, the subsequent insistence of the *Parlement* of Paris on the summons of the Estates General involved a real sacrifice of one of its most cherished traditional privileges and paved the way for the eventual recognition of the principle of popular consent to taxation through properly representative institutions.

If the scope and significance of the "aristocratic revolt" of the years 1787 and 1788 may have been exaggerated, recent research has also led historians to be more guarded in their interpretation of the so-called "feudal reaction" of the prerevolutionary period. In his recent Wiles lectures Professor Cobban has gone so far as to describe this term as a misnomer and he is surely correct when he maintains that a good deal of peasant discontent before 1789 must be ascribed to the penetration of urban financial interests into the French countryside and to the growing commercialization of agriculture. The renovation of the registers of feudal dues which used often to be regarded as an aggressive and reactionary move on the part of the landed nobility against a defenceless peasantry is now seen more as a defensive response to real financial difficulties attributable to rising general prices and higher taxation, as a consequence of the growing adoption of the methods of scientific agriculture and as a by-product of stricter forms of estate management. Much of the hostility against seigneurial exactions expressed in the *cahiers* [lists of grievances] was directed not so much against the landed nobility as such, but rather against its middle class agents, to whom the collection of such obligations was often farmed out, and more particularly against the feudal law-yers (*feudistes*), especially those who were employed on a commission basis. It was not, however, a general practice among *seigneurs* in the eighteenth century to employ *feudistes* on these terms—many and probably a majority paid these experts regular salaries and thus did not afford any artificial stimulus to the collection of feudal arrears or to the revival of obsolete obligations. One reason for the renewal of the land registers (or *terriers*) at this period was to facilitate the collection of existing seigneurial and feudal dues rather than to resuscitate those which had long fallen into disuse. Sometimes the primary aim was simply to reduce the expense of costly legal proceedings against recalcitrant tenants who could often successfully resist the payment of dues when these had not been strictly defined. Where, as in the West of France, the payment of feudal dues and rents was a collective obligation and where the land was divided among a wide range of tenantry, some of whom were middle class non-residents, the renovation of the registers of feudal dues actually tended to prevent the absentee tenants from defaulting and thus helped to alleviate the burdens of the resident community of peasants. . . .

The third major issue which has been reconsidered by historians in recent years is that of the social and professional aspirations of the upper échelons of the French bourgeoisie in the prerevolutionary period. It has been argued that the nobility had, in the second half of the eighteenth century, so used its influence in government circles as to close careers to talent in the higher ranges of the law, the church and the army and that it was the resulting exasperation of the more wealthy and intelligent members of the middle class which made the demand for social and political equality irresistible in 1789. It is no part of my purpose to investigate the merits or limitations of this interpretation in detail. I should doubt myself whether it applied to the richer merchants and financiers, whose objectives were not so much careers open to talent as the attainment of noble status, which was well within their grasp. Once nobility had been achieved the characteristic reaction of the successful merchant or financier was to become assimilated as quickly as possible to the nobility by accepting its social values and traditional outlook. It is worth remembering that the merchant economy of the period was still in principle compatible with the external forms and social attitudes of semi-feudalism, and that there were few if any "captains of industry" in eighteenth-century France. Does this mean, as Professor Cobban suggests, that the revolutionary bourgeois can be identified with the class of venal officers and the members of the liberal professions? It would be an interesting conclusion, but the evidence for its validity has still to be produced.

What I shall attempt in the concluding part of this lecture is rather to explain the reasons for the economic and social attitudes of the French nobility which lay behind the various expressions of its caste exclusiveness. The classic examples of its class consciousness at this period were the increasingly aristocratic composition and demeanour of the *Parlements*, the stricter regulations for the grant of *les honneurs de la cour* [honors of the court] imposed in 1759 and the much debated royal declaration of 1781 limiting direct commissioned entry into the army. These demonstrations of aristocratic conservatism can perhaps best be understood by considering the situation and attitudes of the high judicial magistracy, the court nobility and the provincial aristocracy, as they were affected by royal policy or economic conditions.

The high judicial magistrates of the sovereign appeal courts or *Parlements* formed only a minute fraction of the nobility as a whole and yet in the eighteenth century they attained a unique position as the foremost champions of its privileges. The political ascendancy of these high court judges within the order of the nobility arose partly from their right to register and to remonstrate against royal legislation, partly from the failure of the Dukes and peers to assert their own claims to aristocratic leadership at the time of the Regency and partly from the increasing recognition among the provincial nobility of the importance of the *Parlements* as protectors of provincial liberties against the crown.

This judicial defence of aristocratic privilege derived, however, not merely from the institutional prerogatives of the *Parlements*, but also from the determination of the magistrates, conscious to some extent of their relative social inferiority, to assimilate themselves, on a basis of equality, with the nobility of ancient descent. Although there could be no doubt, in strictly legal terms, about the noble status of the judicial magistrates, their social origins were diverse. Many of the magistrates owed their nobility to wealth derived from commerce but invested by their ancestors in the purchase of the expensive sinecure office of king's secretary, tenure of which conferred privileged status forthwith and hereditary nobility after the expiry of twenty years. Some were the sons or grandsons of men who had started their careers as humble officials in the subordinate provincial courts and who had later purchased judicial office as councillors in one or other of the *Parlements*. Owing to the mechanism provided by the sale of public offices it had become possible, and not infrequent, for members of the middle ranges of the Third Estate to attain hereditary nobility in two generations and even for families of peasant stock of outstanding ability to do so in three generations.

A recent study of the social origins and family connections of the members of the *Parlement* of Paris between 1715 and 1771 has demonstrated not only how overwhelmingly aristocratic its composition was at that period but also how comparatively recent this noble status had been acquired. Of the 590 judicial families surveyed no less than 512 were already noble when their first representatives had entered the corporation. In 1715, 90 per cent of the Parisian magistrates possessed either personal or hereditary nobility and in 1771, on the eve of Maupeou's reforms, that proportion was still unchanged.

Significantly, however, 241 of these magisterial families had derived their noble status and privileges from the comparatively recent purchase of the office of king's secretary and their members were thus regarded as "new men," in the sense that their ancestors had had no previous connections with the legal profession. Despite the concern which most of the *Parlements* displayed in the eighteenth century about their recruitment from aristocratic and judicial families the infiltration of "new men" into their ranks continued. Even when, in the middle years of the century, the *Parlements* of Nancy, Grenoble, Aix and Toulouse conformed to the example set by the *Parlement* of Rennes by excluding commoners from their ranks, this did not mean that their members were henceforth drawn exclusively from the traditional magisterial families. It has been shown that of the 426 lay councillors of the *Parlements* appointed during the last fifteen years of the *Ancien Régime* no less than 266 were *hommes nouveaux* ["new men"] in this sense. Like the French nobility as a whole, therefore, the judicial aristocracy at this period had social origins which cannot be reconciled with the traditional view that it had become a closed and self-perpetuating caste. . . .

CAPITALIST AND PROPRIETARY WEALTH AND THE DEFINITION OF THE BOURGEOISIE

George V. Taylor

There was in the economy of the old regime a distinct configuration of wealth, noncapitalist in function, that may be called "proprietary." It embodied investments in land, urban property, venal office, and annuities. The returns it yielded were modest, ranging between 1 and 5 per cent, but they were fairly constant and varied little from year to year. They were realized not by entrepreneurial effort, which was degrading, but by mere ownership and the passage of calendar intervals. Risk was negligible. Although bad harvests lowered rents in kind, they never destroyed capital, and the rents in money, like annuities and salaries of venal office, were payable regardless of natural hazards. In the proprietary sector investments were almost fully secure.

Historically and functionally, proprietary wealth was aristocratic. Under the old regime, gentility required a stable fortune that left one free to live with ease and dignity on his revenues. In the fortunes of the Toulouse nobles

George V. Taylor, "Noncapitalist Wealth and the Origins of the French Revolution," *American Historical Review*, LXXII, no. 2 (January, 1967), 471–475, 477, 479–480, 482–484, 486–489. © George V. Taylor. Edited by the author and used by permission.

studied by [Robert] Forster and of the magistrates of the Paris Parlement studied by [François] Bluche it was precisely land, urban property, venal office, and annuities that furnished the income on which these families maintained their way of life. Two considerations discouraged nobles from investing in commerce. First, the social values of aristocracy included a notorious aversion to business as practiced by merchants, merchant manufacturers, and bankers. To invest in "trade" was to risk losing status. The only industries that nobles felt entirely free to develop were those rooted in the land and its resources and growing out of certain exploitations of the medieval fief—mines, metallurgy, paper, glass, and canals—and in developing these they adopted practices and forms of organization substantially different from those employed by the merchants. Second, the risks inherent in business endangered the solidity and continuity considered essential to wealth meant to support a family for several generations. Fundamentally, the fortune that best served the interests of an aristocratic family was an endowment. Like an endowment, it was carefully managed, and risk was kept to a minimum. The preference for this kind of wealth, based on ingrained social attitudes that have powerfully retarded French economic growth, survived the Revolution. . . .

The fondness for land penetrated all levels of French society. Profoundly rural, most eighteenth-century Frenchmen had an atavistic attachment to the soil, and "living nobly" was habitually identified with at least seasonal residence in the country. The aristocracy by tradition and the wealthy urban groups by emulation showed an incurable esteem for rural property. The novelist Stendhal, raised in the 1780's at Grenoble, recalled his father, an *avocat au parlement*, as a man constantly preoccupied with acquiring rural land and expanding his holdings. His father's wigmaker (*perruquier*), on missing an appointment with a client, would explain that he had been visiting his "domain," and his excuses were well received. People bought land yielding 1 or 2 per cent with funds that could have been deposited with merchants at 5, and borrowed at 5 to buy land that yielded 1 or 2. This passion for land was by no means limited to Grenoble. Nobles, *avocats*, *procureurs*, financiers, officials, and merchants in all parts of France bought and held urban and rural properties that qualified them for local acceptance, advancement, and privileges. There were shopkeepers, artisans, and even peasants who invested in land and *rentes* that gave them small incomes for old age. In every town those without a business or profession who lived on such investments were taxed on a separate roll, that of the bourgeois, and in 1789 in most towns they voted as a separate electoral group of the Third Estate. A study by Vovelle and Roche shows that the qualification bourgeois disappeared during the Revolution from official acts, and that persons listed under the old regime as bourgeois reappeared in documents of the Directory and the Consulate as *rentiers* and *propriétaires*, demonstrating as well as anything can that before the Revolution the fiscal group called bourgeois was noncapitalist.

Nearly all wealthy landowners exploited their land indirectly, through tenants. They saw their properties not as profit-making enterprises but as sources of rental income. Rent, in fact, was at the center of all calculations. It was what determined the value of a property: as rent increased, the value grew proportionately, so that, curiously enough, the rate of return on capital remained about the same. Generally speaking, rental income seems to have ranged between 2 and 4 per cent of capital value, and Necker wrote in 1784 that the net revenue from land was $2\frac{1}{2}$ per cent, which is to say that, as an investment, land provided the low but assured return typical of proprietary wealth. When an eighteenth-century proprietor set out to increase the revenue of his properties he thought not in terms of increasing the productivity of the soil but of raising the rent, and in the late eighteenth century a significant rise of the peasant population made this easy to do. As land hunger grew and candidates for leases multiplied, rents rose handsomely. Labrousse has found that, from the base period 1726–1741 to the "intercyclic" period 1785–1789, rural money rents advanced by 98 per cent, and in a paper on the royal domains submitted to the Assembly of Notables in 1787 mention was made of "the Revolution which, in twenty years, has nearly doubled the revenues of all land." Where the rent was paid in kind, as in *métayage*, the rise in rents is difficult to measure, but there is no doubt that it took place. Forster has written that in the Toulouse region the old phrase "half-fruits" that signified the owner's share was a euphemism; at the end of the century the owners took as much as three-fourths. It is perhaps possible to say that the French landowner of the old regime was an exploiter of persons rather than of the soil. The circumstances of the prerevolutionary period did nothing to change his traditional attitudes. Indeed, by enabling him to raise his income without raising production they reinforced them. . . .

In the proprietary scale of preference, the passion for property in office was nearly as strong as that for property in land. A venal office was a long-term investment. Usually it brought a low but stable return, and, as long as the owner regularly paid the *droit annuel* (in earlier times the *paulette*), he could, under restrictions applicable to each office, sell it to a buyer, bequeath it to an heir, or even rent it out to someone, such as a judge, who, though admitted to practice, was unable to buy the required *charge*. The number and variety of venal offices that existed at the end of the old regime is incredible. An investigation that Necker launched in 1778 disclosed no less than 51,000 venal offices in the law courts, the municipalities, and the financial system, and their capital value, as revealed by voluntary declarations made under an edict of 1771, totaled 600,000,000 livres, although this should be increased by as much as 50 per cent because the declarations, taxable at 2 per cent per annum, were notoriously undervalued. These offices included those held by the personnel of the parlements and their chancelleries, the judges of the other royal courts, and the multitude of clerks, beadles, sergeants, surveyors, assessors, and concessionaires that surrounded these courts. They also included the offices held by the notaries and *procureurs*, who could practice their professions only by acquiring the appropriate *charges*. They did not, however, include the offices of the royal household, venal military appointments, or places in the financial companies and the higher financial concessions like those of the *receveurs généraux des finances*, and for these we should probably add another 200,000,000 or 300,000,000 livres to the total indicated above. Also excluded from these figures were the offices held by guild officials, inspectors, and masters, and particularly by the wigmakers. Given the present state of research we have no precise idea of how many adult males owned offices, but it would not be surprising to find that they came to 2 or 3 per cent of the total. . . .

In addition to land, urban properties, and office, proprietary wealth was invested in *rentes*. In the broadest sense, a *rente* was an annual revenue that one received for having transferred something of value to someone else. A *rente foncière* was rent for land. A *rente hypothécaire* was an annuity the payment of which was secured by property. A *rente perpétuelle* was an annuity of indefinite duration, terminated only when the debtor chose, on his own initiative, to refund the principal and thereby free himself from paying the *rente*. A *rente viagère* was a life annuity: the principal was entrusted to someone who paid the annuity until the person or persons named in the contract died; at that point the principal became finally and irrevocably his. Because the *rente viagère* was essentially a speculation that destroyed all or part of the capital accumulated for a family endowment, most of those living on proprietary wealth believed it reckless and immoral, and a man who converted his fortune into life annuities was considered to have defrauded his heirs. . . .

It should now be clear that there was a fairly consistent pattern of noncapitalist wealth, that it was traditionally aristocratic, and that "feudalism" is a bad name for it. It was governed by institutional survivals and social values that opposed the progressive and expansive tendencies of capitalism, preferring rent to profit, security to risk, tradition to innovation, and, in terms of personal goals, gentility to entrepreneurial skill and renown. It displayed nearly all the traits of what Rostow has called a traditional society, one dominated by landowners and their values and governed, as far as production was concerned, by pre-Newtonian modes of thought. All these institutions, values, and fixations promoted, as Rostow has suggested, a "long-run fatalism" and a "ceiling on the level of obtainable output per head." In England, no doubt, such deterrents to growth existed, but in ways that are not yet clearly explained they were being outflanked or overcome. In France, however, they flourished. The question of why there should have been such a disparity deserves much more study than it has received.

Compared with proprietary wealth, eighteenth-century commercial capitalism seems a vastly different thing. In commerce, banking, and domestic industry fixed assets were negligible, and investments were put into circulating wealth. Goubert has written of the Motte family of Beauvais:

One is tempted to write that what was always important to those merchants-born [*marchands-nés*] was wealth in motion, the rather intoxicating impression that must have come to them from the merchandise, credits, and cash that moved, circulated, fluctuated, and constantly transformed themselves: a kind of ballet of linens, paper, and money.

This engaging description of commercial wealth is justified by entrepreneurial records in many archives. At Lyons merchants rented the houses and warehouses in which they did business. With the *armateurs* of Bordeaux and Marseilles, ships were short-term assets; bought by a syndicate organized to finance the voyage, the ship was sold at the end of the venture, sometimes at auction, sometimes simply to the syndicate the *armateur* had formed for the next voyage. Industrial machinery was simple and made mostly of wood. In textiles, which accounted for about two-thirds of industrial production by value, it was owned chiefly by the artisans to whom the work was distributed, and when merchants loaned it to them it was not serious enough to warrant carrying in the accounts. All this explains why the ledgers of the old regime carry no accounts for depreciation costs. The day of heavy fixed commercial and industrial investment was yet to come.

Risk, nearly unknown in the proprietary sector, was a central fact of business life. The merchant speculated in commodities, paper, and credit, and, no matter how prudent he was, his fate depended largely on events he could not control. Shipwrecks, acts of war, sudden changes in style, unforeseeable bankruptcies, or unfavorable shifts in exchange rates could wipe him out, and if it was bad luck that broke him it was largely good luck that made him rich. Established merchants, known for caution and probity, went under, while new men, starting with borrowed money and the savings of a clerk's salary, became well to do. Commerce, therefore, was a zone of fortune building and social mobility. But because it lacked the stability of the proprietary sector, it was dangerous for established wealth. "All that I have seen," wrote the Comte de Villèle,

... leaves me with the opinion that every man with an acquired fortune who desires only to keep it, must keep at a distance from people, of whatever class or profession they be, who strive to make a fortune ... he must avoid all business, all relations with them, because they will not fail to make him their dupe. Furthermore, to each man his *métier*, as the proverb says: look at the proprietor trying to speculate, and at the merchant trying to enter agriculture.... Never have I participated in the least speculation.

Finally, in contrast to proprietary wealth, business capital gave low dividends in prestige. The public image of the merchant that Molière exploited rather brutally in *Le bourgeois gentilhomme* was profoundly ignoble, and it afflicted the merchants themselves with feelings of inferiority that probably troubled them more than the contempt they actually encountered. To some extent their unhappiness was self-induced. In 1700–1701 merchant deputies to the Council of Trade complained that merchants were held in low esteem, that the public ignored the superior status of a wholesale merchant or banker, and that because of this their sons avoided business and their daughters preferred nonmerchants as husbands. "Our young people," wrote one of them, "concentrate on the social graces rather than on the really substantial things in life, [and] our children are ever fearful lest it become known that their fathers were once merchants." About thirty years before the Revolution the Abbé Coyer wrote: "Only the Merchant perceives no luster in his career, & if he wants to succeed in what is called in France *being something*, he has to give it up. This misunderstood expression does a lot of damage. In order to be *something*, a large part of the Nobility remains nothing." The merchants felt that the intense practical training of business, the constant supervision and attention it required, and its remoteness from the leisure and finesse of the proprietary round of life kept them from cultivating the social and intellectual qualities that brought respect. Savary, whose *Le parfait négociant* remained throughout the eighteenth century a desktop oracle of business practice and morality, warned merchants not to educate their sons in the liberal arts and not to let them mingle with young nobles and men of the robe in the *collèges*, because the self-esteem they would acquire in those milieux would ruin them for trade. Because these attitudes existed, anyone who remained in business, no matter how creditably he lived, suffered some discount in prestige. Even in the values of the Third Estate, diverse as they may have been, esteem was associated with proprietary wealth. Capitalism, which offered neither the assurance nor the standing that went with land and office, was simply a way, direct and dangerous, of getting rich. . . .

There is no conclusive way of comparing the mass value of proprietary and business wealth in prerevolutionary France. Beginning with what passed in those days for statistics, supplementing them with estimates made by well-informed men who say little about their derivation, making inferences on assumptions which, though reasonable, can be endlessly debated, one concludes that the traditional modes of property—land, buildings, office, and *rentes*—accounted for more than 80 per cent of French private wealth. This indicates a substantial preponderance for the proprietary sector. It is in no way astonishing. The day of heavy fixed industrial investment in factories and railroads, which would have altered the balance, lay far ahead. Meanwhile, most Frenchmen lived on the land, which yielded most of the taxable income and the gross national product. That is why the *économistes* not unreasonably attacked agricultural problems first, often to the neglect of the others.

For our purposes it is desirable to know the relative weight of the two kinds of capital not only for the society as a whole but in the upper Third Estate. Unfortunately, studies of the notarial records are not sufficiently advanced to show this. For the moment, all one can do is count persons, and from this it appears that even in the most heavily commercialized cities the proprietors and professional men in the Third Estate outnumbered the merchants. At Bordeaux, the second most active port, there were 1,100 officials, professionals, *rentiers*, and property owners against only 700 merchants, brokers, and sugar refiners. At Rouen, a prime center of industry, banking, and maritime and wholesale trade, the administrative and judicial officers, professionals, and proprietors-*rentiers* outnumbered the merchants and brokers by more than three to one. At Toulouse, an agricultural, legal, and ecclesiastical capital, the ratio was about eleven to four, but the four included merchants who for the most part traded on small capital and in little volume and did much retail business, so that one hesitates to call them capitalists. There is, however, a further consideration. Because the merchants and industrialists owned, along with their commercial capital, considerable proprietary wealth, we could, with better data, divide them fractionally between the two sectors, and, by such a procedure, the share of commercial and industrial capital in the upper Third Estate would seem much lower than the impression we get by counting heads.

Soundings like these are merely straws in the wind, but they drift always in one direction. They confirm what seems to have been implicit in the consciousness of eighteenth-century France—that even in the well-to-do Third Estate proprietary wealth substantially outweighed commercial and industrial capital. This would not have surprised a Frenchman of the old regime and should not surprise us. The reason for stressing it here is to lay the ground for an assertion that is fundamental in analyzing the causes of the Revolution: there was, between most of the nobility and the proprietary sector of the middle classes, a continuity of investment forms and socioeconomic values that made them, economically, a single group. In the relations of production they played a common role. The differentiation between them was not in any sense economic; it was juridical. This situation, in the historiography of the Revolution, has received practically no serious attention and remains, in Orwellian language, an "unfact." The reason for this is that it contributes nothing to what Cobban rightly calls "the established theory of the French Revolution," the theory that the Revolution was the triumph of capitalism over feudalism. In that context the configuration of proprietary wealth that pervaded both the second and Third Estates has no place and remains unwanted, unused, and therefore, in effect, unknown.

It deserves, however, to be recognized, and its claims are strengthened by bringing forward a second unfact: that a substantial number of nobles participated as entrepreneurs in commerce, industry, and finance. There was indeed, before the Revolution, a *noblesse commerçante*, though not, perhàps, the one that the Abbé Coyer called for in 1756. Provincial, military, and court nobles, peers, and members of the royal family invested in the General Farm, speculated on the Bourse, and developed and exploited mines, canals, and metallurgical establishments, including the great foundry of Le Creusot. On the other hand, there was, to reverse the phrase, a *commerce anobli*, a sizable group of merchants ennobled through the municipal offices of certain cities and the two thousand or more venal offices that conferred nobility on the buyers. For the most part, these ennobled merchant families were in a transitional stage. As enterprises were liquidated, or generations arose that were no longer trained for business, they dropped out of trade to live, as other nobles did, on their revenues. All the same, merchants or not, they were nobles and sat in the noble assemblies of 1789. To sum up, there were nobles who were capitalists. There were merchants who were nobles. As the proprietary wealth traditionally identified with aristocracy extended far down into the Third Estate, so the capitalism traditionally identified with the wealthy Third Estate penetrated into the second, and into its highest ranks.

This means that the old diagram by which we envision prerevolutionary society must be changed. There was a clear juridical boundary that separated nobles from commoners, and a commoner crossed it by registering a legal document, his letters of nobility. On the other hand, the frontier between capitalist and proprietary wealth ran vertically through both orders. The horizontal line marked a legal dichotomy, the vertical line, an economic one. To think of them as coinciding, even roughly, is to misunderstand the situation completely. The concept of two classes, at once economically and juridically disjunct, can be sustained only by ignoring the weight of proprietary wealth in the Third Estate and that of capitalism in the second, or, in other words, by continuing to ostracize them as unfacts. . . .

THE PEASANTRY ON THE EVE OF
THE FRENCH REVOLUTION

Georges Lefebvre

In 1789 the French peasants already held a significant portion of the soil of France; perhaps 30 to 40 per cent on the average, sometimes very much less, sometimes very much more. That is why in comparing them to the serfs of

Georges Lefebvre, "The French Revolution and the Peasants," from *Etudes sur la Révolution française* (Paris, 1954), translation by Ralph W. Greenlaw (ed.), *The Economic Origins of the French Revolution* (Boston, 1958), 76–78, 80–81. © Presses Universitaires de France. Used by permission.

central and eastern Europe who were forced to render uncompensated labor to their lords and to the English agricultural laborers who were free but who were reduced to living on their wages alone, one can describe the French peasants as small independent landholders.

In general nothing is said in discussions of land distribution about those who actually exploited the land—as if it could be assumed that those who owned the land and those who cultivated it were one and the same! This fact is the more striking in that the arrangements under which land was cultivated in France assuredly helped to establish for the French peasant a certain degree of independence with the result that a study of the system of cultivation seems to have the effect of reenforcing conclusions already drawn from a study of the distribution of land ownership. In central and eastern Europe the lords of the great estates had either kept or built up a very extensive domain which they exploited by means of forced labor imposed on their serfs. In England the great landholders by the process of dividing up and parceling out the common lands which was called "enclosure" had created extensive holdings which they exploited by means of agricultural day laborers. In France, the great landholder very rarely undertook the exploitation of his lands directly nor did he have recourse to the practice of enclosure and as a result he rented out his lands either for a monetary rent or on a share-cropping basis in various sized parcels but usually small, and usually as isolated segments of either tillable land, meadow land, or vineyard. Along with the peasant landholder accordingly there were to be found farm tenants and share-croppers and along with them peasants who supplemented their own holdings with lands (of different kinds or for different purposes) which they rented. Finally there were also agricultural day laborers who lived principally on their wages but who generally found some little corner or other of land to rent. In total there existed a very much greater variety of social conditions and differences in degree of independence than one would think from merely taking into consideration the actual ownership of property.

But these rather optimistic conclusions must be rather drastically qualified when two sets of facts which are ordinarily neglected are taken into account. From the point of view of its social and economic implications, the mere size of a piece of land either owned or farmed signifies nothing by itself. It assumes significance only if one compares it to the size of the average amount required to support a family of average size and thereby assure it of economic independence. The second fact that must be considered is that the total number of owners or tillers of land has significance only if compared to the total number of heads of families—a comparison which unfortunately involves a very large margin of error because of the lack of a methodical census. But however imperfect may be the results of these there is no room for doubt as to their general import. The proportion of those who tilled the land, and to an even greater degree the number of peasant landowners, who could live independently, without working for others, was very small in all parts of the country. Accordingly there was a very much larger group of peasants who owned or rented land but who did not have enough to live on and therefore were obliged either to carry on a trade or business or to hire out from time to time as day laborers in order to supplement their income. And finally there was a more or less considerable number of rural inhabitants who had only their wages to live on and when there was no work or the price of bread was too high, there was nothing left for them to do but to resort to begging. . . . In certain regions such as maritime Flanders or in the vicinity of Versailles, heads of families lacking any property or rented land whatsoever amounted to an enormous majority (70 to 75 per cent). In lower Normandy they amounted to at least a third if not more, and on the other hand, in areas where the pattern of land tenure was different, as on the plain of Picardy, the majority of owners and cultivators had only an amount that was clearly insufficient. At the end of the Old Regime, furthermore, the population was increasing very fast and accordingly the agrarian crisis was growing more acute.

This is manifest by the ardor with which the peasants encroached on the common lands or forests in order to build themselves a cottage or to clear small areas so as to add to their tillable land. The *cahiers* very often demanded the sale or lease of portions of the royal domain or even at least a part of the church lands. In this respect the agricultural proletariat and the peasants who already held land, but only an insufficient amount, were in agreement at least in principle. But the crisis also inspired complaints against the whole system of farm land tenure which seemed to come mostly from renters and share-croppers. They called for the dividing up of the great leaseholds and large blocks of land rented to agricultural entrepreneurs for profit, or at least they demanded that the number of small plots available not be decreased. Also they protested against the aggravation of the terms imposed on the leasers of land made possible by the heightening of competition induced by the greater pressure of need. In Picardy the "ill-will" which dated back to the sixteenth century or earlier intensified into a fury against anyone who had the misfortune to replace an evicted tenant. The petitions which were presented during the Revolution; the practices of certain rural communities the boundaries of which included a large proportion of nationalized church lands for which they succeeded in setting up a successful system of collective purchase so that they could be parceled out to small holders; certain practices with respect to communal lands like the *"portions ménagères"* in Flanders and Artois which were let out only on life tenure for a rent paid to the community; or the temporary allotting of certain communal lands in Lorraine; all of these practices leave no doubt as to what was the more or less conscious ideal of the peasant masses. Each one was to have his share; a limited inequality does not seem to have been repugnant to them, especially since some of them were already above a condition of dire need, but there was a certain amount of land which was sufficient to support a family and no one ought to have more than that. Accordingly unused lands, those making up part of the royal domaine, those of the clergy (and later on those of the émigrés) were to serve to provide for the most unfortunate of the community. . . .

It is necessary at this point to recall that the "indigent" and the poor farmer only succeeded in subsisting thanks to the collective rights which, of course, the peasant in easy circumstances or even rich, benefited from as well as they, and even, ordinarily, very much more. There were, for example, the right of grazing cattle on lands where the grain had already been harvested and unenclosed fields; certain rights of usage of the forests; the enjoyment of the common rights of the community, such as the right of gleaning in harvested fields, and the right to collect stubble. . . . All the thinking of the poor peasant . . . tended to limit the rights of individual property in order to defend collective usages which permitted him to live and which he regarded as a property right as sacred as that of others and one which existed to prevent the provisions necessary for his existence from becoming inaccessible to him. It little mattered to him that new arrangements would have increased production since it was he who would have had to pay the price of that progress, while all the benefits—or at least at the beginning—would have accrued to the large-scale farmers who either rented or owned their land and who produced for the market. In short, he opposed with all the force at his disposal the transformation of agriculture into a more capitalistic enterprise.

To free himself from the bother of managing his estates and to assure himself of an increasing or at least a constant income, the seigneur leased out the right to collect the income from his feudal rights just as he farmed out in a block the right to his half of the crop of his share-croppers, or consolidated his leases in the hands of a large-scale leaseholder. This situation was not new, very far from it, but it became more and more frequent. But the one who under this arrangement was to actually collect the payments owed by the peasants naturally was rigorous in exacting them and attempted to increase them. In addition he speculated on the sale of the commodities which came to him as payments in kind. Nothing was more characteristic in this respect than what happened in the case of the forests and the seigneurs' right to graze cattle on the village lands which was peculiar to the eastern region of France and especially to Lorraine. The seigneur would lease out his right to cut wood and his tenant applied himself with zeal to the task of keeping out the peasants; he also leased his right to graze cattle, but whereas when he exercised it himself the peasant suffered very little since the seigneur only occasionally took advantage of it, when he leased out the right to a wealthy leaseholder who was sometimes even an important cattle dealer, everything changed and the village lands were invaded by an enormous herd. As a result the intrusion of capitalism into agriculture was made in part under the cover of feudal rights and made them very much more unbearable. It also perverted their very nature because they had been created to support a seigneur who lived in the midst of his peasants and now they passed into the hands of capitalists who thought only of deriving a profit from them.

But they also increased the income of the seigneur and thereby increased the value of his feudal rights in his eyes and his repugnance to abandon them. Even redemption itself would not have been agreeable to him for where could he invest the capital which he would have received from it? And what form of reinvestment would have offered the same security? The rise in prices combined with the new manner of capitalist exploitation of his feudal rights promised an indefinite increase while money loaned was subject to the risk of loss. But there was a basic conflict between the general intrusion of capitalism into agriculture and the maintenance of feudal rights and the payments made for the use of the land. The suppression of the common right to graze cattle in harvested fields, the fencing in of lands, and the freedom to plant various crops at will could only be obtained quickly if all lands were reassigned in such a way that the domain of the great proprietor, instead of being made up of scattered fields, was consolidated into a compact holding. This is what had been done in England beginning in the fifteenth and six-teenth centuries and especially in the eighteenth century and also in Germany in the first half of the nineteenth century. But in England that operation had been preceded by the disappearance of feudal rights in their literal form and the commutation of labor and monetary obligations into a rent of a fixed amount which had become of less and less importance as the purchasing power of money declined. . . . In France, on the contrary, the feudal rights and monetary obligations remained in existence; certain ground rents were still collected in kind and the conditions which had permitted enclosure in England did not therefore prevail. . . . Moreover, the peasant would have opposed it resolutely and the royal government, which had its own interests and which was not as in England and in the monarchies of Eastern Europe subordinate to the aristocracy in law and fact, would never have consented to be constrained by the interests of that class. But it never had to take a stand on the issue because, as we have said, the seigneurs were too attached to their feudal rights to contemplate a general enclosure law. They did not fail to recognize its advantages and certain of them did carry out some partial redistributions by purchase or escheat when they had the opportunity, but this practice was always exceptional in the eighteenth century. Thus the few edicts of enclosure did not extend to all the provinces and exerted only a limited influence. They sufficed to irritate the peasant but did not succeed in giving to agriculture the impulsion in the direction of capitalism which it had received in England.

IDEAS OF REFORM AMONG THE
FRENCH LOWER CLERGY, 1787–1789

Maurice G. Hutt

The convening of the Assembly of Notables and the prolonged conflict between the government and the *Parlement* of Paris gave rise to a ferment of discussion throughout France during 1787 and 1788. This increased after the publication of the [decree] on 8 August 1788 which gave 1 May 1789 as the date for the opening of an Estates-General. The public debate was greatly encouraged by, and indeed largely carried on in, the innumerable pamphlets which appeared after the king had, in July, invited informed persons to submit memoranda on the proper form and functions of such an assembly. Amid this "avalanche of proposals, complaints, protests and far-fetched schemes" there were a considerable number of pamphlets written by members of the lower clergy. . . . The nature and content of these pamphlets are a valuable indication of the attitude of at least a considerable section—and this an influential section—of the lower clergy on the eve of the Revolution. . . .

The pamphleteers complained bitterly of the gulf between upper and lower clergy, between bishops, abbots and canons on the one hand and curés and vicars on the other. "Let them [the curés' superiors in the hierarchy] allow us to protest forcefully against this distinction between first and second orders which is injurious to both, and which they are not ashamed to call the higher and lower clergy." The lower clergy were poor, hard-working in their vital role yet helpless in the hands of their superiors. The Church was immensely wealthy: its revenue from landed property and the tithe alone amounted to some 150,000,000 *livres*. But if "the corps of the clergy [was] worthy of respect, the administration of its goods [was] vicious." The system of holding benefices *in commendam* [until the appointment of a regular incumbent] resulted in further increases of revenue to bishops and other favored clerics who already prospered as a result of the landed property attached to their offices. "Abbeys, which by their vast size offer an almost necessary source of corruption because need alone cannot consume them," were given to prelates "who already are rolling in wealth." The *commendam* system more than any other single abuse split the clergy into rich and poor. "The clergy of France are divisible into two classes: the officiating incumbent and the commendatories; or to speak more clearly, curés exercising their functions surrounded by the poor who demand their tithes, and the commendatories who have taken these tithes from them." The whole system ought to be abolished, suggested several pamphlets, together with the

Maurice G. Hutt, "The Curés and the Third Estate: The Ideas of Reform in the Pamphlets of the French Lower Clergy in the Period 1787–1789," *Journal of Ecclesiastical History*, VIII (1957), 74–79, 81–83. © Maurice G. Hutt. Used by permission. Quotations translated by editors.

Concordat of 1516 which had given rise to it. Pluralism, "an inexhaustible source of intrigues and attendance at the courts of princes," "unknown in the splendid centuries of the Church . . . [and] as contrary to sound morals as to the law, since a benefice is not awarded except for work . . . ," pluralism must be swept away and with it the system whereby "some die from hunger while others are stuffed with wealth."

The diversion of revenues intended for religious houses into the hands of secular clergymen—for this is the essence of the *commendam* system— undoubtedly increased the gulf between rich and poor clergy, but it was an abuse perpetrated (or so it might seem at first sight) at the expense of the unpopular regular clergy. Far more apparent to the curé and bitterly resented by him was the diversion into the hands of others . . . of tithes which ought to have been paid to him. The *gros décimateurs*, as the tithe-owners were called, had certain obligations, the chief of which was the payment of a *portion congrue* [annual wage] to the incumbent. . . . The *portion congrue* had been raised in 1768 to 500 *livres* for curés and 200 *livres* for vicars. . . . In 1786 the *portion congrue* was raised to 700 *livres*. But this was still unsatisfactory. . . . His increased salary resulted in the congruist being moved into a higher class for the purposes of clerical taxation. The increase in 1786 moved him higher still, and by this time the real value of his salary had sadly declined. . . . "No one can fail to recognize that at the prices to which all the necessities of life—food and clothing—had gradually risen over the years, 700 *livres* was not adequate for a man who had to live at home, and to feed and pay a servant. . . . Who would dare say that 700 *livres* can feed and support two persons?" Taxation took 60 *livres*, a housekeeper the same, and food, including special food for fast-days, 200 *livres*. Heating, drink and corn took another 380 *livres* and still the curé had to find not merely for his own needs, for salt, spices and linen, but also provide alms for the poor whom the lord of the parish and the owner of the tithes only too rarely helped. The *portion congrue* must be raised and this could best be done, suggested some pamphlets, by *bénéfices simples*, benefices which, being "without any obligation save that of conscience," formed merely an additional source of income to favored clergy, and represented another grave abuse in the Church. But far more pamphlets attacked the very basis of the system. Why should the tithe go to the [large benefice holders] "the majority [of whom] are only famous do-nothings [who] spend the heritage of the poor for their own luxury and pleasures." "Let the curés . . . be provided with landed property of the church, and the curés and vicars no longer be dependent for their livelihood on the tithe owners." . . .

The financial position of the lower clergy was made worse by the fact that they were over-taxed. . . . It was not impossible for a bishop to escape taxation altogether with a diocesan office's connivance. The curé who complained could not hope to have justice done him by the *chambres supérieures de décimes* [high chambers for the tithe] . . . which heard appeals in cases which the diocesan offices could not judge themselves. In these appeal courts "we [the curés] have but one representative, who has only a weak voice and who in almost every diocese is chosen by the bishop, and who is loyal to him and the office." . . .

This was the basic trouble. "If up to the present time the lower clergy have not had sufficient resources, if they have supported practically the whole burden of clerical taxation, even though they possess only a very small portion of the Church's goods, it is because they have never been adequately represented [in the administrative organization of the Clergy of France] and because the upper clergy have always been able to lay down the law." The upper clergy were not merely unduly rich and idle, but they also had in their exclusive control the Church's administration. Despite their vital importance in the religious role of the Church—"nothing is more admirable or more obviously useful than a good curé in the midst of his parish" was bishop Thémines's tribute—and despite their security in office and status as ordinaries of their own curés, the curés were no longer consulted by the bishops as they had been in the pristine days of the Church. . . .

Resentment against the wealthy, powerful upper clergy on the part of the curés was greatly enhanced by the fact that during the eighteenth century high office in the Church had come to be the perquisite of the aristocracy. Comment was bitter upon what one pamphleteer terms "the aristocratic ascendancy of the nobility within the clergy." Charity and humility were the necessary qualities of a bishop, not nobility of birth. "Let us leave to the nobles their right of bearing the sword against enemies of the state. . . . But if they wish to be soldiers of Jesus Christ let them forget their titles and pretensions." Noble chapters ought to be subjected to the same rules as all other chapters in the future. "Thus a count of the Lyons chapter would have to add to the proof of his sixteen quarterings of nobility that of twelve years of [pastoral] work; the latter title would doubtless be just as valuable as the former."

This resentment against an aristocratic episcopate was no doubt largely due to class antagonism purely and simply. "It is the revolting haughtiness with which they treat the curés, the commoner priests and the monks"—the "haughtiness" natural to their class—which helped to make the prelates unpopular. But pride was not the only fault of the aristocracy which was out of place in the Church. The aristocracy loved court and Parisian society. The result was non-residence on the part of many prelates. This meant far more than that the bishop took out of his diocese the wealth that might otherwise have helped to stimulate trade there. . . . Far more important was that "your being far off brings about the perishing of souls whose salvation is entrusted to you" just as "your luxurious living kills the poor whom it deprives of bread." . . .

It may be concluded from a study of these clerical pamphlets that the motive of the protesters was not a selfish one but a genuine desire to have the Faith better taught and their own flocks better cared for. Certainly there were those among the lower clergy who declaimed against the undue wealth of the prelates and abbots because they themselves could never attain to such luxury. But there was, far more important, a deeply rooted objection based on moral grounds. The regular canon Ducastelier voices this objection in the opening words of his pamphlet: "The gold in the temples corrupts everything." "It is time to bring ecclesiastics back to their primitive state, to remind them of the principles of the evangelical law." . . .

SUGGESTIONS FOR FURTHER READING

ELINOR G. BARBER, *The Bourgeoisie in 18th Century France* (Princeton, 1955); HENRI CARRÉ, *La Noblesse de France et l'opinion publique au XVIIIe siècle* (Paris, 1920); ALFRED COBBAN, *The Social Interpretation of the French Revolution* (Cambridge, Eng., 1964); JEAN EGRET, "L'Aristocratie parlementaire française à la fin de l'ancien régime," *Revue historique*, CCVIII (1952), 1–14; ADELINE DAUMARD and FRANÇOIS FURET, *Structures et relations sociales à Paris au XVIIIe siècle* (Paris, 1961); FRANKLIN L. FORD, *Strasbourg in Transition, 1648–1789* (Cambridge, Mass., 1958); ROBERT FORSTER, *The Nobility of Toulouse in the Eighteenth Century: A Social and Economic Study* (Baltimore, 1960); NORMAN HAMPSON, *A Social History of the French Revolution* (London, 1963); JEFFRY KAPLOW, *New Perspectives on the French Revolution: Readings in Historical Sociology* (New York, 1965); GEORGES LEFEBVRE, *Les Paysans du Nord pendant la Révolution française* (Paris, 1924; 2nd ed.; Bari, Italy, 1959); EMILE LÉONARD, "La question sociale dans l'armée française au XVIIIe siècle," *Annales: Economies—Sociétés—Civilisations*, III (1948), 135–149; PHILIPPE SAGNAC, *La Formation de la société française moderne*, 2 vol. (Paris, 1945–46); HENRI SÉE, *Economic and Social Conditions in France during the Eighteenth Century* (New York, 1927); ALBERT SOBOUL, *France à la veille de la Révolution*, 2 vol. (Paris, 1960).

Chapter Two

THE ENLIGHTENMENT

THE ENLIGHTENMENT refers to the European intellectual movement of the eighteenth century which sought to destroy long-held "myths" in order to arrive at a clearer understanding of man's physical and moral universe. Criticism of the old was the prelude to discovery of the new, and the Age of Enlightenment might as appropriately be called the Age of Criticism.

In the first selection, Crane Brinton detects "desertion," or what we now term "alienation," of intellectuals as a recurring trait of prerevolutionary societies. The *philosophes* were dissatisfied with existing conditions of the Old Regime and criticized modes of thought and institutions which appeared to them to be antiquated, irrational, useless, or unjust. Reason independent of faith, with utility as its standard, interest in the present world as opposed to heaven, progress in ameliorating man's present state—these were the ideals of the Enlightenment. The Enlightenment began primarily as a critique of traditional, revealed Christianity which was thought to be in conflict with scientific and historical truths. Some of the titles of works by the seventeenth-century forerunners of the Enlightenment alone give a sufficient idea of its initial direction: Fontenelle's *Conversations on the Plurality of Worlds* (1686) and *History of Oracles and the Cheats of the Pagan Priests* (1687), and Pierre Bayle's *Miscellaneous Thoughts on the Comet* (1682). The first work was a satire on popular misconceptions of the planetary systems and the religious reaction against the Copernican system. The second took its inspiration from the rediscovery of classical antiquity and pagan religions which seemed to contain superstitions and frauds which the *philosophes* compared to Christianity. The third was a critique of the whole notion of tradition as a valid source of knowledge: "It is pure illusion to claim that a notion that has passed from one century to the next, from generation to generation, cannot be entirely false." Religion was subjected to a rigorous examination by science and history. Hence the Enlightenment represents a far more thorough break with the past than either the Renaissance or the Protestant Reformation. The first revived classical antiquity but managed to allow this revival to coexist with Christianity; the second rejected papal authority, yet substituted for it the authority of the Bible. Although each accorded the individual a larger role, both movements operated within the Christian tradition. By contrast, the Enlightenment meant an attack on the foundations of Christianity because it substituted reason for authority and tradition.

In a society where censorship was the rule, the Enlightenment was forced to carry on its polemic surreptitiously—through the use of dialogues, travel literature, and encyclopedias. Because the Church maintained that she had been entrusted with revealed truths incomparable to pre- or non-Christian religions (truths which could be attained only through faith, which the Church must preserve from generation to generation), she felt justified in using the arm of the state to impose censorship and imprisonment and thus protect mankind from error. The *philosophes* contested the supernatural basis of these claims to authority, and hence there developed the second major theme of the Enlightenment campaign—"crushing the infamous thing" and establishing civil rights and tolerance. The "infamous thing" was the "fanaticism" identified with the Church and the state, which supported it. This was the message of Voltaire in the middle decades of the eighteenth century.

The second selection, by Professor Peter Gay of Columbia University, illustrates the complexity of the *philosophe*'s relationship to the society he lived in and to the tradition he was abandoning. Although Professor Gay emphasizes the anti-Christian elements in the Enlightenment, he also takes pains to show that this movement was gradual and almost unconscious: "France was a Christian culture that was rapidly losing its Christian vocation without being fully aware of it," and "the *philosophes* . . . much as they wished to change it, were at home in their world."

In the third selection, Professor R. R. Palmer of Princeton University, substantiates the claims of both Professors Brinton and Gay. Through statistical analysis of the Jesuit *Journal de Trévoux* from 1702 to 1760, he concludes that the editors were not so rigorously opposed to the Enlightenment as has often been imagined and that their journal shows a marked increase in the publication of "art and letters," "practical and technical works," and "social studies," as opposed to the earlier predominance of religion and history—a tendency which reflects the general trends of the Enlightenment itself. Thus, Professor Palmer illustrates the corollary of Professor Gay's point that just as the *philosophes* were not totally removed from their society, so the Jesuits were not totally immune to the developments of the Enlightenment. At the same time, the marked increase in literature on the social sciences indicates the growing concern and implicit dissatisfaction with the state of society which Professor Brinton sees as the foreshadowing of desertion. The analyses of these three scholars complement each other and thereby show the Enlightenment in its true complexity.

Although the Enlightenment may appear modern by reason of its criticism of religious intolerance and its campaign on behalf of basic human freedoms, it was no harbinger of democracy. Everett C. Ladd, Jr., of Connecticut College, examines the political doctrine of two eminent *philosophes* and makes it clear that not only was Voltaire a proponent of absolute monarchy, but also that two thinkers traditionally considered more liberal and democratic, Helvétius and d'Holbach, were monarchists as well. Professor Ladd's study indicates still another instance of the *philosophes*' acceptance of the world they lived in.

The causal relationship (if any) between the Enlightenment and the Revolution is an important and difficult question. For a long time it was the contention of the Counterrevolution that the *philosophes* actually plotted the downfall of the Old Regime. The connection between the actions of Robespierre and the thought of Diderot and Rousseau, and the whole philosophical "sect" indiscriminately lumped together, was deemed apparent and certain. The facts that the *philosophes* were by and large not democrats and that the one work which openly avowed popular government—*The Social Contract*—was Rousseau's least read work before the Revolution, seem to refute the idea that the *philosophes* caused the Revolution. Yet Professor Henri Peyre of Yale University, a leading authority on modern French literature, elucidates in an ingenious fashion how the influence of an author and the interpretation of his work is often at variance with what he originally said. For the historian of ideas, the deformation of thought and its popularization are as important as, if not more important than, the correct inter-pretation of the ideas of "great thinkers."

Durand Echeverria's study of the role of America in the French Enlightenment shows that if the *philosophes* did not openly espouse democracy, they celebrated it vicariously through their avid interest in and sympathy for the American Revolution. But it was not only the *philosophes* who espoused it; no event stimulated more general interest. The American Revolution diffused democratic ideals among the reading public. To paraphrase Professor Gay, "The French were rapidly becoming democratic without being fully aware of it."

The Enlightenment marks a significant revolution in modern European thought. Its proponents were substituting new criteria of thought and behavior which departed more radically from tradition than the principles of their Protestant or Renaissance forebears. Although its break with the institutions and beliefs of the Old Regime was less thorough and more indirect than has been thought, it nevertheless became the public creed of the Revolution and of nineteenth-century liberal and radical thought.

༄

DESERTION OF INTELLECTUALS AND NOBLES AS A PREREVOLUTIONARY PHENOMENON

CRANE BRINTON

We must . . . be clear as to what we are talking about before we attempt to use the desertion of the intellectuals as a symptom. Intellectuals we may define without undue worry over preciseness as the writers, artists, musicians, actors, teachers, and preachers. Further subdivision into the small group of leaders who initiate, or at least stand prominently in the public eye, and the larger group who grind over material they get from the leaders, is not of major importance here. What is important, and somewhat puzzling, is the general position of the intellectuals in our Western society since the Middle Ages. Clearly we must not posit agreement among its intellectuals before we decide that a given society is reasonably stable. Even in the thirteenth century, in which so many of our contemporary thinkers find an enviable unanimity as to fundamentals of belief, the amount of bickering among the intellectuals was in reality very considerable. . . .

[But] quantitatively, we may say that in a society markedly unstable

From the book *The Anatomy of Revolution* by Crane Brinton, pp. 45–48, 50–51, 53, 43, 56–58, 52. © 1952 by Prentice-Hall, Inc., Englewood Cliffs, New Jersey. Used by permission.

there seem to be absolutely more intellectuals, at any rate comparatively more intellectuals, bitterly attacking existing institutions and desirous of a considerable alteration in society, business, and government. Purely metaphorically, we may compare intellectuals of this sort to the white corpuscles, guardians of the bloodstream; but there can be an excess of white corpuscles, and when this happens you have a diseased condition.

Qualitatively, we may discern a difference of attitude, partly, no doubt, produced by the numbers and unity of these intellectuals in attack, but partly produced by a subtler reality. Victorian England, for instance, was a society in equilibrium, an equilibrium that looks in retrospect a bit unstable, but still an equilibrium. Here Carlyle upbraided a generation addicted to Morison's Pills instead of to heroes, Mill worried uncomfortably over the tyranny of the majority, Matthew Arnold found England short of sweetness and light, Newman sought at Rome an antidote for the poison of English liberalism, Morris urged his countrymen to break up machines and return to the comforts of the Middle Ages, and even Tennyson was worried over his failure to attain to anything more useful than a high, vague, and philosophical discontent. . . .

. . . If we look at that famous group in eighteenth-century France which stood at the center of the great Enlightenment, [we have] first the impression of immense numbers of intellectuals, great and small, all studying matters political and sociological, all convinced that the world, and especially France, needs making over from the tiniest and more insignificant details to the most general moral and legal principles. Any of the textbooks will give you the roll—Voltaire, Rousseau, Diderot, Raynal, d'Holbach, Volney, Helvétius, d'Alembert, Condorcet, Bernardin de St. Pierre, Beaumarchais—rebels all, men leveling their wit against Church and State or seeking in Nature a perfection that ought to be in France. You will hardly find active literary conservatives like Sam Johnson or Sir Walter Scott, or even literary neutrals, men pursuing in letters a beauty or an understanding quite outside politics. Even the now almost forgotten opponents of the *philosophes*, even the pessimists who deny the doctrine of progress, are doctrinaire intellectuals, as unreasonable devotees of *la raison* as the radicals.

Literature in late eighteenth-century France is overwhelmingly sociological. If you look in the yellowing remains of French eighteenth-century journalism, if you try to reconstruct the chatter of salons and clubs, you will find the same chorus of complaints and criticisms of existing institutions; the same search for Nature's simple plan of perfection in politics. There is both a bitterness and a completeness in this chorus of complaint that you will not find in Victorian complaints. Statistically, one might establish the fact that there were proportionately more intellectuals "against the government" in eighteenth-century France than in nineteenth-century England. . . .

To what did our successfully revolutionary intellectuals desert? To another and better world than that of the corrupt and inefficient old regimes. From a thousand pens and voices there are built up in the years before the revolution actually breaks out what one must now fashionably call the foundations of the revolutionary myth—or folklore, or symbols, or ideology. Some such better world of the ideal is contrasted with this immediate and imperfect world in all the ethical and religious systems under which Western men have lived, and notably in Christianity. It is not quite accurate to assert that for medieval Christianity the other, ideal world is safely put off to heaven. Yet it is clear that with the Reformation and the Renaissance men began to think more earnestly about bringing part of heaven, at any rate, to this earth. What differentiates this ideal world of our revolutionaries from the better world as conceived by more pedestrian persons is a flaming sense of the immediacy of the ideal, a feeling that there is something in all men better than their present fate, and a conviction that what is, not only ought not, but need not be. . . .

. . . A great deal of energy has been expended on the question as to whether this revolutionary ideology "causes" revolutionary action, or whether it is merely a sort of superfluous decoration with which the revolutionists cover their real acts and real motives. Most of this discussion is in the highest degree futile, since it is based on a crude notion of causation altogether untenable in fruitful scientific work beyond a very simple level. There is no more point disputing whether Rousseau made the French Revolution or the French Revolution made Rousseau than in disputing whether egg or chicken came first. We note that in our prerevolutionary societies the kind of discontents, the specific difficulties about economic, social, and political conditions that hardboiled moderns focus on are invariably accompanied by a very great deal of writing and talking about ideals, about a better world, about some very abstract forces tending to bring about that better world. It is, indeed, the *expression* of ideas, rather than particular ideas—which may vary enormously in different revolutions—that makes the uniformity. We find that ideas are always a part of the prerevolutionary situation, and we are quite content to let it go at that. No ideas, no revolution. This does not mean that ideas *cause* revolutions, or that the best way to prevent revolutions is to censor ideas. It merely means that ideas form part of the mutually dependent variables we are studying. . . .

In France, the work of Cochin has shown how what he called the *sociétés de pensée*, informal groups gathered together to discuss the great work of the Enlightenment, gradually turned to political agitation and finally helped steer elections to the Estates-General of 1789. Though the official school of historians in the Third Republic has always distrusted the notion that their great revolution was planned at all in advance, it is difficult for an outsider not to feel that Cochin has put his finger on the essential form of group action which turned mere talk and speculation into revolutionary political work. Freemasonry, even French republican historians admit, had a place in the preparation of the revolution. Masonic activity in eighteenth-century France was clearly no dark plot, but it certainly was far from being purely social, recreational, or educational. Almost all the ambitious nobles and bankers, almost all the intellectuals, were freemasons. Even at the time, clerical conservatives were shocked at what they considered the subversive aspects of freemasonry. . . .

When numerous and influential members of such a class begin to believe that they hold power unjustly, or that all men are brothers, equal in the eyes of eternal justice, or that the beliefs they were brought up on are silly, or that "after us the deluge," they are not likely to resist successfully any serious attacks on their social, economic, and political position. The subject of the decadence of a ruling class, and the relation of this decadence to revolution, is a fascinating and, like so much of historical sociology, a relatively unexplored subject. We can here do no more than suggest that this decadence is not necessarily a "moral" decadence if by "moral" you mean what a good evangelical Christian means by that word. Successful ruling classes have not infrequently been quite addicted to cruel sports, drinking, gambling, adultery, and other similar pursuits which we should no doubt all agree to condemn. It is a reasonable assertion that the virtuous Lafayette was a much clearer sign of the unfitness of the French aristocracy to rule than were Pompadour or even Du Barry. . . .

The salons in which the old regime was torn apart—verbally, of course —were often presided over by noblewomen and attended by noblemen. Princes of the blood royal became freemasons, and if they did not quite plot the overthrow of all decency, as frightened Tories like Mrs. Nesta Webster seem to think, at least sought to improve themselves out of their privileges and rank. Perhaps nowhere better than in France is to be seen one of the concomitants of the kind of disintegration of the ruling class we have been discussing. This is the deliberate espousal by members of the ruling class of the cause of discontented or repressed classes—upperdogs voluntarily siding with underdogs. It is not altogether cynical to hazard the guess that this is sometimes an indication that there is about to be a reversal in the position of the dogs. Lafayette is in some ways a good example of this kind of upperdog, since he seems to have been an unintelligent and ambitious man, whose course was largely determined by fashion. Lafayette tried to do what his own circle would most admire, and since he could not dance well—and his circle admired good dancing—he went to fight for freedom in America, which was also something his circle admired. But ruling classes cannot profitably fight for freedom—freedom, that is, for the other fellow.

Once again, however, it is necessary to point out that the existence of rebellious radicals in the upper classes is only one symptom in a complicated syndrome. Such upper-class mavericks must be relatively numerous as well as conspicuous in a society in disequilibrium. They, and the wasters and the cynics, must *set the tone* for the class. . . .

The present upperdog can be shown—perhaps for propaganda purposes *must* be shown—to have acquired his preponderance by an accident, or a particularly dirty trick, while God or nature was temporarily off duty. . . . The French were told by no less a person than Siéyès that all their trouble came from the usurpations of the Franks over a thousand years ago. French noblemen in 1789 were descendants of barbarous Germans, while French commoners were descendants of civilized Gauls and Romans. Revolution was but restoring the conditions of 450 A.D. Marxism explained the exploiting class without recourse to such pseudo-historical notions. And yet there is plenty of reference in Russian revolutionary agitation to the usurpation of land by the nobles, to their Varangian, or Tartar, or Western, or at any rate foreign origins. Present evil as well as future good needs the strengthening force of what Sorel called the "myth." . . .

THE PHILOSOPHES AND THEIR ENVIRONMENT

PETER GAY

The *philosophes* were men of letters. This is more than a phrase. It defines their vantage point, and eliminates the stale debate over their status as philosophers. As men of letters who took their craft seriously, they devoted to their writing an incessant care which is one of the secrets of their style. Their output was enormous, and they sent less to the printer than they threw away. They knew the pleasure of self-criticism, and the sweeter pleasure of criticizing others. Grimm corrected Diderot, Diderot corrected Voltaire, and Voltaire corrected everybody. Rousseau, far from tossing off his masterpieces in a fit of feverish inspiration, struggled with them for years; Voltaire rewrote untiringly, and treated first editions as drafts to be recast in the next printing; Diderot poured early versions of articles into his letters to Sophie Volland. While there is no single Enlightenment style, all *philosophes* had style.

This devotion to the art of writing gave the *philosophes* the strength that comes from membership in a respectable guild; it gave them, for all their quarrels, common interests and a common vision. No matter how varied their concerns, they were men with a single career. To attribute two

Peter Gay, *The Party of Humanity, Essays in the French Enlightenment* (New York: Alfred A. Knopf, 1964), pp. 117–124. © by Peter Gay. Used by permission.

careers to Voltaire—the irresponsible *littérateur* before the Calas case, the grim reformer after—is to misunderstand the unity of his life. Of course, the *philosophes'* versatility opens them to the charge of dilettantism, and it is true that they sometimes tried to teach what they had not learned—as writers will. But the range of their knowledge was extraordinary. Diderot translated works on medicine and ethics; wrote articles on crafts, industry, philosophy, theology, history, politics, classical and modern literature; rode editorial herd on a stable of willful encyclopedists; broke new paths in the bourgeois drama, in dramatic and art criticism, the novel and the dialogue. Voltaire took an informed and passionate interest in all the countries of Europe and all the countries of the mind.

Yet the *philosophes* were never so deeply engaged in politics to neglect literature, and they were never so deeply engaged in literature to neglect the society in which they lived. While they were literary men, they were neither bohemians nor alienated artists. While their view of their world was critical, and especially in religion, disruptive, they knew and loved the world they wished to change. Rousseau in some moods rejected it altogether, and asked for man's total regeneration, but it is significant that his fellow *philosophes* treated him as a madman long before his clinical symptoms became obvious. When they denounced civilization, they did so urbanely.

The *philosophes*, then, much as they wished to change it, were at home in their world. To divide the century into two sharply defined forces— the subversive *philosophes* against the orthodox—may be convenient and dramatic, but it is also much too simple. There were moments of crisis when two parties crystallized and Catholics squared off against unbelievers, but subtler and more pervasive than hostility were the ties that bound the *philosophes* to their society. They edited respectable magazines, flattered royal mistresses, wrote unexceptionable entertainments, and held responsible posts.

Nor was their attachment to the existing order based solely on calcula- tion: they shared with literate Christians a religious education, a love for the classics of Roman and French literature, and an affection for the pleasures of cultivated leisure. Seeking to distinguish themselves, they did not wish to abolish all distinctions. When they participated in politics, they often sup- ported one orthodox party against another: Montesquieu, the *parlements* against the king; Voltaire, the king against the *parlements*. While they helped to prepare the way for the Jacobins, they were not Jacobins themselves.

Their attachment was strengthened by their association with a spectrum of would-be *philosophes*, half-*philosophes*, or Christians liberal enough to tolerate, or even to enjoy, men whose doctrines they rejected. Hangers-on, who basked in borrowed glory or second-hand notoriety, smuggled *philo- sophes'* letters, arranged for theatrical claques, and offered true friendship in a quarrelsome world. Strategically placed officials stood between *philosophes* and the severities of the law, and good Christians who dabbled in higher criticism or polite anticlericalism spread philosophic doctrines in respectable circles. In brief, the *philosophes* were deeply embedded in the texture of their society.

Yet this did not prevent them from being at war with it at the same time. The *philosophes* never developed a coherent political program or even a consistent line of political tactics, but their polemics called for a France profoundly different from the country in which they lived—France after, not before, 1791. The regime could make concessions: boredom, a lost sense of purpose, could make many a bourgeois, priest, or aristocrat receptive to subversive propaganda. But aggressive deism or materialism, doctrines of the rule of law, complete toleration, and subordination of church to state—these tenets could not be assimilated by the old order. To neglect either side of their dual situation is to make the *philosophes* more revolutionary or more conservative than in fact they were.

This tension, which is yet not alienation, places not only the *philosophes* in their century, it places the century itself. To say that the eighteenth century was an age of contradictions, is to say nothing: all ages have this characteristic in common. We must be specific: eighteenth-century France was a Christian culture that was rapidly losing its Christian vocation without being fully aware of it.

"One day," writes Paul Hazard, "the French people, almost to a man, were thinking like Bossuet. The day after, they were thinking like Voltaire." This is doubly wrong. The *philosophes* had much opposition among the educated and the powerful. While the writings of Montesquieu, Voltaire, and Diderot have survived, those of their adversaries have not, but survival is an unreliable guide to the intellectual map of the past: in the age of Louis XV Christianity had many a persuasive and intelligent defender. Moreover, we cannot properly speak of a "French people" in the eighteenth century. Most Frenchmen were wholly untouched by the Enlightenment and lived, as it were, in an earlier century. They believed in witches, applied spells, used home remedies long condemned by physicians, displayed a trust in authority long discarded by the educated, lived and died happily ignorant of the battles between Cartesians and Newtonians.

Yet for men sensitive or educated enough to be aware of intellectual currents, the eighteenth century was a time of turmoil. A whole complex of ideas and experiences, usually lumped together in the slippery word "secularization," came together in the reign of Louis XV to haunt thinking men. The literature of travel offered the spectacle of happy and civilized non-Christian cultures; the demands of international politics forged secular rather than sectarian alliances; the growth of the European economy stimulated the desire for worldly goods; the great discoveries of science suggested the appalling possibility of a universe without God.

Secularization did not mean the death of religion. Eight Frenchmen out of ten—perhaps nine—were uncontaminated by skepticism. Even the businessman or artisan, who greatly benefited from advances in technology, rarely allowed them to affect his faith. Still, what Troeltsch has called the "Church-directed civilization" was crumbling. Christians lived by the image of hierarchy: as God, his angels, and his creatures were arranged in an order of rank, so by analogy the skies, the family, law, society, the Church, were naturally hierarchical. Now, as natural scientists demonstrated that the hierarchies of terrestrial and celestial motion, or the spheres of the heavens, were absurd, other revolutionaries were exposing the absurdity of other hierarchies.

In this time of trouble the two great hierarchical institutions, the Church and the nobility, did little to counteract this exposure. It is easy to exaggerate the worldliness of the eighteenth-century cleric or the uselessness of the eighteenth-century nobleman. Too much has been written about the atheist abbé and the idle marquis. There were many aristocrats who served their country ably, and who rose above the interests of their order to advocate truly national policies. Yet as the history of eighteenth-century France demonstrates, the French aristocracy was on the whole unwilling to make the sacrifices necessary to integrate it into a state that required some centralization of power and some revision of the tax structure. Born in an age that had given it a social function, the aristocratic caste was losing its vocation, as embittered renegades like the marquis D'Argenson did not fail to point out.

A similar loss of vocation threatened the Church. Thousands of priests fulfilled their offices with devotion; even some bishops believed in God. But in a time when natural philosophers were offering alternative explanations of the origins of man, the nature of evil, and the purpose of life, the Church needed a firmness of character, adroitness, and above all a unity that it could not muster. Many a young man of talent went into the opposition, and used the dialectical skill and classical learning imparted by his priestly instructors for their destruction.

Still, for all the impiety of the age, religion survived, and one reason for its survival was that the famous war between science and theology did not take place in the simple form familiar to us from the Whig Interpretation. The warfare began not between theology and science, but theology and some philosophical consequences drawn from science. It was not necessary to accept d'Alembert's positivism to be a good mathematician; or to be driven by Voltaire's anticlerical spleen to be a good Newtonian. Science, travel, politics, wealth, the great secularizing forces, did their work by indirection, as it were, behind the century's back.

Still they did their work, and they did it in the eighteenth century. In a celebrated book Paul Hazard has expended much learning to establish a crisis in the European conscience before 1715. It is true that practically all the most aggressive ideas of eighteenth-century propagandists had a prehistory, but they did not touch a significant number of people until well after Newton's death in 1727. The typical seventeenth-century scientist was a good Christian: he was a Pascal, not a Hobbes. By separating theology from natural philosophy, or by ingeniously arguing that natural philosophy *supported* theology, seventeenth-century scientists concealed from themselves, as much as from others, the revolutionary implications of their work. It is a commonplace, but one all too often forgotten, that the geniuses from Galileo to Newton lived comfortably with convictions that eighteenth-century *philosophes* would stigmatize as incompatible. John Donne's famous and too much quoted lament that "new philosophy calls all in doubt," was the exceptional response of an exceptional man. In general, the imagination of the seventeenth century was unaffected, or generously expanded, by the new universe glimpsed in the new instruments. For Newton, God was active in the universe, occasionally correcting the irregularities of the solar system. The Newtonian heavens proclaimed God's glory.

This happy marriage of theism and science was not dissolved until the eighteenth century, when the discoveries of the age of genius were pushed to their logical conclusion. "Once the foundation of a revolution has been laid down," d'Alembert wrote in the *Encyclopédie*, "it is almost always in the next generation that the revolution is accomplished." Several brilliant French mathematicians, d'Alembert among them, generalized Newton's laws of gravitation far beyond Newton's wishes. By the last quarter of the century, Lagrange and Laplace had established, in elegant equations, the stability of the solar system. The goal of eighteenth-century science had become evident: Newton's physics without Newton's God.

The crisis of secularization, then, was slower and subtler than we have been led to believe. It was also more pervasive. It was not confined to educated Christians, tormented by the startling conclusions of physicists. It was a problem for the *philosophes* themselves. It is not surprising that their anguish has received little attention—they covered it well with urbanity and noisy anticlericalism.

But anguish there was. The *philosophes* had two enemies: the institutions of Christianity and the idea of hierarchy. And they had two problems: God and the masses. Both the enemies and the problems were related and woven into the single task of rethinking their world. The old questions that Christianity had answered so fully for so many men and so many centuries, had to be asked anew: What—as Kant put it—what can I know? What ought I to do? What may I hope?

Science itself did not answer these questions. It only suggested—ever more insistently as the century went on—that the old answers were wrong. Now, the *philosophes* were products of Christian homes and Christian schools. If they became enemies of Christianity, they did so not from indifference or ignorance: they knew their Bible, their catechism, their Church Fathers, their apologetics. And they knew, because it had been drummed into them early, the fate that awaits heretics or atheists in the world to come. Their anticlerical humor therefore has the bitter intimacy of the family joke; to embrace materialism was an act of rejection.

The struggle of the *philosophes* was a struggle for freedom. They did not fully understand it, but to the extent that they did understand it, they knew their situation to be filled with terror and delight. They felt the anxiety and exhilaration of the explorer who stands before the unknown. . . .

THE FRENCH JESUITS IN THE AGE OF ENLIGHTENMENT

R. R. PALMER

Too often we think of the eighteenth century in France as a time when two distinct groups were pitted against each other, a group of *philosophes* who favored new and enlightened ideas and another group, mostly clerical and frequently Jesuit, who stood directly across the path of intellectual advancement. This view of the matter is essentially that of the *philosophes* themselves. It has perpetuated itself among us, with modifications, because few historians outside of France have examined the Catholic writers of the period. We have easily supposed that these writers were the obscurantists that the *philosophes* called them, because we have generally approved of the liberal and critical spirit which the *philosophes* preached. But this very spirit must in the end prompt us to reconsider. We must consult the Catholic writers if only to restore the balance. By doing so we may also learn more precisely what the "enlightenment" of the eighteenth century was. It was not simply the war cry of a party or an issue that divided men into two camps; it was a readjustment of ideas that affected all educated persons, including those who remained faithful to the church.

From the huge body of Catholic writings of the time, the *Journal de Trévoux* is worth singling out for special study. It was edited by the Jesuits of the college of Louis-le-Grand, the famous school (part of the University of Paris) where Voltaire, Diderot, and many other notables received their education. The journal was launched under the auspices of the Duc de Maine, Louis XIV's natural son, who wished to emulate his father as a patron of letters and to make famous his principality of Dombes, a small district

R. R. Palmer, "The French Jesuits in the Age of Enlightenment," *American Historical Review*, XLV (1939), 44–46, 49, 51–58. © R. R. Palmer. Used by permission of the author.

north of Lyons. At Trévoux in Dombes, therefore, the journal was published until 1731. The editors took as a model the *Journal des savants*, the only older French periodical of this kind. The purpose of both journals was to make the new learning available to general readers by giving excerpts, abridgments, and critical judgments of new books and to promote knowledge by serving as a forum where the learned world could communicate by letters and miscellaneous announcements. The Jesuits, being an organized body engaged in teaching and research and having as regular correspondents their fellows throughout Europe, America, and Asia, were in an especially favorable position for editing such a journal. In addition, the new editors declared their purpose to be the defense of the Catholic religion. But they announced that, except on the matter of theological error, they would treat the works of heretics and unbelievers in an unpartisan spirit.

Beginning in the first month of the eighteenth century, January, 1701, and continuing, as a Jesuit organ, until April, 1762, a few months before the Society of Jesus became illegal in France, the *Journal de Trévoux* covers the important years of the rise and spread of the Enlightenment. Its circulation cannot be estimated, but its success may be judged from the fact that in the mid-century reprints and translations of whole volumes were published in Italy and Holland. Two booksellers about 1750 considered reprinting the complete collection of all numbers since 1701; various individuals proposed making a general index; a large anthology of selected articles was issued by an admirer. In 1762, when the government proscribed the Jesuit order, it sought to induce the editor, Berthier, to continue publication privately, offering a property right in the journal to him and his heirs. From such indications it seems fair to assume that the *Journal de Trévoux* was one of the most widely read and highly valued periodicals in France. It reflects to some indeterminate extent the changing interests of the reading public to whom it was addressed. It reveals more definitely the intellectual life of the Rue Saint-Jacques, to which, then as now, much of France looked for its schooling.

In sixty-two years the editors turned out 150,000 printed pages and dealt with some twelve thousand items, most of which were printed books. It is desirable to know what these twelve thousand books and other items were about, and what kinds of items rose or fell in importance during the sixty-two years. This knowledge may be had only by classification and counting. Statistical method, not usually very helpful to the historian of ideas, seems here to have a legitimate use. The items in question are sufficiently similar to be counted; they are numerous enough for chance vagaries to be minimized; and the period in question is long enough to establish a trend. . . .

The reader . . . will see that the Jesuit editors dealt with all kinds of subjects, and he may note, if interested, that the *Journal de Trévoux* is a rich storehouse of eighteenth century bibliography. . . .

The most striking fact is . . . seen to be the decline in religious items, only halted after 1750. This is the most uniform and constant trend to be observed in the whole period. Does it mean that the people whose sentiments the *Journal de Trévoux* reflects were really becoming less religious? Some answer is furnished by examining the constituent categories under "Religion." . . . The loss is shown . . . to have been most steady and most sweeping in doctrinal religion. There are rises in 1710 and in 1730, probably due to the Jansenist troubles; after 1730 the fall is sudden and pronounced. Applied religion, after vicissitudes, is exactly the same in 1760 as in 1702. Apologetic more than doubles but even in 1760 accounts for hardly more than two of every hundred items recorded. What the figures show, therefore, is a waning of theology. The readers of the *Journal de Trévoux*, whatever their private sentiments, lost interest in the more intellectual and disputatious side of their religion.

Intellectual interests were shifting to new fields. This is no surprising discovery. It is more surprising to find that history and philosophy, as defined in our categories, were not among these fields. Both . . . were proportionately smaller in all years after 1730 than in 1702. The situation incites to further analysis. Let us distinguish the more erudite from the more popular elements.

PROPORTION OF HISTORICAL AND PHILOSOPHICAL ITEMS TO TOTAL ITEMS
(PERCENTAGES)

	1702	1710	1720	1730	1740	1750	1760
Historical writings	7.3	5.8	10.7	9.3	9.3	8.8	7.8
Auxiliary historical sciences	13.3	11.7	8.6	11.4	7.2	6.2	6.9
Formal philosophy	3.8	.6	3.2	2.8	1.4	2.1	1.1
Popular philosophy	1.0	.4	.2	.5	1.9	1.5	1.8

It is apparent that the loss in history was due chiefly to loss in the learned historical auxiliaries, and in philosophy entirely to loss in works classified as "formal." This conclusion is more in keeping with what we know of the Age of Enlightenment after 1730. The fact remains, however, that, so far as the *Journal de Trévoux* gives us evidence, the relative popularity of history was highest in 1720, and that philosophical works, in the *philosophe* sense, remained relatively so few as to be quantitatively negligible.

Science was clearly one of the matters to which reading people, and our Jesuit editors, gave increasing attention. It is the only subject . . . which . . . shows a continual rise in number of items from 1702 to 1750 and the only one not to suffer diminution in the lean year 1730. The most marked increase, in absolute numbers, occurs in the twenty years from 1730 to 1750. It was in these years that the Newtonian system established itself in France. "Natural philosophy" became almost a popular avocation. The literary deigned to enter the laboratory; Voltaire and Mme. du Châtelet, for example, performed many serious scientific experiments together. Proportionately, however, according to the *Journal de Trévoux*, interest in science declined sharply after 1740. By 1760 science had lost even in absolute numbers.

This relative setback to science, like the earlier setback to history, was due to the advance of younger competitors, namely, "Art and letters," "Practical and technical works," and "Social studies." It is the rise of these subjects that distinguishes the age of the *philosophes* after 1730 from the learned age that preceded it. In 1730 . . . Religion, History, and Science were far in the lead. In 1760 the three "younger competitors" had grown so substantially that the six categories were more nearly equal than at any preceding time, all of them falling between 9.9 and 20.1 per cent of the total for that year. This dry fact may be interpreted thus: as the relative recession of religion left more room for other interests, the forces stored up in earlier works of science and history began to spread; science and history were certainly not less important in 1760 than in 1730—the difference is that they were diffused through other fields.

The rise of the new categories is perhaps best explained by changes in French society. As the country became more wealthy, more people had the leisure and inclination to read, people who as a class had not read much before and who had formed no habits of laborious education. Such people, mostly bourgeois but including many who were legally noble, wished to feel that they shared in the enlightenment of the age. More perhaps than any other thirty years in French history, the years from 1730 to 1760 saw the education of the middle class. The writings favored by the new readers were not the old tomes of the professionally learned. The new demand was for lightness of touch, for authors who would not make their readers feel ignorant, for information which, while instructive, was also agreeable. A great body of readable literature therefore arose. Sometimes, indeed, legitimate popularizing went to lengths that suggest our own works on progressive education, as in a certain *Système nouveau par lequel on peut devenir savant sans maître, sans étude, et sans peine* [*A New System whereby One may become Wise without a Teacher, without Studying, and without Difficulty*], in which, to quote the title page further, reasoning supplanted the teacher, amusement replaced study, and familiar explanations removed the need for effort.

The items classified as "Social studies" show the new trend. The sudden rise in 1750 of books on education is significant of the new spirit, though this category is so small that no generalization may safely be drawn from it. Geographical works, though hardly increasing in proportion, continued to fascinate many readers, some of whom no doubt continued to think, like Montaigne contemplating the cannibals, that all human customs were relative. The category "Law, politics, and economics" increases less than we might have expected, being only 6.1 per cent of the total in 1760. The change, however, escapes numerical analysis. In the early years of the century the typical works were the acts of the French parlements or intricate treatises, often in Latin, on the laws of the Holy Roman Empire. In the later years there were many more works dealing with the ideal background in the laws of nature and reason. Three developments were taking place here: the penetration into social studies of ideas presumably based on science, the transfer of emphasis from works intelligible only to experts to works which any enlightened person could persuade himself he understood, and the growing belief that existing positive law was not natural or reasonable—that is, the rise of social discontent.

The increase in "Art and letters" between 1740 and 1750 is the largest and most rapid of any recorded in the tables. It is not easy to interpret. It may have been due simply to the policy of the new editor, Berthier, who took charge of the *Journal* in 1746. It includes, moreover, under "Art" for 1750 and 1760 a considerable number of notices of prints and pictures whose artistic merit may be questioned. These prints nevertheless indicate the trend to popular enlightenment. It was possible, by the mid-century, for more people than ever before to have an accurate idea of how unknown persons and distant places looked. And as for the change in editorial policy, since it was meant to make the *Journal* more popular, it reflects, though with exaggerated suddenness, a change in the reading public. . . .

This brief interpretation of the facts . . . leaves untouched at least two important questions. One is how accurately the notices in the *Journal de Trévoux* reflect the whole production and circulation of books in France. Were there, for example, in reality more writings against traditional religion than the figures in our category "Popular philosophy" suggest? Did the Jesuit editors exercise a kind of censorship in choosing books to notice or review? No answer can be given, for no one knows what the total production of all books on all subjects was. The quantity of antireligious writing can never be measured, because some such writings were surreptitious, and much of such writing entered into books chiefly or ostensibly on other subjects. This, however, can be said, that the editors of the *Journal*, far from keeping silence, usually called attention to such writings in the optimistic belief that they would thus neutralize their venom. All the leading *philosophes* are reviewed in the *Journal de Trévoux*. It appears, upon consideration, that the *Journal de Trévoux* indicates as well as any other periodical of the time, and perhaps better, the general state of the book market and the distribution of reading interests. It was directed to no special class or kind of people but to all educated persons in France, over all of whom the Jesuits wished to maintain their influence.

The other question not touched here is the attitude taken by the editors to the works they reviewed. Their purpose was avowedly to protect the

Catholic faith. How far did this purpose color the ideas that they set before their readers? This question obviously requires a more intensive study than has been made here. The author believes that the bias was not very marked, or rather that it was so definite and explicit, being an absolute belief in Catholic authority, that on matters where this issue did not specifically arise the editors could be, when compared to Jansenists, *philosophes*, and other enthusiasts of the time, relatively balanced and judicious. For example, as late as 1740 we find them opposed to the cosmology of Newton but not on unreasonable grounds, since they admitted Newton's mathematical conclusions but complained of being unable to understand attraction, the void, and forces that operated through a perfectly empty space. When a clap of thunder occurred on Christmas, 1736, and a rumor spread that the sun had been knocked off its course, the editors of the *Journal* published a reassuring letter in which it was pointed out that, while both Descartes and Newton allowed a readjustment of the sun's position to be possible, no scientific observer had in fact noticed any irregularity. By such means they instilled the fundamental idea of the time, the belief in uniform laws of nature. In 1751, reviewing the *Encyclopédie*, they noted certain plagiarisms which had to be acknowledged and so provoked the wrath of the *philosophes*, but their general judgment was by no means unfavorable, and they encouraged Diderot and his colleagues to proceed. The outcries of the *philosophes* must not be taken too seriously. All critical reviews then had trouble with authors. Criticism was not yet distinct from polemics, and authors, more then than now, expected to be praised.

The antagonism became more definite after 1750. The *philosophes* became more bold, and the defenders of religion more suspicious of the enlightened ideas. This new departure is reflected in the increase between 1750 and 1760 of works classified as "Applied religion," which include sermons, devotional manuals, episcopal letters, etc., calculated to protect the faithful against the perils of the age. But in the early period the line was less sharply drawn. So far as we mean by the "enlightenment" of the eighteenth century something other than overt denial of the authority of the church, we must conclude that up to 1750 the Catholic authorities did little to hinder it, that this enlightenment was a general spread of ideas in which persons of many kinds took an active and willing part, and that the Jesuit *Journal de Trévoux* may well have been one of its agents.

THE POLITICAL PHILOSOPHY OF HELVETIUS AND D'HOLBACH

Everett C. Ladd

There has been considerable disagreement concerning the form of government to which Helvétius and d'Holbach were committed. They have been described most frequently as champions of "enlightened" monarchy. Dissents from this position, however, have been numerous. Kingsley Martin, for example, has argued that within limits Helvétius was a democrat. Wickwar placed Helvétius among the most ardent defenders of enlightened despotism, but thought that d'Holbach took a more liberal position, somewhere between Helvétius and Rousseau, as an advocate of a constitutionally limited monarchy. Naville concurred in this judgment. Keim observed that at times Helvétius seemed to hope for the establishment of a federated republic, while at other times he moved very close to Voltaire's position on the possibility of an intelligent, philosophic monarch. That this confusion has occurred is attributable in part to the presence of passages in the writings of our *philosophes* supporting each of these positions. In fact, certain of these positions are clearly wrong, and none of them can stand alone as an adequate description of the essential orientation of our *philosophes*. Neither Helvétius nor d'Holbach were democrats, though there were democratic elements in their political doctrine. Neither favored enlightened despotism, if one understands by the term a form of government which emphasizes reform at the expense of freedom. And though both placed their hopes primarily on enlightened, limited monarchy, this position must be understood much less as a commitment to a particular system of government, than as a product of (1) their reluctance and inability to explore seriously the question of what form of government would be required to realize the objectives which they set up; (2) their faith in the process of enlightenment; (3) their skepticism about the possibility of any form of government other than monarchy at the time; and (4) their interpretation of the preceding three centuries of French history in which French kings had struggled to dominate the feudal nobility and clergy, both objects of their most violent opposition. Before considering each of these, we must first describe in more detail the position taken by our *philosophes* on the form of government best suited to maximize the happiness of society.

D'Holbach undertook in a number of his works to examine systematically each of the three classical forms of government, to determine the strengths and weaknesses of each. The dangers of monarchy were all too

Everett C. Ladd, Jr., "Helvétius and d'Holbach, La Moralisation de la politique." © The *Journal of the History of Ideas*, XXIII (1962), 226–231. Used by permission of the *Journal of the History of Ideas* and the author.

evident: public welfare frequently had been sacrificed to the ambition and greed of the king and his court. And even if one succeeded in "enlightening" a monarch, there were no assurances that his successor would not be a tyrant. Yet if monarchy could be bad, the alternatives could be far worse. Aristocratic government elicited his strongest disapproval; the nobility was self-seeking and self-centered, willing to sacrifice the common good on the altar of self-interest, inanely jealous of undeserved privileges. Society would be reduced to a morass of plots, intrigue and civil war by the struggle for power among the aristocratic elite. In the end, a few families would become masters of the state, sharing the spoils. Instead of just one tyrant, the people would have many; and while one man may have his moments of charity, group interests are always reduced to their lowest common denominator. His condemnation of democracy, however, was as categorical:

The authority is without power, because it is too divided. It is not respected because each individual, thinking himself its agent, acts as though he had acquired the right to abuse it. . . . A sovereign people, flattered by demagogues, become their slaves and the instrument of their wicked designs. Turbulent citizens divide into factions . . . civil wars tear to pieces a society which, blind in its attachments and its hates, often elevates its most cruel enemies. . . . Finally, worn out by its own excesses, the people delivers itself to slavery . . . and thinks itself fortunate to have exchanged license for chains.

It "escapes from freedom." He rejected out of hand all possibility of popular government. The uneducated and those without property would not be allowed to exercise political power. Even the merchants and manufacturers, though entitled to the full protection of the State, were not true members of it, and could not be until they had acquired landed property: "It is the soil . . . which makes the citizen. . . . The land is the physical and political base of the State."

D'Holbach did not preclude, however, all possibility of representative government. He referred favorably to a "mixed" government in which intermediate political bodies—assemblies—would function as instruments of resistance to despotism. He developed the idea of a monarchy limited by a representative power in the *Politique naturelle*, in a discussion of the advantages which a form of federal arrangement might bring to the large state. In such states, he observed, the population is widely scattered; local restraints tend to break down, and a more elaborate governmental machine is needed. There is a greater tendency for these states to fall under despotic government. It would be advantageous, then, to divide such states into provinces with certain powers of self-government, uniting these under a monarch and a general assembly. This representative body would be composed of deputies chosen by elected provincial assemblies. Suffrage would be limited to those who possessed landed wealth. It seems doubtful, however, that d'Holbach saw these assemblies as anything more than consultative bodies, and he gave no indication of how they would have any effective power. He spoke of their activity in very vague terms: The people would "speak" to the monarch through these assemblies, "making known" its needs and grievances. As Naville has observed, d'Holbach's assembly "would act as a kind of permanent session of the Estates General."

D'Holbach, then, favored limited monarchy. At times he demonstrated full awareness that it was not enough merely to enlighten the monarch, to open his eyes to the coincidence of his interests with those of his subjects. Like Helvétius, he had developed a quite sophisticated conception of interests; and he did not believe that men would always determine their actions by a somewhat questionable ultimate harmony of the individual with the general interest. It is for this reason that he emphasized the importance of legislation. And this is why he referred to a system of representation noted above, to the threat of revolution, and to pluralism of a sort: The representative body, however, was to be only consultative; his conception of pluralism was vague to say the least; and the threat of revolution was a theoretical and hardly reliable sanction. D'Holbach maintained that fear is the only obstacle which society can effectively raise against the passions of its leaders; that society must set boundaries to its confidence, must limit the power that it delegates to the ruling elite, and should reserve for itself enough authority to prevent corruption and abuse by that elite; that the record of history testifies to the fact that man is continually tempted to abuse power. He never developed his argument, however, beyond this promising statement of principles.

At first reading, Helvétius appears to give strong, if not compelling support to the claim that he must be considered a democrat. His uncompromising environmentalism, his insistence that all men have equal mental faculties and differ in ability only because their environments are not equally good, is clearly egalitarian. Of greater significance, he anticipated with considerable clarity Bentham's conclusion that the greatest happiness for the greatest number could be realized only through representative democracy; that to bring the "moral aptitude of the governors" to its maximum, sovereign power must be given to those whose interest it is that the general happiness be maximized—the people. All men, he argued, seek only their own interests. Thus, in a monarchy, where all governmental power is in the hands of one man, government tends to secure those things which the monarch believes to be in his own interest; in an aristocratic state, it is the interest of the body of nobles which is satisfied. In "the government of all," however, the self-seeking of the rulers is directed toward the greatest happiness for the greatest number:

... every action conformable to the interest of the greatest number is just and virtuous; consequently, the love of power, the moving principle of the inhabitants, must compel them to the love of justice and of talents. . . . It cannot therefore be wonderful, that this form of government is always cited as the best.

In another section, Helvétius proposed that France be made a federal republic, to enable the people "to oppose efficaciously any ambitious project of their neighbors or of their fellow citizens." These passages remain isolated, however. As unequivocal as they seem, they represent occasional insight rather than a fully reasoned commitment. For the most part, Helvétius was content to direct his efforts to the enlightenment of monarchs. He believed that it was possible for monarchs to see, much more clearly than they had, that their interests were in harmony with those of their subjects. His repeated exhortations testify to this. In a highly revealing passage, Helvétius asked:

Suppose in Portugal more respect were paid to the property, the lives, and the liberty of the subjects, would the government be less monarchical? Suppose they were to suppress the inquisition, and the *lettres de cachet*, and limit the exercise and authority of certain places, would they thereby change the form of government? No: they would only correct the abuses. . . . Are the monarchs of Europe to be compared to the stupid sultans of Asia, to those vampires who suck the blood of their subjects, and whom all opposition exasperates? To suspect a virtuous prince of adopting the principles of oriental despotism is to do him the most atrocious injury. A discerning sovereign will never esteem an arbitrary power. . . .

The vampires of Europe were expected to get the not-so-subtle hint. They were expected to be ashamed and repentant. Through this clever verbal maneuver Helvétius was to secure reform. The princes would be seduced through the appeal to their pride; they would be convinced through the cogency of his argument. Helvétius, then, placed his hopes for reform primarily on enlightened monarchy. It is nonetheless true, however, that far from rejecting out of hand the desirability of popular government, as did d'Holbach, he declared it to be theoretically superior to all other forms.

Our *philosophes* removed all trappings from the monarch. They brought him down to earth, a man, no more virtuous or talented than his fellows. They required him to rule in the best interests of all members of the society on pain of losing his right to rule. For the rest, they left him his throne. Their willingness to rely on the monarchy for reform, despite the anti-monarchical implications of their thought, must be understood in terms of the several factors noted above. First, Helvétius and d'Holbach shared the limited but still substantial confidence of their fellow *philosophes* in the process of enlightenment. The assumption, after all, of the possibility of a more rational man in a more rational society was central to their attack on the "irrationality" of the old order. We must take care, however, that we do not give undue emphasis to this point; for their optimism was tempered by a self-interest psychology and a concomitant theory of interests, and a full awareness that in the sweep of history monarchical abuses had rarely been deterred by a recognition of the ultimate harmony of interests. Much more important was their inability to conceive of an alternative to limited monarchy which would be both practical and desirable. D'Holbach questioned the practicality and desirability of any other form of government; Helvétius only the former. Helvétius did not seriously expect any change from the monarchical structure of the governments of Europe. Certain reforms were palpably necessary, and he wanted immediate action. The king was there, and he considered it to be immediately practical to look to him. Neither *philosophe* constructed a defense of monarchy, but instead accepted it on pragmatic considerations.

Still another factor in the willingness of our *philosophes* to place their hopes on the monarchy is their conditioning by the French political experience. By the time opposition to royal power developed in England in the XVIIth century, Parliament had been securely established as the major contender in the struggle for power, and was able to serve as the effective alternative around which opponents of the monarchy could rally. Such a situation was impossible in France. There, the lines of battle were drawn between the royal and aristocratic parties. Opposition to royal absolutism failed in large part because it was in alliance with a medieval particularism which was in no way compatible with strong, centralized national government. In their struggle against the clergy and the firmly entrenched feudal nobility, and the privileges which these interests defended, our *philosophes* looked to a strong monarchy. Peter Gay's description of Voltaire's royalism as "the result not of detachment from practical affairs and addiction to geometrical speculation, but of involvement in French politics and an intimate knowledge of French history," could as well have been applied to Helvétius or d'Holbach.

One final factor of particular significance in understanding their positions should be noted: Our *philosophes* had little interest in seriously exploring the question of what institutional structure would be required to secure the values which they had postulated. Helvétius expressed this most succinctly when he wrote: "There are, therefore, only two forms of government, the one good, the other bad. . . ." Any government which maximizes the happiness of all members of the society is good government; any which does not is bad. This is, of course, far too facile. That good government must be defined in terms of good actions is not in question; it is no less true, however, that it must in addition be defined in terms of institutional structure; and that the former cannot be securely realized without the latter. Helvétius and d'Holbach sought *"la moralisation de la politique"* ["the moralization of politics"] and were really unwilling and unable to go far in building an adequate constitutional structure. Our criticism should not be too harsh, for there are mitigating circumstances. Still, our *philosophes* must answer for the fact that they ultimately offered nothing beyond pious wishes to make certain that the monarch would work for the greatest happiness of all members of society.

THE INFLUENCE OF
EIGHTEENTH-CENTURY IDEAS ON
THE FRENCH REVOLUTION

Henri Peyre

The problem of the effect of the Philosophy of Enlightenment on the French Revolution is one of the most important problems that confront the pure historian as well as the historian of thought and of literature. It is without doubt the most complex of the thousand aspects involved in the study of the Revolution, that is to say the origins of the modern world. . . .

There is for one thing a long and devious current of ideas which first springing forth as a swift and turgid torrent in the sixteenth century, becoming a more or less tenuous water-course in the great period of the reign of Louis XIV, and finally like a river encircling the most obdurate islets of resistance within its multiple arms, seems to have engulfed the eighteenth century in the years 1750–1765. More and more clearly, those who set forth and develop these ideas take it upon themselves to influence the existing facts, to change man by education, to free him from out-moded superstitions, to increase his political liberty and his well-being. In no way do they dream of a general cataclysm and several of them are not insensitive to the refined amenity of the life that surrounds them or to the exquisite blend of intellectual boldness and voluptuous refinement that characterizes their era.

Suddenly, this pleasant eighteenth-century security, "*Table d'un long festin qu'un échafaud termine*" ["The table of a long feast ending in a scaffold"], as Hugo's beautiful image calls it, crumbles. The Revolution breaks out, and within a few years, rushes through peaceful reforms, produces a profusion of constitutions, sweeps aside the old regime, devours men, and causes heads to fall. This great movement is certainly confused, turbulent and irrational like everything that men accomplish by collective action. However, lawyers, officers, priests, and journalists play a part in it that is often important. These men had grown up in an intellectual climate that had been established by

Henri Peyre, "The Influence of Eighteenth Century Ideas on the French Revolution," © *Journal of the History of Ideas*, IX (1949), 63–66, 68–71. Used by permission of the *Journal of the History of Ideas* and the author.

Montesquieu, Voltaire, Rousseau, Raynal and Mably. May we accurately reach a conclusion of "*Post hoc, ergo propter hoc*"?

It would not have been so difficult to answer such a question if partisan quarrels had not needlessly clouded the issue. Frenchmen are incapable of viewing their nation's past dispassionately or accepting it as a whole. . . . It is a curious fact that the great majority of their political writers from Joseph de Maistre, Louis de Bonald, and Auguste Comte himself, to Le Play, Tocqueville, Taine, at times Renan, Barrès, Bourget, Maurras and many others, has pronounced itself hostile to the "great principles of '89" or at least to that which was drawn from these principles. Three fundamental assertions are the basis of most of the anti-revolutionary arguments. (a) The Revolution was harmful and anti-French; it could only be attributed to foreign influences that perverted the French genius of moderation, restrained devotion, and obedience to the hereditary monarch. It was caused by foreign influences that contaminated eighteenth century thought: Locke, the English deists, the Protestants in general, the Swiss Rousseau, etc. . . . (b) These corrupting ideas were introduced among the French people who had been sound and upright until then, by clubs called "Sociétés de Pensée" and by secret groups of conspiring intellectuals, the Freemasons for example and the *philosophes* themselves, who formed an authentic subversive faction. (Augustin Cochin, *Les Sociétés de Pensée*, 1921.) (c) The Revolutionary spirit is the logical outcome of the classical spirit strengthened by the scientific spirit. This spirit delights in abstraction, generalizes profusely, and considers man as a creature apart from his environment, isolated from his past; it lacks the subtle empiricism which characterizes the English reformists; it is ignorant of everything touching reality. Accordingly it sets out to make laws for universal man, without regard for France's age-old traditions or the local conditions of these provinces. This contention advanced with talent and a semblance of thorough documentation by Taine has beguiled a great number of excellent minds because of its specious clarity.

These contentions have not stood the test of serious scrutiny by literary historians trained in more rigid methods since the dawn of the twentieth century. . . .

So let us differ with those who claim a priori that the Revolution sprang from the teachings of the *philosophes*, only in order to justify their condemnation of both the Revolution and the teaching. But in opposition to this group, the admirers of the *philosophes* and even more the admirers of Rousseau, who was not exactly one of the *philosophes*, have taken up the cudgels in an attempt to deny the responsibility or even the guilt of the eighteenth-century political writers in the upheaval that ensued. . . .

Professional historians generally tend to limit the part played by ideas in world events: the best of them devote, apparently for the sake of form, one or two chapters to the literature, painting and music of the periods studied by their manuals. But the history of civilization and culture is still very clumsily related to general history. Historians prefer to emphasize the purely historical causes of the Revolution: financial disorder, ministerial blunders, or the hostility of *parlements* that had been alienated by encroachments upon their prerogatives, etc. Perhaps in doing so they are choosing the easiest way. Their history does grasp the events, the things that change, that is, the things that would be presented in today's newspapers as facts or news: a tax-measure, a famine, the dismissal of a minister, a change in the price of bread, or a treaty. But it often fails to apprehend the slow subterranean movements which minds inclined to be too matter-of-fact find intangible, until they or e day make their appearance as acts that make news or usher in a historical era. . . .

One must also remember the fact that the history of ideas is not simply the exposition of theoretical views expressed in philosophical writings, but at the same time the history of the deformations undergone by these ideas when other men adopt them, and also the history of the half-conscious beliefs into which ideas first clearly conceived by the few promptly transform themselves. . . .

It is not even necessary to have understood a book or even to have read it through in order to be profoundly influenced by it. An isolated phrase quoted in some article or a page reproduced at some time in an anthology, may have done more to spread some of the opinions of Montesquieu, Proudhon, or Gobineau than thirty re-editions of their writings bought by private libraries and commented upon by ten provincial academies.

In 1933 Daniel Mornet published on the subject sketched here his work entitled *Les Origines intellectuelles de la Révolution française*, which is a study of the spread of ideas justly termed a model of intellectual probity and discretion. Henceforth no one can consider this historical and philosophical problem without owing much to this solid book. The author has avoided the error of so many other writers who make the Revolution inexplicable by drawing a rough contrast between 1789 and 1670 or even 1715. He has followed the slow progress of the spread of new ideas from 1715 to 1747, then from 1748 to 1770, the date when the philosophic spirit had won the day. He has made very searching inquiries into the degree of penetration of the reformist spirit among the more or less learned societies and academies, in the letters of private individuals, in provincial libraries and even in educational curricula. His conclusions are new in many respects because of the exact information they offer and because they show those who are misled by the perspective of a later day into the error of limiting the group of *philosophes* to five or six names, that writers half-unknown to us (Toussaint, Delisle de Sales, Morellet, Mably) were among those most widely read in the eighteenth century. With fitting reserve they tend to show that the thought of the century, by itself, would never have caused the

Revolution if there had not been misery among the people as well; and that misery which was not a new thing at the time would not have brought about the Revolution if it had not had the support of opinion that had long been discontented and desirous of reform. . . .

In order to revolt against one's lot, one must be aware of his wretched condition, which presupposes a certain intellectual and cultural level; one must have a clear conception of certain reforms that one would like to adopt; in short, one must be convinced (and it was on this point that the books of the eighteenth century produced their effect) that things are not going well, that they might be better and that they will be better if the measures proposed by the reformist thinkers are put into practice.

Eighteenth-century philosophy taught the Frenchman to find his condition wretched, or in any case, unjust and illogical and made him disinclined to the patient resignation to his troubles that had long characterized his ancestors. It had never called for a revolution nor desired a change of regime; it had never been republican and Camille Desmouslins was not wrong in stating: "In all France there were not ten of us who were republicans before 1789." . . .

Without enlarging upon what is already rather well known we may say that eighteenth-century writers prepared the way for the Revolution, without wishing for it, because:

a. They weakened the traditional religion, winning over to their side a great number of clerics, and taught disrespect for an institution which had been the ally of the monarchy for hundreds of years. At the same time they had increased the impatience of the non-privileged groups by uprooting from many minds the faith in a future life which had formerly made bearable the sojourn in this vale of tears that constituted life for many people of low estate. They wished to enjoy real advantages here on earth and without delay. The concept of well-being and then that of comfort slowly penetrated among them.

b. They taught a secular code of ethics, divorced from religious belief and independent of dogma, and made the ideal of conduct consist of observation of this system of ethics, which was presented as varying in accordance with climate and environment. Furthermore they gave first importance in this ethical code to the love of humanity, altruism and service due society or our fellowmen. The ideas of humanity, already present in the teaching of Christ, in Seneca and Montaigne but often dormant, suddenly exert fresh influence over people's minds.

c. They developed the critical spirit and the spirit of analysis and taught many men not to believe, or to suspend judgment rather than accept routine traditions. In D'Argenson, Chamfort, Morelly, Diderot, Voltaire of course, D'Holbach, Condillac and many others, and even in Laclos and Sade, we will find the effort to think courageously without regard for convention or tradition, that will henceforth characterize the French intellectual attitude. From this time on, inequality with respect to taxation, the tithe paid to the Church, and banishment or persecution for subversive opinions will shock profoundly the sense of logic and critical spirit of the readers of the *philosophes.*

d. Lastly, these very thinkers who have often been depicted as builders of Utopias are the creators of history or the historical sense, or almost so. Montesquieu studiously examined the origins of law and constitutions and saw men "conditioned" by soil and climate in contrast with the absolute rationalists who were foreign jurists and not Frenchmen. Boulainvilliers and many others of lesser fame studied France's past. Voltaire's masterpiece is probably his work on general history. The result of this curiosity about history was two-fold: it encouraged faith in progress and convinced numbers of Frenchmen that it was their task to fulfill humanity's law, to endeavor to increase the sum of liberty, relative equality, "enlightenment" and happiness in the world; it also proved to many men of the law who examined old documents and the titles of nobility and property, that the privileges of nobility were based on a flimsy foundation. The respect that these bourgeois or sons of the people might have felt for the aristocrats was accordingly diminished, at the very moment when the bourgeois saw the nobles not only accept with admiration but take under their protection destructive writings produced by the pens of commoners: sons of tailors (Marmontel), vine-growers (Restif), cutlers (Diderot) and watch-makers (Rousseau). And the history of the origins of royal sovereignty itself seemed to them scarcely more edifying than that of the feudal privileges. . . .

THE IMAGE AND INFLUENCE OF AMERICA IN THE FRENCH ENLIGHTENMENT

DURAND ECHEVERRIA

By 1783 there had emerged three fundamental interpretations of the westward expansion of European civilization into the new frontier environment of America: one, that of [Corneille] De Pauw, that it constituted a moral and cultural degeneration and debilitation; the second, that of [Simon] Linguet, that it was a cancerous and monstrous outgrowth threatening the life of the European mother-body; and the third, temporarily raised to dominance by the war and the libertarian movement, that this western expansion was the most vigorous and advanced manifestation of western man's accelerating drive to an enlightened and just social order.

The oversimplification of all these interpretations produced a gross distortion of the image. In spite of the greatly increased flow of information on America into France, the supply of facts was by far inadequate to give a balanced picture or to support the top-heavy superstructures of hypothesis. Moreover, the reporting of the facts was inaccurate because of the carelessness, inexperience, and ignorance of the reporters.

The main cause of distortion, however, was that the image was a reflection not of reality but of domestic preoccupations. The basic problem in France in the 1770's and 1780's was the urgent need for the reorganization of an antiquated and inefficient social and political order. The impression, which both fate and Franklin fostered, that America had achieved a social revolution along the very same lines that the French liberal reformers were advocating for France quite naturally produced an irresistible urge to magnify and misinterpret the success of the American Revolution. America was for the French "the hope of the human race" because she furnished the chance to prove for all time the idea of progress: that man, once granted the free use of his enlightened reason, could not fail to create a golden age of prosperity, justice, and happiness. . . .

. . . From the end of the seventeenth century, a few writers . . . identified the British colonies with the ideas of religious freedom and political liberty. The Quakers had attempted to make converts in France as early as 1656, and when William Penn received his charter for Pennsylvania from Charles II in 1681 he caused his agent in Rotterdam, Benjamin Furly, to distribute on the continent tracts in French as well as in Dutch and German in order to recruit colonists. Furly's pamphlets are of interest as probably the first work in French identifying the British colonies with political and religious liberty.

Durand Echeverria, *Mirage in the West: A History of the French Image of American Society to 1815* (Princeton, 1957), pp. 77–78, 15–18, 34–35, 38–47, 70–71. Reprinted by permission of Princeton University Press. © Princeton University Press, 1957.

Pennsylvania, he told the French, was a haven where a man could live in plenty and peace, an asylum for the poor and oppressed of Europe, a refuge for "ingenious spirits of low estate." But he offered them something more than escape, for he also promised liberty, representative government by secret ballot, taxation only by their own consent, the right to make their own laws, and, above all, religious freedom. Furly was an influential figure and a friend of such men as Leibnitz and Jean Le Clerc. That he had an influence on representatives of the critical, skeptical, and rationalistic thought of the first decades of the century is indicated by Le Clerc's eulogy of Pennsylvania in 1712. He wrote of its fertile lands, its rapid growth, its religious freedom, and its virtuous and industrious inhabitants. Of New Jersey, then Quaker territory, he told an amusing incident. "A man one day asked one of the proprietors of New Jersey if there were any lawyers there. The other replied no. Then he asked him if there were any doctors. The other answered no. Finally he asked whether there were any theologians, and the other said no again. 'Happy land!' exclaimed the man. It deserves to be called 'paradise.'" . . .

John Locke's *Fundamental Constitutions of Carolina*, drafted for the Earl of Shaftesbury in 1720, were more important ideologically and were second only to the legislation of Penn in identifying in the French mind the British colonies with enlightened government. The *Constitutions* were repeatedly cited by Voltaire as a successful application of the principle of religious toleration; but even before Voltaire ever mentioned the Carolinas a group of 370 French-Swiss, attracted by promises of religious freedom and representative government as well as of economic opportunity, had founded in 1731 a small colony in South Carolina.

Voltaire's *Lettres philosophiques* (1734), which marked the real beginning of the legend of the "Good Quaker" in French literature of the century, was the first widely read work to identify Pennsylvania with religious toleration. In the first four letters, "Sur les Quakers," Voltaire, though he did not spare the Quaker eccentricities, expressed great admiration for the sect's Early Christian simplicity and its preference of morality over theology, which corresponded so well to his own deism. The fourth letter, on Penn and Pennsylvania, described Philadelphia as a city so prosperous that it even attracted citizens from the other colonies. The laws framed by Penn were, he said, so wise that none had ever been changed, and the just treatment of the Indians had made of these "so-called savages" devoted and grateful friends. Most of all, he stressed the spirit of equality, the religious freedom, the peace, and the absence of priests which blessed that happy land. "William Penn could boast," he wrote, "of having brought to the world that golden age of which men talk so much and which probably has never existed anywhere except in Pennsylvania." All this was of course merely a literary device to express effectively his own pacifism, deism, and anti-clericalism.

Montesquieu shared Voltaire's admiration for Penn as a legislator and called him "a veritable Lycurgus." The *Encyclopédie* further contributed to this picture by including three articles on Pennsylvania, Philadelphia, and the Quakers, all by De Jaucourt, which were drawn almost entirely from Voltaire and Montesquieu. Thus, in the first half of the century Pennsylvania became established in the minds of French liberals as a land where *bienfaisance*, the spirit of benevolence and humanitarianism, reigned as an operative political principle. . . .

After 1770, there were increasing signs that America was coming to be associated with the civil and political liberty of the individual citizen. There was of course the long-standing tradition, created by Penn, Voltaire, Montesquieu, and Locke, which identified the colonies with religious liberty and representative government. Frequently writers attributed American prosperity to the practice of religious toleration. Moreover the *Economistes*, in spite of their absolutist politics, favored a number of liberal and humanitarian reforms, particularly religious liberty, freedom of the press, public education, and the abolition of slavery. . . .

Too much could easily be made of the importance of the British colonies in French thought in the early 1770's. . . . In the years from 1767 to 1775 the Americans had somehow come to symbolize the dream of a new order, in which men would escape from poverty, injustice, and corruption and dwell together in universal liberty, equality, and fraternity. . . .

"The shot heard round the world" sounded as sharp and clear in the Gardens of the Tuileries as if it had been fired on the Place Louis XV. The Age of Revolutions had begun, and the literary symbol of America fashioned by the Physiocrats and *Philosophes* was transformed almost overnight into a popular enthusiasm which fired all of France. The spark of ignition was the news that Washington had forced General Howe to evacuate Boston. The Count de Ségur was spending that summer of 1776 in Spa, and he witnessed the impact of the achievements of the *Insurgents* on international society gathered there:

Their courageous audacity electrified everyone and excited a general admiration, especially among the young, who always were in search of something new and eager for a war. In that little town of Spa, where there were so many tourists, accidental or voluntary deputies, as it were, from all the monarchies of Europe, I was particularly struck to see burst forth in everyone so keen and universal a sympathy for the revolt of a people against their king. The serious English card game whist was suddenly replaced in all the salons by a no less sober game which was christened "Boston."

Nor was the enthusiasm confined to the nobility and the fashionable. One observer wrote the following December, "We have fanatics here of every sort—even women who are mad about the *Insurgents*." . . .

The fad, both in its frivolous and serious aspects, hit the provinces as hard as Paris. When two Boston ladies appeared in Bordeaux in the first weeks of May 1777, they were welcomed by local society, and when they strolled in the Allées de Tourny dressed in a curious mixture of Boston and French styles they were surrounded by all the fashionable ladies and beaux of the city, who showered courtesies upon them. On December 13, 1777 thirteen citizens of Marseille, "in admiration for the heroism of the *Insurgents*," formed a coterie to hold thirteen banquets each year in honor of the thirteen United States, at which exactly thirteen toasts were to be drunk to the Americans and a specially composed song of thirteen verses was to be sung.

Yet this enthusiasm was much more than just a fad. It permeated the army and sent Lafayette and the other adventurous volunteers to suffer with the Americans at Valley Forge. It was stronger than ever before among the *Philosophes*, who carried it into the circles of Free Masonry, the Academy of Sciences, the various salons, and the Court. It filled the newspapers and burst forth in verse, in plays, in novels, and in a flood of new books on America.

This new Americanism was different from that which had existed before the war. America was no longer a mere parable for philosophers; it had become a popular movement spreading down into the lower classes and out to those members of the bourgeoisie who were usually little interested in the polemics of the Physiocrats and *Philosophes*. Americanism now had a new emotional content which revealed that it had somehow caught the imagination of the people and had become identified with certain powerful social drives within the nation. Yet the anatomy of this enthusiasm was complex and its origins various.

Nothing could have more easily excited the interest of the public than a revolt against England. The humiliation of the Treaty of Paris of 1763 was recalled with undiminished rancor in 1776, and the Americans, as bold challengers of the despotism of hated Albion and as underdogs in an unequal struggle, aroused spontaneous sympathy in the French. To the young men particularly, the American war seemed an exciting opportunity to win honor and advancement. The romantic adventure of Lafayette, who attracted from all sides admiration and sympathy, contributed to this atmosphere of chivalric fervor; it was no wonder that suddenly a crowd of young men and adventurous nobles were trying by every means possible to follow his example. The thrill of something new and different appealed to everyone, especially to the women. Thus some of the motives were superficial, though nonetheless effective.

Real political forces, however, lay behind the support of America, for both the royal government and the *Philosophes* had strong reasons to hope for American victories. In spite of an initial reluctance to make official commitments and a definite distrust of American republicanism in the Court, Vergennes' ministry was very pleased to see a revolution which would bleed England militarily and economically, whatever its outcome, and which, if successful, would throw open to French trade the rich American market. Consequently, the government furnished secret aid through Beaumarchais, winked at the volunteers, and later, when Burgoyne's defeat at Saratoga made the gamble worth while, joined the Americans in a military alliance which rendered war with England inevitable.

For their part, the liberals and intellectuals identified the American struggle against British oppression with their own battle against autocracy. The word *liberté* was a constant refrain in every panegyric of America, and to a great extent the American example was used as an excuse to express ideas which otherwise could not have been voiced. As Condorcet, the philosopher and mathematician, later recalled, "Men whom the reading of philosophic books had secretly converted to the love of liberty became enthusiastic over the liberty of a foreign people while they waited for the moment when they could recover their own, and they seized with joy this opportunity to avow publicly sentiments which prudence had prevented them from expressing." The American war was for the *ancien régime* a sort of Pandora's Box out of which poured a cloud of books and articles advocating equality, republicanism, liberty, and constitutionalism, and attacking both the aristocratic principle and monarchical absolutism. Unquestionably the popular support of the United States was in large part actually a disguised demand for reform of the existing French social and political order. . . .

SUGGESTIONS FOR FURTHER READING

General: ERNST CASSIRER, *The Philosophy of the Enlightenment* (Princeton, 1951); PETER GAY, *The Enlightenment: An Interpretation; The Rise of Modern Paganism* (New York, 1966), and *The Party of Humanity: Essays in the French Enlightenment* (New York, 1964); PAUL HAZARD, *The European Mind, 1680–1715* (New Haven, 1952), and *European Thought in the Eighteenth Century: From Montesquieu to Lessing* (New Haven, 1954); DANIEL MORNET, *French Thought in the Eighteenth Century* (New York, 1929), and *Les Origines intellectuelles de la Révolution française* (Paris, 1933); Special: ROGER BICKART, *Les Parlements et la notion de souveraineté nationale au XVIIIᵉ siècle* (Paris, 1934); H. DANIEL-ROPS, *The Church in the Eighteenth Century* (London, 1964); PIERRE FRANCASTEL (ed.), *Utopie et institutions au XVIIIᵉ siècle; le pragmatisme des lumières* (Paris, 1963); FRANÇOIS FURET et al., *Livre et société dans la France du XVIIIᵉ siècle* (Paris, 1965); HENRY GUERLAC, "Three Eighteenth Century Social Philosophers: Scientific Influences on their Thought," *Daedalus*, 87 (Winter, 1958), 8–24; BERNARD DE LACOMBE, *La Résistance janseniste et parlementaire au temps de Louis XV* (Paris, 1948); JEAN MCDONALD, *Rousseau and the French Revolution, 1762–1791* (London, 1965); GORDON H. MCNEIL, "The Cult of

Rousseau and the French Revolution," *Journal of the History of Ideas*, VI (1945), 197–212; ALBERT MATHIEZ, "Les Doctrines politiques des Physiocrates," *Annales historiques de la Révolution française*, XIII (1936), 193–203; R. R. PALMER, *Catholics and Unbelievers in Eighteenth Century France* (Princeton, 1939); BURDETTE C. POLAND, *French Protestantism and the French Revolution: A Study in Church and State, Thought and Religion* (Princeton, 1957); BOYD SHAEFER, "Bourgeois Nationalism in the Pamphlets on the Eve of the French Revolution," *Journal of Modern History*, X (1938), 31–50; CHARLES VEREKER, *Eighteenth-Century Optimism* (Liverpool, 1967); HENRY VYVERBERG, *Historical Pessimism in the French Enlightenment* (Cambridge, Mass., 1958); GEORGES WEULERSSE, *Le Mouvement physiocratique en France (de 1750 à 1770)*, 2 vol. (Paris, 1910), and *La Physiocratie sous les ministères de Turgot et de Necker* (Paris, 1950); Biographical: JANINE BOUISSOUNOUSSE, *Condorcet, le philosophe dans la Révolution* (Paris, 1962); ELIE CARCASSONE, *Montesquieu et le problème de la constitution française au XVIIIᵉ siècle* (Paris, 1926); ALFRED COBBAN, *Rousseau and the Modern State* (London, 1934); PETER GAY, *Voltaire's Politics: The Poet as Realist* (Princeton, 1959); D. W. SMITH, *Helvétius: A Study in Persecution* (Oxford, 1965); CONSTANCE ROWE, *Voltaire and the State* (New York, 1955); ROBERT SHACKLETON, *Montesquieu: A Critical Biography* (London, 1961); ARTHUR M. WILSON, *Diderot: The Testing Years, 1713–1759* (New York, 1957).

Chapter Three

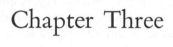

THE DECLINE
OF THE
OLD REGIME
AND
THE DEBACLE OF
FRENCH FOREIGN
POLICY

DECLINE WAS APPARENT in almost every quarter of the Old Regime's administration. Finances were inadequate to meet the rising national debt; ministerial reform was too weak and interrupted to increase the resources of the treasury; the control Louis XIV had exercised over the nobility was gone; and governmental authority over the vehicles of noble resurgence—the *parlements* and assemblies of notables—was insufficient to allow the government to carry out reform programs. The hegemony which France had enjoyed in Europe under Louis XIV was lost in the Seven Years' War. France's financial and military aid to the American colonies, which was vital to the success of the Revolution, simply increased the French national debt to a point where only a revolutionary solution was possible.

The weakness of royal authority stands as both symbol and reality of the decline of the Old Regime. The legacy of Louis XIV's fifty-four years of effective personal rule was an absolute monarchy without an absolute successor. The strength of France's government at the beginning of the eighteenth century was also its weakness, for everything depended on the character and competence of the monarch. Louis XV was unwilling and unable to assume the role. As the late English historian G. P. Gooch indicates in the first selection, France had no independent legislative body or legal tradition which would provide freedom to her subjects and assure the smooth functioning of the government in the absence of a competent ruler.

If it was the weakness of the monarchy that enabled the aristocracy to reassert itself in the *parlements*, as the late English historian Alfred Cobban shows, it was the weakness of monarchical support that prevented ministers from carrying out financial reforms, as Douglas Dakin's examination of the career of Turgot illustrates. Acquiescence to Austrian influence within the royal court and indiscriminate rivalry with Britain, as recounted by the diplomatic historian Albert Sorel who died in 1906, led to France's defeat in the Seven Years' War of 1756–1763 and the loss of Canada to Britain.

In the end it was the financial and economic crises which became the gravest challenges to the Old Regime. Alphonse Aulard, the French historian of the Revolution who died in 1928, examines the financial contribution of Louis XVI's government to the insurgent American colonies. Writing after World War I, when France found herself in a position of similar indebtedness to the United States, Aulard's account focuses solely on the loans and grants to the colonies as a cause of France's financial difficulties. One should include France's chronic deficit and the expenses incurred in keeping an army and navy at war with Britain in this same period as factors leading to the ultimate plight of the royal treasury.

In the last selection, C. Ernest Labrousse, the French historian of the Old Regime economy, sketches the effect of the "Revolutionary cyclical downswing" which followed a decade of depression in a century of general prosperity. During this crisis from 1787 to 1791, profits declined and unemployment was severe. The bad harvest of 1788 aggravated widespread misery. An increase in taxation was impossible and the government was blamed for all these misfortunes. The inability of the Old Regime to finance itself left only one recourse open, the calling of France's national representative assembly or Estates General which would convene for the first time since 1614 to bargain over royal taxation.

$$\mathcal{O} \text{XXX} \mathcal{O}$$

LOUIS XV: THE MONARCHY IN DECLINE

G. P. Gooch

The tragedy of [Louis XV's] life—and the tragedy of France—was that he inherited a calling which he disliked and a political system which demanded more initiative than he could supply. France possessed institutions but no constitution. Eighteenth-century English rulers and statesmen inherited laws and precedents to guide them, from Magna Carta to Habeas Corpus. The sovereign was head of the State, but with the coming of the Hanoverians he ceased to be the effective head of the government. The latest English champion of dynastic autocracy by divine right was James II, who demonstrated that it could not last. Henceforth the monarch could neither rule without Parliament nor override its settled will. Limited monarchy was the invention of seventeenth-century England and in the eighteenth it became an axiom. The British Constitution embodied Montesquieu's ideal of the separation of powers. In France, on the contrary, there could be no appeal to the past, since there were no recognised sign-posts. Instead of freedom slowly broadening down from precedent to precedent there had been retrogression, for the States-General had ceased to meet. In claiming and exercising full sovereignty on the ground that nothing less would meet the demand for unity, internal order and national strength, Louis XIV had been thought successful, but it soon became clear that the system could only be operated by a successor as able and industrious as himself. A young monarch of average ability, good intentions and a feeble will would not suffice: the ship needed a captain, not a mere figure-head. While Frederick the Great visited every part of his scattered dominions every year, halting his carriage in the village street and talking to everyone who wished to speak to him, Louis XV migrated from palace to palace in the environs of Paris, seeing little of his kingdom and his subjects, even in the capital. . . .

The consequences of a *dilettante* on the throne were inevitable. "There was the most intolerable incoherence in despotism," declares Sorel, who

G. P. Gooch, *Louis XV; The Monarchy in Decline* (London, 1956), pp. 76–82, 244–247. © Longmans, Green & Co. Ltd. Used by permission.

always weighs his words, "irresolution in omnipotence, anarchy in centralisation. All the powers were in conflict and each worked for itself. The Generals were paralysed by the fear of dismissal at any moment. There were party intrigues in the camps, where many of the officers owed their place to purchase or favour. The dikes were beginning to crumble." The popularity of *Louis le Bienaimé* which followed his illness at Metz was as brief as a straw fire.

Judged by the low standards of his age Louis XV was not a bad man. His chief duty, as he saw it, was to preserve the system of autocracy unimpaired. A reference by an indiscreet courtier to the States-General provoked a sharp rebuke. "Never say that again" snapped the King. "I am not cruel. But if my brother spoke like that I should not hesitate to sacrifice him to public order and the peace of the realm." Convinced that his authority was from God, he regarded himself as master of the lives, fortunes, and property of his subjects and above the reach of criticism. Most of the courtiers shared that conviction, which came to be challenged only by the bourgeoisie as the reign advanced. Lacking any profound sense of obligation to his subjects he felt he had done enough when he distributed bread after a bad harvest, money after a fire, pensions for elderly officers, and dowries for poor girls. Despite such occasional largesse, he was generally believed to care for little but his pleasures— not harsh but insensitive, not heartless but possessing an organ with a sluggish beat. He wished his subjects well but took no steps, either by innovation or renovation, to secure their welfare.

His second main task, as he conceived it, was the preservation of the Catholic faith from attacks by its enemies and the outward observance of his religious duties. Like his predecessor he said his prayers night and morning, heard mass every day, followed processions, and knelt in the road if the viaticum passed by. Like Louis XIV he detested Jansenists and Protestants. He spoke contemptuously of the *Philosophes*, whose writings he never read, as *ces gens-là* [those people], though he reluctantly consented to appoint Voltaire a Gentleman of the Chamber and Historiographer and allowed him to stand for the Academy. Louis XIV had few intellectual interests and his successor fewer still. The ferment of ideas which made Paris "le café de l'Europe", as the Abbé Galiani called it, was as remote from his field of vision as if it were located in another planet. The impression he produced was that of a spectator sitting at his ease in the royal box, not that of the conductor of the orchestra. . . .

Louis XV had made an auspicious start, for the nation looked with hope and confidence to the pretty lad after an era of almost incessant war, military disasters, and crushing taxation. How deeply rooted was monarchical sentiment appeared when he hovered for a few days between life and death at Metz in 1744. In the frequent conflicts between the crown and the *Parlements* public opinion was far from unanimous on the side of the latter. "When the people is not downtrodden," testified Bernis, a shrewd observer, "and when the course of justice is not interrupted by Court tempests and the ferment of the *Parlements*, the public is always on the side of the King. The distinctive character of the nation is to love its master, respect his authority, and defend it against all comers whenever it does not play the tyrant." There was nothing of the tyrant either in will or in deed about Louis XV, but it was hardly less fatal to the prestige of the monarchical system to have such a dissolute trifler on the throne. France lost her respect for her rulers in the eighteenth century and has never recovered it. That the machinery was worn out nobody attempted to deny. "All the symptoms point to great changes and revolutions in government," wrote Lord Chesterfield on a visit as early as 1753, and from 1750 the word revolution became a term in common use. At the close of the reign a placard was affixed to the Palais Royal, the residence of the Orleans branch of the Royal Family, summoning the colourless Duke to play his part. "Show yourself, great Prince, and we will place the crown on your head." Paris was flooded with broadsheets and satires, to which the Chancellor Maupeou replied in brochures distributed gratis in the streets and parks. The people believed that the most unpopular of the Ministers cared little about the reform of the judiciary, and his attack was attributed to his love of power and his hostility to the *Parlement*. In the closing phase of the reign there was talk for the first time of the sovereignty of the people, fundamental laws, the right of resistance, the English Constitution, and the [English] Revolution of 1688. The roar of the avalanche could be heard in the distance. . . .

The legacy of Louis XV to his countrymen was an ill-governed, discontented, frustrated France. Viewed from a distance the *ancien régime* appeared as solid as the Bastille, but its walls were crumbling for lack of repairs and the foundations showed signs of giving way. The Absolute Monarchy, the privileged *Noblesse*, the intolerant Church, the close corporation *Parlements*, had all become unpopular, and the army, once the glory of France, was tarnished by the rout of Rossbach. Though there was little thought of republicanism, the *mystique* of monarchy had almost evaporated. "He goes to Crécy and to Choisy," wrote a pamphleteer at the close of the reign; "why does he not go to St. Denis?" Now he had gone, and he had taken dynastic autocracy with him in the funeral cortège. The educated bourgeoisie, which was to supply the leaders of the Revolution, resented the shackles of a caste system which barred its advance towards a position in the State commensurate with its growing numbers, intelligence, and wealth. When the Abbé Sieyès asked in his famous pamphlet in 1789 what the *Tiers État* had been and answered with the monosyllable *Rien* ["nothing"], he was scarcely exaggerating the political and social anomaly. The Revolution occurred because the *ancien régime* failed to make reasonable adjustments in good time, and in the era of Absolute Monarchy it is impossible to acquit the ruler of the major responsibility. No one could say that Louis XV lacked warning, for the air was thick with complaints. Though he cared less and less for appearances as he grew older, in the deeper levels of consciousness he was aware of the general malaise though not of its full volume. He knew that he was no longer loved and realised that he had never deserved the affection of his subjects. "A complacent egoist and mediocrity, criminal only because he was a King," is the verdict of Jobez at the close of his six stout volumes on the reign. He left France less suffering and therefore less unhappy than his predecessor but far more degraded in the eyes of the world. He had let his people down. In 1715 there had been hope of recovery, in 1774 there was little or none. "I am far from believing that we are approaching the century of reason," wrote Grimm in 1757. "I almost believe Europe is menaced by some sinister revolution." "I see all the states of Europe rushing to their ruin," echoed Rousseau in 1772; "all the peoples groan." The shrill voice of Cassandra was heard in the land. While England, Prussia, Austria, and Russia were advancing from strength to strength, France was going downhill. . . .

THE DIPLOMATIC REVOLUTION
AND THE DEBACLE OF FRENCH
FOREIGN POLICY

ALBERT SOREL

Louis XIV had left France odious to her neighbors and distrusted by all Europe. The men who succeeded him needed great prudence and wisdom to allay the fear and jealousy inspired by his long reign of conquest and war. Fortunately, the moderation required of them remained the most adroit and advantageous of policies for France. France kept Alsace, Franche-Comté, Flanders, and Roussillon. Beyond this expanded frontier she was no longer threatened by the same enemies. The treaties of Utrecht had modified the entire balance of power. . . .

Henceforth, it seemed that France had only to maintain her status on the Continent. There she was the most compact power, and her principal enemy was greatly reduced. She was surrounded by states weaker than herself that sought her aid and feared her. She was in a position to resume the role of moderator of Europe and guardian of peace for which Richelieu had prepared her. Her superabundant strength and flush of vigor, the essence of health for great nations, could be carried into the other hemisphere.

Albert Sorel, *L'Europe et la Révolution française*, 8 vol. (Paris, 1885–1904), I, 288–294. Translation by Louise Apfelbaum.

The future of her greatness henceforth lay in the colonies, but there she encountered England. In this new theater their rivalry became even fiercer than in the days of the Hundred Years' War. All of France's resources were needed to continue a struggle which spread over the entire world. She ought not to have advanced her armies towards the Rhine when she was simultaneously committed in Canada and the Indies. Peace on the Continent was the prerequisite for winning the magnificent fortune awaiting her in America and Asia. If she wanted it she had to renounce her Continental ambitions, and she was capable of doing so, for her defenses were formidable. No one around her would dare fire a cannon without her permission. But unfortunately she did not have the wisdom to do so, and in attempting both to establish colonies and to reorganize the kingdoms of Europe, she compromised her power in two worlds at the same time.

The French wanted colonial conquests but they could not refrain from making European ones. England was to profit from this, for Austria became her natural ally against France and was to tie down the French armies. But the French could still contain Austria—they had Prussia, Savoy, Poland, and Turkey, if needed. Diplomacy could accomplish this, but this did not satisfy French policy. Her enmity for the House of Hapsburg outlived the reasons for their rivalry. . . . Containing it was not enough; only its annihilation would provide satisfaction. "It is always a fundamental rule for statesmen," wrote d'Argenson, "to reduce that power to the point where the Emperor is no greater a landowner than the richest Elector." Charles VI died in 1740 leaving only a daughter [Maria Theresa]. The opportunity seemed favorable, and loudly sounding the kill, the French went to war at the head of all the other fortune hunters. They were going to "make an emperor and conquer kingdoms." But the Bavarian who was crowned was a mere puppet emperor, and Marshal de Saxe was considered lucky to preserve for France what Louis XIV had already conquered. The sole result of the coalition was to aggrandize Prussia.

France, however, was defeated at sea, and she left to his own resources the capable Dupleix, who, with a handful of men, founded an empire [in India]. And that was not the worst: after first leaving Canada exposed in order to conquer Silesia for the King of Prussia, France lost it simply for the sake of returning that province to the Queen of Hungary. France had played into England's hands in the War of the Austrian Succession, and into those of Austria in the Seven Years' War.

Frederick was the most uncertain of allies. In 1755 he cynically defected and sided with the English, who had just resumed the war against France. England had Prussia, so it was important that France have Austria to maintain the equilibrium. When Maria Theresa offered her alliance, France accepted, and thus the famous treaty of May 1, 1756, was concluded. The object of their alliance was purely defensive, a fact that France failed to grasp. Though changing partners, she did not cease being their dupe. Louis XV became the defender of Austria with the same blindness that had made him become her adversary. The war on the Continent, at first of secondary importance, became the principal concern, and France fell from the rank of foremost power to that of a second-class state without even attaining the indirect results for which she had sacrificed her most precious interests. Frederick kept Silesia, while France lost Canada, abandoned Louisiana, and turned over her Indian empire to the British. Louis XV had conducted a policy whose sole aim was to defeat England in such a way as to assure that country's triumph.

"Above all," wrote Bernis to Choiseul, then Ambassador to Vienna, "see to it that the King does not remain in servile dependence upon his allies. That would be the worst of all."

Such was the state of France during the last years of the reign of Louis XV. The alliance of 1756, originally a clever expedient, became the most disastrous political system of all. Without gaining territory, France lost her preponderance in Europe. Previously she had grouped around her all those who were disturbed by Austrian power. Forced to choose between them and Austria, she let the latter do as she pleased. Most humiliating of all, immediately after a war in which she lost everything by catering to Maria Theresa's hatred for Frederick, she saw these two irreconcilable Germans come to an understanding without her knowledge, reach an agreement at her expense, and share, in collaboration with Russia, the spoils of Poland, one of her oldest dependents.

France's only remaining ally was Spain. They were allied in 1761 by the Family Compact, the only beneficial accomplishment achieved during these years of disaster. The alliance endured because both countries had the same enemy to combat—England. Victorious but still jealous and ever on watch, England was, to the eighteenth-century French, the hereditary enemy and implacable rival. Treaties with her were considered only truces, and hostilities were forever brewing. An age-old hatred, inflamed by continual wounds to French pride, nurtured the desire for revenge. Contemporaries compared the relationship between England and France to that of Rome and Carthage. One famous political writer said that "England has adopted the same principle of not letting us recover; of ceaselessly watching our ports, shipyards, and arsenals; of spying on our projects, preparations, and slightest movements and cutting them short by haughty insinuations or threatening shows of force."

This represented a great decline. Louis XV's incoherent efforts at secret diplomacy to repair the errors caused by his official policies sprang only from the futile disquiet of a mind weary of itself. His agitation simply betrayed his weakness. This man of feeling sacrificed and consumed in a thankless and questionable effort all the forces of a soul capable of conceiving and, perhaps accomplishing great things under a different regime. Gérard de Rayneval, one of the most enlightened and able secretaries in the Ministry of Foreign Affairs, wrote that there developed

among all nations the opinion that France no longer had either strength or resources. Envy, which up to then had been the motivating force behind the policies of all the courts towards France, deteriorated into contempt. The government of Versailles enjoyed neither credit nor influence at any court. Instead of being at the center of all great affairs as it had been, it became a passive spectator. Its approval or disapproval was no longer held of consequence.

The nation sensed this decline and was all the more irritated because the new state system upset all its traditions. National propaganda had for a century striven to incite feeling against the House of Hapsburg. The need to bring about its downfall, even through Protestant alliances, especially with Prussia, was considered a principle of statecraft in the public mind. Learned in school, these truths were judged to be as obvious as the philosophy of the Enlightenment and the rules of classical tragedy. Richelieu had never been so greatly honored nor the treaties of Westphalia so widely admired. The War of the Austrian Succession stirred and reawakened these great memories. France was fighting her two traditional rivals at the same time. Napoleon was to say that the battle of Fontenoy [in 1745] kept the monarchy alive for another forty years. Confronted with Frederick's defection at the beginning of the Seven Years' War, the public became aware of the need to turn the tables and contain Prussia. It could understand and applaud the Austrian alliance. It believed that France, having rid herself of the Prussians, could now assemble all her resources against the English. But when France saw that the war effort was being carried into Germany and that France was fighting not for herself but for the House of Hapsburg; that Canada was being sacrificed for Silesia; and that under the pretext of avenging Maria Theresa's losses, she was exposing her own shores to English attack, she ceased to understand and felt betrayed.

FRANCE AND THE FINANCING OF
THE AMERICAN REVOLUTION

ALPHONSE AULARD

... The American insurgents were very hesitant to turn to France. The memory of the Seven Years' War stood between the young nation and the old kingdom. In North America, French and English colonists had mercilessly fought and killed each other ... and since the war there had been no love lost between them. When the first difficulties arose between the colonies and their mother country, Franklin wrote to his son from London on August 28, 1767, "I fancy that intriguing nation would like very well to meddle on occasion, and blow up the coals between Britain and her colonies; but I hope we shall give them no opportunity."

Once the revolution began, these sentiments changed quickly. If Louis XVI's ministers looked with pleasure on England's embarrassment and saw it as an occasion to avenge the humiliation of 1763, the enlightened public was moved by nobler feelings. There was immediate sympathy in France for those courageous rebels who hated despotism and who wished to be free or die.

In May, 1777, Franklin wrote from Passy to Doctor [Samuel] Cooper that the French, who were under the yoke of despotism, were enthusiastic about American liberty and the constitutions of the newly freed English colonies. "There are," he said,

such numbers everywhere, who talk of removing to America, with their families and fortunes as soon as peace and independence shall be established, that it is generally believed we shall have a prodigious addition of strength, wealth, and arts from the emigration of Europe; and it is thought that to lessen or prevent such emigrations, the tyrannies established there must relax, and allow more liberty to their people. Hence it is a common observation here that our cause is the *cause of all mankind*, and that we are fighting for their liberty in defending our own.

The time had passed when Franklin considered France a scheming nation and when the French accused the Virginians of bloody disloyalty.

Lafayette says in his *Memoirs* that it was then that his heart *was committed*. Many other French hearts were won over at that time, and the public spectacle of this allegiance caused the Americans to feel that they could, without dishonor, ask for aid from a nation which had only recently been their enemy and which now displayed such chivalric sympathy for them.

Alphonse Aulard, "La dette américaine envers la France," *La Revue de Paris*, trente-deuxième année, 1925 (III), pp. 319–327, 334, 336–338. © *La Revue de Paris*. Used by permission. Editors' translation.

This loyal and deep change of heart must be remembered in order to understand the origin of the monetary debt.

The financial aid began even before any American emissary, or at least any authorized emissary, arrived at Versailles. By the fervor of his written memoirs and his engaging words, the enthusiastic adventurer Beaumarchais caught the imagination of the lethargic Louis XVI and perhaps even that of the cold, calculating Vergennes, the Minister of Foreign Affairs.

On May 2, 1776, Vergennes wrote a letter to the king . . . in which he requested him to sign an authorization for him to "furnish a million *livres* to aid the English colonies. . . ."

. . . The King of France had already spent a million *livres tournois* on the Americans' behalf when Silas Deane . . . arrived at Versailles in the first days of July, 1776, the first of the political agents whom Congress was to send to France. . . .

Congress increased to three the number of these agents at Versailles. Arthur Lee and Benjamin Franklin, who were in England, became Deane's two colleagues, and arrived in France in December, 1776. The personal success and popularity of Franklin are well known. He was the persuasive advocate of his country's cause before French public opinion and the King of France.

These three envoys were virtual plenipotentiaries and tried to obtain far more than Deane had requested. In a letter to Vergennes on January 5, 1777, they pointed out that "the private purchase made by Mr. Deane . . . is rendered ineffectual by an order forbidding their exportation." They asked for outright assistance, eight ships of the line completely manned, with guns and cannon to be sent under convoy. . . .

The three American envoys continued to insist on military aid, offering in return to help France in reconquering Canada, and to ask for other subsidies and loans.

Finally, the certainty that England would negotiate with the rebellious colonies and the enthusiastic sympathy of France decided the king and Vergennes to take the crucial step.

On February 8, 1778, Vergennes and the American plenipotentiaries signed two treaties, one of commerce, the other of alliance. . . .

Before the conclusion of the treaties and the entry of France into the war, the king made a gift to the United States in the sum of 3 million *livres*, including the million granted to Beaumarchais.

Then followed a combination of loans and gifts, and in 1781, the king freely gave 6 million *livres* more. The various expenses involved in the loan of 1 million *livres* from the farmers-general were so great that the Americans in fact received only about 850,000 *livres*. In another gift, the French government assumed the difference so that the Americans had to pay back only what they had actually received.

Another and rather small generous gesture was made, but one which, because of a secret detail, . . . was as unknown to historians as it was to contemporaries. The register entitled *Decisions of the King, 1760–1792* at the French Ministry of Foreign Affairs [shows an entry] for December 7, 1780, under the heading "Affairs of America," that reads, "Deane, one of the envoys of the United States of America who signed the treaties with the King, extraordinary aid of 24,000 *livres* out of secret contingency funds. . . ."

Along with the gifts, there were loans made once the treaties were signed, namely:

In 1778, 3 million *livres*, paid in four installments of 750,000 *livres* each, once every three months.

In 1779, a million paid in four installments of 250,000 *livres* each, at irregular intervals.

In 1780, 4 million, in five installments, four of 750,000 francs and one (the last) of a million.

In 1781, 4 million more, paid in roughly the same manner.

In 1782, 6 million, in three installments, two of 1,500,000 *livres*, one (the last, on July 5) of 3 million.

Altogether 18 million *livres* were loaned. The repayment of this capital of 18 million was set for January 1, 1788. Moreover, in May, 1781, the king borrowed 5 million florins—the equivalent of 10 million *livres tournois*—from the States General of Holland for the United States on his security and responsibility.

In this whole matter of gifts and loans, it may be gathered that Louis XVI was more disposed towards generosity than was his minister Vergennes, because the king was more influenced by French public opinion. . . .

. . . At the end of November, 1780, Congress decided to ask the king for 25 million as a loan to provide for the maintenance of an army of 32,000 enlisted men until the end of the war.

Washington then sent Colonel John Laurens to France to ask for the dispatch of more men, but above all for subsidies of money. In these instructions, dated January 15, he wrote, "Without [money], we may make a feeble and expiring effort the next campaign, in all probability the period to our opposition. With it, we should be in a condition to continue the war, as long as the obstinacy of the enemy might require."

It was in vain that Franklin, who saw the straits of the royal treasury at first hand, tried to calm the impatience of his compatriots. On December 5, 1782, in a letter to [Robert R.] Livingston in which he announced an imminent loan of 6 million, he wrote:

It is vain for me to repeat again what I have so often written, and what I find taken so little notice of, that there are bounds to every thing, and that the faculties of this nation are limited like those of all other nations. Some of you seem to have established as maxims the suppositions that France has money enough for all her occasions and all ours besides, and that if she does not supply us it is owing to her want of will, or to my negligence. As to the first, I am sure it is not true; and to the second, I can only say I should rejoice as much as any man in being able to obtain more; and I shall also rejoice in the greater success of those who may take my place.

Franklin was, in addition ... very tightfisted and ever vigilant. On February 6, 1782, Vergennes decided to put at his disposition what remained of the Dutch loan amounting to 4,264,291 *livres*. Franklin replied that the accounts were wrong, and that 6,450,981 *livres* remained. He attached a statement of what he had received, and in which an installment of 2,210,000 *livres* was presented as a private loan. Vergennes had to answer him firmly that this sum would be deducted from the Dutch loan. . . .

Once the peace was signed in 1783, no further loan or outright grant was accorded the United States. . . .

The time for the first payment on the interest arrived on January 1, 1785. The date for the first installment on the principal arrived on September 3, 1786, that is, three years after the signing of the peace treaty. . . .

This moment passed without France's demanding anything, however solemnly the commitment was made on both occasions by the United States. The financial distress of France's allies was such that no one even dreamed of asking for the smallest sum. The American states were not paying the taxes which Congress imposed on them.

In 1785 the American treasury took in only $375,000. In 1786 its financial embarrassment was such that, for some time, Congress could not even pay its ambassadors their salaries.

On the eve of the Revolution, the royal government had received from the United States only the interest from the Dutch loan which it had contracted for them. This interest, amounting to 400,000 *livres* a year, was paid regularly to France beginning in 1784. . . .

. . . The opinion of the French elite did not make these calculations: it would have protested against the attitude of a demanding creditor towards those heroic rebels who were both victorious and poor. The debt was not spoken of to the Americans, and rarely did the French speak of it among themselves. . . .

By 1789 the United States had received from France gifts totaling 9 million *livres* plus approximately 3 million in forgiven interest, a total of 12 million as an outright gift. In addition they had received 34 million in loans.

Today 46 million is a small sum in the budget of a great state. It was a large sum then. [Marcel] Marion, the historian of French finances, believed it possible to say that at the end of the Old Regime, France's income was 236 million *livres* and her expenses 283,162,000 *livres*. These terms of comparison show the relative importance of the monetary aid accorded the United States by the King of France.

The Americans felt it, and Lafayette, who had gone off to fight for them, was scarcely more popular in the United States than Louis XVI, who had given or loaned them important sums. On December 17, 1782, in a letter in which he excused himself to Vergennes for having signed the preliminaries of peace without including him—in spite of his instructions—Franklin said, "I believe that no prince was ever more beloved and respected by his own subjects than the king is by the people of the United States."

No doubt he wanted to excuse himself, but he did express a true sentiment, one general in America.

In order to lend, the royal government had to borrow, and thus began or accelerated the ruin of its finances. This ruin was completed by the other enormous expenses which the war brought once France had entered it.

If the American Revolution prepared the French Revolution by spreading principles and an example, it also prepared it by the financial disorder that resulted from France's assistance. Without this assistance the Old Regime might perhaps have lasted a few years more. . . .

THE PARLEMENTS OF FRANCE IN THE EIGHTEENTH CENTURY

ALFRED COBBAN

If we compare the French monarchy in the eighteenth century with practically any other European monarchy of the same period, the striking fact that emerges is the comparative effectiveness of the limitations on royal power in France, and this in spite of the fact that, in the absence of other checks, organised opposition to the crown was concentrated in a single institution. The royal courts of law, known as the *parlements*, stood out in proud isolation as the last great relics of the medieval French constitution. The *parlement* of Paris still retained much of the prestige won in the centuries when it had co-operated with the monarchy in the glorious task of building up the unity of France. . . . On the model provided by Paris twelve other *parlements* and four sovereign courts had in due course been established in the provinces between the fifteenth and the eighteenth centuries. The *parlement* of Paris,

Alfred Cobban, "The *Parlements* of France in the Eighteenth Century," *History*, n.s., XXXV (1950), pp. 64, 67, 69–80. © *History*. Used by permission.

however, by virtue of its priority in time, its situation, and the vast extent of its jurisdiction, covering one-third of the country, was by far the most important. . . .

The powers of the *parlements* fell into three categories. First came their strictly judicial duties as law courts. Secondly, they had a wide range of police powers, which brought them into rivalry with the royal *intendants*. Most important of all, in the eighteenth century, were their political claims. Registration by the *parlements* was the traditional method of promulgation for royal decrees, each court having the exclusive right of registration within its own *ressort* [jurisdiction]. When a *parlement* found cause for objection in the king's decrees it drew up *remonstrances*. The king could reply to these by *lettres de jussion*, ordering that his decrees should be registered, and if the *parlement* remained recalcitrant its resistance could be overridden by the procedure of *lit de justice*. In the last resort, if the *parlement* refused to recognise the *lit de justice*, reiterated its remonstrances, or suspended its sessions in protest, the crown could take action against individual magistrates by *lettre de cachet*, ordering imprisonment or removal to another town, or in extreme cases the exile of the court as a whole. . . .

The *parlements*, indeed, were destined to play the leading part in the new Jansenist controversy. Endemic throughout the reign of Louis XV, it became particularly acute in the 'thirties as a result of the wave of religious enthusiasm produced by a very inconvenient, though well authenticated, outbreak of miracles at the tomb of the Jansenist deacon Pâris. Conflict between the *parlements* and the church was further intensified by the policy of the archbishop of Paris, Christophe de Beaumont, a virtuous, charitable, not very intelligent prelate, and a fanatical partisan of the bull *Unigenitus*, who ordered his clergy to refuse the last sacraments to all persons suspected of Jansenism, unless they could produce a *billet de confession* signed by a priest who had accepted the bull. Since opponents of the bull could not be prevented from dying, a better means could hardly have been found of maintaining a continual flow of incidents and perpetuating unrest. The *parlements* protected the Jansenist clergy and took legal action against those who obeyed the archbishop's orders to withhold the sacraments. The court being largely under the influence of the *dévot* [clerical] party, the royal council supported Christophe de Beaumont. It attempted to still the Jansenist agitation by decree after decree, but never persisted long in any one policy. We need not trace the long series of *remonstrances, lits de justice* and exiles, followed by weak royal withdrawals. In turn the *parlements* successfully resisted the archbishop of Paris, the crown and the papacy. Finally they turned their main attack against the Jesuits, the traditional enemies of Jansenists and Gallicans alike. The story of the fall of the Jesuits is too well known to require re-telling. In 1764 the king yielded to pressure from many quarters, and the long campaign of the *parlements* reached its triumphant conclusion. With the dissolution of the Society of Jesus in France the struggle came to an end, and Jansenism ceased to occupy the centre of the political stage.

In their embittered warfare with the church, the *parlements* had undermined one important pillar of divine-right monarchy, and given a lesson in successful disobedience. At the same time they were engaging in direct warfare with the monarchy through their constant opposition to all attempts on the part of the royal administration to reform its finances. It is hardly too much to say that every project for financial reform between 1715 and 1789 broke on the rock of the opposition of the *parlements*. After various indecisive skirmishes, a serious dispute arose with the appointment, in 1745, of possibly the ablest financial minister of the century, Jean-Baptiste de Machault, to face the problem of financing the War of the Austrian Succession. Since existing taxes, with all the exemptions allowed to the privileged classes, could evidently not produce sufficient revenue, the obvious solution lay in a new tax which should be free from such exemptions. In 1749, therefore, Machault presented an edict creating the *vingtième*, a tax on income to be imposed on all proprietors. The battle against the *vingtième*, begun by the *parlements*, was taken up by the clergy, who through the influence of the *dévot* party at court succeeded in obtaining exemption for the property of the church. In effect this meant the ruin of Machault's plans. The *vingtième* was subsequently so riddled with exceptions that it became little better than merely another tax upon the unfortunate peasantry. It was a long time before another controller-general was found to attempt a fundamental reform. . . .

It may fairly be said that the *parlements* presented an unyielding barrier against which the reforming spirit of the century broke itself in vain. The writings they condemned, though packed with plans for reform, were far from revolutionary. In the royal administration there was a machine ready made for putting the plans of the reformers into operation. A reforming bureaucracy is a rare thing in history, but such was the French bureaucracy in the eighteenth century. For the frustration of reform, and its eventual translation into revolution, the *parlements* bear no small share of the responsibility. In the words of Aulard, "If they prepared the Revolution, . . . it was not only because they weakened the monarchy by the fact of their disobedience, it was also because they prevented it from evolving and creating new institutions better related to the spirit of the time."

With the successful resistance of the *parlements* to ministerial attempts at financial reform, and their triumph over the clergy, symbolised in the destruction of the Society of Jesus, it may be said that one stage in their history in the eighteenth century was completed. . . .

The *Grandes Remonstrances* of 9 April, 1753, may be regarded as opening the second stage in the campaign of the *parlements* against the monarchy. In these the *parlement* of Paris speaks of *"une espèce de contrat"* ["a kind of contract"] between the sovereign and the people, and asserts that "if subjects owe obedience to kings, kings for their part owe obedience to the laws." They now cease to rely mainly on their historical claims and begin to appeal to the rights of the nation, of which they regard themselves as the representative. If we are looking for an agency through which the ideas of the contractual school of political thought could have been brought into the minds of the members of the revolutionary assemblies, among whom, it must be remembered, a large proportion were *avocats*, here is a much more palpable one than the little-read and less understood *Contrat social* of Rousseau. Nor should we turn to the *philosophes* or physiocrats, whose writings were more strongly influenced by the ideas of the newer utilitarian trend of thought. It is not unreasonable to suggest that the *parlements* played a large part in spreading the idea that the people is the only rightful source of power. On the eve of 1789 they were even talking, however inappropriately for such bodies, of liberty and equality—"that man is born free, that in origin men are equal, these are truths which do not need to be proved"; and of the authority of the general will—"One of the first conditions of society is that the individual will shall always yield to the general will." . . .

The fall of Choiseul, and his replacement by Maupeou in 1770, was to lead to a revolutionary change. For the first time Louis XV had given his confidence to a strong minister, who was determined to crush opposition. He had an equally determined colleague in the abbé Terray, who, as controller-general, proceeded to deal with what had become a critical financial situation by a wholesale repudiation of obligations and a forced loan. These measures, which were in effect a declaration of royal bankruptcy, were directed mainly against the wealthy *bourgeois*, for whom the *parlements* had no love. To these steps, therefore, they offered only a perfunctory resistance. But the king had now a minister who was prepared to take the initiative and crush the opposition of the *parlements* once and for all. Maupeou flung down a deliberate challenge, to which the *parlement* of Paris replied by suspending its sessions, and refusing to resume them, although four times summoned by *lettres de jussion*. In January 1771, Maupeou proceeded to have the magistrates exiled and their offices confiscated. A royal court was substituted for the *parlements*, taking their name and functions. Protests showered upon the ministry, but undeterred, Maupeou next turned the axe against the provincial *parlements*. At the same time, the opportunity was taken to divide the huge *ressort* of the *parlement* of Paris by the creation of six new courts. Maupeou also had plans for fundamental judicial reform. To begin with, the purchase and sale of offices in the new *parlements*, and the taking of *épices*, [gifts to insure special consideration] were forbidden. Further projected legal reforms were destined not to be realised until his secretary, Lebrun, was able to introduce them in the year VIII [1800], under the consulate of Bonaparte. Freed from the opposition of the *parlements*, however, Terray was able to introduce important financial reforms. By 1774 he had reduced the deficit to manageable proportions. . . .

The *parlements* soon showed the use they intended to make of their victory. Turgot, who had been made controller-general, initiated a programme of reform. A former *intendant*, he belonged to that administrative magistracy which the *parlements* regarded as their natural enemy. As his measures appeared they encountered a series of protests from the *parlements* and refusals of registration, until the hostility they aroused gathered so many forces into the opposition that the king abandoned him. Turgot's was the first of a series of attempts at financial reform, continually frustrated by an increasingly close alliance of all the privileged interests, with the *parlements* in the vanguard of resistance. . . .

So long as Necker, who succeeded Turgot, attempted no reforms, and pursued his policy of borrowing on an unprecedented scale, he encountered no serious opposition from the *parlements*, and their demand for the *états généraux* was forgotten. When he took the first step towards reform their hostility revived and it became impossible for him to obtain the registration of further loans. Recognising defeat, he put forward proposals which he knew the royal council would reject, thus enabling himself to resign with honour and the reputation of having sacrificed office to his desire for reform. Calonne, who became controller-general in 1783, also met with little opposition while he continued the policy of borrowing. When the sources of loans began to dry up, and he was faced with the urgency of new taxation, he attempted to circumvent the inevitable opposition of the *parlements* by calling an assembly of notables. This device, however, proved fruitless and his successor, Brienne, reverted to the attempt to obtain registration for fresh taxes from the *parlements*, with the usual result.

Having tried conciliation, and even corruption, in vain, Brienne, or rather his colleague Lamoignon, fell back on strong measures in the form of a revival of the policy of Maupeou. On 8 May 1788, the process of *lit de justice* was used to set up forty-seven new courts to take over practically the whole judicial business of the *parlements*, with a *cour plenière* at Paris to verify and register the laws. The conflict was now frankly a political one, between the supporters of the absolute monarchy and the privileged classes led by the *parlements*. The words unconstitutional and anti-constitutional, which are hardly met with before 1788, become frequent. Open revolt breaks out in several of the provinces. With clergy, *noblesse*, *bourgeoisie* and the mobs of the towns all on the side of the *parlements*, the crown once again gave way. The queen reluctantly abandoned her support of Brienne, and public opinion forced back into office the one man whose genius was supposed to be equal to the task of solving the financial problems of the country. On 23 September 1788, Necker recalled the *parlements* and abandoned the scheme of Lamoignon. All parties were agreed that there was only one final recourse now: the *états généraux* were summoned for the following year. . . .

Yet the moment of the triumph of the *parlements* was the moment of their downfall. It was at this point that the falsity of their whole position was revealed. When they registered the royal decrees convoking the *états généraux*, they added the condition that the forms of 1614 should be observed. They followed this up by rejecting a proposal in favour of the right of the *tiers état* [Third Estate] to deliberate on all subjects. In so doing they revealed themselves as the mere spokesmen of the privileged orders, and brought the fundamental opposition of interests between themselves and the *tiers* to the surface. Protests against the attitude of the *parlements* poured out. The leaders of the *tiers* launched a violent campaign against them, stirred up popular agitation, and directed the mob against the *parlements* in their provincial strongholds. Neither the privileged classes, nor the *bourgeoisie*, it must be observed in passing, realised how dangerous a game they were playing, in letting loose popular passions just at the time when a series of bad harvests, following on a period of economic regression, had produced an economic crisis of the utmost severity. Without the economic crisis, indeed, the political crisis might not have been possible. Most sections of the country were suffering from it, and since the royal administration was still the responsible government of the country, they all tended to place the blame for the economic ills, the real sources of which they failed to understand, on the king's ministers.

The *frondeur* [rebellious] *parlements* had blocked the road to reform for so long, while at the same time exciting the demand, that now they were faced with revolution. Not for themselves had they laboured to bring down the absolute monarchy. Now was seen what Mirabeau had prophesied in a letter of April 1788, to Montmorin—"Suddenly the *parlements* by the force of circumstances will be reduced to their true stature." . . .

TURGOT AND THE FATE OF HIS
SIX EDICTS

Douglas Dakin

Although for a long while Turgot had discussed his projects with the King, it was not until January 1776 that the Edicts were submitted at intervals to the Council, where they were debated in Louis's presence. Anticipating the

Douglas Dakin, *Turgot and the Ancien Régime* (London, 1939), pp. 233–244, 247. © Methuen & Co., Ltd., and Octagon Books, Inc. Used by permission.

numerous objections that the Ministers and others round the King would raise, and fearing that every effort would be made to misrepresent his proposals, he took the wise precaution of composing for Louis a *mémoire* outlining their scope and explaining in simple language their necessity and justification. He was following his wonted method and, indeed, the only one that was possible, for again it was a question of appealing to the King in the name of humanity and of justice, of overcoming his timidity, of making him resolute, and of counteracting the intrigues and insinuations of other advisers.

One of the Six Edicts, in the form of a Declaration dated 5 February, suppressed all dues levied upon grain, cereals, and pulses in Paris with the exception of a number of relatively trivial impositions upon inferior grains, which were left as perquisites for the porters and measurers. Earlier legislation, as we have seen, had not applied to Paris, the letters patent of 2 November 1774 having merely reserved to the King the right to declare the grain trade free in this city when circumstances permitted. The surviving restrictions upon commerce in grain and flour in Paris and its environs detracted from the freedom accorded elsewhere. . . .

Another edict was complementary to the Declaration of 5 February. It suppressed a multiplicity of officials of the ports, quays, halls, and markets of Paris, many of whom were notoriously corrupt. On several occasions these office-holders had been deprived of their benefices, only to be reinstated a short while afterwards, the Government as usual making a little profit in employing this habitual fiscal expedient. The offices in question had been abolished once again in 1759, but had been restored provisionally the next year until the holders could be compensated. Turgot's edict really executes that of 1759 which had fixed the indemnity. In doing this it provides that taxes formerly levied by these officials should in future be collected by the *ferme général* [tax farming system], the proceeds being devoted to the compensation of those who had lost their employments. Turgot thus arranged matters so that this particular reform occasioned no loss to the Treasury. The other measure, however—that suppressing the dues on grain—meant a diminution in revenue of 52,000 *livres* annually; but this deficit he had already made good as a result of the reform of the levy of impositions in Paris.

A third edict abolished the *Caisse de Poissy*. This institution, purporting to facilitate the cattle and the meat trade, was really nothing more than a means of levying an imposition, very little of which found its way to the Treasury. Originally established in 1690, and re-established in 1707 to meet the rising expenses of the War of the Spanish Succession, suppressed again after the Peace of Utrecht, and finally restored in 1743, the *Caisse de Poissy* was supposed to advance money to the butchers to enable them to pay the dealers, and the dealers in turn to pay the farmers, who normally were compelled to wait a long time for their money. But all that the financiers of the *Caisse* did in practice was to advance money to the wealthier butchers who had no need for credit and, in doing this, to levy a commission which increased the price of each beast by 15 *livres*. Upon all advances they received a profit of 92 per cent per year, their total earnings (there were 100 of them) being 1,500,000 *livres* annually. There was really no justification for the *Caisse*: numerous petitions had denounced it, and very few people had the effrontery to defend it. . . .

Such were the . . . lesser Edicts. They were relatively trivial measures designed to reduce slightly the cost of living for the wage-earners in Paris, to promote a little more the freedom of trade, and, in doing these things, to provide, if all went well, a small gain to the Treasury. Substantially of the same nature as numerous other reforms for which Turgot was responsible, they were not in any way an outrageous attack upon property. For all the owners of offices concerned were adequately compensated, and the lesser financiers received much more lenient treatment than they might have expected, for example, from the Abbé Terray.

"Your Majesty," wrote Turgot in 1776, "has known for a long while my thoughts concerning the guilds. . . ." Already he had attacked restrictions upon labour, and also the monopolies enjoyed by the commercial and industrial communities. In November 1774 he had freed the citizens of twenty-three imperial towns from the *droit d'aubaine*, under which the property of certain deceased aliens escheated either to the Crown or to the seigneur. For he believed that this archaic survival "debarred from settling in France a great number of skilled men, industrious artisans, capitalists, and useful merchants who desired nothing more than to make France the centre of their activities. . . ."

There were other pressing reasons for abolishing the guilds. In the first place, the majority of them were saddled with debts, some the result of loans raised to meet the demands of the Treasury, and others the outcome of ill-managed corporate transactions. Fortunately the communities in Paris possessed sufficient assets to meet their liabilities, but outside Paris the situation was not such a happy one, and, as Turgot told the King, a thorough examination of the finances of the provincial guilds must be made before the Treasury could take over responsibility without incurring heavy losses. In the second place, the guilds increased the price of food. In times of normal grain prices, for example, the people of Paris ought to have been able to buy bread at 2 *sous* 2 *deniers* the *livre*: as it was they were called upon to pay 2 *sous* 9 *deniers*, or well over 10 per cent too much. Finally, the guilds were constantly involved in litigation, and this not only conduced indirectly to high prices, but also involved numerous individuals outside the communities in heavy and ruinous legal costs. In this particular abuse one vested interest was linked with another; as Turgot warned the King, the *gens du palais* were sure to defend those institutions that provided them with steady employment and a lucrative reward; and, as usual, they would aver that they were protecting the masses, this time from the sharp practice of traders and merchants, who, if left uncontrolled, would flood the markets with inferior commodities at outrageous prices.

Of all Turgot's reforms, the most eagerly awaited was that suppressing the *corvées* [compulsory road repair]. "The provinces," Condorcet wrote to him as early as September 1774, "are expecting the same good work that you accomplished at Limoges. . . ." By December he was ready to raise the question in the Council, and Louis, on being shown the information that had been collected, was quick to feel the grave injustice of the *corvées*. Probably this was the occasion when he presented to the King the memorandum to which he refers in 1776. "When I had the honour more than a year ago to read to Your Majesty a first *mémoire* on the suppression of the *corvées*, your heart seemed to decide the matter immediately. Your resolution soon became common knowledge; the provinces came to hear of it; and from that moment it became impossible not to abolish this imposition. . . ."

His projected reform of July 1775 was based upon three general principles: first, the intendants, in consultation with the engineers, were to compose annual budgets for public works in the *généralités*, and these, having been sanctioned by the Council, were to be registered in the *Cours des aides*; secondly, the sums thus approved were to be levied on all landowners, no matter what their status, in proportion to their incomes; finally, all such taxation was under no circumstances to be paid to the Treasury, but was to remain in the hands of the local officials of the *ponts et chaussées* [highway administration]. In this way Turgot hoped to obviate the danger that an imposition to replace the *corvées* might be diverted to other needs. The project in general was approved by the intendants, several of whom had interesting comments to make. Corée of Franche-Comté and Fontette of Caen, while favouring the measure for the regions where the unreformed *corvées* prevailed, preferred the systems they had introduced themselves. Journet of Auch feared that the imposition might prove unjust, but only for the reason that the *cadastre* [land register] in his *généralité* [fiscal region] was highly defective. A number of replies expressed the fear that the privileged classes, with the connivance of the *Cours des aides*, might quickly gain exemptions from the tax, with the result that a heavy burden would fall upon the *taillables*. Calonne of Metz and Esmangard of Bordeaux went so far as to suggest that the *Cours des aides* should not be given cognizance of the imposition, which should be levied solely upon the royal authority.

It was on 6 January that Turgot presented the Edict to the King, who immediately gave it his approval. The preamble contains a summary of all his earlier writings denouncing the inveterate abuses and injustice of the *corvées*. . . .

Throughout the remainder of January the Six Edicts were debated in a committee of the Council, and, although the detailed provisions do not seem to have been known to the public until the second week in February, the general principles aroused considerable discussion throughout the kingdom. The magistrates began their offensive before receiving the texts for official registration; they took no trouble to ascertain the scope of the Edicts; and even when finally they were given this knowledge, they simply ignored it, preferring to misrepresent the measures and the ideas of the man responsible for them. Although it was the Edict abolishing the guilds that more than any other infringed their professional interests, they concentrated their attack upon the legislation suppressing the *corvées*, for the simple reason that they could enlist the support of the clergy and the nobility. Both Malesherbes and Véri frequently warned Turgot of the danger he was running. Yet neither of these sympathizers went so far as to advise him to withdraw. Véri, in fact, gave him constant encouragement, endeavouring at the same time to convince Maurepas of the necessity of a firm policy at this juncture in the interests of the royal authority.

Turgot first tried to reason with the *Parlement*. Early in January he arranged an interview with d'Aligre, the premier president, hoping to convince him of the utility and justice of the Edicts. D'Aligre was unbending; a warm conversation ensued, ending with the threat of unflinching opposition on the one side and of the determination to prevail upon Louis to hold a *lit de justice* upon the other. For Turgot to have given way would have meant an end to all reform. Then again, as a King's Minister he considered it his duty to uphold the monarchical prerogative against the attacks of the Magistracy; for, from the very beginning, it was not exclusively a question of his Edicts, but of the nature of sovereignty. That was a point which Maurepas failed to grasp firmly. While on the one hand he knew that it was expected of him to promote Louis's authority, yet on the other he was prone to listen too carefully to those who were forever telling him that he was the one to protect the throne from the wild designs of visionary reformers.

It was Conti who came forward to lead the magisterial opposition. Standing to lose 50,000 *livres* annually if the guilds were abolished, and welcoming always any opportunity to weaken the royal power, he adopted an uncompromising attitude. . . . It was d'Eprémesnil, a young, headstrong, and excitable magistrate, who proposed the vote of censure and who gained a passing fame in denouncing the economists as "an absurd, fanatical, dangerous sect, the more dangerous as they now had one of the King's Ministers at their head." He compared them to the Jesuits, and held up Necker for admiration as an orthodox economist. Conti expressed his agreement with these opinions, and before leaving asked to be informed when the Edicts were to be laid before the Parlement, adding that if he were unable to come in his carriage, he would be brought on a litter.

The magistrates had been encouraged by the knowledge that matters were not moving smoothly in the committee of the Council. It was Miromesnil . . . who was at once their informer, their accessary, and yet to some extent their instrument. A man of little talent and of little mind, by nature a petty Machiavellian, he became in spite of his mediocrities the mouthpiece of the privileged classes. Mistaking in the first instance the feebleness of Maurepas and of the other Ministers for a spirited opposition to Turgot's Edicts, oblivious of the real issues at stake, and having his own magisterial reputation to regain, he did everything to encourage the opposition of the Parlements. Here was a vicious circle: Maurepas and the Ministers grew ever more alarmed, and Miromesnil ever more convinced that he was acting for the best. The Ministers hardly knew which way to turn. They resented the attack that Turgot's measures had brought upon the Government, and yet were delighted to see him in difficulties; and though on the one hand they were reluctant to give him the firm support that might have gone far to silencing the magistrates, on the other their position compelled them to show a little fight in face of common danger. Therefore, early in February they half-heartedly advised the King to proceed with the Edicts, to allow time for remonstrances and, if need be, to hold a *lit de justice*. Even Miromesnil concurred in this advice, hoping to modify the Edicts at a later stage. . . .

The Edicts were submitted to the Parlement on Thursday 7 February. That suppressing the *Caisse de Poissy* was registered immediately. A number of the magistrates spoke in favour of the remaining Edicts; but the majority were resolute against them. Conti was true to his word; he attended every session of the *Parlement*, and he sat upon the committee appointed to compose remonstrances. At any moment he might have withdrawn his opposition had the Ministers pronounced wholeheartedly in Turgot's favour; but, encouraged by Miromesnil's stubborn resistance to Turgot in Council, he felt assured of success, and was convinced that Maurepas, who continued petulantly to censure the Edicts in public, would desert the Comptroller-General. . . .

THE FISCAL AND ECONOMIC CRISES
AT THE END OF THE *ANCIEN RÉGIME*

ERNEST LABROUSSE

In many respects, the Revolution certainly appears to have been a revolution of extreme poverty, as Michelet had guessed and contrary to the thesis of Jaurès, which Mathiez was to take up. Not that Jaurès and Mathiez denied the reality and the influence of poverty. But, according to them, it played only a relatively small and occasional role. This might be true if the economic crisis of 1789 were really what it seems at first sight: a simple "crisis of subsistence," which was precipitated by a hailstorm, and to which propitious heavens were to put an end, with the connivance of the "new men" of the National Assembly and the Gallicans on its Ecclesiastical Committee. Poverty would thus seem to be a kind of meteorological incident. The economic collapse of 1788–1790 was unfortunately on another scale. It afflicted all of the French economy, from grain crops and wine to textiles and building—an economy still deeply shaken by the difficulties it was just beginning to overcome and by the cruel blows of 1785. The cyclical crisis of 1789 was doubtless a cause of the Revolution, and, as one would expect, so was the pre-revolutionary economic depression, but to a much higher degree than Jaurès and Mathiez realized. Both crisis and depression had a profound effect on the events of 1789 and 1790. And they were not without influence on institutions, nor did they fail to provoke lasting, sometimes definitive changes in the most important fiscal and social laws. On these grounds they are real causes.

At the immediate source of the Revolution was a financial crisis, itself a consequence of the debts acquired during the war in America. One can say in broad terms—as others have—that without the war in America there would not have been a financial crisis nor a convocation of the Estates General, nor a Revolution—at least not at the time and in the shape in which it broke out. The Revolution, considered as an event, thus is grounded not only in an economic reality having financial consequences but in a recession. Without war—no "American" debt, no massive increase in expenses and no ills to begin with; but with the recession—no resources, no possible increase in returns and no remedies to these ills, or rather very troublesome resorts and remedies. An increase in the important taxes on consumption had to be abandoned after the 10-per-cent increase of 1781. The *brevet de la taille* [rate of the *taille*] remained fixed after 1780. The last *vingtième* was imposed in 1782 and discontinued in 1787. The spontaneous increase in revenue from the tax

C. Ernest Labrousse, *La Crise de l'économie française à la fin de l'ancien régime et au début de la Révolution* (Paris, 1944). Translation in Clough, Gay, Warner (eds.), *The European Past* (New York: Macmillan, 1964), I, 415–419. © Presses Universitaires de France. Used by permission.

on consumer goods was not sufficient. No doubt the yield from the *aides* increased with the substitution of state control for tax-farming, with the rapid rise in population, and the even more rapid growth of the cities, those great consumers of wine and liquor, and finally with the spread of an economy of trade. The peasant masses, emigrating to the cities, had to pay a tax on the wine they drank in taverns, whereas the wine from their own vineyards, consumed in a closed economy, was tax-exempt. The crisis in wine-growing was itself to increase the *aides*, as it forced the farmer to convert into brandy, which was taxed at a higher rate, sizable quantities of unsold wine. The taxes on consumption held their own or even rose. But the returns would have been very different in an expanding economy of rising prices, which would automatically have increased the revenue from taxes at the wholesale level proportional to prices. This in turn would have induced the farmer to cultivate more land, that is, to multiply the amount of taxable products. And, on the other hand, with an increase in profits, it would have been possible to re-establish the taxes on consumption of 1781 as well as to increase the *brevet de la taille*. To be sure, rewriting history is a strange practice. Let us assume as a hypothesis that at the time of the war in America and in the years following, there existed a state of affairs similar to that at the beginning of the next century, that is, an economy in full expansion: is it so very bold to say that under those circumstances it would have been easier to meet the deficit? or at least that the increase in public returns could easily have served as security for loans to be issued in the future? The Comptroller General would not have had to overcome both the costs of the war and the fast-decreasing revenue from the *taille*. He could have deferred summoning the Assembly of Notables and appealing to the privileged—that is, practically speaking, those people benefiting from rising farm rents, the income from lands which at that time was the only large category of increasing revenue; but these were the very people who obstinately avoided taxation. It would not have been so urgent for the *Ancien Régime* itself to undertake fiscal reforms, namely to survive through self-denial, or to call on the nation to make its Revolution.

The financial consequences of the prerevolutionary depression and of the revolutionary crisis were therefore very serious. They prevented or made difficult the adjustment of receipts to expenditures. What the State received remained insufficient. But, again because of the depression and the crisis, the amount that a taxpayer had to pay became excessive. The tax rate was not reduced, far from it. Though it remained fixed after 1782, we must remember that it was raised, though moderately, at this date as well as in 1781. It was not so much that the fiscal burden increased, but that those who were obliged to bear it were weaker. The drop in prices brought with it a drop in the volume of business transacted, which itself involved a more than proportionate drop in profits: so much so that the tax, though it might hypothetically remain the same, quickly assumed fantastic dimensions in comparison with a fast-vanishing profit. A universal and automatic "fiscal reaction" aroused the majority of the nation against it.

This relatively little known "fiscal reaction" was itself paralleled by a much better known "seigniorial reaction," a seigniorial reaction, some of whose origins may also be found in the economic difficulties which dominated the reign of Louis XVI. The seigniorial proprietor had hoped to gain, through an increase in the amount of taxes he collected in kind, a compensation for the decline in monetary revenue which had resulted from the fall in prices. And above all the lessees of manorial rights—no doubt the most frequent example—used this method to counteract the effects of the economic decline, when, confident in a rising economy, they had agreed to renew seigniorial leases at a high price. As was true of royal taxes, the seigniorial tax was thus also increasing without regard to profits which were decreasing, at any rate on lands subject to this tax, for example lands subject to the *champart*.

But besides the "seigniorial reaction," as it is usually defined, which perhaps applied only to a small fraction of the lands, another seigniorial reaction, universal and automatic, affected all tenants: whether they paid the *champart* or the *dîme* (in this context, equivalent to seigniorial rights). Those who owed a tax in kind, proportional to the gross product, paid, on this account, a relatively increasing tax because the profit, the net product, had fallen proportionally lower than the total volume of business or gross product. As a result, at a time of economic decline or crisis, the tax proportional to the gross product necessarily became a progressive tax on the net product. Here again the tax-payer felt an added burden, even though the amount he paid remained the same.

The universal and prolonged fiscal reaction and the universal and prolonged seigniorial reaction set the majority of the farmers and cultivators against the monarchical tax and against feudalism, not only at the time of the great economic crisis of 1789, in which these two reactions culminated, but during the preceding ten years. The proletariat was no better off. The day laborer, who was working fewer days and was raising a larger family, also had to pay taxes, which at first increased and then remained constant but in both instances were progressive because these taxes were levied against a declining income. If, as was often the case, the laborer also worked a parcel of land which he might own or rent, his income also had to bear the growing pressure of the seigniorial rights, which had reached their maximum during the crisis of 1789.

Thus, it can also be said that even if the tax remained stable and unchanging, that was enough to make it overwhelming. Open the *cahiers*! See what they have to say about the crisis! Taxes must be blamed. Taxes were responsible for hindering the growth of agriculture and crushing the share-cropper and the farmer. The *aides* must be blamed for ruining the wine-grower by causing underselling which devoured profits. Private taxes or seigniorial rights gave rise to similar complaints. Were not these simply the old complaints? Perhaps. Were they foolish complaints in that they held taxes responsible for the crisis? Certainly. But these complaints were genuine and were justified insofar as they denounced the disproportion between profits and taxes, and between wages and taxes. The provoking increase in royal and seigniorial taxes finally was met by something more than complaints. The offices of the tax-farmers as well as the toll-house gates were put to flames. Grain, collected in kind, was repossessed from the seigniorial granaries. From the farmer to the day laborer, a whole people were in agreement, driven to unite through a common decline in agricultural revenues, and by a joint resistance to the fiscal and seigniorial reaction. The cities joined in crying out against the taxes on food and drink and against the nobles and manorial lords who had monopolized the grain collected in kind. As a result, there occurred not only such events and incidents as the "class war" of 1789 and 1790, but also comparatively lasting laws such as those which abolished the *gabelle* and which transformed and lightened the taxes on food and drink, and finally some permanent laws such as those which abolished the *dîme* and put an end to feudalism. . . .

It does not matter that a free economy is by definition not a controlled economy: when economic difficulties arise contemporaries ascribe them to the government. It has already been mentioned that taxes were accused of being responsible for the crisis. Taxes are politically instituted: though at first the *taille* and the *aides* were the accused, the Comptroller General, the ministry and the regime were ultimately held responsible. Especially since taxation, as might be guessed, did not appear to those affected as the sole villain. From all sides, there arose the discordant clamor of recriminations. If a depression and a cyclical crisis occurred, it was not only because the fiscal burden was excessive, it was also because expenditures were excessive. The deficit and the ruin of public credit, far from being perceived as consequences, seemed to contemporaries to be causes: causes of the general uncertainty, of the timidity of capital, and of the ruin of the spirit of enterprise. Why was there the prolonged economic contraction, the long period of fall or fluctuation in the price of grain, or the prolonged collapse in the price of wine? Because the State mistakenly discouraged export. There was overproduction; the government could have put a stop to it but abstained from action. Why did it not revive the prohibition against planting new vineyards? Why again was there, in 1789, such a rapid and wild rise in the price of grain? It was conceded that the bad harvest was in part responsible: but the people accused the monopolists and the government, which had allowed too much wheat to leave the country in 1787 and had not allowed enough to enter in 1788. Marat was to denounce Necker, in particular, as a speculator. If agriculture lacked capital, it was not because the farmer's profit was declining, but because fiscal inequality, exceptions and privileges concentrated the wherewithal of economic activity in the cities. The economic ills were considered political in origin. The remedy was also to be political: a liberal "system of laws."

SUGGESTIONS FOR FURTHER READING

General: C. B. A. BEHRENS, *The Ancien Régime* (London, 1967); PAUL H. BEIK, *A Judgment of the Old Regime: Being a Survey by the Parlement of Provence of French Economic and Fiscal Policies at the Close of the Seven Years War* (New York, 1944); HENRI CARRÉ, *La France sous Louis XV, 1723–1774* (Paris, 1891); JOHN LOUGH, *An Introduction to Eighteenth Century France* (London, 1960); JAMES B. PERKINS, *France under the Regency, with a Review of the Administration of Louis XIV* (Boston, 1892), and *France under Louis XV*, 2 vol. (Boston and New York, 1897); GASTON ZELLER, *Aspects de la politique française sous l'ancien régime* (Paris, 1964); Special (foreign policy): SAMUEL FLAGG BEMIS, *The Diplomacy of the American Revolution* (New York and London, 1935); ALBERT, DUC DE BROGLIE, *L'Alliance autrichienne* (Paris, 1897); C. CHAMBRUN, *A l'école d'un diplomate, Vergennes* (Paris, 1944); PIERRE MURET, *La Prépondérance anglaise, 1715–1763* (Paris, 1949); GASTON ZELLER, *Histoire des relations internationales*, vol. II–III: *Les Temps modernes*, 2 vol. (Paris, 1953–55); (finance and politics): EDGAR FAURE, *La Disgrâce de Turgot (12 mai 1776)* (Paris, 1961); JACQUES GODECHOT, "Les Relations économiques entre la France et les Etats-Unis de 1778 à 1789," *French Historical Studies*, I (1958), 26–39; HERBERT LÜTHY, *La Banque protestante en France de la révocation de l'édit de Nantes à la Révolution*, 2 vol. (Paris, 1959–61); MARCEL MARION, *Histoire financière de la France depuis 1715*, Vol. I, 4 vol. (Paris, 1914–1925); (assemblies): L. BERTHE, "Les Assemblées provinciales et l'opinion publique en 1787–1788," *Revue du Nord*, XLVIII (1966), 185–200; HENRI CARRÉ, *La Fin des parlements (1788–1790)* (Paris, 1912); ALBERT GOODWIN, "Calonne, the Assembly of French Notables of 1787 and the Origins of the 'Révolte Nobilitaire,'" *English Historical Review*, LXI (1946), 202–234, 329–377; JEAN EGRET, *Le Parlement de Dauphiné et les affaires publiques dans la deuxième moitié du XVIIIe siècle*, 2 vol. (Grenoble, 1942), and *La Pré-Révolution française, 1787–1788* (Paris, 1962); JEAN-DOMINIQUE LASSAIGNE, *Les Assemblées de la noblesse de France au XVIIe et au XVIIIe siècle* (Paris, 1962); MICHEL PÉRONNET, "Les Assemblées du clergé de France sous le règne de Louis XVI (1775–1788)," *Annales historiques de la Révolution française*, XXXIV (1962), 8–35; JULES FLAMMERMONT, *Le Chancelier Maupeou et les parlements* (Paris, 1883); J. H. SHENNAN, "The Political Role of the Parlement of Paris, 1715–1723," *Historical Journal*, VIII (1965), 179–200, and "The Political Role of the *Parlement* of Paris under Cardinal Fleury," *English Historical Review*, LXXI (1966), 520–542.

Chapter Four

FRANCE
MAKES A
REVOLUTION

I N THE HISTORY of modern Europe 1789 is a key date, and may even be said to inaugurate "modern" history itself. From one point of view, the French Revolution was but one phase of a wider intellectual and political upheaval in Western Europe and North America that began about 1760 and to which the name *Democratic*, or *Atlantic Revolution* has been applied.[1] Certainly France did develop a revolutionary solution to her internal problems from the large stock of ideas then current—social contract, natural rights, inequity of privilege, absurdity of medieval survivals in an age of Enlightenment—but it was her practical application of these ideas that was eventually exported to the rest of Europe by the Revolutionary armies after 1792. More than any other event since the Protestant Reformation, the French Revolution was international in its ideology: it vaulted political and linguistic boundaries, rallying men to its cause or forcing them to take up arms against it.

At the same time, however, the Revolution remained essentially French. As Professor Rudé demonstrates in the first selection, its origins lay in the political, social, and economic conditions of late eighteenth-century France, and the inability of the Bourbon monarchy to deal with them effectively. Stemming from the growth of a new and ambitious social class, as well as from a general consciousness of the abuses of the Old Regime, the Revolution was precipitated by an economic and financial crisis, one that the privileged classes would not allow the monarchy to resolve without sacrificing its "absolute" power. The clash between the king and an aristocracy at first supported by most of the country prepared the way for the convocation of the Estates General in May, 1789, the passage of sweeping reforms, and the gradual alienation of many of those who had demanded that the monarchy be reformed.

Reduced to its fundamentals, the principles of 1789, the Revolution was first of all a modernizing process, the guiding spirit of which may be called "rationalization." This meant an attack on existing institutions as being outmoded, inefficient, inequitable, and irregular, and which involved an attempt to make them effective, fair, and coherent. The "Gothic" structure of the past, the product of centuries of tradition and custom, yielded before the pickaxes of eighteenth-century utilitarianism, just as the Bastille was razed after its fall on July 14, 1789. The Declaration of the Rights of Man and Citizen proclaimed in August has been styled the "death certificate of the Old Regime"; it was also the birth certificate of a new era. By 1791 French institutions had been drastically remodeled to conform to its principles. France was endowed with her first written constitution, one that established a limited but still viable monarchy.

But the unwillingness of the monarch to abide by the restrictions placed upon him, dramatically revealed by his unsuccessful flight to Varennes in June, 1791, vitiated the new constitution even before it could be put into effect. Then the

---

[1] For a detailed exposition of this thesis, see R. R. Palmer, *The Age of the Democratic Revolution*, 2 vol. (Princeton, 1959–64), and Jacques Godechot, *France and the Atlantic Revolution of the Eighteenth Century, 1770–1799* (New York, 1965).

outbreak of foreign war, desired by both the monarchy and the Girondins of the Legislative Assembly, for different reasons, imperiled all that had been accomplished. Beginning with the overthrow of the king in August, 1792, France underwent another and far-reaching Revolution: the liberal, bourgeois, and decentralized regime was transformed into a centralized, authoritarian, and popular government.

Actively supporting this Second French Revolution led by the National Convention were the *sans-culottes*—the small shopkeepers, tradesmen, and artisans —of Paris. In the second selection, the French historian Albert Soboul describes the social composition and motivation of this social group, which has been called the "mainspring of the Revolution." Far from being the "scum" of society, the *sans-culottes* were respectable citizens who wanted to defend the gains of the Revolution, protect and extend small property, combat "aristocrats" and ensure social equality and their own physical survival in a period of war, rising prices, and scarcity. Between 1792 and 1794, they swelled the ranks of the army, filled the public administration, and through their popular societies and demonstrations, helped to maintain the forward momentum of the Revolution. Much against its will, they pressured the Montagnard Convention into organizing the Terror to repress the enemies of the Revolution and institute the stringent measures which characterize 1793–94, Year II of the Republic.

The Terror marks the apex of the Revolution. But after victory abroad and pacification at home were achieved, and the *sans-culottes* themselves brought under control by the Committee of Public Safety, the democratic Republic of Robespierre was eventually overthrown in its turn in July, 1794. The pendulum of politics, which had caused the elimination of the absolute monarchists of 1789, the liberal monarchists of 1790–92, the moderate republicans of 1792–93, and now the radical republicans, was to swing back toward the conservative republicans of the Thermidorian reaction and Directory (1794–99), the regime of Napoleon (1799–1814), and the "absolute" monarchy of the Bourbon Restoration.

The favorable re-examination of the Directory that the English historian Albert Goodwin presents in the last selection is part of a trend that has developed in the past thirty years to see the harried constitutional republic in a more sympathetic light. Too often considered a "parenthesis" between the Convention and the Consulate, the Directory is presented by Goodwin as a capable group of men who had to grapple with the crucial problems of internal order while waging (and winning) a struggle against Old Regime Europe.

But because the Directory could not return to the policies of the Terror or rely on the popular crowd (broken by 1795), it was compelled to turn to the army for support. Napoleon Bonaparte, its most popular general, who had helped save the Thermidorian Convention in 1795, returned from Egypt to overthrow the Directory in November, 1799, and declared that the Revolution was over.

In a sense it was, for Napoleon sought to consolidate rather than innovate. But its ultimate consequences still shape the destiny of France. Besides the tradition of spectrum politics—the wide range of political ideologies from Left to Right— the Revolution also created what might be called "permanent illegitimacy," the inability of any French regime to establish itself firmly in the hearts of all

Frenchmen by securing their loyalty and respect. The monarchy, inefficient and incapable as it had become by 1789, still represented a centuries-old tradition which the entire country could accept, if not always hold in the highest esteem. The fall and execution of Louis XVI brought this to an end. The remaining years of the Revolution, and indeed the years since 1793, witnessed the constant search for a new basis of political authority, of legitimacy, to which all Frenchmen could rally. One constitution has succeeded another, but none has served as more than a resting place until a crisis, foreign or domestic, has swept it into the dustheap. In this sense the Revolution is not yet over.

⁓◌ɰɰɰ⌐⌐

WHY WAS THERE A REVOLUTION IN FRANCE?

George Rudé

. . . The system of government devised by Louis XIV had, under his successors, lost a great deal of its vigour and its ability to maintain the loyalty and respect of their subjects. This . . . was due in part to the indolence and personal failings of Louis XV and, in part, to the tendency of the bureaucracy, staffed by privileged office-holders, to become almost a law unto itself. Meanwhile, as the middle classes became more prosperous and more self-important, they could hardly fail to become more resentful of the extravagance, inefficiencies and petty tyranny of a Court and government to whose upkeep they largely contributed but over which they had no control. Yet Louis XVI, on ascending the throne, was eager to bring about substantial reforms in the administration, to reduce the expenditure of the Court, to free trade of petty restrictions, to ease the tax-burdens on the peasantry and promote a measure of self-government, by means of local assemblies, in the provinces. Unlike his predecessor, he had a high sense of personal responsibility; besides, in Turgot, he had a minister who enjoyed the esteem and affection of both the "enlightened" and the industrious middle classes. Yet the whole scheme collapsed and Turgot was out of office after a couple of years. Why? Because Turgot's reforms, though welcome to the middle classes, ran counter to the vested interests of the *Parlements*, the higher clergy and aristocratic factions at Court. In this his experience was similar to that of Machault and Maupeou before him and of Calonne, Brienne and Necker after him; and it proved once more that no far-reaching measures of reform were possible, however well-meaning the King or honest and able his

From pp. 71–82, *Revolutionary Europe, 1783–1815* by George Rudé. Copyright © 1964 by George Rudé. Reprinted by permission of Harper & Row, Publishers, and of William Collins & Sons, Ltd.

minister, so long as the privileged orders were left in possession of their powers, through the *Parlements* or their influence at Court, to obstruct their operation. These, then, were the limits beyond which reform could not go— sufficient to whet the appetite of some, to irritate others and to satisfy none. Sufficient, too, to draw further hatred on the privileged orders and contempt on the monarchy that appeared to shield them.

Besides, if the middle classes were growing richer, their hopes of achieving their social ambitions were becoming more slender. The obstacles to the free exercise of trade and manufacture by onerous internal tolls, *péages* (private tolls on rivers, canals and bridges), and the inquisitions of government inspectors were long-standing grievances; but now a new grievance was being added, as during a period of "feudal reaction" the avenue to social and political advancement was becoming progressively closed. The merchant or financier, enriched by banking, manufacture or colonial trade, could no longer count, after (say) the 1750's, on crowning his career by the purchase for himself or his children of a hereditary office of State or a commission in the army. Such posts . . . were becoming the sole preserve of the aristocracy: the *Parlements* were closing their doors against middle-class intruders; and, with few exceptions, noble birth had, by 1789, become the sole essential qualification for holding high office in the army, Church or administration. It is perhaps the more remarkable that the French middle classes—if we except the writers, lawyers, pamphleteers and journalists among them—waited so long before fully venting their grievances. It was only when prodded into action by the *Parlements*, the higher clergy and nobility that, as we shall see, they began seriously to lay claim to social equality and a share in government.

Again, the picture of growing peasant prosperity painted by Tocqueville was by no means universal. While one in three of the French peasants owned their land outright, the larger part of these proprietors owned tiny parcels of land that, even in years of good harvest, were quite insufficient to feed their families: Arthur Young wrote that, in Champagne and Lorraine, he had, "more than once, seen division carried to such an excess that a single fruit tree, standing in about 10 perch of ground, has constituted a farm, and the local situation of a family decided by the possession." There were, too, the even greater number of share-croppers and landless labourers, who purchased their bread in the market and who could never, under the most favourable of circumstances, hope to have more than the most meagre of shares in rural prosperity. The small proprietors, poor tenants and cottagers had the added grievance that improving landlords and wealthy peasants, stimulated by the urge to increase agricultural production, were enclosing fields and common lands, and encroaching on the villagers' traditional rights of gleaning and pasture. A more general grievance was . . . the recent tendency of landlords to rake up old rights attaching to their lands and to impose new or added obligations to those already exacted from their peasants. What Tocqueville had not noted, and only recent research has brought to light, is that it was precisely in these closing years of the Old Régime that the general prosperity of agriculture was grinding to a halt, and that a prolonged depression was beginning to take its place. This developed in two main stages. After 1778, the year France entered the American War, there was a recession as the result of which prices fell— gradually in most industrial and farm products, but reaching crisis proportions in wines and textiles. During these years, the net profits of small tenant farmers, peasant proprietors, wine-growers and other share-croppers tended, because of the heavy and sustained toll of tax, tithe and seigneurial exaction, to fall out of all proportion to the fall in prices, while large landed proprietors were cushioned against loss by means of their feudal revenues. Then, on top of this cyclical depression, came the sudden economic catastrophe of 1787–89, which took the form of bad harvests and shortage, with the price of wheat doubling within two years in the main productive regions of the north and reaching record levels in 27 of the 32 *généralités* in mid-summer 1789. The crisis hit the bulk of the peasantry both as producers and as consumers; as proprietors, tenants, share-croppers or labourers; as wine-growers, dairy-farmers or wheat-growers. From agriculture it spread to industry; and unemployment, already developing from the "Free Trade" treaty of 1786 with England, reached disastrous proportions in Paris and the textile centres of Lille, Lyons, Troyes, Sedan, Rouen and Rheims. Another result was that wage-earners and all small consumers, in both town and countryside, were compelled by the rapid rise in food-prices to increase their daily expenditure on bread from perhaps half to three-quarters, or even four-fifths, of their earnings. Thus, peasants and urban craftsmen and workers were drawn together in common hostility to government, landlords, merchants and speculators; and these classes entered the Revolution in a context of increasing poverty and hardship rather than of "prosperity." . . .

But, of course, it needed more than economic hardship, social discontent, and the frustration of political and social ambitions to make a revolution. To give cohesion to the discontents and aspirations of widely varying social classes there had to be some unifying body of ideas, a common vocabulary of hope and protest, something, in short, like a common "revolutionary psychology." In the revolutions of our day, this ideological preparation has been the concern of political parties; but there were no such parties in eighteenth-century France. In this case, the ground was prepared, in the first place, by the writers of the Enlightenment. It was they who, as Burke and Tocqueville both noted, weakened the ideological defences of the Old Régime. The ideas of Montesquieu, Voltaire and Rousseau, and those of many others, were, as we have seen, being widely disseminated and absorbed by an eager reading public, both aristocratic and middle class. It had become fashionable, even among the clergy, to be sceptical and "irreligious"; and the writings of Voltaire had combined with the struggles within the Church itself (Gallicans against Jesuits, Richerists and Jansenists against the increasing authority of the bishops) to expose the Church to indifference, contempt or hostility. In the 1750's, Parisians had demonstrated against their Archbishop's refusal to allow priests to administer the sacrament to dying Jansenists; and Hardy, the bookseller-diarist of the University quarter in Paris, reported similar expressions of anti-clericalism in his Journal in the 'eighties. Meanwhile, such terms as "citizen," "nation," "social contract," "general will" and the "rights of man"—soon to be followed by *"tiers état"*—were entering into a common political vocabulary. As Tocqueville observed, it was often the pillars of the administration itself—ministers and Intendants—that first initiated a wider public in the use of these phrases; but it was neither they, nor the *philosophes* themselves, nor the fashionable society and men of letters of the salons, that brought them down to street-level and transformed abstract speculations into popular slogans and rallying-calls for political action. This was partly the work of the pamphleteers of the Third Estate in 1788 and 1789; but, long before that, the ground had been well and truly prepared by the tracts and remonstrances published by the *Parlements* who, in their prolonged duel, from the 1750's onwards, with ministerial "despotism," quoted freely, and almost indiscriminately, from the writings of the *philosophes*. So we find the *Parlement* of Paris, in its grand remonstrance of 1753, asserting its right, as an "intermediate body," to be the guardian of a "kind of contract" between the King and his people. The law, claimed the *Parlement* of Toulouse in 1763, must be subject to "the free consent of the nation." In 1760, the *Parlement* of Rouen had insisted that "the right of acceptance (of laws) is the right of the nation"; and, in 1771, it repeated that the fundamental laws of the realm should be "the expression of the general will." And, in 1788, the *Parlement* of Rennes quoted almost textually from Rousseau and the American Declaration of Independence in proclaiming: "That man is born free, that originally men are equal, these are truths that have no need of proof." What was new in all this was that the *Parlements* were not just writing political tracts, as the *philosophes* had done before them, but were deliberately setting out to influence public opinion and to marshal active public support in their struggles with the Crown.

But, when all this has been said, it is still doubtful if (say) in January 1787, any intelligent Frenchman or foreign observer could have found good reason to predict that a revolution was close at hand, and still less to foretell the form that such a revolution would take. It is easy for us, with our superior knowledge after the event, to see that such reason existed; yet, even so, there was still an important element lacking. It still needed a spark to bring about an explosion and it needed a second spark to bring about the particular alignment of forces that ushered in the revolution of 1789.

The first spark was the government's declaration of bankruptcy following the American War. Opinions may vary as to the extent of the influence of the American Revolution and of its Declaration of Independence on the course of events in France; but there can be no two opinions about the cataclysmic results that flowed from France's participation in the war. In 1781, Necker, the Controller General, had, in a famous *compte rendu* of the nation's finances, assured the government's creditors that there was a favourable balance of 10 million livres; in 1786, three years after the war ended, his successor, Calonne, estimated a deficit of 112 million livres. The sum represented nearly a quarter of the total State revenue and called for drastic remedies. Calonne decided that it would be useless to resort to the old time-worn expedients: short term loans already amounted to 400 million livres; the *taille* had been fixed at its present level in 1780 and was already high enough to provoke peasant discontent; and it seemed unwise to increase the taxes on consumers' goods at a time of recession and of falling industrial profits. The minister, therefore, proposed to the King that government expenditure should be cut (always a popular measure with all but those at Court); that the operation of the stamp duty should be extended; and that the *vingtième* (which many landowners evaded) should be replaced by a land tax on the annual production of the soil, to be paid in kind by all landowners and assessed and collected by local assemblies of owners representing all three estates. As a sop to large cultivators, it was further proposed to revive Turgot's former measures for free trade in grain, and to extend them to the export market.

The proposals had much to recommend them: if put into operation, they would have wiped out the deficit and assured the Treasury of a regular income. But, having learned wisdom from experience, the King and his minister knew that they would meet with resistance from the privileged orders: they were being asked to surrender a part of their fiscal immunities; the Church, in particular, valued its right to be taxed by means of the *don gratuit* (voluntary gift); and the provincial *Parlements* might resent any encroachment by the new local assemblies on their own jurisdiction. Besides, the business community—and, therefore, the Third Estate—might equally object to the stamp duty, whose main burden would fall on their shoulders. To forestall trouble it was, therefore, decided to submit the proposals not to the Paris *Parlement*, as was usual in such cases, but to a specially convened assembly of Notables—a mixed body of all the estates, which was composed of prelates, nobles, members of the *Parlements*, Intendants, councillors of State and members of provincial estates and urban corporations; and which had the advantage of being hand-picked by the King and of not having met for 160 years. Furthermore, it was convened in both haste and secrecy, and the objects of the meeting were not made public in advance.

The results were far less encouraging than was hoped. Calonne succeeded in estranging all parties. The die-hards, though in a minority, naturally resented the attacks on privilege; and the majority opposed the proposals on other grounds. The liberal aristocracy in particular (among them the Marquis de Lafayette), who played a large part in the proceedings, were not opposed to a more equitable distribution of taxes and made no objection, in principle, to the stamp duty, the land tax and the provincial assemblies; but they profoundly distrusted Calonne, whom they suspected of trying to buttress ministerial authority by means of the new assemblies and by manipulating a tax whose amount and means of assessment had not been sufficiently circumscribed. When Calonne tried to break the deadlock by an open appeal to public opinion, the King was appalled by such a breach of decorum, dismissed the minister and replaced him by Loménie de Brienne, Archbishop of Toulouse. Brienne was a *protégé* of the Queen and had the further advantage of popularity (he was known for his liberal, Physiocratic opinions) and of enjoying the confidence of the Notables and the clerical order. Yet, though he had been one of Calonne's sternest critics, circumstances compelled him to present a programme that differed only in detail from that of his predecessor: he modified the stamp duty and made the important concession of fixing an upper limit of 80 millions to the estimated yield of the land tax. The proposals were well received, but he failed to win the full authority for their enactment that he had hoped for. The Notables, possibly encouraged by the spate of pamphlet literature which their meeting had evoked, decided that such radical fiscal measures lay beyond their full competence and should be referred to the Paris *Parlement* for their approval—or, better still (the suggestion was Lafayette's), to the States General, which had not met since 1614. On 25 May, the Notables were dismissed and Brienne had to face the *Parlement*, after all.

It was, in fact, once more the judicial oligarchy of *parlementaires*, and not the Notables or the older aristocracy, that raised the banner of rebellion and provoked what has been called the "aristocratic revolt." Not that the *Parlement* at this time represented a solid body of reaction. Its main court—the *cour des pairs*—consisted of 144 members, including 7 Princes of the Blood, 7 ecclesiastical peers and 27 lay noblemen; the rest were the rank-and-file *conseillers* of the *Enquêtes* and *Requêtes*, mainly young men: of 72 whose ages have been recorded, 59 were under thirty-five years of age. They were divided between those who sought every favourable opportunity of asserting the privileges (ancient or usurped) of the *Parlement* and other "intermediate bodies" against the increasing claims of government and a smaller group, who, inspired by the *philosophes* and the American Revolution, were eager for far-reaching constitutional reform. The spokesman of the former, in the debates that followed, was Duval d'Eprémesnil; and of the latter Adrien Duport, supported, on occasion, by Lafayette's friend, the Duke of La Rochefoucauld among the peers, and the King's cousin, the Duke of Orleans, among the Princes of the Blood; all three were to play a prominent part in the Revolution of 1789. Though divided as to their ultimate aims, the two groups were drawn together by the circumstances of the moment: they were both suspicious of ministerial "despotism" and both hoped to realize their various purposes by means of the States General. So when Brienne turned to the *Parlement* to register his decrees, it raised no objection to the liberation of the grain trade and welcomed the new provincial assemblies; but it rejected the stamp duty and land tax and insisted that the States General be summoned to deal with the financial crisis. Brienne was equally obdurate: he had other reforms in mind—a reform of local government, the restoration of the provincial estates, judicial and army reform, and civil rights for Protestants—and he feared (with some justice) that the States General, if convened, would either serve as a diversion or submerge his own moderate measures in others of a far more radical intent. So the King's authority was invoked to call a *lit de justice*, which overrode the *Parlement's* objections, promulgated the fiscal decrees and exiled the Paris magistrates to the northern town of Troyes.

But it was the *Parlement* that won the day. The provincial courts, to whom Brienne now turned, were far more consistent than the Parisians as champions of aristocratic privilege and local immunities; they rejected almost every one of the minister's proposals and rallied to the support of their Paris colleagues; and Brienne had no option but to yield. The *Parlement* was re-instated in September, the decrees on the stamp duty and land tax were withdrawn, and it was agreed by all concerned that the existing *vingtième* (though expected to yield a substantially lower revenue) should be prolonged until 1792. The magistrates' return from exile was acclaimed by noisy and enthusiastic demonstrations in the City of Paris, anti-royalist tracts began to circulate, and Arthur Young reported the opinion that France was "on the verge of some great revolution in the government."

The "revolution" that Young predicted was, however, not so much one of the middle classes and the people as one that would be likely (as he put it) to "add to the scale" of the nobility and clergy. And such a view seemed amply justified by the events of 1788. In the previous October, the Paris *Parlement* had agreed to register further loans in return for the government's promise that the States General should meet in 1792. But negotiations broke down again in November, and the Duke of Orleans, by now a popular figure, and two other magistrates, who had been particularly outspoken in the debates, were exiled. This prompted the *Parlement*, in May, to court further popularity by issuing a declaration condemning the whole system of arbitrary government, including the obnoxious *lettres de cachet*. Brienne replied by ringing the law courts with troops and forced the *Parlement* to surrender two of its leaders (d'Eprémesnil was one) to royal justice. Meanwhile, the Keeper of the Seals, Lamoignon, issued six edicts, which suspended all the *Parlements*, vested the greater part of their appellate jurisdiction in forty-seven new tribunals, and transferred their powers of registering royal edicts to a "Plenary" Court. Thus it was intended not only to punish the *Parlements* for their disobedience, but to drive a wedge between them and the rest of the "political nation"—particularly the liberal aristocracy and the host of middle-class *avocats* and lawyers, to whom the new measures would open new avenues of preferment.

But the plan miscarried and, far from dividing its critics, stirred up something like a nation-wide rebellion against the government. The clergy, when invited to vote an extraordinary *don gratuit*, re-asserted their own immunity from taxation and protested against the suspension of the *Parlements*. The dukes and peers of the realm added their protesting voices to those of the clergy; and the general order of the nobility, though long resentful of the social pretensions of the *noblesse de robe*, found the moment opportune for declaring their support. In Paris and the provinces, both middle classes and "lower orders," fired by the militant declarations of the *Parlements*, joined in the common hue and cry against the "despotism" of ministers. The "patriots," as champions of "the nation" against both privilege and "despotism," had been inclined, like Mirabeau and Lafayette (but unlike Duport and Barnave), to pin their hopes on ministerial reform; but now, seeing Lamoignon's *coup d'état* as a veiled threat to the coveted States General, they tended to line up behind the *Parlements* instead. Besides, many of the Third Estate had been disappointed by the half-heartedness or alienated by the illiberalism of ministerial reforms; and of 500 protesting pamphlets published in the four months following the edicts of May 1788, one half were the work of "patriot" scribes. Meanwhile, riots broke out at Bordeaux, Dijon, Grenoble, Pau, Rennes and Toulouse—all cities with a tradition of provincial separatism and aristocratic self-rule. In Dauphiné, where Barnave and Mounier were active, *noblesse* and Third Estate co-operated in reviving the long-moribund estates of the province; in Brittany, the estates united in common protest against ministerial "despotism." At Grenoble, massive riots, launched by the lawyers' clerks and supported by the townsfolk and visiting peasantry, prevented the suspended magistrates from leaving the city for five days. At Rouen, where the nobility exploited the people's anger over the high prices resulting from the restoration of free trade in grain, the Intendant and military commander were attacked in the streets and besieged in their houses. In both cities, the army proved unreliable: egged on by young officers of the provincial *noblesse* and irritated by Brienne's new disciplinary regulations, it refused to fire and fraternized with the riotous townsmen.

Overwhelmed by this national movement of protest, the government was compelled to surrender. The States General were promised for May 1789; Brienne was replaced by Necker; Lamoignon's judicial reforms—and, for that matter, all other projected reforms—were withdrawn; and the

Parlements were recalled soon after. The result was hailed as a triumphant victory for the people at large—not least by the Paris tradesmen, journeymen and apprentices of both City and *faubourgs*, who had found an additional cause for demonstration in the sudden upward movement in the price of bread. The "aristocratic revolt" (for such it was in essence) had triumphed all along the line: with the support of the nonprivileged classes, it had forced the government to withdraw its taxation proposals and to reinstate the *Parlements*; the States General would meet in May; and the States General, it was confidently believed, would solve all the nation's problems. But many believed (and some hoped and others feared) that, by striking further blows at the "despotism" of ministers, it would proportionately increase the authority, status and advantage of the privileged orders.

Yet these calculations proved to be ill-founded, and the revolution that emerged from the convening of the States General turned out to be of a very different kind from that envisaged by many of the pamphleteers of 1788 and Arthur Young's informants of October 1787. Chateaubriand later wrote that "the patricians began the revolution and the plebeians completed it"; and Robespierre said something similar. In a sense it was true, and many historians have accepted the verdict. But the revolt of the nobility was, perhaps, a curtain-raiser rather than a revolution, for it was the prelude of a revolution which, by associating the middle and lower classes in common action against King and aristocracy, was unique in contemporary Europe. This was by no means what liberal aristocrats or middle-class "patriots," or anyone else, had intended or foreseen. . . .

THE "MAINSPRING OF THE REVOLUTION": THE PARIS SANS-CULOTTES

Albert Soboul

. . . If in times of crisis, the complex and solid mass of the Parisian sans-culotterie provided the impetus behind the more violent episodes in the Revolution, in calmer times, less worried about the provision of its food, it paid only a fluctuating attention to political affairs. Not every sans-culotte

Albert Soboul, *The Parisian Sans-Culottes and the French Revolution, 1793–4* (Oxford: Clarendon Press, 1964), 42–54. © Oxford University Press, 1964. Used by permission of the Clarendon Press, Oxford.

was a militant. A study of the sectionary political personnel in the Year II [1793–94] will give us a more complete and more balanced social description of the Parisian sans-culotterie.

For this study, the most important material has been taken from the collection of dossiers forming the alphabetical series of papers of the Committee of General Security. Based primarily on the repression of Prairial Year III [1795], in some respects they throw as much light on the Thermidorean psychology of the property-owning classes as on the terrorist mentality of the sans-culottes themselves. We need, therefore, to be very careful about accepting the many denunciations contained in these documents. As the class struggle intensified during the spring of the Year III, the least word was exaggerated and used as evidence to justify arrests, explaining why so many people were arrested as *septembriseurs* when it is perfectly clear that they had taken no part whatsoever in the massacres of September 1792. Bitterness and personal vengeance were given free rein. There was also the very real fear experienced by many of the *honnêtes gens* [well-to-do] in the Year II of seeing themselves deprived of their social and political status: the repression was particularly severe for this reason. The numerous files dealing with disarmament and arrests present an equally valuable documentation, the only one which gives us direct information on the political personnel of the Sections as a whole.

The nature of this evidence does not, by any means, enable us to make an exact statistical study—the age of the militant sans-culottes is rarely indicated; their profession is often omitted; the vocabulary is loose and misleading. Any study of the social composition of the sans-culotterie is, therefore, beset by many uncertainties. At the end of the eighteenth century, manual workers were frequently referred to, rather disdainfully, as *le peuple* by the propertied-classes, aristocrats and the bourgeoisie. The bookseller Hardy writing in his *Journal* unites under the same phase—*menu peuple*—the non-propertied-classes and the lower middle class Parisians who were, in fact, often property-owners—small tradesmen and workshop masters as well as *compagnons*, labourers and the destitute. In fact, there are as many shades of difference between the lower middle-classes and the proletariat as there are varieties of social conflict. Jean-Jacques Rousseau had written in his *Confessions* that he had been born "in a family which distinguished itself from the 'people' by its manners and social customs." Robespierre's host, the cabinet-maker Duplay, provides another example of this kind of attitude. The remark of his daughter, wife of the [deputy] Lebas, recalling that her father had never, out of a sense of his bourgeois dignity, eaten with any of his *serviteurs* (referring to his workmen) has often been quoted. Jaurès reminds us that Duplay received not less than ten to twelve thousand *livres* from house-letting alone, not to mention the earnings from his own trade. The vocabulary reflects the faint lines of demarcation between social groups and the indelible mark imprinted upon those who belonged to the artisan class: it was the trade or guild which supplied the qualification, not the kind of work a man did, nor yet what his position was in his chosen profession. The "cabinet-maker" Duplay certainly had his connexions with the working population, but he was nevertheless a furniture-contractor on a large scale. Had he ever used a jointing-plane in his youth? Or his father? Or his grandfather? It may appear to be only a small detail, but the question would have to be considered before we could write a true social history of the Revolution. The head of a business concern kept his professional qualification and still described himself as a "cabinet-maker" or a "carpenter" even when he was employing dozens of workers. This was the case with the "fan-maker" Mauvage, a militant sans-culotte in the Section du Faubourg-du-Nord: we have to study his dossier carefully before we discover that he owned a factory which employed sixty people. The same word is used to describe social realities which are basically different, and we have to decide in each case exactly where these artisans and shopkeepers belonged in the social hierarchy. At what point does the work of a craftsman become a business concern? More often than not, the documents of the period fail to distinguish between the *compagnon*, the small craftsman and the contractor: the degrees of difference between them are multiple, and the transition from one to the other is graded into many stages. Any attempt to fix a rigid system of classification upon so fluid a society must be arbitrary. In any case, it would not be possible to make a really satisfactory study if we were to rely solely on the political documents: we need to determine the financial resources of the militants. However, the absence of fiscal documents for the Parisian Sections makes this extremely difficult. Intensive research into the notarial records might perhaps compensate for this loss, at least for those sans-culottes whose social standing bordered on the edge of the middle bourgeoisie. As for the records dealing with the lowest strata of Parisian society, they have disappeared altogether unless reference to them can be found in the dossiers of the anti-terrorist repression.

The political personnel of the Parisian Sections in the Year II may be divided, according to their functions and their social background, into three categories illustrating the social diversity of the sans-culotterie. The personnel of the *comités civils* [administrative committees] represented the oldest, most stable and most prosperous category, and were often considered as belonging to the middle bourgeoisie. A later institution, the *comités révolutionnaires* [revolutionary committees] were more popular in origin. The personnel of these committees were very soon paid for their services. From March 1793 to Fructidor Year II, they suffered from the repercussions of political upheavals, becoming more and more democratic until the autumn of 1793. The third category was that of the ordinary militant sans-culottes, mostly to be found after the autumn in the *sociétés sectionnaires* [popular societies in the Sections], representing the most popular elements of the sans-culotterie.

Created by the municipal law of 21 May–27 June 1790, and composed of citizens with the necessary qualifications for voting, the *comités civils* were largely renewed after 10 August 1792. Most of the *commissaires* [commissioners] on these committees kept their posts from this date to the Year III, some of them even escaping the reprisals in Prairial. Their purely administrative function provided them with the opportunity to stand aloof from political terrorist activities. Moreover, although the committees received money from the municipality for their expenses, the *commissaires* were for a long time unpaid. It was only on 6 Floréal Year II [25 April 1794] that the Convention voted the payment of three *livres* a day in recognition of their public services. This allowance came too late for the personnel of these committees to be democratized. The *commissaires civils* belonged mostly to the higher ranks of the sans-culotterie. The money which they earned from their workshops, or from their business interests, permitted them to devote their time to their administrative tasks.

The *comités révolutionnaires*, at first paid only their expenses, but later salaried, were more democratically recruited than the *comités civils*. They represented the more popular elements of the sans-culotterie. Few of the *commissaires* lived off their own incomes—only 20, or 4.6 per cent. of the total number of 454; whereas 26.2 per cent. of the members of the *comités civils* did so. Amongst them only 4 were *rentiers* in the full sense of the word (0.8 per cent.); 11 belonged to the liberal professions (2.4 per cent.), and 6 were former shopkeepers or artisans (1.3 per cent.). Although there were few heads of business concerns, there were also no really popular elements. Manufacturers, contractors, or mastercraftsmen accounted for 13 (2.8 per cent. as compared with 2.3 per cent. for the *comités civils*). On the other hand, we find 22 wage-earners, operatives, *compagnons* or apprentices, and 23 domestic servants or former domestic servants—a total of 9.9 per cent. The liberal professions were represented by 52 *commissiares*—artists, sculptors, painters, musicians, and schoolteachers: lawyers were relatively few. To this group we can add 22 lower-grade civil servants (*employés*), 7 of whom were employed by the Post Office (4.8 per cent.).

Here again, most of the *commissaires* were craftsmen or shopkeepers: 290 out of the total of 454, or 63.8 per cent. of the personnel of the *comités révolutionnaires*. Altogether, 206 *commissaires* (45.3 per cent.) could be considered as having some connexion with the artisan class; 84 were engaged in commerce (18.5 per cent.). The craftsmen are relatively more numerous than in the *comités civils*: for many of them, expenses of three, and later of five *livres* a day, compensated for the decline or total loss of their trade: this is substantiated by the number of craftsmen connected with the luxury or art trades. The 28 shoemakers form the most important group (6.1 per cent.), followed by the 18 cabinet-makers (3.9 per cent.), then 16 wig-makers or hairdressers (3.5 per cent.). But there were 42 *commissaires* connected with some branch or other of the art trade (9.2 per cent.). A group of 37 *commissaires* were builders (8.1 per cent.), and 29 were timber-merchants or furniture-makers (6.3 per cent.).

Amongst the 84 persons engaged in trade, 41 described as merchants appear to have held a status above that of an ordinary shopkeeper. Ten wine merchants, whether wholesale or retail traders, headed the list, to which we can add six who sold soft drinks. The sale of drinks played an important part in the political life of the Sections. Another 15 dealt in the provision of food supplies: there were 6 grocers, 3 pastry-cooks, a baker, a fruiterer, also 2 restaurant-owners and 2 inn-keepers.

Scattered hints in individual dossiers sometimes enable us to discover the social standing of these *commissaires*. Many craftsmen and shopkeepers who had been more or less ruined by the loss of customers found a means of livelihood in the salaried duties of a *commissaire*. This explains the large numbers of wig-makers, hairdressers and shoemakers to be found on the *comités révolutionnaires*, as well as the domestic servants who had lost their positions, particularly numerous in the committee of the Section du Bonnet-Rouge in what used to be the *faubourg* Saint-Germain. Noel, a wig-maker from the Section de Bon-Conseil had lost his job "because of the Revolution," and he had three children and an old mother to care for. A similar case was that of Jean-Baptiste Moulin, also a wig-maker, *commissaire* of the Section de la Republique and a juror on the Revolutionary Tribunal from 22 Prairial Year II. Arrested in the Year III, he defended himself by the following statement: "having lost my position as a wig-maker I was forced to enter the *comité de surveillance* in my Section so that I could live." Miel, a sans-culotte from the Section des Marchés held in custody since 5 Prairial, had according to the *comité civil* in Messidor Year III "accepted a place on the *comité révolutionnaire* so that he could procure the means of livelihood for himself, his wife and his children."

If many of the *commissaires* found that their duties rewarded them with an income which they could no longer derive from their occupations, some on the other hand, still enjoyed either a modest income or a situation of some importance. Lambert, a *commissaire* in the Section de l'Arsenal, was a former domestic servant living on his small private income. Etienne Fournier, *commissaire* for the Section de l'Indivisibilité who had been a crockery-dealer, enjoyed an income of 1,700 *livres*, the yearly salary of an ordinary *employé*. In the Section Révolutionnaire, *commissaire* Tarreau considered that his position as a jeweller did not give him "what one might call a fortune"; "it only provided me with the everyday necessities of life to keep my wife and children." This meant that Tarreau's social status lay about halfway between the wealthy and the popular classes. The dyer Barrucand from the Section de l'Arsenal, "conqueror of the Bastille," a *commissaire* dealing with the manufacture of pikes, member of the *comité révolutionnaire*, admitted that he was worth 21,600 *livres*. He had bought a house valued at 47,300 *livres*: doubtless, to do this, he must have borrowed money and sold his silverware, but this does not mean that he was any the less comfortably situated.

Other *commissaires* were important business men. In the Section des Gardes-Françaises, Maron, a plaster-manufacturer, employed twenty workmen in the quarry which he owned. As for Mauvage, *commissaire* in the Section du Faubourg-du-Nord, a really militant sans-culotte, we have seen that he was responsible for a fan-making concern employing sixty workers: nevertheless, he still called himself a "fan-maker." Some profited from their circumstances to put themselves on their feet financially and to rise in the social scale. Candolle, *commissaire* in the Section de l'Arsenal, previously a porter, became a wine-merchant. Larue, a member of the *comité révolutionnaire* of the Section des Lombards, did even better—an apprentice mason in 1789, he had become a building-contractor by the Year II. According to those who informed against him in the following year, "The Commune had given him work on various projects which helped him to make his money."

Although the *comités révolutionnaires* drew more upon the popular classes than the *comités civils*, they still reveal very much the same social pattern—from wage-earner to the large employer. The sans-culotterie did, indeed, represent a coalition of socially heterogeneous elements.

If we look at the third category of the political personnel in the Sections in the Year II—that of the militants, we arrive at the same conclusion, with the slight difference, however, that the wage-earning element in this group is more important. Out of the total number of 514 militants counted (and by the word "militant" we mean every citizen who played an active political role, whether in the popular society or in the general assembly, and who, for this reason, became a victim of the reaction of the Year III), 64 were wage-earners—*compagnons*, operatives, apprentices, journeymen or day-labourers—a percentage of 12.4. If we add to this list domestic servants, odd-job men, office-boys and shop-assistants, 40 in all (7.7 per cent.), the popular element forms 20.1 per cent. of the militant group, as opposed to 9.9 per cent. of the personnel of the *comités révolutionnaires*, and 0.8 per cent. of the *comités civils*. As a contrast, we find only one *rentier* and one landlord, 8 shopkeepers or retired traders (1.9 per cent.), whereas on the *comités révolutionnaires* and *comités civils* this group represented 4.6 per cent. and 26.2 per cent. respectively. The number of contractors or manufacturers is also quite small—only 4, or 0.7. On the *comités civils*, this percentage rises to 2.3 per cent. and to 2.8 per cent. on the *comités révolutionnaires*. As for the liberal professions, they are represented by 35 militants (6.8 per cent.), to which we can add 45 *employés*, making a total percentage 15.5. This group of *employés* is particularly important for, more often than not, they formed the life-blood of the *sociétés sectionnaires*.

The shopkeeper and, above all, the artisan class predominate amongst the militants, although the proportion is lower than for either of the two committees—81 tradesmen (15.7 per cent.), and 214 craftsmen, (41.6 per cent.). Amongst the tradesmen, 34 (6.6 per cent.) are described as merchants. The 18 engaged in the grocery trade were the most numerous, but the 10 wine-merchants are placed on top of the list, confirming the importance of their contribution to the political life of the Sections.

Among the 214 artisans, the shoemakers form a compact group of 41 militants (7.9 per cent. of the whole), followed by 24 hairdressers and wig-makers, and 20 tailors: should we, perhaps, establish a relationship between the militant activity of these small craftsmen and their professional difficulties? The building trade accounts for 30 militants (5.8 per cent.), there were 29 engaged in the timber and furniture trades (5.6 per cent.), but only 23 from the art and luxury trades (4.4 per cent.). Thus the trades which demanded fewer professional qualifications provided a large number of militants. For the *comités civils* and *comités révolutionnaires* the proportion was reversed: the artisans were really an *élite* to which the sans-culottes in many of the Sections looked for leadership.

Although the wage-earning element predominated amongst the militants, there were also many citizens who were comfortably situated, financially and socially. In the Section des Droits-de-l'Homme, Varlet possessed an income of 5,800 *livres*. In addition to his salary as a postal clerk, this *enragé* [revolutionary extremist] had a small income of his own, and could obviously be regarded as a representative of the middle classes. François Mercier in the Section Marat, formerly an assistant in a hat shop, was a juror on the Revolutionary Tribunal. He had invested the 12,150 *livres* which he had inherited from his mother in 1780 in a life insurance policy. He said that he had taken an interest "in the business affairs of different people," and had also saved from his income, and from his fees as a juror, the sum of 9,430 *livres*. In the Year III, he stated that he was worth 21,580 *livres*. Bouland, an active militant from the *société de Lazowski* and the Section du Finistère, who never stopped "condemning the activities of merchants," had bought a house at the beginning of the Revolution in the boulevard Hôpital. Damoye, a saddle-merchant in the Section de Montreuil was arrested in Pluviôse Year III for his terrorist activities in the previous year. In his defence statement, he described himself as a well-to-do property-owner, adding that "he has his living to think of, and, for this reason, has suffered great anxiety since he was put under arrest two months ago." In the Year IV, the same man was asked for a forced loan of 3,000 *livres* (hard currency). Damoye was a typical example of the bourgeois sans-culotte.

Thus, if we analyse the composition of the political personnel of the Sections in the Year II, as well as the part played by the *faubourg* Saint-Antoine and to a lesser extent by the *faubourg* Saint-Marcel in the revolutionary movement and the important *journées* from July 1789 to Prairial Year III, we must conclude that the revolutionary *avant-garde* of the Parisian sans-culotterie did not constitute an industrial proletariat, but a coalition of small master-craftsmen and *compagnons* who worked and lived with them. This explains certain characteristics of the popular movement, as well as certain contradictions, arising from the ambiguous situation in which the sans-culottes often found themselves.

The small master-craftsman, working and living with his *compagnons*, very often a former *compagnon* himself, exercised a decisive ideological influence on the latter. Through him, bourgeois influences penetrated into the world of the workman. Even if he was in conflict with him, the small work-shop *compagnon* inevitably derived many of his ideas from his employer, and often living and eating under the same roof had basically the same attitude to the great problems of the day. It was the lower middle-class craftsman who fashioned the mentality of the worker. However, having said this, many small problems remain to be solved. In particular, we must distinguish between the "independent" craftsman of Paris and the "dependent" crafts-man, the classic example of the latter being the silk-weavers of Lyons—*le canut lyonnais*. Juridically free and head of his concern, possessing his own machine, even in a position to hire his own labour, the latter has all the appearance of an employer. But economically he is only a wage-earner, strictly dependent upon the merchant who supplies him with the raw material and who distributes the finished article. The interests of the "dependent" craftsman and the *compagnon* are the same—confronted with merchant capitalism they demanded price-controls and a basic minimum wage. But they did not go so far as to work out a direct relationship between the nature of the work and the rate of pay: wages were determined by the cost of living, not by the value of the work done. The social function of labour is not clearly understood. The dependent craftsman stands in an intermediate position between the *compagnon* and the independent craftsman aspiring towards the status of a lower middle-class citizen.

As for the wage-earning worker in the large manufacturing concerns, more important in the centre of Paris between the Seine and the *barrières*, less widespread in the *faubourgs*, they sometimes showed a more independent spirit which, to some extent, foreshadowed that of the proletariat of the great modern industrial concerns: the Réveillon affair, which turned into a riot on 28 April 1789, was a case in point. But more often than not the wage-earners in these larger manufacturing ventures had begun employment in small workshops. The spirit of the craftsman which they retained was strengthened by the environment in which they lived—a small minority of factory-workers surrounded by far greater numbers of *compagnons*. Labour as a whole carried the imprint of lower middle-class artisan mentality, and like it, the Parisian labour-force shared its bourgeois ideology. Neither in thought, nor deed, could the Parisian workman become an independent element during the Revolution.

There was a serious contradiction in this situation which affected the sans-culotte's attitude to his work, his position in society and his political activity. Although they shared their mode of living with their *compagnons*, craftsmen still owned their workshops, their equipment, and looked upon themselves as independent producers. The fact that they exercised authority over *compagnons* and apprentices accentuated their bourgeois mentality. Nevertheless the system of small production and direct sale was diametrically opposed to the ideas of the merchant bourgeoisie and commercial capitalism. In consequence, these craftsmen and shopkeepers who formed the more articulate section of the sans-culotterie cherished a social ideal which was incompatible with the evolution of the economic system. They campaigned against the concentration of the means of production, but they were themselves property-owners. When the more extreme sans-culottes demanded a maximum of wealth in the Year II, the contradiction between their own social position and this demand escaped them. They expressed their feelings in passionate outcries and bursts of revolt, but never in a coherent programme. The same was true of the individuals and political groups which shared their outlook—Jacques Roux, Hébert, even Robespierre and Saint-Just.

Failing to define their place in society as a working population, the sans-culottes had no clear and precise idea of the nature of labour itself. They did not appreciate that it had a social function of its own; they only considered it in relation to property. The bourgeoisie in a century of enlightenment had restored the arts and crafts to their rightful place, they had given an incomparable impetus to the forces of invention; but, concentrating their attention mainly upon the problems of technique and production, they had not conceived of the idea of labour as part of the social structure. From 1789 to 1794, the bourgeoisie had never thought about labour problems in themselves or in relation to the workers, but always with regard to the interests of their own class: the Le Chapelier law is evidence of this. If the Convention decreed the General Maximum on 29 September 1793 after constant pressure from the sans-culotterie, it was, as far as the montagnard bourgeoisie were concerned, simply a tactical move. Price-controls were related essentially to food supplies; salaries were not in any way determined by the amount of work a man performed. Divided between a predominantly artisan economy and nascent industrialism, lacking all sense of class-consciousness, how could the Parisian labour-force fail to be influenced by the bourgeoisie into whose hands it had largely entrusted the defence of its interests in the vital struggle against the aristocracy: its attitude to the problems of labour could only reflect prevailing political and social conditions. For the bourgeoisie, property was the key to the problem. The Declaration of 1793, like that of 1789, had established it as the first of the imprescriptible Rights of Man, after the abolition of feudalism had made it an absolute right. For the sans-culottes

in the Year II, the problem of labour was not their primary social preoccupation. They were far too aware of their interests as consumers—it was not the
question of strike-action or demands for higher wages which roused the
sans-culotterie, but the question of food supplies. A rise or fall in the cost of
the main products of popular consumption, grain and, above all, bread,
which accounted for at least half of the family expenditure, was the decisive
factor which tightened or eased the wage-earner's budget. The sans-culottes
looked for a fixed system of price-controls on basic commodities; the demand
for a sliding-scale of prices was exceptional. This perspective reflects economic
and social conditions, as well as the ideology of the period.

Price-controls on basic commodities were demanded with all the more
insistence by the militants because they were subjected to pressure in their
respective Sections, not only from wage-earners, but also from the thousands
of destitute Parisians, tormented by hunger. Hunger—an essential factor in
all popular movements—was the cement which held together the artisan,
the shopkeeper, and the workman, just as a common interest united them
against the wealthy merchant, the contractor, the noble, and the bourgeois
monopolist. From a sociological point of view, the term "sans-culotte" may
appear to be vague, but from the standpoint of the social conditions of the
time, it reflects a reality. It is true that the political motives explaining popular
behaviour must not be excluded—particularly hatred of the nobility, the
belief in the "aristocratic plot," the desire to destroy privilege and to establish
equality before the law. How else can we account for the enthusiasm and
disinterestedness of the sans-culotte volunteers? But the riots of February
1793, like the popular movement of the following summer, do not entirely
fit into the general pattern of the bourgeois revolution: to quote Robespierre
himself, these events were due to the popular demand for cheap and shoddy
goods. The aim of the maximum, so stubbornly insisted upon and finally
imposed on 29 September 1793, was to provide the wage-earners with their
daily bread, not to facilitate the problems of national defence: the permanent
motive behind popular action is to be found in the hardship of everyday life.
In the last analysis, it can be said that economic fluctuations provided the
rhythm of the revolutionary movement.

On 1 Prairial Year III, the tailor Jacob Clique from the Section des
Gardes-Françaises was arrested for having said: "One would think that the
buyers and the farmers are plotting together to sell everything as dearly as
possible in order to starve the workman." Questioned about this statement, he
replied: "I am embittered by misfortune. The father of three young children,
without any resources, my daily work has to provide a living for five people.
I was given hardly any work throughout the difficult winter we have just
faced." Political demands were linked in a confused way with the demand for
bread. "Under Robespierre," the cabinet-maker Richer from the Section de
la République was alleged to have said on 1 Prairial, "blood flowed and there

was enough bread to go round. Today, blood no longer flows and there is a shortage of it. It seems, therefore, that we must spill a little blood before we can get bread." The sans-culottes could not forget that during the Terror, despite every difficulty, there was no shortage. The political behaviour of the terrorist is intimately linked with the demand for bread, and it was this dual factor which cemented the unity of the Parisian sans-culotterie.

THE DIRECTORY—A REVALUATION
Albert Goodwin

The French Executive Directory which assumed office on 11 Brumaire year IV (2 November 1795), and was destroyed by Bonaparte's *coup d'état* of 18 Brumaire year VIII (9 November 1799), has been traditionally regarded by historians as a byword for corruption, governmental incompetence and political instability. Its rule is usually associated with the financial bankruptcy of 1797, defeats of French armies in the field, administrative chaos at home and the Directors' policy of self-perpetuation in office by means of a series of "purifications" of the elected Assemblies. In 1799 the Directory is supposed to have been ripe for dissolution and France ready for Bonaparte. It is the purpose of this paper to suggest that such an interpretation does not do full justice to the governmental record of the Directory between 1795 and 1799, and that it represents an over-simplification of the situation in France on the eve of 18 Brumaire. . . .

. . . The usual indictment may be said to be based on four main charges —that the personnel of the Directory was both corrupt and incapable; that its administration of the finances brought the country within measurable distance of ruin; that its foreign policy involved an indefinite postponement of the prospects of a general peace; and, finally, that the Government could not even fulfil the first condition of effective rule by securing public order and individual freedom at home. . . .

On the score of venality there is ample authority for the view that the Directors themselves were, with perhaps a single exception, reasonably honest. The corruption of Barras was, of course, notorious and remains indefensible. The evidence against the rest, however, is slight. Certain passages in Thibaudeau's Memoirs suggest that Reubell, who for some time virtually controlled Directorial finance, deserved censure, and some suspicion was apparently directed against Merlin de Douai and La Revellière. It is true

Albert Goodwin, "The French Executive Directory—A Revaluation," *History*, vol. XXII, no. 87 (December, 1937), 201–218. Copyright by Albert Goodwin. Used by permission of the author and *History*.

that Reubell's reputation for financial integrity was not unblemished, since he had suffered disgrace for peculation under the Terror, and he was well known to be avaricious. On the other hand, there is no real evidence against him of corruption while a Director, and it should also be remembered that the Commissions of Inquiry specially appointed by the Councils to investigate his guilt in August 1799 completely exonerated him as well as Merlin and La Revellière. . . . The rest of the Directors seem never to have been the objects of contemporary criticism on the ground of their dishonesty.

How far is it true to say that the Directors were individually men without ability? For the present purpose it is only necessary to consider the members of the original Directory and three others—François de Neufchâteau, Merlin de Douai and Treilhard. . . . The others may be disregarded because of the shortness of their period of office—Barthélemy was in power three and a half months, Gohier less than six months, Ducos and Moulin four and a half months. The usual opinion of the original Directory . . . is that they were a group of mediocrities. If only the highest standards are applied, such a judgment would not be unfair. But if the ordinary criteria of capacity are accepted, then the Directors must be credited with more than average ability. Mature they were bound to be since article 134 of the constitution insisted that they should be at least forty years of age, and although the manner of their nomination left something to be desired, they were all men of wide experience, most of them with special aptitudes and qualifications for the conduct of the departments of government they controlled. The least remarkable from the point of view of sheer ability were Le Tourneur and Barras. Le Tourneur was entirely devoid of political gifts, and in all matters of policy he followed without question the lead of his school-friend Carnot. He did, however, possess a good knowledge of the technical side of naval affairs. . . . Similarly, it would be hard to think of any revolutionary leader, apart from Fouché, better fitted to organise the police than Barras, whose whole life had been spent in intrigue. Nor is it accurate to regard Barras as a political cipher. Especially when resolute action was needed, Barras could be counted on, as he had already shown on 9 Thermidor and 13 Vendémiaire. . . . Luck alone cannot account for his survival till 18 Brumaire.

La Revellière was in many ways a curious mixture, half crank, half fanatic, a botanist, student of Rousseau, high priest of the new revolutionary cult of Theophilanthropy and a believer in the *juste milieu* in politics. A sincere republican, he was consumed with a hatred of priests and aristocrats, and yet he had small liking for the rural or urban proletariat. In foreign policy he was an advocate of the war of propaganda and conquest. . . . His special sphere in Directorial policy was education, the *fêtes nationales* and manufactures.

Carnot, . . . a former member of the Committee of Public Safety, and famous as the "Organiser of Victory," . . . was a paragon of executive efficiency, and had real genius in the administration of war. He proved a failure as a Director, and for obvious reasons. He had a biting tongue and alienated his colleagues by his cynicisms. He was a convinced pacifist at a time when both Reubell and La Revellière, for different reasons, were keen supporters of foreign war. He disappointed the expectations of his Jacobin friends by evolving in the direction of the Right. Lastly, although he had little or no talent for politics, he was never satisfied to confine himself to his departmental duties. Still, he can hardly be described as a mediocrity.

There is general agreement that Reubell was a man of great ability. An Alsatian barrister of eminence, he had a good command of modern languages and an encyclopædic knowledge. He owed his ascendancy over his colleagues to his industry and his strength of will. Utterly devoid of scruple and severely practical, he may be described as the main driving force behind Directorial policy. At one time he maintained a close supervision over the three most important departments of government—justice, finance and foreign affairs. Subsequently, however, he was content to delegate responsibility to ministers of proved capacity, such as Merlin and Ramel, and concentrated his own attention on the conduct of diplomatic affairs. In this sphere he identified himself with the policy of conquest and expansion which he hoped would culminate in the acquisition of the natural frontiers. As Reubell was only eliminated from the Directory by lot in May 1799, his influence upon policy was exerted throughout, and gave it a much-needed continuity.

Of François de Neufchâteau, Merlin and Treilhard, it is only necessary to say that the former was a distinguished administrator whose work as Minister of the Interior conferred lasting benefits on the French state and anticipated many of the Napoleonic reforms, and that Merlin and Treilhard were the leading juris-consults of the day. Any government which could count on their services might well have considered itself fortunate.

The subject of Directorial finance is both technical and controversial. Here attention can only be directed towards one or two points which serve to modify the severe criticisms usually passed upon it. The two leading events upon which discussion has centred are the collapse of the Assignats in 1796 and the repudiation of two-thirds of the public debt in September 1797. Both these occurrences were, in some ways, regrettable, but, by themselves, do not entail an utter condemnation of the finance of the period. . . .

The immediate financial problem to be faced by the Directory was how to arrest the continued fall of the Assignats. One of the last acts of the Convention had been to establish by the law of 21 June 1795 a sliding scale of depreciation for contracts and other debts, the value of which was to be fixed according to the quantity of Assignats actually in circulation at the time of the signing of the contract. This experiment failed because it was not applied to all contracts and because the treasury had not a sufficient reserve. The first important proposal made by the Directory was for a forced loan payable in specie, corn, or in Assignats taken at 1 per cent. of their face value (6 December 1795). The manufacture of Assignats was to be discontinued and the plates broken on 21 March following. As the Assignats were worth less than 1 per cent. of their nominal value, and as receipts for payments of the forced loan were to be accepted in payment of direct taxes, this plan really amounted to a timid attempt at deflation and an effort to increase the revenue from taxation. The over-valuation of the Assignats and the lack of specie for their conversion, however, effectually ensured the failure of this scheme.

The next experiment—the issue on 18 March 1796 of *mandats territoriaux* —was devised by the Finance Minister, Ramel-Nogaret. These *mandats* were in effect a new form of paper-money which it was hoped would gradually displace the Assignats and be immune from depreciation. To render them attractive to the public they were to entitle the holders to obtain *biens nationaux* at the fixed valuation of twenty-two years' purchase of the annual value of 1790. Unfortunately, however, a committee of the Council of Five Hundred made the Assignats convertible into *mandats territoriaux* at one-thirtieth of their nominal value. Thus, although the new facility provided for the acquisition of unsold national property prevented the *mandats* from depreciating immediately, they were bound to collapse eventually because of the over-valuation of the Assignats in terms of the new paper-currency. It had been thought that the capitalists would eagerly take up the *mandats* in order to acquire the estates of the Belgian monasteries, but the more cautious of them hesitated to buy property so near to the frontier before the conclusion of a general peace, while the speculators preferred to discredit the *mandats* in order to effect purchases at a later stage at less cost. An additional difficulty was that the new currency was not immediately available, since the government only issued *promesses de mandats*. For these reasons the *mandats* failed to gain general acceptance, and despite the efforts of the government to force their currency, they quickly fell to a discount. In the course of July, August and September 1796 laws were passed whereby the *mandats* were to be accepted by the government in payment for taxes and in exchange for *biens nationaux* at their market price only. The *mandats* were finally withdrawn from circulation by a law of 4 February 1797. Thus failed the Directory's main effort at stabilisation. The failure was not, however, without its re-deeming features, since it at all events prevented the inflation from getting completely out of hand, and it did in fact result in the resumption of a metallic standard.

In its essentials, the "repudiation" of 1797 was a comparatively simple operation. The law of 9 Vendémiaire year VI (30 September 1797) enacted that one-third only of the public debt should be consolidated and entered on the Grand Livre as a sacred charge, and that the capital of the other two-thirds should be redeemed by the issue to stockholders of bearer bonds (*bons des deux tiers mobilisés*). By way of compensation, the state guaranteed that interest payments should in the future be made subject to no deductions as they had been in the past, and that the *bons des deux tiers* should be available for the purchase of national property. . . .

. . . It must be admitted that the bankruptcy demolished the incomes of the rentier class. An example will suffice to show the extent of the injury and to elucidate the actual nature of the operation. A rentier with a capital of 3000 livres invested in the public debt which before September 1797 had given him, at 5 per cent., 150 *livres* interest, now received 50 *livres* as interest on one-third of his capital (*tiers consolidé*) and a nominal holding of 2000 *livres* in *bons des deux tiers mobilisés*. In the final liquidation of 30 Ventôse year IX (21 March 1801), when the two-thirds were converted into perpetual annuities at the rate of 1/4 per cent. of their capital value, the 2000 *livres* would be exchanged for an annuity of 5 *livres*. The net result was that instead of receiving 150 *livres* interest, the fundholder received 55 *livres*, which meant that 63.34 per cent. of his capital had been destroyed. In this way the state repudiated in all nearly 2,000,000,000 *livres* of public debt. The consequent shock to public credit may be imagined. . . .

It is, however, necessary to say in defence of the consolidation that bankruptcy in France had really been made inevitable by the misguided financial policy of the Constituent Assembly. The issue of the Assignats and the failure to levy sufficient taxation to balance the budgets had compromised the efforts of all subsequent administrations to grapple with financial shortage. The repudiation of 1797 was, in fact, only part of a larger scheme to effect reforms in the French budget. By reducing governmental expenditure from 1,000,000,000 to 616,000,000 *livres*, Ramel was able, for the first time in the history of revolutionary finance, to establish a balanced budget. Part of this economy was achieved by drastic reductions in the military estimates, but the main saving came from the consolidation of the public debt. The financial end in view was, therefore, sound enough in the circumstances, although the means were not. Finally, the responsibility for the final liquidation of 21 March 1801 must be borne by the Consulate. The real bankruptcy only came after the Directory had fallen.

One aspect of Directorial finance, also mainly due to Ramel, which deserves more general recognition, was the recasting of the whole system of direct and indirect taxation. Concentrated in the short interval of peace between the preliminaries of Leoben and the war of the Second Coalition, these reforms present several points of interest. The new legislation relating to direct taxation was to be one of the most lasting achievements of the revolution, for it survived down to 1914. . . .

The first direct tax to be reorganised was the tax on trade licences (*contribution des patentes*). This had been re-established in 1795, not for fiscal purposes, but as a means of preventing unjustifiable trade practices. Some changes were introduced in the method of its assessment in 1796, and the final adjustments were made by the law of 22 October 1798. The land tax (*contribution foncière*) assumed definitive shape in the law of 23 November 1798, the new tax on doors and windows in that of 24 November. The latter duty, payable in the first case by the owner, but ultimately by the tenant, encountered considerable opposition, on the ground of its English origin. It may be regarded as a first approximation to an income tax, and . . . was . . . doubled (1 March 1799) and then quadrupled (23 May 1799) as a means of meeting renewed war expenditure. . . . Lastly, on 23 December 1798, the *contribution mobilière et personelle* which was partly a poll tax and partly a tax on movable property was entirely reconstructed. These four direct taxes . . . formed the essential structure of the French taxation system down to the outbreak of the World War. . . .

Some of the features of the legislation on direct taxation reappeared in the revival of the indirect taxes. . . . Some of the new duties, such as the highway tolls, imposed on 10 September 1797, were again adopted from England. And hardly less permanent . . . were the new mortgage, registration and stamp duties (November–December 1798). Other indirect taxes which proved indispensable were those on powder and saltpetre (30 August 1797), on gold and silver ornaments (9 November 1797), playing-cards (30 September 1798) and tobacco (22 November 1798).

A tendency to exaggerate the financial straits of the government may have inclined historians to accept with greater willingness Sorel's thesis that continued European war became a necessity to the Directors. . . . On Sorel's view, war would ensure that the French armies would be occupied and prevented from interfering in politics at Paris, that the cost of clothing and feeding the troops would be borne by the foreigner, and that the empty coffers of the republic would be replenished by the confiscations and forced contributions levied on the conquered countries. Several unjustifiable assumptions have, however, to be made if this position is to be upheld. . . . French industry might very well have absorbed the returned French armies —they need not necessarily have been put on half-pay. Nor should generalisations about the financial resources which the government drew from the activities of its armies abroad be accepted without caution. It requires to be proved that the war provided on balance a net income for the Directory. What figures we have point in the opposite direction. Moreover, if the main danger to the executive government was felt to be the existence of a class of ambitious generals, the real solution would have been not to prolong but to curtail the war, and thus to put an end to the extravagant pretensions and illicit gains of the commanders. There could be little doubt that the country as a whole wanted peace, and the Directors knew it. . . .

Nor does the actual diplomacy of the period disprove the contention that the Directors were not averse from the conclusion of a satisfactory peace.

The failure of the conference at Lille in July 1797, when Malmesbury had Pitt's instructions to spare no efforts for peace, was not entirely the result of the purge of the moderate party in the *coup d'état* of Fructidor or of the over-bearing attitude of the Triumvirate. The breakdown must be placed at the door of Barras and Talleyrand, whose secret intrigues both before and after Fructidor did so much to prevent the English and French governments from reaching a frank understanding. Malmesbury at the outset agreed to the preliminary conditions put forward by the French agents. Recognition was given to the Republic, the annexation of Belgium and the French treaties of alliance with Holland and Spain. At the same time, however, he excepted secret treaties and made no promise about a "general restoration" of con-quered colonies. The French negotiators, Le Tourneur, former Director, Admiral Pléville Le Pelley and Maret, accepted Malmesbury's reservations, although these were quite inconsistent with the public articles of the Spanish treaty and the secret treaty with Holland. This initial ambiguity, with regard to the surrender of Dutch and Spanish colonies, was never explained to the Directory by its representatives. When, therefore, Malmesbury claimed the Cape and Ceylon, the Directory refused to consider his demands. Neverthe-less, such was England's desire for peace that the government was even prepared to surrender the colonial conquests without compensation. Mean-while, as the result of a ministerial reshuffle of 16 July, Talleyrand had become Foreign Minister. His English connections, his hopes of profitable speculative dealings on the London exchange and his sincere desire for peace all inclined Talleyrand to smooth away difficulties. He and Barras accordingly encouraged Pitt to believe that the French government, in return for hard cash, would not insist on the surrender of the Cape and Ceylon. Pitt consequently did not press the need for immediate concessions on his colleagues, and still reposed considerable faith in the prospects of the triumph of the moderates in Paris.

The precise effect of the *coup d'état* of 18 Fructidor upon the Lille con-ferences was that Le Tourneur, Maret and Colchen were replaced by Treilhard and Bonnier, who were instructed to present Malmesbury with a virtual ultimatum. It was to the effect that if he had not powers to cede all the English colonial conquests, he was to leave France, and not to return until he had. This new move, so far from being "a raising of the French terms," marked a reversion to the original demands. The Directory had not been informed that these conditions would be unacceptable from the British point of view, and it is clear that the Directors thought that Fructidor would enable them to impose this settlement. The ultimatum was conceived not as a means to end the peace negotiations, but as a way of exacting the full price from an enemy known to be in great difficulty. Malmesbury, having no authority to make the concessions, left Lille on 17 September with little or no hope of return. The resumption of negotiations was finally prevented by the battle of Camperdown. . . . It was the secret intrigues of French agents at

Lille which stiffened the English resistance before Fructidor, and which, after the *coup d'état*, were the cause of French intransigence.

On the other hand, the approval which, under strong provocation from Bonaparte, the Directors gave to the preliminaries of Leoben and the final treaty of Campo Formio, cannot be regarded as indicative of the pacific views of the Directors. It is fairly certain that those treaties would have been rejected by the Directory if its hands had not been tied, and indeed the best interests of France demanded that Bonaparte's policy should have been set aside. The Directors had, in each case, ample room for dissatisfaction. At Leoben, Bonaparte, anxious to monopolise the credit of having concluded peace, speeded up negotiations in order to prevent the official French negotiator, General Clarke, from arriving in time to share the discussions. In the public articles of the preliminaries of peace Bonaparte renounced the left bank of the Rhine, towards the acquisition of which Reubell's foreign policy had been mainly directed, and in the secret articles, by retaining the Duchy of Milan and suggesting the partition of Venice, he definitely disobeyed his instructions for the first time since the inception of the Italian campaign. In addition, it is clear that Bonaparte virtually conceded all that Thugut, the Austrian minister, wished to obtain. The principle of the integrity of the Empire was upheld, access to the Adriatic won, and the surrender by Austria of Belgium and Milan amply compensated for by her acquisition of part of Venice. When the articles of Leoben were read to them three of the Directors—Reubell, Barras and La Revellière—declared they were inacceptable, and the Minister for Foreign Affairs—Delacroix—also reported unfavourably on them. Yet on 30 April 1797 Reubell alone refused to sign the ratification of the preliminaries. . . . The Directors were compelled to accept Leoben because the French public, acquainted only with the public articles, had received the news with an enthusiasm which it would have been dangerous for the government to have damped, and, moreover, the rejection of the terms would have entailed an admission that Bonaparte's advance into Austria had in actual fact placed him in a very serious military position.

These incidents were paralleled by the negotiations at Campo Formio. Bonaparte withdrew from Austrian territory without waiting for the ratification of the Leoben preliminaries by his home government, and again ignored his instructions. He had been ordered by the Directors to renew the war rather than surrender Venice, and also to insist on the compensation of Austria in Germany. The actual terms of peace, however, conceded most of the advantages to Austria. As a result of the exchange of territory, her position was strengthened both in Italy and Germany, a check was placed on the ambitions of her rival Prussia, and she had the prospect of still further compensations if France succeeded in wresting the left bank of the Rhine from the representatives of the Empire in the projected congress at Rastadt. On the other hand, France deserted her ally Prussia, assumed a share of responsibility for the extinction of Venice, and erected in the Cisalpine Republic an uneasy neighbour whom it would be essential in the future to protect. Once more the Directors submitted, but most unwillingly. They could not afford to forfeit the position they had just won after Fructidor, nor did they wish to see a revival of the European coalition against France, as seemed not unlikely after the failure of the Lille conferences.

The net result of this double surrender on the part of the Directors was to deprive them of the initiative in French foreign policy and to substitute the Italian policy of Bonaparte for that of the natural frontiers as canvassed by Reubell. Moreover, in the years which followed Campo Formio the Directors did much successful work by assimilating the conquered territories in Belgium and on the left bank of the Rhine, by protecting the Italian republics and by exerting further pressure on Great Britain. In fact, for a whole year after Fructidor, French influence on the Continent was virtually unchallenged, and the real reverses suffered by French arms and diplomacy and the revival of the second Coalition must be ascribed not to Directorial incompetence, but to the initiation of the Egyptian expedition—a venture devised by Bonaparte and Talleyrand.

It is less easy to defend the inability of the Directors to secure internal peace and security. Here at least the record of the Directors was one of almost complete failure. This failure, however, only repeated the lapses of monarchical and previous revolutionary governments. Nor should it be overlooked that the task of maintaining public order in the provinces had become immeasurably more difficult under the Directory in consequence of the revival of royalism, the appearance of banditry, and the adoption of conscription, (5 September 1798). Conscription was applied at an unfortunate moment—just at the time when the French armies had sustained a series of severe defeats and when the prospect of starvation was greater among the fighting forces than at home. Evasion of the law and desertion both helped to swell the number of brigands, who were able to organise "reigns of terror" in various parts of the country. It is customary to blame the government for having done nothing to face up to these difficulties. A long series of measures designed especially to grapple with brigandage, however, affords little support to this criticism. One of the first acts of the Directory after its acceptance of office was to add a seventh ministry—that of general police— to the six ministries provided for in the constitution, and to institute exhaustive inquiries into the state of the *garde nationale* and the gendarmerie. This investigation revealed defects which were, to some extent, remedied by a law of 17 April 1798 reforming the gendarmerie. Other administrative gaps were filled by the laws prescribing capital punishment for robbery with violence on the high roads and in private houses (15 May 1797), the law enforcing increased penalties against gaolers who connived at the escape of their prisoners (25 September 1797), and the law reforming the personnel of the criminal courts (10 January 1798). It must be admitted that these changes did not affect substantial improvement, but it is evident at least that the problem had been taken in hand. . . .

It only remains to summarise the reasons for thinking that the instability of the Directory has perhaps been exaggerated. This political insecurity has been ascribed partly to the Constitution of the year III, and partly to public hostility to the Directors and the general desire for a strong executive government on the eve of Brumaire. . . .

. . . There is something to be said for the view that the main constitutional difficulties of the Directors were in the course of time solved. The necessity of having a majority of at least three to two for the transaction of business may have opened the way to differences of opinion among the Directors, but after Fructidor (4 September 1797) the Triumvirate of Barras, Reubell and La Revellière removed this source of weakness. It was not until Reubell retired on 16 May 1799 and was replaced by Sieyès that this solidarity of the Directors was shaken. Similarly, the lack of any power to dissolve the Councils did not seriously hamper the Directors, since resort could always be had to systematic corruption at the annual election of one-third of the Councils or to a *coup d'état*. Although the right of initiating legislation lay with the Council of Five Hundred, the Directors were not deprived of the power of giving effect to their policy, since the machinery of Directorial messages to the Legislative Assemblies proved an adequate substitute. Moreover, the formal absence of the power of initiation often provided the government with ready-made excuses when public opinion showed itself at all critical. Nor was the tenure of the Directory as a whole or of individual members of it really insecure. The life of the Directory was fixed at five years (Article 137)—a period which exceeded that of the Councils by two years and that of the Assemblies of 1791 and 1793 by three. As only one Director retired annually by lot, the political complexion of the executive could not be effectively altered by the Councils except after a wait of three years, and even then only on the unlikely assumption that the majority in the Councils remained stable. Finally, the substitution of three Consuls for five Directors at Brumaire left the form of the executive government very much the same.

Nor can French public opinion immediately before Brumaire be described as actively hostile to the Directors. The prevailing feeling was one of apathy rather than of antipathy. The initial reforming zeal of the revolutionaries had dwindled, people in the provinces had lost interest in electoral devices, and once the tide of victory against the foreigner had turned in favour of France the cry of "The country is in danger" had lost its meaning. Now, in a situation of this kind the government in actual possession of power is not usually in a weak position, and it is doubtful whether in 1799 there was a general feeling in France that the overthrow of the Directory would do much to improve conditions. Hardly less widespread than apathy was fear

... of extremes, whether royalist or Jacobin. Fortunately for the Directors, the only formidable opposition to their rule came from precisely these two sources. For this reason the Directors had an easy means of prolonging themselves in office by *coups d'état* directed now against the Right, now against the Left. This "seesaw policy" far from being an indication of the essential instability of the government can be regarded as a source of strength. Not only was it effective, it was also consonant with the best interests of the country at large. As the representatives of moderate republicanism, the Directors could in this sense lay claim to a good deal of popular support.

Whether or not Frenchmen were willing on the eve of Brumaire to exchange the republican constitution of the year III for a military dictatorship cannot be decided with certainty. The difficulties encountered with the Council of Five Hundred at St. Cloud on 19 Brumaire, the cries of "Outlaw him" which greeted Bonaparte and the well-known sympathies of the Parisian troops, at least make it clear that the constitution was still regarded as a bulwark against dictatorship. Bonaparte's military prestige had been somewhat tarnished by his abandonment of the army in Egypt and little was known of his political and administrative ability. As a peacemaker, he still enjoyed the reputation he had gained at Leoben and Campo Formio, but Sieyès evidently thought that he would be willing to accept subordinate political office. . . . The theory of an "inevitable" military dictatorship has had a long innings; has not the time arrived when it should be abandoned? France in the autumn of 1799 was economically prosperous, the danger of invasion had already been averted, the reforms of Ramel and Neufchâteau were beginning to bear fruit, and the fear of reviving Jacobinism, dating back to the law of the hostages, might easily have been dealt with in the usual way. In religious matters . . . although the desire for a restoration of the altars may have been pressing, there was considerably anxiety lest with it there should be associated a return of the church lands.

If Bonaparte had been forty instead of thirty, would he not have remained faithful to his original idea of becoming a Director?

SUGGESTIONS FOR FURTHER READING

Documentary: JOHN HALL STEWART (ed.), *A Documentary Survey of the French Revolution* (New York, 1951); J. M. ROBERTS and R. C. COBB (eds.), *French Revolution Documents* (New York, 1966–); Historiographical: PAUL FARMER, *France Reviews Its Revolutionary Origins* (New York, 1944); General: GEORGES LEFEBVRE, *The French Revolution*, 2 vol. (New York and London, 1962–64); J. M. THOMPSON, *The French Revolution* (Oxford, 1944); CRANE BRINTON, *A Decade of Revolution, 1789–1799* (New York, 1934); M. J. SYDENHAM, *The French Revolution* (London, 1965). Special Studies: JACQUES GODECHOT, *Les Institutions de la France sous la Révolution et l'Empire* (Paris, 1951); NORMAN HAMPSON, *A Social*

Interpretation of the French Revolution (London and Toronto, 1963); ALFRED COBBAN, *The Social Interpretation of the French Revolution* (Cambridge, Eng., 1964); GEORGES LEFEBVRE, *The Coming of the French Revolution* (Princeton, 1947); BEATRICE F. HYSLOP, *French Nationalism in 1789 According to the General Cahiers* (New York, 1934); M. J. SYDENHAM, *The Girondins* (London, 1961); CRANE BRINTON, *The Jacobins* (Cambridge, Mass., 1930); DONALD GREER, *The Incidence of the Terror During the French Revolution* (Cambridge, Mass., 1935); and *The Incidence of the Emigration during the French Revolution* (Cambridge, Mass., 1951); SEYMOUR HARRIS, *The Assignats* (Cambridge, Mass., 1930); ALBERT MATHIEZ, *La vie chère et le mouvement social sous la Terreur* (Paris, 1927); ALBERT SOBOUL, *The Parisian Sans-Culottes and the French Revolution, 1793–4* (Oxford, 1964); R. R. Palmer, *Twelve Who Ruled* (Princeton, 1941); JOHN B. SIRICH, *The Revolutionary Committees in the Departments of France, 1793–1794* (Cambridge, Mass., 1943); ALBERT MATHIEZ, *After Robespierre, The Thermidorean Reaction* (New York, 1931); GEORGES LEFEBVRE, *The Thermidoreans and the Directory* (New York, 1964); ANDRÉ LATREILLE, *L'Eglise catholique et la Révolution française*, vol. I (Paris, 1946); BURDETTE C. POLAND, *French Protestantism and the French Revolution* (Princeton, 1957); Biographical: J. M. THOMPSON, *Leaders of the French Revolution* (Oxford, 1929); LEO GERSHOY, *Bertrand Barère: A Reluctant Terrorist* (Princeton, 1962); MARCEL REINHARD, *Le Grand Carnot*, 2 vol. (Paris, 1950–52); J. SALWYN SCHAPIRO, *Condorcet and the Rise of Liberalism* (New York, 1934); LOUIS MADELIN, *Danton* (London, 1921); DAVID DOWD, *Pageant-Master of the Republic: Jacques-Louis David and the French Revolution* (Lincoln, Neb., 1948); LOUIS GOTTSCHALK, *Jean Paul Marat: A Study in Radicalism* (New York, 1927; reprinted, 1967); J. M. THOMPSON, *Robespierre*, 2 vol. (Oxford, 1935); GEOFFREY BRUUN, *Saint-Just: Apostle of the Terror* (Boston and New York, 1932; reprinted, 1966).

Chapter Five

THE
COUNTERREVOLUTION

THE HISTORY of the Counterrevolution has long suffered from the vehemence of partisanship; pro-Revolutionary historians have decried it, whereas conservative historians have regretted its failure. Perhaps not unsurprisingly then, some of the most significant recent contributions to the field have been made by British and American historians, who are relatively free from commitments for or against the Revolution.

The Counterrevolution was not a concerted, organized movement against the events of 1789 and later, but rather spontaneous, interrupted, and often confused manifestations of resistance, revolt, and attack. The formal Counterrevolution began with the emigration of the princes of the blood in the summer of 1789 which the late French historian Emmanuel Vingtrinier describes in the first selection. Led by the Count of Artois, the princes eventually settled in Turin and there attempted to organize a counterrevolutionary committee for inciting rebellion within France and appealing to the courts of Europe for military intervention. Here the first difficulties were encountered: the courts of Europe were unwilling to take action because of their own diplomatic intrigues and the continued presence of the King and Queen within France. Vingtrinier deals with the first period of the Counterrevolution, when neither Emperor Joseph II nor Leopold II was willing to intervene against France. It was only after the failure of the king's flight to Varennes in June, 1791, the accession of Emperor Francis II, and France's declaration of war on Austria in April, 1792 that the European powers mobilized. At Valmy on September 20, 1792, they began their first of nineteen more years of defeats.

Of the approximately 130,000 émigrés (0.5 per cent of the population) in the period 1789–1799, roughly a third had succeeded in crossing the borders by the end of 1792.[1] This first sequence of departures consisted mostly of aristocrats and clergy who, fearing for their lives, property, and freedom of expression, often emigrated (as in the case of army officers) to join the émigré princes. The remaining two-thirds of the emigration occurred after 1792, mostly during 1793 because of the war, the invasion of the northeast, the fall of the Girondins, and the Terror. It is ironical that in the Republic which followed the fall of the Monarchy, the emigration not only markedly increased but became, by and large, lower class in composition. To quote Donald Greer, "the change in the social complexion of the emigration . . . reveals a curious paradox, for in 1793, the year of the birth of modern democracy [in France] the emigration became democratic."[2]

In the second selection, André Latreille, the French Church historian, describes what most historians today recognize as a major turning point of the Revolution. The Civil Constitution of the Clergy, voted by the Assembly on July 12, 1790, led most of the bishops, as much as half of the lower clergy, and large numbers of the faithful to oppose the Revolution. In the spring of 1791, Pope Pius VI condemned both the Civil Constitution of the Clergy, which demanded an oath

[1] Donald Greer, *The Incidence of the Emigration During the French Revolution* (Cambridge, Mass., 1951), Appendix.
[2] *Ibid.*, p. 35.

of allegiance to the state as the new ecclesiastical sovereign as well as to the principles of the Revolution contained in the *Declaration of the Rights of Man and Citizen*. Hence to accept the Revolution, to swear the oath, or to recognize the curés who *did* swear the oath, was to become schismatic toward the Church; to be loyal to Rome was to be a "nonjuror" or "refractory," and eventually *suspect*. Thus began the unfortunate break between the Church and the revolutionary tradition characteristic of French history since 1789. More immediately, the ranks of the Counterrevolution were swelled, the king decided to flee, and war became inevitable. Hopes for conciliation and peaceful assimilation of the Revolution were lost.

In the third selection, the American sociologist Charles Tilly compares the social structure of revolutionary and counterrevolutionary communities in southern Anjou—the seat of the Vendée uprising in 1793. Though the most noticeable statistic in his study is the wide divergence between the percentage of priests taking the oath in a revolutionary district (64.7) and a counterrevolutionary district (5.3), Tilly also emphasizes less-known differences in social structure (percentage of bourgeoisie to peasantry) to explain the origins of the Vendée Counterrevolution.

Another unfamiliar aspect of the Counterrevolution, now being extensively investigated by British and French historians, is the role of counterrevolutionary espionage. Harvey Mitchell, Professor of History at the University of British Columbia, is one of the first historians to unravel the Dropmore papers (for a long time discredited as specious). From them he has deciphered a coherent interpretation of the underground correspondence among Francis Drake, an agent of the British government, and the Comte d'Antraigues, an émigré in the service of the French royal government in exile, and secret agents in Paris. The correspondence indicates both the degree of sophistication that espionage had attained during the Revolution and the conflicting political aims of the several parties involved. The later organization of the Paris Agency, *les Amis de Paris*, and the *Institut Philanthropique* eventually were able to win over members of the army, negotiate with representatives and deputies, and set up a secret network throughout the Departments to gain control of the local organs of government in an attempt to overthrow the Directory. The Paris Agency was eventually counterinfiltrated and the "Brottier conspiracy" was unmasked and its members were arrested and prosecuted.

The Terror of 1793–1794 produced reprisals during the counterrevolutionary reaction after the fall of Robespierre in July, 1794. The proscriptions against émigrés and priests were followed by laws allowing the churches to re-open and the émigrés to return. The oath of loyalty was rendered palatable to the orthodox, and suspects were no longer those disloyal to the Revolution but rather former members of the Departmental Committees of Public Surveillance. This is the subject of the fourth selection by Professor Godechot of the University of Toulouse, an authority on the French Revolution. The Red Terror of the Revolution found its counterpart in the White Terror of the Counterrevolution; former Revolutionary terrorists now fell victim to Counterrevolutionary mob violence.

The Counterrevolution can be seen to have had a dialectical involvement with the Revolution. It preceded the Revolution, even caused it through the noble, clerical, and parliamentary resistance to reform. Its activity during the Revolution was ironically one of the latter's impelling forces. The eventual success of the princes in forming a coalition only provoked Revolutionary ardor, universal conscription, and a crisis which led to the fall of the Girondins and the furthering of the social revolution. The converse, of course, was also true. The Civil Constitution of the clergy may have been the decisive factor in the development of the Counterrevolution. After Robespierre came the Thermidorian reaction, the White Terror, and the Directory. Thus both the Revolution and the Counterrevolution abetted each other by their mutual abrasions. This, of course, was not the aim of either. For the true Counterrevolutionary, as for the Revolutionary, compromise was not possible in the 1790's and his intransigence defeated his own objectives. Both the true colors and despairing vindication of the most extreme form of Counterrevolution can be found in their writings, which Professor Paul Beik of Swarthmore College analyzes in the final selection. By 1799 the theorists had abandoned conciliation at a time when the Revolution had assumed a more tolerant, less radical form within France. Resigned to the fact that the restoration they desired was no longer feasible nor the ploy of conciliation useful, the counterrevolutionary impulse to condemn the Revolution and champion its own position was stronger in the face of defeat.

Successful in 1814, the Counterrevolution was still forced to continue its ideological struggle against the principles of 1789 throughout the nineteenth century and into the twentieth. Though it compromised to a small degree with some aspects of the Revolution, it remained traditionalist, royalist, and later nationalist. The importance of the Counterrevolution must be measured not in its immediate, tangible results, but in its curious involvement with the Revolution of 1789–1799 and its subsequent viability despite repeated failures.

⚘

COUNTERREVOLUTIONARY POLITICS: THE EMIGRATION AND INTRIGUES OF THE PRINCES

Emmanuel Vingtrinier

[In July, 1789,] the Prince of Condé . . . decided to leave the kingdom with his entourage. Since the king had chosen to surrender to his enemies rather than to accept the services of the princes of the blood, "honor" obliged the latter to "abandon everything." The victor of [the battle of] Johannisberg [of 1762] would go abroad, prepare his revenge, and undertake a counter-

Emmanuel Vingtrinier, *La Contre-Révolution. Première période, 1789–1791.* 2 vol. (Paris, 1924–25), I, pp. 34, 62–63, 69, 72–73, 80, 82–83, 77–79, 369, 372; II, 64–67. © Emile Paul. Used by permission. Editors' translation.

revolution. "We are no longer able to serve from within," he told the king. "We are going to attempt more effective action from without." Louis XVI heard his cousins' farewells, and "by an order exacted from his weakness," the Condé family left to prepare for their departure.

The Count of Artois and the princes of Condé could not prolong their stay in Brussels [where they first halted]. It did not suit Emperor Joseph II to allow a nest of plots and conspiracies to hatch in his states, close as they were to the French border. The brother of Louis XVI had requested the King of Sardinia, Victor Amadeus III, his father-in-law, for permission to settle in Turin. Then, with their large entourage, the princes made their way through Germany to Switzerland, and at each stop heard reports of the tragic events which afflicted France. . . .

By this time, the princes had become determined to attempt a counter-revolution. In his presumptuous frivolity, the Count of Artois dreamed of returning to his country with arms in hand, and there to play a role worthy of a grandson of Henry IV. . . .

Offering less and less resistance, Victor Amadeus finally allowed the émigrés to conspire in his capital and under his protection. . . .

They flattered themselves that the Revolution would be promptly repressed, but they were not at all in agreement on the means. Some wanted to appeal to foreign powers by invoking the solidarity of sovereigns, to strike hard and be done with it as quickly as possible. Others felt that the intervention of foreign troops, rather than rallying "all true Frenchmen," would be likely to increase even further the headiness of independence and unite the entire nation against the monarchy. To their way of thinking, the princes should stir the discontent of the provinces against the [National] Assembly, discover which were the most faithful, and appeal to well-disposed people of all classes. But the reestablishment of the Old Regime could not be realized without resistance and struggle. From the beginning most of the émigrés expected to use force to effect the Counterrevolution, and some of the younger ones were already entertaining mad dreams of revenge. . . .

The Count of Artois . . . soon formed a permanent "Committee" organized solely for the frightful enterprise of directing the Counterrevolution. The responsibilities of the Committee were almost limitless: it was to concern itself with French affairs, to gather all types of information, to establish contacts in the most sympathetic provinces, to direct the agents whom it sent there, and finally to pursue the negotiations which would be undertaken with foreign courts. . . .

From the beginning they faced a major difficulty, the lack of money. The finances of the Count of Artois were in even worse condition than those of the State: he was 21,850,000 *livres* in debt, while the revenues from his appanages and ancestral estates reached only 3,600,000 *livres*. Preparations were made to send someone to Spain to solicit subsidies from King Charles IV.

But without further delay, the Committee worked through emissaries and a "vast correspondence" within France to increase the number of discontented and to recruit determined partisans. They began with Dauphiné. Agents went from chateau to chateau and pointed out to the nobles the evils that the Revolution had already caused and the even greater ones which would follow if the audacity of the revolutionaries met no resistance. Demanding their word of honor not to betray the secret, they disclosed the plan formulated by the princes to return to France to reestablish order, and exhorted them to take part in the Counterrevolution.

It was in the eastern and southern provinces especially that the Committee tried to make its influence felt. In addition to Dauphiné, the areas of Provence, Languedoc, Lyons, Franche Comté, Burgundy and Alsace, which lay close to Piedmont, Spain, Germany, and Switzerland, were, more than the rest of France, within reach of either emissaries or invading armies. And so the princes hoped to find conditions there all the more favorable since these provinces had suffered the most during the recent disturbances.

Finally, on the advice of Calonne, [the former controller general of finances under Louis XVI,] and with the thought of preparing the way for foreign intervention, the Count of Artois appealed to the nobility to leave France, and the Prince of Condé gave orders to the Marquis of La Queuille, a deputy from Riom who had remained in Paris, to invite the nobles to come to Piedmont and "form regular corps." . . .

When Joseph II received letters [requesting help] from the [Count of Artois] and Madame Elizabeth, [the sister of Louis XVI,] written to "wring tears from the driest heart," he remained unmoved. The eloquence of the Count of Artois seemed "most unusual" to him. In his reply, the Emperor did not in the least conceal his "way of seeing things." He recalled some old advice given to his sister, [Marie-Antoinette,] which she had not followed. He found faults in the conduct of the king and listed them. He spoke of the Netherlands, which he himself had just lost, and of his war against the Turks, which was not over. Finally, reaching the heart of the matter, Joseph II asserted that he had received "no plea or request from the king, who, if he wished, had so many means of transmitting them." "By what right then," he added,

would another have to take the smallest step or raise his voice against all that has been decided and sanctioned by the most unquestionable authority in the world, namely the king, together with the nation, legally represented by its deputies? . . . Your Royal Highness, with all the princes who thought it their duty to leave France, are only citizens, though very distinguished ones, but who are not a legal body or have any right not to submit to everything which the king and the nation find worthy of decreeing. If you desire the happiness of France, the king, the queen and everything to do with them . . . , do not fail in the only means by which you can given them peace and happiness—by getting together and putting an end to this kind of opposition party called aristocratic . . ., which is weak in itself and incapable of carrying out the good it seeks and desires, and which can only be harmful. . . . Would it be by a civil war of province against province, or of provinces against the capital, of troops against troops, or citizen against citizen, that you think you could cure the evils of your country and improve the position of the king? What a mistake! You would destroy them all. . . .

The Imperial reply, received in Turin on November 7, [1789,] exasperated the princes, as much by the truths which it expressed in a coldly moralizing tone, as by the scant respect which Joseph II showed for their persons. They considered it "terrible, repulsive, and even insulting." This initial failure, however, did not discourage them. . . .

The departure of Louis XVI had to be obtained at all costs. The days went by while [the princes] waited for a reply from the Tuileries [to their suggestion that Louis XVI leave France]. "The king will not leave if he is not forced to do so," declared [the Count of] Vaudreuil. And since excellent news had been received from the eastern provinces, "Let the Salon Français, [a royalist club in Paris,] abduct him," he exclaimed, "and take him to Alsace."

As for the great powers, what exactly was known of their feelings? Calonne, the "dupe of Pitt's assurances," with his "inexpressible levity," had continued to maintain against all reason "that we should rely only on England and Prussia for support of the Counterrevolution." But San Martino di Front, the Sardinian ambassador to London, informed Victor Amadeus that the government of George III, far from intending to reestablish the power of Louis XVI, rejoiced over the abasement and discredit into which the first crown of Europe had fallen. England's armament and her deliberate quarrel with Spain [in 1790 over Nootka Sound] had no purpose other than to detach this nation from France and to cause the disruption of the Family Compact. . . .

Victor Amadeus no doubt took the interests of his son-in-law very much to heart, but he himself could not risk the enterprise without the support of one of two great powers. . . . "The king, your father-in-law, is full of zeal," [a royalist agent wrote to the Count of Artois,] "but the Emperor of Spain must move before he can act."

In August, [1790,] Bombelles, [the French ambassador to Venice,] had gone to see [the new ruler of Austria,] Leopold II, at Adelsburg and show him all the advantages he would secure by helping Louis XVI, and had received "the most satisfactory replies." Since then the new sovereign had neither answered the pleas of the Count of Artois nor spoken of French affairs. Gherardini, his minister in Turin, also maintained an absolute silence. At Vienna, Prince Kaunitz, in an interview with [the Sardinian ambassador,] the Marquis of Brême, spoke of Jacobin propaganda and of the need for the monarchies to protect themselves from the revolutionary contagion, but he never came to a practical conclusion. To the Baron Castelnau, an envoy of the Count of Artois, he had said in a surly tone: "When a person has important business at home, he would be unwise to become involved in that of others." Was there only "weakness or bad faith in all the cabinets of Europe?" Castelnau, it is true, had been carried away by his zeal and committed some blunders. Orders were then sent to Armand de Polignac at Venice to go in person to Vienna and attempt to divine the personal intentions of Leopold, which might not be in complete conformity with the views of his old Chancellor, [Kaunitz]. In any case, it was known at the court of Turin that Marie Antoinette put her greatest hope in her brother. So Victor Amadeus for his part wanted to sound out the future Emperor without causing suspicion. . . .

On orders from the King of Sardinia, the Marquis of Brême went to Frankfurt in the first days of October, [1790,] to represent his sovereign at the coronation of [Leopold II] and above all to try to learn his feelings, as well as those of the German princes regarding French affairs. The Piedmontese ambassador wasted no time in doing so.

From the letters of Queen [Marie Antoinette], Leopold II suspected that Victor Amadeus was about to allow his hand to be forced by his son-in-law. Giving an audience to Brême, he told him frankly that

I am very much afraid that, much against the will of King Victor Amadeus, whose wisdom I know, the French at his court will succeed in being too precipitate about the time necessary for success. They should be persuaded that they cannot undertake anything as long as the royal family is in the hands of its enemies. Precipitous action would plunge a dagger into the hearts of these unfortunate rulers. . . . I have heard Frenchmen daring enough to say that nothing would change since the Count of Artois remains. I do not think so, and I shall never be my sister's murderer. . . .

. . . Victor Amadeus sensed the bitterness of the Imperial warning. Already, Brême, after a conversation with the Elector of Cologne, had informed his master that very little hope was left that the cause of the émigré princes would be supported by the members of the Empire. Moreover, there was, as the king saw, no "indication that the other powers" wanted "to take an active part" in the efforts at Counterrevolution being prepared in Piedmont. . . .

But at the same time, obeying his own inclinations, and believing that there was going to be a great change in the political system which would break the Franco-Austrian alliance, Victor Amadeus decided to write directly to the Emperor. With maladroit haste he assured him that he would never act except in accord with him when and how he [Leopold] so chose. This was the first step toward the alliance with Austria which was to be so disastrous for the House of Savoy.

At the moment when the King of Sardinia finally gave up supporting the enterprises of the émigrés without participation by the Emperor, the royalist committees in Lyons and Provence were clamoring for the aid of foreign forces, which was absolutely indispensable, they said, if they wished to act before the departure of [Louis XVI].

The princes could no longer hide the fact that it was impossible to satisfy their wishes. Nevertheless, the Count of Artois and especially Condé, less resigned than ever, persisted despite the warnings of their best friends, to seek to penetrate France in the shortest time possible.

THE CHURCH AND THE COUNTERREVOLUTION

André Latreille

[In 1790] the National Assembly began its debate on the plans for church reorganization proposed by its Ecclesiastical Committee. On July 12, 1790, it approved all the provisions which constituted the Civil Constitution of the Clergy.... Dominating the whole Constitution is the statist postulate that the sovereign alone possesses the power to make changes he considers appropriate, not only in ecclesiastical organization but also in worship. If there were theologians and canonists within the Gallican Church who were in favor of every attempt at compromise and willing to allow the reorganization of church jurisdictions or the election of bishops, for example, they constantly warned the Assembly that it could not fail to deal with the spiritual authority following canonical forms, "without fundamentally damaging religion."

The first president of the Ecclesiastical Committee, Bishop de Bonald, had already said in regard to the reform of convents that

What I do not consider legitimate in the exercise of this authority is that by itself, it casts down barriers which it did not erect... before the institution which alone in the spiritual order has the power to bind and loose on earth has spoken.

All the bishop-deputies took the same position in regard to the Civil Constitution of the Clergy. Three months after the vote, a remarkable

A. Latreille, J.-R. Palanque, E. Delaruelle, and R. Rémond, *Histoire du catholicisme en France*, vol. III (Paris, 1962), pp. 83, 86–89, 91–95, 98–99. © Editions Spès, 1962. Used by permission. Editors' translation.

pamphlet by the thirty bishops who still sat in the Constituent Assembly (and from which only Talleyrand and Gobel were excluded) and entitled *Exposition of the Principles of the Civil Constitution of the Clergy* proclaimed:

If the civil power wishes to make changes in the religious order without the consent of the Church, it contradicts its principles and does not destroy them. It contradicts its principles and destroys the means which could assist in putting its ideas into effect.

We wish to know the desires of the Church so as to reestablish a necessary harmony between the civil and ecclesiastical powers, and by their union, to preserve peace of mind and public tranquility. . . .

. . . The two archbishops sitting on the Royal Council advised that the decrees be ratified, but only because they considered open resistance impossible and still cherished hopes of a compromise *with* the Holy See. So, before knowing the feelings of either the episcopate or the Pope, Louis XVI gave his approval on August 24, 1790. Yet neither the maxims nor the traditions of the court of Rome, nor the disposition of the reigning Pope, made acquiescence by the Holy See appear likely.

By the end of October, the Gallican episcopate had undertaken its responsibilities. Nearly all the bishops (eighty-three to be exact) rallied to the *Exposition of Principles* written by the bishop-deputies, while reserving the right of final decision to the successor of St. Peter, who, placed at the center of Catholic unity and communion, had to be the interpreter and voice of the wishes of the universal church. Eight months would pass before Pius VI issued his opinion on March 10, 1791—eight interminable months during which his silence left the faithful of France uncertain, during which the Assembly multiplied the laws intended to hasten application of the Civil Constitution, eight months of irreparable delays!

The Constituent Assembly, strengthened after its first victory over the king, was naturally not inclined to abandon any of its claims to legislate alone in ecclesiastical matters.

On November 27, to hasten things along, it decided to compel, under penalty of revocation, "all bishops, former archbishops, curés and other public functionaries," to take an oath "to be faithful to the nation, the law and the king, and to maintain with all their power the Constitution decreed by the National Assembly and accepted by the king."

This was the constitutional oath destined to remain famous in history, sowing discord in church and state, and leading to the rupture of the harmony between the two powers which had so often been exalted as indispensable to the success of the Revolution.

Of 160 prelates, only seven agreed to take it, of whom four—Brienne, Jarente, Savine, and Talleyrand—were heads of dioceses, and who, in any case, were completely discredited by their unbelief and morals. . . . All the others refused. It remained to be seen how many of the lower clergy and faithful would follow the example given them. Public opinion was less clear than it seems to us today. Rome's silence need not be considered—the good country curé was not accustomed to looking so far away, and the voice of the Pope did not reach him easily. He was often quite alienated from his bishop by numerous legitimate grievances and by a different way of looking at the political crisis. He waited for "the light of those whose life he shared and whose wisdom he admired, without having to seek his doctrines outside his diocese." He questioned a canonist or cleric in a neighboring town, but the feelings expressed were quite contradictory. Even if he did not take into account either the material and moral advantages which ecclesiastical reorganization promised him, or (if he refused) the threat of being considered a "disturber of public order" and an enemy of national regeneration, he still hesitated to cut himself off from his parishioners, to abandon his post, the parish, and presbytery to which he was closely bound. This was especially the case when the local authorities, insisting on retaining him, were willing to close their eyes to the reservations which he might attach to his oath. Insofar as it is possible to see clearly through the innumerable local studies and attempts at overall statistics, we are led to estimate that half, or slightly more, of the parish clergy—that is to say, a third of the entire clergy—immediately adhered to the Civil Constitution. This was a considerable proportion, but like any average, the result of extreme variations—from the Vendée and Bas-Rhin Departments, where 90 per cent refused, to the Var, where 96 per cent accepted—and which indeed conceals inexplicable "cases"—in Haute-Saône, in contrast to four refusals and 152 acceptances, it is calculated that 352 priests, that is two thirds of the total, made reservations or immediately reneged on their promise. . . .

The pontifical judgment was at last rendered on March 10, 1791, in a lengthy document, the papal brief *Quot Aliquantum*, addressed to Cardinal de La Rochefoucauld and the bishops who had signed the *Exposition of Principles*. Pius VI declared that the Civil Constitution had "as its aim and effect the destruction of the Catholic religion." It dealt a fatal blow to the divine constitution of the Church by its clauses relative to the canonical institution of bishops, the election of priests, and the functioning of episcopal councils. It sought to overturn the fundamental idea of faith that the Roman Pontiff had supreme jurisdiction over the entire Church. The Sovereign Pontiff took the occasion of this examination of doctrinal and disciplinary questions, which the Assembly had illegitimately taken up, in order to pronounce a severe judgment on the principles it had proclaimed. Thus he publicly censured—having already delivered an unpublished address in consistory—the Declaration of the Rights of Man, which was guilty of granting to the citizen

this absolute liberty which not only assures the right of not being disturbed for one's religious opinions, but which also accords this license to think, write, and even to print without impunity anything in religious matters that the most unbalanced mind may suggest. This is a monstrous right which, nevertheless, appears to the Assembly to flow from the equality and liberty natural to all men.

But what could be more rash than to establish among men an equality and an uncontrolled liberty that seemed to strangle reason? What was more contrary to the rights of God the Creator, who limited the liberty of man by His prohibition of evil, than "this liberty of thought and action which the National Assembly grants to social man as an imprescriptable right of nature?"

Thus, with fearful solemnity, the theses of the Roman Church came into conflict with the principles of modern liberalism, an antagonism that would occur so frequently after 1789. The Gallican bishops would, with much dignity and moderation, attempt to explain their conduct in their reply to the letter, distinguishing between the level of natural right and that of political action. In the very terms of the Holy Father, they reproved a liberty and equality contrary to the dictates of reason and dogma, but as citizens who desired not to contradict popular aspirations in the civil order, they believed it possible to establish a veritable realm of public liberty within an hereditary monarchy:

And without difficulty have we recognized this natural equality which excludes no citizen from places to which Providence calls him because of his talents and virtues. Political equality may be expanded or restricted, depending on the form of government. And we have believed that our opinions were free, as are those of all citizens, in these rather broad questions which God Himself has declared open to discussion among men.

As far as the Civil Constitution was concerned, the Gallican bishops, having anticipated the Pope in his condemnation, found no difficulty in adopting the line of conduct prescribed by him. . . . Henceforth, there were two churches confronting each other in the kingdom. In more than one locality, two bishops or two priests would anathematize each other before a divided population, which could understand their opposition only in its own way. The average man, in effect, did not grasp the relative distinctions in ecclesiastical discipline. As long as mass was said as usual in the parish church and the sacraments dispensed, he was little concerned to know whether the priest who officiated had legal jurisdiction or why the taking of a political oath could make him schismatic. He was more inclined to judge priests on the sympathy which they inspired as persons and on the attachment which he himself felt toward the Assembly and the Revolutionary cause. On one side were those who took the oath, and on the other those who did not; those who, in disdain, were called "juring" or "refractory," or who, in admiration, were styled "civic" or "good" priests. Under these conditions, the antagonists had to compete for the favor of the authorities and rival each other in polemical argument before the faithful.

The conflict began at the level of the episcopal town and spread to the smallest parish. For several months at Blois, the new bishop of the Loir-et-Cher Department, Grégoire, who was master of the cathedral and the episcopal palace, and who enjoyed the support of the municipality and the clubs, had to face the former incumbent, Thémines, who fled to another part of town and hurled interdicts against the "intruders," as the jurors who dared to assume priestly functions in place of the nonjuring clergy were called. The struggle lasted until the day when the pressures of the Jacobin club and the orders of the directory of the Department forced Thémines to yield, and he emigrated to Savoy. So troubled was the atmosphere that the number of legitimate bishops who departed increased. Until the administering of the oath, only about ten of them had emigrated. In 1791, particularly after the incidents which marked the Easter observance, the vast majority left. They hoped to be gone for a short time, until the day when order was restored and the confidence of the people had returned. There can be no doubt that in this way the resistance of orthodox priests was disorganized, and the latter were long left in very difficult conditions. By the last months of the Constituent Assembly, the old Gallican Church was decapitated.

The unrest spread to the lower ranks, but there the resistance often had more success. If a community did not want a constitutional curé, it was not enough for the National Guard to install him by force. The parishioners turned their backs on him and continued to receive sacraments from clandestine priests who officiated in private chapels or in convents, thus instigating a virtual boycott against him. As long as these sources of resistance within the convents survived—the civic oath was not imposed on members of religious orders, but only on the secular priests, curés, and teaching orders—as long as the patriots' forces were not coordinated by an organized network of popular societies in communication with one another, as long as the administrative decentralization created by the Constituent Assembly paralyzed the transmission of orders, the refractory clergy enjoyed a relatively easy time. . . .

That the disobedience of a Catholic majority imperiled public order and even the operations of the new administration is self-evident. Already the correlation between religious rebellion and lack of patriotism was being drawn: investigators noted that in the West—the Vendée and Deux-Sèvres Departments—the peasants refused to obey any and all fiscal laws. That this situation was the result of calculated machinations by the nonjuring clergy is more doubtful. The bishops who remained in France, particularly the directory of eight bishops which [Archbishop] Boisgelin directed at Paris, were not content with recalling the traditional teachings on submission to established authority, but also warned the faithful against "the human pressures [which] ought to have no place in the zeal that inspires religion."

But the nonjurors were already divided into moderates and firebrands, and the latter did not fail to throw discredit on the entire work of the Revolution and on the cowardly compromises of prelates who were considered too political. In many dioceses, the clergy had to ask instructions of an émigré bishop, hence presumably one of aristocratic bent, and such foreign communications caused suspicion at a time when the obvious maneuvers of the nobles massed in the Rhineland or Savoy, and the intrigues and provocative declarations of the émigrés, began to raise the threat of war. On November 29, 1791, the Assembly passed a decree stipulating that a cleric who had not taken the oath within a week would be considered as being "suspect of revolt against the law and of having evil intentions against the country," deprived of all salaries and pensions, and removed from communities where troubles had broken out.

For the first time the term *suspect* appeared in Revolutionary legislation —it was destined to become a great weapon of the Terror in designating extremely vague categories of citizens who were presumably guilty of treason for vengeance by patriots. . . .

A SOCIOLOGICAL ANALYSIS OF COUNTER-REVOLUTION: THE VENDÉE

Charles Tilly

. . . When explaining the existence of a phenomenon, a sociologist is likely to begin by asking of exactly what kind of social unit (traditional bureaucracies? marginal individuals? high-ranking cliques?) it is characteristic. He is likely to proceed immediately to an analysis of the distinguishing characteristics of such social units (elaborate hierarchy? dual allegiances? powerful controls over membership?) and thus to a systematic comparison of units which display the phenomenon with otherwise comparable units which do not. He tends to search for reliable evidence (often, but by no means necessarily, in the form of quantitative measures) that the differences actually exist. Then he seeks to explain the phenomenon in question in terms of the distinguishing characteristics of the unit in which it appears. This leads him to an analysis of the way the elements of that unit fit together, or the subsumption of the case at hand under some broader generalization, or (more likely) both.

There is nothing occult, or even uncommon, about such a logical procedure. The important elements to retain are: the careful identification of the units of analysis, the concern for the identification of reliable differences, the use of generalizations already established, the stress on systematic comparison. These have obvious implications for the study of a counter-revolution. The most powerful new questions they lead to are these: (1) What were the real differences between the areas in which the counter-revolution sprang up in 1793 and those which remained calm, (a) under the Old Regime, (b) during the early Revolution? (2) What was distinctive about both the organization and the composition of the *groups* which actively supported the Revolution, and those which actively resisted it, over the period 1789–93? (3) What significant changes in the social situation occurred during the same period? (4) Is there any general knowledge available that helps to assemble coherently the answers to these three questions and the fact of counter-revolution?

These questions are by no means already definitely answered, but the very fact that they are now being asked is leading to rapid increases in our understanding of the Vendée.... Within the section of Anjou south of the Loire, some 700 square kilometers in area, appeared the most concerted counter-revolutionary outburst of 1793, as well as sharp divisions between the areas and the groups supporting and opposing the counter-revolution. A valid explanation should account for these divisions. It should also relate them to the process which culminated in counter-revolution.

Even asking the prior question—"Precisely what *are* the divisions to be explained?"—is quite useful. Although characterizations of the rebels are legion, the only studies remotely approaching the careful description of the supporters of revolution and counter-revolution in the West are Donald Greer's valuable compilations, by department and social category, of individuals officially designated as émigrés, and of people executed during the Terror. Those studies yield the following statistical description of these two categories of presumed opponents of the Revolution for all of western France:

Category	Per cent of All Émigrés	Per cent of Those Executed
Clergy	35	2
Nobility	23	2
Upper middle class	5	3
Lower middle class	2	3
Working class	10	41
Peasants	20	48
No status given	5	1
Total	100	100

Even when taken for individual departments, these figures provide only the most unreliable of guides to the divisions to be explained, since they necessarily mix counter-revolutionary and revolutionary sections of departments; since they comprehend only opponents, not supporters, of the regime; since the categories themselves do not correspond closely to the major social divisions in the West; since they do not indicate which categories had more than their shares of execution and emigration; and since neither emigration nor execution is tantamount to participation in the rebellion. We need other social categories, finer geographic divisions, further measures of opposition and support.

There are, as it happens, quite a few materials in the archives which will with careful handling turn themselves into measures of this sort. Eighteenth-century records of births, deaths and marriages, voting lists for 1790 and 1791, and population enumerations from the early Revolution all make possible some estimates of the distribution of occupations and its variation from one section to another, in Southern Anjou. Rosters of the National Guard, records of enlistments in the army, local election returns, and some curious *listes des bons patriotes* provide some information as to the identities of the supporters of the Revolution. The lengthy interrogations of refugees and prisoners during the counter-revolution, the registers made up from them, and the captured rosters of counter-revolutionary army units offer information on the character of the rebels. Some of the more easily handled items of this sort are in the following table, summarizing tentative findings for all of Southern Anjou:

PER CENT DISTRIBUTION BY MAJOR SOCIAL CATEGORY

Category	Estimated Occupational Distribution of Adult Males Rural Communes	Army Volunteers 2792	Bearing Arms with Rebels (Revolutionary Sources)	Bearing Arms with Rebels (Counter-Rev. Sources)	Aiding Rebels (All Sources)
Noble	0.29	0.0	0.61	0.0	1.95
Priest	1.28	0.0	0.0	0.0	8.87
Bourgeois	8.03	28.96	14.72	1.62	21.00
Hired hand	14.28		6.75	9.43	3.68
		4.52			
Other peasant	44.77		20.86	53.91	37.88
Weaver	10.62		31.29	14.56	8.44
		66.51			
Other artisan	20.73		25.77	20.48	18.18
Number identified	—	221	1121	841	801

The statistics ... suggest ... the nearly total absence of peasants, nobles and priests from the patriotic camp. They raise serious reservations about the depiction of the Vendée as a "peasant" rebellion. They tend to confirm Greer's general conclusions about the victims of the Terror in the West. And the discrepancies between the revolutionary and counter-revolutionary sources of information about the rebels (undoubtedly affected by the fact that the counter-revolutionary sources are communal rosters, while the revolutionary ones are mainly the minutes of interrogations and depositions) bring into play some absorbing new problems. Not the least of the fruits of this sort of investigation are the inquiries it stimulates concerning the actual social relations among the diverse groups actively opposing the Revolution. It leads naturally to an analysis of the structures and relations of the revolutionary and counter-revolutionary parties of Southern Anjou.

In order to understand the party divisions, however, one must understand the regional divisions. . . . For most of the period of the Revolution that concerns us here, the province of Anjou (alias the department of Maine-et-Loire) was divided into districts averaging some 60,000 persons, which were subdivided into cantons, themselves generally composed of three or four communes and four or five thousand people. The districts, cantons, and communes provide a convenient standard set of units for a wide variety of comparisons.

Given these units for comparison, the first task is the uneasy one of designating them as "revolutionary" and "counter-revolutionary." . . . In the Vendée, one may . . . map the reported incidence of armed opposition to the Revolution in the first weeks of 1793's great outbreak. The same can be done with the counter-revolutionary incidents of 1790 and 1791. Likewise, it is possible to map the residences of the rebels identified in the documents already discussed, and to use the numerous claims for reward presented during the Restoration by Vendean veterans for the same purpose. These various tests agree with each other fairly well, and therefore identify the groups of communes, cantons and districts whose characteristics must be compared.

. . . The following table [compares] the most uniformly counter-revolutionary district of Southern Anjou (Cholet) and the most undividedly revolutionary district (Saumur):

	Counter-Revolutionary	Revolutionary
Number of reported rebels per 1,000 population	9.83	0.04
Émigrés reported per 1,000 population	4.1	7.1
Per cent of priests taking Civil Constitution oath	5.3	64.7
Army enlistments per 1,000 population, 1791-92	2.3	7.0

The table has the virtue of being disconcerting. Considering that emigration is so widely taken as a sign of opposition to the Revolution, that the counter-revolutionary sections of Anjou have so often been portrayed as teeming with resident nobles in *bonne entente* with their peasants, and that the persecution of the clergy is supposed to have driven so many of them out of the country, one might have expected a much higher rate of emigration for those sections. Not so. This ... leads to a re-examination of the question of noble residence, and to the (tentative) conclusion that the gentlemen were actually more numerous in the revolutionary sections of Southern Anjou, as well as to the hunch, plausible but untested, that emigration was most frequent where a determined counter-revolutionary minority met a determined revolutionary majority. One of the advantages of using systematic comparison and well-defined measures is that the results so often prove one's easy assumptions wrong.

Despite a few such contretemps, however, the general result of a variety of comparisons is to reinforce the conclusion (a) that there was a relatively well-defined boundary between revolutionary and counter-revolutionary sections of Southern Anjou; (b) that the two areas differed significantly in political behavior for several years before the counter-revolution; (c) that it therefore makes sense to investigate further the contrasts in social organization between the two areas defined in this way.

At this point, a sociological view of the problem is especially useful. Many commentators, especially those mainly concerned with writing descriptions, rather than histories, of the region, have detailed their intuitions of a drastic difference between an isolated, backward Vendée and a more dynamic, urbane world around it. Between the Mauges and the neighboring Saumurois on the east, the difference is great. Distant, wide horizons succeed the plateau cut with valleys and ravines; wastes and orchards disappear, replaced by rich fields of hemp and vineyards. After a dark, rather hard Anjou comes a bright, light, sunny, blooming, flowering Anjou, a country of small property, a country of substantial people, individualistic, conscious of their liberty, egalitarian, a place where the Vendean insurrection was never able to take serious root. The intuition of a contrast appears in a slightly different form in the frequent assertion of the intense isolation of the Vendée. But no one could seriously hold that the West as a whole, the setting of such cities as Nantes, Angers, La Rochelle, Niort, Laval, Saint-Malo or Le Mans, was completely rural or completely isolated. Nor was the counter-revolution simply the response of the most "backward" sections to the Revolution. One element of the contrast, to be sure, was the difference between localized, subsistence agriculture (in the Vendée) and market-oriented, rationalized agriculture (in the surrounding area). But another, often neglected, element is the eighteenth-century development of nuclei of trade and manufacturing in the midst of the traditional farming areas. One more statistical fragment, again comparing the extreme districts of Southern Anjou, shows the result:

ESTIMATED OCCUPATIONAL DISTRIBUTION OF ADULT
MALES; RURAL COMMUNES (PER CENT)

Category	Revolutionary	Counter-Revolutionary
Noble	0.47	0.16
Priest	1.42	1.10
Bourgeois	1.69	8.43
Hired hand	29.19	11.26
Other peasant	51.11	41.13
Weaver	2.35	21.27
Other artisan	13.77	16.64

The important fact to notice is the higher proportion of artisans and bourgeois (largely merchants and petty manufacturers) in the counter-revolutionary section, surrounded by peasants little involved in the money economy (as the low proportion of hired hands suggests). To put the matter all too baldly, such a social situation is much more favorable to violent local conflict between "old" and "new," "backward" and "progressive" than is a uniformly advanced, or a uniformly backward, social setting. In fact, it is not far off the mark to say that throughout the West, the peaks of counter-revolutionary activity were not in the backward sections so much as the junctions of rural and urban ways of life.

Even if this simple formula explained the variation from revolutionary to counter-revolutionary sections of the West, it would still be necessary to analyze the changes in the social situation from 1789 to 1793. This returns us to one of the traditional issues, but from a new direction. Rather than asking whether the *cahiers* of the Vendée asked for any reform (when, after all, each commune was asked explicitly to state its grievances), we may ask whether there was any significant difference in the *cahiers* of the two sections of Southern Anjou that were later to disagree so acridly over the Revolution. The answer: yes. On almost every significant issue on which there was a difference, the counter-revolutionary section made fewer demands for reform. In this case, a statistical criterion does barbaric injustice to the pithy content of the cahiers, but is still convenient. 63 per cent of the revolutionary communes opposed the *droit de chasse* [hunting rights], while 13 per cent of the counter-revolutionary communes opposed it. On the question of reform or suppression of the manorial courts it was 31 per cent against 22 per cent. When it came to opposing the fiscal rights of the seigneurs, it was 52 per cent versus 15 per cent. 14 per cent of the *cahiers* of communes from the revolutionary area proposed the sale of church lands, and 26 per cent complained about the tithe collected by outsiders, while the figures for the counter-revolutionary territory were 2 per cent and 11 per cent. In short, in regard to issues that mattered a great deal in the years to follow, there were already notable differences in the positions taken in 1789 by the spokesmen of communities of the two sections of Southern Anjou.

Nevertheless, clearly defined revolutionary and counter-revolutionary *parties* did not form in the area until later. To summarize very briefly, a nucleus of revolutionary leaders, drawn especially from the mercantile bourgeoisie, emerged fairly early in the section that joined the counter-revolution, and steadily increased its share of the available public offices, and its control of the political apparatus. The organized opposition to the revolutionaries crystallized much more slowly, locally and erratically. That opposition was a good deal more heterogeneous than the revolutionary nucleus. A series of public issues drove more and more of the population into commitment to one party or the other, and increasingly drastic conflict both reinforced that commitment and drove the parties further apart. This happened somewhat independently within most localities of the Vendée. . . . The level of conflict mounted erratically to the apex, counter-revolution.

COUNTER-REVOLUTIONARY ESPIONAGE: FRANCIS DRAKE AND THE COMTE D'ANTRAIGUES

HARVEY MITCHELL

Normal channels of communication between Britain and France were closed in 1793, after the beginnings of hostilities between the two countries, and the British ministry was hard put to it in consequence to acquire not only military information but also information about the various French political groupings and the policy of the French government. The only people in France who could be immediately helpful to the ministry were the opponents of the Revolution. Despite the fact that they employed their agents primarily to sow the seeds of counter-revolution, the gathering of intelligence counting as a secondary object, the resources of the royalists in France were more extensive than anything the British government possessed and, although rather reluctantly, it was prepared to make use of them. Among its various sources of information, the best known, yet the most mysterious, is the series of bulletins forwarded by Francis Drake, British minister at Genoa, to the Foreign Office. Twenty-eight of these were published a little more than fifty

Harvey Mitchell, "Francis Drake and the Comte d'Antraigues: A Study of the Dropmore Bulletins, 1793–1796," *The Bulletin of Historical Research*, XXIX (1956), pp. 123–130, 134–136, 143. © *Bulletin of Historical Research*. Used by permission of and revised by the author. This material appeared in somewhat different form in the author's *The Underground War Against Revolutionary France; The Missions of William Wickham, 1794–1800* (Oxford, Clarendon Press, 1965).

years ago by the Historical Manuscripts Commission in the *Dropmore Papers*, the first being dated 2 September 1793, and the last 14–22 June 1794. . . .

The first point to be noted is that the Dropmore bulletins do not stand alone. They are only part of a much larger series . . . scattered through various collections of documents . . . for which the two most important sources [in Britain] are the Drake Papers recently acquired by the British Museum, and the Foreign Office correspondence with Genoa.

Why should Drake be the intermediary in this correspondence? Francis Drake was appointed minister plenipotentiary to Genoa in July 1793, and was instructed not only to obtain intelligence about naval movements in the Mediterranean but also to acquire information about the state of France. Less than a month after his arrival at Genoa he sent two alleged extracts of the proceedings of the Committee of Public Safety to Grenville [the British Foreign Minister], adding that he would be able to send a similar bulletin by every post if the minister gave his approval. He guaranteed that the source of the bulletins was reliable and promised more important and interesting news in the future. He closed his despatch with a request for secrecy so as to prevent any disclosure regarding the writer of the bulletins. . . .

Although Drake kept the identity of his correspondent a secret from the Foreign Office, claiming that he did not know who he was, there is no doubt that he not only knew the name of his correspondent, but also was in constant touch with him. It is clear from the Drake Papers in the British Museum that his correspondent was in fact the Comte d'Antraigues. . . .

D'Antraigues was a man of great resource, imagination, and intrigue. In 1788, when he published his [*Memoir on the Estates-General*], he was merely giving formal sanction to ideas that he had long been nurturing and which can be most conveniently identified with those by the provincial [nobility] for whom the future of the monarchy was inseparable from a candid admission of their primacy in any political readjustment. For d'Antraigues, as for them, the real destroyers of privilege were the misguided but nonetheless calculating groups of [constitutional monarchists], who, he suspected, despite evidence to the contrary, were working together to uproot the social order. Even more formidable, however, were the partisans of [the Baron de] Breteuil whose success, d'Antraigues feared, would mark the consolidation of ministerial despotism and the final decline of the [nobility]. Convinced that the Constituent Assembly would bring France to disaster and that the monarchy was the captive of his enemies, d'Antraigues gave up his seat in the Assembly and in 1790 left France for Switzerland where he put his facile pen at the service of the princes on whose behalf he wrote several counter-revolutionary pamphlets, violent in tone and total in their rejection of moderation. Though his sympathies lay with the princes, he never felt absolutely bound to subordinate his own views to theirs, seeking instead to impose his own concept of counter-revolution upon them. He thought he could do this best by cultivating the support of Spain; and the opportunity of doing so occurred in 1791 when he met Las Casas, the Spanish ambassador at Venice. Like d'Antraigues, Las Casas was a firm opponent of any tendency that would strengthen the Spanish monarchy at the expense of the privileged orders. The two joined forces in an effort to increase their power and influence over their respective courts; and to this end d'Antraigues put at Las Casas' disposal the information he was receiving from his agents in Paris and his friends in the south-east. At the outset the chief agents in Paris were the chevalier Despomelles, a lieutenant-colonel under the old régime who had been interested in army reform and had worked on the *Journal général de France* published by the abbé de Fontenay; Pierre-Jacques Lemaître, a [lawyer] and until 1790 [clerk] at the [Council of Finances]; and possibly Carlos Sourdat, a former magistrate from Troyes. They were joined in later years by the abbé Brottier, Duverne de Presle, a one-time naval officer, and la Villeurnoy, a former [master of requests]. Using invisible ink and code, the Paris agents sent their letters to d'Antraigues in Switzerland where he deciphered and doubtless edited them; thence they were sent to Las Casas in Venice; Madrid was their final destination. Even when Las Casas was transferred from Venice in May 1793, the route of the correspondence remained unaltered. But in November d'Antraigues took up residence in Venice as the comte de Provence's representative to the republic. It was at this time that Drake arranged with d'Antraigues to allow Whitehall access to the correspondence. It should also be noted that d'Antraigues made similar arrangements with the courts of Vienna and St. Petersburg.

The bulletins that Drake received from d'Antraigues over a period of nearly three years cannot be isolated from their personal correspondence, which elucidates many of the matters discussed in the bulletins. From the very beginning of the correspondence d'Antraigues' letters reveal that he had two principal objects in mind. His first aim was to wrest some form of recognition from Britain for Louis XVII and for his uncle as regent; his second was to stress the necessity of British aid to the Vendéan rebels. . . .

The longer the British withheld aid from the Vendée and refused to commit themselves to unqualified support of the Bourbons, the more virulent became the criticism of what were labelled Britain's Machiavellian designs. . . . In his replies to d'Antraigues, Drake defended British policy. He explained that his government had prevented the comte de Provence from reaching Toulon because consultation with London should have preceded such a drastic step, and suggested that concerted assistance to the Vendée would be possible only if the royalists, instead of continuing to operate from their narrow ideological base, broadened their outlook to include men from all parties opposed to the Convention. He assured d'Antraigues that a small invading force, which, in the circumstances, was all the British government could muster, could not achieve success unless internal aid prepared the preliminaries of a landing. When, in the winter and spring of 1794, the bulletins reported feverish preparations in the Vendée for a large scale offensive, he warned d'Antraigues that Britain could not be held responsible if the impending action failed.

The main issues in d'Antraigues' wish-and-fear world arose from his suspicion of Britain's attitude towards the royalists. According to Drake the prime consideration was the restoration of order in France. "When this is effected," he wrote, "the rest will follow." While d'Antraigues believed that recognition of the princes was a pre-requisite to success in the Vendée, Drake argued that the British government would recognize them only after more concrete evidence of success. To d'Antraigues, Britain's refusal to recognize the royalists could mean only one thing: that the destinies of Britain's French policy had been entrusted to his most hated political opponents, the constitutional monarchists. . . .

Early in 1795 d'Antraigues resumed his efforts to obtain effective British aid for the Vendée and recognition of the comte de Provence as regent. The Convention was earnestly trying to bring the civil war in the west to an end, and the Vendée, exhausted, without resources and full of despair, was more disposed to listen to its overtures. As d'Antraigues surveyed the scene in the Vendée, the conferences some of its leaders were having with representatives of the Convention alarmed him. Once more he pointed out that the Convention's emissaries were emphasizing that Britain was sympathetic to the constitutionalists and was ignoring the legitimate claims of the royalists. Britain, he urged, must clarify her position towards the armies in the Vendée by stating that the royalists were and would continue to be the sole beneficiaries of her aid. Hesitation would only increase the suspicion of the Vendée and throw it into the arms of the republic. At the same time, d'Antraigues took care to show that, while the possibility of a truce could not be underestimated, the Vendée was still a viable theatre of war. . . .

The question of the Comte de Provence's status was still pressing. The death of Louis XVII had made a declaration from his successor imperative. Grenville, realizing that such a declaration would be forthcoming, and fearing the intemperate language which Provence's advisers would be likely to urge him to use, sent Lord Macartney to Verona to persuade him to issue a moderate manifesto, which would make some concessions to the Revolution. But the Verona Declaration, as Provence's manifesto came to be called, had been drafted before Macartney's arrival. Although d'Antraigues had misleadingly assured Drake that the Declaration would be "absolument dans le sens désiré par l'Angleterre," ["just as England desired"] it was conceived in a sense exactly opposite to the recommendations Macartney carried with him. Vengeance was its keynote, repudiation of the Revolution its promise and the sovereignty of the king, surrounded by benevolent and wise ministers, its only "concession" to constitutional monarchy. Towards the end of August 1795 d'Antraigues revived the charge that the British government was working with the constitutionalists, and that the British agents who, he supposed, were promoting their interests were retarding the work of the counter-revolution. This theme began to show signs, in the first half of 1795, of replacing the advocacy of the Vendée in importance. . . .

The story of the Drake-d'Antraigues correspondence is now completed. Did d'Antraigues achieve any of his objects? On the question of Louis XVIII's recognition the British government maintained an unswerving attitude: recognition would follow only if there were evidence of a widespread movement in France in his favour. On the question of the Vendée, the British included d'Artois in their plans in the summer of 1795 [on the ill-fated expedition to Quiberon Bay] and it was no fault of theirs if d'Artois put his safety before the pleas of his fellow royalists. As to the charge that Britain was co-operating with the constitutionalists, it is true that by the autumn of 1796 Wickham [the British minister in Switzerland] had evolved a plan of counter-revolution which rested on their recommendations, though he had done so reluctantly, and only after he failed to persuade the "pure" royalists to see the necessity for uniting with them.

It is more difficult to estimate what influence d'Antraigues' version of French policy had on the Foreign Office. The bulletins appeared to be the only source of information regarding the discussions of the Committee of Public Safety, and any scrap of intelligence was valued. Grenville regarded the bulletins as important enough to send them to George III, but there is no evidence that they had any influence on British policy. Essentially the ministry was very cautious. It was aware that d'Antraigues was motivated by an abiding hatred of the constitutionalists and a fear that Britain was as willing to co-operate with them as with the royalists. As for Drake, Grenville felt that he should subordinate his mission to Wickham's. Thus, d'Antraigues' efforts to influence the British government through Drake failed during this crucial period.

The correspondence permits us also to catch a glimpse into the tortured minds of the royalist émigrés. Although they were the central antagonists of the Revolution, they were fated to remain on the sidelines as observers, important in their own minds but awkward allies, obsessed with the fear that they would be by-passed. D'Antraigues shared these fears to a high degree. The only force that bound the royalists together was a hatred of the Revolution, but it did not conceal serious divisions among them. The jealousies and recriminations which characterized the discussions of Louis XVIII's ministers were already legendary, and d'Antraigues felt no special loyalty to them. His primary aim was to possess a measure of power under the restored monarchy, and therefore the fear that France would be able to consolidate the Revolution with the consent of Europe dominated his thoughts.

COUNTERREVOLUTIONARY TERROR

Jacques Godechot

The fall of Robespierre on 9 Thermidor provoked a profound and spontaneous wave of reaction which had not been foreseen by those who had contributed to it. There were, in effect, Thermidorians of the left and extreme left who had reproached Robespierre for wanting to halt the Revolution and mitigate the Terror. Such was the case, for example, of Billaud-Varenne, Collot d'Herbois, and Vadier. But the Thermidorians of the left were very quickly outstripped by the former Dantonists, Girondins, and even the Feuillants. A great wave of clemency swept over France, and the prisons were opened and emptied.

At first, demands were limited to the release of prisoners and suspects. But when these suspects were freed, they wanted to avenge their imprisonment and their relatives who had been condemned to death and executed. A new stage, that of reprisals, opened in what has become known as the White Terror.

The White Terror began very slowly after 10 Thermidor, and it accelerated during 1794 to end in the summer of 1795 after the royalist failure of 13 Vendémiaire (September 4).

What were the characteristics of the White Terror? Louis Blanc, a republican who wrote his *History of the Revolution* while in exile in London after 1848, said that the "White Terror surpassed in horror even the September massacres, the mass shootings at Lyons, and even the mass drownings of Carrier." While this view seems excessive, there can be no question that the White Terror was particularly atrocious, for if it had fewer victims than the Red Terror, at least the latter had a justification—that of saving France and the Republic which was threatened on all its borders and torn from within by serious uprisings. In contrast, the White Terror had only private vengeance as its aim. Nor did the massacres of the White Terror resemble those of the Red Terror. In the Red Terror they were atrocious but legalized: those found guilty of helping the enemy or of conspiracy were condemned to death and executed. In the White Terror, by contrast, the man whose property, person, or family had suffered from the Red Terror took vengeance on those he accused (often wrongly) of having been responsible for his suffering.

The White Terror usually took the form of assassinations and massacres, whereas the Red Terror, except in the case of the massacres at Nantes and the shootings at Lyons, followed forms that were legal if harsh.

Jacques Godechot, *La Contre-Révolution, doctrine et action, 1789–1804* (Paris: Presses Universitaires de France, 1961), 264–272. © Presses Universitaires de France. Used by permission. Editors' translation.

The White Terror developed in stages: from 10 Thermidor, Year II (July 28, 1794), the date of Robespierre's execution, until the beginning of January, 1795, the White Terror was scarcely noticeable. This was the period of mass release of prisoners. But beginning in January, 1795, the White Terror took on a more pronounced tone. It was largely the consequence of the law of 20 Nivôse, Year III (January 10, 1795), which authorized the return of émigrés who worked with their hands and who had left France after May 31, 1793. In other words, this law authorized the return to France of both the Alsatian peasants who had fled during the withdrawal of the Austrians, and the Lyonese workers who had emigrated or merely gone into hiding during the repression. It also permitted the return of the émigrés from Marseilles and Toulon, as well as fugitives from the West. It was the émigrés from the South, in particular, who benefited from this law, which explains why the White Terror was especially active in southeastern France.

Another law, passed somewhat later on 3 Ventôse, Year III (February 21, 1795), on a motion by Boissy d'Anglas, authorized the reopening of the churches, while proscribing the external signs of worship. The priests, even the refractory, were then allowed to return if they took the oath of fidelity to liberty and equality, instituted after August 10, 1792, and which had never been prohibited by the Pope. They could freely exercise their religion. Many, of course, returned or came out of hiding, but along with them, a certain number of émigrés or deported refractory priests also returned who did not take the oath of "liberty and equality" and strengthened the royalist party.

On 5 Ventôse (February 23, 1795), another law was proposed, this time by Merlin of Douai. It ordered that all members of district, Department or municipal administrations, or of Watch Committees, who had been dismissed or suspended since 10 Thermidor, be put under surveillance in their home town under penalty of six months' imprisonment. This law was very important for the history of the White Terror, for its effect was to gather in their local commune all those dubbed Terrorists, and consequently to mark them for reprisals by freed suspects. . . .

The White Terror, however, did not extend throughout all of France. The reaction, of course, manifested itself to some degree everywhere in various forms, but the White Terror raged only in the region bounded by the Saône, Rhône, Mediterranean coast and the frontier of the Alps and Jura. It was particularly violent in the area of Lyons, in the valley of the Rhône, and in Provence. . . .

Numerous émigrés returned after 9 Thermidor and before laws were passed authorizing them to do so. The refractory priests arrived in droves, and the location of Lyons, so near to the Swiss and Italian borders, explains why their return was easy. In addition to these returned émigrés and refractory priests, there were numerous deserters from the armies of the Rhine and Italy who converged on Lyons.

Within Lyons itself, some were thinking not only of avenging the terrible repression which Lyons had suffered in 1793, but of going even further and preparing a royal restoration in favor of Louis XVII, who was still imprisoned in the Temple and thought to be in good health.

The man who took charge of the operations was an English agent sent to Switzerland at the end of 1794, [William] Wickham. Wickham directed all the royalist intrigues in France which aimed at the restoration of a constitutional monarchy. It was thought, however, that the accession of Louis XVII with a constitution similar to that of 1791 would raise no difficulties. Wickham was the great dispenser of the funds that England provided, supplying them to the royalist organizations in France. He installed an agency at Lyons, and later organized another in Swabia under the direction of the former leader of the Lyonese insurrection, General Précy....

When the death of the young Louis XVII became known at Lyons, a great number of Lyonese went into mourning and walked openly in the streets with a mourning band on their arms. The theaters were closed and there were all kinds of demonstrations of grief.

Wickham would have liked General Précy, then a refugee at Turin, to lead a new insurrectionary movement, but the memory of the ferocious repression of 1793 was still too painful. If Lyons was royalist, it no longer wanted to take the initiative for an insurrection.

On the other hand, private reprisals multiplied, and were carried out by a group of royalists known as the "Company of Jesus."... At Lyons the "Company of Jesus" gathered together the *muscadins* (royalist dandies), those youths who were preparing the Restoration, as well as those who sought revenge....

Assassinations became increasingly numerous when the decree of 22 Germinal (April 11) decreed that Terrorists be disarmed. When it was known at Lyons, the moderate municipal government carried out an operation involving the search of many homes. All apartments and houses, particularly those where former Terrorists lived, were visited. There was an extensive roundup of Terrorists, who were imprisoned and then tried. During the trial of an ex-member of the Revolutionary Commission of Vaise, the crowd broke into the courtroom and displayed its hostility. The court session was halted since the judges did not want to pronounce a death sentence under pressure of this demonstration. The crowd then invaded the prisons and massacred the prisoners. A first slaughter took place on May 4, and was followed by new invasions of other prisons, with more than 120 victims in all. There were new massacres in September, but this time the victims were Terrorists. No doubt there were far fewer victims at Lyons than Paris, but the toll of slain was high nonetheless in proportion to the number of prisoners and inhabitants of Lyons. Elsewhere, the prisons having been opened, those prisoners who were not murdered escaped, allowing a great number of Terrorists to flee and go into hiding. Many of those held as ordinary criminals or felons also fled. . . .

In Franche–Comté and especially in the Jura, the White Terror raged with less violence. Nevertheless, the Terrorists of the Ain Department, arrested by order of the representative on mission, Boisset, were murdered as they were leaving the town of Bourg-en-Bresse on April 19. Some massacres also took place in the prisons of Lons–le–Saunier on May 25–26. On June 1, a convoy of prisoners, composed almost exclusively of Terrorists, was massacred by a band of masked individuals, either *muscadins* or members of the "Company of Jesus." These incidents marked the White Terror in Franche–Comté, and were less serious than those which erupted in the southern Rhône valley and in Provence.

In these regions, the White Terror came as the consequence of actions by representatives on mission. Beginning in February, 1795, the representatives Girod-Pouzol, Cadroy, Mariette, and Chambron made some decisions which facilitated the reprisals of returned émigrés or freed suspects. For example, they ordered that the seat of the criminal tribunal of the Bouches-du-Rhône Department be transferred to Aix-en-Provence, a particularly royalist town. This tribunal had been triumphantly removed from Marseilles by the Jacobins after August 10, 1792. The same representatives ordered the disarming of the Terrorists of the district of Arles. They closed the popular societies, dismissed the Jacobin National Guard, and reorganized it to include moderates who were soon dominated by the royalists. . . .

At Toulon on May 17, there was a revolt by the Jacobins, who halted returned émigrés, some of whom wore the words "Long live Louis XVII!" on their hats. The Jacobins were masters of the town for four days, and the representative on mission, Brunel, who was unable to reestablish order, committed suicide in despair. The Jacobins of Toulon decided to march on Marseilles in order to free their comrades imprisoned there, but the representatives on mission gathered together the "Companies of the Sun," the National Guard and the royalists, and dispersed the men from Toulon. Forty were killed and 300 taken prisoners, and of the latter, 47 were executed.

The march of the Toulon Jacobins on Marseilles produced a kind of "great fear" throughout Provence. The Toulon offensive exacerbated the struggle between royalists and Terrorists. At Aix-en-Provence, the representative Isnard declared to the crowd: "If you have no arms, if you have no guns, then dig up the bones of your fathers and use them to exterminate the brigands." After such exhortations, it is no surprise that the massacres spread. . . .

COUNTER-REVOLUTIONARY THOUGHT

Paul H. Beik

The most popular elements used by members of the Right in explaining the coming of the revolution were, in order of importance, (1) the enlightenment, (2) conspirators, (3) Providence, and (4) changing material conditions accompanied by changed ideas. The enlightenment as a cause appeared earliest and increased steadily. Conspirators and Providence were less used in 1789 but increased thereafter. The combination enlightenment-conspirators-Providence appeared often enough to be called a favorite explanation on the part of the Right; we shall qualify this statement later, but for the moment it may be noted that Barruel suggested it before May, 1789, and greatly elaborated it in subsequent years, when the same theme was being taken up by D'Antraigues, Provence, Du Voisin, De Maistre, and De Bonald. Needless to say, not all of these three elements were equally valued by those who used them, and some of our protagonists used only two out of the three (Sabatier used enlightenment and Providence, clearly valuing the former more highly; Ferrand used conspiracy and enlightenment). Realistic explanations based on naturally evolving conditions and ideas were by no means the exclusive property of those who shunned the enlightenment, conspiracy, and Providence, as we saw in the case of De Bonald. Almost everyone at one time or another referred to such elements, and to mistakes by specific persons, and we have already noted that everyone held the enlightenment responsible to some extent. On the other hand, it is probably true that the absolutists were less secular-minded in their explanations. The enlightenment-conspiracy-Providence formula was exclusively theirs, except for the agile D'Antraigues, and they started earlier and worked harder at condemning the enlightenment.

Concerning the problem of what to do about the revolution once it had become a fact, the Right may be said to have produced four main themes, two of them before the fall of the monarchy and two afterward. The first, visible in the writings of Calonne and Ferrand even before the opening of the Estates General, was the urge to halt the revolution while the aristocracy was still in control. Except for Calonne, who was an absolutist only in the most formal sense, this tendency belonged to the aristocratic limiters. The second theme, concerning the need to go back and begin again even at the cost of forceful counter-revolution, was more general, although the period of its dominance, to August, 1792, was still one in which a majority of the Right's major publications accepted limitations on absolutism.

Paul H. Beik, *The French Revolution Seen From the Right, Social Theories in Motion, 1789–1799*, *Transactions of the American Philosophical Society*, n.s., XLVI, pt. i (1956), 109–111. © American Philosophical Society. Used by permission.

Gradually there grew also the theme of intervention by the European powers, until from 1792 this became a well-developed doctrine in support of a kind of Holy Alliance. There were European values, the argument ran, which transcended nations; there was a European standard to which the French or any other people could be held accountable. This was a major theme of the whole Right. It found its best expressions in De Maistre's "European character" and in De Bonald's "constituted societies" but the idea was not theirs alone. We have seen it in the writings of Ferrand, Montlosier, D'Antraigues, Sabatier, Calonne, Montyon, and Barruel. Cosmopolitanism was thus by no means the exclusive property of the revolutionists. Nor was nationalism of a sort; but where the revolutionary cosmopolitanism, besieged by a hostile Europe, led to intensified nationalism at home, a different problem can be seen in the thought of the Right. They too felt the tension between cosmopolitanism and nationalism, but in their need to save France from partition they were able to fall back upon traditionalism, as they had done in defending their other desires. It would be a mistake to emphasize too strongly the factor of nationalism in the thought of the Right. The potential was there, but, lacking the principle of popular sovereignty which could so easily lead to deification of the nation, and feeling more akin to still-conservative Europe than did the embattled revolutionaries, they gave it little attention.

Concerning a fourth theme, whose significance we shall discuss more fully in the sections which follow, the Right moved toward agreement only by narrowing itself. The issue was rejection of all or part of the revolution. After the fall of the monarchy the idea of no compromise with the moderates appeared more and more frequently as absolutism revived, until among our examples only Montyon accepted the revolution's first stage, while Montlosier and Calonne had left the old Right . . . and were ready to compromise with the revolution.

If the ideas which we have been following are real evidence of human experience they reflect an important episode in French history, the failure of what in Anglo-Saxon usage would be called "conservatism." The term, despite its origin in French counter-revolutionary literature, is less at home in the French language than in the English, and with reason, considering what the English accomplished in passing by way of oligarchy into liberalism and democracy. Our sources, collected to show how the French Revolution looked from the right, have shown the formation of the Right: not a political party, but a point of view expressing the alienation of part of the society. We do not mean to hold the Right responsible for the differences between France and England, or to conclude that England provided the norm for other countries. Our sources provide only a partial explanation of the difference, even from the French side, but they come from one of the most crucial events in the formation of that difference. They show what became of French conservatism during the revolution; how, indeed, it became reaction, or, in less harsh terminology, how it lost touch with the socially and politically possible.

Let us recall that the political issue *par excellence* in the thought of the Right concerned representative government, and that the main social issue was the threat to the society of ranks and corporate interests. At the end of the old regime the outstanding political problem had been what to do with an absolutism so immobilized by the complex of corporate groups that its very functioning as a government was threatened. Those whose duty was to make absolutism work were forced to take measures menacing to powerful organizations in the old society. The aristocracy's answer, long prepared in historical and constitutional theories and after the Seven Years War stimulated by the *parlements'* struggle for public opinion, was to support the Estates General, that is, representative government linked to the old society. If these rival tendencies of the crown and aristocracy may be called "conservative," such usage has at least the justification that each in its way supported changes defensively, in the hope of avoiding worse. Actually the aristocracy's victory in this first stage of the revolution may just as well be described as that of a very moderate, oligarchical, political liberalism. . . .

As the revolution progressed, a new Right was formed, increasingly resourceful in the defense of social hierarchy but less and less inclined to support representative government. . . .

We reach here the crucial point in our argument. Absolutism had recaptured the Right, but at a price. No longer was it the absolutism of former centuries which had from time to time modernized France in collaboration with the Third Estate. That kind of absolutism, rare enough in past practice but always a potential force, had gone out in a bloodless revolution with the defeat of the *Cour plenière* in 1788. The new official absolutism was dedicated to the defense of the old regime socially as well as politically. It was as if this payment had been exacted by the aristocracy for their adherence. As is evident in the philosophies of, for example, De Bonald and De Maistre, representative government of the kind which the aristocracy had finally won in the summer of 1788 was abandoned, but the crown was to defend the old society. Moreover if De Maistre and De Bonald had renounced parliamentary government, they had by no means given up older aristocratic limitations on the power of the king. If they had retreated, they had retreated no further than Montesquieu, and intended the spirit of the laws to be aristocratic. The practice of government suggested in their theories was one in which the king was to be bound hand and foot by the aristocracy. In return, he was granted an immense theoretical dignity, with every possible scientific and religious sanction. The creativeness which served the absolutist revival produced real innovations, but innovations in defense of the past as it should have been. More than ever the doctrine of absolutism claimed to serve the people, claimed more subtly, scientifically, imaginatively, and logically that the king was the embodiment of the general will. The theory of absolute monarchy reached its perfection at the moment when the actuality had ebbed to the level of Louis XVIII in exile, and his promises, and even those promises included restoration of the main elements of the old regime.

Thus the social philosophy which had become the dominant and official view of the Right after the fall of the monarchy was no longer akin to the conflicting conservative programs of absolutism and the aristocracy on the eve of the revolution. It had the recalcitrant elements of both but the concessions to modernity of neither. It was no longer the oligarchical liberalism which had been dominant in the aristocracy and to which Louis XVI had yielded; nor was it the reforming absolutism which had once known how to appeal to the people. Moreover it was weaker for having abandoned these possibilities. The appeal to the people which had once helped the king was to profit an adventurer, for enlightened despotism, abandoned except in theory by royalism, was to be taken up by Bonapartism. . . .

The answer to Bonapartism, if there was to be one, certainly required every effort of the upper classes to unite in a program designed to promise peace without reaction. Perhaps it was impossible to undo even part of the damage which had resulted from the inopportune quarreling of France's political and social leaders in 1788. By 1795 it was certainly too late to proceed along this line without concessions to the propertied beneficiaries of the revolution, peasants and bourgeoisie. Conceivably, however, these might have been withheld from the Bonapartist possibility by a bold extension of what had once been the aristocratic program for limiting absolutism. It was the lure of such an extension which made rebels of Calonne and Montlosier, men whose premises, interpretations of the revolution, and social realism indicate willingness to save essentials by compromising beyond the first victory of the aristocracy. These men were not friendless after leaving the Right. There had always been Anglophiles of the stamp of Mounier, Lally-Tolendal, Bergasse, and Malouet, as well as the Swiss, Mallet du Pan and the *bête noire* Necker. Their position, which we have illustrated only to the extent that Cazalès, Montlosier, and Calonne approached it from the right, had the overwhelming handicap that revived and officially entrenched absolutism made impossible its basic strategy: cooperation of the aristocracy and the propertied in a representative system. Our sources indicate, moreover, that instead of extending and liberalizing the original aristocratic tendency, the experience of revolution had satisfied many of the aristocrats with the new absolutist program. Among our examples only Montyon remains to remind us of the aristocracy's short-lived hopes of 1789. Thus although the further development of aristocratic limiting did take place, and was in due time to characterize the Restoration, this movement was only one side of the conflict which was splitting the French upper classes as the revolution neared its binding by Napoleon. . . .

SUGGESTIONS FOR FURTHER READING

FERNAND BALDENSPERGER, *Le Mouvement des idées dans l'émigration française (1789–1815)*, 2 vol. (Paris, 1924); PAUL BEIK, *The French Revolution Seen from the Right: Social Theories in Motion, 1789–1799*. *Transactions of the American Philosophical Society*, n.s., XLVI, Pt. 1 (Philadelphia, 1956); ALFRED COBBAN, *Ambassadors and Secret Agents: The Diplomacy of the First Earl of Malmesbury at the Hague* (London, 1954), and "The Beginning of the Channel Isles Correspondence, 1789–1794," *English Historical Review*, LXXVII (1962), 38–52, and *Edmund Burke and the Revolt Against the Eighteenth Century* (2nd ed.; London, 1960); MARCEL FAUCHEUX, *L'Insurrection vendéenne de 1793, aspects économiques et sociaux* (Paris, 1964); W. R. FRYER, *Republic or Restoration in France? 1794–7. The Politics of French Royalism, with Particular Reference to the Activities of A. B. J. D'André* (Manchester, Eng., 1965); JACQUES GODECHOT, *The Counter-Revolution* (to be published by Howard Fertig, Inc., New York); ANDRÉ LATREILLE, *L'Église catholique et la Révolution française*, vol. I (Paris, 1946); LOUIS MADELIN, *La Contre-Révolution sous la Révolution* (Paris, 1935); ALBERT MATHIEZ, *After Robespierre: The Thermidorean Reaction* (New York, 1931); HARVEY MITCHELL, *The Underground War Against Revolutionary France: The Missions of William Wickham, 1794–1800* (Oxford, 1965), and "Vendémiaire, a Revaluation," *Journal of Modern History*, XXX (1958), 191–202; BERNARD PLONGERON, *Les Réguliers de Paris devant le serment constitutionnel. Sens et conséquences d'une option, 1789–1801* (Paris, 1964); JEAN VIDALENC, *Les Emigrés français, 1789–1825* (Caen, 1963).

Chapter Six

NAPOLEONIC
IMPERIALISM

IT IS A CURIOUS FACT that two men so far apart ideologically as Edmund Burke and Maximilien Robespierre should both have predicted that a general would seize control over the French Revolution. Writing in his *Reflections on the Revolution in France*, the English conservative spoke of "some popular general, who understands the art of conciliating the soldiery, and who possesses the true spirit of command" becoming "master of [the] whole republic." The French Jacobin, for his part, warned as early as December, 1791, that "in times of troubles and factions, leaders of armies become the arbiters of the fate of their country, and tilt the balance in favor of the party that they have embraced. If they are Caesars or Cromwells, they themselves seize authority." Although neither Burke nor Robespierre lived long enough to see his prophecy fulfilled, the man each feared assumèd power in November, 1799, when General Napoleon Bonaparte overthrew the Directory with the help of the army and established a Consulate.

The significance of this *coup* and an analysis of the fascinating yet elusive character of the man who was to dominate France and much of Europe are presented in the first selection by the late Professor of the History of the French Revolution at the University of Paris, Georges Lefebvre. No admirer of Napoleon, Lefebvre discerns the qualities—the imperious will, the inexhaustible energy, the romantic touch of destiny—that made it possible for Napoleone Buonaparte, son of an impoverished Corsican noble, to emerge as Napoleon I, Emperor of the French.

Within three years of coming to power, Napoleon had succeeded in bringing the Revolutionary wars to an end, first by his victory over Austria at Marengo and the subsequent Treaty of Lunéville (1801), then by the settlement with Britain embodied in the Treaty of Amiens (1802). At the same time, the Concordat with the Papacy, promulgated in 1802, ended the bitter religious schism that had divided France. His successes enabled him to become Consul for life, and his administrative and financial reorganization of the country combined with his mastery over the army enabled him to govern more effectively than Louis XIV ever had.

If, as Felix Markham shows in the second selection, Napoleon was the heir of the Revolution and sought to preserve its legacy of civil equality, abolition of "feudalism," and religious toleration, he had no use for its democratic principles or economic liberalism. Power and order were his bywords, and Napoleonic imperialism at home meant obedience to the law, payment of taxes, and military service—all for the greater glory of France and Napoleon. And while seeking to consolidate his power by synthesizing the best features of the Revolution, as in the Napoleonic Code, he was not averse to creating a new aristocracy (thereby conciliating survivors of the Old Regime) and dignities like the Legion of Honor. Virtually all his creative achievements, such as the establishment of the Bank of France and the Civil Code, were accomplished by the time he was proclaimed Emperor in 1804. Thereafter his rule was marked by unending wars of conquest and increasing despotism.

Napoleonic imperialism abroad had both advantages and weakness. This is made clear in the selection by the late French historian, Louis Madelin. As he admiringly describes it, the spirit of the Empire was one of order and efficiency, bringing the benefits of the Revolution to conquered lands, while also subordinating them to purely French interests. Madelin reluctantly admits that the Continental system, designed to exclude English goods and thereby bring Britain to her knees, conscription, and the struggle with the Papacy did much to alienate non-French peoples from their "liberator."

Though he seemed to dominate Europe in 1807, had annexed vast areas to his Empire, reorganized Germany and Italy, and broken the latest coalition against him, he could never completely master the Continent. England still remained outside his grasp, the Spanish "ulcer" soon began to drain the strength of the Empire, and the quarrel with the Pope weakened his supremacy. The forces of nationalism which the French Revolution had released and which had made Napoleon's conquests possible, now began to be turned against him, first in Spain then in Russia during the disastrous campaign of 1812, and in Germany in 1813. By 1814 Napoleon had been forced back across the Rhine, and Paris, center of the Revolution, had been taken by the Allies. Napoleon was compelled to abdicate and go into exile. Though France escaped relatively lightly by the Peace of Paris, Napoleon's desperate gamble to return to power in the Hundred Days of 1815 resulted in his great defeat at Waterloo. France's renewed humiliation was made worse this time by the loss of strategic border territory, a huge indemnity, and an Allied army of occupation.

In the final selection, the American historian Hans Kohn assesses the relation of Napoleon to the new force of nationalism which was to dominate nineteenth-century Europe. Napoleon never quite understood its power, and in the long run, it helped bring him down. Kohn emphasizes the ambition of the Emperor as a key factor in his unceasing wars, and stresses that the pose he adopted on St. Helena of having been a supporter of liberalism and nationalism formed the basis of the Napoleonic legend.

This legend grew with the passage of time, and the forces seemingly contained by the Treaties of Vienna of 1815 were to burst out even before the Emperor died in 1821. They culminated in the series of revolutions of 1848, and the assumption of power by his nephew in 1851. By his conquests, Napoleon I prepared the breakup of the Old Regime throughout Europe over the next century.

NAPOLEON SEIZES CONTROL OF THE REVOLUTION

Georges Lefebvre

That the Revolution resorted to dictatorship was not a matter of chance— internal necessity drove it in that direction, and not for the first time. Nor was it accidental that it should have ended in the dictatorship of a general. But it happened that the general was Napoleon Bonaparte, whose temperament, even more than his genius, seemed incompatible with peace and moderation. This was an unforeseeable event which was to swing the balance to "eternal war."

The republicans had long wanted to reinforce governmental authority. . . . Unfortunately, the process of revision established by the Constitution of the Year III [1795] required a delay of at least seven years. The *coup d'état* of 18 Fructidor [September 4, 1797] had provided an opportunity which Sieyes, Talleyrand, and Bonaparte considered exploiting, but one they allowed to slip by. However, in the Year VII [1799] there were thoughts of creating another such opportunity. Without realizing it, the republicans were following a tendency which, since the beginning of the civil and foreign wars, had been driving the Revolution towards the institution of a permanent and all-powerful executive, that is, towards dictatorship. This was because it was a social revolution, and the dispossessed aristocracy did not confine itself to insurrection alone. Using enemy gold, the aristocracy exploited the hardships of war, especially the monetary and economic crisis, which was an endless source of discontent, to turn the population against the government. The French did not want to return to the Old Regime, but they suffered hardships and considered their leaders responsible for them. At each election the counter-revolutionaries hoped to seize power. In 1793 the Montagnards had seen the danger and prolonged the life of the Convention until a peace was concluded. The Thermidorians claimed they were restoring an elective system, but all too soon they had resorted to a Jacobin expedient, the Two-thirds Decree [of 1795, which kept most of them in office]. Then the Directory, menaced by the elections of the Year V, had returned to dictatorship on 18 Fructidor. But as long as the Constitution of the Year III remained in force, this dictatorship was brought into question annually and required one *coup* after another. But it could not establish itself securely. The principles of 1793 might be revived and made permanent until peace was at last established and the counter-revolution persuaded to accept the new order. In this way the dictatorship of Napoleon was closely connected to the history of the

Georges Lefebvre, *Napoléon*, "Peuples et Civilisations," vol. XIV (5th ed.; Paris: Presses Universitaires de France, 1965). © Presses Universitaires de France, 1936. Used by permission. Translation by John S. Whitehead.

Revolution. Whatever he may have said or done, neither he nor his adversaries could ever break this connection, a fact the European aristocracy understood perfectly.

As in 1793, the Jacobins of the Year VII proposed instituting a democratic dictatorship while relying on the *sans-culottes* to impose it on the Councils. Taking advantage of the crisis that preceded France's victory at Zurich, they succeeded in forcing the government to pass several revolutionary measures: a forced loan, a prohibition on substitutes for conscripts, a law of hostages, and . . . requisitioning. These ran counter to the self-interest of the bourgeoisie and impelled it to take action. . . .

Once popular force was discarded, only the army remained to institute the dictatorship of the bourgeoisie. On 18 Fructidor, Year V, the Directory had already made use of it. The civil authorities had not lost any of their control even if they did suffer some casualties. This time things were very different because it was not royalists but true republicans who were to be driven out. Only a popular general had a chance of carrying it off, and the unexpected return of Napoleon gave him the opportunity. The will of the nation which was invoked to justify 18 Brumaire played no part in it. The nation rejoiced to learn that Bonaparte had returned to France, because it knew he was an able general. Still, the Republic had conquered without him and the triumph of [General] Masséna redounded to the credit of the Directory. The real responsibility for the *coup* lies with that part of the republican bourgeoisie called the "men of Brumaire," the most prominent of whom was Sieyes. They had no intention of surrendering to Bonaparte and chose him only as their instrument. And yet they brought him to power without setting any preconditions, without even deciding the essential features of the new regime in advance—proof of their inconceivable mediocrity. Bonaparte would not repudiate the "notables" since he was no democrat either, and only their cooperation would permit him to govern. But on the evening of 19 Brumaire, when they had hastily organized the provisional Consulate, they should have had no further illusions. The army had followed Bonaparte and him alone. He was therefore the master. Whatever he and his apologists may have said, his power was from the start a military dictatorship and consequently absolute. It was he who would decide the questions on which the fate of France and Europe depended.

Who was this man? No real portrait of him can be drawn because his personality changed so strikingly from that of the studious officer and dreamer of Valence or Auxonne, and even from that of the young general who, on the eve of the battle of Castiglione [in 1796], still held councils of war, to that of the Emperor in his last years, intoxicated with his own omnipotence and infatuated with his own omniscience. But the essential characteristics appear throughout his career; power could only accentuate some or diminish others.

Short with small legs, rather muscular, ruddy, and still lean at age thirty, his body was vigorous and always alert. The sensitivity and strength of his nerves were admirable, his reflexes lightning fast, and his capacity for work unlimited. He could sleep at will. But there was another side: damp cold left him feeling tired and gave him coughs and urinary trouble. Opposition provoked a frightening rage. Despite long, hot baths, extreme sobriety, and a moderate but constant use of coffee and tobacco, overwork occasionally produced brief moments of weakness that left him in tears. His brain was one of the finest that has ever existed, for he remained always at attention, tirelessly grasping facts and ideas, his memory recording and classifying them, his imagination playing freely with them. Without tiring, his permanent inner tension enabled him to conceive political and strategic schemes which erupted in sudden flashes, comparable to those of a mathematician or poet. These usually came at night in the form of a sudden insight which he himself called a "mental spark" and the "presence of mind after midnight." This intellectual vitality, shown through his flashing eyes, illuminated a face that was still rather "sulphurous" when the "sleek-haired Corsican" came to power. It was this vitality that made him unsociable and not, as [Hippolyte] Taine would have us believe, the incomprehensible brutality of a somewhat depraved condottiere savagely let loose on the world. He did justice to himself when he said, "I am not really too bad a man." This was true, for he proved generous and even amiable towards those who managed to get close to him. But there could be no common bond or true understanding between ordinary men, who performed their duties all the more quickly so they could enjoy rest and pleasure, and Napoleon Bonaparte, who was all effort and concentration. From his mental and physical makeup sprang that irresistible impulse to action and domination called his ambition. He looked at himself with candor: "They say I am ambitious, but they are mistaken; I am not, or at least my ambition is so closely bound up with my being that the two cannot be distinguished." Who could have said it better? More than anything else, Napoleon was a temperament.

From the time when he was at [the royal military school at] Brienne, still a child, a poor and ridiculed foreigner, he drew strength from the pride within him and from his scorn for others. But by making him an officer, destiny served his instinct to command without having to discuss amazingly well. If as a military commander he could receive information and even take advice, he alone was master and he was the one who always made the decisions. Bonaparte's instinctive taste for dictatorship was transformed into a habit of his profession. In Italy and Egypt he brought it with him into government. In France he wanted to be considered a civilian, but his mark was indelible. If he often consulted, he was never able to tolerate a free opposition; worse, before a group of men accustomed to discussion, he lost his composure. This is why he persecuted the "Ideologues" with such a furious hatred, while the crowd, confused, undisciplined yet still formidable, always inspired as much fear as contempt in him. It was as General Bonaparte that he won power and as such that he exercised it—costumes and titles changed nothing.

Nevertheless, there were several men beneath his uniform, and his fascinating attraction is as much the result of this diversity as the variety and brilliance of his gifts. He burned with the same appetites as the others when he was the Bonaparte of the Year III, wandering penniless amidst the Thermidorian carnival, rubbing elbows with the powerful of the day, the wealthy men and beautiful women. Something of this always remained with him—a certain pleasure in subjugating those who had treated him haughtily, a taste for ostentatious magnificence, and a concern to heap wealth on his family, the "clan," which had suffered from the same poverty. He also uttered some memorable phrases, worthy of a bourgeois gentleman, as when he said on his coronation day, "Joseph, if our father could see us!" Still, he was moved, and far more readily, by a nobler urge, that of knowing and understanding everything. Of course, it served him well, but it was one he satisfied first without harboring any ulterior motives.

As a young officer, he was a tireless reader and compiler, as well as a writer. If he had not gone to Brienne he might easily have become a man of letters. Having chosen the path of action, he remained a thinker, and this warrior would never be happier than in the quiet of his study, among his papers and files. This trait tended to recede as his thought grew practical, and he boasted of having repudiated "ideology." He nevertheless remained a man of the eighteenth century, a rationalist, and a *philosophe*. Far from depending entirely on intuition, he relied on reason, knowledge, and methodical effort: "I habitually consider three or four months in advance what I should do and expect the worst" and "Every operation ought to be carried out according to a system, because chance does not guarantee success." He considered his flashes of insight to be the natural result of his patience. He had an entirely classical conception of the unified state, all of one piece, based on a simple and symmetrical plan. At rare moments he even showed an intellectualism that appears in one of his most striking traits—his dual personality, his ability to step back and watch himself in action and to reflect sadly on his own destiny. Learning of Josephine's infidelity, he had written to Joseph from Cairo, "I need solitude and isolation. Greatness bores me, my emotions are exhausted and glory is insipid. At twenty-nine I have nothing left." Walking at Ermenonville with Girardin, he would soon say: "The future will learn whether it might not have been better for the repose of the world if neither Rousseau nor myself had ever been born." When Roederer, who was visiting the abandoned Tuileries with him, sighed, "General, this is sad," Bonaparte, First Consul for two months, replied, "Yes—like greatness." And so, in a startling way, intellectualism introduced the Romantic sadness of Chateaubriand and Vigny into his firm, hard mind. But this never lasted more than a fleeting moment and he quickly returned to reality.

Everything seems to have made him follow a realistic policy, and everything in its execution was indeed realistic, down to the smallest detail. In his rise to power, he ran the gamut of human passions and learned to play on them. He knew how to exploit self–interest, vanity, jealousy, and even dishonesty. He had seen what can be gotten from men by exciting their sense of honor and arousing their imagination. Nor did he fail to understand how terror might be used to subdue them. With a sure eye he discerned in the work of the Revolution what was dearest to the nation and what was most useful for his despotism. To win over the French, he presented himself as both a man of peace and a god of war. This is why he may be classed among the great realists of history.

But he was one only when it came to action. Within him lived still another man, one who had traits of a hero and who must have been born during his school years out of his desire to dominate a world that he felt disdained him, and especially to equal the half-legendary figures in Plutarch and Corneille. What he aspired to most was glory: "I live only for posterity"; "death is nothing, but to live vanquished and without glory is to die every day." His gaze was fixed on the rulers of the world like Alexander (who conquered the East and dreamed of conquering the world), Caesar, Augustus, and Charlemagne (who created and restored the Roman Empire, the very name of which conveyed the idea of a universal power). Empire was not a concrete idea, one that might serve as a guide, measure, and goal for a political effort. But, these men were examples to stimulate the imagination and gave action an indefinable charm. He showed less interest in the accomplishments of heroes than in the great personal energy that produced them. He was an artist, a poet of action, to whom France and mankind were only his instruments. On St. Helena he expressed his feelings about greatness when, recalling his victory at Lodi and his sudden awareness of the will to power, he said magnificently, "I saw the world fall away from beneath me as if I were being carried into the air." This is why it is vain to seek the ultimate goal of Napoleon's policies or the limits he might reach—there were none. To his followers who were disturbed about this, he reported that "I always replied that I had no idea what they were," or, more meaningfully despite the facetious way he said it, "The place of God the Father? Oh, I would not want it —it has no future." In a psychological form, here again is that dynamic temperament which made such an impression from the very first. Here is the Romantic Napoleon releasing his energy and considering the world simply as a place where he could act dangerously. But the realist in him could not be seen only in the means he used, but also in the way he fixed his ends by taking everything into account. And if he was motivated by his imagination and a taste for glory, he did know where to stop.

If, however, as Molé correctly observed, Napoleon escaped from reality, which his mind was so capable of grasping, his origins are as much responsible as his personality. When he arrived in France he felt like a foreigner there, and until he had been expelled from Corsica by his compatriots in 1793, he remained hostile to the French. To be sure, he was sufficiently imbued with their culture and spirit to take his place among them, otherwise he would never have been able to become their leader. But he had not had the time to become part of the French community and to absorb its national tradition to the point of considering its interests as the measure and goal of his own action. He remained something of a rootless individual and a classless one as well; for he was neither quite a gentleman nor quite a commoner. He served the king and the Revolution without becoming attached to either. This was one cause of his success, since he was thus perfectly free to rise above parties and appear as the restorer of national unity. He drew on no principles that might have served as a norm or limit from either the Old Regime or the new. Unlike Richelieu he was not restrained by a dynastic loyalty which would have subordinated his will to the interests of his master. Nor was he restrained by a civic virtue which would have placed him at the service of the nation.

A parvenu soldier and a pupil of the *philosophes*, he detested feudalism, civil inequality, and religious intolerance. Seeing enlightened despotism as the reconciliation of authority and political and social reform, he made himself its last and most illustrious representative. In this sense he was a man of the Revolution. His fierce individualism, however, never accepted democracy, and he repudiated the great hope of the eighteenth century which had stimulated the Revolutionary ideal—that of a humanity one day civilized enough to be its own master. Concern for his own security did not even make him prudent as happened with other men because, in the common meaning of the expression, he was disinterested, dreaming only of heroic and perilous greatness. A moral check remained, but he did not share the dreams of other men. If he understood passions and turned them effectively to his own ends, he obeyed only those which enabled him to subjugate them, and he downgraded all those which inspired others to self-sacrifice—religious faith, civic virtue, love of liberty—because he considered them obstacles. Not that he was insensitive to these feelings, at least in his youth, because they easily led to heroic action. But circumstances turned him in another direction and bottled him up within himself. In the splendid and terrible isolation of his will to power, moderation had no meaning.

NAPOLEONIC IMPERIALISM AT ITS ZENITH: THE GRAND EMPIRE AND THE CONTINENTAL SYSTEM

Felix Markham

At the end of 1807 the Napoleonic Empire stood in its most imposing form, before intervention in Spain had revealed the cracks in the structure. It is a convenient moment to consider its organisation and character.

The elaborate coronation of Napoleon in Notre Dame in December 1804, blessed by the Pope in person, marks a further stage in the reaction of the Napoleonic régime against the principles of the Revolution. It is true that he was crowned "Emperor of the French," not King of France, and the term "République Française" remained on the coinage until 1808; but the court ceremonial of the *ancien régime* was revived and an imperial nobility created. Many of the courtiers of Louis XVI, and the palace servants, returned to serve the new court. After the establishment of the Empire, and still more after the Austrian marriage, more and more of the old *noblesse* rallied to the new régime, and filled the court offices and the administration.

In 1804, six Grand Imperial Dignitaries, (Grand Elector, Arch-Chancellor, Arch-Treasurer, etc.) were created, and the military Grand Officers, including the new Marshals of the Empire. In 1806, hereditary ducal fiefs, carved out of the Italian territories, were given to certain soldiers and civilians, e.g. Ponte-Corvo to Bernadotte, Benevento to Talleyrand. The way for the full reintroduction of hereditary nobility was paved by the elevation of Marshal Lefebvre as Duke of Danzig in 1807, with a grant of lands within the territory of the Empire. In 1808, a regular hierarchy of titles was established—Prince, Duke, Count, Baron and Knight; their titles were to be hereditary, if they were supported by an income adequate to the rank. Napoleon had deliberately selected Lefebvre for the first hereditary dukedom, in order to soften the blow to the principle of equality: for Lefebvre was an old veteran of the Republic, plebeian in origin and married to a former washerwoman. Napoleon viewed the creation of an imperial nobility as an act of policy, intended to efface the prestige of the old *noblesse*, to promote a fusion of the new and the old aristocracies, and to attach everybody of importance to his person and his fortunes. But it was a policy which defeated its own purpose; the more he lavished titles and grants out of the Civil List and the profits of war, the less his followers had to look for in the way of advancement, and the less they were inclined to risk death or confiscation in further adventures. In the final débâcle of the Empire, many of the former royalists proved to be more faithful to him than his marshals and the bourgeois ex-revolutionaries.

Napoleon was obsessed with the problem of making his dynasty legitimate and permanent. It was for this purpose that he sacrificed and divorced Josephine, to whom he was genuinely attached, and married the Austrian Archduchess Marie Louise (1810), the niece of Marie Antoinette. The birth of the King of Rome (1811) gave him immense satisfaction, and he acquired the rather ridiculous habit of referring to Louis XVI as "*mon oncle.*" He put too much reliance on the marriage-tie with the Habsburgs, and was reluctant to believe that his father-in-law, the Emperor Francis, would turn against him in 1813. But he was never deceived for long into thinking that the problem was solved. His real thoughts are revealed when he said: "Conquest has made me what I am, and conquest can alone maintain me." . . .

Napoleon believed that power could only be exercised through fear and constant supervision. "Abroad and at home, I reign only through the fear I inspire." He told his brother Louis, King of Holland, that "a prince who, in the first year of his reign, is considered to be kind, is a prince who is mocked at in his second year." He acted on the principle that most men are actuated by low motives. At St. Helena he said: "Men must be very bad to be as bad as I think they are." He was skilful in keeping his followers in awe of himself, in playing them off against each other and maintaining a constant state of jealous rivalry for his favours. It is estimated that he dictated about 80,000 letters and orders during the fifteen years of his rule—an average of fifteen a day. One of his civil servants has written that "the Emperor exercised the miracle of his actual presence upon his servants, however far they might be away from him." . . .

The desire for absolute obedience grew on him with power. One by one his more independent advisers were got rid of—Roederer, Chaptal, Talleyrand, Fouché—and replaced by second-rate men who knew only how to obey. Chaptal said of him that "he wanted valets, not counsellors." Napoleon tried to train up a younger generation of administrators through a system of appointing junior *auditeurs* to the Council of State, and even to the end of the Empire, he allowed considerable freedom of debate at the sessions at which he presided. But after Tilsit it was noted that his imperiousness and intolerance of opposition had increased. Metternich, then ambassador in Paris, observed in October 1807: "There has recently been a total change in the methods of Napoleon: he seems to think that he has reached a point where moderation is a useless obstacle." The letters he wrote at this period show a brutal contempt for human nature, which portended disaster. As early as 1806, his Minister of Marine wrung his hands and said: "The Emperor is mad, and will destroy us all." . . .

Napoleon preferred to legislate through the Senate. On paper, the Senate had acquired important new functions in the Constitution of the

Year XII, that of the Empire. Two standing committees of the Senate were set up, the "Committee for Individual Liberty" and the "Committee on Liberty of the Press," which could consider cases of arbitrary arrest or suppression of freedom of speech, and denounce the ministers concerned. The first committee was successful in a handful of cases; the second was debarred from considering papers and periodicals, and handled only eight cases in ten years.

The Ministry of Police, which had been suppressed in 1802, was revived in 1804, under Fouché till 1810, and then under Savary, more heavy-handed and less subtle than Fouché. The system of "*lettres de cachet*" of the *ancien régime* was openly revived by a decree of 1810, which established state prisons, and allowed detention without trial on the authority of the Privy Council. Napoleon had not only his daily police bulletin, but his "black cabinet" for the censorship of correspondence, and his own secret agents, who kept him informed on the state of public opinion. Censorship of the press had been established by a decree of January 1800. Napoleon was firmly convinced that he could not dispense with it, but he preferred to disguise it. By 1811, there were only four papers in Paris, and one for each Department. In 1810, dissatisfied with the control of the censorship of books by the police, he set up a separate official censorship under a director-general; the following year he ordered it to be more lenient and less arbitrary and pettifogging in its methods. The theatre was also under police control, and the arts were regimented by government favours and rewards. It is only fair to add that the Napoleonic censorship was relatively mild, and was continued under the parliamentary régime of the Restoration. . . .

Napoleon paid much attention to education, mainly as a "source of power," through the control of men's minds, and as a means of providing trained administrators. The Revolution had produced grandiose schemes on paper for free state education, but by 1800 primary education had sunk to a level lower than in 1789. Secondary education had made some progress with the founding of the Polytechnique in 1794, and of some hundred Central Schools. These were, however, boycotted by bourgeois families as being too irreligious. In 1802, they were reorganised, and government control was exercised through a Director of Public Instruction under the Ministry of the Interior. In 1803, the St. Cyr officers' school was founded, and the Technical School, the best trades-school in Europe at the time, was expanded. . . .

After a long discussion in the Council of State, a constitution for a "University of France" was produced in 1808. This was not a university in the proper sense of the term, but rather a Ministry of Education, which, under its Grand Master, was to control and license all teachers. Napoleon conceived it as a sort of lay Jesuit order, to control and combat private, clerical education, which had recaptured the field of primary education and still occupied half the field of secondary education. But Napoleon made the mistake of appointing Fontanes, a clerical and crypto-royalist as Grand Master, and the University was permitted to license religious teaching bodies. Fontanes used his authority to favour religious education and purely classical studies. Primary education made little progress, but by 1813 the system of secondary education in France was the most advanced in Europe, with 6,000 students in University faculties. . . .

Friendly relations with the Pope had not lasted long, since the Concordat was based on a misunderstanding on both sides. Napoleon meant to control the Pope and the bishops as his "moral Prefects," and with his growing appetite for domination after Austerlitz and Tilsit, revived the pretentions of Charlemagne, and even the cæsaropapism of Constantine. At St. Helena he said: "I should have controlled the religious as well as the political world, and summoned Church Councils like Constantine." Pius VII was no political prelate, but a devout priest who, although eternally grateful to Napoleon for the "restoration of the altars," was determined to preserve the spiritual free-dom of the Church and the temporal independence of the Papacy, even at the price of martyrdom. This underlying conflict of ideas might not have come to a head but for the strategic importance of Italy in Napoleon's campaigns. In October 1805, during the Austerlitz campaign, French troops, falling back from Naples on Masséna's army in Lombardy, occupied Ancona in the Papal states. The Pope sent an angry letter to Napoleon, threatening to break off diplomatic relations, which arrived at a critical moment before the battle of Austerlitz. He suspected the Pope of joining his enemies when he was in difficulties, and never forgave this insult. In January 1806, when the Bourbons had been expelled from Naples, and Eugène in-stalled as Viceroy in Italy, he wrote to the Pope: "Your Holiness is sovereign of Rome, but I am its Emperor. My enemies must also be yours." After Tilsit, he summoned the Pope to join the Continental blockade and close his ports to the English. When the Pope refused, he occupied the Papal states in February 1808. Finally, in 1809, during the Wagram campaign, he pro-claimed the annexation of Rome to the French Empire. He wrote to Murat that "the Pope is a madman who should be shut up." The Pope was arrested in the Vatican, and imprisoned in Savona. Napoleon had unwisely forgotten what he had said to his agents before the Concordat: "Treat the Pope as if he had 200,000 men."

Despite this outrage, there was no open unrest against the Emperor in the French Church, and a majority of the French bishops supported Napoleon in his attempts to reach agreement with the Pope in his isolation in Savona, and later at Fontainebleau. Pius held firm, and countered by refusing to confirm the appointment of bishops. After Moscow, Napoleon relaxed his terms and offered Pius the Treaty of Fontainebleau in 1813, which the Pope signed and then refused to ratify. In January 1814, the Pope was allowed to return to Rome without conditions.

The consequences of the quarrel between Pope and Emperor, though serious, have often been exaggerated. It undermined Napoleon's moral position in France and Europe, and increased the fanaticism of the guerrilla opposition in Spain, Italy and the Tyrol. But most Catholics were able to recognise that this was a quarrel over temporal, and not spiritual, questions; and the origin of the religious conflict in Spain was not so much the treatment of the Pope, as Napoleon's policy of introducing the Code Napoléon, involving the suppression of the ecclesiastical endowments and monasteries.

The economic recovery of France under the Consulate was checked by the renewal of war from 1803 onwards. It is difficult to assess the financial and economic position of the Empire, since between 1803 and 1814 the French economy was mobilised for war, and sacrificed to the needs of Napoleon's "Continental System." The finances of the Empire remained strong, at least until 1813, thanks to the sound system of taxation and finance constructed by Gaudin under the Consulate, and to the profits of successful wars garnered by Napoleon. The *droits réunis*, established in 1804, revived the indirect taxes of the *ancien régime*—a rationalised salt-tax and taxes on liquor and tobacco. In 1811, tobacco became a state monopoly. These taxes yielded a large and increasing revenue up to the end of the Empire. The war indemnities and contributions levied by Napoleon on conquered and vassal states were paid into a separate fund, the *domaine extra-ordinaire*, under the personal control of the Emperor. . . .

It is easy to exaggerate the drain on French manpower caused by Napoleon's wars. Before 1813, a large proportion of the heavy losses, e.g. in Spain and Russia, fell on allied and vassal states. A reasonable estimate of the number of Frenchmen conscripted between 1800 and 1814 would be 2 million out of a population of 28 million. Judged by the standards of twentieth-century wars, this was not an excessive proportion.

Napoleon paid great attention to economic questions, partly because he had been deeply impressed by their political repercussions in the anarchy of the Revolution. "I fear insurrections caused by shortage of bread," he said. "I would fear them more than a battle of 200,000 men." The workers were harshly regimented, but elaborate measures were taken to ensure the food supplies of Paris and to provide relief in times of unemployment. The Empire effectively exorcised the menace of popular insurrection provoked by hunger. . . .

In economics, as in naval strategy, Napoleon's sense of reality deserted him, and he acted on doctrinaire principles and prejudice. There was a strong tradition in France of mercantilism and protection inherited from Colbert, and the physiocrats of the eighteenth century stressed the importance of agriculture as the source of true wealth, as contrasted with the artificiality of commercial wealth. Napoleon had been deeply impressed by the collapse of the paper money of the Revolution, the "*assignats*," and he regarded

England's huge national debt as a symptom of fragility and weakness. The idea behind the Continental System—that of attacking England's credit by stifling her exports, and so draining her gold reserves—was already a commonplace in the Revolutionary wars, and Napoleon carried this idea to its logical conclusion. From 1793 onwards, the French Republic had excluded British goods, and from 1803 to 1806 Napoleon had continued and expanded this policy into a "coast-system" reaching as far as Hanover.

After Trafalgar, direct naval action against England was indefinitely postponed; but with the collapse of Prussia in 1806, Napoleon saw the opportunity of extending his coast system into a Continental system of exclusion, through control of the Baltic coast. The Berlin Decree of November 1806, which inaugurated the Continental System, declared that "the British Isles are in a state of blockade"; all commerce with them was prohibited, and all goods belonging to, or coming from, Great Britain and her colonies were to be seized. After Tilsit, Russia and Austria adhered to the System, and Portugal and Spain were occupied the following year. Writing to his brother Louis about the Decree, Napoleon said: "I mean to conquer the sea by the land." The English government immediately retaliated by a series of Orders in Council, declaring all neutral ships which obeyed the Berlin Decree to be lawful prize, and requiring them, if they intended to avoid capture by English cruisers, to be furnished with a license in an English port. Napoleon intensified the pressure on neutrals by the Fontainebleau and Milan Decrees (October and December 1807), which declared that neutral ships obeying the Orders in Council would be treated as English ships, and seized.

During 1808, the System appeared to exert considerable pressure on England, as shown by the drop in her exports, despite an immense development of contraband trade; but in 1809 Portugal, Spain and the Spanish colonies escaped from Napoleon's control, Turkey signed an agreement with England, and Russia was already beginning to break away from the System. In 1809, the U.S.A. lifted the embargo imposed in 1807 on belligerents who had seized neutral ships. Moreover, Napoleon soon began to waver in his application of the System, under pressure from French economic interests. The ports were ruined, industry was starved of raw materials, revenue was falling off, and there was a glut of wheat. As early as March 1809, he began to sell licences for export to England, and a system of licences, with high tariffs for colonial goods, was regularised by the St. Cloud and Trianon Decrees of 1810. By the irony of fate, it was Napoleon's export of wheat to England in 1810 which eased her serious situation in 1811, when she was faced with a crisis of over-production and unemployment, combined with a bad harvest. It is true that the Continental System was never designed to starve Britain of food supplies (and in normal years this would have been impossible, as she depended on foreign wheat only to the extent of one-sixth of her total consumption); but Napoleon undoubtedly missed a chance in 1811, when the cutting off of supplies from the Continent might have created a revolutionary situation.

Napoleon, however, regarded the Continental System as having a double purpose—as a weapon of economic warfare, and as a permanent protectionist policy, designed to divert the axis of European trade from Britain to France. If, at first, he could mobilise considerable support in Europe for his attack on the "English tyranny of the seas," especially after the seizure of the Danish fleet at Copenhagen in 1807, he forfeited it by his blatant subjection of the economic interests of Europe to those of France. "My policy is France before all," he wrote to Eugène in 1810. The line taken by Napoleonic propaganda, that Europe must unite and suffer temporary deprivation in order to attain freedom from British commercial domination, became less and less convincing when it was clearly seen that there was little to choose between French and British economic imperialism. Licenses were reserved for French traders, with an exception in favour of the Americans, who resumed trade with France at the end of 1810. This concession embroiled the United States with Britain, but it annoyed Napoleon's Continental allies, and particularly the Tsar.

Finally, the Fontainebleau Decree of October 1810 caused great popular unrest, with its special courts for trying cases of contraband and orders for the public burning of English manufactured goods. As Metternich observed: "This mass of ordinances and decrees which will ruin the position of merchants throughout the Continent will help the English more than it harms them.". . . If he had been successful in the Russian campaign, Napoleon would no doubt have made a supreme effort to bring Britain to her knees by the Continental System. As it was, the System was more or less abandoned in 1813, since Napoleon desperately needed the money to be gained from licences.

Napoleon had not only roused the people of Europe against the Empire by his Continental System, he had also lost the confidence of the French middle class, the main beneficiaries of the Revolution and the class which had put him into power. The prolonged economic depression which hit France in 1810–11 was ascribed by them to the Continental System; and from this period dates their indifference to the fate of the régime and the dynasty which was strikingly apparent in 1814. The middle classes had shared his protectionist views and continued obstinately to hold them through the nineteenth century, but they abandoned Napoleon when he ceased to gain them profits. . . .

There was also a basic internal contradiction in the Napoleonic autocracy in France. As the middle classes had gained most in wealth and power from the Revolution and the Empire, they would sooner or later demand a share in the government. As soon as the tide of victory turned, even the servile

Legislature began to demand reforms and liberties in 1813. Both in religion and in politics, the character of the constitutional monarchy of the Restoration and the July Monarchy is already taking shape under the Empire. Napoleon was well aware of this problem when he said: "All this will last my lifetime, but my son will have to govern very differently."

THE SPIRIT OF THE NAPOLEONIC SYSTEM

Louis Madelin

"God is patient because he is eternal," say the priests. Napoleon did not consider himself ephemeral, but neither did he think he was eternal. A half-century's time was all he wanted. "Ah! if I could have ruled France for forty years," he said to Gourgaud [on St. Helena], "I would have made it the finest empire that ever existed." But since he knew full well by 1811 that he would not rule for forty years, he was impatient. He wanted things to be done well, but quickly. And because . . . he gave his officials "the impression that he was always present in their offices" (to use the expression of one of them), they were accustomed never to put off until the next day anything that could be decided, prepared, and executed immediately. When a young prefect arrived at Amsterdam, Hamburg, Rome, or Barcelona, he was at work within twenty-four hours and never let up. He quickly became familiar with things and people, saw what had to be done, reformed, created, constructed, and rapidly built up his files. But he did not shut himself up in them because he knew before six months, or perhaps six weeks, were out, the Emperor would ask him, not only for drafts of plans that were precise, clear, and practical, but also for the results he had already achieved. Such a prefect could not afford to show either indifference or ignorance in any matter. Even a hasty inspection of the inventory of that collection in the French National Archives . . . which contains the records of Napoleonic administration beyond the "natural boundaries" is cause not only for awe, but also for deep respect for the all-consuming and creative activity that the prefects displayed in the "new Departments." Almost all of them were young, and, as a result, eager and energetic. They could bear the fatigue to which officials who were equally capable but older succumbed. They came and went, rode horseback, delivered dispatches, and in a single day, traveled from office to construction

From Louis Madelin, *Histoire du Consulat et de l'Empire*, vol. X, *L'Empire de Napoléon*, pp. 323–328, 355–364. Copyright by Librairie Hachette, Editeur, 1946. Used by permission. Editors' translation.

site, from festival to council meeting, consulting all helpful persons while not wasting a useless minute in idle talk. . . .

Make order prevail and restore discipline—that was their first task. Of course, not all shared the thinking of a Napoleon who virtually desired an insurrection because he considered it inevitable and useful, since, in the end, order would be respected. "Every conquered people must revolt once," he wrote to Joseph on August 17, 1806, "and I would regard a revolt at Naples just as a father regards an outbreak of smallpox among his children, provided that it does not enfeeble the patient. It is a salutary crisis." As realism carried to an extreme, the severity is frightening. His officials, however, did not abandon hope of making their authority triumph without the help of that "salutary crisis" and strove to spare those under their administration an outbreak of "smallpox" that could always have unhappy results. . . .

The French had made their revolution to establish a new order. But the other peoples to whom they brought it "ready-made" were spared the cruel sufferings that they themselves had endured, and enjoyed only its benefits. On the other hand, government was harsh and rarely allowed the discontented the time to rise in revolt. The preponderant role played by the "solid director of police" in Holland, Germany, Tuscany, and the Roman States is striking. Saliceti, himself Minister of Police at Naples, demanded that one be sent to Rome just after its annexation. But these were the disciples of Fouché, from whom they had learned their skills, and all could agree with him in saying, "Better to prevent than to repress."

"Peoples show their love by respect," Napoleon wrote to his brother Louis. It is striking that "love" did in fact follow "respect" once France had disappeared from the countries she governed. Within a few years she came to be considered their "guardian." This was so because everywhere she had effectively organized and often established *justice*. . . .

Its great instrument was the Napoleonic Code. Today we are accustomed to seeing only its faults, but we must remember that it represented light and order in the dark legislative confusion of Europe. All the new principles are contained in it, and wherever the French penetrated, it was the Code which was established, first and foremost. This was what led the Emperor to insist to everyone that, as soon as the French came into possession of a territory, it be imposed on those under their jurisdiction. "Establish the Napoleonic Code," he wrote in 1806 to Joseph, who had just been installed on the throne of Naples. "In this way, estates that are too large will disappear along with feudalism." "This was what made me preach the Civil Code everywhere and led me to establish it in the first place," he added. And the Code had to be applied in its entirety. There could be no question of "retouching" it, he wrote to Louis, or, in the brutal expression he used in a letter to Joachim Murat, King of Naples, of "castrating" it. Not only did he impose it on "his kings," Joseph, Louis, Jerome, and Joachim, but he also hoped to see it adopted by the German courts in the Confederation of the Rhine. "The Romans gave their laws to their allies. Why should France not have hers adopted?" He wanted the Code to be introduced into the constitutions of Italy, Westphalia, and Warsaw. And he meant not the Civil Code alone, but all the French codes issued since 1804. . . .

After a few years, foreign nationalities not only submitted to the Code, but eventually came to regard it as beneficial. A German historian would later write of French rule in Westphalia that "rarely has a country received such good laws as this short-lived kingdom!" These laws were the laws of France, and they were now bestowed upon a third of Europe. . . .

[But] the "system" was also burdensome and sometimes offensive since it was based on the principle of uniformity, a consequence of the habits of French centralization, one that in any case antedated Napoleon. One day, when voices were raised in the Council of State to suggest that Piedmont be made an exception to the law abolishing the feudal regime everywhere, Napoleon sharply opposed the suggestion: "Even if you annex the Pillars of Hercules and Kamchatka," he cried, "the laws of France must be extended to them." Some have been astonished that so great an enemy of "ideology" should make the same mistake as Condorcet did in 1791 when he declared from the rostrum of the Legislative Assembly that "a good law should be good for all men just as a theorem is true for all. . . ." Yet, since Napoleon often showed that he was an opportunist, it is hard to understand how he, as someone of Italian blood, could not only have professed but also pressed to its limit a concept that was so peculiarly French. . . .

The answer is that Napoleon was, above all, a man of authority, and by all evidence, authority was served by such a system. But, just as Colbert had done, Napoleon further aggravated the excesses of the system of centralization which, even in France, often had damaging consequences. . . .

It is certain that this was a great source of friction for foreign nationalities. It is not true . . . that a "good law should be good for all men. . . ." That the metric system should be imposed on all Europe in 1809 and that everyone now be compelled to use "meters," "kilos," and "francs" was in practice a good idea that no one denied, but it was one that irritated the common people because they found it confusing.

Administration was uniform throughout the 130 French Departments. The organization adopted in the Year VIII (1800) formed its basis: prefects and subprefects; first presidents and directors; rectors in academies and head-masters in *lycées*; supervisors, inspectors and subinspectors of forests, mort-ages, wills, and probate; engineers and assistant engineers in charge of bridges and mines; professors wearing the same gowns with their academic palms; judges clothed in the same black or red robes; functionaries appearing in similar uniforms—all these met at Rome and Paris, Amsterdam and Bor-deaux, Mainz and Lyons, Laibach and Rouen. The same official newspaper was published in five languages . . . and the same national holiday, August 15, was celebrated from Zara to Hamburg, and from Brest to Cologne. . . .

But some functionaries, who were completely infused with the excessive spirit of centralization that prevailed in this system, forever dreamed of "perfecting" it even more. The expression attributed to Fontanes, Grand Master of the University, is well known: "We must be able to say 'At this same hour throughout the Empire, all *lycée* students are doing the same Latin theme.'" There is a curious letter in the French National Archives in which Martial Daru, intendant of the crown at Rome, noted wistfully (if not indignantly) . . . that the clock on the imperial palace of the Quirinal "did not yet mark the same hour as that of the Tuileries," an annoying discrepancy that would have to end as quickly as possible. . . . In otherwise perfectly realistic quarters of this system, an ideology existed that could imagine that if the clockface of the Quirinal could be made to read like that of the Tuileries, a patrician of Rome or a shepherd in Latium would be transformed into a French citizen. . . .

But this was not what aroused the common man. His resistance sprang from more tangible grievances—the Blockade and its consequences, and conscription and its hardships. The Blockade . . . of course annoyed "old France" by depriving her of colonial products and English goods, but its inconveniences had their compensations. Favored by the "Continental System," her industry had until 1811 reached a high degree of prosperity. Freed from English competition, she manufactured almost to excess, pouring her goods throughout the Continent which the Imperial victories had opened and virtually delivered to her. But the Napoleonic states beyond the old frontiers suffered severe consequences from this famous "Continental System." To profit from it, not only the annexed areas but also the states integrated into the "Federative Empire" would have had to be included in a customs union that allowed their products to move without hindrance throughout Napoleonic Europe, and hence would have given their industries unprecedented development like those of France. It would have been expedient for the Emperor to match his political confederation with a "commercial confederation" which one of his officials, Crétineau-Laroche, had advocated as early as 1806. "Its bases," he said, "would be established on the needs and surpluses of each state, on the industry appropriate to it—that is, one that it could carry on with the greatest advantage for both the other confederated states and itself." But, in contrast, the Emperor, who was most anxious to assure purely French industry a special prosperity, often forced the countries of "his confederation" to sacrifice many of their industries to the requirements of the French, which were favored to the point of abuse. . . .

While he would not allow French goods to pay the slightest duties upon entry to other Napoleonic states, he shut France tight against those of his own confederation. But one Bavarian . . . noted that "only the cooperation of all the peoples of the Continent could provide the quantity of goods and manufactured products that would enable them to do without those from England." The Emperor remained deaf to all pleas, and seemed unable to imagine, even in the distant future, the European "Zollverein" that his vassal states demanded. Perhaps he thought that by gradually *integrating* into "France" the territories which had until now been simply attached to the "Federative Empire" he could, as he had with Holland, make their annexation more desirable by doing away with the French tariff barriers against them. But meanwhile, the confederated states, including his own "Kingdom of Italy," continued to be sacrificed, and thus to suffer the effects of the Blockade without securing the advantages it brought to the inhabitants of "old France."

Conscription ... weighed cruelly on the French population, but the conscripts, whether they came from the Rhine or the Pyrenees, from Provence or Brittany, were called to fight beneath the same national flag and in their country's service. It was different for the unhappy Italians, Illyrians, Germans, and Dutch, who were called simply to fill the Imperial armies beneath banners that, a short time before, had been alien to them. This conscription ... was generally detested ... from the banks of the Tiber to those of the Elbe.

The Blockade and conscription were the greatest grievances that Napoleonic Europe felt toward its terrible master. But the two things did not arouse the same animosities everywhere.... The Rhinelanders submitted more willingly to conscription than even some Frenchmen did because they saw great advantages to themselves in the formation of a strong army. And the Germans became rather easily resigned to serving since they had all been born soldiers. The Neapolitans and Romans who ... had little to eat and wear did not consider the Blockade a source of great evil, but the inhabitants of the Hanseatic towns felt the same hatred as the Dutch toward the odious Blockade. They too were merchants and suffered by being deprived of sugar and coffee. But they also considered it abominable that merchandise that might have made them wealthy was burned before their eyes. In short, they felt it was ruining them. The Neapolitans and Romans who did not have such feelings against the burning of merchandise did, on the other hand, feel strongly about conscription ... since, by nature and habit, they disliked fighting. And the Dutch, who were merchants to the depths of their souls, already suffered from the Blockade on one hand; moreover, since they had not been soldiers for some time, they were as much appalled by conscription as the Italians. If the struggle of the Emperor against the Pope scarcely moved either the Dutch or Germans, it troubled, scandalized and aroused the Belgians and Italians throughout the peninsula, especially those of Rome. But the Continental Blockade and conscription, which were strengthened each year, were measures suitable for a state of siege, and, as consequences of the war, would disappear with it. Indeed, the Emperor expected to have become reconciled with the Pope by then. The truth was that, for the moment, annexed Europe generally despised Napoleon as the cause of all their difficulties. In all these countries the remark of one brave Dutch patriot might often be heard, *not only* in Amsterdam, *but* in Hamburg, Rome, Naples, and Barcelona as well: "Napoleon's best can only be bad in Holland."

Napoleon knew this, but he had such faith in the power of his "system," the effects of his prestige, the merits of his administration, and the advantages it brought and so much confidence that time would increase them, that he paid little heed to this resistance. What he said of Rome, namely that in five years the city would acclaim him once he was crowned at St. Peter's and had climbed to the Capitol, he might have said of the other countries he governed. A certain *fusion* would gradually take place between these "new Frenchmen" and the old, as had happened, over centuries between Provençals, Gascons, Bretons, Auvergnats, Flemings, Lorrainers, Alsatians, and Burgundians on the one hand, and the Frenchmen from the banks of the Seine with whom the kings of France had united them. And it is indeed true that the first signs of this possible fusion could be seen. In the upper ranks of society there were marriages between Frenchmen and former foreigners, who had now become "Frenchwomen." . . . The children of such unions, the Emperor thought, would serve as bonds. Again, "fusion" might also result from the "fraternity of arms" among soldiers who, having served under the same banners, would become accustomed to considering them their own, and who, having marched, fought, suffered, and triumphed side by side, would carry the same glorious memories back to their homes. When in December, 1810, Lacépède demanded that the Senate raise 120,000 men drawn from throughout the enormous Empire, he saw it as a means of amalgamating nationalities. "The Empire," he declared, "now contains many peoples who for a great number of years have been far removed from the idea that one day they might bear the name of Frenchmen. Keen insight has found a great political means of tightening the bonds among all these peoples who have become French. In the European system the Empire serves as a broad base that will attract neighboring states and so assure their present rest and their future security." Other factors came into play. To his schools in France . . . Napoleon summoned young Italians, Croats, Germans, and Dutch of all social classes. In three, five, seven or ten years, these young men would return home thoroughly gallicized and would be "good Frenchmen." And, in fact, is it so impossible that things should not have worked out this way? Already, under the aegis of this Empire, which had been born of a crisis of rising nationalism, a kind of international, "European" society was taking shape. The French who had until now usually remained home, crossed their frontiers far more eagerly once they knew that they would find the flag of France waving over the Castel Sant'Angelo [at Rome], the port of Hamburg, and the Amsterdam stock exchange. On the other hand, those who had recently been foreigners, filled not only government positions, but also the armies of the Empire. . . . In the long run, would fusion not have taken place as a result of all this, and would contact not have led to interpenetration? . . .

The experiment, which was a long-term affair, could not be completed. Napoleon fell too quickly for us to know whether it would have borne all the fruits he expected of it. But an entirely different consequence resulted once the Emperor had fallen. Before twenty years had passed, the foreign nationalities freed from his domination would recall the benefits they had known without having fully appreciated them. Brought once more beneath the yokes of lesser men, sometimes returning to a state of disorder, or more simply falling back into the inertia of the Old Regime, they suffered far more than before. Having seen the great flash of light, they would in their new darkness recall the days when, often against their will and at the cost of temporary unhappiness, the Man had awakened them to a full life. Nationalism would awaken, great hopes would stir their hearts, rouse them to action, quicken their blood, and exalt their spirit. Even if it had been for only a few short years, and whether directly or indirectly, Germans, Belgians, Rhinelanders, Swiss, Illyrians, Italians, and even Spaniards were not men of the Great Empire for nothing. Detested in 1810, 1811, and 1812 by so many of his European subjects, Napoleon would then appear as a kind of posthumous liberator, and many of those who denounced his power would honor his memory.

But this was not yet the case in 1812. The annexed areas in large part only submitted to his authority. But he believed that "Rome was not built in a day," that all would eventually fall into place. For he had faith in his star and hopes for the future. Like Cardinal Mazarin he might say, "Time and I . . ." and perhaps "I—and time. . . ."

NAPOLEON AND THE AGE OF NATIONALISM

Hans Kohn

. . . For the French people the Revolution meant a full awakening to nationalism; for Napoleon its influence was different. He abandoned his Corsican patriotism to embrace the Revolutionary cause. Was he swayed by

Reprinted from *The Journal of Modern History*, vol. XXII, no. 1 (March, 1950), pp. 22–23, 26–27, 29–31, 37, by permission of the University of Chicago Press and the author. Copyright 1950 by the University of Chicago Press. The article comprises Chapters 15–17 of the author's *Prelude to Nation-States: The French and German Experience, 1789–1815* (Princeton, N.J.: Van Nostrand, 1967).

the promise of liberty it held out to French and Corsicans alike? Political liberty soon came to have as little meaning for him as did nationalism, but he sensed the dynamic possibilities in this enthusiastic upsurge of a great people. . . .

. . . Napoleon understood the dynamism of the French Revolution, this immense release of energy, this gateway to ceaseless activity and boundless ambition. His personality was admirably suited to his time. In a period which exalted the individual and his opportunities Napoleon . . . was an extreme individualist, for whom France and Europe, nation and mankind, were but instruments of his destiny.

The same quest for an efficient government that brought about the Revolution in 1789 helped Napoleon to power ten years later. The French longed for a strong man who would safeguard the main achievements of the Revolution in orderly security and stabilize the new frontiers and glorious conquests in peace. Of all the institutions of the young republic, the army alone possessed the prestige and the power to achieve this. Of its young generals, Buonaparte appeared the most promising. He did not disappoint the country's expectations. A man of rare vitality and capacity for work, of penetrating intelligence and prodigious memory, he proved a great administrator and organizer, continuing the line of enlightened monarchs of the eighteenth century and surpassing them by far, the last and the greatest of them. Like them, he did not understand and had no use for nationalism and the new popular forces. Like them, he believed in the state, in direction from above, in efficiency and rational order. But unlike the greatest of them, he did regard himself less the first servant of the state than its master. The state was the vehicle and instrument of his personal destiny. His primary end was not the welfare of his subjects or the *raison d'état* of France, and not, except for brief moments, the perpetuation and glory of his dynasty. All these limited goals he accepted and from time to time promoted each one or all of them, but they did not satisfy or contain him. His ambitions knew no definite limits; his activities had no fixed and stable direction. He felt his will was strong enough to triumph over the nature of man and the nature of things alike. To him, the impossible was only "a phantom of the timid soul and the refuge of the coward." Despite his youthful Rousseauan nationalism, he was an eighteenth-century cosmopolitan for whom civilization was one and the world the stage; in other respects he anticipated the twentieth century. He set the earliest and greatest example in modern times for the potentialities of the cult of force that found so many adherents in the extreme movements of socialism and nationalism a hundred years after his death. The words of this eighteenth-century man of genius sound sometimes like pronouncements of our times: "There is only one secret for world leadership, namely, to be strong, because in strength there is neither error nor illusion: it is naked truth." "Succeed! I judge men only by the results of their acts." He was a dynamic force, for whom "the world is but an occasion to act dangerously." Though his daring had ultimately to fail, it built much that lasted.

Unlike the typical eighteenth-century man, Napoleon did not know moderation, nor could his temperament accommodate itself to peace. He did not believe in harmony but in mastery, not in compromise but in struggle and decision. In 1803, after the Treaty of Amiens, France had everything it could desire, but Napoleon was unwilling for it to become a great state among other states and for himself to be a king equal to other kings. He had to be the first of all, the emperor of the Occident, the successor to Charlemagne and to Caesar; soon his ambitions went beyond the legacy of Rome, to Byzantium and to Asia. His triumphs he owed to the disunity of his adversaries, to their hesitation and half-measures. But his *hubris* drove him on until he succeeded in arousing the peoples, in overcoming the jealousies and pettiness of the rulers, in uniting Europe—not under his leadership but against him. He was repeatedly offered favorable peace conditions that would have left France in possession of many of its conquests; he rejected them. His stake was everything; the alternative was nothing. He could not resign himself to the French nation-state of the nineteenth century. He did not belong to the age of nationalism. . . .

When Napoleon in 1804 assumed the title of "Emperor of the French," many regarded this step as a betrayal of the Revolution. The Revolutionary hero seemed dead, buried under glittering uniforms and high-sounding titles, church incense and court ceremonial. Beethoven tore up the dedication of his *Third symphony* to General Buonaparte and replaced his name by the lament, "To the memory of a great man." Stendhal, watching the coronation ceremonies in Paris, looked with disgust at the emperor as a new Caesar and called his accommodation with the pope "an alliance of all the charlatans.". . .

In reality, Napoleon never ceased to incarnate truly one aspect of the French Revolution: its universalism and its quest for efficient government. To other aspects like nationalism and liberalism he often paid lip service, but he found little use for them in his actions. His own nature drove him to disregard or misinterpret the forces of liberty long before he became emperor. He did not revive the title of king, because it seemed to imply an abdication of popular sovereignty, while the title "Emperor" flattered the nation and its desire for glory without alarming it unduly. It preserved the feeling that national sovereignty was unimpaired . . . and did not recall the struggle with the royal government for liberty. . . .

Napoleon was ready to use national aspirations as far as they seemed to fit into his system, without having any sincere desire to satisfy them. He never thought seriously of an independent Poland or an independent Italy, though from time to time he gave vague encouragement to those who believed in them. For him nations had no reality of their own. He created and dissolved new states incessantly and shifted frontiers and rulers restlessly. Nor did he encounter opposition from nationalism in the beginning. The people dissatisfied with his rule were less moved by national sentiments than by dislike of alien troops who stayed on and lived off the land and in many cases behaved without tact or restraint. They were motivated much more by loyalty to religion or to traditional ways of life than by nationalism. Only toward the end of his reign did Napoleon succeed, against his will and intention, in arousing nationalism in some of the people subject to or threatened by his rule. Thus indirectly and unwittingly Napoleon became a midwife to to the birth of the age of nationalism on the continent of Europe.

At the end of 1811 Marshal Davout, the commanding officer in Hamburg, warned Napoleon of the mounting national sentiment in Germany and of the dangers to French rule that this growth of German nationalism involved. Napoleon rejected the warning; he did not believe in the possibility of nationalism and in his rebuke pointed to the peaceful character of the German people. Germany seemed to him quiescent and obedient. "If there were a movement in Germany, it would ultimately be for us and against the small princes." Whatever understanding of nationalism there was in Napoleon's mind applied to Italy. He was the first to create an Italian republic and later a kingdom of Italy and thus to give a powerful impetus to the slowly awakening demands for Italian unity and nationhood. Later on, he was to say that he had planned eventually "to create a single state out of this great peninsula." Yet while he had the power, he divided Italy up arbitrarily and repeatedly, according to what he believed were the momentary interests of his empire and his dynasty. On behalf of these interests, he might, if his empire had survived, have crowned a second son king of Italy and united the country around his throne.

Only when all hopes for empire and dynasty had vanished and Napoleon himself was a captive on St. Helena did he begin to build up consistently a legend about his intentions and plans to promote the liberty of nations and the happiness of Europe. This legend deeply influenced the thought of following generations and prepared the way for a brief rebirth of empire and dynasty. In a famous passage, he espoused simultaneously the cause of national unity for the four great continental peoples, the French, the Spanish, the Italians, and the Germans, and the cause of a united Europe where the same views and interests, laws and principles, would prevail throughout the continent. Even then, his words betrayed the vagueness of his thinking on these issues. His decisions were dictated by changing strategic needs. Against England and Russia, Napoleon wished at times to consolidate France, Spain, and Italy into a compact Latin bloc that would be an impregnable barrier against "all the nations of the north." He asked himself why no German prince had used the German demand for unity to his own profit. "Certainly, if heaven had willed that I be born a German prince, I would infallibly have governed thirty million united Germans; and from what I think I know of them, I believe that, once they had elected and proclaimed me, they would never have abandoned me, and I would not be here now." ...

The cult of force and of limitless empire dominated Napoleon's mind to the last: his dream did not change on St. Helena. With greater sincerity he told Benjamin Constant a few months before he had to leave France: "I wished for the empire of the world, and to insure it unlimited power was necessary to me. To govern France alone, a constitution may be better." The age of nationalism rejected the emperor of the world and demanded constitutions. ...

Napoleon appeared as a "violent anachronism" in the age of nationalism; at its beginning, for the protection of their liberty, tranquillity, and diversity, the other peoples united against him and overthrew his new order of conquest and uniformity. Their resistance sealed his fate. In the first war of nationalities he perished. But his violence aroused dark passions hostile to the Enlightenment, which had formed the background of his own ideas. Napoleon was still a rational classicist whom Goethe and Hegel greeted as an embodiment of the world spirit, but the superman in him broke the bounds of the human and the humane. Romantically, a man alone against the world, he rose above the common law in the certainty of his historical mission. What would happen if a whole people followed his lead and—without the safeguards of respect for reason and the essential oneness of men of all classes and nations—also rose above the common law, ready to stand alone against the world, and bear this burden in equal certainty of historical mission?

SUGGESTIONS FOR FURTHER READING

Documentary: SOMERSET DE CHAIR (ed.), *Napoleon's Memoirs* (New York, 1948); J. CHRISTOPHER HEROLD (ed.), *The Mind of Napoleon* (New York, 1955); JOHN E. HOWARD (ed.), *Letters and Documents of Napoleon* (London, 1961–); Historiographical: PIETER GEYL, *Napoleon, For and Against* (New Haven, 1949); General: GEOFFREY BRUUN, *Europe and the French Imperium, 1799–1814* (New York, 1938); JACQUES GODECHOT, *L'Europe et l'Amérique à l'époque napoléonienne* (Paris, 1967); ROBERT B. HOLTMAN, *The Napoleonic Revolution* (Philadelphia, 1967); LOUIS MADELIN, *Histoire du Consulat de l'Empire*, 16 vol. (Paris, 1937–54); FELIX MARKHAM, *Napoleon* (New York, 1963); GEORGES PARISET, *Le Consulat et l'Empire (1799–1815)*, vol. III of ERNEST LAVISSE (ed.), *Histoire de France contemporaine* (Paris, 1921); FÉLIX PONTEIL, *Napoleon Ier et l'organisation autoritaire de la France* (Paris, 1956); J. HOLLAND ROSE, *The Life of Napoleon I* (New York, 1901), and *The Personality of Napoleon* (London, 1912); J. M. THOMPSON, *Napoleon Bonaparte* (New York, 1952); Special: J. CHRISTOPHER HEROLD, *Bonaparte in Egypt* (New York and London, 1962); A. B. RODGER, *The War of the Second Coalition, 1798 to 1801* (Oxford, 1964);

DAVID G. CHANDLER, *The Campaigns of Napoleon* (New York, 1966); HENRI LACHOUQUE, *Napoleon's Battles: A History of His Campaigns* (London, 1966); HAROLD C. DEUTSCH, *The Genesis of Napoleonic Imperialism* (Cambridge, Mass., 1938); HERBERT BUTTERFIELD, *The Peace Tactics of Napoleon, 1806–1808* (Cambridge, Eng., 1929); ANDRÉ FUGIER, *Napoléon et l'Espagne*, 2 vol. (Paris, 1930); H. A. L. FISHER, *Napoleonic Statesmanship: Germany* (Oxford, 1903); OWEN CONNELLY, *Napoleon's Satellite Kingdoms* (New York, 1965); ELI F. HECKSHER, *The Continental System* (Oxford, 1922); E. TARLÉ, *Le Blocus continental et le royaume d'Italie* (Paris, 1931), and *Napoleon's Invasion of Russia, 1812* (New York and Toronto, 1942); HENRY H. WALSH, *The Concordat of 1801: A Study of the Problem of Nationalism in the Relations of Church and State* (London, 1933); E. E. Y. HALES, *Napoleon and the Pope* (London, 1962); ROBERT B. HOLTMAN, *Napoleonic Propaganda* (Baton Rouge, 1950); FÉLIX PONTEIL, *La Chute de Napoléon* (Paris, 1943); LORD ROSEBERY, *Napoleon, The Last Phase* (London, 1900); RALPH KORNGOLD, *The Last Years of Napoleon* (London, 1960); Biographical: CAROLA OMAN, *Napoleon's Viceroy: Eugène de Beauharnais* (New York, 1968); LOUIS MADELIN, *Fouché*, 2 vol. (Paris, 1900); OTTO WOLFF, *Ouvrard* (London, 1962); [ALFRED] DUFF COOPER, *Talleyrand* (London, 1932).

Chapter Seven

THE RESTORATION
AND FALL
OF
THE BOURBONS

THE FRENCH RESTORATION can best be viewed as an attempt to reconcile the traditions of the Old Regime with the Revolution. Napoleon's defeat in the spring of 1814 might have led to merciless indemnities and recriminations against France and her total exclusion from European affairs. Such hostility would have perpetuated in only a different way the division between France and the rest of Europe characteristic of the Revolutionary period. But such was not the case. As early as December, 1813, the Allies' Declaration of Frankfurt informed the French that the war was being waged against Napoleon rather than them. In the first selection, Georges Lacour-Gayet, the late French diplomatic historian, describes Talleyrand's success in achieving recognition for France at the Congress of Vienna in the face of many obstacles and establishing her role as a recognized power in Europe.

After Napoleon's abortive attempt to regain power in the Hundred Days of 1815, France was invaded by more than a million Allied soldiers and was burdened by a large indemnity. But within three years she had freed herself and regained the confidence of her European neighbors. The main task remaining for the restored Bourbon monarch was to restore domestic tranquility. Louis XVIII's determination not to become the "king of two peoples" captured the theme and ambition of his reign. But when he dated the Charter of 1814 in "the nineteenth year of our reign," he consciously stressed its continuity with the Old Regime. The reinstatement of the old nobility, even if it lost its old privileges, the honoring of its indemnity claims in 1826, and the proposed inheritance law restricting fragmentation of property, revived social distinctions which had ceased to exist since 1789. The pre-eminent position of the Church, legislation such as the law of 1825 against sacrilege and the influence of the Jesuits—all recall the union of throne and altar which the Revolution had abolished. Professor Frederick B. Artz, long-time professor of French history at Oberlin College, explains how much the electoral system during the Bourbon Restoration was in keeping with the French tradition of royal absolutism. Similarly, the French historian Guillaume de Bertier de Sauvigny of the *Institut Catholique* of Paris and Notre Dame University shows in the third selection to what extent the nobility had regained its social and political dominance in what the bourgeoisie, recalling the 1780's, termed the "feudal reaction."

Yet a careful reading of both Bertier de Sauvigny and Artz will show that this is only one side of the Restoration. If privilege was revived, the seigneurial system was in fact forever destroyed. Political power was still based on class distinctions, but distinctions of wealth rather than of birth. The monarchy was restored, but it was a monarchy limited at least in principle by the Charter and by a bicameral legislature composed of a Chamber of Deputies and a Chamber of Peers based on the English model. If suffrage was far from universal, it was at least more extensive than in any other European country at the time. If elections were tampered with, at least they were held. Although censorship of the press existed, there still was probably more freedom of press than in any previous regime. Despite tendencies toward clericalism, greater freedom of worship existed than during the Old Regime or the Revolution and far-reaching debate took place between liberals and traditionalists on the relationship of Church and State.

But the inability to resolve the tensions between the Old Regime and the Revolution emerges as the fundamental characteristic of the Bourbon Restoration and explains its failure. After the initial reaction against Bonapartism and Jacobinism in the White Terror, a period of relative calm followed from 1816 to 1820, when moderates from among both Royalists and Liberals controlled the Chambers. In 1820 the assassination of the Duke of Berry, heir to the throne, led to the dismissal of the moderate minister Decazes, and pushed the monarchy further to the right during the last years of Louis XVIII. Although the reform of the electoral law in 1820 initially worked to the government's advantage, the accession to the throne in 1824 by the Count of Artois, the old leader of the Counterrevolution, strengthened the liberal opposition. Through a series of unpopular laws and the appointment of a very unpopular minister, Polignac, Charles identified the monarchy with the Old Regime and lost the support of the electorate. In the fourth selection, Professor Vincent W. Beach of the University of Colorado describes the political collapse of the Restoration in 1830. When the country refused to return a Chamber which would support royal policy, Charles and his minister decided to invoke Article XIV of the Charter against the Charter: "The King is the supreme head of state . . . and makes the ordinances necessary for the execution of the laws and the security of the State." The use of this provision to dissolve the newly elected Chamber precipitated the Revolution.

In the last selection, Professor David H. Pinkney, of the University of Washington, sees the social and economic malaise of the last years of the Restoration as a more basic cause of the Revolution. This "conjuncture" of social and economic forces overpowered the politics of boldness in 1830 as similar forces overwhelmed royal indecision in 1789. The people, who had participated in the revolutions of 1789 and 1793, once again rallied to help overthrow a regime that they blamed for their misery, only to substitute once again another regime which would fail to rule in their interest.

TALLEYRAND AT THE CONGRESS
OF VIENNA

Georges Lacour-Gayet

Talleyrand arrived in Vienna on September 23, 1814, and stayed at the Hotel Kaunitz, which he had rented for the French legation.

On the following day he began his visits to members of the diplomatic corps. In the midst of his round of polite exchanges, he realized that the Allied

G. Lacour-Gayet, *Talleyrand*, vol. II (Paris, 1930), pp. 430–432, 434, 437–438, 440. © Editions Payot, Paris, 1930. Used by permission. Editors' translation.

representatives were still motivated by the spirit of the Treaty of Chaumont [against Napoleon], and intended to maintain control of the convening Congress for themselves and themselves alone. Talleyrand, for his part, was determined to abide by the spirit of his instructions. As he wrote the Duchess of Courland on September 27, "I will not abandon the ideas of moderation and calm which it is the noble position of the king to have prevail." Nevertheless, he let it be understood that the plan to ostracize France and the lesser states was contrary to the very character of such international deliberations. Metternich and Nesselrode, with whom he had personal relations, did not want to offend him, and made their sentiment felt among their English and Prussian colleagues. They invited Talleyrand to a preliminary conference at the Chancellery of Foreign Affairs. On that day the Prince unobtrusively forced open the door to a citadel which had until then remained jealously closed.

At this session, his colleagues used the expression "Allied Powers" familiar to them. "I repeated," said Talleyrand,

the words "Allied Powers" with a little astonishment and even anger. "Allied," I said, "and against whom? It is no longer against Napoleon—he is on the island of Elba; it is no longer against France—peace has been made; it is surely not against the King of France—he is the guarantee of an enduring peace. Gentlemen, let us speak frankly. If there are still Allied Powers, I have no place here. . . . And yet if I were not here, you would have great need of me. I am perhaps the only one who asks for nothing. In large measure, that is all I want for France. . . . I do not want anything, I say again, and I offer you much. The presence of a minister of Louis XVIII here hallows the principle on which the whole social order rests. Europe's first need is to banish forever the notion that rights can be secured by conquest alone, and to revive the sacred principle of legitimacy from which order and stability spring. . . . If, as is already rumored, some privileged powers would like to exercise dictatorial control over the Congress, I must say that, confining myself to the terms of the Treaty of Paris, I could not consent to recognize any supreme power at this meeting, and I would not heed any proposal emanating from it."

The audience remained silent for a few moments. Then, the Prince having made some concessions to pride, "which he saw threatening [the Congress]," it was decided that [Friedrich von] Gentz, a member of the [Austrian] Aulic Council and Secretary General [of the Congress], would destroy the protocols of the preceding sessions and draw up an agenda for the day's session. Talleyrand signed the minutes along with his colleagues, and this memorable session was to be, if not in fact, at least in law, the first official and plenary conference of the Congress of Vienna. Henceforth, France participated in all the conferences held among the great powers.

At the end of October, 1814, Talleyrand could write to Paris that the Bourbon House, which had returned to France five months before, and France, which had been conquered five months earlier, were already restored to their rank in Europe and had reassumed their proper influence in the most important deliberations of the Congress. The Prince was within his rights in claiming for himself the glory of Cardinal Richelieu, who had raised the name of the king to its rightful place among foreign nations. But at the Congress of Vienna, this glory only satisfied his own pride.

In a letter which the Prince sent to Madame de Staël on October 2, he wrote, "The success of Bonaparte was not the only detestable thing about him. . . . It was his principles which were horrible; they must be forever driven from Europe. . . . I do not know what we will do here, but I promise you noble language."

The "horrible principles" of Bonaparte were at the moment in great favor at Berlin and St. Petersburg. The King of Prussia wanted to annex Saxony, while the Emperor of Russia reserved Poland for himself. Talleyrand wrote to the Duchess of Courland that "your Prussians passionately love the usurping power of Bonaparte; they hate only his success." . . .

. . . The Prince, in his repeated interviews with the representatives of Austria and England, did not cease to denounce the greed of Russia and Prussia. He succeeded in arousing their uneasiness and gaining their support for his idea of Central European equilibrium. His persistent tactics resulted in a diplomatic agreement. On January 3, 1815, France, Austria, and Great Britain signed a secret treaty for a defensive alliance. Each of these powers pledged to raise a corps of 150,000 men if one of them were attacked. It was against Russia and Prussia that these precautions were taken.

The following day, January 4, Talleyrand was able to write to Louis XVIII:

Now, Sire, the coalition is dissolved and will be so forevermore. Not only is France no longer isolated in Europe, but your Majesty already has a federative system which fifty years of negotiations would not have given him. She works in harmony with two of the greatest powers, three states of second rank, and soon with all the states which follow principles and maxims other than revolutionary principles and maxims. She will truly be the leader and soul of this union, formed for the defense of principles which she was the first to proclaim. . . .

Prince Talleyrand took part in all the discussions of the Congress. Nevertheless, his diplomatic activity concentrated especially on the three questions of Saxony, Poland, and Naples which he had made his domain. Faithful to his principle, he demanded nothing for France. To him, there was no need to take up the [Paris peace] treaty of May 3 again. Though making allowance for his point of view, we may rightfully wonder whether it would not have been a wise precaution to raise the question of those areas on the left bank of the Rhine which France had surrendered. The secret alliance of January 3 might have allowed the ambassador of Louis XVIII to win two great powers to his cause. The Rhineland, which twenty years of French rule had detached from Germany, might have received a special status in international law. If it had become a neutral state with a status similar to that of Switzerland, it would have become a buffer zone between Germany and France. There is no evidence that Talleyrand considered this scheme. All the territories on the left bank were to be awarded to Prussia. In the reactionary work of the treaties of Vienna, the creation of a Rhenish Prussia was a virtual engine of war directed against France. Nine years after Jena, France had a power on her flanks which continued to speak of vengeance.

But the circumstances in which the final act of the Congress was signed must not be forgotten. Napoleon had returned from Elba and his reappearance had the immediate effect of reestablishing a close harmony among all the members of the Congress. On March 20, the Emperor reentered the Tuileries palace; on the 25th, the Big Four powers reformed their alliance; on the 27th, Talleyrand acceded to it.

When Talleyrand learned that the Emperor had landed in the Juan Gulf, he could only regret that the Congress had not heeded his proposal of October. Then he had written: "There is a rather certain plan of removing Bonaparte from Elba. No one yet has any sure idea of where he could be put. I proposed one of the Azores. It is five hundred leagues from any land." And, in December, he had said that it was necessary "to hasten and be rid of the man of Elba and Murat, [the King of Naples]." An energetic and immediate decision had to be taken regarding the man he characterized as a "bandit" and "brigand." "I will do everything in my power to prevent us from being lulled to sleep here, as well as to have the Congress pass a resolution which will demote Bonaparte from the rank which inconceivable weakness allowed him to retain."

The French legation itself immediately drew up the draft of a declaration against Napoleon, and on March 13, the draft was adopted by the Congress. A few words are enough to indicate its spirit: "The powers declare that Napoleon is excluded from civil and social relations, and that as an enemy and disturber of the peace of the world, he is liable to public vengeance." The Prince transmitted this text to the Duchess of Courland with a kind of fierce joy: "I do not believe, dear friend, that any document like the one I am sending you has ever appeared before. History furnishes no example of a similar rejection by the whole human race." ...

On June 10 the Prince left Vienna [to] rejoin the wandering court of Louis XVIII. He had decided on his line of conduct in advance. A few days earlier he had written to the Duchess of Courland, "I shall do my duty, but I will not allow myself to be shaken from my line of conduct by the fancies, intrigues and nonsense of the emigration." He arrived at Aix-la-Chapelle on June 19, and began to receive news of the great battle which had begun the day before. He learned that Wellington and Blücher had joined forces and that Bonaparte had been defeated. ...

THE ELECTORAL SYSTEM IN FRANCE DURING THE BOURBON RESTORATION, 1815–30

Frederick B. Artz

The basis of the political régime in France from 1815 to the July Revolution of 1830 was the Constitutional Charter of 1814. This curious document, which the wits of the time said had been—like Louis XVIII—"brought back in the baggage of the Allies," contained in its terms the most absurd contradictions. The preamble had been dated by Louis XVIII as "of the nineteenth year of our reign." It spoke of the Charter as a "concession" of the king, who, though all authority in France resided in his royal person, had nevertheless decided to follow in the footsteps of his illustrious ancestors in granting certain new institutions to the French people. So, although the text of the Charter contained an enumeration of democratic principles in line with the ideals and principles of the Revolution—which made it all in all the most liberal instrument of government to be found anywhere in continental Europe—yet its preamble, wholly in the spirit and terms of the Ancien Régime, flatly contradicted these principles of free government. It was these glaring inconsistencies, especially as they came up in such practical questions as ministerial responsibility, the censorship of the press, and the extension of the franchise, that determined the currents of political life until, failing a peaceful settlement, a revolution in 1830 brought a new adjustment.

The electoral system which supplied the membership of the chamber of deputies was the only place in the whole system of government which gave political expression to the conflicting principles and interests of the French people. This accounts for the lively interest in the electoral problem. Certainly no question, not even the problem of the censorship of the press, was more debated when political questions were discussed at all. All seemed to agree on the necessity of a high property qualification for voting. Even so thoroughgoing a radical as Benjamin Constant says of this: "Those whom poverty keeps in eternal dependence and who are condemned to daily work are no more enlightened on public affairs than children, nor are they more interested than foreigners in our national prosperity, of which they do not understand the basis and whose advantages they enjoy only indirectly. Property alone, by giving sufficient leisure, renders a man capable of exercising his political rights." This is hardly the view one would have expected, but the excesses of the Terror had evidently entirely discredited the idea of universal suffrage. The question was never debated in the chambers.

Reprinted from "The Electoral System in France during the Bourbon Restoration, 1815–1830," by Frederick B. Artz, *Journal of Modern History*, I (1929), pp. 205–213, 215–218 by permission of The University of Chicago Press. © 1929, *Journal of Modern History*.

The questions usually discussed—now that the principle of limitation had been admitted by all—were the conditions of age and of income, the advantages of direct and indirect elections, and the question whether the electors should meet in several *collèges d'arrondissement* or in one *collège de département*. And though fine arguments were used on both sides, each party was really less interested in creating an electoral law that would in itself be reasonable than in finding one that would assure a majority for itself in the chamber of deputies. Hence in the first years of the Restoration, when the current of a widespread royalist reaction was strong, the Ultra-Royalists worked to lower the qualifications for suffrage. Later, with the rapid growth of a Liberal opposition, the Ultras changed their tactics entirely and worked for a stricter limitation of the suffrage. The Liberals made much capital of this reversal of Ultra opinion, but they were guilty of the same thing.

The basis of the electoral system, fixed by the Charter, held that to be eligible for election to the chamber of deputies, a man must be forty years old and pay a direct tax of 1,000 francs. If, however, there could not be found in any given department fifty persons of the required age and income, the number might be filled up from the largest taxpayers under the 1,000-franc limit. For the right to vote a man must be thirty years of age and pay a direct tax of 300 francs. Half of the deputies representing any department must be chosen from eligibles residing within that department; the other half might be selected from eligibles residing anywhere in France. The system of indirect election in two stages, which had been in use since 1799, was maintained. The qualified voters were divided into two degrees. The electors in the first degree were eligible to vote only in the collège d'arrondissement. Those in the second degree were to vote in the departmental collège. The admission to the latter was limited to the proportion of one elector to every thousand inhabitants, and the members must be chosen from the 600 most heavily taxed individuals in the department. The presidents of all the electoral collèges were to be named by the king (Article 41). By royal ordinance of July 13, 1815, and September 5, 1816, the age of electors was lowered from thirty years to twenty-one, and that of parliamentary candidates from forty years to twenty-five. Also the membership of the chamber of deputies was raised from 258 to 402. The collège d'arrondissement elected candidates equal to the total number of deputies to be sent up by the whole department. Eight days later, the departmental collège met, and in this final election at least half of the deputies chosen must be from the list sent up by the collège d'arrondissement. One-fifth of the membership was renewed each year. Louis XVIII, and later Charles X, kept the right granted by an imperial decree of 1806, which allowed the monarch to add to the electoral collèges those who had rendered "special service to the state." Following this principle, an ordinance of July 21, 1815, authorized the prefects to add twenty members to the departmental collège and ten to the collège d'arrondissement. This greatly increased the government's influence in election. In theory the persons so nominated had rendered "special service to the state," but in practice a reputation for holding "healthy opinions" far outweighed other considerations. It is easy to see by the correspondence of the ministry of the interior what great importance the government attached to this measure, and the efforts it made to get every possible gain out of it. In 1815 one of the prefects writes to the minister of the interior:

Sir, in conformance with the instructions contained in your confidential letter, I have just appointed a commission among whom is a lawyer who enjoys public esteem for his uprightness and his excellent sentiments. The assembling of these reliable men makes it possible for me to please the government by making a choice of men devoted to the king and the country. . . .

This abuse was continuous through the whole period of the Restoration. An average departmental collège numbered about 200 electors, and the effect of introducing into such a body twenty electors pledged to vote for the ministerial candidate speaks for itself. A part of the royal ordinance of September 5, 1816, again raised the age of parliamentary eligibles to forty, at the same time reducing the membership of the chamber of deputies to 258.

The next electoral law was that of February 5, 1817. This abolished the whole system of indirect elections and conferred a direct vote on every male citizen of thirty years or more who paid a direct tax of at least 300 francs. There was hereafter only one type of electoral collège which was to meet in the chief town of the department. The secretary and the ballot tellers were to be named by the collège. The Liberal framers of this law had had the fixed intention of devising a scheme whereby the ascendancy at future elections might be given to the middle class. The success of the Liberals in electing their candidates to the chamber of deputies—twenty-five were returned in 1817, forty-five in 1818, and the same number in 1819—pushed the Royalists to devise a new law which they succeeded in getting passed during the conservative reaction following the assassination of the Duc de Berri in 1820. This law of 1820 restored the collège d'arrondissement and allowed the members of the departmental collège to vote in both collèges. The membership of the chamber of deputies was raised to 430, of whom 258 were to be elected directly by the collèges d'arrondissement, composed of all the qualified taxpayers, and 172 by the departmental collèges, which were to be made up of the most heavily taxed inhabitants equal in number to one-quarter of the whole body of electors in the department. The Ultras who were the framers of this law hoped that it would keep the control of the chamber of deputies in the hands of the large landowners. They seem to have forgotten entirely that the taxes on rights of incorporation, unknown before the Revolution, were now counted as direct taxes, and so the law allowed large numbers of lawyers and manufacturers the right to vote. Two further acts complete the legislative side of the electoral history of the Restoration: the Septennial Act of June 9, 1824, which abolished the annual renewal by one-fifth of the chamber of deputies and provided for an entire renewal of the chamber every seven years; and Martignac's law of July 2, 1828, which provided for an annual revision of the voting registers, an attempt to put some check on the power of the prefects.

Let us turn to the practical working of the system. . . .

It was not the custom for the candidate to do extensive campaigning, and there was apparently almost no interest in elections until after 1824, when, with the accession of Charles X, a real danger of a counter-revolution gradually aroused public opinion. In referring to the elections of 1824, a pamphlet published that year in Bordeaux compares French conditions to those prevailing in England in this regard:

In France, campaigning is limited to intriguing in secret. One may wish to be named, but pride and self-respect forbid that this be made known in public. Ask a man in public if in the bottom of his heart he desires ardently to become a member of the chamber of deputies, he will answer you that he has never dreamed of such a thing.

The names of the candidates did not even appear in the newspapers, and until nearly the end of the Restoration an election was in many districts hardly more than *une affaire de salon ou de café*, that is, merely an affair of personal relationships. The election of the successful candidate was looked upon as the bestowal of an honor from the ruling class. He had not yet come to be the appointed mouthpiece of his constituency. Democracy in government was not yet even understood. After the organization in 1817 of the Liberal "Comité Directeur" under Laffitte, Manuel, and Constant, public political speeches, at least in the larger towns, became somewhat more common. The custom arose also of sending out letters to prominent electors. Conservative opinion disliked this thoroughly and fought it. "The demagogic effrontery with which at the last election in Paris," said the *Conservateur*, "a candidate appealed for the vote of a certain part of the electors; those printed letters scattered in profusion about the rooms of the election hall, in game rooms and goodness knows where else, with their appeals addressed in the name of the nation to all the friends of liberty, asking them to vote for 'the friend of the people.' One recalls the election of Robespierre and other friends of the people." After 1824 the "Comité Directeur" of the Liberal opposition announced through handbills:

In order to aid the electors to surmount the difficulties which they meet, an office will be open every day at 22 Quai Pelletier from 11 to 4. Here electors may receive advice for nothing.

The *Constitutionnel* for November 8, 1829, announced:

Last evening there was held a large gathering of defenders of the constitutional monarchy. In this assembly were all the constitutional ex-deputies at present in Paris, beside a crowd of well-known citizens. They drew up a list of liberal candidates for the departments.

The Liberal society, "Aide-toi, le Ciel t'aidera," founded in 1827, organized electoral committees over France on a much larger scale. . . .

The electioneering often took the form of an attempt to force the prefects to revise the list of electors and to enforce the proper posting of these lists. There was undoubtedly a great deal of dishonesty on the part of the prefects in the preparation of the lists. From the archives of the police one may see what elaborate electoral statistics were kept of nearly all the electors of an arrondissement. These tabulations of opinions, influence, and personal ambitions of the voters, at least as the police saw them, were available for the use of the prefects and were much used by them. Every time an election was held the Liberals protested that the lists of electors were falsified. Their exasperation is well displayed in an article in the *Constitutionnel*, February 26, 1824:

Innumerable protests are being made all over France against the manipulation of the electoral lists. Many electors are being deprived of their rights. Some with white hair and bent with age have been refused because they had not baptismal certificates at hand, even though they were born before 1794. Others are refused because they cannot show proper papers for possessing lands which have been in their families for years, others for having falsely represented their tax returns, and others finally merely because the authorities claim that their first names were not exactly as in the government records. . . .

The king himself sometimes intervened in elections. In 1816 Louis XVIII issued the following proclamation: "The king expects of the electors that they direct all their efforts to keep from the polls all the enemies of the throne and of legitimacy." The next year Louis XVIII explained to the municipal council of Paris his hope that "his people would justify by their choice the confidence he had placed in their care and wisdom." A proclamation of 1820 called on all loyal voters "to keep from holding the noble office of deputy, the fomenters of trouble, the artisans of discord, the propagators of unjust accusation against the government of the king, his family, and himself." Finally, in June, 1830, Charles X issued the following:

Frenchmen, the last chamber of deputies misconceived my intentions. I must count on your co-operation to do good. Oh that a single sentiment would move you! It is your king who demands it, it is a father who calls on you.

Evidently neither Louis XVIII nor Charles X had any real conception of free and representative government.

The church was also used as a means of enforcing the choice of the government in elections. The bishops frequently issued orders to vote for the Royalist candidates and certain bishops openly used their priests as electoral agents. In fact the whole machinery of government was employed to get votes, and methods were used which—to borrow an expression from the president of the royal court at Grenoble—were "très peu délicats." These abuses became so notorious that in 1828 Martignac sent out a committee to investigate electoral methods and usages. . . .

But even had the electoral system been honestly handled, it was really not fitted to give any adequate expression of public opinion. Following the electoral law of 1820, there were in all France in 1829 only 88,275 electors to a population of about thirty-two million. And these electors were distributed in the most unequal way. The department of the Seine had 10,000, while Corsica had only thirty. Moreover, between a third and a half of the electors never went to the polls. Out of 72,199 eligibles only 48,478 voted in 1815, 47,427 in 1816. In 1819, out of 4,800 voters of the Seine-Inférieure, 2,500 voted, and of 1,700 voters of Eure-et-Loir, only 938 voted, and these figures are typical. As it was often hard for the country voters to get to the polls, their abstentions from voting were always larger than those of the town dwellers, so that in practice most of the votes were cast by the wealthy bourgeoisie. . . .

The majorities which decided elections were generally very small, often not more than ten votes. If of 88,000 voters a third abstained from voting, and a tenth of the remainder formed the majority, the chamber of deputies represented less than 6,500 voters out of 32,000,000 French people. . . .

In conclusion: the narrow limitation of the suffrage, the widespread abstention from voting, the extensive pressure and manipulation used by the government in all elections, together with the lack of experience and understanding of what either a real electoral system or even what free government itself actually is—as a result of all these the chamber of deputies failed to represent anything more than a very small segment of the people. Still the Restoration furnished the French with their first extended experience in democratic government under peaceful conditions.

FRENCH SOCIETY UNDER THE RESTORATION

Guillaume de Bertier de Sauvigny

Was French society, as the theory behind the Civil Code would have it, "dust composed of equal and separate atoms"? No, of course not. Besides family ties which resisted all upheavals, there were numerous principles of distinction and community which divided the French into classes or social groups. More than today, outward distinctions like costume and language differentiated them.

The social distinctions of the Old Regime, which were founded on legal privileges, no longer existed, but it was easier to erase them from the law than from custom, and they continued to mark clear-cut groups within society. Money was another factor of social discrimination, and its importance was reinforced by the Constitution, which made it the basis of political power. The individuals who could pay 300 francs in direct taxes to vote and 1000 francs to be eligible for office formed a new class of privileged persons in the nation. A deputy from the Gironde Department wrote to Villèle in 1827 that "the foundation of all our laws is wealth; the condition for prominence is gold; and the reward desired by all is riches. It is, therefore, at the altars of fortune, and there only, that those who desire to play a role in the fate of their nation today make their sacrifices." A third principle of social distinction was superimposed over the others—that of profession—and among the people of Paris, it has been observed, occupation more than wealth drew individuals as well as families together. Certain professions, such as the clergy, the military, and civil service, were sufficiently special to characterize a social group, and even within each, hierarchy created numerous divisions. Yet the other professions had quite ill-defined boundaries. In what category, for example, would one place the banker who was engaged in large-scale trade or who financed an industrial enterprise, the merchant who controlled a number of cottage industries, the military man and the civil servant who continued to direct the working of their lands, the small craftsman who sold the products of his own labor, and the peasant who did weaving at home or who spent part of the year in carting and peddling?

Three other factors also contribute to the confusion of the picture. First, politics, for in high society, the liberals did not associate at all with the royalists. A Lafayette, for example, who was a noble, an émigré, and a great landed proprietor, was estranged from the class of his birth because of his political associations; on the other hand, great bourgeois royalists like the

G. de Bertier de Sauvigny, *La Restauration* (2nd ed.; Paris, 1963), 244–250. © Librairie Ernest Flammarion. Used by permission. Translation by Ann New.

banker Jauge became part of the [aristocratic] society of the Faubourg Saint-Germain. Secondly, Parisian society was considerably different from that of the provinces, and the principles of social distinction were quite diverse from one province to another. Finally, the Revolution and Empire had unleashed a general upward movement at all levels of society, one which quickly shifted individuals and families about on the scale of values of wealth and profession. Under the Old Regime, tradition demanded that sons follow the profession of their father; now children desired to outdo their parents, and parents made the greatest sacrifices in order that their children might realize the ambitions which they themselves could not attain. Louis Veuillot recounted a naive dialogue between his parents which is a curious echo of the dreams of young Julien Sorel: "'My poor Marianne,' my father said, 'you are mad. Have you ever seen the sons of workers like ourselves become notaries?' 'Why not? Napoleon was a corporal and he certainly became Emperor.'" Imaginary or true, this quaint scene illuminates the profound attachment of the masses to the memory of the Emperor, and illustrates the great social revolution of the nineteenth century.

In the final analysis, aside from the hierarchies of Church and State . . . , in this society, with its infinitely varied and changing character, there were actually only two classes whose individuality can be defined in terms both precise and general enough to be applicable to all of France—the nobility and the industrial workers. But what about the middle class? It certainly existed and its hour of complete triumph was drawing near, but there is a problem in defining it in a society where it was swelling rapidly with all those individuals who were not engaged in manual labor. How can the middle class be described without a detailed discussion of the various professions? And the scales of social prestige varied considerably from province to province. This was even true for the rural classes: . . . what did the vine growers of Côte d'Or . . . have in common with the peasants of Vivarais . . . ? Moreover, developments were so slow among the peasantry that our fifteen-year period does not reveal any feature which was not already true of the end of the eighteenth century and which would not remain so until about 1850.

The existence of the nobility was recognized by Article LXXI of the Charter: "The old nobility reassumes its titles; the new retains its. The king creates nobles at will, but he grants them only ranks and honors without exempting them from any of the social responsibilities and duties of society." In addition, the creation of the Chamber of Peers, which organized an aristocratic power alongside the royal power and the nation's elected representatives, seemed to promise the nobility a more regular and effective political influence than it had enjoyed even under the absolute monarchy. This was so only in appearance, however, as can be seen by considering the differences which distinguished the noble chambers of the old Estates-General —truly representative of the nobility of the kingdom which had elected them—and the Chamber of Peers, a mere emanation of royal power which could, at its pleasure, introduce members of common birth.

The ordinance of August 19, 1815, which established an hereditary peerage and a kind of hierarchy of titles within the upper chamber, at least assured this body a certain additional independence, though without doing anything to make it more representative. "We no longer have, or we do not yet have, an aristocracy," said Royer-Collard in February, 1816. "We shall have to wait for it. The aristocratic power created by the Charter is still only a fiction; it resides solely in the virtues, courage, and enlightenment of men to whom it has been entrusted. It will become a reality only when it becomes the faithful expression of a superiority that is truly recognized."

What superiority? Intelligence and culture? But these are not easily come by. The authority which comes with positions in the government? But no one dreamed of reinstituting what Napoleon had sought to create, a Russian-style "table of ranks." That of services rendered? But the hereditariness which was accorded the peerage considerably limited the openings in this area. The size of one's wealth, therefore, remained the basis of political power in the electoral system stemming from the Charter. Landed wealth in particular seemed by its nature to give the aristocracy an indispensable basis of power. This became its goal and it made attempts to weaken the effects of the equal division of property stipulated in the Civil Code.

An ordinance of August 25, 1817, determined that no one would be admitted to the Chamber of Peers if he had not previously acquired a *majorat*, that is, a clear title to an inalienable and indivisible piece of property destined to pass to his eldest son along with his title of peer. The value of this *majorat* had to be in keeping with the hierarchy of titles: 30,000 francs' worth of revenue for a duke, 20,000 for a count, and 10,000 for viscounts and barons.

Subsequently a way was sought to extend these arrangements to all the nobility: the titles of nobility granted by the king would only be transmitted to a son on condition that a *majorat* totaling 10,000 francs for a marquis and 5,000 francs for a viscount be created (February 10, 1824). But even these conditions were still too onerous for the great majority of nobles, who had large families. In 1826 only 307 *majorats* had been formed outside the peerage, and of this number, 105 dated from the Empire. The famous law on inheritances proposed in 1826 was conceived by its promoters as a remedy to this situation. As is well known, however, it was rejected by the Chamber of Peers itself.

The noble families, which no longer had the king's generosity to maintain their rank, launched an assault on the budget of the state, trying to obtain priority for all the paid positions within the state, even those which the old aristocracy would have felt unable to accept without losing prestige. Thus, numerous men of noble birth became police officers, justices of the peace, tax assessors and collectors, inspectors, ministerial employees, highway inspectors, and even postmasters. The Polytechnic School received the sons of noble families in larger numbers than it would during the July Monarchy: 70 as against 47. For the first and last time in the history of modern France, the prestige associated with birth and name was linked to political and administrative power. Of 164 prefects named under the Restoration, 122 were nobles from the Old Regime, as were 250 of the 545 subprefects and general secretaries of the prefectures. The state gained a class of civil servants of exceptional integrity—if not of always obvious ability—one accustomed to putting honor of service before material interests. In spite of the vituperation from the opposition against the wealthy members of the ministerial majority, and what a Balzac novel might lead one to believe, there were never fewer political-financial scandals than in this period. In the entire corps of prefects and subprefects, there were only two cases of dismissal for dishonesty during these fifteen years.

On the other hand, this arrangement did not serve the purposes of the bourgeoisie, which saw itself deprived of one of the principal results of the Revolution. It vented its disappointment by complaints about the "feudal reaction," which must be considered one of the main causes of the failure of the Restoration as far as the middle classes were concerned.

This question was closely connected with the vexing problem of titles of nobility, the importance of which can scarcely be realized today. The old aristocracy held only a very few titles granted regularly by royal brevet or letters patent. Its members, when they did not take a manorial title attached to their land, simply styled themselves "knight" or "esquire." With the return of the king, they therefore found themselves, from the point of view of titles, at a great disadvantage in relation to the nobles created by the Empire, for whom every title was based on an official government act. "The old nobility reassumes its titles," stated the Charter, but the majority of the nobles of birth, who were only children in 1789, had never had any to begin with! By common agreement, then, they "reassumed" their titles as they pleased, with only the title of duke being reserved to a formal nomination by the king. A certain number of nobles cared to regularize these new titles by securing new letters patent, but since the formalities were difficult to fulfill and the registry fees high, most of them did not bother and were content to be self-styled marquises, counts, viscounts, or barons, which came to be called "courtesy titles."

This same preoccupation with assuming a rank which lacked a basis in law gave the particle de [of] an importance and significance which it never had under the Old Regime. There was not a Dubois or a Dupont who, for the sake of his career, did not want to be called Dupont or Dubois of something. How lucky were those, like the minister Decazes, who, by the simple device of adding an appropriate space, could have the much desired prefix appear in their names. The deceptions and absurdities which this rush to become noble provoked can readily be imagined. The parents of the great Balzac—honest common people if ever there were any—believed it necessary, on the occasion of the marriage of their second daughter to a Monsieur *de* . . ., to have two different announcements printed: on one they called themselves *de* Balzac, as they would be called in the society their daughter was entering; while on the other, they remained simply Balzac, for the sake of their old friends who might otherwise mock the family's new pretensions. Is this simple fact not delightful and more revealing of the spirit of society than long treatises?

As for industrial workers, the exact number is very difficult to ascertain. Statistics from 1820 indicate 4,300,000 persons earned their living from industry, compared to 22,251,000 in the other professions. But these figures represent families and not individuals. Moreover, as has already been noted, many farmers might devote part of their days to industrial work. Another indication comes from the statistics of the military review boards, which counted an average of 228 "industrial workers" as compared with 516 farmers, out of every 1,000 recruits.

The condition of the worker varied considerably from craftsman, to proletarian in large industry, to rural worker-farmer. The last had the advantage of living at home and hence of being able to live more cheaply. However, their salaries would undergo a continual decline as a result of the pitiless competition of large, concentrated industry, which would inevitably lead to their disappearance. For example, the muslin workers of the Tarare region, who earned between 40 and 45 *sous* a day in 1820, earned no more than 28 or 30 *sous* fifteen years later. The prices paid in Rouen in 1815 for a dozen handkerchiefs varied, depending on the size, from 5 to 30 francs; they eventually fell to 1 franc 50 and 4 francs 50. Moreover, the living conditions of this class of workers differed greatly from one region to another, like the conditions of the peasantry to which they continued to belong.

The aristocracy in this world of labor was composed of the workers in urban trades, who retained the organization traditional to the crafts which was so favorable to the development of the best human qualities. The working day was certainly long, but since its duration was generally limited to the daylight hours, the long evenings during winter afforded considerable leisure; moreover, a break for meals, from 9 to 10 and from 2 to 3, was generally observed; finally, Sunday was free, as were religious and special holidays. The workingman was often given lodging by his employer, and ate and worked with him. Or, if he was a member of a *compagnonnage* (trade guild), he lived with young people of his own age in the hospitable lodgings of a "mother" society where he could find a family atmosphere. His wages were generally sufficient to assure him a comfortable existence: in Paris, in 1820, a locksmith earned 5 francs a day, a roofer 4 francs 50, a stonecutter 3 francs 50, and a carpenter 3 francs 25. Thus there were in Paris, as certain inventories taken of the property of the deceased attest, some workers who were able to amass a small store of capital for themselves in government annuities, private loans, real estate, and even rural lands.

CHARLES X, POLIGNAC, AND THE APPLICATION OF ARTICLE XIV OF THE CHARTER

VINCENT W. BEACH

It is going too far to assume that Charles asked Polignac to head a ministry for the express purpose of executing a *coup d'état*. The papers of Ferdinand de Bertier as well as other sources indicate that a parliamentary majority in support of the new ministry was not beyond the realm of possibility. . . . Polignac, however, was not a leader who could weld a group of ego-maniacs into a workable coalition, and the parliamentary majority never materialized. . . .

From November 17, 1829, until the July Revolution of 1830, Polignac was prime minister in name as well as fact. . . . Fifty-eight years old when he became prime minister, Polignac had spent 30 years of his life outside France. The truth was that he had no real comprehension of the institutional changes wrought by the Revolution. In common with Charles X, he had remained attached to the customs and traditions of the pre-Revolutionary era. The king, who was 72 years old, was annoyed and saddened by the continuous assaults on the prerogatives of the crown; he wanted a president of the council whom he loved and trusted—one on whom he could depend to carry out his wishes. Polignac seemed to fill the bill. . . .

In a memorandum in Polignac's handwriting entitled *Mesure urgente* dated September 10, 1829, written just a little over a month after he organized the last ministry of Charles X, Polignac expressed his views quite clearly. The abuses of the press, the absence of distinctions between the old and new nobility, and the special privileges of the middle class were injurious to society as a whole, declared the president of the council. Even the ministerial system which he headed came under fire. Polignac maintained that in a government in which seven cabinet members had a certain amount of independent

Vincent W. Beach, "The Polignac Ministry: A Re-Evaluation," *University of Colorado Studies in History*, 3 (1964), pp. 95–98, 102, 118, 127, 130–132, 136–137, 141–142, 144–146. © Vincent W. Beach. Used by permission.

authority in their areas of responsibility, the king's power was in danger of being frittered away. Complaining that ancient and long respected customs were being attacked with audacity, he wrote: "It may be difficult, but it is not impossible for us to return some day to a system which incorporates aristocratic principles and closes the doors of the chamber of deputies to mediocre men driven by turbulent and revolutionary passions." . . .

The most violent royalists were urging that Charles apply Article XIV of the Charter which declared the king to be "the supreme head of the state and competent to issue regulations and ordinances for the laws and the safety of the state." . . .

Charles X had been considering the application of Article XIV of the Charter since the Polignac ministry took office. Indeed, Polignac's discussions with the king in January, 1829, indicated quite clearly that the president of the council visualized a basic reconstruction of political and social institutions pretty well in keeping with the king's desires. . . .

The electoral colleges were scheduled to convene on June 23 and July 3, and August 3 was the date set for the opening of the new legislative session. During the election campaign, the opposing parties marshalled their arguments and presented their programs to the some 90,000 men who participated in the direction of French affairs. The liberals and constitutional royalists had as their prime aim the re-election of the 221 deputies who had voted for the hostile address in reply to the speech from the throne. The king and the council were determined to elect a majority of men to the chamber who would go along with an institutional reorganization which would place the preponderance of power in the hands of Charles X and his friends. . . .

On June 23, the *collèges d'arrondissement* assembled, and before the end of the month it was known that the opposition had triumphed. Although the departmental colleges had not yet met, it was already obvious that the king and his faction would not have a majority in the chamber. When the departmental colleges assembled on July 3, they confirmed the earlier trend; the ministry was for certain faced with a hostile lower house. The 20 departments in which the voting had been delayed until July 12 and July 19 also elected a preponderance of deputies opposed to the government, adding to the magnitude of the ministry's setback. . . .

The 90,000 voters and 5,000 electors had rejected the advice of their king and elected a chamber hostile to the government. The government had the support of the bureaucracy and of officialdom in general, not to mention the active aid of the prelates of the church. All things considered, the crushing defeat of the government at the hands of the well-to-do property owners was amazing. Of 428 deputies elected, some 270 were to be counted in the opposition while the government elected only 145. Of the 221 who voted for the hostile address, 202 were returned to the chamber. Some 13 other deputies could not be counted in either group.

Charles could not conceal his disappointment, and the ultra faction was momentarily stunned. The result was scarcely believable to members of the extreme right. The editor of the ultra-royalist *Drapeau blanc* printed the statement which follows:

The results of the elections must open the monarch's eyes. No doubt about it, the Revolution triumphed. Charles X is on the road that his unhappy brother was forced to take, and at the end is the scaffold. The electors have voted for the knife to his throat; safety for them and for France lies only in the unchangeable will of the king.

The *Drapeau blanc* expressed the sentiments of the king perfectly. . . .

When the cabinet met at the Tuileries the next day, Polignac reported to the king that the ministry was unanimous in its view that Article XIV [of the Charter] was applicable in the existing situation. . . . There was not the unanimity which Polignac suggested. Charles and Polignac, however, decided on new appointments to the ministry, and the president of the council's close friendship with the king placed him in position to exercise great influence at decisive moments. . . .

Thus, the constitution, in effect, was to be changed, and the election machinery rigged in such fashion as to guarantee the king a majority in the chamber of deputies. Charles and Angoulême approved these measures in principle when they were presented to them, and cabinet meetings between July 10 and July 25 were dominated by the discussion of the final form of the ordinances. In a little speech to the members of the council, Charles X tried to justify the decrees which cost him his throne.

The men of the left are completely dominated by the spirit of revolution. In attacking the ministry, they are seeking to destroy the monarchical system. Unhappily, I have had more experience along these lines than you who are not old enough to have witnessed the events of the Revolution. I remember quite well what happened then. The first concession by my brother was the signal for his destruction. They also made protestations of love and fidelity to him. They, too, merely asked him to dismiss his ministers. He yielded and lost everything. . . . If I dismissed you, they would finish by treating us as they treated my brother. . . . Rather than be conducted to the scaffold, we will fight, and they will have to kill us with arms in our hands. Thus, gentlemen walk firmly along the road that we have marked out. . . .

Because the ordinances, signed on July 25, indicate exactly what Charles X had in mind, a detailed analysis of their content and significance is in order. The first decree suspended the liberty of the press.

No newspaper or periodical or semi-periodical, established or about to be established, without discrimination as to the matters discussed therein, shall appear, either in Paris or in the departments, except in virtue of an authorization, which the authors and the printer thereof shall have separately obtained from us. . . . Works published without authorization shall be immediately seized. . . . Authorization must be renewed every three months. . . . It can be revoked. . . .

The second ordinance dissolved the chamber of deputies, a decree obviously within the area of authority delegated to the king by the Charter.

On the third ordinance the king and his faction were depending for the creation of a new French political structure. This decree dealt with the electoral machinery and had as its objective the establishment of a system that would guarantee the election of deputies who would support the program of the government. It reduced the number of members of the lower house to 258 (from 428) and stated that "the deputies shall be elected for five years and in such a manner that the chamber may be renewed each year by a fifth." This was an improvement over the Septennial Law which it replaced, and there was no quarrel with shortened terms or annual renewal. The Charter provided that an individual, to be eligible for membership in the chamber of deputies, must pay a direct tax of 1,000 *francs* and that a citizen, to be able to vote at all, must pay a direct tax of 300 *francs*. . . .

The fourth ordinance provided that the district electoral colleges would meet on September 6 and the departmental colleges on September 13. The chamber of peers and the chamber of deputies of the departments were to convene on September 28. A fifth ordinance restored to the council of state certain extremists who had been relieved of their positions during the Martignac ministry.

Such were the decrees published in the *Moniteur* on July 26, 1830. If they could be made to prevail, the quarrel between the king and the chambers would be resolved. The king would be supreme. . . . Within hours of the publication of the decrees on Monday, July 26, resistance developed, and by the end of the week it was clear the Charles X and the Polignac ministry were finished. Charles abdicated in favor of his grandson, the Duc de Bordeaux on August 2, and the liberals, who had been most active in undermining the regime, hurriedly invited Louis Philippe to become king. By-passed were the men who had done the fighting at the barricades. Some of them wanted a republic; others were Bonapartists hoping for a comeback. With only 9,000 army effectives in the vicinity of Paris, and not all of these loyal to the regime, the government was unprepared for strong resistances to the ordinances.

Not only did the dynasty go down, but the men who, with Charles, shared responsibility for the events of July had sacrificed their political future and, for a few years, their freedom as well. The overthrow of Charles X was no fluke, no accident of circumstance. True, it seems incredible that the king, with the army, the police, the courts, and the church hierarchy seemingly at his beck and call, was unable to save his throne. Basically, of course, a king who offends a significant portion of the general population is certain to offend many of those on whom he directly depends for support, and this proved to be the case in July, 1830. It seems that the liberals, who had aroused the masses so effectively, had also dampened the enthusiasm for Charles X of a significant number of aristocrats and churchmen who had served as main props of the regime. The men who held the key positions in the institutional structure on which he relied seemed paralyzed, and either did not rally to his defense or were quite ineffective in their efforts. Polignac, who as first minister should have been the driving force, seems to have lost his nerve completely once resistance to the ordinances developed.

Only a handful of the 428 members of the chamber of deputies assumed an active role in the revolt, and fewer still hoped for the downfall of the regime. Despite their bitter diatribes in the chambers, they seemed to want Charles X without the ultras. But the insurgents, becoming more radical by the moment, could not be satisfied by the repeal of the ordinances, and it became necessary to ditch Charles X to prevent the establishment of a republic. The republicans and others in the mob could not, for the most part, meet the existing qualifications for voting and officeholding, and they were threatening to establish a much more democratic regime, a development which the upper-middle-class businessmen, who had been dominating the chamber of deputies, determinedly opposed.

The significance of the Revolution of 1830 is to be found not only in what it changed but in what it prevented. With the July ordinances Charles hoped to complete the construction of a political and social structure in which the members of the old nobility would be the main props, but the middle-class business interests successfully prevented this step and not only retained but added to the privileges which they had enjoyed since the Revolution. Jacques Laffitte, Casimir Périer, Adolphe Thiers and François Guizot, at one time or another, served as first ministers of France during the reign of Louis Philippe, something they could never have hoped for while Charles X remained king. And the overthrow of the legitimate line left room for some Bonapartists to make a comeback, since, in the general purge following the July days, most of the state and departmental offices changed hands.

Thus, the well-to-do members of the chamber of deputies who made Louis Philippe the King of the French were rewarded for their efforts, but the men who had fought at the barricades and hoped for a republic (or an empire) found little comfort in the relatively minor changes made in the Charter of 1814. They still could not vote or hold office, and they renewed the struggle in 1848, only to find the cards stacked against them once again.

A NEW LOOK AT THE FRENCH REVOLUTION OF 1830

DAVID H. PINKNEY

Among the revolutions in France since 1789 one, the Revolution of 1830, has been singularly neglected by historians in this century, and neither in this century nor the preceding one has it attracted much attention from any but the political historians. The economic and sociological dimensions of the event have been generally ignored. Consequently, the Revolution of 1830 is ordinarily seen as a political movement arising out of the unpopularity of Charles X and his ministers and out of their attempt to arrogate the sovereign power to the crown. . . .

This conventional history, written in the single dimension of politics, leaves much unexplained, many questions unanswered.

Why did the workers of Paris risk their lives in July 1830? To defend the Charter of 1814 as many contemporaries fatuously pretended to believe? To defend the abstract principles of 1789? To re-establish the Republic, which was to some a distant memory, to most only a hazy ideal?

Why did the same limited electorate of substantial property owners change from strongly pro-royalist and pro-government in 1824 to pro-liberal and anti-government in the next general election less than four years later and become revolutionaries in 1830? Was this startling reversal owing solely to the ultra-royalists' political policies? Even in 1824 the electorate knew pretty well what these policies were, and then it approved them.

Why did the provinces accept the Revolution so readily? Why did Charles not appeal to the provinces to support him against revolutionary Paris? The history of the Great Revolution would certainly suggest this course. . . .

The basic fact seen from the vantage point of economic history is that the Revolution of 1830 occurred during a depression that wracked the French economy from 1823 to 1832. The popular resort to violence came when food prices in Paris, and in the provinces, too, were at a level that tens of thousands of workingmen could not afford to pay.

The reversal of the prosperity that France had enjoyed after 1817 was first evident in 1826. In that year industrial prices, moving upward for nearly a decade, fell off. Wages in industry declined as much as 10 per cent. In some places unemployment was considerable—11,000 looms were idle in Lyon in the spring of 1826; in the same year 3000 construction workers unable to find work in Paris returned to their homes in central France. These economic reverses although locally serious produced no widespread distress, but in

David H. Pinkney, "A New Look at the French Revolution of 1830," *Review of Politics*, XXIII (1961), 490–501. © *Review of Politics*. Used by permission.

1828 and the following years a crisis stemming from a succession of bad crops, turned recession into grave depression. From 1827 through 1830 there was but one good crop of wheat, only two of potatoes. In 1828 the price of wheat was 40 per cent above the price in 1825, in 1829 60 per cent above, and it never dropped below that level in the next three years. The price of bread to the consumer rose even more—as much as 125 per cent between 1825 and 1829.

The French workingman in the 1820's spent a third to a half of his income on food, and bread was the staple of his diet. A rise in the price of bread cut sharply into his budget and forced him to reduce other expenditures. One of the few other expenditures that his meager budget could afford was on clothing, and reduction of that expenditure, in turn, affected the textile industry. The cotton, wool, and silk industries, all fell into doldrums that continued through 1831. The iron industry was affected in 1829. The demand for coal declined. For the first time since the beginning of the Restoration the middle class saw prices and profits drop and stay depressed.

Middle class opinion blamed the government for the crisis. One might infer this from the experience of our own time, our own practice of holding our government responsible for depression or recession, but proof of it can be found in the parliamentary debates and the press of the time. This dissatisfaction seems to have found expression, too, in the parliamentary elections. In 1824 in a period of full prosperity the electorate chose a large majority of rightists, supporters of the government. Essentially the same electorate in 1827 returned a majority on the left, strongly hostile to the government. In 1830, with the depression much worse, the same voters elected an even larger majority of leftists. A few weeks later they calmly sanctioned a violent revolution that ended the regime that they blamed for their economic difficulties. The depression surely had something to do with this political reversal.

Urban workingmen suffered much more than their employers from the depression. Not only did their cost of living rise disastrously but their wages dropped, and the curse of unemployment fell upon thousands. There were many variations from industry to industry and from region to region, but in general, Labrousse maintains, between 1826 and 1830 wages declined from a quarter to a third. Unemployment was common by 1827–28 and in the summer of 1828 and the following years it assumed serious proportions. Police reports, prefectoral and procureur-general reports in these years all attest to the generalization and persistence of unemployment throughout the nation. The large foundry at Chaillot in Paris cut its force from three to four hundred to one hundred. The royal tapestry factory, La Savonnerie, let go half its workers. In October, 1828, the Minister of the Interior instructed the prefects to discourage workingmen from coming to Paris in search of employment.

The worker found his standard of living under triple pressure from rising prices, declining wages, and unemployment. The result was want, distress, and, as the depression continued and deepened, dark and desperate poverty for tens of thousands of Frenchmen. In Paris the police reports of the time are unanimous that when the price of a four livre loaf of bread exceeded 12 or 13 sous, most of the working population of the city was underfed. The price had been at $11\frac{1}{2}$ sous in 1826. By the end of 1828 it stood at 19 sous, and it never fell below that high level until 1832, when the government fixed the price by law. News of each rise in price was received in the poor quarters of Paris as a veritable sentence of death. Death from starvation was not unknown in the city, and certainly many deaths attributed to other causes really stemmed from prolonged privation. The great cholera epidemic in 1832 had its heaviest incidence in the poor, starved quarters of the capital. In October, 1828, the Commissioner of Police in the Faubourg Saint-Antoine wrote: "Rise in the price of bread . . . produced . . . bitter complaints; the approach of winter frightens the people and with good reason. . . . Soon the father of a family will not earn enough to buy bread and how can he provide for clothing his children and for payment of his rent?"

To thousands in Paris the difference between life and death was the bread card distributed by the police and by relief offices that entitled the holder to bread at reduced prices. In July, 1830, (significant date!) 227,000 Parisians applied for this relief. The population of the city was only 755,000. . . .

What was the connection between misery and revolution? . . . It is certain that *les misérables* in the depression of the late Restoration blamed the government, the King, and the Jesuits for their plight. A police report of October 21, 1828, recorded:

A hand lettered poster has been put up at the port of entry to the rue Saint-Nicolas, quarter of Quinze-Vingts: "Vive Napoléon! War to the death on Charles X and the priests who want to starve us to death." Several workers applauded it. . . . The same signs have been distributed in the rues de Charenton and de Charonne, in the faubourgs Saint-Marceau and Saint-Martin. In cabarets and shops there is talk that the people must join to march on the Tuileries to ask for work and bread. . . .

Distress and desperation found overt expression in riots, demonstrations, concerted violence scattered over all France, especially in the departments north of the Loire River. After 1828 food riots and rebellion against tax collectors became the principal subject of reports from the procureurs-general. In the eighteen months ending in December, 1827, only three incidents were mentioned, but in 1829 ninety incidents were reported, twenty-five in the month of May alone. These included holding up grain convoys, extortion of grain from peasants and tenants, forced sales of grain at "fair" prices, destruction of *octroi* barriers, and the sacking of offices of tax collectors. At the same time the number of labor disturbances increased—strikes, petitions, demonstrations for higher wages or more work. This agitation was most intense in the spring, summer, and fall of 1829 and again in spring of 1830. . . .

The political significance of this is unmistakable. . . . The government was blamed for the troubles of the time. "The King and the Jesuits," cried the rioters, "force up the price of wheat." At Saint-Germain-en-Laye a crowd gathered to protest the high cost of bread shouted, "Vive la République" and "Vive Napoléon!" In the same years rioters in two villages raised the tricolor. Signs and handbills demanding bread insulted the King and acclaimed the days of the Revolution, when the Law of the Maximum had kept the price of bread low.

The prolonged depression created a situation favorable to revolution. It exasperated bourgeoisie, workers, and peasants alike with the Bourbon government, and in producing popular disorder it accustomed men to violent resistance to authority. Economic distress alone would probably not produce a political revolution, but the height of economic distress coinciding with a political crisis and a provocative act by the king did. . . .

Sociology provides a second vantage point from which to view the Revolution. . . . The capital suffered from a social disequilibrium produced by an influx of population greater than the city could assimilate into its normal life. There were not enough jobs for all. Thousands were forced into the most menial, most unstable jobs and obliged to live in part at least on public relief and private charity. Housing capacity fell far short of needs; newcomers and many others were forced to live in garrets and cellars, in teeming apartments and crowded furnished rooms. All the essential urban equipment lagged behind the growing needs of the waxing population; streets were inadequate for the growing traffic; there were not enough sewers, not enough water, not enough schools, not enough hospitals.

A consequence of this imbalance was the development of a population living on the margins of the city's life—insecure, wretchedly housed, undernourished, in poor health, even physically inferior, and resentful against the society that had no place for it. Resentment readily became overt, and it was ordinarily expressed in crime.

What do these generalizations . . . signify for the Revolution of 1830? The first three decades of the nineteenth century brought a formidable increase in the population of Paris, coming after centuries of very slow growth. Between the censuses of 1801 and 1817 the number of inhabitants rose more than 30 per cent; between 1817 and the next census in 1831, more than 10 per cent. If the latter census had been taken in 1830 before the Revolution, the second percentage would certainly have been notably higher. In 1830 at least a quarter of a million more people lived in Paris than had lived there just thirty years earlier.

In those thirty years neither the city's economy nor its urban equipment expanded to accommodate so explosive an increase. Few houses were built in the workers' quarters. No major street construction was completed in the old and crowded districts. Few streets had underground sewers, and the river still served as the principal collector sewer. Not one house in five had running water.

The meaning of all this in human terms is eloquently expressed in statistical records and in literary evidence. In July, 1830, the number of persons aided by public relief, we have seen, exceeded 225,000; more than one person in every four in Paris was living on the very edge of subsistence. Swarms of beggars were a constant reminder of shocking poverty. The *Journal des Débats* for November 27, 1828, reported: "Beggars pursue passers-by in the streets, besiege the doors of churches, penetrate into houses, impose on storekeepers, and everywhere present the striking contrast of abject misery beside wealth and abundance." The death rate for all France in the 1820's was about 25 per 1000. In Paris it was 32 per thousand in 1828, 33 in 1829, 35 in 1830. In the age group of twenty to thirty-nine years, which included most of the immigrants, the death rate between 1826 and 1830 averaged a frightening 48 per 1000, almost double the rate for the country as a whole. These figures would be even higher in the crowded, poverty-stricken quarters of the center of the city. The death rates in the various arrondissements of Paris in the 1820's varied directly with the degree of poverty in each. Infant mortality in the Rue Mouffetard, for example, was double that of the fashionable Rue du Faubourg Saint-Honoré. . . .

The number of suicides and the number of homicides increased sharply in the final years of the Restoration, and both were expressions of the growing sickness of Parisian society. Most involved the poor and the miserable of the city. Between 1830 and 1835 nearly two-thirds of the bodies brought to the Morgue remained unidentified and unclaimed. In death as in life, these unfortunates were on the margins of society—unwanted and rejected in life, unknown and unmourned in death.

The high percentage of illegitimate children is another evidence of a large part of the population living beyond the law, unassimilated to society. More than one third of the births in Paris in the latter 1820's were illegitimate.

This pathological behavior becomes more comprehensible if one looks at the housing in which these people were obliged to live. About half the city's population crowded into the central quarters comprising only about one-fifth of the city's area. Here hundreds of houses of about twenty feet frontage, five stories, and no courtyard, housed thirty, forty, even sixty persons. Here deaths from cholera in 1832 were double the average rate for the entire city. . . .

Paris in 1830 had a fourth, perhaps even more, of its population living both physically and morally on the edges of civilized life—thousands were beyond the edge and most passed readily from one side to another. In this mass crime was normal—a kind of settling of accounts between the outcasts and the society that had no place for them. It was only another step to revolution—a mass settling of accounts.

The connection in 1830 between misery, both economic and moral, and rejection by society, on the one hand, and revolution on the other, has not been conclusively proved, but there are a number of significant links. Geographically there is a close correlation between the worst slums where the Parisian savages lived out their miserable lives and the bitterest street fighting in 1830. A similar correlation exists between the areas of high incidence of cholera in 1832, which attacked the poorest quarters, and the street fighting in June of that year. . . .

Here we are face to face with insurrection that sprang not from simple economic distress. It was the protest of the outcast against a society that had no honorable place for him and his children. Perhaps, too, it was the action of the rootless, amoral individual who in existing society could find self expression only in violence.

SUGGESTIONS FOR FURTHER READING

General: FREDERICK B. ARTZ, *France Under the Bourbon Restoration, 1814–1830* (Cambridge, Mass., 1931; reprinted, New York, 1963); PAUL BASTID, *Les Institutions politiques de la monarchie parlementaire française, 1814–1848* (Paris, 1954); S. CHARLÉTY, *La Restauration*, vol. IV of ERNEST LAVISSE (ed.), *Histoire de France contemporaine* (Paris, 1921); GUILLAUME DE BERTIER DE SAUVIGNY, *The Bourbon Restoration* (Philadelphia, 1967), and "Population Movements and Political Changes in Nineteenth Century France," *Review of Politics*, XIX (1957), 37–47; A. GAIN, *La Restauration et les biens des émigrés*, 2 vols. (Nancy, 1929); JEAN-JACQUES OESCHLIN, "Sociologie, organisation et stratégie de l'ultra-royalisme," *Politique*, n.s., no. 3 (1958), 231–259; EMMANUEL BEAU DE LOMÉNIE, *La Carrière politique de Chateaubriand de 1814 à 1830*, 2 vol. (Paris, 1929); JEAN LUCAS-DUBRETON, *Le Comte d'Artois, Charles X, le prince, l'émigré, le roi* (Paris, 1962); DAVID H. PINKNEY, "The Myth of the French Revolution of 1830," in DAVID H. PINKNEY and THEODORE ROPP (eds.), *A Festschrift for Frederick B. Artz* (Durham, N.C., 1964); FÉLIX PONTEIL, *La Monarchie parlementaire* (Paris, 1949); SOUTADE-ROUYER, "Les Notables en France sous la Restauration," *Revue d'histoire économique et sociale*, XXXVIII (1960), 98–110; JOHN HALL STEWART, *The Restoration Era in France: 1814–1830* (Princeton, 1968); GEORGES WEILL, *Histoire du parti républicain en France (1814–1870)* (Paris, 1928); Special: (diplomatic) GUILLAUME DE BERTIER DE SAUVIGNY, *France and the European Alliance, 1816–1821* (Notre Dame, Ind., 1958); HENRY A. KISSINGER, *A World Restored: Matternich, Castlereagh and the Problems of Peace, 1812–22* (Boston, 1957); HAROLD H.

NICOLSON, *The Congress of Vienna, a Study in Allied Unity, 1812–1822* (London, 1946); JACQUES-HENRI PIRENNE, *La Sainte-Alliance; organization européenne de la paix mondiale,* 2 vol. (Neuchâtel, 1946–49); (political and ideological) FREDERICK B. ARTZ, "Bonapartism and Dictatorship," *South Atlantic Quarterly,* XXXIX (1940), 37–49; DOMINIQUE BAGGE, *Les Idées politiques en France sous la Restauration* (Paris, 1952); EZIO CAPPADOCIA, "The Liberals and Madame de Staël in 1818," in RICHARD HERR and HAROLD T. PARKER (eds.), *Ideas in History* (Durham, N.C., 1965); IRENE FOZZARD, "The Government and the Press in France, 1822 to 1827," *English Historical Review,* LXVI (1955), 51–66; NORA E. HUDSON, "The Circulation of the Ultra-Royalist Press under the French Restoration," *English Historical Review,* XLIX (1934), 687–697; GEORGE A. KELLY, "Liberalism and Aristocracy in the French Restoration," *Journal of the History of Ideas,* XXVI (1965), 509–30; JEAN LUCAS-DUBRETON, *Le Culte de Napoléon, 1815–1848* (Paris, 1960); FRANK MANUEL, *The New World of Henri Saint-Simon* (Boston, 1956); STANLEY MELLON, *The Political Uses of History: A Study of Historians in the French Restoration* (Stanford, Calif., 1958); (religious) SIMON DELACROIX, *La Réorganisation de l'Eglise de France après la Révolution (1801–1809)* (Paris, 1962); ERNEST SEVRIN, *Les Missions religieuses en France sous la Restauration, 1815-1830,* 2 vol. (Paris, 1948-59); CHARLES H. POUTHAS, *L'Eglise et les questions religieuses sous la monarchie constitutionnelle (1814–1848)* (Paris 1961).

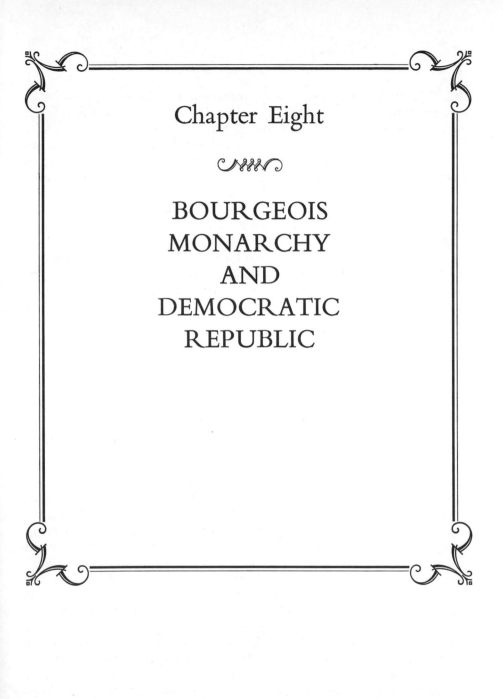

Chapter Eight

BOURGEOIS
MONARCHY
AND
DEMOCRATIC
REPUBLIC

BEGINNING IN 1789, France underwent a series of experiments in government that ran in two similar cycles: absolute monarchy, liberal monarchy, democratic republic, and authoritarian empire. The second cycle opened with the Bourbon Restoration in 1814 and was to end with the fall of the Second Empire in 1870. The liberal July Monarchy and the democratic Second Republic occupied the interval between them, and were in turn separated by the Revolution of 1848. Neither of these regimes was to survive, the one because it failed to remain true to its origins by making the necessary political reforms, the other because its initial unity was broken by class conflict. Both regimes were also affected by what has been called the "Napoleonic legend" and the attempts made by the nephew of the great Napoleon to regain his family heritage. From this point of view, both regimes were merely preludes to the restoration of the Empire. Orleanists and Republicans alike were to be subject to a Bonaparte after 1851.

None of this could have been foreseen when Charles X was toppled in the Revolution of 1830. As the French historian Jean Lhomme seeks to prove in the opening selection, the revolution deposed one ruling class (the landed aristocracy) and installed another (the upper bourgeoisie), and made few and not very substantial changes in the Charter of 1814. Lhomme stresses the bourgeois control over the new regime, Louis-Philippe's affinity for this class, and its refusal to grant any concessions to those below it. Lhomme's traditionalist view of the "bourgeois" July Monarchy has come under increasing challenge in recent years,[1] but the limited suffrage and the unwillingness to bend before demands for electoral and parliamentary reform remain valid as causes of growing discontent by the late 1840's.

The man who for the last eight years of the reign was to be the king's first minister and the symbol of the intransigence of the regime was François Guizot. Guizot has generally had a bad press since 1848, and in the second selection the English historian Douglas Johnson attempts to present him in a more favorable light. The author stresses the continuity, historical consciousness, and detachment of Guizot's thought, characteristics that caused him to be considered "un-French" in his own day. Though sympathetic to Guizot as a calm thinker and sound intellect, Johnson is not blind to his faults, especially his failure to appreciate the changes in social and economic conditions that were taking place in France. Despite such a reappraisal, Guizot is still likely to be considered a smug defender of the middle classes, who had no understanding of the "social question," and whose admonition to "get rich" ("by work and thrift") seemed so derisory to the working class.

There was another cause for discontent with the July Monarchy: the growth of romanticism, symbolized by the success of Hugo's *Hernani* in 1830, led to dissat-

---

[1] See, for example, René Rémond, *The Right Wing in France from 1815 to de Gaulle* (Philadelphia, 1966). Rémond calls the July Monarchy a government of élites of all kinds, not simply that of a single class. The statistical study of Patrick L.-R. Higonnet and Trevor B. Higonnet, "Class, Corruption, and Politics in the French Chamber of Deputies, 1846–48," *French Historical Studies*, vol. V, no. 2 (Fall, 1967), 204–224, emphasizes the continued importance of the aristocracy and noble birth in the political life of the period.

isfaction with the stuffy and pacific regime of Guizot and Louis-Philippe. The connection between romanticism and the Industrial Revolution is analyzed in the third selection, by Albert J. George, Professor of French at Syracuse University. He links the rise of romanticism to improved printing techniques which made mass production of books possible, an increase in literacy, and a change in taste among the reading public, which preferred prose to poetry and the social novel to the old-fashioned romance. He also recognizes that this transition was indicative of changes in the structure of French society, especially the development of a large urban working class and the rise of the "social question," which was to dominate the thought of mid-nineteenth-century philosophers and writers.

The Revolution of 1848, which overthrew the July Monarchy and established a democratic Republic on its ruins, is considered in the selection by the American historian Peter Amann. Amann questions such long-held views of the Revolution as that of the democratic solidarity of the working class, its peacefulness, and its "romanticism." He also casts doubt on the intensity of class conflict traditionally seen in the violent June Days, when the uprising of Parisian workers was crushed by the conservative Constituent Assembly. Emphasizing the importance of rural as well as urban revolution, and the impact of industrialization and population growth, he seeks to present the picture of a country applying eighteenth-century solutions to twentieth-century problems.

But the year 1848 is one of the most extraordinary in the history of France. In January, King Louis-Philippe and his minister Guizot were firmly in power, governing in accord with the wishes of a wealthy electorate of some 250,000 persons, and Louis-Napoleon Bonaparte, who had twice sought and failed to overturn the regime, was in exile in England. By December, Louis-Philippe was living in exile in England, and Louis-Napoleon was President of the Republic, elected to office by some 5,500,000 votes from all classes of French society. If anyone won the Revolution, it was neither the Conservatives nor the Republicans but the nephew of the Emperor.

How could such a thing happen? As the French historian André-Jean Tudesq indicates in the final selection, one of the principal reasons was the existence of the Napoleonic legend. By 1848, Napoleon had become all things to all men: the heir of the Revolution and the guardian of order, the symbol of French military glory, and the person who had made the peasantry secure and prosperous. Based on Napoleon's own writings in exile, spread by song and poetry, and amplified in the memories of old soldiers, the legend had become a political force to be reckoned with by the 1840's, when Louis-Philippe sought to capitalize on it by returning the ashes of the Emperor from St. Helena. It was this force that Louis-Napoleon exploited when he campaigned for office in 1848.

Yet it should also be stressed that Louis-Napoleon did not rely on the legend alone for his victory. He had not been involved in the political maneuvering of the Provisional Government or the repression of the Parisian uprising in June; his "socialist" tendencies appealed to the working class; and he had an effective propaganda machine working for him in his campaign. Conservatives like Thiers, seeing him as the likely victor, followed rather than led him. Louis-Napoleon, who never doubted his destiny, was to exploit the mistakes of the conservative

National Assembly elected in 1849 and seize power in his own "18 Brumaire" in December, 1851. His long years of waiting and scheming were over.

~~~

BOURGEOIS SUPREMACY DURING THE JULY MONARCHY

JEAN LHOMME

In three days, July 27–29, 1830, the insurrection [against Charles X] was victorious. The course of the fighting need not be described here, but its results deserve to be examined. The ruling class, the landed aristocracy, was quite small and could not hold out long when all the other classes were leagued against it. At best only the army was on its side, and though important, it was poorly commanded by [Marshal] Marmont. . . . The forces confronting the army were, of course, not composed of the upper (*grande*) bourgeoisie, which was unaccustomed to street fighting and which was in any case also quite small, but by a few leaders directing the troops drawn from two main groups, the workers on the one hand, and the lower and middle bourgeoisie of the National Guard on the other. . . .

The workers' participation in the uprising greatly astonished contemporaries, and afterward the bourgeois press, perhaps more out of necessity than conviction, congratulated them. . . . "It is the people who have done everything in the last three days, and the successful results of the struggle belong to them," wrote the *National* on July 30. . . .

The interim that followed the "Three Glorious Days" was taken up with delicate negotiations in which the Duke of Orleans and the heads of his latter governments—notably Thiers and Jacques Laffitte—participated. It culminated in the comic scene on the balcony of the Hôtel de Ville when the Duke and Lafayette embraced each other, and Louis-Philippe succeeded Charles X.

This represented a triumph for the upper bourgeoisie, but how was it possible for those who had not really fought for them to have gained the fruits of victory? For many of their allies, the workers and petty bourgeois, the normal outcome should have been the proclamation of the Republic. They would have to be content with such platonic satisfactions as the return of the tricolor flag as national emblem and the fact that Louis-Philippe would be "King of the French" rather than "King of France." . . .

Until the July Revolution the dominant class had been the landed

Jean Lhomme, *La Grande bourgeoisie au pouvoir (1830–1880): Essai sur l'histoire sociale de la France* (Paris: Presses Universitaires de France, 1960), pp. 34–44, 71–75. © Presses Universitaires de France, 1960. Used by permission. Editors' translation.

aristocracy; after the July Revolution it was the upper bourgeoisie. [They represented] a descending and an ascending class. For the moment the other classes played only a secondary role. The workers and petty bourgeois who fought at the barricades and even formed the shock troops of the revolution were not the ones who received the rewards. . . .

[The aristocracy] was "descending" in that it lost the powers which had been concentrated in its hands until now. . . . History offers few examples of so rapid and complete a displacement. Elsewhere there were violent reactions and resistance; here only acceptance and resignation, nothing more. The landed aristocracy had long awaited the return of the legitimate king, Louis XVIII. But disappointed by many of his policies, it had placed higher hopes in his successor, Charles X, who represented the aspirations of all the Ultras. The fall of the last Bourbon sent a shock wave through their ranks, for it was all too easy to understand and foresee that this also meant the fall of the traditional nobility.

What would the members of the landed aristocracy do in the face of this change of rulers and regime? Some would completely abandon the struggle and cease fighting the "king of the barricades." They closed their salons in the Faubourg St. Germain and (in the familiar phrase) "retired to their lands." These, of course, remained the exceptions, for the lure of pleasure, self-interest, and habit kept most in Paris. Others decided to continue the struggle, which might be planned and carried out in many ways. Some disappeared from the Chamber of Peers, because they had either been excluded from it or refused to take the oath of allegiance to the new king. They would act against the July Monarchy by word and pen. . . . Those of their colleagues . . . who decided to take the oath, as 104 did on August 10, 1830, would remain members of the peerage. Along with some deputies they would form a Legitimist party that remained a source of opposition throughout the July Monarchy. But they also faced republicans in the Chambers, and despite the prestigious talents of Berryer, their role continued to be small and unobtrusive. They were but one factor in the parliamentary struggle, though they did succeed in securing or strengthening agricultural protection, which was so necessary to their interests. Finally, some members of the aristocracy used salons and songs against the regime of Louis-Philippe and the upper bourgeoisie. . . . But it must not be forgotten that even in a country like France, such weapons could achieve little. . . .

The aristocrats had lost the struggle. It is all too easy to have predicted that they would retain only that share of political and social power that the victorious upper bourgeoisie wanted them to have. This proved to be such crumbs as the right to produce songs and caricatures, a right allowed the powerless who might be punished with a few days prison if they abused it.

The July Monarchy was even clever enough not to leave the landed aristocracy a weapon that it might have used in such a sentimental and nostalgic country: it was denied the prestige of misfortune. The faithful who had followed the old king into exile were few, and the government of Louis-Philippe carefully avoided making martyrs of those who remained. Two instances of this policy may be cited. When the ministers responsible for the July Ordinances, Polignac and Peyronnet, were brought to trial and the Parisian populace demonstrated in favor of the death penalty, the Chamber of Peers wisely limited their sentence to life imprisonment. Another example was the abolition of hereditary peerage in 1831, a measure that may be considered in various ways, but can hardly be called "bloodthirsty."

. . . All in all, the persecution was neither systematic nor very severe. Only once was there a really serious incident, the fault of the Legitimists themselves. They had made it an annual ritual to commemorate the murder of the Duke of Berry on February 13, 1820. On February 13, 1831, when the July Monarchy was barely six months old, a memorial service was held at the Church of St. Germain l'Auxerrois [in Paris], where a portrait of [his son] the Duke of Bordeaux, the "miracle child," was displayed. A popular counterdemonstration sparked by this excessive zeal resulted in the pillaging of the church. The Archbishopric of Notre Dame suffered the same fate the next day. Those responsible for this disorder were not hard to find, and the aristocracy henceforth knew what fury it might provoke if it attempted to return to the past.

. . . Stripped of its political and social power, and even deprived of any prestige it might gain from misfortune, could the aristocracy not at least have continued the struggle with a last weapon, an economic one? . . . Until about the time of the Revolution and Empire, fortunes had traditionally been based on land. Landed proprietors not only represented *wealth*, but were virtually the *only* persons of wealth. No doubt the eighteenth century —to go no further back in time—had seen the creation of fortunes based on trade, tax, farming, and judicial professions, like that of notary. Yet these were exceptions to the rule that land formed the most highly esteemed, most generally recognized, and most commonly acquired source of wealth. This is why we have referred to a *lan*ded aristocracy, for the respected nobility drew most of its income from land. . . . But it was precisely around 1830 that its wealth was being diminished both absolutely and relatively. Absolutely, but not simply because the pensions dispensed from the royal coffers by Charles X ceased, since these were negligible sums. The nobles spent a good part of their time on their estates, but made little effort to improve them. Stendhal [in his *Memoirs of a Tourist*] claimed that the nobles spent two-thirds of their income on their estates or in Paris, while devoting the other third to improving their land. But this was a dream, not a reality. All contemporary observers noted the poor agricultural methods, especially on the large estates that belonged to the landed aristocracy.

Their landed wealth also declined relatively, which is even more remarkable. Beginning in 1830, incomes drawn from the land were no longer the only important ones. Alongside them were appearing incomes derived from industry, banking, and more generally, from "business," as was the case with the Périer family. Characteristically, this income and the fortunes made from it did not enter aristocratic pockets, but rather, these forms of enrichment were typical of another class, the upper bourgeoisie.

. . . If the decline of the landed aristocracy was both so sudden and complete, it was because the supremacy of this class rested on insecure foundations. The values it promoted were for the most part outmoded. If it was able to maintain itself for almost fifteen years, this was due to exceptional circumstances that are readily ascertainable—the long domestic disorder and endless foreign wars that had brought great fatigue in their wake. The regime of the Restoration bore the stigma of defeat and foreign occupation, but most Frenchmen accepted it as a promise of peace abroad and stability at home. As long as nothing more was demanded of it, the landed aristocracy, supported by the Bourbons, was able to appear responsive to the will of the nation, but the day that it had to face up to a new situation, it immediately collapsed. . . .

Another proof of its decline was the apathy that met the attempted *coup* by the Duchess of Berry in 1832–33. A mad attempt, poorly conceived and managed, but one that might have galvanized its energies. The aristocracy was content to make ironic remarks about the police measures of Louis-Philippe and his ministers. There was little risk in doing that. . . .

As a class, the landed aristocracy no longer had a role to play in the social history of France. It represented only an increasingly negligible and uninfluential force. . . . One class lost its supremacy. Another replaced it. . . .

This was the upper bourgeoisie. . . . The rise of this new class quickly became apparent, for it was a banker, Jacques Laffitte, whom Louis-Philippe chose to head the first government of his reign. The date, November 2, 1830, is an important one. For the first time since 1815—in fact, for the first time even long before that—a ministry was headed by someone without a title of nobility. Moreover, that someone was a banker. Truly, the reign opened under the sign of Mammon, and such a choice symbolized an entire political, social and, most important, an economic program.

Still, Laffitte did not remain in power long—only until March, 1831. He was blamed, and not unfairly, for failing to repress the outbreaks that led to the sack of the Church of St. Germain l'Auxerrois and then that of the Archbishopric on February 13–14, 1831. But one banker, Casimir Périer, immediately succeeded another. And the distinction historians make in this regard when they call one a member of the "party of movement" and the other a member of the "party of resistance," has little merit. . . . Both Laffitte and Périer were typical representatives of the upper bourgeoisie, the class which had attained power and would seek to gain the maximum advantage from it.

[This class] held several advantages at this time. The men who composed it were "new"; that is, they had until now been kept from important positions by the members of the landed aristocracy, and under the Restoration they could play only secondary roles. They were not responsible for the blunders of the preceding regime, and the July Ordinances were not their doing.

Most of Louis-Philippe's friends were from this class and he himself was most closely associated with it. Beneath his consciously bourgeois appearance, the new king was fully aware of his rights and was strongly authoritarian. He would unfailingly choose his ministers from the same class, the upper bourgeoisie. He would eventually give his entire confidence to Guizot, who held power for the long period from October, 1840, to February, 1848. Though not a businessman, Guizot became the tireless and probably the most systematic defender of the interests of the upper bourgeoisie.

Finally, the upper bourgeoisie benefited from having opposed the Bourbons. Allowances were made for this opposition to the vanquished regime. With the landed aristocracy eliminated, its power would pass to others, and quite naturally to those who appeared worthy of it. Here the members of upper bourgeoisie had a serious claim to consideration, since the way they handled their own affairs seemed to qualify them to conduct public business, and precisely to the degree that they had achieved success. There is no need to elaborate on this assimilation of public affairs into private business or to stress the temptation to serve their own interests under the guise of the general good that these new men thus faced. . . .

In 1830 chance . . . placed political power in the hands of the upper bourgeoisie. For eighteen years the beneficiaries of this historical accident made a double effort, both to retain this power and to organize it.

The opposition from Right and Left had to be disarmed. On its right, the upper bourgeoisie faced some relics that it could defeat without much difficulty. The task was more deliberate where the Left was concerned.

The principal political measure against the Right was the abolition of the hereditary peerage in 1831. Although Article XXIII of the Charter of 1830 maintained the hereditary peerage, the logic of the new regime led to its suppression. The king himself feared that heredity would favor an aristocracy that would remain too independent towards him. Casimir Périer, his prime minister, was of a different opinion, but felt that public opinion was too strongly in favor of suppressing it, and so left the task to the legislative branch. . . .

The Chamber of Deputies voted to abolish it by a large majority. The Chamber of Peers followed suit, thanks to the naming of a "batch" of new peers who tipped the scales. The law was enacted on December 29, 1831.

A few months before, on April 19, another law was passed, this time against the Left, or rather in order to satisfy the most vehement of its demands, the liberalization of the electoral system. Under the Restoration, a man had to pay 1,000 francs in direct taxes in order to serve in Parliament and 300 francs in order to vote. . . . The new law reduced the tax paid as a qualification for election to 500 francs and lowered the age of eligibility from 40 to 30. It also set 200 francs and the age of 25 as the prerequisites for voting. Payment of 100 francs (the *demi-cens*) enfranchised members of the Institute and retired military officers having pensions of at least 1,200 francs.

The law as passed caused deep disillusionment in many circles because only a small fraction of those individuals with "capacities" [e.g., doctors, professors, magistrates, notaries, and members of learned societies] were given the ballot. . . . Those who continued to allow the new regime the benefit of the doubt considered the law a concession. The hope was expressed within the middle classes that this would be the first of many. But in fact—and this is important—it was the *one and only* concession made. Despite their repeated demands, the middle classes were unable to secure any other political advantage than this throughout the entire length of the reign. That their surprise should have developed into hatred, and their favorable opinion into outright opposition, is understandable.

In any case, the effect of the law of 1831 on the composition of the electorate was relatively small and resulted in a mere doubling of the number of voters, as the following statistics show:

Election	Electorate
June–July, 1830 (last elections under the Restoration)	94,600
July, 1831 (application of the law of April 19, 1831)	167,000
June, 1834	171,000
November, 1837	199,000
March, 1839	201,000
July, 1842	220,000
August, 1846	248,000
April, 1848 (elections to the Constituent Assembly of the Republic under universal suffrage)	9,600,000

The increase in the number of voters was due only in small part to the natural increase in population, for it did not grow substantially, rising from 32,500,000 in 1831 to 35,400,000 in 1846. The real reason was the increase in general wealth. . . .

With some 200,000 voters, France thus permitted only a relatively small number of individuals to vote, generally members of the upper bourgeoisie or landed proprietors. And the reforms of 1831 were of more advantage to the former than the latter, since those bourgeois whom the increase in moveable wealth and profits from industry had raised to the ranks of the electorate were always more numerous. Landed proprietors could hardly expect a similar increase in their incomes. Reduced to second place, they were no longer the dangerous adversaries of the upper bourgeoisie and might eventually become their allies.

Thanks to the two laws of 1831 just described, the upper bourgeoisie might for a moment think that it had eliminated the opposition of the Right and mollified that of the Left. Actually, it retained a monopoly over the electorate and elective offices. At the price of a modest sacrifice and through a minor reform, the doubling of the electorate, the bourgeoisie thought that it could retain political power for itself alone.

But once these results were secured, they had to be perpetuated. Such was the attitude of the well-to-do, who looked at the order they had established, found it good, and refused to change any part of it. And their resistance would prove effective, for it would require nothing less than the February Revolution of 1848 to break it. Meanwhile, for eighteen years the upper bourgeoisie took an entirely negative position. It refused to make any changes in either the electoral system or the parliamentary regime.

Electoral reform was demanded by the Left for reasons of principle, as well as by the Right, which hoped to embarrass the government. Moderate and more far-sighted supporters of the regime also desired it. They understood the need to make some sacrifices and the impossibility of turning back the tide of demands indefinitely. They envisaged a new reduction in the tax payment required of a voter combined with an increase in the number of those enfranchised by reason of their "capacities." A petition circulating in Paris called for the enfranchisement of all members of the National Guard. In 1835 it gathered 60,000 signatures; in 1840, more than 200,000. Reviewing the National Guard on June 14, 1840, Louis-Philippe heard the cry of "Long live Reform!" for the first time. In 1842, in rejecting a move by [the deputy] Ducos in favor of an increase in the number of "capacities," Guizot voiced his expressive ideas: "The voter who pays 300 francs in taxes perfectly represents the voter who pays 200 or 100 francs. He protects him, covers him, speaks and acts naturally for him, for he shares and defends the same interests." Lamartine replied that there was no need for statesmen—barriers would do the trick. . . .

But Ducos's motion was rejected all the same, just as that of Duvergier de Hauranne would be on the very eve of the February Revolution. Duvergier proposed that the tax qualification for voting be lowered to 100 francs, and that numerous "capacities" be added, including those of municipal councillors of communes with more than 3,000 inhabitants. The result would have been to increase the size of the electorate by about 200,000 persons. But Guizot secured its defeat when the Chamber of Deputies voted 252 to 154 against it. All this deserves to be stressed since the reforms outlined by Duvergier de Hauranne were obviously quite moderate, discontent was growing in the country—it was at this moment that Lamartine coined the famous phrase, the "revolution of contempt"—and the so-called banquet campaign had already begun. The part played by the prohibition of a banquet scheduled for February 22, 1848 [in precipitating the Revolution] is well known. The next day Guizot resigned, and the day after that Louis-Philippe abdicated. . . .

A RECONSIDERATION OF GUIZOT

DOUGLAS JOHNSON

All the statesmen and politicians of nineteenth-century France need to be reconsidered; it is doubtful whether any deserves reconsideration more than Guizot. Neither historians nor history have been fair towards him. He was a man who achieved eminence in many different ways, as a journalist, a historian, an educationalist, a diplomat, a writer on theological matters, an administrator of the French Protestant church and one of the great orators of France, as well as being a political leader. . . .

[But] he is invariably thought of as a politician whose intellectual preoccupations are not to be set against his outstanding characteristic, which is that of failure. At best therefore Guizot is thought of as a superior mediocrity, a dull dog, a man whose importance is only grudgingly admitted . . . at worst Guizot is thought to typify class oppression and corruption, and by his deliberate perversion of parliamentary institutions and deliberate encouragement of middle-class egoism, he is still considered, as he was once called, "the evil genius of the French bourgeoisie." . . . There seems to be a general supposition that behind his eloquence and industry there lay a fundamental incapacity, and that behind his austere exterior there was even a certain dishonesty.

These suppositions have persisted, although many legends about Guizot have been exploded. It has for a long time been known that the phrase "get rich" could only be thought of as an example of political immorality when removed from its context, which was either "get rich by work and thrift," an exhortation to which no one could have taken exception, or an appeal

Douglas Johnson, "A Reconsideration of Guizot," *History*, vol. XLVII, no. 161 (October, 1962), 239–253. Copyright 1962 by Douglas Johnson. Used by permission of the author and *History*. French passages in the text have been translated by the Editors.

to the Chamber to better the moral and material conditions of France, which was equally far from having any sinister implications. It has also been clear from Guizot's correspondence with intimate friends . . . that he was far from being the distant and disagreeable Huguenot so frequently presented in the textbooks, but was instead a man of great warmth of personality, capable of inspiring and of experiencing deep affection. It has been evident too for some time that the charge that Guizot maintained himself in power by corrupt elections and packed parliaments needs to be modified. Not only have historians been content with slight evidence and the conviction that there existed examples of corruption although they could not cite them, but they have also supposed that there is only one ideal form of parliamentary government, by which the French system of the 1840's must be judged. Guizot himself commented on the fact that although all his government's papers had fallen into the hands of his opponents after 1848, little was found to confirm the two charges which had been most frequently against him, those of corrupting parliamentary life and of pursuing a timid foreign policy. Yet in spite of this knowledge, the conventional picture of Guizot both as a man and as a statesman has tended to persist.

In this tendency, historians are following in the tradition of Guizot's contemporaries, many of whom were continually hostile to him. They sought to belittle him by suggesting that he was of no importance, "a man of pasteboard," or "a telegraph" worked either by Louis-Philippe or by de Broglie; they suggested that he was unpatriotic and emphasized his pro-English sentiment by calling him "Sir Guizot" or "Lord Guizot." . . . They attacked his personal character, making him out to be "a thin, yellow, anxious, shriveled person, foreign to any pleasant or gracious aspect of existence," clinging to office out of an arid love of power. It is true to say that Guizot was never popular and this is undoubtedly a fact of some importance. In 1848, for example, his unpopularity helps to explain why the opposition was so determined to get rid of him and why many conservatives were reluctant to defend his government. . . . Yet it is difficult to believe that Guizot could have been so unpopular and still capable of remaining a minister and even of becoming chief minister. . . . Guizot . . . was always anxious to compose a public countenance which was severe and correct. It was this public countenance which was disliked and which one must try to penetrate.

Guizot's connections with the pastors of the Protestant *Eglise du Désert* (both his grandfather and one of his great-uncles were pastors), his birth in the Protestant center of Nîmes and his unusually cosmopolitan education in Geneva, which must have been one of the few parts of imperial France where it was possible to study foreign languages and literature, were particularly significant. They emphasized an un-French side to his character which made him always somewhat remote from the French scene. As a young man, living after 1805 in Paris, he showed no interest in the military ceremonies of the capital or in the military prowess of the Empire. At a time of intense French nationalism he was mainly preoccupied with foreign literature; he was a journalist, but ... had no knowledge of the public for whom he was writing. Under the Empire he became an intellectual when the government had no use for intellectuals, with the Restoration he was a journalist and professor when the government was attacking both the press and the university, with the July Monarchy he was a minister and an upholder of the established order at a time when it was both facile and modish to be amongst the critics and opponents of this society. If one considers his Protestantism, then one has to notice how far he was from being at ease amongst many of his co-religionists and how he always possessed an admiration for Catholicism which was not generally shared by them.... In all these ways, and in others, he was continually resisting movements of opinion within France, frequently at odds with general opinion in the country. As foreign minister he never understood the enthusiasm that existed in France for Mehemet Ali and the Egyptian cause during 1840, as he never understood the excitement over the British and French disagreement in Tahiti and the hatred engendered by the British missionary Pritchard who opposed the French Protectorate.... He never understood that Thiers' bellicose gestures gave him a certain popularity, however much they may have merited ridicule. In short, as a politician who did not understand the nature of public enthusiasms, he seems to have had many of the characteristics of a foreigner amongst the French.... It might be that this very detachment in the long run causes such a politician to be isolated and to make mistakes, but at the same time it often enables him to look with greater clarity on a situation with which he feels less involved. However, one should not think of Guizot's "separateness" as only important so far as politics was concerned. Perhaps the outstanding feature of his career was the continuity of his activities.

In 1814 Guizot, then professor of modern history at the University of Paris, accompanied his colleague, the philosopher Royer-Collard to the Ministry of the Interior, becoming secretary-general to the Ministry when the abbé de Montesquiou was minister. The Hundred Days caused Guizot to quit this position and return to his university teaching, but after Waterloo he resumed administrative functions, first at the Ministry of Justice and later at the Conseil d'Etat. It was in 1820 that the victories of more violent liberals and the assassination of the Duc de Berri provoked a political reaction which removed Guizot from his position as a ministerial adviser. He then concentrated on his university lectures, the subject of which was the "Origins of Representative Government." In 1822 Villèle stopped the lectures, and Guizot concentrated on his writing and began his study of seventeenth-century history. The coming to power of Martignac restored him to the university and to the success of his lectures on civilization, whilst the society *Aide-toi le ciel t'aidera*, which prepared for the elections, recalled him to more active politics. When, in the 1840's, matters of international diplomacy began to be particularly important, Guizot himself became a diplomat (being ambassador in London from February to October 1840) and a specialist in foreign affairs. 1848 was a repetition of 1814 and 1822. Once events had interrupted his political career, and he had made his escape to London, Guizot simply resumed his study of the English revolution where he had earlier abandoned it.... Thus when one form of activity was stopped he turned to another. He was never reduced to idleness and he was never silenced.

But this was not simply an example of industry; it was also a demonstration of consistency. He always believed that the issues of the day could only be understood if they were considered within their intellectual framework. Nineteenth-century France was distinguished by its confusion of problems and ideas and by the great uncertainties which hung over it. It was necessary therefore to find the pattern within the complexity, to distinguish the different tendencies and to understand the nature of the contradictory forces. Intellectually Guizot was always trying to stabilize and fix things which were constantly in motion, and it was in fulfilling this function that his "un-French" remoteness from the scene was a source of strength to him. It was this which distinguishes him as a political thinker....

Guizot emphasized the need for politicians to understand the principles and laws on which society was based, to work out a theory of society and a theory of institutions. He believed that politics, like history, could not avoid becoming philosophical, and he was severe in his criticism of those politicians who had but one opinion, which was "to distrust all opinions, to move among them, selecting something from each, taking this to reply to that, and that to reply to this, and thus each day gain some wisdom to suffice for the needs of the moment." As a historian Guizot not only believed that a knowledge of history was desirable insofar as it gratified man's imagination and his desire for knowledge, but he also and more particularly thought of history as having a function to perform in society.... Guizot was not a rationalist, trying to devise institutions by reflection only, or trying to find formulae sufficiently abstract to be accepted by everyone: he thought historically and he sought to write history so as to discover the general and hidden fact which lay enveloped beneath all the external facts.... History ... must make sense....

Guizot's work forms a whole. It is this that explains his long eminence, his "strange preponderance." Possessing as he did great gifts as a writer and orator, his major contribution was to construct an intellectual system around the issues affecting French society. In this way he made himself indispensable, one might almost say unavoidable. He gave a distinction and a sense of purpose to activities which were otherwise without them. Policies which were the day-to-day affairs of an uninspired governing class, could be placed by Guizot in the movement of world history. . . . Whilst foreign affairs were surrounded by an unthinking excitement, Guizot stood apart and insisted on finding a foreign policy appropriate to French interests and resources. . . . It is of course true that he sometimes lost his detachment and forgot that his rôle was to indicate decisions according to principles. Thus between 1840 and 1848 he often allowed himself to be controlled by an uncertain parliamentary majority so as to become inactive and to magnify the difficulties of legislation. During the same period, as minister for Foreign Affairs, he sometimes forgot the principles of policy, because unduly bound up with personalities and, like many French ministers, overnervous of diplomatic movements directed against him. However, since Guizot was primarily distinguished by his intellectual system, it is by this that he should be judged.

It possessed three major weaknesses. Firstly, there was obviously a strain in being an intellectual and a practical man of affairs. Too often the principles which were elucidated were those which were convenient. In France it was evident that the return of the Bourbons and the provision of the Charter had been both largely accidental. If these sources of authority has been established only accidentally, then how could their authority be accepted on principle? A theory of sovereignty had to be worked out. There were two rival schools: there were those who placed it in the people. In practical terms this was the conflict between Louis XVIII returning to France because he was the rightful king, and the Napoleonic Senate claiming that they invited him to accept their constitution. In 1814 this conflict had been avoided rather than resolved and, if it was not to recur, then some theoretical solution had to be found. Guizot was one of those who rejected both theories and who presented a third, stating that sovereignty existed nowhere on earth. He maintained that no one man, no group of men, nor all men together could claim to possess the rightful sovereignty of a state or nation. The only rightful sovereignty was that of justice, truth and reason, and the task of political science was to discover which form of government could best attain this sovereignty. Guizot believed that representative government was the form of government best suited to this task. . . .

As a theory, Guizot's sovereignty of reason was subtle rather than profound and most resembles a form of expertise. It ignored any idea of individual rights; it was a theory of representative government but not a theory of representation; it was a counter-sysytem rather than a system. But, above all, since the best government was the government which governed most justly, government was an affair for experts rather than the product of a particular society. There is thus a distinction between government and society. Guizot himself noted this phenomenon in France, writing in 1852. "There are two Frances, that of the political classes and that of the popular classes. They do not know each other and each acts for itself, without concern for the other." Yet he never seemed to see that such a situation was in keeping with his own theories. In much the same way, Guizot saw the upper middle class as playing a political rôle in the state without reference to its economic interests. . . .

The second major weakness in Guizot's intellectual system was that it was eclectic. . . . He pointed out that with the restoration of the Bourbons, for the first time since 1792 the France of the *ancien régime* and the France of the Revolution could meet in conditions of liberty. He accepted both the past and the present in order that what was good in both the *ancien régime* and the Revolution might be maintained, and what was bad in both be eliminated. The Charter was for Guizot a drawing together of the achievements of history, it was a climax to French development.

This view of affairs enabled Guizot to accept the simultaneous existence of a legitimate monarch, the outstanding characteristic of the *ancien régime*, of a restricted form of parliamentary government, the outstanding feature of the early, constitutional revolution, and of a centralized administrative system which had been perfected under Napoleon. Unlike Royer-Collard, he did not believe that the aristocracy had ceased to exist. After it had in 1815 accepted the loss of its privileges, and in 1830 the fall of the Bourbons, it could still play a vital part in French affairs. . . . As the historian of civilization Guizot believed that the eclectic character of European civilization was its outstanding characteristic; no single element had been dominant, all the principles of social organization had borne fruit, whether theocratic, monarchical, aristocratic or democratic. Rome provided municipal institutions and the idea of law; the Christian church provided moral influence; the German invaders brought with them the modern spirit of liberty as well as the bond between a leader and his followers which became feudalism. Guizot saw this variety of forces as responsible for the distinctive diversity of European civilization. . . . Eclecticism saps any sense of reform or of creation. New developments cannot easily be appreciated; the past obscures the present. Above all, this eclectic strain in Guizot's thought meant that he had no ideal. It was this that young men found most unsatisfying in the July Monarchy. . . .

But perhaps the greatest weakness of Guizot's thought was that, at a time when thought was becoming increasingly social, he based his theories and generalizations concerning human nature upon a hypothetical individual man. This is most clear in his historical work when he stresses the importance of "moral likelihoods" in judging both theories and evidence. . . . Throughout his historical work Guizot assumes that there are certain self-evident truths. He believes that men have a natural tendency to elevate themselves to a sphere superior to their own, that they are shocked by the spectacle of disorder, that they only accept a superior if there is a legitimate reason why this superiority should exist. In his political thought, when he dealt with man's desire to have institutions which linked him to the past or with the individual's approach to sovereignty, in his religious thought, particularly when stressing man's devotion to the supernatural, there are similar, basic assumptions. Even in diplomatic affairs this method of reasoning is evident. Over the Swiss crisis of 1847, for example, Guizot is convinced that the Swiss population would turn away from extremism only when it had experienced civil war, because human nature needed such experience to reinforce its natural tendencies.

Thus at the heart of Guizot's reasoning there is much that is vague and instinctive; he proceeds too readily from assumption to assumption. It is therefore not surprising to find Guizot as baffled as anyone by the spectacle of divided France. . . . And while other public men could afford their moments of incomprehension, Guizot could not. His mission was to understand and to explain; when he failed to do so he had little else to offer. In politics he could do little more than hope that the possessing classes would not be too egotistical and that the poorer classes would not be envious; he had nothing to offer but a warning about pride. In history he could not put forward any satisfactory explanation for change and development. . . .

It can of course be said that to explain Guizot's failure in terms of his intellectual inadequacies, rather than in terms of personal shortcomings, is is only to change the emphasis. He remains a failure. This of course is true, but one might quote Guizot's own remark, made in 1861, "Who, in our time, has not fallen?" he asked. In fairness to Guizot there are certain things which must be added. . . . The difficulties of governing France, like the difficulties of economic development in France, are to be largely explained by a varied social structure and by a historical development which had created new divisions and intensified old ones. In this situation, as Guizot believed, there was no single or self-evident way in which representative government could be organized. It has sometimes been said that there was no essential difference between Guizot and Thiers during the July Monarchy, and the royalist leader, Berryer, later recalled how, in the days of their rivalry, each had "claimed to be playing the same tune differently." Yet in fact there was an essential difference. Whilst Thiers acted from day to day, observing the situation attentively, and always taking every opportunity to increase his support and to make himself more "ministrable," Guizot, as one can see from his speeches and letters, tried to justify his government in terms of principle and to make his leadership an intellectual leadership.

It was during the July Monarchy that France began to resemble a modern state and that the government began to provide the equipment necessary for economic development. In this, the period from 1840 to 1848 is of vital importance, and if one considers the very heavy expenditure incurred by the government in those years, it is ironical to think how they were accused of doing nothing. . . . When one remembers the law of 1833 on primary education, the freedom of the press, the importance and vitality of the parliamentary debates, and the way in which the whole period was alive with intellectual speculation, it seems inappropriate to dismiss the "liberalism" of Guizot as a sham. In foreign policy, whilst the opposition indulged in emotions and struck appealing attitudes, Guizot's policy was always reasonable and usually realistic. When one remembers the excitement caused by French policy at Tahiti, when the British government protested against the expulsion of the Reverend Mr. Pritchard and the French opposition protested against Guizot's supposed subservience to England, one can only agree with Guizot's remark to Brougham, "For war to have come of it, the mad would have had to become the masters or the wise to have become mad." Without going into the wearisome details of the Spanish marriages it would seem that it was Palmerston rather than Guizot who lost his sense of proportion over the affair. Guizot expressed his astonishment that the marriage of the youngest son of the French king to the younger sister of the Spanish queen taking place simultaneously with the marriage of the Spanish queen to a Spanish noblemen, should give rise to indignation in England; he was convinced that there was nothing certain or predictable in Spanish affairs and he saw no reason why the estrangement between England and France should be permanent. The historian shares his astonishment and history confirms his conviction. . . .

Guizot can be compared to many French statesmen. He has some resemblances to Mounier, the old constitutionalist, to de Tocqueville, to Emile Ollivier, and to certain politicians of the Third Republic. Yet it remains true that none of these men, however admirable they were in particular ways, possess anything like the diversity of talents or the consistent determination which were Guizot's. In every respect he was, as Sainte-Beuve put it, "a considerable man of whom there is much to say."

THE ROMANTIC REVOLUTION AND THE INDUSTRIAL REVOLUTION IN FRANCE

Albert J. George

For more than a century scholars and critics have argued over French romanticism. Quantities of ink have flowed in an endless series of analyses of trends, themes, and more particularly, conflicting definitions. The following paper

A. J. George, "The Romantic Revolution and the Industrial Revolution in France," *Symposium*, VI (1952), pp. 281–282, 284–289. © *Symposium*, Syracuse University Press. Used by permission.

... will simply indicate that a number of factors stemming from the Industrial Revolution seem to have materially altered the course of French romanticism. The arrival of the machine age, changes in the technology of printing, the slow spread of education, and the creation of a huge audience of limited literacy, all combined to influence the direction Romanticism would take after 1830.

The Industrial Revolution came slowly to France. In 1800 France still had an economy based on agriculture and commercial capitalism. For at least twenty years more, wars, economic chaos, and depressions like that of '97 kept France behind England. Revolution, the blockade, and the Bourbons, each in its own way stemmed the importation of the new machines and the new ideas.

But Napoleon had unwittingly set the stage for the advent of the Industrial Revolution. Under him manufacturers first realized the profits to be gained from mechanization, and large amounts of capital swelled the coffers of Army suppliers. The Empire saw the introduction of machines like the Douglas, the Ternaux, or the Jacquard. Later, during the Restoration, hand labor even disappeared in some areas, and the number of machines jumped from 15 in 1815 to 625 by 1830. Railroads began to crawl over the nation, and factories sprang up everywhere. The Industrial Revolution would now have hit France explosively except for the three depressions that plagued the Restoration (1816, 1818–19, 1826–27), but by 1830 even the unobservant knew that the old France was fast disappearing.

With the Industrial Revolution came the factors that were to influence literature, some of them the prerequisites for a literature on a mass basis. First it should be noted that France had no factory for the industrial production of ink until Pierre Lorilleux established one at Paris in 1818. More important, paper was made by the age-old process of hand-dipping until Robert invented the paper-making machine in 1798. His apparatus, however, did not operate commercially until 1812, and not until 1833 did France possess enough of them to supply printers with large amounts of cheap paper.

Even had paper existed in quantity, antiquated printing processes limited book production. As late as 1800, publishers used a barely modified Gutenberg press, and the printer's devil still patiently swabbed type. In 1817, Ganal invented the inking roller to speed up the new Stanhope press (1818), then the Clymer (1820). Finally in 1834, Joly contributed the cylindrical press, and printing was ready for mass production.

Meanwhile, the position of the author had changed. The Revolution had killed the patron system, leaving writers completely dependent on the public. Sales became not only a measure of popularity, but of economic stability. An author had to submit manuscripts which a publisher considered salable, manuscripts that would attract large numbers of readers and simultaneously insure further publication and a decent income.

His audience, however, had changed, too. The compact, sophisticated elite of pre-1789 had vanished. What remained of it counted less for the professional writer than the horde of potential buyers whose unpredictable whims could condemn a book. And the literary least common denominator of this mass was low. In 1789 there had been only 72,747 students in the colleges, a fact which agitated the Constituent Assembly, but produced only unimplemented legislation. Napoleon tried to spread secondary schooling and, in turn, the Bourbons encouraged primary education, but the greatest spread of literacy came from the rise of mutual schooling, from the "athénées," the "instituts," and the "musées." 100 of these in 1802 grew to 990 in 1821. The most notable advances occurred within the lower middle class, progress which the July Monarchy encouraged until France attained the highest literacy rate in Europe. More people than ever could read and write, but barely so. In literary terms, if the average Frenchmans' ability to appreciate prose style was low, in poetry it was non-existent. The literary strength of the old regime diminished as it spread through the nation. . . .

From this condition stemmed the embarrassment of the French romanticists. The dynamics of literary revolution required them either to continue their experimentation, or, in turn, to become a second classicism.

And a new factor deepened their embarrassment. By 1830 the advent of the mass audience had changed the national literary taste. People read more than ever, especially the country folk, fed by some 3500 colporteurs, but their taste would have enraged Boileau. They preferred almanacs like the Liégeois or the "Grand Grimoire," editions of which ran into the thousands. Prose tales about Gargantua, Till Eulenspiegel, Collet the bandit, les Quatre fils Aymon, or Richard sans peur enjoyed an unbelievable popularity. . . .

Paris might boast an intellectual elite, but literary France had outgrown its capital. . . . Conservative, resistant to change, the provinces languished in the literary doldrums, far less sophisticated than Paris. . . . Simple prose that told an exciting tale, seemed the recipe for literary success in the provinces, particularly if the story contained elements of realism well within the audience's capacity to understand. The heroine's reputation might teeter on the brink of disaster during a breath-taking struggle but virtue had to triumph over vice.

Such facts were not ignored by publishers. A depression in bookselling that began during the Revolution and lasted through the Restoration, made it imperative for writers to appeal to large audiences in order to interest publishers, for the latter, even more than authors, had sensed the great change in taste. . . .

About this time the Industrial Revolution caught up with printing, providing a means of reaching the new mass audience at low prices, a means that would be applied to prose, not poetry. Furthermore, the Industrial Revolution endowed the writers with a considerable amount of the content for which they had been seeking. Along with the presses and paper-making machines came other factories, and in their wake trailed the more sordid offshoots of the revolution. An industrial proletariat swelled cities, increasing the number of potential readers but also presenting France with apparently insoluble social problems: female and child labor; landless, salaried, and underpaid workers at the mercy of profit-minded owners. Crowded slums vomited forth the underprivileged children of incredible squalor, alcoholism, prostitution, and an alarming rate of illegitimacy, horrible conditions which drove workers to the despair of violence in their first reaction to the new age. Some tried to smash the hated machines, but cooler heads recommended unity, not on the lines of the outmoded "compagnonnages," but of modern unions. Labor strife broke out early, as in the bloody Lyon riots of 1831, and books like Bigot de la Morogue's "De la misère des ouvriers" publicly acknowledged the shameful effects of the factory system.

Thus, about 1830, romanticism possessed artistic freedom, the means to reach a large and expanding audience, and a new material for plots more startling than any of the old horror tales.

At precisely this moment, the unity of romanticism broke over the dangerous question of the acceptance of prose and the new era. Veterans of the early struggle, almost all poets, adjusted their principles to allow themselves a measure of material reward. Most had already dabbled timidly in prose, and they were now prepared to live in uneasy peace with their age. They had established solid reputations and were content to retire from rebellion. Hugo . . . with Musset, Vigny, and Lamartine had begun this literary revolution which they abandoned about 1830. They had smashed a spineless neo-classicism; they had given verse a suppleness long absent; and they had posed the principle of experimentation that would transform the old conception of poetry. Sensing the magnitude of their act, they all loudly proclaimed their virtues. . . .

[But] it remained for another generation, that of the Petit Cénacle, to explore the possibilities of the poetic revolution. These youngsters reached literary maturity during the first days of the era of prose, when a poet not only could not make a living but probably would not even be published. The age belonged to the bourgeoisie triumphant, practical-minded, materialistic in outlook, and devoid of great artistic sensibilities. To young poets the new world looked ugly, scarred by factories, inhabited by a strange class of factory workers, and dominated by what they considered a completely illiterate and money-mad middle-class.

The France of Louis-Philippe made the young men hostile by rejecting their verse and misunderstanding their aims, an attitude which produced bitter hate in the frustrated poets. The doctrine of art for art's sake lay implicit in the romantic revolution; it had been specifically indicated in the "Etudes françaises" and the preface of the "Orientales." . . .

This flight from reality the young men accomplished in their revival of the poetic revolution. . . . It was left primarily to the Petit Cénacle to fulfill the promise of the "Orientales," and to furnish the Symbolists and the Parnassians with the means to create a modern poetry. . . .

The older men, on the contrary, had apparently retreated down the thorny sides of Parnassus. They welcomed the means the Industrial Revolution had given them to reach a mass audience. A Lamartine might never love the people, but he, along with George Sand, Hugo, and many others elected to embrace utilitarianism and the doctrine of the Messiah. The first two entered politics to better social conditions, but others, a Balzac or a Stendhal, worked almost exclusively with the novel. The shift was to prose and with it came the second great accomplishment of romanticism: the creation of the basis of the modern novel. . . .

The romance had hitherto labored under the curse of the classical aestheticians. Prose was a poor relation of poetry and the theater, fit only for the back-stairs maid or to amuse Madame during a very idle moment. But as the new public grew, so did the social and artistic acceptability of the romance. The less sophisticated cared little for the niceties of verse; they had no poetic tradition, and their literary common denominator was low indeed. A few writers would notice this and capitalize on it, a Stendhal or a Balzac. These two especially would consider seriously the genre they preferred and their subsequent revision of ancient practice and theory would result in another prose form: the modern novel. . . .

Their work stemmed from the romance but contained changes of importance which the age itself suggested. Writing for a practical middle class of low intellectual curiosity which had inherited the nineteenth century, these men adjusted their art. A sense of change, born perhaps of the Revolution, gave their work a time-perspective and a sense of development unknown in the romance. Plots might be as exciting as ever, but they were now situated in contemporary or near-contemporary settings known to the reader, a change which transformed local color into realism, the life familiar to the average man. This seemingly unimportant shift inevitably entailed a modification in characters, since these had to match the milieus described. The ordinary citizen replaced more heroic personages and, as these authors manipulated the real and the average, they turned to a study of men and manners. Far more than the romancers, they dealt with personalities as manifest in society. Consequently the fundamental problems of their art changed. Because the point of narration lay within their stories, they had to dissolve ideas into personal relationships, necessitating a shift from single to multi-faceted characters, from allegory to symbol. Plot became subordinate to behavior as writers focussed on character analysis or social results rather than pure action for action's sake, and the need to portray real people in everyday situations forced authors to employ motivations familiar to most readers. The old box-car construction of the romance was replaced by a structure possessing greater unity, less dependent on the use of coincidence as a transition between episodes. The outlines of a new genre appeared atop the vestiges of a traditional genre as the need to show actual life in turn dictated the sequence and importance of episode.

And not only did structure change, so did content. . . . Necessarily, in their descriptions of the age, authors referred more and more to the poor workingman in the crowded slum or the underpaid factory girl, who earned immortality from Daumier and Lamartine. Opposite them stood the greedy factory owner and the harsh boss. A long line of new characters paraded through the pages of the novel: Stendhal's rioting union man, Balzac's stock market manipulators, the newspaper writer, the "Figaro"'s Bohemian bousingo, Gaudissart, the travelling salesman, Nucingen, the spectator, David Séchard, the inventor of a paper-making machine, or even Julien [Sorel], a young man lost in a hostile world.

Around them crystallized a sequence of new themes. Many of these were manipulated according to the political ideas of a writer and, consequently, were treated in either a favorable or unfavorable light. Lamennais' "Le Livre du peuple" in a sense marked the official entry of the people into literature as a major factor, and most all writers followed this example. The factory loomed ever larger as a symbol of the age, of either progress or modern slavery. The machine, particularly the locomotive, and its social effects, became a favorite even in the poetry of a social hermit like Vigny. The plight of the proletariat furnished grist for George Sand's mill, even affected a purist like Gérard de Nerval. The passion for speculation, for forming new enterprises, became a stock theme of Balzac. Occasionally these characters and themes even served as the butt of savage mockery . . . , a fact which confirms a widespread use that became more general as the age of Louis-Philippe matured. No reader thought it strange that romanticism passed from a hedonistic *carpe diem* to Eugène Sue's socialist reforms. Economic nationalism, the evils of the factory system, the theme of the modern dispossessed, and the picture of the restless crowd formed the new artistic clichés. The use of the new themes expanded as the Messianic urge motivated writers more powerfully. The new characters, and what they stood for, made up a noticeable part of the stock in trade which contemporary reform-minded writers employed to make themselves understood by their audience. . . .

That the course of Industrial Revolution and the development of romanticism in France are contiguous is beyond question, and, likewise, the fact that they are inextricably and specifically related seems beyond doubt. Yet, to demonstrate a determinism or a causality in any direction, however enticing, would lead beyond the safety of the facts. Nevertheless, it seems possible to conclude, without teleological implications, that the Industrial

Revolution opened the way for a mass literature, and that the very machines which fashioned that age split romanticism into two factions, one of which continued the poetic revolution which the first generation had begun. To the other it presented new possibilities for artistic expression. It helped focus attention on prose, thereby aiding the shift from the romance to the novel and further contributed to the novelist a new set of characters and themes; to both prose and poetry it gave new and striking images. In short, it seems to have been a major factor in the development of French romanticism.

THE CHANGING OUTLINES OF 1848

PETER AMANN

For over [a century] the French Revolution of 1848 has proved a source of embarrassment to historians. A certain awkwardness clung to early accounts by narrators who had themselves played a part in the Revolution, since their apologies were chiefly concerned with shifting the blame for the demise of the regime. Later generations of republican historians faced other difficulties: committed as they were to the French revolutionary tradition, they found the undeniable failure of 1848 hard to explain without dishonoring the prophets of the tradition or questioning the efficacy of revolution as a means of social change. The Revolution proved little more grateful to conservatives. Beside the Great Revolution, 1848 seems a pale example of Revolutionary violence. It can be ridiculed, but humor is frowned upon in scholarly circles. The best that conservatives could do was to look upon the Second Republic with "hopefulness and sorrow": hope, because France had managed to survive even this crisis; sorrow, because chance and force had prevailed over all "patriotic efforts." At the other end of the political spectrum, the current Marxist-Leninist position is even more uncomfortable. To maintain that the proletarian revolution failed because economic and class conditions had not yet matured, the Communist historian must close his eyes to the fact that France's social evolution in 1848 was probably as "advanced" as Russia's in November 1917. To judge from a random sample of modern European history texts, American historians also tend to face 1848 with ambivalence, which may reflect current United States distaste for revolution on one hand, support of political democracy on the other. . . .

Against the broad background of what some historians have called "the springtime of the peoples," the generosity and selflessness of the French

Peter Amann, "The Changing Outlines of 1848," *American Historical Review*, vol. LXVIII, no. 4 (July 1963), pp. 938–949, 951–953. Copyright by Peter Amann and used by permission.

revolutionary masses have been standard fixtures. Louis Blanc's own description of

one hundred thousand workers, armed from head to foot yet starving, guarded Paris with heroic devotion. The blood-thirsty followers of the red flag who were then in control of the streets made sure that no one would so much as lose a hair. The homes of the rich were guarded by the poor and men in rags stood watch at the doors of those who slandered them . . .

has set the tone, though its rhetoric may make us squirm. In an attenuated form, these sentiments can be found in many of the semipopular accounts inspired by the centenary. I do not want to suggest that this interpretation is pure invention. Once the fighting was over, the victors were good natured enough in contrast to the lynch spirit that had characterized the Parisian populace nearly sixty years earlier after the capture of the Bastille. No revolutionary terror, formal or informal, no September massacres or revolutionary tribunals followed in the wake of the February Days. Postinsurrectionary vandalism was hard on Paris street lights but easy on private property and on persons. Historians like to cite the low crime rate in the spring of 1848 as further evidence of revolutionary self-restraint. It should be noted, however, that Marc Caussidière, the revolutionary police prefect, credited this achievement less to mass idealism than to the efficiency of his improvised police force. The oft-quoted remark by Marche, speaking for the Paris working class in February 1848, offering three more months of misery as the workers' contribution to the Republic, though probably apocryphal, is at least satisfyingly symbolic of the patience and moderation of the revolutionary masses. Yet these same workers, patient where their own interests were concerned, could not contain their generous anger when the cause of Polish liberty seemed at stake in May.

How should this somewhat rosy picture be shaded? Perhaps one might begin by questioning the depth of such international democratic solidarity. It must be remembered that 1848 marked the renewal of severe economic crisis accentuated by the February Days themselves. In the midst of widespread unemployment arose a strong nativist reaction against foreign workers who were pre-empting "French jobs." . . . The "liberation armies," composed of German, Italian, and Belgian residents in France and organized on French soil, were encouraged by the authorities less for motives of international solidarity than because this armed exodus rid the country of an unwanted labor force of aliens. In Rouen news of the Parisian revolution had set off working-class demonstrations with cries of "Long live the Republic! Down with the English!" The subsequent mass expulsion of English skilled workers and technicians from the Rouen area occasioned indignant if ineffectual outcries in the British Parliament. While the expulsion of the English eliminated an industrial aristocracy of the Norman textile industry and the French railroads, the agitation against the unskilled Flemings who occupied the lowest rung of the economic ladder in the department of Nord was no less vocal, even though in this instance mass deportations were avoided. . . . In sum, virulent xenophobia, feeding on economic insecurity, was more characteristic of the urban masses than was any sentiment of international fraternity.

A second modification must be made in the overidealization of the *peuple* by considering the widespread popular outbreaks against the nascent machine age, outbreaks that may have surpassed the scope of the earlier and much better-known Luddite riots in England. At least three forms of this industrial sabotage . . . were by-products of the French Revolution of 1848: in Paris bands of unemployed printers smashed the mechanical printing presses on which they blamed their plight, demanding the reintroduction of hand presses. After several days of machine breaking, organized printing workers took the lead in putting a stop to the movement. Secondly, on a much vaster scale, the recently built railway lines radiating from Paris came under attack by mobs led by teamsters, innkeepers, and others whose livelihood the railroads had endangered. While the violence was particularly widespread in the Paris outskirts, it expanded along the two major lines to Normandy and the Belgian frontier and was marked by burning railroad trestles and station houses. Thirdly, in a number of textile centers stretching from Normandy to Champagne, factory workers, probably encouraged by the owners of obsolete workshops, broke up power machinery and in some cases set the mills on fire. . . .

. . . The Revolution of 1848 was more than a fraternal banquet: it unleashed a wave of violence that sought to redress social grievances which had nothing to do with revolutionary ideology. It would indeed have been astounding if, after two years of bread shortage and unemployment, the "people" had really played the role of plaster saints *en blouse* assigned to them by republican mythology.

Much has been made of the ineffectiveness of the revolutionary leaders of 1848, their imitativeness, their verbosity, their bombast. . . . No doubt the revolutionaries of 1848 did fail, and perhaps . . . harsh words are fully justified. One may speculate, however, whether those revolutionaries who were carried away on the night of August 4, 1789, or the Bolsheviks who began their governmental career by abolishing the death penalty were any less "messianic" . . . than the leaders of 1848. Perhaps the difference between these eighteenth- and twentieth-century romantic idealists on one hand, and the "forty-eighters" on the other, was that the former were given an opportunity to learn through experience, whereas in 1848 such opportunity was cut short by the disaster of the June insurrection.

Even were we to admit the romantic incapacity of the revolutionary leadership, the militant rank and file of revolution cannot be accused of romanticism. Gustave Flaubert, who had made a point of going to Paris on February 23 in order to study the Revolution "in its artistic aspect," has left us some brilliant satirical pages in his *Sentimental Education*. . . . It is difficult to view the revolutionary club movement in Paris on any but the novelist's terms: mild pandemonium, a touch of pathos, and total lunacy. . . .

The political clubs sought to fill three not always compatible roles. First, through lectures, speeches, and discussion they sought to indoctrinate a semi-literate electorate in the traditions of the republican movement. . . . Secondly, the clubs inherited the ideal of direct democracy through popular pressure from the *sociétés populaires* of the Great Revolution. Finally, and this was by far their most time-absorbing activity, the clubs turned themselves into electoral and party machines that would give direction to the 300,000 Parisian voters in particular and the 10,000,000 French voters in general who had been turned loose without direction, organization, or political experience. . . .

Contrary to historical folklore, most clubs went much too far in being down to earth: the minutes are filled with eternal discussion of the registration and enrollment of National Guards, with voter registration and voting procedures, with the scrutiny and nomination of officer candidates to the National Guard and to the Constituent Assembly elections. Indeed, to such an extent did many clubs come to function like Democratic ward clubs, that upon the heels of the national elections interest of members dwindled, and many of the Parisian political clubs seen to have disappeared altogether. In short, even if the indictment of the revolutionary leadership as impractically romantic may be valid, among the lower echelons of the club movement an excessive preoccupation with narrowly practical politics was much more characteristic.

A third major thesis . . . views the Revolution of 1848 as a case study of the kind of bourgeois-proletarian class struggle that Karl Marx had envisaged in the *Communist Manifesto* and indeed spelled out in *The Class Struggles in France (1848–1850)*: "If . . . the French proletariat, at the moment of a revolution, possesses in Paris actual power and influence which spur it on to drive beyond its means, in the rest of France it is crowded into single, scattered industrial centres. . . ." Here again is a generalization that cannot be simply dismissed. It is true, for example, that the provisional government, save for the two outsiders Louis Blanc and Alexandre Martin, better known by his *nom de guerre* Albert, was composed of politicians very conscious indeed of bourgeois values and aspirations. It is also true that most of the short-lived reforms benefiting the working classes that were made into law in the first months after the February Revolution were imposed upon the government by popular pressures. It may further be argued that the savage repression of the June insurgents reflected the inflexibility of an entrenched middle class toward lower-class demands. It is not surprising that twentieth-century historians have concluded that "in the social turmoil appeared the first features of modern Marxism.". . . .

. . . A proletariat of factory workers certainly did exist in French textile centers such as Rouen-Elbeuf in Normandy, the Lille-Roubaix-Tourcoing complex in northern France, the mill towns of Alsace, and the silk center of Lyons. Paris, however, was in 1848 dominated, not by large-scale mechanized industry, but by craft workshops to the point where the ratio of employer to workers was about one to five. The survey undertaken in 1848 under the auspices of the Paris Chamber of Commerce indicates that, though the city contained some modern mechanized enterprises including railroad repair shops, most of its labor force was to be found in traditional occupations such as cabinetmaking or in the completely non-mechanized building trades. Whatever class conflicts may have existed in Paris, they were unlikely to focus on the struggle of the relatively insignificant capitalist employers against their proletarian employees. . . .

Upon closer inspection, even the traditional symbol of class dichotomy, the insurrection of June 1848, dissolves into a conflict of bewildering complexity. Rémi Gossez . . . has shown that though manual workers were predominant on the side of the insurgents, the part played by retail merchants, foremen, small employers, cabaret keepers, and so forth, was not inconsiderable. The insurrectionists also included large contingents of the *Lumpenproletariat*, to use the Marxist terminology, which according to all the rules should have been a counterrevolutionary vanguard. On the other side of the barricades among the forces of order, though shopkeepers, white-collar workers, professional men, and intellectuals predominated in the ranks of the National Guard, a very substantial minority of manual workers was also to be found there. Factory and workshop owner-managers were inconspicuous on either side; they were more intent on standing guard over their establishments than on serving in the ranks. In Gossez's view, tension between worker and shopkeeper, tenant and landlord, the reciprocal hostility of peasant soldier and city dweller of peasant origin, as well as purely personal vendettas, distorted any "classical" pattern of class struggle. . . .

I take issue, finally, with a fourth generalization which views the Revolution of 1848 as a strictly urban and chiefly Parisian phenomenon—in sharp contrast to the revolutionary linkage of city and countryside in 1789. On one level this interpretation cannot be challenged: while there had been rural disorders for some time, the July Monarchy was toppled, not by grain riots in the countryside, but by revolutionary action in the streets of the capital. . . .

The Second Republic saw . . . at least three distinguishable waves of agrarian revolution. While these never reached the scope of the great fear of 1789, they were substantial movements which, taken as a block, constitute

the last *Jacquerie* in France. . . . In contrast to 1789, however, no synchroniza-
tion of the agrarian with the Parisian revolution was ever achieved.

The first of these agrarian movements paralleled the assault on the
railroads and on the powers looms, a desperate last sally by economic groups
that were being by-passed. In rural terms this was the last stand of the poorer,
economically backward regions of peasant France—the Alpine departments,
the departments of the Massif Central and those of the Pyrenees, together
with some adjacent areas—reacting to the pressure of population, the weight
of indebtedness, the disintegration of collective property and communal
privileges, the collapse of cottage industry in the general economic depression. The news of the fall of the monarchy set off widespread attempts to
regain collective rights of which peasants had been deprived since the Revolution of 1789. Particularly in the departments of the Pyrenees whole villages
rose up in arms against administration of the Forest Codes of 1827 and 1837
which had deprived them of customary cutting rights dating back, in some
cases, to the thirteenth century. In a number of areas these risings soon
turned against the local moneylenders, which in Alsace meant large-scale
anti-Semitic outbreaks. Both the erosion of communal rights and the dependence on the usurer were peasant problems that predated the Revolution of
1848. The February Days merely roused false hopes of direct redress of these
grievances, hopes deceived by the appearance of mobile columns of regulars,
sent in the name of the Republic.

Peasant reaction to the imposition of the 45 per cent surtax by the republican regime in Paris is more widely known. This second wave of peasant
outbreaks beginning in March 1848 was directly related to the political
decisions in the national capital. Resistance developed in those regions least
able to pay, that is, in the same area where the first wave of violence had
barely subsided. The same mobile columns that had repressed the initial agrarian movement were now turned to the collection of the new land tax. The
scope of this military operation in the French countryside should not be
underestimated: about fifty thousand regulars were involved, a larger
number of army personnel than was at General Louis Eugène Cavaignac's
disposal in suppressing the June insurrection in Paris. . . .

Throughout the same backward areas of southeastern, central, and
southwestern France that had seen the two earlier waves of agrarian outbreaks in 1848, a political radicalization of the peasantry took place in
1849. . . . In 1848 political radicalism had been an urban phenomenon. The
June insurrection disillusioned its urban supporters with the Republic. The
"demo-socs" of 1849, despite superficial resemblance to the radicals of 1848,
appealed instead to a peasant clientele in terms of peasant needs, chiefly
cheap credit. Most of the eighteen departments in which they gained a clear
majority, and the twenty-three others where they garnered more than 40 per
cent of the vote, were agricultural departments of the southeast, center, and

southwest. Peasant radicalism died hard: the 25,000–30,000 peasants of the Alpine departments who resisted Louis Napoleon's *coup d'état* by force of arms did so, not in support of an alien constitution, but in behalf of a revolutionary peasant republic in the making. . . .

Any tenable explanation of 1848 must take into account the confluence of several distinct trends in nineteenth-century French society, some of which have not attracted historians' attention until recent years: the industrialization of the country; the pressure of a rising population; the economic depression of the 1840's; the French revolutionary tradition itself.

Economic historians are agreed that by 1848 France had built up substantial industry of the British type behind the tariff walls of the post-Napoleonic regimes. Up to the middle of the century, however, industrialization had merely raised new problems without solving old ones. Contemporaries tended to deplore conditions in the new mill towns . . . though they might differ on remedies or prospects for the future. At the same time the new industrialization, particularly in textiles, had seriously undercut the cottage industries which had traditionally supplemented the incomes of large sections of the peasantry. As late as 1848 industrialization had not yet reached the "take-off" point . . . and was unable to absorb the growing rural overpopulation.

In spite of all that has been said about the laggard nineteenth-century French birth rate, this rate produced a steady population growth between 1750 and 1850. This increase, by wiping out the material gains realized by the peasants from the Great Revolution, sharpened a universal land hunger. In the "underdeveloped" southwestern department of Ariège, for instance, a population density of fifty persons per square kilometer prevailed in 1846 as compared to a mere twenty a hundred years later when the department was still largely agricultural and forest land.

These problems of industrialization and population growth were underlined and accentuated by what French economic historians deem to have been the last great economic depression of the preindustrial type (characteristically beginning with a crop failure and only gradually spreading to industry) which after the 1848 Revolution turned into the first modern depression, paralyzing commerce and industry by a crisis of confidence and hence of credit. In dealing the deathblow to cottage industry and thus to the prosperity of the countryside, the economic crisis of 1846–1850 forced the large-scale internal migrations that helped to set the stage for the economic "take-off" of the 1850's.

In 1848, however, any solution still lay in the future. In the face of fundamental problems brought on by industrialization and population growth and heightened by economic crisis, the French revolutionary tradition provided little constructive insight. Its basic doctrines, fashioned in the successful struggle against the hierarchical society of the eighteenth century, had been only superficially refurbished to meet the novel problems of the nineteenth century. Post-Napoleonic attempts to readapt the doctrine lacked analytical acumen, precision, and, above all, universal acceptance. The great common core of the tradition in 1848, its faith in political equality, was no answer to the problems of the new age. A determinist might maintain that among available French ideologies only Bonapartism provided the kind of dynamic pragmatism that this crisis called for, even though this may be the wisdom of hindsight or excessive charity on the part of historians in awarding to Louis Napoleon full credit for French economic growth.

In 1848 France faced critical social problems that became closely linked in the depression following 1845. While these problems, though but dimly perceived as a general malaise by contemporaries, helped to create the revolutionary situation in mid-nineteenth-century France, the Revolution itself, drawing on a largely irrelevant tradition, was unable to provide an adequate solution. . . .

THE NAPOLEONIC LEGEND IN FRANCE IN 1848

André-Jean Tudesq

In Europe national feeling has very often been expressed through hero worship. In mid-nineteenth-century France, the "great man" was first and foremost a military leader, and national feeling still identified itself with the warrior ideal. The growth and glorification of the figure of Napoleon was the product of the collective French imagination, and represents an idealization of the martial life, one which had already developed under the Old Regime, or even by the end of the French Middle Ages, around the names of Joan of Arc, Duguesclin, and Bayard.

The attitude that many adopted toward Napoleon and the treaties of 1815—though they did not attempt to translate it into action—appeared in 1848 as the best measure of French national feeling, whose symbol and most popular expression was the cult of the Emperor, the memory of Napoleon.

The profound influence of the Napoleonic legend on the constitutional development of the Second Republic would reveal its importance in the ideological and emotional behavior of the nation. The popular view of events appears, in this instance, more important as a source of feeling and action than does the hard reality of the facts. . . . This study will first analyze

A. Tudesq, "La Légende Napoléonienne en France en 1848," *Revue Historique*, LXXXI (juillet–septembre, 1957), pp. 64–65, 67–73, 75–76, 78–80, 82–85. Copyright by Presses Universitaires de France, 1957. Used by permission. Editors' translation.

what the memory of Napoleon represented in the mind and thought of the men of 1848, as well as its most important manifestations. From these observations it will seek to determine how Napoleonic ideology, or ideologies, took shape. Finally, it will attempt to describe the geographical diffusion and social differentiation of the Napoleonic legend in 1848.

The memory of Napoleon had persisted and the Napoleonic Legend had spread under the July Monarchy, especially after 1840. In 1848 Napoleon appeared to some as the heir and representative of the first Revolution, and most saw in him the incarnation of the national genius. He also represented the tradition and guarantee of the principle of order.

To the men of 1848 Napoleon seemed the heir of the Revolution because he symbolized the least discussed aspect of that period—foreign policy. A phrase of Napoleon's uttered on St. Helena was frequently quoted . . .: "In fifty years, Europe will be either republican or Cossack." Popular logic deduced that Napoleon, the enemy of the "Cossacks," was therefore a republican. But the terms "Republic" and "Revolution" were synonymous in the minds of the men of 1848. . . . Napoleon appeared as the man of the Revolution because his adversaries were the counterrevolutionaries, especially in 1815. . . . So, during the February Days, the two cries, "Long live the Republic, long live Napoleon," were heard, and on February 22, some thousand individuals parading from the Panthéon to the Madeleine passed before the Vendôme column and shouted "Long live Reform, long live Napoleon." On the 23rd and 24th, the workers assembled in the Place de Grève acclaimed the Republic and Napoleon in the same breath. During the June Days, the rebels in the Place Saint-Sulpice added "Long live Napoleon" to their shouts of "Long live Barbès." . . .

Napoleon was hailed as a national hero not only because was a soldier of the Revolution, but also because his victories and the mastery—even if it was temporary—that he gave France in Europe satisfied national pride and the desire for glory. Even the progressive bourgeoisie, which was generally cool to the imperial cult, saw this side of him. Ledru-Rollin's secretary, Alfred Delvau, wrote: "Napoleon, the nemesis of kings, made France great; Louis-Philippe made it little."

This recognition of him as the national hero had been confirmed by the return of Napoleon's ashes in 1840. It was reconfirmed in 1848 when at the end of May, the problem of admitting the descendents of Bonaparte to the political assemblies was debated. The remarks of the Minister of Justice, Crémieux, were applauded by the Assembly: "The glory of Napoleon," he said, "belongs to France . . . and we gladly accept what is popular in this glory. . . . The fame of Napoleon remains one of the great memories of the history of a people and covers it with an immortal brilliance."

In that same debate, continued on June 2, Piétri, the representative who had proposed that the proscription of the Bonapartes be ended, declared that "the great imperial era recalls not a throne but the power and greatness of France." The martial spirit and military glory appear to be the national ideal that governing classes tried to inculcate into the masses. . . . Military glory was thought to purify the nation and could even excuse despotism. Thus, referring to the Empire in his declaration to the voters of the Aude Department in April, 1848, Dezarnaud . . . declared: "It was a glorious despotism . . . that the greatest man of the age made understandable, even without excusing it. He at least loved France for itself, though he oppressed it." Not everyone had such reservations, and Garnier-Pagès recognized and deplored the fact when he wrote in his *History of the Revolution of 1848* that "the peasants and ignorant workers recall only the glory they helped achieve and pay for; and the amputated limbs of their fathers are only marks of conquests and valor." In their electoral declarations many candidates recalled either that their fathers had fought in the imperial armies or that they themselves had been soldiers of Napoleon. Generally it was the armies of 1815 and the time of defeat that were evoked with the greatest fervor, perhaps because national feeling was stimulated by defeat. . . .

But in addition to the popular view of Napoleon as the "Little Corporal" or soldier of the Revolution, there was another aspect of the Emperor in 1848, that of the man of French tradition and order. This was largely the result of written works, beginning with those of Napoleon himself, which sought to give their readers the interpretation he himself wanted drawn from the facts available. Thus emerged the figure of a Napoleon who was linked to the French monarchical tradition. For example, Duvergier de Hauranne, studying centralization in France, could write that "it was not simply the work of the Empire, but the work of centuries, begun by Richelieu, continued by Colbert and Turgot, and completed by the Revolution and Empire." . . .

Finally, another factor drew the men of order to the memory of Napoleon, and it seemed most important to them—the name Napoleon meant the restoration of internal peace. [Robert-Antoine de] Beauterne wrote that . . . "what remains of the order reestablished by the Empire is still what for the moment protects us against anarchy." But this same opinion was expressed by Voltairians and bourgeois republicans. Thus, in 1848 Jules Favre could justify his adherence to the candidacy of Louis-Napoleon Bonaparte by saying that, "in preferring Monsieur Bonaparte to his opponent, I feel that the prestige and popularity of this great name would greatly serve to consolidate the Republic by conciliating the parties.". . .

The presence and intensity of the Napoleonic feeling shown in various guises has been shown, but how did this sentiment, this memory remain alive and strong until 1848, when Napoleon had been gone from France for 33 years and dead for 27? . . . Of the writings that contributed most, if not to create then at least to perpetuate the Napoleonic legend, foremost were the *Memoirs*. In his *Memoirs* dictated on St. Helena, the Emperor knowingly distorted the truth on many points in order to make his own viewpoint and interpretation of the facts prevail in future generations. After his death, there were numerous editions of his works, a sign that they were indeed in demand. Though the exact number of copies printed is unknown, the chronology of editions either of complete works or of selections can be traced. Among the latter the most common was the last will of Napoleon, and in this document could be found the request that Louis-Philippe would carry out in a grandiose way: "I desire . . . that my ashes rest on the banks of the Seine among the French people whom I so greatly loved." It also contained a profession of faith: "I die in the Apostolic and Roman religion into which I was born." Between 1821 and 1833, fifteen editions of the will alone were printed. . . .

But the works of his companions on St. Helena also won popular success. There were six editions of the *Memorial of St. Helena* of Las Cases between 1823 and 1842, not to mention selections, making it one of the best sellers in the first half of the nineteenth century. During the Restoration, the publication of memoirs or war experiences by men of the imperial era won liberal public opinion—which he had betrayed in his lifetime—over to the memory of Napoleon. . . . Historians and apologists added their own special note by identifying their persons with that of the Emperor. In the case of Napoleon it might be said that history was born only after legend, and Hippolyte Castille, in a book written in 1852, could state: "Napoleon grew from year to year. History moves slowly—it is more the the work of time than of the historian. . . . The history of Napoleon is the history of all France, and like Caesar's, it is the history of a people." . . .

Romanticism helped to spread the Napoleonic legend. The Emperor became one of the patriotic themes of the epic literature reviving in the nineteenth century. Casimir Delavigne and the two poets from Marseilles, Barthélemy and Méry, accustomed the bourgeoisie and middle classes to hearing the Imperial era celebrated, but it was Victor Hugo above all who was carried away by his enthusiasm for Napoleon, and to such a point that his imagination led him to believe he was destined to complete the work of Napoleon. However, his readers and admirers then formed a very socially limited public, and in 1848 he appeared as a conservative, suspect to Parisian republicans.

The principal written source of the Napoleonic legend was song, generally transmitted by word of mouth. Here one name stands out, that of Béranger. In 1848 Béranger, in what may seem a surprising estimate, was considered the best French poet of his day. He owed must of his fame to the songs he devoted to what he called "the greatest poet of modern times, Napoleon." The influence of Béranger in the development of the Napoleonic legend would be a study in itself, but suffice it to say that his songs, as well as the prints of Charlet and Raffet . . . popularized the figure of the Little Corporal throughout France, even more than did the works of Balzac, Hugo, or the battle paintings of Horace Vernet or Charles Langlois.

These songs and prints penetrated the lower classes of the nation only to the degree that an echo had already been awakened in the popular mind. Popular legend had preceded the poets. Oral tradition strengthened the imperial cult within families and at school, so that living memories explain the persistence of the imperial cult better than the written sources do.

There were few families which did not have former soldiers of the Imperial army in them. This is attested by an author who had little sympathy for it, Garnier-Pagès, who wrote that in 1848 the name of Napoleon "was strongest in the hearts of old soldiers who had retired to their homes, and who spread and strengthened it through legendary tales." . . .

[So], the most important popular source was the living memory which made the man of 1848 a participant in the imperial epic. Active service in in Napoleonic campaigns, especially in the voluntary levies of 1814 and 1815, were often mentioned in the declarations of candidates in the elections of 1848. . . . The two principal themes were the man's presence at the side of the Emperor, and his struggle against invasion and abandonment of the army when Napoleon ceased to be its leader. General Higonet, a candidate in the Cantal Department, declared: "As a volunteer at the camp of Boulogne, I took part in the great battles of the Empire with the Emperor." General Rullière in the Haute-Loire Department stated: "I began my career as a grenadier in the Imperial Guard, and on the day of Wagram, the Emperor named me adjutant-major of the Young Guard." . . . Recollections of 1815 remained in the minds of the generation that lived through that period . . . and were associated with the memory of Napoleon in the collective mentality. Those alive in 1815 helped create the legend by the stories they told to their families, at school and in cafés.

But other events encouraged the Napoleonic legend in the years just before 1848. The pacific government of Louis-Philippe apparently favored a rebirth of enthusiasm for Napoleon because it considered this an outlet for the warlike French imagination. Thus the bourgeoisie which in 1830 had used the memory of Napoleon to fight the Ultras and to raise the people of Paris against Charles X, employed the posthumous glorification of the Emperor against the party of the counterrevolution. But we may also wonder if it did not also use the imperial cult—which it consciously adopted—to divert popular feeling from social demands.

The completion of the Arch of Triumph in Paris, the creation of a Napoleon Museum at Versailles, and the reinstallation of Napoleon's statue atop the Vendôme column on July 28, 1833, were so many events that perpetuated the memory of the Emperor. But most important was the return of his ashes from St. Helena—which they brought to the Invalides by a son of Louis-Philippe in 1840. . . .

. . . Ernest Legouvé . . . recalled in his *Last Memoirs*, that "those who saw that day will never forget it. . . . Everywhere along the route there was a vast crowd lining the highway and greeting each forward step of the advancing funeral procession with enthusiastic shouts." Balzac estimated the throng gathered on the Champs Elysées at 8,000 persons. . . .

These manifestations of the Napoleonic legend, this persistence of the imperial cult may be considered relevant facts or examples, but not capable of true analysis. Yet there is also evidence of a statistical kind—the partial elections of June 4 and the Presidential elections of December 10, 1848. To be sure, the partisans of Prince Louis-Napoleon Bonaparte were not all admirers of the imperial regime, and many of his opponents invoked the memory of Napoleon I against his nephew. But the political reasons that motivated the candidacy of a Bonaparte need not be discussed here; what is important is the impact this candidacy had on the people and the mass of the country, which voted for a candidate simply because he bore the name of Napoleon I. . . . The geographical and social diffusion of the Napoleonic legend may be seen from the distribution of the votes in the election of December 10. . . .

First, it must be observed that the regions that voted least for Louis-Napoleon Bonaparte were those where the Legitimists had retained their greatest influence, where the royalists had held out longest during the First Republic, and where the White Terror had been fiercest in 1815—Brittany, Provence, and Lower Languedoc. Still, this explanation is not enough, for the Chouan country of Vendée and Charente voted *en masse* for Bonaparte. . . .

. . . His heaviest vote came from central and west central France, from Charente-Inférieure to Puy-de-Dome, from Dordogne to Indre-et-Loire, from the north of the Paris Basin and from the southeast of the same Basin. More revealing were the almost spontaneous by-elections of June 4, 1848, which showed the great persistence of the imperial cult in the Yonne and Charente-Inférieure Departments. . . . Economic as well as emotional or ideological considerations need to be considered in explaining the particular spread of the Napoleonic legend.

The imperial cult remained strong among the peasantry because the Napoleonic era had been a period of rising prices for them, one that ended in 1817, almost simultaneously with the Empire, and so the Restoration coincided with a decrease in the profits of the rural classes. . . . At Paris, in June, 1848, Napoleonic enthusiasm was greatest in the working class areas. . . .

The republican bourgeoisie does not seem to have followed its troops under the July Monarchy in their admiration for the Emperor. In a work on France and her destiny published shortly before the February Revolution, Henri Martin wrote that "Napoleon misunderstood the nature of his mission because he misunderstood the genius of modern times and the progress of the human mind." Criticizing the idea of Empire, he went on to say "Here again is that idea which has so often frustrated the destinies of Europe." The same thought can be found among the republicans of the *National*— used, it is true, against the candidacy of Louis-Napoleon Bonaparte. Thus, for example, in an article that appeared on November 6, 1848, the policy of Bonaparte was raked over the coals in this way: "What does the name mean? In foreign policy it means conquests, the coalition of Europe, in a word, war with all its risks, including the ruin of industry and trade. . . . Moreover, the name bequeathed his descendants by the Emperor recalls the cruelest attacks on liberty. This name, taken in the sense that history gives it, is the very denial of all the progress we have achieved and of all our liberties." The radical position, expressed by the newspaper *Réforme*, also proved no partisan of the imperial regime. Its issue of May 27 eulogized the men "who had not acted under the Empire, believing that glory could not be used to pay the funeral expenses of liberty." Finally, the third social group which showed little enthusiasm for Napoleon was composed of educated workers, primarily craftsmen, who were concerned with political questions. On June, 19, Proudhon's newspaper, the *Représentant du Peuple*, printed a poem written in December, 1840, and never before published, entitled "Return of the Ashes of Napoleon Bonaparte, Emperor." It was accompanied by a preface that read: "Above all, the ignorant and credulous crowd must be saved from the consequences of its mad enthusiasm, put on guard against deceptive advice, and shown that the democratic principles of all humanity have never had more implacable enemies than the Corsican of bloody memory." . . .

[But] on the whole, the conclusion can be drawn from the elections of December, 1848, that the majority of Frenchmen took part in the imperial cult. . . . Thus the Napoleonic legend appears as the most popular expression of national feeling. It stemmed from the conjunction of a simple, abstract idea—national glory—and an overly common emotional condition, which awoke different reactions in individual consciences. So as classes, generations, ages, and tempers differed, they saw an ambiguous meaning in the name "Napoleon," one that part of the bourgeoisie—and not the least part—used to stir public opinion.

The memories of the imperial *grognard* wore down the old prejudices toward the military when the military became a protector of the internal order. Beginning in 1848, the Right would gradually rally to the army, a change due in part to the Napoleonic legend. But in 1848 we reach the end of the Napoleonic legend as an expression of national feeling. From then on, Bonapartism as a mixture of revolution and counterrevolution, or rather as a counterrevolutionary ideology, would be born, one that could develop only after a revolution. . . .

SUGGESTIONS FOR FURTHER READING

Bibliographical: PETER AMANN, "Recent Writings on the Second French Republic," *Journal of Modern History*, XXXIV (1962), 409–429; General: PAUL H. BEIK, *Louis Philippe and the July Monarchy* (Princeton, 1965); PIERRE DE LA GORCE, *Louis-Philippe* (Paris, 1931); S. CHARLÉTY, *La Monarchie de juillet*, vol. V of ERNEST LAVISSE (ed.), *Histoire de France contemporaine* (Paris, 1921); PAUL THUREAU-DANGIN, *Histoire de la Monarchie de juillet*, 7 vol. (Paris, 1884–92); PHILIPPE VIGIER, *La Monarchie de juillet* (Paris, 1962); JEAN DAUTRY, *1848 et la IIe République* (2nd ed.; Paris, 1957); Special: SHERMAN KENT, *Electoral Procedure under Louis Philippe* (New Haven, 1937); JOHN J. BAUGHMAN, "Financial Resources of Louis Philippe," *French Historical Studies*, IV (1965), 63–83; CHARLES H. POUTHAS, "Les Ministères de Louis-Philippe," *Revue d'histoire moderne et contemporaine*, I (1954), 102–130; IRENE COLLINS, "The Government and the Press in France during the Reign of Louis-Philippe," *English Historical Review*, LXIX (1954), 262–282; ARTHUR L. DUNHAM, *The Industrial Revolution in France, 1815–1848* (New York, 1955); ADELINE DAUMARD, *La Bourgeoisie parisienne de 1815 à 1848* (Paris, 1963); LOUIS CHEVALIER, *Classes laborieuses et classes dangereuses à Paris pendant la première moitié du XIXe siècle* (Paris, 1958); JOHN J. BAUGHMAN, "The French Banquet Campaign of 1847–48," *Journal of Modern History*, XXXI (1959), 1–15; GEORGES DUVEAU, *1848: The Making of a Revolution* (New York, 1967); PRISCILLA ROBERTSON, *Revolutions of 1848: A Social History* (Princeton, 1952); ALEXIS DE TOCQUEVILLE, *Recollections* (New York, 1959); *Congrès historique du centenaire de la Révolution de 1848, Paris, 1948* (Paris, 1948); ALBERT CRÉMIEUX, *La Révolution de février* (Paris, 1912); PAUL BASTID, *Doctrines et institutions politiques de la Seconde République*, 2 vol. (Paris, 1945); JEAN LUCAS-DUBRETON, *Le Culte de Napoléon, 1815–1848* (Paris, 1960); ANDRÉ-JEAN TUDESQ, *L'Election présidentialle de Louis–Napoléon Bonaparte* (Paris, 1965); DONALD C. MCKAY, *The National Workshops* (Cambridge, Mass., 1933; reprinted, 1961); PIERRE MARTINO, *L'Epoque romantique en France, 1850–1830* (Paris, 1945); PIERRE MOREAU, *Le Romantisme* (Paris, 1932; reprinted, 1957); JEAN RENÉ DERRÉ, *Lamennais, ses amis et le mouvement des idées à l'époque romantique, 1824–1834* (Paris, 1962); ROGER PICARD, *Le Romantisme social* (New York and Paris, 1944); DAVID O. EVANS, *Le Socialisme romantique, Pierre Leroux et ses contemporains* (Paris, 1948); ALBERT J. GEORGE, *The Development of French Romanticism; The Impact of the Industrial Revolution on Literature* (Syracuse, N.Y., 1955); Biographical: CHARLES ALMERAS, *Odilon Barrot, avocat et homme politique* (Paris, 1950); DOUGLAS JOHNSON, *Guizot: Aspects of French History, 1787–1874* (London and Toronto, 1963); T. E. B. HOWARTH, *Citizen-King, The Life of Louis-Philippe, King of the French* (London, 1961); JOHN ALLISON, *Monsieur Thiers* (New York, 1932); EDWARD GARGAN, *Alexis de Tocqueville: The Critical Years, 1848–1851* (Washington, 1955).

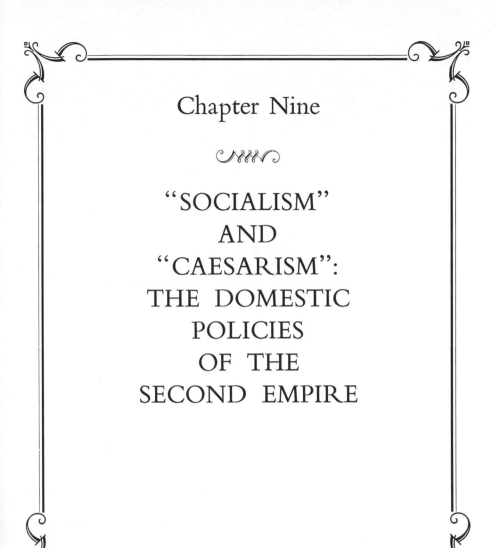

Chapter Nine

"SOCIALISM"
AND
"CAESARISM":
THE DOMESTIC
POLICIES
OF THE
SECOND EMPIRE

THE MOST VARIED judgments have been made about Louis-Napoleon Bonaparte, who governed France first as President of the Republic, then, from 1852 to 1870, as Napoleon III, Emperor of the French. He has not lacked detractors, from Victor Hugo, who dubbed him "Napoleon the Little," to the English historian, Sir Lewis Namier, who used the epithet the "first mountebank dictator." But he has also attracted admirers, from the scientist Louis Pasteur, who remarked that his reign would "remain among the most glorious in our history," to the French historian Albert Guérard, who praised him for his "unfailing gentleness. . . . quiet intellectual courage [and] profound generosity." The cause of these diverse assessments lies in the contradictions within the man himself—his desire for power and his distaste for violence, his "socialism" in economic and social affairs and his "Caesarism" in politics, and the imagination and daring of his schemes and the conspiratorial way he put them into effect. The perplexed reader can only echo the desire of Napoleon III's cousin Mathilde, who declared that she would have liked to "break open his head to find out what was inside."

In domestic affairs, as Georges Pradalié shows in the opening selection, the Second Empire marked a sharp break with the past. During this period France began to be transformed from a still predominantly agricultural country into a modern industrial power. This radical transformation of her finance, transportation, trade, and industry, the author demonstrates, was due to the initiative of the Emperor and his circle. A "socialist," as he described himself, or a "Saint-Simon on horseback," as he has often been called, Napoleon III forced the country to modernize its traditional economic structure by expanding credit, building railways, lowering tariff barriers, and stimulating productivity. But it must be noted that his economic liberalism, notably the free trade agreement with England in 1860, alienated the protectionist support he had previously enjoyed.

Nor did Napoleon III's social and economic policies have their desired effect. Always concerned with improving the lot of the working class while seeking to keep it politically docile, the Emperor, by fits and starts, launched a program for the physical and moral improvement of the worker. The Dutch scholar Hendrik Boon analyzes these policies and their weaknesses in the second selection. He shows both the aims of the Emperor and the devious way in which he sought to put them into effect, as well as the lack of gratitude that a maturing working class displayed toward its benefactor. More than concessions, the workers wanted to be able to run their own affairs, a fact the Emperor did not quite grasp.

An era of great economic and social change, the Second Empire also had a profound significance for the constitutional history of France. In the third selection, the French political scientist Marcel Prélot traces how the regime gradually evolved from the authoritarian ("Caesarian") government of 1852 modeled on the First Empire, to a virtual "constitutional monarchy with universal suffrage" by 1870. And despite its sudden collapse, Prélot discerns in the Empire a successful training ground for the mass electorate created by the Revolution of 1848, and claims that without this experience, the parliamentary system of the Third Republic would have been impossible.

This favorable view of Napoleon III is complemented by the final selection, in which Theodore Zeldin, Dean of St. Antony's College, Oxford, and specialist in the political history of the period, seeks to dispel the "myth" he feels has grown up around the Emperor. Though its tone is apologetic, it concentrates on explaining how the Napoleonic election "system" worked, and how the electorate was persuaded (by one means or another) to support the government at the polls. Zeldin is compelled to admit that the system was breaking down by 1870 because of a decline in the Emperor's energies and the rise of an effective opposition stimulated by his own reforms. Whether Napoleon III can indeed be styled one of the "great statesmen of the century" is, of course, debatable.

Ironically, in September of 1870, only a few months after the Liberal Empire had been proclaimed and overwhelmingly ratified by a plebiscite, it collapsed without a shot being fired in its defense. As in 1814 the cause was defeat on the battlefield, not internal unrest, and fittingly Sedan brought to an end the second cycle of French political regimes that had opened at Waterloo more than a half century earlier. Twice France has passed through a series of constitutional experiments, and twice her emperors died in exile, leaving young sons who would never reign. But France could never again return to her pre-industrial state or limited suffrage: the Second Empire had set her firmly on the path to modernity.

THE ECONOMIC TRANSFORMATION OF FRANCE UNDER THE SECOND EMPIRE

Georges Pradalié

... In 1852 France was still a country with poor roads, few canals, and a skeletal railway system whose development had come to a virtual halt. The economic world of the country was a narrow one, dominated by local consumption, "with each region living strictly off itself. . . . Its basic feature remained what it had been for centuries—an antique system of agriculture centered around small, sleepy villages. The king's officials were forced to come to terms with, if not actually surrender to, the local 'notables' and legal specialists."[1]

Georges Pradalié, *Le Second Empire* (2nd ed.; Paris: Presses Universitaires de France, 1963), pp. 48–59, 62–63, 65–68. © Presses Universitaires de France, 1963. Editors' translation.

[1] Marcel Blanchard, *Le Second Empire* (Paris, 1950), p. 53.

France was basically a country of peasants and artisans, a "country of carters, bargemen, craftsmen, itinerant journeymen, and peasants who spent half their time engaged in basic cottage industries. Above all, it was a nation of free farmers living out their narrow, limited, parochial and peculiar lives under the watchful eyes of the local 'notables' and the strictures of their priests."[2] It was a country governed by the "notables" whose narrow outlook had thrown up a high protectionist wall around the nation's economic life. It was a country where banking facilities were inadequate and those with savings invested them in real estate, one where notaries and usurers were the only sources of credit. The state was concerned primarily with the conduct of justice, diplomacy, police, and war, and, despite the creation of ministries of Public Works, Trade, and Agriculture, it seldom intervened in economic affairs.

But all of these features which were part of the society of Louis-Philippe's day, as well as those of previous generations, would soon begin to disappear, and a new society quite unlike it would emerge. The birth of such a new society was not unique to France: England had already begun her economic revolution, as had Belgium, the German Rhineland, Saxony, and Silesia. The years from 1852 to 1870 were a period of great economic transformation throughout Western Europe and the United States. They were a period when capitalism underwent tremendous expansion, due in large part to the discovery of gold in California in 1848 and in Australia in 1851. A considerable quantity of the metal came into circulation, filtering through London, but most of it finding its way to France. As a result, gold replaced silver as a means of exchange, and the reserves of the Bank of France rose from 122,500,000 francs in 1847 to 1 billion in 1869.

This influx of gold and the increase in the money supply stimulated business. The economic transformation was also encouraged by technological discoveries like the Bessemer steel process that increased production and lowered prices.

What was unique to France, what distinguished her from England, for example, was the fact that this economic transformation was the deliberate result of policies put into effect by the Imperial government. Around Napoleon III there had formed a group of individuals infused with an innovating spirit who were both men of ideas and men of action, businessmen as well as economic theorists.

The Emperor had always been preoccupied with economic questions. Imprisoned in the fortress of Ham, he closely studied the questions of sugar production and interoceanic canals, drawing up plans for one across the Isthmus of Panama. These old interests of his had been reinforced by his stay in England. There he had seen a major country in the process of economic

---

[2] *Ibid.*, p. 54.

transformation, became acquainted with businessmen and economics, read the works of liberal economic theorists like Ricardo and Bentham, and closely followed the Parliamentary debates leading to free trade. Napoleon III was far more aware of economic problems than the kings and ministers who had preceded him.

There were political and social aspects to his economic policies. The Emperor wanted to win the entire country over to his government by increasing the general prosperity, and sought to make France forget politics and her loss of liberty. Finally, he seems to have hoped that in this way he could solve the "social question": economic prosperity would bring an end to unemployment, the curse of the working class, and enable workers to receive higher wages.

This policy was marked by a dichotomy between two kinds of liberalism —economic and political. The Emperor cared little for the political variety, but under him economic liberalism would triumph. Just the opposite had been true under the July Monarchy, when the notables had been liberal in their politics and conservative in economic affairs.

The kind of men who gathered around the Emperor explains how he was able to put his ideas into practice. These notables loyal to Orleanism were hostile to them. The administrative bodies and most officials belonged to the traditionalist school and quietly opposed the daring ideas of the Emperor. The Council of State, for example, was always suspicious of Napoleon III's innovating spirit. The Council of State, the Emperor told [Alfred] Darimon, "certainly contains a great many enlightened men, but reform frightens them. They always find some law to put in my way." That body blocked even the most useful measures, such as the organization of agricultural credit.

Since the Emperor was thus confronted with the hostility of all his officials, he was forced to find other intermediaries he could trust and who understood him. Most of his advisers belonged to the Saint-Simonian school. Stripped of its utopian features, the doctrine of Saint-Simon [1760–1825] appears to be primarily a movement that put economics before politics. . . . His doctrine called for power to be taken from the nobles, priests, and lawyers and given to industrialists, the master technicians of production. The Saint-Simonians believed that the unlimited development of production would increase the well-being of all and solve the social question. To accomplish this it was first necessary to expand credit, build railways, and abolish customs barriers between states.

There were numerous Saint-Simonians around the Emperor, notably the two Pereire brothers, who established the *Crédit Mobilier*; Paul Talabot, a graduate of the *Ecole Polytechnique* and founder of the P.L.M. railway line; and Michel Chevalier, another graduate of the same school and principal theoretician of a liberal economy. Besides these there were a few Jewish bankers like [Achille] Fould, or important administrators such as [Claude]

Vaïsse, prefect of the Rhône Department, and [Georges] Haussmann, prefect of the Seine.

Almost at once after the *coup d'état* [of December, 1851], financial circles began to recover their confidence. The 3 per cent government bonds which had fallen to 32 francs 50 centimes in 1843 and reached 54 francs 75 centimes before the *coup*, now climbed to 67 and would reach 86 in 1852. This was due to the mobilization of credit, for as early as February, 1852, land banks had been founded, and in November the *Crédit Mobilier* of the Pereire brothers was established, which soon gave a great impetus to large-scale enterprise.

The government's role was far more concrete and effective in the area of railways. Eight days after the *coup d'état*, a decree authorized the construction of a belt line on the right bank within the fortifications of Paris. On January 5, 1852, a decree authorized the concession of a line between Paris and Lyons.

In 1853 Haussmann was named prefect of the Seine and the vast program of public works in Paris began. Finally, Napoleon III became concerned with lowering customs duties, and by the *senatus-consultum* of December 25, 1852, he could modify tariffs on his authority alone.

The flood of precious metals that poured into Europe offered a favorable opportunity for the modernization of France, but its circulation and application to business were even more important. To assure this, the country had to be provided with the banking facilities that it lacked. Until now most credit had been obtained from big banks, that is, from a group of Parisian houses, mostly Protestant or Jewish, like the Rothschilds and Fould, which were primarily concerned with investing in state loans, and which financed companies and business simply for their own profit. With their limited capital they failed to carry on an essential function of credit institutions, namely the bringing together of business firms and investment funds.

But in 1852 the *Crédit Foncier* and the *Crédit Mobilier* were founded. The first fulfilled the long-expressed desire of agricultural circles, one most genuinely felt in 1843, when the average rate of interest on mortgages reached 9 per cent. The decree-law of February 28, 1852, authorized the creation of societies for land credit that would provide long-term loans repayable in annual installments. Three large firms were authorized: the *Banque Foncière* of Paris, with a monopoly in the area of the capital; the *Société Foncière* of Marseilles, which had a monopoly in the area of Aix-en-Provence; and the *Société Foncière* of Nevers, with a monopoly over three Departments. But the Paris bank was soon incorporated with those of Marseilles and Nevers, giving birth to the *Crédit Foncier* of France.

Crédit Foncier lent on long-term first mortgages, repayable in annual installments, and secured its capital through the issue of bonds guaranteed by its mortgages. Its governor and subgovernor were named by the state.

By 1870 the investments it had made since its founding had given it interests in more then half of France's urban property, both in mortgage loans and in loans to local communities. But its operations did not really benefit agricultural holdings, since the *Crédit Foncier* lent only paltry sums for such projects as drainage. On the other hand, it gave powerful support to urban property and the great public works projects in the towns.

Both industry and commerce had lacked a large credit institution. In November, 1852, the *Société Générale du Crédit Mobilier* was founded with a capital of 60 million francs divided into shares of 500 francs. Among its founders were the Pereire brothers, Emile and Isaac, members of a Jewish family of Portuguese ancestry living in France for two generations, who were Saint-Simonians, former editors of the *Globe* newspaper, and important founders of railways. Fould and Morny were also among its original members. . . . The bank sought to "orient" and "direct" the entire economy as the original Saint-Simonians had dreamt. *Crédit Mobilier* came to be the commanding company for industry, and aided in the creation or management of large-scale enterprises.

But how could the *Crédit Mobilier* secure the sums necessary to finance French industry and commerce? The system it used resembled that of the *Crédit Foncier*: it obtained its capital by issuing stock, thus borrowing with one hand what it lent with the other. Its credit was secured by the whole system of closely knit enterprises brought together in its own system.

It had phenomenal success, its shares quadrupling in price between 1853 and 1856. It became the model of a large business bank, with national and even international activity, and gave an extraordinary impetus to large-scale enterprises. The national network of railways also benefited from its credit, and it assisted in their creation. It helped the Eastern, Western, Southern, Great Central, Ardennes, and Pyrenees lines, so much so that the Pereires became administrators for most of France's major companies, whose shares were sold by the bank. Its activity extended to foreign rail lines like those of Northern Spain, Switzerland, Austria, and Russia. The *Crédit Mobilier* also engaged in ocean transport: it created the *Compagnie Maritime Transatlantique* for transoceanic travel; it cooperated in forming the large insurance companies; it organized the coal mines in the Pas-de-Calais Department; and it financed the real estate companies of Paris. In 1863 the Pereire brothers may have controlled 19 companies with 3,500,000,000 francs in capital. But the *Crédit Mobilier* also attempted to become a bank of issue, thereby drawing down upon it the wrath of the vigilant Bank of France, while the great Rothschild bank had been hostile to it from its very beginnings. Finally, a considerable part of its investments had been tied down, especially after 1863, in land purchases at Marseilles, so that its credit was weakened. In 1867 the Pereires had to resign from it, and the company was eventually dissolved in 1871. . . .

Founded in 1863 the *Crédit Lyonnais* would be primarily a kind of regional bank, with branches from Dijon to Marseilles, and under the direction of that extraordinary entrepreneur [Henri] Germain, it would extend its operations to the rest of France. The *Société Générale* was created in 1864 to foster trade and industry; its purpose was to finance middle-sized enterprises and it sought to "democratize credit." Stock corporations eventually were legalized through reforms embodied in a law of 1867.

At the beginning of the Second Empire, France still had only 3,600 kilometers [2,200 miles] of railways in operation, divided among 18 small companies. Between 1852 and 1856 the main lines in the French network were completed: the Paris-Belgium and Paris-Strasbourg lines in 1852, the Paris-Marseilles line in 1855, then the Paris-Tours-Bordeaux-Bayonne, Paris-Caen lines, and finally the Bordeaux-Toulouse line in 1856.... By the end of the Empire, 23,500 kilometers [14,570 miles] of the main lines had been constructed, most of the modern French system.

These great endeavors were not state projects, but the state encouraged, hastened, and participated in them in the most direct way. Under the July Monarchy the question was long debated as to whether railways should be a state undertaking or be left to private enterprise. Eventually a system of privately financed lines had been adopted. But, distrustful of large business firms, it chose relatively small ones to run them: for example, four or five companies were to operate the Paris-Marseilles route. Then the Second Empire replaced this patchwork with one of cohesion by creating large companies that would develop railways much more economically. This allowed each line to make good its losses on the less profitable lines with profits from the more successful routes. In March, 1852, a decree approved the merger of the Paris-Orléans, Central, Orléans-Bordeaux, and Tours-Nantes lines. In this way, six large routes were formed: the *Compagnie du Nord* (formed in 1857 and linking routes in the Northeast); the *Compagnie de l'Est* (formed in 1854, composed of the Eastern lines); the P.L.M. (the Paris-Lyons-Mediterranean line); the *Compagnie d'Orléans* (also established in 1857, for the Orléans route); the *Compagnie de l'Ouest* (for the Western lines); and the *Compagnie du Midi* (for the Southern route). The length of the concessions was set at 99 years, with the state guaranteeing a minimum rate of interest—generally 4 per cent—for half the life of the concession.

Railways wrought a profound change in France's way of life. The economy of agricultural regions changed from one oriented toward filling local needs to one of production for export. Before the advent of railways, Languedoc, for example, had produced virtually everything its inhabitants needed—grain, oil, fruit, wine, meat, wool, and silk. But with the new transport, wine gradually become the sole crop. The revolutionary effect of the railway in the other agricultural regions of France was the same. It also aided industry by bringing together coal and iron ore, and coal and wool....

And railways led to the final triumph of Parisian centralization: all the great lines, except that of the South, originated in Paris, had their terminals there, and drained off men and goods to the capital to the detriment of the provinces. . . .

It was in the context of a policy of prosperity created by the regime that the major free trade measures were taken in the 1860's. The Franco-British trade agreement of January 23, 1860, grew out of negotiations between [Eugène] Rouher, Minister of Commerce, and Michel Chevalier, representing France, and Richard Cobden, for Britain. It eliminated all prohibitions on such important items as cotton and wool, thread and cloth, and ready-made clothing. Customs duties were not to exceed 30 per cent *ad valorem*, and would fall to 25 per cent after October 1, 1864. For their part, the English admitted free commodities which hitherto had been subject to a moderate customs duty, while tariffs on wines were slashed by four-fifths. Export taxes on coal were eliminated. By the treaty, which was signed for ten years, the two signatory states accorded each other most-favored-nation status.

Similar trade agreements multiplied. One was signed with Belgium in 1861, another with Prussia and the other states of the Zollverein in 1862. Between 1864 and 1866, the system became the basis of France's relations with European powers, notably Italy, Switzerland, Sweden, the Netherlands, Spain, Austria, and Portugal. These various treaties eliminated tariffs on raw materials and substituted lower tariffs for complete prohibitions.

This policy came under bitter attack from the leaders of industry and agriculture, and was possible solely because the Emperor desired it. Only a few free trade theorists like Michel Chevalier, representatives of export industries such as the deputies of the Gironde Department who spoke for the shippers and winegrowers, and few rare men of the Left, like Jules Simon, who defended the interests of the mass consumer, supported it. The overwhelming majority of "notables" was firmly opposed to it, making it one of the prime factors in their disillusionment with the Empire. But this lowering of customs barriers stimulated the development of foreign trade, which quadrupled under the Empire. . . .

In [industry] progress was even more spectacular than in agriculture, for the industrialist profited from technical discoveries since he had the necessary capital to introduce them into his own industry. The Second Empire was the period of the formation of industrial capitalism, when investment of capital in industry more than doubled. . . .

Scientific discoveries produced the greatest transformation in the chemical industry. Thus it was that in 1854 Sainte-Claire Deville discovered aluminum, which would be a new metal in industrial life. Chemistry also transformed the dye and perfume industries, and led to the cheap production of sodium: a kilo of sodium that had cost 7,000 francs in 1840, fell to only 6 francs by 1870.

Increasingly, power was furnished by the steam engine. At the beginning of the Empire, there were only some 7,200 steam engines in France with a horsepower of 90,000; by its end, there were 24,787 steam engines with some 305,000 horsepower.

More and more coal was being consumed: consumption rose from 7 million tons in 1848 to 21,500,000 tons in 1869. France's coal mines produced 4,500,000 tons in 1850 and 13,500,000 in 1869. This rise can be explained by improved mining techniques, new methods of mine ventilation and hydraulic machines that allowed miners' cages to be raised and lowered. Deeper pits were dug and output per man increased.

But it was the metals industry that saw the most remarkable changes. The English technique of using coke in iron smelting had taken a long time to penetrate France, where charcoal was the traditional fuel. Only in 1853 did the production of iron made by coke surpass that made by charcoal. But thenceforth progress was quite rapid, all the more so since the blast furnace had been perfected with the introduction in 1858 of Cowper's hot blast stove. As a result, iron production increased from 406,000 tons in 1850 to 1,400,000 tons in 1869. With the introduction of the Bessemer process in 1855, steel output rose spectacularly from 283,000 tons in 1850 to 1,014,000 tons in 1869. Iron and steel were being used in railway tracks, construction, machinery, as well as in the building of the central market of Paris (Les Halles) in 1863. The price of iron fell and the iron industry became the basis of economic life.

Until now textiles had been France's basic industry, and as in England, the one in which progress had been most spectacular. Under the Second Empire, there were fewer important improvements made in it, although the Alsatian industrialist [Josué] Heilmann had invented the automatic combing machine in 1845. New machinery for cloth printing was also developed in Alsace, and the sewing machine made its appearance. Invented by a Frenchman, [Bathélemy] Thimonnier, who had no success in getting his device used in France, it became widely adopted only when the American version created by Singer was introduced after 1857.

The spread of mechanization is far more characteristic of the Second Empire than new inventions. Though the cotton industry was entirely mechanized, woolen manufacturing in many regions remained in the hands of artisans, and silk was almost always produced by craftsmen.

At mid-century, France was still largely rural, and hardly a region existed where linen and wool were not spun and woven, especially by craftsmen working at home on their farms. But three major areas dominated the textile industry, which became increasingly mechanized: the Nord Department, Alsace, and Normandy. At towns like Roubaix, Tourcoing, Lille, and Armentières, a highly mechanized industry developed because of the proximity of coal. All forms of wool, linen, and cotton manufacture from combing to spinning and weaving were carried on. In Alsace, calicos continued to enjoy the same success they had had in the eighteenth century, but manufacturers were compelled to perfect new techniques. It was Normandy that remained most faithful to the old methods, and so it was there that economic crises were severest. And beginning in 1860, the textile industry suffered great difficulties, due in large measure to the American Civil War which dried up the cotton supply.

It may therefore be said that during the Second Empire a profound transformation of all forms of industry took place, and France experienced her Industrial Revolution.

THE SOCIAL AND ECONOMIC
POLICIES OF THE EMPEROR

Hendrik Boon

The second of December, 1851, marks the real beginning of the personal rule of Louis Napoleon Bonaparte; the transformation of the republic into an empire, which was to follow a year later, was only a change in name that did not alter the real conditions of power. Thus the prince attained his aims through a *coup d'état*, and now at last held the power he had so long desired. Now it was up to him to demonstrate whether he could succeed and move with greater assurance than had the preceding regimes. But, above all, the time seemed ripe to reveal his personal plans and to show the country the path he wished to follow. Intelligent observers shared the thoughts of the Austrian ambassador, who after the *coup* remarked, "There is Louis-Napoleon who has just arrived with his valise full of schemes worked out during his long years in prison and exile."

At first he occupied himself with becoming the true master of the country. If the opposition in Paris was overcome in a few days, the acceptance of the *fait accompli* was not so easy in several Departments. There repressive measures were indispensable: workers' societies were dissolved or prosecuted, and the leaders of the opposition imprisoned or deported. Special commissions purged the country of all centers of resistance. Thus the personal regime of Louis Napoleon Bonaparte opened with repressions and deportations. No doubt the president did not fully realize the extent of the measures his subordinates had taken—as always the servants went farther than

H. N. Boon, *Rêve et réalité dans l'oeuvre économique et sociale de Napoléon III* (The Hague: Martinus Nijhoff, 1936), pp. 65–70, 146–156. © Martinus Nijhoff, 1936. Reprinted by permission. Editors' translation.

their master might have desired. But when he learned how numerous the prosecutions were, he wanted to mitigate their severity, and he ordered rather arbitrary reviews of the decisions. But the damage was already done. The socialist workers and their associations had been the first and often the only victims of the repression, which was directed by conservatives. In their eyes, the regime was reactionary, and the accomplishments of the Empire never completely succeeded in erasing their first painful impression. The maintenance of a strong, cohesive authority which Louis Napoleon desired was interpreted by his partisans in their own way. Even his most intimate friends, like Persigny, had little enthusiasm for the president's social inclinations.

Once these repressive measures had firmly established his authority and there was no longer any chance that the spirit of rebellion would rise, the president dared to reveal his plans for social pacification and economic improvement. Was he capable of accomplishing the task he had set for himself? From his writings and previous life, we know the ideas he held dear, especially the Napoleonic idea of supporting individual effort by a timely assistance from above. He was an authoritarian democrat. With the principle of authority solidly established at the top, he wanted to have it exert power that would be stimulating and beneficial. It would bring about all economic and social improvements. Economic improvements would be achieved through a policy of active intervention and large-scale public works; social improvements through legislation—enacting the measures that the republican legislatures had considered but not dared to impose on the country. . . .

On December 15, 1851, shortly after the installation of his new ministry, the Prince-President sent to the prefects through the Minister of the Interior a circular ordering that work on all public projects be suspended on Sundays and recognized holidays. This circular only demonstrated the government's good will—the idea of passing laws requiring compulsory rest in private enterprises was unthinkable.

Another decree issued during the first month of the dictatorship regulated cafés and cabarets. The measure was inspired by Louis Napoleon's observations both in England and later in his own country. Beyond its preoccupations with morality, the decree had an ill-concealed political significance: "Considering that the ever-increasing number of cafés, cabarets, and taverns is a source of disorder and immorality," the prefects were given virtually absolute authority over these establishments. They could not open without his authorization and he could always close them to protect morality and prevent public gatherings. But no decree could change the mentality of the regular customers of cafés or curb drunkenness. Louis Napoleon proved to be as much concerned with the financial condition of the population as with its morals: the government pawnshops were reorganized to make them better able to protect the population from the usury of moneylenders, and branches were opened in Paris.

One measure that clearly shows the kindheartedness of Louis Napoleon was his institution of "chaplains of the last rites." Many of the Paris poor were deprived of the last rites of the church at their burial because they lacked the money to pay for them. So special vicars paid by the state and known as "chaplains of the last rites," were attached to the large cemeteries of Paris. At the request of the deceased's family they followed a coffin that was not accompanied by a priest, led them to the grave, and recited the last rites of the church. In this regard, one of Louis Napoleon's close friends recalled how [in exile] at Arenenberg, he had reflected on the obligations of society towards the poor and miserable: "I often think of the duties society owes the disinherited, and the more I reflect on them, the more I am convinced that there is still much more to do in this respect. If I should one day attain power, I will not fail to use it to right these wrongs."...

The most important measure that Louis Napoleon took during these months of dictatorship was the decree depriving the Orleanist branch of part of its property.... Louis Napoleon [now] wanted to erase the unfavorable impression produced by this move against a family that was still very much esteemed in certain sections of the country, by setting aside the revenues from it for works of undeniable usefulness. Thus he at last had the enormous sums necessary to accomplish some of the reforms and improvements he considered most needed. Each article of the decree is, in effect, the execution of his program, and of all the decrees in this period, this is certainly the one dearest to him.

Of the anticipated revenue, 10 million francs were allotted to the mutual aid societies; another 10 million were used to improve workers' housing in the large manufacturing towns; 10 million more went to establish land credit banks in the Departments which needed them and which would comply with the conditions prescribed by the government. Finally, 5 million were set aside to establish a retirement fund to aid the poorest parish priests.

Such legislation—the development of mutual aid societies, workers' housing, a retirement fund—indicates the scope and extent of the legislation of the authoritarian Empire. Add to this the execution or the modification of laws passed by the preceding regimes, such as the legislation on arbitration boards and workers' passbooks, and the picture of the principal social measures of the first years of the Empire on which Louis Napoleon Bonaparte had actively contributed or collaborated to some degree is nearly complete.

Is it right to credit the Emperor with such an active role in the social legislation of his government? The personal part Napoleon played in the law making is not easy to determine, and the dry, formal phrasaeology of the laws does not help us to decide who was ultimately responsible. What is certain is that he did not dominate the entire administration as his uncle had, and though his will may have been equal to the task, his knowledge was not. Still he dominated the government, and no power in the country could interfere with his plans. Though he received advice and information, he made all the decisions himself. In 1854 he told a visitor that he did not allow his ministers to discuss state affairs. Several times a week he met with his cabinet to consider an agenda that he himself had fixed. He presented it with administrative questions which he wanted his advisers to debate so that he might become fully informed, and he usually listened while rarely taking part himself. The final decisions were made in his study with only the minister concerned present. It was within the walls of this small private study that most decisions on the social measures of his reign were taken. We learn little from documents about this exchange of ideas. At times a speaker in the Chamber who hoped to flatter his master would extol the role the Emperor had played in the preparation of a proposed measure. This was often a hint to the obedient representatives that they should be discreet in criticizing a proposal dear to their sovereign's heart. The warning was not superfluous, since the quite conservative majority of the Chamber showed little appetite for the reform measures of the Emperor. Napoleon could therefore understand all the difficulties inherent in a government in the daily operation of the great administrative machine. The experience of power soon taught him that it was one thing to dream of improving society while on the banks of peaceful Lake Constance, and quite another to make laws for a great country like France. . . .

. . . The working class movement, stifled by the measures which the government took after the *coup d'état*, only appeared dormant. Normal economic development and the increasing importance of mechanization and large industrial enterprises, tended to make working conditions virtually the same everywhere. The local differences in working-class conditions diminished as distances shortened. When the workers in the large urban areas began to realize how numerous they were, the birth of a working-class movement became imminent.

In the long run, the Empire could not expect to restrain such a growing mass. Napoleon III knew this full well and hoped he could direct the movement before it grew too strong. His basic aim was to satisfy the material and social demands of the working class, demands which seemed justified to him, and thereby both rally the workers to the Empire and deflect their political demands. Moreover, it was certainly easier to bring about the reforms he so very much desired with the active cooperation of the workers themselves than to rely on the machinery of an authoritarian state bureaucracy which opposed them. The workers first had to be given the opportunity to air their demands, for the imperial police had until now blocked every attempt by the workers to join together to discuss their affairs. But it was impossible for the Emperor to enter into direct contact with them without revealing his plans.

In order to approach them he used his cousin, Prince Napoleon, as an intermediary. The latter understood the social aims of the Emperor perfectly and helped him as best he could. Their friendship had begun at Arenenberg, where Louis Napoleon had found pleasure in talking with his young cousin about his social ideas. The relations they established then lasted throughout their lives, even though they frequently had serious differences of opinion. But if Prince Napoleon often embarrassed the Emperor by his provocative speeches and unjustified criticisms, they were in full agreement on social questions. From his prison at Ham, Louis Napoleon had often written to his cousin on social problems that preoccupied him, and together they had studied the question of pauperism. Their lengthy correspondence reveals many disagreements over political issues, but never any over social questions. Working with the Emperor, Prince Napoleon, who had many connections with the opposition, endeavored to establish contact with the workers. Armand Levy, a journalist, acted as his go-between. Some newspapers now suggested the idea that the workers demand social improvements from the Emperor, who would certainly receive such demands favorably.

The thinking of this Palais Royal group which gradually gathered around Prince Napoleon is best demonstrated by a series of small, cheap "working men's pamphlets" in orange covers, sold in the workshops. The distribution costs may have been borne by the Prince, but they were probably written by the workers themselves. The frankness with which the workers dared to state their demands is startling, and since all publications were still strictly censored, this is the best evidence that they were authorized by the government. Their demands were quite diverse: some demanded trade unions while others wanted to restore the old guilds. All mention the Emperor's willingness to grant all the concessions the workers sought. "We reaffirm that the government, faithful to the word of the prisoner of Ham, will allow the working men to organize." The workers themselves had to prove that they had come of age, and with considerable boldness, they petitioned Napoleon: "We have the firm hope that you will finally authorize the delegations mentioned in the most popular of your works, so that each day the people can inform Your Majesty of their desires and needs."

The government took up the idea of workers' delegations, although in a different form from that desired by the authors of the pamphlets. In September, 1861, a request was addressed to the Emperor that he facilitate the visit of a certain number of workers to the expositions being held at Florence and London. Once the request was drawn up, it was supported by the members of the Palais Royal group. Sending delegations of working men to a universal exposition was not new, but until now they were always sent by employers. This time the choice of their representatives would be left to the workers themselves. It is impossible to say who first proposed this innovation, since the idea had been in the air. What is certain is that once the idea was broached, the Emperor immediately grasped its importance. As president of the imperial commission for the exposition, Prince Napoleon was entrusted with organizing the elections. But the prefect of police, who looked with suspicion at the meetings of workers to elect their delegates, sought to prevent them by declaring that he could not be held responsible for any disorder that might occur. A formal order from the Emperor was necessary to overcome his hostility. It was the first time that Napoleon III had revealed his hand publicly.

The troubles that the authorities so greatly feared did not materialize. The workers proved themselves worthy of the trust of the Emperor, who wanted them to choose their representatives in complete freedom, without supervision. As a result, more than two hundred delegates eventually crossed the Channel to London, where they saw much that aroused their admiration and envy. In the reports which they drew up on their return, they demanded the same freedoms as their English comrades. Some have maintained that the section of their report which expressed their desires for social reform was not prompted by the government, which had merely wanted to give them the opportunity to study foreign industry. But the government would have been extraordinarily naive to suppose that working men could travel abroad and not return with some demands. The secret aim of the Emperor was to learn the workers' precise demands so that he would know how they could be satisfied. In this respect, Napoleon III's desire appears to have been realized—the reports did not yet reveal that spirit of class conflict which was to be so inimical to the Empire. On the contrary, they almost always revealed the workers' desire to see the end to the antagonisms between employers and workers, who should naturally share common interests.

Another consequence of the workers' delegations, one the Emperor had probably not foreseen, was the birth of an international association of working men. There can be no question that the organization of the International was the direct consequence of the contacts made between the French and English workers during the universal exposition at London. Thus Napoleon III was indirectly responsible for the origin of this mighty force of modern history. Though he had not anticipated it, the Emperor at first applauded its creation, for Napoleon III cherished plans for international organizations. His scheme for a European congress had just failed. In his youth he had had noble dreams of organizing the masses: "Without organization the masses are nothing; disciplined, they are everything. Without organization they can neither speak, nor make themselves heard; they can neither listen nor act." . . . The subsequent measures taken on the Emperor's initiative reveal the drift of his thinking. Napoleon hoped to win over the working class largely through a few major laws that would satisfy the demands drawn up by the delegates when they returned from the London Exposition. New legislation on labor unions became an urgent necessity since the Emperor had vitiated the force of existing laws by ending convictions for those engaging in strikes.

The old imperial officials understood the thoughts of the sovereign only imperfectly. The first draft of the law, prepared by the Council of State, granted workers the right to organize only under numerous restrictions which made it virtually meaningless. The Emperor's advisers had watered down his scheme as much as possible. As a result the plan disappointed all those who had expected serious reforms. That this first draft ran counter to the wishes of the Emperor is shown by a conversation that Napoleon III had with one of the opposition deputies. The sovereign became indignant when he learned that the proposed law would not improve the condition of the working man, and specifically voiced his intention not to be satisfied with half-measures, but to grant them full freedom. To make his own ideas prevail, he entrusted [Emile] Ollivier, one of the opposition deputies, with drawing up a new plan. Ollivier's later claims that he had suggested the law to the Emperor are therefore exaggerated. He simply redrafted the bill presented by the Council of State, omitting the word "union." The Chambers bowed before the will of the sovereign and approved the new draft more in resignation than with enthusiasm. . . .

Even in the final version, however, the law failed to satisfy all the workers' demands. If workers were allowed to form unions and to strike, they were still denied the right to assemble. The law acknowledged the temporary right to strike for specific purposes, but it refused to allow union activity. A great deal also depended on the spirit with which the law was enforced.

Having chosen the path of allowing greater freedom, the Emperor had to follow it. But there were signs that those close to him hesitated to grant new concessions to the workers. . . . Only the weight of his own personal influence enabled the two great laws of 1868 to pass. Freedom of assembly, a natural accompaniment to the freedom to organize that Napoleon III wished to grant his people in order to foster the development of workers' benevolent and mutual societies, was limited to non-political meetings. Despite this restriction, the law encountered such resistance in the Legislative Body that the Emperor had to order Rouher to make sure the deputies obeyed. The same was true for the law allowing freedom of the press. This legislation was to unleash a flood of criticisms against the Empire.

The measures aimed at encouraging credit and cooperative societies among the workers were more successful, and here the Emperor's personal initiative had foreshadowed legislation. In 1862 the Empress founded the Society of the Prince Imperial. The institution was to some degree the realization of a dream that Louis Napoleon had cherished since he became President—to found a bank that lent on faith. In establishing this society, the Emperor sought to provide credit to those who lacked but deserved it, "to put capital within the reach of the honest and hard-working craftsman, to disprove the old axiom that only the rich can obtain credit." The Emperor suffered from the illusion that a good reputation was a form of collateral that served as credit and security. The Society of the Prince Imperial made loans that permitted workers to purchase tools and implements or acquire supplies in times of temporary economic crisis. Its capital, secured through subscription, soon reached almost two million francs. The Emperor and Empress alone contributed 100,000 francs. The loans were repaid with great regularity, proof that the workers were faithful to their pledged word. In any case, a loan was made only when two solvent individuals guaranteed it.

Besides worker credit, Napoleon III also encouraged the cooperative movement which was making great strides among the working class. Here the great obstacle was the legislation on corporations. A preliminary change in the law resulted from the trade agreement [with England]. The Emperor had promised to free industry from all the restrictions that had handicapped it, but this initial modification still raised obstacles to the creation of corporations. Realizing the inadequacy and ineffectiveness of the measure, the Emperor pledged himself in a speech opening the Legislative Body in 1865 "to eliminate all obstacles that hindered the creation of societies intended to improve the condition of the working class." He announced his firm intention to attempt a great experiment by establishing cooperative societies, and the promised law passed after rather lengthy discussion. Corporations were given almost complete freedom to organize, and government authorization was no longer necessary. Impartial observers considered it one of the best laws enacted under the Empire. . . .

The Emperor was more concerned with the development of the cooperative movement than with the details of legislation, which he gladly left to his subordinates. To encourage the movement as much as possible, he founded an imperial fund for cooperative societies, with a capital of a million francs, half of which he personally subscribed. This institution would help the societies to function. Unfortunately, it had scant success since it was founded on a strictly commercial basis, and had few clients who were sufficiently solvent. Napoleon III also facilitated the creation of a silk workers' cooperative society at Lyons, by allotting them an advance of 100,000 francs from the Society of the Prince Imperial. . . . Cooperation was in the air, and Napoleon III only stimulated a movement advocated by the most intelligent thinkers of his age. Despite a few failures, the movement grew rapidly.

The Emperor had far less success in his attempts to influence the budding labor movement. He had looked with favor on the formation of the International, which even fitted in with his own views. But the new association gradually manifested signs of open hostility towards the Empire. Its leaders realized that many workers reproached them for their apparent understanding with the Empire, and in foreign congresses, the members of the International began to show growing antipathy to it. An open conflict developed when the report of the French delegates to a congress at Geneva was banned in France. The government's attitude is demonstrated by the reply that the representatives of the International received at an audience they had requested to protest this step. Rouher told them that the ban would be lifted if they agreed to insert a few words of praise for the Emperor "who had done so much for the working class." The workers refused to give the Empire this satisfaction, and as a result prosecutions soon began. Two trials halted the development of the International in France. The workers' spirit of independence is admirable, but their refusal to grasp the hand that Napoleon III offered them would long retard the realization of their social objectives. The Third Republic often proved even more hostile than the Empire had. . . .

In general, it is fair to say that the labor policy of Napoleon III failed completely. If he had assured the laboring man work, strikes still took place. The relaxation of repressive legislation resulted in the development of a workers' organization unalterably opposed to the Empire. The workers did not respond to the advances made by the Emperor's intermediaries. It was not enough for him to satisfy their material and social demands. If Napoleon III had detected the symptoms of the movement which was about to appear, not only in France but throughout the world, he did not succeed in securing any benefits from the favors he had shown the workers.

Perhaps the task he sought to accomplish was beyond his power, perhaps beyond that of any mortal. One socialist, [Albert Thomas], after having described the material benefits that Napoleon III had bestowed upon all classes of society, rightly asked, "Who could delude himself into thinking he could always contain or even successfully direct these two great historical forces—working class demands and national aspirations? Such was the tragedy of the Second Empire. In their spontaneous development these forces one day turned violently against the dynasty that claimed to control them." . . .

THE CONSTITUTIONAL SIGNIFICANCE
OF THE SECOND EMPIRE

MARCEL PRÉLOT

... The centennial of 1852 passed almost unnoticed. The second "December 2"—or rather the third, since the Napoleonic legend considered the day of Austerlitz as the first—has little meaning in the public mind. It seems the date of a simple constitutional formality, of a proclamation which had appeared inevitable, not only since the *coup d'état*, but from the beginning of 1851. At that time the [National] Assembly had let itself be disarmed, and Thiers ... had declared, "The Empire is made. ... The word will be used whenever it is desired."

It was desired at the end of the Assembly's session. Compared to Napoleon I, Napoleon III wasted little time. It took fifty-three months ... for Citizen Bonaparte to become Emperor; twelve were enough for the Prince-President. But what the victor of Marengo founded, the occupant of the Elysée Palace restored.

Constitutionally, Napoleon III had to insist on it. In this context, December 2, 1852, takes on a precise historical significance. It becomes part of that series of reversals which make up two-thirds of the history of nineteenth century France. Her "constitutional development" ... was really accomplished by a series of restorations. Weary of having introduced so many novelties and of having conquered so many lands in twenty-five years, the France of the treaties of Vienna drew back within herself, and in a sense recapitulated her own history. She no longer innovated, she restored. The Bourbon Restoration of 1814, the Napoleonic restoration of 1815, the Orleanist restoration of 1830, the Girondin restoration of 1848, the Bonapartist restoration of 1851—all foreshadowed the attempted restorations of the Bourbons and the July Monarchy, which collapsed due to the obstinacy of the Count of Chambord and the failure of [Marshal] MacMahon.

... In his suggestive *History of France*, Jacques Madaule has aptly observed that "Napoleonic prestige did more for Napoleon III than the doctrines of the authoritarian Republic. It became apparent some decades later that Bonapartism without Bonaparte had little hold on the French people." Twenty years before, following the July Days, the subtle question of quasilegitimacy had been discussed: Was Louis-Philippe king "because of" his Bourbon blood or "in spite of" it? Both answers were debatable. Napoleon III had no doubts at all that his rise to the Presidency and later to the imperial throne occurred because he was a Bonaparte.

Marcel Prélot, "La Signification constitutionnelle du Second Empire," *Revue française de science politique*, vol. III (janvier–mars 1953), pp. 33–44, 47–48, 50–56. Used by permission of the *Revue française de science politique*. Translation by Hans D. Kellner.

. . . After less than forty years, Napoleon III succeeded his uncle. . . . The course of events had simply restored to the Bonaparte-Beauharnais family the scepter which was rightly theirs. But the Prince-President, in order to stress the regularity of his succession, titled himself the third of his line. In this way he recognized the ephemeral title given the son of the head of the family by the Chambers in a last outburst of vanquished patriotism. Thus, Napoleon III based his reign on hereditary right. . . .

. . . The Napoleonic restoration led to the rebirth of imperial institutions. . . . In his proclamation of January 14, 1852, the Prince-President himself declared: "I have thought it logical to prefer the precepts of genius to the specious doctrines of men with abstract ideas. I have taken as my models the political institutions which once, in similar circumstances at the beginning of this century, strengthened a tottering society and raised France to the heights of prosperity and greatness. I have taken as my models the institutions which, instead of disappearing at the first sign of popular agitation, were overturned only by a coalition of all Europe. In short, I am saying that since France has for fifty years functioned only by virtue of the administrative, military, judicial, religious, and financial organizations of the Consulate and Empire, why should we not also adopt the political institutions of that era? Created by the same spirit, they must contain the same qualities of nationalism and practical utility."

We can detect a measure of deception, even of bluff, in these words. But it is impossible not to see in the Constitution of 1852 the logical extension of the ideas of [Abbé] Sieyes which Bonaparte had digested at length and which comprised the Constitutions of the Years VIII, X, and XII. There is some justification in this. Pierre de la Gorce saw in the constitutional draft of 1851 "the half-visible imprint of the powerful mind, however distorted and dim it may have been," of the former vicar-general. Of all French constitution makers, Napoleon III was no doubt the only one who knew in advance, at the moment he laid the foundations of a political structure, precisely what that structure would be. He condensed his ideas into five concise propositions and submitted them to a plebiscite in December, 1851:

1. A responsible chief named for ten years.
2. Ministers dependent on the executive power alone.
3. A Council of State composed of the most distinguished men, to draft the laws and lead the discussion in the Legislative Body.
4. A Legislative Body to discuss and vote on the laws, one elected by universal suffrage without *scrutin de liste* which distorts the election process.
5. A second assembly composed of all the illustrious persons of the country acting as a balancing force to protect the fundamental compact and the public liberties.

Without even a change of name, these were the organs of the First

Empire as they existed in 1807 after the absorption of the Tribunate into the Legislative Body: the Emperor and his ministers, and the three assemblies —Council of State, Legislative Body, and Senate. It was also the same basically unequal distribution of power that permitted the Emperor to dominate completely the system which he conceived and shaped to suit his own purposes.

In his exercise of executive power, the Emperor was free and independent. He commanded both the army and navy; he declared war; he made peace, treaties of alliance and commerce; he named all officials; he made the regulations and decrees necessary for the execution of the laws; he declared a state of siege, provided he informed the Senate; he authorized all public works by decree; he not only held the power to pardon, but also to amnesty, a power generally reserved to the legislature (Article 1 of the *senatus-consultum* of December 25, 1852); and justice was dispensed in the Emperor's name.

If he shared lawmaking powers with the Legislative Body and the Senate, the Emperor nevertheless controlled them. He was master of the law as the King in the limited monarchy had never been; that is, he held the initiative in the drafting of a law and after its passage, he controlled its "promulgation," which had previously been called "sanction." In principle, the Emperor alone decided whether a bill would be drafted, or submitted to a vote in the Legislative Body. There was only one exception: the Senate had the right to initiate *senatus-consulta* and bills of great national importance. However, given the timid behavior of the "gerontocracy," the Emperor had virtually exclusive control over initiative. Only the Emperor possessed the right to make a law enforceable. Without his promulgation, no law or *senatus-consultum* had any force. Thus, the imperial veto was absolute and not merely "suspensive." . . .

Compared to the Emperor the other branches of government seem to be subordinate and complementary institutions, mere tools of his reign. Article III [of the Constitution of 1852] stated this clearly: the Emperor "governs *through* the ministers, Council of State, Senate, and Legislative Body."

The ministers were first of all "the honored and powerful assistants of the head of state." "Honored" in several ways—in costume, salary, and housing. "Powerful" because in an essentially hierarchical regime the head of a department held wide discretionary powers. But still "assistants," since each was answerable only to the head of state for his authority. Thus, there was no solidarity among them—they acted individually. To be sure, the Emperor called them together, but they formed no council in the sense of a deliberative collegiate body. The Prince-President noted that such a practice could be "a daily obstacle to the special prerogative of the head of state, the expression of policy emanating from the Chambers and therefore subject to the frequent changes which prevent any sense of continuity, any application of a regular system." Neither collegiality, nor homogeneity, nor ministerial solidarity existed. One other characteristic distinguished the regime from a parliamentary government: the ministers were selected from outside the Legislative Body, they could neither be discussed there nor (for better reason) be censured. They could belong only to the Senate because that house did not participate in the drafting of laws. The minister who sat in the Senate might speak only as a Senator, not as a minister. In practice the application of these rules of subordination went even further than the literal propositions suggest. "The ministers," wrote Pierre de la Gorce, "held their portfolios, but they held them in trust, almost in bond, as long as they were merely the servants of a master who was complicated, mysterious, and stubborn, and who inspired to draw all power to himself."

The Council of State collaborated in the work of both the executive and legislative branches. A true "council of the state," that is, of the government and the legislators, it was styled "the principal mechanism of the new organization" in the proclamation of January 14, 1852. Composed of an elite of distinguished and practical men, numbering between 40 and 50, the Council drafted the bills in special committees and closed sessions to avoid the fatal delays of oratorical display. At its discretion it could review the amendments added by the Legislative Body and reject them without showing cause. . . . The Council also approved the budget, article by article. . . .

The Legislative Body participated in the exercise of legislative authority, and the Senate in constitutional affairs. The respective positions of these two assemblies resurrected from the Year VIII differed greatly from the chambers of a bicameral legislature. "The Senate and the Legislative Body," Emile Ollivier would say as the system was collapsing, "move in two different spheres: constitutional laws were reserved for the former, ordinary laws for the latter, so that a Constituent and Legislative Assembly stood juxtaposed instead of forming two legislative chambers."

The Legislative Body took part in the drafting of ordinary legislation. It debated the laws and voted them, but while the Council of State and Senate were shown constitutional and imperial favor, the lone elected assembly was surrounded by distrust and restrictions. The greatest preoccupation was to prevent the Legislative Body from increasing its authority and becoming a Chamber of Deputies. As a result, it could not settle issues that it discussed—a logical restriction since the initiative belonged to the Emperor. The Legislative Body could amend only with the approval of the Council of State; similarly, its budgetary rights were restricted. It even had no freedom in its own chamber. Its presiding officers, named by the Emperor, not only directed the debates, but also watched over the deputies. When Emile Ollivier entered the Legislative Body as a republican, he held an important post at the palace and had a great number of connections, but when he tried to shake the hand of a fellow deputy, the man turned his back and murmured, "Careful! Morny is watching us." There was no rostrum because tribunes stimulated eloquence. The deputies were obliged to rise in their places; thus the wings of lofty oratory were clipped. Besides, who could hear them? The public galleries were narrow and uncomfortable. Five members could force the assembly into a secret session. No stenographic record was kept of the debates, and the government distributed a colorless official summary which the press was required to publish in full or not at all. This discretion would insure "that the nation's representative would take the grave questions of state seriously." The Legislative Body thus resembled a kind of large general council. Composed of 260 members, it was small enough to guarantee calm deliberation and a firm hold by the administration over the legislators whose election depended on the government.

The Senate took part in constitutional affairs. . . . The proclamation and preamble of January 14, 1852, described it as an assembly "composed of all the illustrious persons . . . acting as a balancing force to protect the fundamental compact and the public liberties . . . and composed of those elements which create a legitimate influence in all countries: a famous name, wealth, talent and public service." The Senate, then, amounted to a gallery of national personalities who entered it at the conclusion of their careers, and who were virtually assured of financial security in the form of a salary of 30,000 gold francs. . . . Princes of the imperial family, cardinals, marshals, and admirals were senators by right. The Emperor named the rest, but their number was limited to 150. Although he declined the privilege, the Emperor could also preside over the Senate. The duties of the Senate included the right to initiate bills of great national importance, as well as to hear petitions and individual appeals concerning the needs of the country. As the *Moniteur* stated, "The Senate should bring to the attention and authority of the Emperor all matters which can contribute to the glory of his reign and the progress of civilization." But above all, the Senate possessed constituent powers; it was as much a decision-making as a law-making body. A decision-making body as long as it respected the "five basic laws," the Senate could modify the constitutional laws by *senatus-consulta*, interpret their meaning, and decide what steps were necessary to execute them. A law-making body, the Senate could withhold constitutional status from laws and decisions made by the government. It would "resist all attacks on the Constitution, religion, morality, freedom of worship, individual liberty, the equality of citizens, the inviolability of property, and the irremovability of judges." It made its decisions after a law was passed and before it was promulgated, whether directed to do so by the government or a direct petition.

In sum, if the regime was tempered to some extent, if it lacked "the brutal simplicity of despotism," it was nevertheless quite authoritarian and strongly personal. Napoleon III, like Napoleon I, was the alpha and omega of a governmental system which was all the more complex since he meant to mask the all too simple realities of a power stretched to the limits tolerable to Frenchmen since the Revolution of 1789. The principles and bodies did not change. . . .

"Universal suffrage is restored." This was the cry of triumph which a year before had foreshadowed that other proclamation: "The Empire is re-established." However, it would be wrong to see the restoration of universal suffrage as a factor in the imperial restoration. These events must be kept clearly separated, for the universal suffrage in question was that of 1848, not of the Year VIII. To be sure, Napoleon I had resorted to several plebiscites, and their frequency reflects the importance he ascribed to the gesture. "The appeal to the people has the double advantage of legalizing the dissolution [of the National Assembly] and of purifying the origins of my power; otherwise it would always have appeared dubious." So said the First Consul in 1802, years before the Emperor in exile on St. Helena elaborated on the same idea, an idea on which he ultimately based the entire legitimacy of his power.

But, in point of fact, universal suffrage did not exist in a concrete form before 1848. True popular participation dated only from the February Revolution, and thus the Prince-President threw in his lot with a real force, not a mere principle. Universal suffrage was a legal means for the heir of the Emperor to accede to power; it was also a process which allowed him to legitimize the *coup d'état* and to restore the throne.

This attitude was the very opposite of that of the Bourbon Restoration. Hereditary right, which was the sole factor considered in the legal succession to the monarchical throne, became simply a guidepost of destiny in the Napoleonic conception. The will of the nation also played its role. The Second Empire was established on popular sovereignty or, as it has been more commonly called since 1848, on democracy.

If it was possible to rank these two inseparable factors, democracy and hereditary right, in their importance in restoring the Empire, popular will would have to be placed before hereditary right. In a letter to the Minister of State dated November 12, 1861, the Emperor declared that, faithful to his origins, he could not "regard the prerogatives of the crown as either an untouchable sacred trust or a paternal legacy which, above all, had to be handed down intact to his son," . . . but rather "as the rights which he [the Emperor] exercised in the public interest, for the peace and prosperity of the country." The Emperor took control of the state with the consent, if not at the invitation, of the general interest. The country realized that it could not by itself organize "its lasting happiness. Its ambitions were limited to its everyday needs. It cannot possibly face up to its great needs or foresee the future as well as an experienced central power can from the height of its observation post. Given the powerlessness of the people to save itself, to create or re-establish order because of the many ambitions which disturb and betray it, it must accept a powerful leader. This power is not there to satisfy private interests, but to channel all forces in the nation towards the single goal of constant improvement."

Granted by the crowd itself and administered for its benefit, this power could, in law and in fact, be almost limitless. A recent historian of that period, Charles Pouthas, describes the reign of Napoleon III as a kind of enlightened absolutism seeking its support directly from mass opinion. . . .

It would be an error, however, to believe that even at this time there was no discussion of imperial desires, real or imagined. In the Legislative Body, aside from the isolated hostility of Montalembert, certain timid pockets of resistance began to appear. Quiet as these were, they proved already sufficiently tenacious to suggest that they would one day again threaten absolutism. Certain issues polarized this discreet dissent. A liberal nucleus began to take shape during the debates on the law establishing the death penalty, legislation on public safety, and the measures taken against Montalembert. Another and overlapping group proved intransigent when public education came into question. Similarly, the presence of very active protectionist elements, as well as the intervention of the "budgeteers" in the technical realm of finance, frequently forced the executive to make significant concessions.

[Jules] Baroche . . . noted with surprise, if not bitterness, that between 1853 and 1858 a conservative, clerical, and protectionist opposition took shape, representing the sentiments and interests of a large segment of the ruling class. At the same time, after the elections of 1857 and the by-elections of 1858, the famous republican group, the "Five," emerged—Emile Ollivier, [Alfred] Darimon, Jules Favre, Eugène Picard, and [Jacques-Louis] Hénon. Thus, the Second Empire saw the two great parties of the Second Republic revive, parties whose bases in the country the author of the *coup d'état* believed that he had destroyed forever: the conservative and liberal Party of Order and the democratic and anticlerical republican party. . . .

In 1860, facing the unequivocal signs of a two-fold renaissance of public opinion and its influence, the Emperor had to respond. He was forced to make a choice, but at that moment he was master of his choice. Forced to choose, because if he allowed events to take their course, they might become irresistible; master of his choice, for his power had not yet been compromized or even really questioned. The Emperor could choose to maintain the Empire intact by reinforcing the police, as he had just done after Orsini's assassination attempt; by adapting institutions to accentuate the ambiguity and technicalities of the work of the Legislative Body; or by allowing the opposition to expend its energy in a hopeless and muffled struggle. On the other hand, the Emperor could recognize the need to accommodate himself to public opinion, face the fact that the tide of liberalism was irreversible, and realize that avoiding the mistakes of Louis-Philippe on the suffrage question did not allow him to repeat the errors of Charles X in regard to the elected chamber. Thus, Napoleon III could open the way to the "liberal Empire.". . .

From 1860 to 1869 the Empire was really, in the apt phrase of Pierre de la Gorce, "the equivocal Empire." "It was no longer the old Empire, not yet the new Empire, but rather a regime undergoing constant variations in accordance with the wishes of the master and the contradictory influences of his servants." . . .

From 1860 to 1870, by a series of *senatus-consulta* and decrees, personal government gave way to parliamentary government. Without recognition of the principle itself, certain parliamentary practices were introduced in bits and pieces. There was a constant effort to maintain a clear separation between the governmental and legislative powers, in order to keep the ministers who conducted affairs of state from having any contact with the Legislative Body. These various measures, none important enough in itself to create a new regime, were, however, sufficient to throw the original system out of balance because of their partial and piecemeal introduction.

Moreover, the concessions only whetted the appetites of the opposition forces and increased their demands. What they basically wanted was the abdication of the Emperor. The "dynastic" opposition wanted a functional abdication and the establishment of a parliamentary regime, while the republicans desired a personal abdication and the departure of the man of December 2, as well. Between 1860 and 1870, progress was constant towards these two goals which were attained step by step.

From the beginning of the Liberal Empire, it was impossible to restore the simple alternatives of unconditional obedience to imperial decisions or opposition to the Empire. The idea of a "third party" was in men's minds even before it appeared in speeches and writings.

In 1861, 91 deputies criticized Napoleon's papal and Italian policy in moderate but outspoken terms. The complicated Roman situation, the repercussions of which were enormous, produced a true religious opposition. This would have been almost inconceivable before.

But the elections of 1863 mark the decisive turning point. Pierre de la Gorce has aptly described the difference in political climate between this election and the one held six years earlier: in 1857 "the Emperor protected material and moral interests from such an unassailable position that the 'men of order' could only follow in his wake. Thus the elections appeared to be but a confirmation of the plebiscite." In 1863, on the other hand, "the country still showed no aspiration to direct its own affairs, but displayed some eagerness to understand them. The religious interests, whom Napoleon had abandoned or feebly defended, summoned all those who had gladly remained silent in the past to their aid."

Despite official optimism, the results were somewhat disquieting. Of the thirty-two opposition candidates elected, seventeen were republicans and fifteen independents. Persigny, the Minister of the Interior, had to admit in a circular to the prefects that "sympathies for former governments" had revived.

In 1869, what had been a minor setback became a real reverse. The authoritarian right, which represented "the Empire intact," had only 80 members; the republican left had grown to 40; the remainder was composed of deputies who did not demand the end of the Empire, but who wanted the liberal institutions of a parliamentary regime. This last group included the independents elected in 1863, anxious Catholics, angry protectionists, and discontented former "official" candidates. Headed by a turncoat republican, Emile Ollivier, this loose group numbered more than 130 adherents. Beside them existed some 40 Orleanist-leaning deputies who formed a "center left" led by [Napoléon] Daru and [Louis] Buffet.

The mystical unanimity with which the Emperor had begun his career was gone, just as the imperial myth was itself dead. In becoming a reality, it had lost its vague and attractive form. . . .

The results of the plebiscite of 1870 showed that the country had not turned against the still popular Emperor; but it obviously meant to have a more active and effective say in public affairs. It could no longer believe that Napoleon could see and do everything singlehandedly. His many unsuccessful programs and resounding defeats made it impossible not to blame them on the old bureaucracy and authoritarian institutions.

In short, the country hoped that Napoleon would "reign" more and "rule" less. All expiring regimes share such hopes. Louis-Philippe's sons had nervously wished for this on the eve of 1848, and now Ollivier was promising that "we shall enable him [Napoleon III] to enjoy his old age."

The very existence of the parliamentary Empire approved by the plebiscite of May 8, 1870, has often been ignored because it was so brief. To be sure, the regime did not last long, but as the end result of a gradual evolution, it lasted long enough for its historical importance to become clear. The Empire, which had begun as a "democracy without freedom," eventually became a *constitutional monarchy with universal suffrage*. The contrast between these two phrases marks a transition and not a parenthesis in the reign of Napoleon III. The Second Empire appears as the authoritarian price of the abrupt institution of universal suffrage. . . .

It is understandable that the men of the generation that lived through the Empire, and those that immediately followed it, were particularly offended by the absence of civil liberties. But with the passage of time, we can see things in a different light, and a much more favorable one. Basically, the Empire was a time of apprenticeship for universal suffrage, a decisive moment in the political education of the peasantry, which comprised the greater part of France's population. The numerous recent studies in electoral geography show that "rural Bonapartism" gave rise to the "rural radicalism" so characteristic of the Third Republic. Both phenomena were reactions against the "notables." The Emperor had been the hero of the "common man"; the republican left replaced Napoleon III as his protector against traditional or economic forces. It was from Bonapartist soil that the "new social stratum" (*nouvelles couches*) of Gambetta sprang. When Gambetta prophetically declared to the declining Empire that "between the Republic of 1848 and the Republic of the future, you are only a bridge, and one we shall cross," he summed up history in an image that would have been perfect if, instead of taking the middle pier of the bridge [the Second Republic] as his point of departure, the great orator had started from the far bank, that is, the July Monarchy.

The Second Empire was indeed a "bridge," but it did not merely link two Republics; it also connected the parliamentary regimes of 1830 and 1875. The trial of the Empire was doubtless inevitable before the durable synthesis of the institutions of the Third Republic could be attained. An authoritarian regime was necessary to contain nascent democracy until it became mature enough to accept the traditional forms of a liberal constitution.

THE MYTH OF NAPOLEON III

Theodore Zeldin

There has . . . grown up a myth about Napoleon III as a sort of counterpart to the legend about Napoleon I. It began with the story that he had been elected president because the royalist politicians thought he would be a tool in their hands, a story that they invented to flatter their own importance. There is, in fact, incontrovertible evidence that they supported him because they saw that he was bound to win; and Thiers, who never erred on the side of modesty, would have stood himself had he thought he had any chance at all. The story that he was allowed to take his seat in parliament in June 1848 because he was considered harmless and an imbecile is also an invention from the same source. Rumours were spread that he could not speak French, that his hobby was rearing eagles in cages, that so conscious was he of his own incompetence that he had opened negotiations of his own accord to secure the return of the legitimist pretender. The politicians who met him, however, quickly saw how wide all this propaganda was of the truth. Montalembert, the leader of the liberal Catholics, was much impressed when he first went

Theodore Zeldin, "The Myth of Napoleon III," *History Today*, vol. VIII, no. 2 (February, 1958), 104–109. © 1958 by Theodore Zeldin. Used by permission of the author and *History Today*.

to see him in October 1848. "I cannot conceive," he noted in his diary, "where his reputation for incompetence comes from."

It is time, therefore, that the abuse of his enemies should be appreciated in its true light and not accepted as impartial history merely because they happened to be distinguished men. What has been said about him should be put aside and an attempt should be made to study the facts and the primary sources. The man, however, cannot be assessed unless his work is also assessed. . . .

His standing as a statesman must depend to a very considerable extent on the way in which the Liberal Empire is interpreted. Napoleon I claimed in exile that his object had always been to establish liberty, and that the Hundred Days were destined to inaugurate a new era of peace and constitutional monarchy. No one has believed him, and quite rightly, for his character and his career made it impossible for him to accomplish such a metamorphosis. Is it right, however, to dismiss the similar claims of Napoleon III? Was he a liberal only in opposition and a despot as soon as he got the reins of power into his own hands?

In truth, he was probably a determined believer in the merits of neither liberalism nor despotism, but an opportunist above all else. He had thought a great deal about the art of success, and he was determined not to repeat the mistakes that had made others, and especially his uncle, fail before him. Politics was for him "the application of history." The task of the statesman was to study history and to discover which of the driving forces in the world had passed forever and which would triumph. Success would come to him who judged correctly which way the wind was blowing and trimmed his sails accordingly; to him who always made sure to lead events and not to be dragged by them. He must represent the aspirations of his epoch; and that is why his flattering courtiers pleased him by saying, "Sire, you are the century." . . .

In 1848 he was, to an extraordinary extent, "the man of the century"; and he did not owe his success simply to the attraction of his name. He represented better than anyone else the French peasantry, whose hearts were on the left but whose pockets were on the right, who were fond of being "advanced" in theory but who, in the practical conduct of life, sought only the traditional rewards for their labour—property and social advancement for their children. Similarly, Napoleon was at once conservative and radical, a lover of peace but also a lover of glory, an unbeliever married to a religious wife—a bundle of contradictions, but of the very contradictions that were innate in the great majority of his subjects.

He was the only politician of the time who could be conservative without being retrograde. The proclamation of universal suffrage had cast terror into the old parliamentary leaders, who hastened to modify and limit it as soon as they returned to power. Napoleon alone knew how to place himself at the head of such an electorate, to lead it in the direction he chose and so to prove that it could be a perfectly harmless and conservative force. When he fell in 1870, no one could seriously think of abolishing universal suffrage; and this is not the least of his contributions to the development of the institutions of his country. . . .

. . . Napoleon made his government work by offering the electorate what it wanted, in return for support on matters to which it was indifferent. The centralization of Louis XIV and Napoleon I placed immense power in the hands of the government, and without the approval or initiative of its head very little could be done. Napoleon III argued that the details of politics mattered little to the peasants, and that they did not care whether there were one or two parliaments in Paris or none at all. He thought that what really interested them was how to finance improvements in their daily existence, how to build roads to their farms and railways to their markets, how to bring water to their villages and how to establish local schools for their children, and how, on top of all this, to find the money to maintain their hospitals and their almshouses, to repair their churches and to embellish their village halls. The centralization of the country required the peasants to pay taxes for these very purposes, but they had to send their money to Paris and then to beg it back from the government. The government was willing to help those who helped it. It redistributed the taxes in the form of subsidies to the villages that voted favourably in the elections. It offered part as a bait, just before the elections, and the rest as a reward if the results were satisfactory. It seemed a good bargain to many who cared nothing for politics and hence the unanimous votes which the opposition attributed to force.

A good deal of force and intimidation was, of course, used but not on the great majority of ordinary men. The system was more subtle than that. Napoleon had by far the best organized party in the country, for he had at his disposal the civil service, which now reached the zenith of its prestige and its power. The prefects, enjoying their hey-day and reproducing in the provinces the glitter of the imperial court, were not simply administrators but the veritable political leaders of their departments. They gave much time to the task of making converts to Bonapartism, wooing the aristocracy with dinner parties and balls, wooing the bourgeoisie with jobs and favours, wooing above all the masses with the gift and the promise of material benefits. They took the credit for the prosperity that the country enjoyed; and it is largely thanks to them that the Second Empire was afterwards remembered as the good old days when men used to play games with golden coins.

They could speak to almost every peasant in the country through the mayors of the villages, appointed by the government and so invested with all the authority that comes from being an official of a centralized state like France. These mayors presided over the elections in the villages; and they made sure that the people understood the "social contract" of the Second

Empire. They did not compel any man to vote for Napoleon or his official candidates, and they did not falsify the returns of unanimous results: they just made it unwise to cast a contrary vote. The system of voting was different from that now used in England. The voter was not presented with a list of candidates and asked to place a cross against one of them. Instead, he was required to put in the box a ballot paper which he had to produce himself, bearing the name of his favourite. These ballot papers were generally supplied by the candidates; but the government had the advantage that it sent the ballot paper of the candidate it supported with the card that entitled an elector to vote. The ignorant, therefore, frequently came to vote with their electoral cards and their government ballot papers, which they put in the box as though they were the only ones that could be used. When some poor peasant came to the village hall with a ballot paper that an opposition agent had given him, the mayor presiding over the box would at once spot it.

"Ah!" he would say. "Haven't you got any other ballot paper apart from that one?"

"Why, yes, Monsieur le Maire."

"Show me."

The elector shows several. The mayor takes the official candidate's and says, "Here, my good man, this is the *good one*; put the others down—." Then the mayor puts it into the box. Or he would say, "Put the ballot paper you've got into your pocket and take this one: this is the *good one*."

Such proceedings took place when the mayor was a paternal figure and the elector a submissive peasant. But sometimes a more arrogant man would march into the voting hall and demand a ballot paper. He is given the official candidate's. He asks for "another one." The mayor says there are no others. The man insists. The mayor gets angry. A row would start and in the end the man would probably be thrown out. Of course, the mayor would receive great sympathy; for was not this desire to vote against his advice a challenge to his authority, a doubt cast upon his knowledge of how administrative business should be transacted? It was for personal reasons, as much as because of their political preferences, that the mayors lost their tempers with organizers of opposition. They looked upon dissent as a personal insult. One mayor, no more pompous than most, thus writes to his prefect: "Yesterday three men travelled over my commune, putting up red posters everywhere in favour of M. Casimir Périer. When I and a gendarme asked them by what right they were putting up notices on the wall of the town hall without my authorization, they replied in an *impertinent* manner, that they had no need of my authorization." This was a slur on his dignity and his rage can be imagined.

The mayors had valuable allies in the schoolmasters, who were likewise agents of the state. Here is a report from one of them to show how they acted: "As secretary of the town hall, entrusted in this capacity with the preparation of all the election documents, I was able to exercise far greater influence on the elections. In conjunction with the village constable, I distributed the ballot papers I received from Monsieur le Préfet to the electors. I strongly supported the candidature of M. Arnaud, the government's candidate. I tried to make the electors understand that we must all without exception consolidate the plans of our august Emperor by a unanimous vote. Despite, this, I was compelled to redouble my zeal and energy owing to the fact that some agitators had led astray a large number of electors and particularly twenty electors at a village not far away, who had been earnestly solicited to vote for M. Dupont Delporte and were completely disposed to vote for the latter and in consequence to reject the government's candidate. Having heard this vexatious news, I went to make them see the error into which they had fallen. To prove to them that the government is good, I gave them knowledge of a letter which Monsieur le Maire of the commune had received from Monsieur le Préfet, in which it is said that a new subsidy of 220,000 francs had just been given to the department to be divided between the communes that had suffered in the floods of 1856. In the presence of this testimony of the solicitude of the government, will you be so ungrateful, I told them, as to refuse it your co-operation: and at once they all threw down the ballot papers that had been given to them and came at once to the town hall to vote for M. Arnaud."

In the course of the reign this system gradually disintegrated, and by 1869 it had pretty well collapsed. Napoleon himself hastened its collapse by his own measures. He found it unsatisfactory despite, and even because of, the almost absolute power that it gave him. One day, talking with the duc de Plaisance of his days as president of the republic, he said regretfully, "Ah! Those were the days!" Plaisance said things did not seem to have worsened for him. "You are quite wrong, my dear duke," replied Napoleon. "At that time it was all life and movement around me; today it is silence. I am isolated, I no longer hear anything." He was expected to do everything himself, but inevitably, in practice, he could not. He had to bear all the responsibility, nevertheless, while his ministers wielded their immense power without adequate control from parliament or from each other. Both he and they soon perceived that such checks were desirable, quite apart from any ideological reasons, simply in the interests of more efficient government. He saw, too, that he could hardly go on preaching liberty to the rulers of Europe when he did not practise it himself. He was getting old, moreover; and yet as things stood, all the achievements of the reign hung on the life of one sick man. He must provide for the future and found institutions that would render his work permanent.

Many of his earliest supporters had no wish to continue with the old system either. They may have been docile enough when he emerged clothed in all the prestige that his immense victories at the plebiscites gave him; but now they thought it was time they should share his power. They could no longer win their elections in their constituencies simply by declaring their loyalty to him, by saying, as did an old veteran of Waterloo, "If you re-elect me, I shall, as before, support the Empire and we will repeat together, 'Long Live The Emperor.'" They now had to meet the powerful challenge of an opposition which promised all the utopian joys the age could imagine. They could no longer defeat them by the old system; so they had to outdo them at their own game and promise even more, with liberty to crown it. In this way did they become supporters of a Liberal Empire, which was thus created not by the opponents of Napoleon but by his old supporters, converted like him. They had the good fortune to find in Emile Ollivier a leader who had one of the rarest and most elevated minds of his day, and who was able to organize them and to bring their vague ambitions to success.

The Liberal Empire was an attempt to break the vicious circle of revolution and reaction in which France had been caught since Louis XVI. It sought to effect progress without revolution, in the belief that reforms could be obtained only gradually, whereas revolutions, being essentially violent, would never achieve their ends because they inevitably created new problems and brought divisions, emigrations and reaction in their train. It held that France could not turn at once from despotism to parliamentary government; and it established a representative form of government as a first step. It was not muddled thinking that led it to maintain that if France wished to imitate nineteenth-century England, she should first start by copying her neighbour's preliminary institutions of the seventeenth and eighteenth centuries.

It is possible to argue therefore that since Napoleon III tackled, and for a time successfully solved, the most fundamental problem in French politics, he can claim a place among the great statesmen of the century. When the prejudice against him has died down, it will very likely be recognized that he came near to achieving as much in politics as his uncle achieved in administration and in war.

SUGGESTIONS FOR FURTHER READING

Bibliographical: ROBERT SCHNERB, "Napoleon III and the Second French Empire," *Journal of Modern History*, VIII (1936), 338–355; ALAN B. SPITZER, "The Good Napoleon III," *French Historical Studies*, II (1962), 308–329; General: MARCEL BLANCHARD, *Le Second Empire* (Paris, 1950); T. A. B. CORLEY, *Democratic Despot: A Life of Napoleon III* (London, 1961); G. P. GOOCH, *The Second Empire* (London, 1960); ALBERT GUÉRARD, *Napoleon III* (Cambridge, Mass., 1943), and *Napoleon III: A Great Life in Brief* (New York, 1955); PIERRE DE LA GORCE, *Histoire du Second Empire*, 7 vol. (Paris, 1894–1905); CHARLES SEIGNOBOS, *La Révolution de 1848*.

Le Second Empire (1848–1859), and *Le Déclin de l'Empire et l'établissement de la IIIᵉ République (1859–75)*, vols. VI and VII of ERNEST LAVISSE (ed.), *Histoire de France contemporaine* (Paris, 1921); F. A. SIMPSON, *The Rise of Louis Napoleon* (3rd ed.; London, 1950), and *Louis Napoleon and the Recovery of France, 1848–1856* (3rd ed.; London, 1951); J. M. THOMPSON, *Louis Napoleon and the Second Empire* (Oxford, 1954); ROGER L. WILLIAMS, "Louis Napoleon: A Tragedy of Good Intentions," *History Today*, IV (1954), 219–226; Special: THEODORE ZELDIN, *The Political System of Napoleon III* (London, 1958); HOWARD C. PAYNE, *The Police State of Louis Napoleon Bonaparte* (Seattle, 1966); GEORGES DUVEAU, *La Vie ouvrière en France sous le Second Empire* (Paris, 1946); DAVID I. KULSTEIN, "The Attitude of French Workers towards the Second Empire," *French Historical Studies*, II (1962), 356–375; ANDRÉ BELLESSORT, *La Société française sous Napoléon III* (Paris, 1932); LOUIS GIRARD, *La Politique des travaux publics du Second Empire* (Paris, 1952); DAVID H. PINKNEY, *Napoleon III and the Rebuilding of Paris* (Princeton, 1958); JEAN MAURAIN, *La Politique ecclésiastique du Second Empire de 1852 à 1869* (Paris, 1930); ARTHUR L. DUNHAM, *The Anglo–French Treaty of Commerce of 1860 and the Progress of the Industrial Revolution in France* (Ann Arbor, Mich., 1930); Biographical: ROGER L. WILLIAMS, *Gaslight and Shadow: The World of Napoleon III, 1851–1870* (New York, 1957); JEAN MAURAIN, *Un Bourgeois français au XIXᵉ siècle: Baroche* (Paris, 1936); HAROLD KURTZ, *The Empress Eugénie, 1826–1920* (Boston, 1964); J. M. and BRIAN CHAPMAN, *The Life and Times of Baron Haussmann* (London, 1957); PIERRE SAINT MARC, *Emile Ollivier, 1825–1913* (Paris, 1950); THEODORE ZELDIN, *Emile Ollivier and the Liberal Empire of Napoleon III* (Oxford, 1963); ROBERT SCHNERB, *Rouher et le Second Empire* (Paris, 1949).

Chapter Ten

"THE EMPIRE MEANS PEACE": THE FOREIGN POLICY OF THE SECOND EMPIRE

THE DIPLOMATIC HISTORY of nineteenth-century Europe can be divided roughly into four periods: (1) a Napoleonic (1800–14), dominated by Emperor Napoleon I and characterized by the struggle of Revolutionary France against a series of coalitions of Old Regime powers; (2) a Metternichian (1814–51), whose spirit was that of the Austrian minister of foreign affairs, Prince Metternich, and which outlasted his fall from power in 1848, being a period of general peace broken by national and liberal revolutions against the Vienna settlement of 1815; (3) a second Napoleonic (1851–70), dominated by Emperor Napoleon III, who sought to undo the treaties of 1815, promote foreign nationalism, and expand French territory and influence; and (4) a Bismarckian (1870–90), dominated by the Iron Chancellor, who aimed at preserving German hegemony, French isolation, and the peaceful solution to international disputes. To some extent the two Napoleonic periods resemble each other in that they focused on the will of the French Emperor, and because Napoleon III sought to avenge the defeat of his uncle and fulfill his presumed plans for the reordering of Europe.

The foreign policy of Napoleon III can itself be divided into two phases: the first, from 1851 to 1860, was marked by general success, victorious wars, and the gain of French prestige and territory; the second, from 1860 to 1870, saw increasing frustrations, diplomatic isolation, and final defeat at the hands of Germany.

Though he proclaimed that the Empire meant peace, Napoleon III fought separate wars against the three powers Napoleon I had battled simultaneously: Russia, Austria, and Prussia. Against Russia, Napoleon III conducted the Crimean War (1854–56), ostensibly to protect Catholic interests in the Holy Land but actually to prevent Russian penetration into the Ottoman Empire and to gain British collaboration. After a long and bloody struggle, the Peace of Paris (1856) proved that France had regained the initiative in foreign affairs and become the diplomatic center of the Continent. Prestige and the humbling of an old antagonist were the chief gains.

The Italian war waged against Austria in 1859 was another kind of struggle. As Louis Girard, Professor of History at the Sorbonne, demonstrates in the first selection, Napoleon III wanted to "do something" for the Italians because he was sympathetic to Italian nationalism. But his plans for Italian unification, which were limited to the elimination of Austrian influence and a reorganization of the country into a confederation, went awry by 1860, and though he received Nice and Savoy for his efforts, the Emperor alienated both Pope and King by his attitude toward Rome. From 1860 until the Empire fell, Napoleon III's Italian policy remained a heavy burden, one that cost him much domestic support.

Napoleon III also engaged in a policy of aggrandizement in the Mediterranean, Far East, and Mexico. In the first two areas he was relatively successful: France expanded in Algeria, showed the flag in Syria, sponsored the Suez Canal, wrung some concessions from China, and gained a foothold in Indochina. But in the New World, Napoleon's scheme for a Mexican Empire collapsed, foreshadowing his own end. "The great idea of the reign," as the English historian,

J. P. T. Bury describes it, was full of promise as long as the United States was torn apart by its Civil War. Once that conflict ended and American influence could be exerted, France was forced out, Emperor Maximilian was executed, and the "great idea" evaporated.

A colonial defeat Napoleon III could perhaps afford; those in Europe he could not. By the mid-1860's, the rising star of Bismarck was to bring ill omens for France. French intervention may have been directly responsible for Italian unification, but Germany was "made" while France remained virtually passive. Bismarck's shrewd manipulation of the German situation compelled France to be first a spectator, then a victim of Prussian military power. In the third selection, Lynn M. Case, Professor of History at the University of Pennsylvania, explains why France failed to act at the critical moment of the Austro-Prussian War of 1866, so that Sadowa represented a sharp defeat for her even though not one French soldier was killed there. The author emphasizes, perhaps over-emphasizes, how important public opinion was in causing the Emperor not to intervene at a time when France might have gained influence and territory.

The final crisis of the Second Empire, that over the Hohenzollern candidature for the Spanish throne, burst suddenly on France in the summer of 1870, only a few months after the creation of the liberal ministry of Emile Ollivier. In the last selection, the English scholar Michael E. Howard traces the genesis of the crisis and shows how Bismarck cynically exploited it against France. In the initial phase, the Empire succeeded in getting the German candidate to withdraw from consideration, but then it snatched defeat from the jaws of victory by insisting on further guarantees. The famous Ems interview between King William of Prussia and Count Benedetti became the incident that precipitated a war for which France was ill-prepared. The ensuing conflict led directly to the fall of the Empire when its troops were defeated at Sedan and Napoleon III taken prisoner.

An advocate of nationalism, Napoleon III was brought down by it much as his uncle had been more than a half a century before. France gained territory by her assistance in Italian unification when the Treaty of Frankfurt was signed in 1871. The legacy of defeat was to hang heavy over the new Third Republic for almost fifty years.

THE SECOND EMPIRE AND ITALIAN UNITY

Louis Girard

Napoleon III was brought to power by universal suffrage and prided himself that in his person he had restored the Napoleonic dynasty, whose program could not help but be different from that of the Bourbons. The Bonapartes reconciled the dynastic idea with the principles of 1789, which is why they thought they could rally the nation around the person of their leader. Included in the Napoleonic tradition was the policy of reaching a concordat with the Church, the idea of confident collaboration between Pope and Emperor, one that the history of the first Napoleon did not entirely justify. And finally, the foreign policy of the Empire aimed at liquidating the effects of the defeat of Napoleon and the people in 1815. The defeat of France had been the signal for an alliance of kings against peoples, whose chief victims were Poland and Italy, and whose symbol was the installation of the Bourbons. Their fall and the restoration of the Empire would lead to the liberation of Europe, since France could not leave this glorious mission to England.

The power upholding the treaties of 1815 was Metternich's Austria. [But] it would be dangerous to act in Germany, where Prussia would be responsible for checking Austria. In Italy, Napoleon III was confronted with a long tradition dating back to Sully and Henry IV. The peninsula had to be liberated from the Austrians and the freedom of the Holy See guaranteed. Once liberated, Italy could move only towards internal reforms that included constitutionalism, something Austria had prevented. . . . In any case, France would have to protect Piedmont, which, though created against her, nonetheless also protected her borders. If Piedmont expanded, the French government would demand Savoy from her. As in Germany, an independent and liberal Italy would take the form of a confederation. From this point of view, the ideas of Napoleon III scarcely differ from those of the ministers of Charles X or Louis-Philippe.

But the crisis of 1848 modified these traditional ideas. First, the hostility of the French towards the Piedmontese dynasty came to an end. While [King] Victor Emmanuel and [Premier] d'Azeglio could be trusted, the Mazzinians, who had appeared on the scene and developed the idea of Italian unification, seemed akin to the "reds" of France. Violent if powerless, they could only plunge Italy into anarchy that would favor an Austrian

Louis Girard, "Le Second Empire et l'unité italienne," *Atti del Convegno Internazionale sul Tema: Il Risorgimento e l'Europa (Roma, 28–31 ottobre 1961)*, Accademia Nazionale dei Lincei, anno CCCLXI-1964, quaderno n. 57 (Rome, 1964), 143–149. Used by permission of the Accademia Nazionale dei Lincei and the author. Editors' translation.

offensive. Their efforts in 1849 had made a French expedition [to Rome] and [its] occupation necessary. The situation was in itself abnormal and temporary, but it had to be maintained because its end meant that either Austria or revolution would return to Rome. It was this situation that brought about the "great refusal" of Pius IX—the unfortunate way he had rejected the advice contained in Louis Napoleon's letter to Edgar Ney,[1] and devoted himself to policies that were thoroughly Austrian in spirit. Nonetheless, in 1848 the idea of the cession of Lombardy to Piedmont, of the autonomy of an Italian confederation whose inhabitants and their princes would be united with each other, and of a Kingdom of Upper Italy with as yet unspecified boundaries began to take hold. But in all this Napoleon III played no part.

Once he was Emperor, he always declared that he wanted to "do something" for Italy. Indeed, the status quo could not be respected, for its continuation would cause an explosion. Piedmont had become part of the western world and henceforth served as a magnet for all the progressive elements of the peninsula. To do nothing would lead to a break with Austria, a Mazzinian revolution, and a conflict with Rome that might result in a schism. Imperial France wanted none of these. But if she took no action, Austria would act in her stead, thereby causing a delayed French intervention. Since France was so strong and free, she had to act first "to prevent revolutions by giving legitimate satisfaction to the needs of the people," and to insure that a middle way between revolution and reaction could be found. This presupposed French support for the moderate, reformist party, both in Piedmont and at Rome. The Holy See had to understand that "canon law was not enough for the protection and development of modern society." Having achieved the separation of civil and canon law, it would have to become reconciled with Piedmont under the aegis of Napoleon III. In this way Italy—and France as well—would be spared the Mazzinian danger. This was, in short, a return to the program of 1848.

The Emperor first attempted to realize this program in collaboration with the rest of Europe at the [Peace] Congress of Paris in 1856. A year later he realized that Austria would never associate herself with a policy that she believed (and rightly so) would spell the end of her domination in Italy. So, in 1858 the Emperor decided that France would intervene alone, a policy formulated at Plombières and involving a military alliance with Piedmont. A series of attempted assassinations, culminating in the dramatic Orsini affair, may have strengthened the Emperor's conviction that he would have to act to prevent the consequences of action by a common front of Italian

---

[1] In 1849 President Louis Napoleon had written to his friend Edgar Ney, expressing his hope that Pius IX, once he was restored to the papal throne, would issue a general amnesty, create a secular administration, institute the Napoleonic Code, and create a liberal government in his domains. [Editors' note.]

and French revolutionaries in refuge at London. Northern and central Italy would form the possible base of operations for revolution to spread throughout Europe. Prolonged French inaction might have justified it. That the revolutionaries had to some extent rallied to Piedmont since 1856 could be only one more argument in its favor.

Thus no one man was responsible for this policy, for none of the preconditions for it had been "trumped up." It was born of a situation and the feeling of urgent necessity. But Cavour, the King, and the Emperor were not men to let it all "go to waste." The novelty was the idea of *provoking* a crisis in order to determine its direction and prevent a spontaneous revolution from creating disastrous conditions.

What were the weaknesses in this plan? It presumed that once Pius IX was freed from Austrian influence he would return to those ideals he had held at the beginning of his pontificate. "Rome is the sticking point," as La Guéronnière would say [in his pamphlet *Napoleon III and Italy*]. The strength of the Mazzinians and their ability to adapt were equally unknown quantities. Napoleon III was a realist in his concern with the national problem in the areas where he was powerful. But his plans revealed uncertainty about areas that included a vast part of Italy; he showed little interest in Naples, while he left the fate of the Romagna and the duchies unsettled. He had not even resolved the very important question of Austrian participation in the future confederation.

Until the last moment he wavered between a diplomatic solution imposed upon Europe by a congress, and a military solution that diplomatic events made rather uncertain. It was to preserve the fortunes of both France and his dynasty, and to avoid leaving them solely in the hands of England that the Emperor intervened. But when the Austrian ultimatum was given he had no choice—previous governments would also have intervened. Still, in marching to the aid of Italy in a war that frightened public opinion and was one that the army had not sought, he had only the republicans, part of the students and workers, and the "left" on his side. He changed the whole tone of his government which, since his *coup d'état*, had been in debt to the conservatives. In this way he broke with his allies in the "party of order," those formerly of the "Rue de Poitiers." [The Catholic conservative] Falloux wondered whether the French were going to Italy "as the sons of St. Louis or of the Directory." As neither, for in an audacious move, Louis Napoleon went off with the army that had carried out his *coup d'état* to impose the terms contained in his letter to Edgar Ney. As the future Marshal Vaillant had said at Rome in 1849, if France "went to do Austria's work," what purpose was there in entering Italy? But it was a break with the policy of the Roman Expedition. . . .

To have allowed the Habsburgs to crush Piedmont would have been a Sadowa seven years before its time. While the imperial declaration of war supplied no precise geographical details, it did refer to [an Italy free to] the Adriatic, a point that would prove unfortunate. The victories at Magenta and Solferino were only doubtful successes, and in addition to the effective resistance offered by the Austrian army, the threat from Germany required that the hostilities be brought to an end. We have reason to believe that French public opinion would not have accepted a general war, though its suddent reversal after Villafranca revealed how changeable it could be.

But [peace] was dearly bought. Austria remained in Italy and difficulties arose in those areas—the Romagna and the duchies—whose disposition had been left undecided. How could they be abandoned to their fate under a restoration? At the same time, Pius IX refused to make any concessions or reforms, and, in any case, the sack of Perugia [by papal forces] was a strange way to have begun.

Henceforth, French parties could be classed according to their Roman and Italian policies. The old parties regrouped around the threatened temporal power of the Church, and even liberal Catholics like [Ambroise] Rendu and Augustin Cochin demanded that the Villafranca agreement be carried out.

Napoleon III attempted to associate himself with what remained of the confederative idea—a vicarate in the Romagna, a prince of the house of Savoy in Tuscany—but his heart was not in it. All this was overtaken by events, and at bottom was he really so surprised? We may doubt it, for he had wanted Italy liberated, she had shown her will, and the Emperor bowed before it. As a result he secured Savoy and Nice. He did envisage a new balance of power: a federation between North and South Italy, one that the Pope would join with what remained of his states. With Austrian participation ruled out, he would have to accept a *modus vivendi* with Victor Emmanuel and Cavour. So read *The Pope and the Congress*, a pamphlet that openly called for the end of the Pope's temporal authority. It spoke only of Rome, and a Rome in which a neutralized temporal power would have lost any real importance. The Emperor was quite clear regarding the Legations, but significantly he left the Marches and Umbria in a void. The idea that Rome might be partitioned [between King and Pope] already existed, but it would be an unequal partition since Prince Napoleon spoke only of the Leonine city when he later addressed the Senate on March 1, 1861. With a few exceptions, the famous pamphlet virtually anticipated the modern solution for the problem of the temporal power. By the end of 1859, Napoleon III had made his decision. At heart he was not deeply interested in southern Italy, while the Po valley and Rome were the two firm points of his Italian policy. His ephemeral scheme for the federation between Naples and Turin quickly showed how inconsistent he was. In short, his attitude in 1860 was still inspired by his idea of a middle way between reaction and revolution, one that would assure a peaceful and lasting solution to the Italian question.

With the aid of Austria and that of the French Legitimists as well, Pius IX, along with Monseigneur de Mérode and [General] Lamoricière, played a die-hard game of "all or nothing," and organized a Vendée and a Coblenz. If he had succeeded, would he have made war on Italy with the aid of Austria and Naples? The thought is absurd, but damns his unrealistic policy of considering Napoleon III as a revolutionary at a time when the [French] occupation of Rome enabled the temporal power to survive. The Emperor could not accept a policy which returned things to the situation before the war. On the other hand, the papal Vendée was met with a Garibaldian insurrection. To be sure, many French "redshirts," like many papal Zouaves, were driven by the lure or need of adventure. French Garibaldians continued to display, if not hostility towards the Imperial regime, then their desire for a revolutionary solution to the political and religious situation. Pushed to its limit—the [seizure of the papal palace of the] Quirinal—their triumph implied the success of the revolution, a kind of denunciation of the compromise between 1789 and Catholic tradition on which the Imperial dynasty hoped to build its future. The Cavourian and Napoleonic compromises were more closely linked than ever, even without the marriage of Prince Napoleon [to the daughter of the King of Sardinia], and as a Napoleon he wished to dose out some punishment to the Bourbons of Naples. Finally, he preferred to have Garibaldi fighting in the South rather than on the borders of Venetia or the county of Nice. The *Opinion Nationale* of Guéroult, the new organ of radical Bonapartism, was terse: "If Garibaldi attacks Rome, France will let him do so in the face of absolutist Europe. If Pius IX leaves Rome, France will withdraw her troops, Italy will occupy it, and the Pope will return." The Emperor might have preferred to let the army of Victor Emmanuel act rather than "absolutist Europe," and he did everything possible to prevent Pius IX from leaving Rome by guaranteeing him his "security," if not that of his states.

He could observe that the Italian "federalists" did not rush to the aid of the Bourbon king. The latter maintained himself in Gaeta only through the presence of French warships, just as the Pope did at Rome thanks to the [French] occupation force. The French Empire did not confuse Mazzinism and "Cialdinism" [i.e., Piedmontese annexation], as the Legitimists did. The advance of the Piedmontese removed the "free corps" of the Old Regime and those of the revolution without his having to intervene. Certainly in 1858, Napoleon III could not have foreseen the possibility of so rapid a unification of Italy, and *who* could have? But in one sense, he was justified by the fact that the miraculous Risorgimento followed so quickly upon the partial expulsion of the Austrians, while neither King nor Pope was swept away by revolution. So, he could easily resign himself to it.

Would the recall of the fleet cruising off Gaeta be a prelude to the recall of the troops stationed in Rome? On February 1, 1861, the *Journal des Débats* came out in favor of unification: "The program of Villafranca was a plan for Italian confederation in which the Pope would have held the honorary presidency. . . . Since then unification has become a reality and federation an illusion. . . . Italy must be Italian. . . . Today confederation would be only an Austrian restoration directed against France." Moreover, the kingdom to be built would offer French investors a profitable area for investment.

But Napoleon III did not want to abandon the Pope to the King. In February, 1861, [the pamphlet] *France, Rome, and Italy* replied to the republican and Bonapartist left. The French government had refused to sacrifice Italy to the court of Rome, but neither would it sacrifice the Pope to the revolution. The federative idea, which the French conservatives were supporting out of desperation after having mocked it before 1859, was outmoded. Conciliation between Pope and King was now imperative. Pius IX was isolated because he had broken with the Italian national movement whose "natural" leader he once was. Italy had been reformed, and it was up to the sovereign pontiff to return to his policy of 1847 by preventing "through reforms that would strengthen his states, the revolutions that would destroy them." He was tied to Italy and the Emperor of the French, and ought to follow their advice, not that of the counterrevolutionary conspirators. Moreover, Europe and the rest of the world were feeling the influence of reason, freedom, and progress—even Russia and Austria were touched by them—and Rome alone could not remain unchanging. Italy was freed but not yet completed. The work would be crowned by conciliation, and the seal set on it by a French evacuation.

This idea that the Roman question would be resolved only by an agreement between the Pope and Italy made good sense. Italian governments had held it since Cavour. Still, it was unwise to speak of the papacy's "saving itself"—the Holy See would eventually adopt a middle way, but not on anyone's orders. It responded by becoming involved in a counterrevolutionary program that ruled out any thought of reform. The Emperor's Italian policy foundered at Rome.

To extricate himself, he therefore had to devise expedients. At first, Napoleon III hoped for the death of Pius IX; then, in despair, he arranged the September Convention [of 1864 with the Kingdom of Italy on French evacuation], which might in some way force a solution. When he obtained the cession of Venetia from Francis Joseph [in 1866], he flattered himself that he had completed his program of liberating Italy. Sadowa, however unfortunate it may have been for Napoleon III, also offered the compensation of excluding Austrian influence and of crushing Rome's hope that the [Italian] kingdom would collapse.

And, in fact, it cannot be denied that the idea of an inevitable reconciliation made progress between 1861 and 1867. The partisans of the temporal power fully understood that for all intents and purposes its fate had been decided. In Italy many clerics and laymen realized the necessity of making Rome the capital of both the nation and the Catholic world. In 1867, developments took place that were to check the progress of conciliation. During the celebration of the Eighteenth Centenary of the Martyrdom of St. Peter, the world's Catholics flocked to Rome, in what [Louis] Veuillot considered a prelude to a counterrevolution which would have the Pope as its mainstay. The "peace congress" [of European republicans] at Geneva replied to this Catholic conclave with a reaffirmation by Garibaldi of the right of revolution. Soon after, he hurled his volunteers against the borders of the Roman state, believing that Italy's rights to the city could not be denied.

Napoleon III could no more accept a move of this kind, one that excluded any reconciliation, any more than he could have accepted the Austrian ultimatum to Piedmont in 1859. Nor could he allow the [Italian] government at Florence to carry out an operation against the Patrimony of St. Peter like that against Naples in 1860.

But if he ignored the suggestions of the French left that France allow developments to take their course, he also avoided submitting to the program of the Legitimist and clerical press which demanded not only that he help the papal troops against the Garibaldians, but also that he wage war on Italy to destroy its unity and restore a federation. Would this action probably have been accompanied by an authoritarian reaction in France, by a new "Roman expedition at home"? In his thinking, the new [French] occupation [of Rome] could only be temporary and would end after the decisions of a European congress—one which never met. But after the solemn pledge [that Italy would "never" take Rome] imposed on Rouher by the majority of the Legislative Body, Napoleon informed his minister that "in politics one should not say 'never.' Suppose that one day the Pope and Victor Emmanuel came to an understanding"—a thought that did not leave him. When [Bishop] Dupanloup came to see him before leaving for the [Vatican] Council [in 1869], he suggested that the cardinals hold a conclave in the event that Pius IX died during its sessions. Might they not elect a conciliatory Pope?

This question adequately characterizes the mixture of foresight, ignorance, stubbornness, and flexibility that marked the Italian policy of Napoleon III. He claimed to know the French better than they knew themselves. It would have been presumptuous for him to say the same thing about the Italians. Dedicated to a program which was virtually the same as that of the moderate party of 1848, he had been surprised by the rapidity of the move toward the idea of unification. After having perhaps exaggerated the dangers for his regime and for Europe of a sudden and violent explosion in Italy, he did not fully realize that the result of expelling the Austrians would mean surrendering the peninsula to Piedmont, the only effective state in Italy. But quickly realizing his mistake, he showed remarkable adaptability. He understood that the old dynasties had no future and that in a confrontation with the King [of Piedmont], only the Pope could survive. Consequently, a free and united Italy could take final shape only through an understanding with the Holy See. He rapidly grasped the outline of this reconciliation and, after all, [the scheme laid down in] *The Pope and the Congress* today seems realistic. The idea was not unique with him—it was shared by all French and Italian liberals, Catholic or not.

How then can we explain the final though relative failure of a policy which would be largely justified in the long run? By his ignorance—which all his generation shared—of the conditions necessary for reform within the Church by the Church itself. Reconciliation became possible only when the entire temporal state disappeared. In short, the Emperor believed that once the King [of Italy] had entered Rome, the Pope would flee or subordinate himself, becoming the most eminent Italian bishop, a misconception that the revolutionary and conservative parties of Europe helped to create. It must not be forgotten that Rouher's pledge of "never" and the arrival of Garibaldi in 1871 to help the armies of the French Republic [against Prussia] symbolized the mistakes and failure of a policy. Compare them to Italy's entry into World War I in 1915 and the Lateran Treaty of 1929 [between the Papacy and the Italian state]. We may well say that in this matter, as in many others, Napoleon showed a better understanding of the ends than the means.

"THE GREAT IDEA OF THE REIGN": THE MEXICAN EXPEDITION

J. P. T. BURY

The Mexican expedition was once called by Rouher "the great idea of the reign" (*la grande pensée du règne*) and subsequently this phrase was used in derision by Napoleon's adversaries. Yet in many ways the conceptions underlying the expedition were imaginative and showed once again that Napoleon was a ruler who had an acute perception of the new forces at work in his time. In the New World, which both he and some of his Saint-Simonian advisers such as Michel Chevalier had visited, he believed that there were still vast reservoirs of wealth to be tapped and he was impressed

J. P. T. Bury, *Napoleon III and the Second Empire* (London: The English Universities Press, Ltd., 1964), pp. 133–139. Copyright © 1964 by the English Universities Press, Ltd. Used by permission.

by the great and growing might of the United States. But he had little more love for this Protestant power in North America than has his successor as master of France a hundred years later, General de Gaulle; and he believed that if the Latin countries were to count in years to come they, too, must take part in industrial advance and build economic empires. Here in the New World there seemed unexpectedly to open an opportunity for France to acquire a rich sphere of economic influence and to construct a barrier in the way of the southward advance of what, in an undated memorandum of the 'forties, Louis Napoleon had called "this colossal power," the United States. This opportunity he seized with both hands, but it proved to be far less golden than he expected and his intelligence services were, not for the first time, faulty.

Napoleon's interest in Central America was, of course, no new development. It goes back at least to his concern with the proposed Nicaraguan Canal when he was a prisoner at Ham. Moreover, it has recently been shown that the canal which he had been invited to sponsor was part of a wider scheme whereby he might become President, not of Ecuador, as Lord Malmesbury erroneously recorded, but of a united Central American state, for which its promoters hoped to secure British protection. In a brochure of the late 'forties, written to forward the canal scheme, he had alluded to the desirability of seeing "Central America become a flourishing and considerable State, which will restore the balance of power by erecting in Spanish America a new centre of industrial activity powerful enough to give birth to a strong feeling of nationality and, by supporting Mexico, to prevent further encroachments from the north." Here already in germ were three main elements in "the great idea": "industrial activity" or economic development, "nationality," and the "balance of power"; in other words, he wished to see the building in Central America of a strong and prosperous nation capable of halting the southward advance of the United States, which had but recently annexed large areas of Mexico. But in 1849 Prince Louis Napoleon envisaged these developments as taking place under English auspices, whereas in 1861 the Emperor Napoleon saw them as a splendid means of enhancing French power and prestige.

In 1848 he had to explain to his Central American friends that he was far too preoccupied with his affairs in France to trouble further with canals in Nicaragua. But his interest in that part of the world was only dormant, and by 1854 it appears that, perhaps under the influence of Chevalier, he had come to the conclusion that the key to the future of Central America lay not in Nicaragua but in Mexico with its known but undeveloped mineral wealth. Mexico, which had won independence from Spain in 1821, was, like many other Latin American Republics, torn by racial and religious dissensions. These involved it in intermittent civil war, which led in 1857 to the triumph of the strongly anti-clerical "Liberals," headed by a man of Indian origin named Juarez, and to the imposition of a secularizing constitution much to the discomfiture of the Creole aristocracy and its clerical supporters. Now, from Napoleon's point of view, order and stable government were essential prerequisites of economic development, and he did not welcome the success of Juarez who in return for American support was ready to grant considerable economic concessions to the United States. Already in 1857 Napoleon had told Disraeli of his "wish and willingness to assist in establishing a European dynasty in Mexico." In 1858 he was ready to listen to one of the Mexican exiles, Hidalgo, who had gained access to him through the Empress, ever a champion of Catholic interests, and who represented that there was a strong party ready to re-establish a monarchy there if only a suitable sovereign and sufficient help were forthcoming from some European power.

Undoubtedly Napoleon's interest was aroused; but if he listened, he did not commit himself. For one thing, the Italian war was soon to be his main preoccupation; for another, the United States had made it plain that they would regard European interference in Mexico as a breach of the Monroe Doctrine.

But by the autumn of 1861 the situation had greatly altered. Italy had been unified apart from Rome and Venetia; the United States was paralysed by the Civil War which had broken out between North and South in April 1861; and in July Juarez, who had taken over a nearly empty treasury, had suspended payment on all debts to foreign bondholders. Juarez's action and the temporary impotence of the United States gave Napoleon his opportunity. The interests of British and Spanish as well as French nationals were damaged by Juarez's refusal to pay his creditors, so that in the autumn the Emperor was able to negotiate a convention whereby the three powers agreed to send a military expedition to put pressure upon Juarez to meet his obligations. At the same time he secretly endorsed the idea of a monarchical restoration and, realizing that a French prince would arouse too much jealousy, countenanced an approach to a younger brother of the Emperor Francis Joseph of Austria, the Archduke Maximilian.

Thus the Mexican adventure began under seemingly favorable auspices. There is little doubt that Napoleon at this stage believed that the show of force by the three powers would be enough to provoke a rising against Juarez, whose government would collapse, and that the Mexican royalists and French diplomacy would then do the rest, re-establishing a monarchy under Maximilian who would grant the desired economic privileges to France.

Unfortunately, the three powers from the first disagreed about the claims they were to present to Juarez and about their ultimate objectives. Moreover, the landing of some 9,000 troops (two-thirds of them Spaniards) on the Vera Cruz coast did not precipitate the looked-for rising. Napoleon, who on the eve of the Italian war had told Cavour to mind his finances and supplies: "One cannot be too careful in one's preparations"—had shown singular credulity in believing the Mexican exiles' stories and extraordinary negligence in not preparing himself with the maximum of accurate information before attempting to implement his "great idea." The Mexicans were no more ready to rise at the call of the European in 1862 than the Annamese [in Indochina] had been in 1858.

The consequence was that the Spaniards, who wanted not a Hapsburg but a Bourbon prince, and the English, who had no interest in overturning the Mexican government, having obtained some pecuniary satisfaction, soon withdrew. The French forces were left in isolation in "that land of yellow fever and black vomit," as Disraeli called it, where for the time being ... they suffered far more from the climate than from the foe.

Thus the first phase of the adventure was over. The French Foreign office had never been eager for embroilment in Mexico and now it might well seem that France, too, could withdraw after securing financial compensation. What followed, however, showed that for Napoleon the financial issue was simply a pretext for securing a foothold in Mexico. He was determined to go ahead with his plans, and, since the show of moderate force had failed, he was prepared, despite warnings from the Spanish general Prim about the difficulties of the enterprise, to use much greater force to achieve his real ends. In July 1862 he personally instructed the French commander, General Forey, to take Mexico City, summon a constituent assembly, advise it to restore the throne and invite Maximilian to become Emperor. Of Catholic interests and France's financial claims Napoleon made no mention.

The French troops were increased from some 2,500 to 20,000 (later to 30,000) and the offensive began in February 1863; but once again the looked-for popular support was not forthcoming. The French forces were checked in front of Puebla in May, as they had been checked before in Rome 1849, and, since this check, too, appeared to be an insult to national honour which had to be avenged, Napoleon was all the more dogged in the pursuit of his "great idea." Moreover, the eventual fall of Mexico City did not mean the collapse of resistance. Nationality in Mexico, as in Spain in 1808, worked against and not for a Napoleon, and Juarez could still harry the French from north and south.

Under such circumstances it was impossible to summon a freely elected parliament to vote for a monarchical regime. The French commander had to resort to a hand-picked Assembly of Notables who duly offered the crown to Maximilian. But when Maximilian, who had accepted Napoleon's earlier overtures with alacrity, at last arrived in Mexico in 1864, he proved to be too weak a personality to dominate an extraordinarily difficult situation. The government he set up was therefore unable to attract any large measure of Mexican support and depended for its maintenance on the French army.

Thus Napoleon's land of promise turned out to be a Serbonian bog. He had had to keep troops in Rome for fifteen years to bolster up the Pope and now it looked as though he might have to maintain a far larger body of men indefinitely in Mexico to prop up Maximilian. Indeed, before leaving Europe Maximilian had exacted a promise that Napoleon would lend him the support of French troops for a certain time, and in 1864 he had been assured that the troops would leave Mexico only by stages and when they could do so without compromising the existence of the new government.

Unfortunately for both Emperors (for Maximilian took the title of Emperor of Mexico), these pledges were untenable. Napoleon's position in Mexico was far less defensible than his position in Rome. In Rome it was clear that he was defending French Catholic interests; in Mexico he had no aim that could be publicly avowed as in the French national interest. French public opinion, critical of the expedition from the first, became increasingly reluctant to grant credits for expenditure which brought no visible return. Yet, obstinate and obsessed by his Mexican dream as he was, Napoleon might still have braved opposition at home but for the ending of the American Civil War in 1865 and the deterioration of the European situation in 1866. In 1862 his decision to carry on with the implementation of the "great idea" was not such folly as it might seem in retrospect; for he could still reckon that the Southern States, whose independence France like England had refused to recognize, might win the American Civil War and that North America would be permanently divided. But in 1865 the victorious Northern States, who had regarded Napoleon's neutrality during the Civil War as unfriendly, were in no mood to tolerate continued French interference in a neighbouring state. They resumed their aid to Juarez and launched a masterly diplomatic campaign against the European intruder. The threat was clear. Napoleon, who could not face war with the United States as well as war with Juarez and revolt in Algeria, was obliged to tell Maximilian that he would have to withdraw his troops by stages, even though the Mexican monarchy was not securely established. The appeals of Maximilian's wife, the Empress Charlotte, who personally crossed the Atlantic to see Napoleon and Eugénie in the summer of 1866, were in vain. By then the Austro-Prussian war had broken out and it was more than ever impracticable for Napoleon to keep 30,000 men locked up in Mexico.

The last French troops left the country of disillusionment in December 1866 and after that the miserable end was not long in following. Already the Empress Charlotte, frantic at Napoleon's treachery and her own failure to win European aid, had gone mad. Six months after the departure of the French soldiers in May 1867, Maximilian, who had changed his mind about abdicating, was taken prisoner by Juarez's men and shot. . . .

The Mexican adventure, so particularly Napoleon III's own idea and commitment throughout all its stages, vividly illustrates the qualities and still more the defects which had already shown themselves in his conduct of policy in Europe—imaginativeness and obstinacy, opportunism and equivocation, wilfulness and negligence. Of all his overseas enterprises it was the most disastrous. It dealt an irreparable blow to his prestige and cast a deep shadow over the remaining years of the Second Empire.

NAPOLEON III AND THE AUSTRO-PRUSSIAN WAR

Lynn M. Case

At the beginning of the year 1866 the French government and the French public were more and more concerned over what seemed to be an impending Austro-Prussian war over Schleswig-Holstein in particular and over rivalry for dominance in the German area in general. Ever since 1815 France had counted on this Austro-Prussian rivalry to preserve the balance of power in Europe. Austria and Prussia would not only check each other, but by their mutual suspicions they would, it was hoped in French circles, prevent the formation of a coalition against France. However, if one of these rivals should seriously defeat the other in a trial of strength, the resulting disruption of the balance of power would adversely alter France's relative position in Europe. Even more, such a victory would probably encourage the victor to compel the smaller German states to transform the loose Germanic confederation into a powerful federation dominated by that victorious power. Such an eventuality would be doubly calamitous to France. Her relative position would be still more weakened, and she would have to consecrate more and more of her wealth and manpower for military defense, especially on the most vulnerable of her borders.

Since an Austro-Prussian war seemed inevitable, Napoleon III had to consider the wisest policy for France in such a contingency. Obviously he must try to keep both sides as equal as possible so that neither could win an overwhelming victory. If they both insisted on fighting to the bitter end, they would then happily wear each other out. Prussia's military advantage was not too well known at that time because, as far as armaments were concerned, Austria was trying to keep up with the Prussians. The probability that most of the other German states would join Austria perhaps made the line-up appear to Napoleon a little too favorable to Austria. He therefore

Lynn M. Case, *French Opinion on War and Diplomacy During the Second Empire* (Philadelphia: University of Pennsylvania Press, 1954), pp. 196–211. Copyright 1954 by the University of Pennsylvania Press. Used by permission.

encouraged Italy to make an alliance with Prussia to counterbalance Austria's German support. This Italian alliance would promise Venetia to Italy and also make her more friendly to France in case France needed friends after a one-sided victory.

But a policy also had to be evolved in case the other contingency arose —that of the complete defeat of one of the two prospective belligerents. In such a case France, in self-defense, would be compelled to intervene. This would mean mustering her forces and entering the war on the weaker side. By doing this France could prevent one dominant nation from upsetting the balance of power and could impose her will in the final settlement—a settlement which would save the weaker contestant and give France a chance to demand her border territories along the Rhine which she had lost in 1815. This territorial compensation Napoleon III had always dreamed of as one of the aims of his reign.

To enter a war at such a psychological moment without being attacked presented, however, the difficulty of carrying public opinion with him. Napoleon knew that opinion seemed hostile to war both in 1854 and 1859 when he had had to take up arms. Yet in both of these instances the enemy (Russia and Austria respectively) had appeared as plausible aggressors, and the French public had supported the wars. But the strong peace settlement during the Polish and Danish crises would certainly have strengthened his misgivings about public support of an unprovoked French counterbalancing intervention into this future German conflict. The Emperor of the French, therefore, needed to know just how much the public would qualify its peace sentiment in case the second alternative materialized. Consequently it would have been surprising if he had not continued to feel the pulse of France through the administrative reports to learn what the people were thinking in the early months of 1866. These reports could give him, and do give us today, a fairly clear picture of French opinion on the eve of the Austro-Prussian War.

In the early period, before 3 May 1866, the manifestations of French opinion were again overwhelmingly opposed to war and to France's participation in one. All the procureur reports mentioning foreign affairs during the month of April, except that from Lyons (covering opinion from January to April), showed either definite opposition to France's entering the impending war or at least alarm at the prospects of war. The report from Rennes is typical of the attitudes reported:

All my information [wrote the procureur general] was in agreement in asserting that at no time has the maintenance of peace been so unanimously desired. This trend of public opinion has been so energetically expressed that the people seemed to refuse to admit that there could be any circumstances urgent enough to oblige the emperor to abandon the wise neutrality he has enunciated. This ardent and absolute desire for peace, pushed almost to the point of obsession with a large number, can be explained by various causes, the principle one of which can be found in the more threatening perils and the more general uneasiness that war would engender for private business interests in these days. . . .

But, in addition to the official reports coming into the minister of justice, evidence of antiwar sentiment was found in the observations of the foreign diplomats in Paris. Wächter from Wurttemberg told how Rothschild and Pereire, representing French financial circles, had pleaded with Napoleon III on 10 April to throw his great influence in the scales of world diplomacy to prevent war. They painted a very somber picture in general if peace were not assured. . . .

. . . By the testimony of Napoleon's procureurs general, of the foreign diplomats, and of the semiofficial press French opinion strongly favored a peace policy up to the month of May.

And in the first week of May two incidents occurred which gave the emperor a chance to see how this opinion was becoming stronger and more emphatic. We have an advance warning of the first impending incident from Count Nigra who, writing to his government on Tuesday (1 May), said:

The French government is concerned about the interpellations which will take place Thursday in the legislative body. . . . It will be asked for an explicit declaration concerning the attitude it will take relative to Italy. . . . But in the face of the [Austro-Italian] military preparations, which the supporters of peace at any price like to present as simultaneous or almost simultaneous, the French government will have some embarrassment in making a reply.

The dreaded parliamentary attack came on Thursday, 3 May, and from the most formidable member of the opposition in the lower house, Adolphe Thiers. In a long and masterful speech he underlined one guarantee which France had received in the treaties of 1815, that of a Germany only weakly united in a loose confederation. That, he said, was the basis of French policy. Germany must be warned against forming a strong federation; Prussia must be told politely but firmly that France will oppose any considerable expansion of the Prussian state. Thiers also denounced France's help in achieving Italy's unification, and he insisted that France should not enter the impending war to protect Italy. Indeed, France should insist that she withdraw her Prussian alliance. If Italy imprudently entered the war, she should have to take full responsibility for her eventual fate.

Go [cried Thiers], go anywhere in France, go into the smallest towns and villages, and you will see whether this policy, which would tend to re-establish the ancient German empire by placing the power of Charles V in the north instead of in the south of Germany, whether that power [Prussia], supported by Italy, would be popular in France. No, there is too much common sense in France ever to welcome such a policy.

But Thiers recognized that sentiment was also opposed to war to protect France's position. "Undoubtedly we agree with the policy of neutrality," he added, "because no one here is foolish enough to insist on plunging into a war to avoid a war." Consequently France was to give Prussia a polite warning, and, if Prussia refused to heed it, to maintain an ominous silence. Thiers's policy, then, was a curious combination of "speak up" and "shut up" with no tolerance for "putting up" a threat of force to back the protests.

Thus Thiers had said all he could to discourage moral support of the Prussian-Italian cause without daring to be caught in the trap of advocating war. But the speech was an open criticism of Napoleon III's tendency to encourage various national aspirations. In a speech just preceding that of Thiers the government spokesman, Rouher, had tried to be as reassuring as possible. If Italy attacked Austria, he declared, it would be at her own risk and peril. As for France, she adhered to "a peaceful policy, a genuine neutrality and freedom of action." Whether it was Thiers or Rouher, the policy— in line with prevailing opinion—was peace. . . .

. . . The emperor was cut to the quick by the courage of Thiers' attack, by the general approval he obtained among Napoleon's own legislators, and especially by the favorable references to the treaties of 1815, which the emperor detested. He finally decided to make an issue of the debate and at the same time send up a trial balloon to ascertain once and for all just what was the attitude of the country and whether at least it might not be lured into intervention for the sake of compensation. He did it in a curious way by a public speech given in Auxerre on 6 May. Its most significant passage was:

> I have, besides, a debt of gratitude to repay to the department of Yonne. It was one of the first to vote for me in 1848 because it knew, like the great majority of the French people, that its interests were mine and that I, like it, detested the treaties of 1815 which they would like to make the sole basis of our policy.
> . . . In your midst I breathe more easily, for it is among the working people of town and country that I rediscover the real genius of France.

The general impression the emperor wanted to make was that he favored the national movements which changed the settlement of 1815, that he wanted a rectification of France's boundaries of 1815, and that he was not averse to a war in central Europe to achieve these ends. Now he could sit back and watch the public reaction, and could see whether the public, looking at the situation in this light, would be less averse to war and France's possible involvement in it. . . .

. . . The procureurs general and prefects . . . three weeks later . . . felt obliged to assert that the people were opposed to his Auxerre speech and to any encouragement of war. Considering that these officials were inclined to look for favorable reactions, this high percentage of admitted unfavorable opinions is impressive. The procureur report from Orleans is typical of the vast majority:

I have to inform Your Excellency [wrote the procureur general], with a deep feeling of regret but none the less faithfully, that the Auxerre speech has not obtained the approval that the emperor's words have always before received. I must say that public opinion appears hostile and defiant. The demonstration in the chamber in the session of 3 May and the speech delivered at Auxerre were so closely connected and yet seemed so opposed to each other that it was a serious matter to see a sort of current draw the public to the side of the chamber and just to that extent draw it away from the emperor. . . .

Napoleon III apparently had his answer: the public had definitely and consciously supported the legislature against the emperor and preferred a policy of peace to one of adventure. Lord Cowley, the British ambassador, in accusing the emperor of wanting war so that he could dictate terms in favor of France and Italy, summed up his impression of the response to the Auxerre speech thus: "But the country did not respond to this ill-concealed, if unavowed, policy. So strong a desire for the maintenance of peace was manifested that the emperor was obliged to change his tactics and propose conferences for the settlement of the differences which were likely to lead to war."

A new proposal on 24 May of a European conference in collaboration with England and Russia was then the emperor's next step. He did not have much hope of the success of a conference, but it would leave the impression with the public that he preferred a peaceful solution. Austria, however, rejected the conference in early June, and the outbreak of war then became only a matter of time.

It is one of the ironies of history that French opinion, by being for peace at almost any price, contributed to the outbreak of the Austro-Prussian War. Bismarck could not have felt safe to unleash a war if he had not been reasonably sure that the French government would be restrained from intervening against Prussia by a strongly pacifist public opinion. Prussian agents and army officers, entering France from Geneva in the months just preceding the war, were seen by the prefects themselves in all parts of the country even as far as Marseilles, Toulouse, and Bordeaux, checking on the antiwar sentiment of the populace and on any secret war preparations by France. As a result of their reports and those of the Prussian military attaché in Paris, von Loe, Bismarck was able to boast to the French ambassador in Berlin, Benedetti, at the start of the war: "Our confidence in the emperor is so great that we are not leaving one soldier on the left bank of the Rhine."

Three days before hostilities started, in the session of 13 June, Napoleon III had read to the legislative body a letter he had written to his minister of foreign affairs, Drouyn de Lhuys, as the vehicle for giving to the public his views on the situation. Here under a sugar-coating of peaceful neutrality he retained a vague suggestion of French intervention in case of an unfavorable disturbance of the balance of power. The letter also suggested to the public that France would demand compensations if one side acquired enough territory to upset the balance of power, that France was assured participation in the final settlement, and the present policy of "attentive neutrality" might require the use of "our strength." . . . Evidence of the public reaction to the conference proposal and to France's attitude during the early weeks of the war shows conclusively that the French people of all classes and of most shades of politics were still strongly opposed to France's engaging in a war. . . .

Then suddenly during the night of 3–4 July came the telegraphic news of the overwhelming Prussian victory at Sadowa. The emperor, his counselors, and the discerning public were stunned by the implications of the news. The European balance of power had been destroyed overnight, and France was on the light end of the balance. La Gorce, contemporary and historian of the period, exclaimed: "We felt that something on the soil of old Europe had just crumbled. . . . Among the people uneasiness . . . in the sovereign's official circle . . . bitter perplexity." The *Times* correspondent wrote home: "The intelligence of the Austrian defeat has produced consternation. You hear it remarked on all sides that this tremendous weapon [needle gun] makes the Prussians almost masters in Europe." Even before the battle of Sadowa, Napoleon III had shown concern over Prussia's initial minor victories. "I saw the Emperor this morning [1 July]," wrote Cowley, ". . . it was clear from His Majesty's tone that the Prussian successes have taken him by surprise and that he is in some alarm at them." After Sadowa, Empress Eugénie expressed her unconcealed alarm directly to the Prussian Prince Reuss: "You have displayed such energy and promptitude in your operations that with such a nation as a neighbor we run the risk one fine day of seeing you at the gates of Paris before we scarcely realize it. I'll go to bed French and wake up Prussian." The Prussian troops, confidently removed from the Rhine area, had helped to make these operations successful. Thus French pacifist opinion had not only contributed to the outbreak of the war but had also unwittingly compassed the defeat of Austria and the disruption of Europe's balance of power.

On the heels of this disconcerting news came Austria's surrender of Venetia to Emperor Napoleon, accompanied by a request for his mediation to end the war. . . .

Not only did Napoleon III accept the mediation offer, but he also immediately made use of it for favorable publicity. Under his own supervision a brief announcement was composed and published in the next morning's *Moniteur*. It read:

An important development has just occurred.

After having safeguarded the honor of his arms in Italy, the emperor of Austria, acceding to the ideas put forward by Emperor Napoleon in his letter to his minister of foreign affairs of 11 June, cedes Venetia to the French and accepts his mediation to bring about peace between the belligerents.

Emperor Napoleon hastened to answer this appeal and immediately addressed himself to the kings of Prussia and Italy to effect an armistice.

The Emperor's knowledge of the moods of public opinion usually seemed unerringly accurate. But on this occasion he overplayed his hand. The change from consternation to loud rejoicing, which this announcement inspired, bordered on the hysterical. The *Moniteur* was hardly off the press before Paris was shouting with joy. Public buildings and private shops and dwellings all over town were decked out with flags. There was enthusiasm everywhere. The stock market jumped four francs. The ubiquitous little lawyer, M. Dabot, was a witness to the celebrating but not a participant. In his diary of 5 July he wrote: "The flags are flying from the windows. Why? From pure national vanity! For the gift is dangerous. Naturally the emperor is going to give Venetia to Italy, and she angered . . . will store up another grudge against France. Well, I'm not going to fly a flag from *my* window." And then at night the streets and buildings were illuminated. The long lines of gas lights which fringed the balconies and roofs created a joyous holiday brilliance. The emperor had kept France from war, and now as the arbiter of a continent he was going to restore peace to the rest of Europe—and perhaps some lost provinces to France. Hopes were high after a previous night of dismay. . . .

. . . The Paris press was more sober in its reception. The non-governmental papers did not forget the Sadowa disaster and discussed the possible difficulties of getting Italy's co-operation. To the extent that they were saner in their appreciation just so were they still failing to reflect general opinion. The semiofficial press, however, took the hint from the *Moniteur* insertion or from some prodding of La Valette, the minister of interior, and further emphasized the glory coming to France and her ruler. The *Constitutionnel* expressed pride that Austria would "so nobly seek out the imperial government." The *France Politique* exclaimed, "Immense victory for humanity, for civilization, and for France." The emperor was hailed as liberator of Venetia, founder of world peace, and arbiter of Europe.

Yet on the same day of the flag flying, public rejoicing, and stockmarket rise (5 July) the fatal council meeting at Saint-Cloud took place. Napoleon knew that his position was weak in comparison with what the public acclaimed it to be. He quickly sensed that his face-saving announcement in the *Moniteur* had worked too well and might embarrass him in some warlike decisions he might have to make. Goltz reported that he tried to have the demonstrations of rejoicing stopped, but it was too late. The council meeting was initially arranged by Drouyn de Lhuys, the foreign minister, in a way to favor his forceful intervention policy. He deliberately excluded La Valette, the minister of interior. Moreover, he managed to see the emperor alone before the meeting opened. He and Randon, minister of war, brought out the seriousness of the Sadowa victory and the necessity for quick action to salvage the situation. To the eastern border 80,000 men could and should be sent at once. France still had a chance to retain Austria and the other German states as allies. Then by mobilization and legislative appropriation she could follow up the initial movement of the 80,000. The decrees for the movement of troops and the summons of the legislature and a note announcing the forceful policy should be published the next morning (6 July) in the *Moniteur*.

For a moment the tragedy at Sadowa and the urgency of the situation completely overwhelmed the emperor. They seemed to have blotted out all his consideration for the peaceful pressures of public opinion. Influenced by the insistent pleas of his two leading ministers and of the empress herself Napoleon indicated his agreement with the policy of forceful intervention.

It was at this point that La Valette, uninvited, walked into the council meeting. Since he was minister of interior, the emperor welcomed him and explained the subject under discussion. La Valette immediately jumped up and opposed vehemently the whole proposal. A mediator, he declared, cannot start out by threatening force. The one who encouraged the Prussian-Italian alliance cannot be the one to urge perjury on the Italian king. And then La Valette advanced what he hoped might be the clinching argument— public opinion. "What would Europe say [including French public opinion] if Italy, forced to justify herself, published documents to show that her treaty with Prussia of 8 April had been, not only approved, but actually promoted by the imperial government?" The emperor was visibly affected. Neither he nor Drouyn de Lhuys replied, but they and the empress deliberately withdrew from the council for a short time. When they returned, Napoleon persisted in his agreement with Drouyn de Lhuys. La Valette, however, would not let the matter rest here. He went on with further arguments about France's unpreparedness, the drain on her men and supplies by the Mexican expedition, the threat that Prussia and Italy would fight rather than submit to forceful intervention. Turning upon the foreign minister, he castigated him for his irresponsible and hazardous policy. The atmosphere became so charged with recrimination that the emperor finally closed the meeting without indicating any change in his previous resolution. By that time, however, he also knew that Rouher, his favorite advisor and minister of state, and Baroche, his minister of justice, were in entire agreement with La Valette.

The night of 5–6 July must have been a sleepless one for the emperor, for he finally brought himself to abandon the war policy of Drouyn de Lhuys and the empress for the peaceful mediation policy of La Valette and Rouher. The importance of this decision in assuring Prussia's complete victory and her dominance in Europe is revealed by Bismarck's admission before the Reichstag (16 January 1874) of the bad situation in which Prussia would have found herself if Napoleon III had chosen the opposite policy of forceful intervention. "France had but few available forces [he declared], but a small contingent would have been enough, along with the large numbers of troops of southern Germany, to constitute a very respectable army. This army would have immediately forced us to cover Berlin and abandon all our successes in Austria." . . .

. . . The more the developments of opinion since January 1866 are studied, the more the conviction grows that public opinion was one of the emperor's most important considerations in his debates with himself that night. He had noted the universal rejoicing at the *Moniteur's* announcement. To threaten force would belie the favorable position the people had attributed to him. Metternich reported thus on the emperor's indecision:

A regular panic seized him at the idea of an Italian rejection [of mediation] and the sight of the illuminations glorifying the triumph of his policy made him feel doubly the weight of the engagements he has assumed and which could throw in his lap a war in two directions. From that moment he began to hesitate and vacillate.

Yet it must have been more than just the celebration of 5 July. . . . He had been preoccupied with opinion all during his reign. Regular reports during the Polish and Danish crises and in the months just before the outbreak of the Austro-Prussian War had clearly informed him of the almost unanimous insistence on peace. The people and the press had both openly condemned his Auxerre speech, and he had recently made further special inquiries of the prefects and the mayors concerning opinion. Perhaps he had forgotten his public for a moment, but in the quiet of that wakeful night the still, small voice must have again spoken loudly in his inner ear. Especially, who were those opposing the policy of force? They were La Valette who, as minister of interior, received and analyzed the prefect reports on public opinion, and Baroche, minister of justice, who received the reports of the procureurs general, and finally Rouher, minister of state, who represented the government in the legislature and who knew the legislators' hostility toward war. They were closest to opinion, they were always the ones to whom he turned for information on opinion. Rouher, to be sure, usually had great influence with Napoleon III, but both La Valette and Baroche were of secondary importance at court. That their advice prevailed over that of the empress, Drouyn de Lhuys, and Randon must be in part explained by the force of opinion they represented. Rothan affirms that "public opinion at that advanced stage of the reign was in fact the great concern of the imperial government." But a more direct acknowledgment of it came from the emperor himself in a conversation he had with the Spanish ambassador, Olózaga, in July 1870 during the crisis over the Hohenzollern candidacy. On that occasion he confessed:

> It cost us a great deal to recognize the state of affairs which the battle of Sadowa created in Germany. We tolerated it, although not without regret. French public opinion was at that time very emphatic in favor of peace, and I was resolved to respect that trend of thought. . . .

Napoleon III, like many responsible chiefs of state in our present-day democracies, faced a perplexing dilemma of following what he thought was his own better judgment or of yielding to the less discerning public demand. He had to choose between the exigencies of the state system and the democratic dictates of opinion. Perhaps he should have been more vigorous and courageous in educating opinion to the point where it would have understood the far-reaching implications of the diplomatic situation. His one adventure in this direction, his Auxerre speech, was certainly inadequate and ineffectual. Yet, if his final decision, made in response to the popular will, brought misfortune to France, the French people themselves must bear their share of the blame. . . .

"RED RAG" AND "GALLIC BULL":
THE HOHENZOLLERN CANDIDATURE

Michael E. Howard

. . . In July 1870 the crisis of the Hohenzollern Candidature broke from a clear sky.

On 30th June Émile Ollivier, the President of the Council, declared to the Chamber that "at no period has the maintenance of peace seemed better assured." He was not alone in his optimism. On 5th July Lord Granville, taking up his duties as Foreign Secretary in Mr. Gladstone's first Cabinet, was informed by the Permanent Under-Secretary that "he never had during his long experience known so great a lull in foreign affairs." Yet the issue which shattered the peace was not a new one. The Spaniards had been seeking a monarch ever since their revolution against their unsatisfactory Queen Isabella in 1868, and the name of Leopold, Hereditary Prince

Reprinted with permission of The Macmillan Company and Rupert Hart-Davis, Ltd., from *The Franco-Prussian War; the German Invasion of France, 1870–1871* by Michael Howard (New York: The Macmillan Company; London: Rupert Hart-Davis, Ltd., 1961), pp. 48–57. © Michael Howard, 1961.

of Hohenzollern-Sigmaringen, had figured very early in the list of possible candidates. He was a Catholic, married to a Portuguese princess and father of a family. His brother Charles had recently accepted the crown of Rumania. His relationship to the Prussian Hohenzollerns, would bring the goodwill of one great European power, and since there also ran in his veins the blood of Murats and Beauharnais it was to be hoped that Napoleon would be mollified as well. In September 1869 his principal Spanish supporter Don Eusebio di Salazar visited Leopold and his father, Prince Charles Antony, to urge all these arguments upon him. But the Prince showed little desire to ascend the unstable throne in Europe, and Salazar went empty away. In February 1870, however, after further canvassing by Bismarck's agents, Marshal Prim, President of the Spanish Council of Ministers, sent him back in an official attempt to renew the offer, and this time tried to enlist William I as an ally. This was a shrewd move. Both Charles Antony and Leopold were disciplined Hohenzollerns, quite prepared to take their orders from Berlin. Neither had yet altered his views about the unattractiveness of the project, but Leopold wrote to William: "I consider it my duty as an Hohenzollern, soldier and subject to submit to the express will of his Majesty, our King, accepting it as the guiding line of my conduct if higher political considerations and the expansion of the power and lustre of our house so demand."

William did not consider that it demanded anything of the sort. He had no wish to see his kinsmen scattered on unreliable thrones whose collapse could only involve him in humiliation. But Bismarck's reaction was different. He saw not only the advantages of a dynastic link with Spain, advantages both commercial and military, but the disadvantages which would arise if the throne were to fall into the hands of a party inimical to Prussia. On 28th May 1870 he wrote to Charles Antony a powerful letter pointing out the vital service he could render Germany by accepting the throne for his son. Charles Antony capitulated and his son Leopold reluctantly concurred. Salazar was sent for and on 19th June Leopold informed William I that he was resolved to accept the call to the Spanish throne. William showed natural umbrage that negotiations on such a vital matter should have continued without his knowledge or consent; but he gave his approval to Leopold's decision, "though with a very heavy heart." By 21st June all was arranged and Salazar telegraphed the good news to Prim.

William could claim, as he later did in the face of French attacks, that he had treated the matter as a private family concern throughout, and had used no influence to induce Leopold to accept the Crown. The same claim, when made before the Reichstag by Bismarck, was utterly false. The idea of the Hohenzollern Candidature may have originated in Spain, but throughout the previous winter Bismarck had actively forwarded it. But for his intervention it would probably have been extinguished by the cold water poured on it by the Hohenzollern princes themselves. But that is no reason to see in his policy, as have so many French historians, a "trap" deliberately laid for France. Bismarck knew quite well that a Hohenzollern on the throne of Spain would be highly unwelcome to France; but if all had gone as he had hoped, Leopold's election would have been over before Napoleon had a chance to intervene. "It is possible that we may see a passing fermentation in France," he wrote in June to one of his agents in Spain, "and without doubt it is necessary to avoid anything that may provoke or increase it ... undoubtedly they will cry 'intrigue,' they will be furious against me, but without finding any point of attack." Once the election was complete France would have no grounds for intervention which did not gravely offend the sovereignty of the Spanish people, and Napoleon would be compelled, as in 1866, to acquiesce in a *fait accompli.*

As it was, things went wrong, and they did so in a manner which, if the French had kept their heads, might publicly and profoundly have humiliated Bismarck. While Salazar negotiated, Prim kept the Cortes in prolonged session in Madrid, until the news of Leopold's acceptance made it possible to proceed to formal election. On 21st June Salazar wired that all was well, and added that he would be back in Madrid by the 26th. By an error in deciphering, this last date was read as the 9th; and rather than keep the Cortes sweltering for another idle fortnight in Madrid, Prim adjourned them until the autumn. No election could be held until they were convoked again, and in the interval there was little hope of Leopold's acceptance remaining secret. As it was, it leaked out within a few days of Salazar's return; and on 2nd July Prim tried to repair the damage by officially informing the French Ambassador that Leopold had been offered and had accepted the Crown.

The news shocked Paris. It was clear that the German Chancellor had been engaged for at least six months in a discreditable and damaging intrigue, and the French Government with good reason was outraged. The Duc de Gramont, a career diplomat who had only recently taken over the Ministry of Foreign Affairs, told the British Ambassador that the affair was "nothing less than an insult to France." The bland and patently mendacious assertion by von Thile, Bismarck's Secretary of State, that "so far as the Prussian Government is concerned the affair does not exist," heated tempers in Paris to a disastrous degree. The other powers of Europe were equally appalled at what *The Times* stigmatised as "a vulgar and impudent *coup d'état* in total contradiction to accepted diplomatic practice in handling such matters"; and had Gramont kept his head and acted as the spokesman of the Concert of Europe, Bismarck might have found it difficult to justify his actions. But Gramont was no Talleyrand. Ollivier and his colleagues were inclined to conciliation, but the Empress, whose hand was to guide Napoleon's pen during the next ten days, was not. Leboeuf assured the Council that the army was ready to fight, and on 6th July with imperial encouragement Gramont read a ministerial statement in the Corps Législatif, which filled the chauvinists with delight. While admitting the right of the Spanish people to chose whomever they wanted as king, he maintained that this right did not extend to disturbing the balance of Europe to the French disadvantage and "placing in peril the interests and the honour of France." "To prevent it," he went on, "we rely at once on the wisdom of the German and the friendship of the Spanish people. But if it proves otherwise," he continued, in a phrase inserted, curiously enough, by the pacific Ollivier, "then, strong in your support and in that of the nation, we would know how to fulfil our duty without hesitation and without weakness." The right wing and its Press roared their approval; and Bismarck, on reading the speech, commented "this certainly looks like war."

On the purely diplomatic level the prospects of a settlement still seemed fair. William I, who disliked the Candidature and certainly did not want war, was at Ems accompanied by only one Foreign Office official, Abeken, and thus was only remotely susceptible to the influence of Bismarck, who was still on his estates at Varzin. Charles Antony and Prim were appalled at the furore which they had unwittingly unleashed, and it needed little persuasion to make them abandon the project. But although William was prepared, privately and as head of the family, to advise his cousins to withdraw, he maintained that this was an affair with which he as King of Prussia had nothing to do; and it was precisely this attitude which Gramont refused to accept. Count Benedetti, the French Ambassador to Berlin, was instructed on 7th July, to demand a categorical statement that the King's Government did not approve of Leopold's acceptance and had ordered him to withdraw it. Having tried, and failed, to humiliate France, Prussia must now undergo a comparable humiliation herself. When Benedetti reported, on 9th July, that William would say only that he would acquiesce in Leopold's withdrawal in the same fashion as he had acquiesced in his acceptance, Gramont replied "if the King will not advise the Prince of Hohenzollern to withdraw, then it will be war at once, and in a few days we will be on the Rhine." He was himself being goaded by fear and by public opinion. If they delayed, he said, the Prussians would gain the lead in military preparations; and, he wired Benedetti a little pathetically on the 11th, "you cannot imagine how excited public opinion is. It is overtaking us on every side and we are counting the hours." He accused Benedetti of not being firm enough. If no definite answer was forthcoming from the King by the 12th, it would be regarded as a refusal of satisfaction.

In Gramont's eyes, and those of his supporters, the question of the Candidature itself had thus become secondary to the more vital point, of obtaining "satisfaction" from Prussia, of a kind which William, fortified by urgent advice from Bismarck, was determined not to give. Thus when on the 12th July Charles Antony, besieged by envoys from Madrid, Paris, and Ems and by letters from Queen Victoria and the King of the Belgians, renounced the throne on his son's behalf, the news was received by Gramont and by the right wing deputies and Press with embarrassed irritation. Ollivier and the Emperor openly declared their delight at what they regarded as an honourable solution; but it was not a view which found much support in Paris. To rest content with such a settlement was generally considered to be shameful. The demand went up, inside and outside the Chamber, for "guarantees." The *Moniteur* suggested that Prussia should be compelled to evacuate the fortress of Mainz. Compared with such views, Gramont's demands were moderate, but they still insisted on the necessary humiliation of Prussia. He suggested to the Prussian Ambassador, Baron von Werther, that William should write Napoleon a personal letter of "explanation"; and he instructed Benedetti to obtain from William not only a declaration associating himself with Charles Antony's refusal, but an assurance that he would not permit the Candidature to be considered again. It was from these instructions that the war was to arise. If such an assurance was not forthcoming France would consider that her just demands had not been met, and would continue with her military preparations.

There was nothing particularly dramatic about the famous interview at Ems on 13th July. Benedetti encountered the King in the public gardens during the early part of the morning, and William, with the courtesy which never failed him, came over to speak to the Ambassador himself, and congratulated him on the news of Leopold's withdrawal. Benedetti had to ignore this olive branch: as instructed he demanded a guarantee that the King would not consent to a renewal of the Candidature. The King refused to bind himself to any course of action in the indefinite future, and the two parted coolly. A little later William received Charles Antony's formal letter of renunciation and sent his aide-de-camp to inform Benedetti, and to tell him—a considerable concession—that he gave it "his entire and unreserved approval"; but when Benedetti requested another interview to raise once more the question of a guarantee he returned the answer that there was nothing further to discuss.

Benedetti, it is clear from his reports to Gramont, was in no way conscious of being discourteously treated, but the temper of the King and of his entourage had risen higher than he realised. They had learned of the agitation in Paris for guarantees, and of Gramont's demand for a royal letter of explanation, and Werther was abruptly recalled for consultations. The report which Abeken wired to Bismarck of the day's events was thus considerably sharper than Benedetti's to Gramont.

His Majesty [he said], having told Count Benedetti that he was awaiting news from the Prince, has decided . . . not to receive Count Benedetti again, but only to let him be informed through an aide-de-camp; . . . His Majesty had now received from the Prince confirmation of the news which Benedetti had already received from Paris and had nothing further to say to the Ambassador. [He concluded] His Majesty leaves it to your Excellency whether Benedetti's fresh demand and its rejection should not at once be communicated both to our Ambassadors and to the press.

From Abeken's telegram two conclusions emerge: first, that the King was considerably irritated by Benedetti's demand, and by the French refusal to consider the question closed; and secondly, that the King himself had the idea of making his rebuff to Benedetti public. Bismarck, in the version of the affair which he gave to the world, was to emphasize these considerations to the point of distortion: but he did not invent them.

Bismarck had viewed the worsening of relations with open satisfaction. A peaceful withdrawal of the Candidature would have meant an open defeat for his policy, and if war with France had to come, now was as good a time as any. The news of Charles Antony's renunciation, which greeted him on his arrival, flung him into the profoundest depression. It was a humiliation, he wrote later, "worse than Olmütz." But no more than Gramont did he consider that the affair was ended. Suspecting what Gramont's next step might be, he telegraphed to Ems urging the King to give Benedetti no explanation of any sort. If anyone should explain themselves it was France; indeed, he informed the King, "the growing exasperation of public opinion over the presumptuous conduct of France" made it necessary "that we should address to France a summons to explain her intentions towards Germany"; and to make this possible he requested the King's immediate return to Berlin.

Events had reached this stage when Bismarck, at supper with Moltke and Roon, received Abeken's telegram from Ems, and saw that with a very little editing Abeken's words, already sharp, could be made to seem so violent that war would inevitably follow. Moltke gave a final assurance that all was ready—indeed, he maintained, it would be better to fight now than in a few years' time, when the French military reforms would be taking effect. Bismarck therefore set about editing the telegram. There was no question of falsification; yet Benedetti's *démarche* was made to appear positively insolent, and his dismissal final. "His Majesty the King," concluded Bismarck's version, "thereupon decided not to receive the French Ambassador again, and sent to tell him through the aide-de-camp on duty that his Majesty had nothing further to communicate to the Ambassador." This, he assured his friends, would have the effect of a red rag on the Gallic bull. Within a few hours a special edition of the *Norddeutsche Zeitung* carrying the telegram was selling on the Berlin streets. As a final touch the telegram was sent to all Prussian representatives abroad, with instructions that they were to communicate it to the Governments to which they were accredited. Nothing was left undone to goad the French into war.

The effect was as Bismarck had anticipated. Both in Berlin and in Paris excited crowds gathered shouting "to the Rhine!" William I cried, on reading the telegram, "This is war!" So did Ollivier and Gramont. War could hardly have been long delayed if Bismarck had carried the King with him in his demands for "satisfaction" from France; but the sad irony is that on the 14th of July, when the news from Berlin reached Paris, the peace party in the French Government had precariously gained the upper hand. On the 13th the Ministers meeting in Council heard for the first time of the instructions which Gramont had sent Benedetti the previous evening; and though they somewhat reluctantly approved them, they added a rider that "the demand for guarantees was susceptible of mitigation and any honourable transaction would be welcome." An urgent despatch from Lord Granville counselling the Imperial Government to rest content with Leopold's renunciation was read aloud and created considerable effect; and a proposal to decree mobilisation was voted down, to Leboeuf's chagrin, by eight votes to four. Not till the following day did Benedetti's despatches and reports of Bismarck's "Ems Telegram" reach Paris; and then, by comparing the two, the Ministers were able to gauge the full extent of Bismarck's distortion and judge the bellicose purpose which lay behind it. Unanimously they consented to mobilization and at 4:40 P.M. the orders went out. Then they had second thoughts, and for six hours they debated an appeal to a Congress of Powers. A note to that effect was drafted and Napoleon prepared a message to Leboeuf to delay the recall of the reserves. "I doubt," grimly commented the Empress, who was attending the Council meeting, "whether that corresponds to the feeling in the Chambers and the country." The harrassed Leboeuf threatened to resign. But as the evening wore on there came the news that Bismarck had officially communicated the Ems telegram to the Governments of Europe. In face of such provocation all thoughts of accommodation disappeared. By nightfall the French Government, like Bismarck himself, was resolved on war.

When next day, 15th July, Gramont and Ollivier, addressing the Senate and the Corps Législatif respectively, demanded the necessary war credits, the voice of the opposition did make itself heard. The veteran Thiers, whose patriotism, political ability and military learning were above reproach and who had until the withdrawal of the Hohenzollern Candidature used all his influence to support the Government, followed Ollivier on the rostrum and, amid constant interruptions, denounced the war. "Do you want all Europe to say that although the substance of the quarrel was settled, you have decided to pour out torrents of blood over a mere matter of form?" The leaders of the Left supported him—Gambetta, Arago, Garnier-Pagès, Jules Favre; but on the solid majority of the Right and the Centre he could make no impression at all. The mastodon trumpetings of Guyot-Montpayroux—"Prussia has forgotten the France of Jena and we must remind her!"

—fitted in better with their mood. Ollivier, in replying to Thiers, accepted the heavy responsibility of the war "*d'un coeur léger*" ["with a light heart"]. He hastened to qualify the unfortunate phrase—"I mean with a heart not weighed down with remorse, a *confident* heart"—but for the rest of his long life he was never to be allowed to forget it. A commission of the Chamber hurriedly examined him, Gramont and Leboeuf. Leboeuf stoutly assured them the army was ready. Better war now, he said, unconsciously echoing Moltke, than in a few years' time when the Prussians would have improved their rifles and copied the *mitrailleuse*—and, he added, before the Opposition in the Chamber had destroyed the army altogether. Gramont, when asked whether France could rely on any allies, replied subtly: "If I kept the Commission waiting, it was because I had with me at the Foreign Ministry the Austrian Ambassador and the Italian Minister. I hope that the Commission will ask me no more." The Chamber was satisfied by Leboeuf's soldierly bluntness and Gramont's diplomatic evasions, and by an overwhelming majority the votes of credit were passed. Outside in the streets the crowds greeted the news with roars of delight, and the demonstrations which the Republicans organized against the vote were drowned.

Thus by a tragic combination of ill-luck, stupidity, and ignorance France blundered into war with the greatest military power that Europe had yet seen, in a bad cause, with her army unready and without allies. The representatives of Austria and Italy, like those of Russia, Britain, and the South German States, made it clear that they could not support France in such a struggle; and opinion in England, naturally gallophobe and sympathetic to the ally of Waterloo, was powerfully swayed when Bismarck released to *The Times* details of the proposals for the absorption of Belgium which Napoleon had so imprudently entertained in 1866. But it was not due simply to the machinations of Bismarck that France had to go, alone and unpopular, to meet her fate.

SUGGESTIONS FOR FURTHER READING

Bibliographical and General: see preceding chapter; Special: FRANKLIN C. PALM, *England and Napoleon III* (Durham, N.C., 1948); EMILE BOURGEOIS and E. CLERMONT, *Rome et Napoléon III (1849–1870)*; (Paris, 1907); LYNN M. CASE, *Franco-Italian Relations, 1860–1865* (Philadelphia, 1932); NANCY NICHOLS BARKER, "Austria, France and the Venetian Question, 1861–66," *Journal of Modern History* XXXVI (1964), 145–154, and "France, Austria, and the Mexican Venture, 1861–64," *French Historical Studies*, III (1963), 224–245; C. SCHEFER, *La Grande pensée de Napoléon III: Les Origines de l'expédition de Mexique, 1858–62* (Paris, 1939); LYNN M. CASE, *French Opinion on the United States and Mexico, 1860–67* (New York, 1936); GERHARD RITTER, "Bismarck et la politique rhénane de Napoléon III," *Revue d'histoire diplomatique*, LXVIII (1964), 291–324; CHARLES W. HALLBERG,

Franz Joseph and Napoleon III, 1852–64 (New York, 1955); WILLARD A. FLETCHER, *The Mission of Vincent Benedetti to Berlin, 1864–1870* (The Hague, 1965); E. ANN POTTINGER, *Napoleon III and the German Crisis, 1865–1866* (Cambridge, Mass., 1966); ROBERT H. LORD, *The Origins of the War of 1870* (Cambridge, Mass., 1924); LAWRENCE D. STEEFEL, *Bismarck, the Hohenzollern Candidacy and the Origins of the Franco-German War of 1870* (Cambridge, Mass., 1962).

Chapter Eleven

SOCIALIST THOUGHT
AND
THE PARIS
COMMUNE

E VER SINCE the French Revolution of 1789, but especially since the death of Saint-Simon in 1825 and the July Revolution of 1830, socialist thought had been progressively developing a more elaborate critique of bourgeois society. To the socialists, the Great Revolution had not brought the liberty, equality, and fraternity it had so proudly proclaimed. It had merely substituted a society based on property for the eighteenth-century society of aristocratic privilege. Property, they felt, was becoming as hereditary as nobility had previously been. Society was perpetuating the domination of an indolent leisure class, protecting it and guaranteeing it the privileges of wealth, while simultaneously ignoring the rights of the working class. The relationship of employer to salaried wage earner was looked upon as simply the modern version of slavery. Liberty, wrote Louis Blanc, consists not only in the right to work but in the power to exercise the right. The competition for employment caused by population growth, economic downturns, and low wages deprived many workers of this right. Moreover, liberty without equality was considered hypocritical, so that not only the subhuman conditions of the worker but also the entire unequal distribution of wealth came under attack. A common strain of criticism ran through Fourier, Blanc, Proudhon, and Blanqui. Privileges, class distinctions, the unjust domination of one class over another, wealth earned without labor, individualism and egoism, the disparity between production and consumption were to them the observable symptoms of social malaise. The intervention of the state conceived as an association of workers was the accepted mode by which "each individual whatever his birth, will be loved, honored, and rewarded according to his works."

The first selection, by the late French historian Maxime Leroy, gives us a succinct account of the development of socialist doctrines from the Revolution to 1870. Keenly aware of the differences separating one thinker from another, Leroy nevertheless stresses a common bond in their critique of property. The mechanism of change was what they least agreed upon—hence the liberal and pacific socialism of Proudhon, who based his hopes on trade unions, and the violent socialism of Blanqui. These two socialist thinkers were the most influential on the Paris Commune.

In the second selection, Edward Mason, Professor of Economics at Harvard, sketches the military and political origins of the Commune and assesses its significance in the history of France. After Napoleon's defeat at Sedan in 1870, a Government of National Defense took power and attempted to continue the war against the Germans. The difficulties this government had in maintaining the defense, its lack of popular support especially within Paris, its economic conservatism which prevented it from taking steps toward requisition, rationing, and confiscation of property thought necessary by the radical opposition, combined with a political liberalism which encouraged clubs and periodicals critical of the government—all led eventually to the insurrection of March 18, 1871. The Central Committee in Paris seceded from the government set up at Versailles and the short-lived (seventy days) Paris Commune of 1871 was established.

To what extent was this Commune actually socialist-inspired or representative of a socialist experiment? Professor Mason, like many authorities, stresses that the Commune was not the product of socialist ideology. Yet he indicates that socialists were active in the Commune and that after 1871 the myth of the Commune continued to inspire socialist and Marxist activity. In this light, the French socialist tradition is seen to owe more to the Commune than the Commune to French socialists. Leroy indicates that Marxism proper was not a force within France until 1870; even within the First International in France, before 1870, Marx was not followed.

The American scholar Samuel Bernstein describes the activity of the First International, unionism, and Proudhonist and Blanquist socialism before March, 1871. Although the First International was not politically effective in creating the Commune, the latter was viewed as its intellectual child.

In the final selection, Professor Eugene W. Schulkind of the University of Sussex, England, describes popular organizations during the Commune. The reader can judge for himself how the thought of these organizations was similar to, and influenced by, utopian socialist thought of nineteenth-century France. Eventually, social preoccupations became secondary to military concerns as the Versailles government began to attack the Paris Commune successfully.

Indirect and limited as socialist influence may have been on the Commune, there does seem to have been some connection between the two. Like the problem of the relationship of the Enlightenment to the Revolution, the connection is difficult to see clearly. To deny completely any relationship, however, seems as unwarranted as to view the Commune as the result of deliberate socialist planning.

Cℛℐℐℐℐ⌒

THE DEVELOPMENT OF SOCIALIST DOCTRINES FROM THE REVOLUTION TO THE COMMUNE

Maxime Leroy

What we call socialism originated in the lower classes during the severe food shortages of 1793 and 1794. In its first appearance as a mass movement, socialism took the form of a criticism of social inequality as symbolized by property. The philosophy of [Gracchus] Babeuf was essentially an attack on individual property. His goal was to destroy it and institute communal ownership on an "all for one, one for all" basis. Babeuf's system was a form of communism in that common ownership was to replace private property. Throughout the vicissitudes of its turbulent history, socialism was destined to remain what it had been from the very beginning—an attack on private

Maxime Leroy, *Les Précurseurs français du socialisme de Condorcet à Proudhon* (Paris: Editions du Temps Présent [now Editions du Seuil], 1948), pp. 14–18, 21–28. Used by permission. Editors' translation.

ownership, with the establishment of common property remaining its goal. Originally a doctrine of the poor, the underfed, and the badly clothed, socialism represented a movement stirred by poverty, under the harsh pressures of real inequities which remain even today (though under different names) the driving, if not the only, force behind the working-class movement. Above all, the socialists hoped to increase wages and secure better living conditions, just as we today continue to speak of a "living wage." The movement gradually became complicated by various ideological demands; but poverty remained at the heart of the measures which Babeuf and his comrades were the first to devise and put into action. . . .

With the increased volume, sophistication, and diversification of [industrial] production, the growing contact between workers and bourgeois, and the strengthening and centralization of worker discipline between 1830 and 1848, socialism inexorably forced its way into the world of economic theory. It was becoming a new economics—the economics of the poor classes, as Proudhon described it. The rudimentary economics of Babeuf was developed by Proudhon in his *System of Economic Contradictions* and by Marx in his *Communist Manifesto* and *Capital*. . . .

. . . The upheaval of 1830 clearly confronted public opinion with what has since been called the "social question," the question that socialism sought to answer. 1830 was a very important date in the history of socialism.

The circumstances surrounding the events of 1830 are quite familiar, so only a brief summary need be given here. At the end of July, 1830, Charles X issued the ordinances illegally suppressing the freedom of the press which the Charter of 1814 had granted as a constitutional liberty. The immediate result was grave excitement: journalists and politicians voiced their fear and anger, and worked together to resist this abuse of authority by the king. Thiers drafted a vehement proclamation, while great waves of unrest spread throughout the city, which was still aroused by the recent elections.

As each of the malcontents realized, the resistance of the bourgeoisie would be ineffective without popular support. The workers in the printing shops, their livelihood threatened by the shutdown ordered by the master printers, stirred and protested in turn, and were finally joined by the entire populace. Without popular participation, the troops of the Duke of Ragusa [Marmont] who were charged with suppressing the disorder could have easily crushed the agitation begun by the journalists.

The victorious bourgeoisie did nothing for the proletariat which had given it such strong support. On the contrary, the bourgeoisie reinforced the penal legislation of the Revolution and Empire against all working-class efforts to attain increased wages. As a result, the workers spoke of the revolution as having been "stolen" from them. There was no social legislation to reduce extremely long working days, or to suppress the inhumane employment of women and small children, or to improve working conditions. The economic philosophy of 1789 continued to prevail. Guizot and Thiers defended this philosophy which Louis Blanc described in this way: "The essence of liberal economic doctrines was to increase the quantity of goods without considering how they should be distributed. These doctrines were ruthless and left the survival of the weak to the mercy of chance." And what chance!

But class consciousness began to take form. In 1833 a worker wrote that henceforth the workers "were conscious of their strength, because the great victory of July could not have been won without their help." But out of this grew a feeling of pride among the working classes, their distaste for the upper classes, a need to obtain guarantees, attempts to raise wages, disorders, and unions. . . .

Socialism, however, did not develop directly from one socialist theorist to another in the period between 1830 and 1848. Religious philosophers and orthodox economists were also among those who contributed to socialist thought. Just as Marx continued and developed the thought of Ricardo, so Saint-Simon extended and expanded that of Jean-Baptiste Say at the beginning of the nineteenth century. Among the nonsocialist precursors of socialism, Lamennais, who vigorously criticized private property, stands out. Without calling for revolution, Lamennais nevertheless contributed to socialist ideas by his attacks against the inhumanity of the economic system described by [Louis-René] Villermé. Another nonsocialist, Lamartine, had, as he put it, a feeling for the masses. His speeches in the Chamber of Deputies, and especially his *History of the Girondins*, aroused and inflamed the masses who submitted to his dictatorship for several weeks in 1848, hoping that it would fulfill their hopes for an extension of the revolution.

Thus a diffuse socialism spread not only through the speeches of Lamartine, but also through newspaper accounts of those by Voyer d'Argenson, the Count of Ludre, and [Etienne-Joseph] Garnier-Pagès, whose brother 1848 would make famous. The following lines which appeared in the *National*, the great liberal newspaper with democratic tendencies, suggest the progress this socialism had made in winning over public opinion: "Industrial and manufacturing property is becoming concentrated and monopolistic, and is tending to form a veritable and powerful feudalism. Landed property, however, is becoming more democratic each day through division of ownership."

Around 1840 a working-class press developed, though it had a modest circulation, while at the same time, the workers intensified their professional organization under the cover of mutual aid societies. Of these newspapers, two—*L'Atelier* and *La Ruche Populaire*—made lasting contributions to the movement.

1848 consolidated these many efforts and shadowy hopes. The hesitant nature of this political movement and its divided character reflected the diversity of its origins. February ended one social cycle, the cycle of the democratic socialism which had sprung directly from the "days" and laws of 1793 and 1794. A new cycle began, at first uncertain in its characteristics and confused in its doctrines, but precise on one point—beginning in 1848 socialism was increasingly a working-class movement. The *Communist Manifesto*, though not influential until after the Commune in the 1880's, when Jules Guesde created French Marxism, would be the doctrinal basis of the movement which he would lead along the revolutionary path to the dictatorship of the proletariat.

In calling this early socialism democratic, we are emphasizing its specific character. It developed out of the spirit of the Declaration of the Rights of Man of 1789. But we cannot hold to this view without making many distinctions which, if examined carefully, may account for the various social difficulties which later arose. This socialism was not only democratic . . . but also Jacobin and even Christian.

Babeuf criticized the Declaration, as did Saint-Simon, Fourier, and Louis Blanc. Although they differed, these various socialists all hoped to replace the regime of 1789 rather than to perfect it. This was their common bond. But they launched their attacks from different vantage points. The underfed Babeuf directed his criticism primarily against inequality. He dreamed of modest but still well-stocked tables and envisioned a Spartan communism. Saint-Simon, a highly cultivated nobleman, was rather indifferent to political liberty, concentrating chiefly upon the organization of production. Hostile to real equality, he placed most of his hopes in fraternity. As for Fourier, he rejected the entire system of 1789 and all its principles, considering them inadequate, abstract, even harmful. Fourier alone was a true adversary of the principles of 1789.

These men lived and thought under a regime which had no enthusiasm for liberty, and nothing spurred them to invoke it. The Constitution of 1789 was based on property qualifications for voting and therefore was hostile to the entire doctrine of liberty and equality. The Terror represented harsh political fanaticism. Indebted to the Jacobins, the followers of Babeuf were dictatorial and terroristic.

If Saint-Simon thought only of organizing production into a hierarchical system having a strongly authoritarian character, Fourier, while dreaming of a society comparable to a vast Abbey of Thélème, where the most delightful license would prevail, did not want passion to have free play. He imprisoned the members of the phalanasteries within a tight bureaucracy, rendered absurd by its minute details. It cannot be said that these first socialists loved liberty, either philosophical or political.

The same spirit permeated the books of these dreamers who observed social reality with varying degrees of perception as it did those secret societies which discussed revolutionary action. The conspirators observed military discipline in order to gain power and forcibly impose new rules of civic discipline and obligatory work upon the old society. "Humanity" was a word frequently used to mean respect for the individual. "Liberty" also figured in the speeches and articles of the day. But, to use Robespierre's phrase, everyone dreamed of the despotism of liberty. Liberty would triumph under the direction of a dictatorial power. One of the most listened-to voices of the era, Louis Blanc, sought a "strong power," a phrase he used in his *Organization of Work* (1839). Buchez, who had a great influence over the workers and who presided over the Constituent Assembly [of 1848], exalted Robespierre, and Louis Blanc also praised him. In his *History of the Girondins*, Lamartine "gilded the guillotine," to quote an expression of Chateaubriand which Saint-Beuve recorded.

Liberty was necessary, but it would have to be imposed by violence and maintained by solid institutions. The most active democrats and socialists of the time expected a popular dictatorship to accomplish the desired extension of the revolution.

From another point of view, the fundamental principle of 1789 was losing all its prestige, and liberty fell into low esteem among the poor because the liberals invoked it as the basis for barring any legal intervention on their behalf. Lamennais condensed this opinion of the poor into a famous phrase: "In relations between the strong and the weak, liberty oppresses and the law emancipates."

Only one thinker of this period, which was so fertile in social doctrines and controversies, used liberty as the basis for his entire critique of society, his projects for its reorganization, his economic ideas, and all his hopes for social liberation. This was Proudhon. Opposed to the Jacobins and communists, he shared their hostility to the liberal economic-political regime. He was as much the enemy of Rousseau as of Robespierre, and he particularly hated the Saint-Simonians, whose program he compared to a masquerade. Without the support of an organized party, his influence was limited, but to an unknown extent, it somehow kept alive a ferment of free criticism within the vast and confused revolutionary movement born in 1830. But not only the author of the famous "memoirs" on property supported the cause of individualism in the 1840's. Despite its Jacobinism, this early socialism was infused with thoroughly liberal traits. This was because of the still persistent influence of the ideology of 1789 which Proudhon sought to interpret. Unexpressed hopes for liberty moved the Jacobin republicans and even the communists during the "bourgeois monarchy." The authoritarian and dictatorial secret societies did not repudiate 1789; they simply dismissed it as a method which was temporarily ineffective. The ideal which it represented would not be achieved quickly. Many violent attacks would be needed to topple the royalists, the bourgeoisie, and the Church—the classes which had been dominant since 1789 and which Fourier referred to as a "new feudalism."

No conclusions can be drawn from such an historical outline of these troubled, confused, and uncertain times except the very ones which the men of the period themselves drew in the aftermath of 1848. The developments which followed these disappointing revolutionary days were partial answers to the problems which they had presented, and to some degree they solidified the new principles which the June Days seemed to have destroyed forever. The Second Empire, which was the eventual result of the June Days and which would eventually end in the tragedy of 1870, granted the lower classes at least part of the social legislation that it had demanded but which the July Monarchy had refused and the February Revolution had vainly attempted to institute. While the Second Empire did make some legal concessions to the growing solidarity of the working class by allowing strikes and public meetings, and even permitting professional organizations, the working class, having painfully learned the lesson of June, quietly intensified its economic and political opposition to the regime. It was during this period that the First International was formed in London, a gathering that affirmed the principles slowly elaborated by socialists over the first half of the nineteenth century. In 1864 under the impetus of delegates from many nations, but dominated by the French, Germans, and English, the class struggle of Karl Marx, the collectivism of Pecqueur, the internationalism and pacifism of Saint-Simon, the liberalism of Proudhon, the cooperative professionalism of Louis Blanc, and the trade unionism of Flora Tristan merged into a single socialist synthesis. After 1871, however, circumstances gradually sharpened its internal differences and broke them down into rival ideologies.

THE PARIS COMMUNE: AN EPISODE IN THE HISTORY OF THE SOCIALIST MOVEMENT

EDWARD S. MASON

The Franco-Prussian War stripped the tinsel and decoration from a reign deeply devoted to surface ornamentation. The march of Prussian feet in the Champs-Élysées furnished the sad accompaniment to the burial of an imperial government whose chief had been imprisoned at the battle of Sedan and whose dissolution the fourth of September had pronounced. A lay figure whose false proportions had been set before the gaping nation by the clever

Edward S. Mason, *The Paris Commune, an Episode in the History of the Socialist Movement* (New York: Macmillan, 1930), pp. 58–62, 117–118, 168–170. © Edward S. Mason. Used by permission.

finger of political stagecraft, Napoleon III had shown himself to be the most buoyant of fair-weather navigators. But the winds of adversity were not to be tamed by donning a startling uniform and appearing before the people with his hand in his coat, in the manner of his illustrious predecessor. He fell amid practically universal applause and the populace accepted with acclamation the designation prepared by that anti-court poet Victor Hugo, "Napoleon the Little."

The Germans marched into France and on to Paris glowing with moral satisfaction at the fall of "Babylon the proud," that cesspool of European civilization. The war had scarcely ended, and the German troops were still overlooking Paris, when the Commune came to confirm them in their certainty that this was the degenerate race. The Commune of 1871 capped the climax of the degradation of France and half of the bitterness of this sanguinary civil war is to be explained by its historical setting. Even France was convinced by the Commune of the moral degeneracy of Paris. . . .

Whether or not the causes of the Commune are, in the last analysis, traceable to the decline of religion and morality in France, and particularly Paris, the events of the eight months which preceded the 18th of March, 1871, had something to do with it. Napoleon and France had entered upon the war with Germany too light-heartedly and with inadequate preparation. A series of disastrous encounters culminated in the battle of Sedan, which led to the capture of the emperor himself along with MacMahon and his army. Although this catastrophe occurred on September 1st, definite news was delayed in reaching Paris. Rather vague though ominous rumors emanating from Brussels and London circulated in the capital on the morning of the third but it was not until four o'clock in the afternoon that the full extent of the defeat was known. A telegram to the empress brought the information to Paris:

The army has been defeated and captured; I myself am a prisoner.

NAPOLEON.

This bombshell, bursting on the city of revolutions, led to the overthrow of the government. The legislative assembly, with a majority strongly conservative and allied to the Emperor, met to deliberate on the form of government demanded by the exigencies of the situation. While it deliberated, the Paris mob acted. Finding its leaders in the Republican minority of the legislature, the frenzied crowds, after invading the special session of the legislative body itself, carried these leaders to the Hôtel de Ville, where the Republic was proclaimed. By six o'clock on the evening of September 4th the new Government of the National Defense was formed and announced to the rest of France. General Trochu, governor of Paris, was maintained in his functions and appointed Minister of War.

The Government of the National Defense, although the product of a spontaneous and unorganized revolutionary movement, found itself at the outset without opposition. It was more secure on its first day than at any other period in its history. The population of Paris and of France, stunned by the magnitude of the military disasters, closed its ranks silently behind the new government. The conservative majority of the Chamber of Deputies, reassembled after the invasion of the mob, faced the fact of the proclamation of the Republic and accepted it. In an able speech Thiers expressed the sense of the majority.

We have only a few moments to remain together; it is necessary to use them. Before recognizing the authority which has just been born, we have to establish certain questions of principle and of fact upon which it is not possible to speak out.

To fight this authority would be unpatriotic. We can not oppose ourselves to it nor can we enter into collusion with it. I pray that God may assist it. Let us separate, let us conduct ourselves as good citizens, devoted to our country. As long as it demands of us nothing contrary to our conscience, or to the true principles of society, our position will be easy. We do not dissolve, but, in the presence of the terrible misfortunes of France, we return with dignity to our homes. It is impossible either to recognize a government born of an insurrection, or to oppose it when it fights against the enemy.

The radical and revolutionary element in Paris, on the other hand, which was to be a thorn in the side of the new government during the siege, and which was later to make the Commune of Paris, acquiesced in the events of September 4th, and in general lent its support. The future leaders of the Commune were present in the mob, rallying their cohorts and inciting the masses to action. There were demands on the part of the crowds surrounding the Hôtel de Ville that certain of these leaders, Delescluze, Millière, Blanqui and others, be taken into the government. But there is no evidence that the revolution of September 4th was planned or organized by any of the revolutionary groups prominent in Paris. In spite of the fact that Rochefort was the only radical included in the Government of the National Defense, the support of the radical as well as the conservative element in Paris was given to the newly constituted authority.

The enthusiasm for the Republic and the government which represented it in the streets of Paris was indescribable. "What a moral victory was this day in Paris," cried the liberal "L'Avenir National." "It would console us for the defeat of Sedan, if anything could console us for such a disaster." Blanqui, the leader of the revolutionary communist party, with a dozen or fifteen of his followers signed a plea for united action in the defense of France, behind the new government.

In the presence of the enemy, no more parties, no more divisions.

With a government which betrayed the nation, co-operation was impossible.

The government created by the movement of September 4th represents republican thought and national defense.

That is sufficient.

All opposition, all contradiction must disappear to make way for national safety.

But in spite of the enthusiasm of the radical element and the tacit support of the conservatives the position of the Government of the National Defense was insecure. With the fall of the emperor the custodian of national sovereignty became the National Assembly, duly elected by the people. The new government supplanted the National Assembly and yet was never given official recognition by it. The Government of the National Defense was the work of a Paris mob and in this mob the revolutionary element was strong. A failure to satisfy the claims of radical groups would mean opposition, more or less strong and more or less organized, from the very people who felt themselves to be, and with some justice, the creators of this government. Falling between these two parties and facing the well-nigh impossible task of fighting a superior force with the inadequate machinery of an incompetent empire, the Government of the National Defense succeeded in making itself one of the most unpopular régimes in the history of 19th century France.

The opposition of the radical groups came first and the next five months witnessed one long series of half-hearted attempts on the part of the government to hold in check insurrectionary movements in Paris. The final outcome of this situation was the Commune of 1871. And the lack of governmental success in repressing the revolutionary element was in large measure the result of its own revolutionary origin. The conservative opposition came later and attributed to the Government of the National Defense not only the responsibility of the disastrous conduct of the war but that of the insurrectionary movements culminating in the Commune of Paris which was but the logical outcome, according to the conservatives, of the illegal assumption of power on September 4th. . . .

The radical opposition in Paris was effective because of the internal political weakness of the government. Itself the product of revolution, the Government of the National Defense had never secured its position by an appeal to the electorate of France. After the insurrection of October 31st, it is true, its position was strengthened by the vote in Paris, but this position still lacked the support of a national plebiscite. The revolutionary origin of the Government of the National Defense together with its unconsolidated legal position was a severe handicap in its dealings with those revolutionary groups in Paris which were in part responsible for its power. This weakness was accentuated, under the circumstances, by its republican and democratic principles, or prejudices, against political repression. Revolutionary clubs, journals, committees, and societies, were allowed to breed and multiply in the capital without interference. The police system inherited from the old régime and thoroughly discredited in a republic proved of little service. It is impossible to say whether a government strong internally would have been able to hold in check the radical opposition fed by military reverses, but certainly the Government of the National Defense left to its successor a situation in Paris made doubly difficult by the strength and multiplicity of revolutionary organizations.

This situation became untenable because the radical opposition gradually secured control of an army, the largest armed force in France, the National Guard of Paris. The population of the capital, hastily and carelessly organized, proved a source of embarrassment during the siege and a source of danger after it. The method of electing officers led only too often to the selection of demagogues and intensified the lack of discipline which is frequently a failure of such military organizations. For the most part congregated inactively in Paris, the National Guard, dissatisfied with its position in the defense, easily fell a prey to the arguments which circulated nightly in the clubs. After the armistice it was the only considerable body of men to retain its arms and its complexion became decidedly more revolutionary with the departure of the conservative middle-class elements from Paris. Without the support of the armed body of the National Guard it is more than doubtful whether the Commune could have been made.

The natural tendency after the Commune was to find the cause of the revolution in the activities of socialist and communist revolutionary societies in Paris, particularly the International. The Marxian interpretation, which has been followed by most of the socialist commentators, has it that the Commune was the product of a proletarian and socialist revolution. Although this is emphatically and notoriously untrue, the part played by revolutionary organizations in Paris was important. Unfortunately it is extremely difficult to evaluate. The International in Paris, disorganized by the prosecutions of 1870, had partially reconstituted its sections by the outbreak of the war. Although seriously handicapped during and after the siege by the poverty of its members it did act as a cohesive influence in amalgamating the opposition. The Committee of the Twenty Arrondissements was in large part the direct creation of the International. The central office at 6 Place de la Corderie was the "local" of a large number of socialist republican political associations and labor organizations and, at the same time, a favorite meeting place for representatives of all the opposition groups in Paris. Members of the International took an active part in the insurrections of October 31st and January 22nd. Other revolutionary groups, the Blanquists, a small though well-knit society, the Jacobins, particularly Delescluze, Pyat and their respective followings, and individual leaders such as Flourens,

Sapia, and Tibaldi, were also actively responsible, together with the radical clubs and newspapers, for a considerable cohesiveness in the ranks of the opposition. The Communal revolution, though certainly not socialist, and not distinctively proletarian, depended upon this organization of the socialist and revolutionary proletarian element.

Finally, the creation of the Federation of the National Guard and its organ the Central Committee was indispensable. Organized on the occasion of the February election, the Federation soon advanced beyond its original purposes and became a powerful force working for the maintenance of the Republic, the dissolution of the standing army and the perpetuation of the National Guard. Controlling the armed forces of the capital the Central Committee set itself up against the government on a number of points and finally came into collision with it on the question of the surrender of military equipment. The National Guard unorganized, or obeying its legal commanders, was not dangerous. In the hands of the Federation and its Committee, it was bound to provoke a revolution.

There is little or no evidence that the form the revolution took was actively present in the minds of those responsible for it. The word "Commune" was bandied about in the clubs, radical newspapers and revolutionary societies before the 18th of March; it acted as the rallying cry in the insurrections of October and January; but no one appeared to have a definite conception of its meaning. An orator at the Club Favier put the matter very well when he said, "I'll wager that even here, at the Club Favier, three quarters of the audience does not know what the Commune means. [Protests, denials, tumult, shouting. 'He's a police spy!' Others: 'Well, go ahead and tell us what it is.'] The Commune is the right of the people, it is equal treatment for all, it is the levée en masse and the punishment of traitors; the Commune, finally, is the Commune." . . .

Civil war was prepared; irreconcilable aims and an uncompromising behavior on both sides had made it inevitable. It required but a few days' time and the natural course of events to bring the National Guard of Paris and Thiers' renovated army to blows.

The ten days which elapsed from the 18th of March till the 28th, when the Commune was installed, saw a spontaneous and unorganized uprising taken in hand by a planless and incompetent committee. Unwilling and afraid to go ahead to overthrow the government, incapable of checking the movement for which it had assumed responsibility, the Central Committee was borne by the flow of events along a course which lay between revolution and legality. Since the program which it proposed to Versailles was obviously unacceptable, and since the moderation of these demands seemed impossible, even if desirable, in view of the pressure from behind, the Committee was faced with the alternative, either of using force or of shifting the responsibility. Rejecting the first it pinned its faith on the mythical and mystic Commune.

Meanwhile sufficient time had elapsed to allow Thiers to rally his disorganized and dispirited troops and begin the formation of an army. The golden moment for revolutionary action had passed.

Thiers, in the face of an admittedly difficult but not impossible situation, had adopted a plan of attack without an adequate examination of his own resources or those of the opposition. The failure of this plan, assisted by incapable direction, was the signal for revolution. Whereupon the government of France, deserting its traditional capital, left Paris in the hands of what was certainly, on the 18th of March, a minority. Safe in Versailles, Thiers pursued the only policy which the intransigent behavior of the Assembly and that of Paris permitted; i.e., preparation for war. Meanwhile he sought to gain time by encouraging the plans of conciliation of the mayors and deputies of Paris.

The revolutionary uprising which had upset the calculations of M. Thiers drew its strength from the proletariat of Paris organized in the battalions of the National Guard. It was socialist in neither its motivation nor its program. The incentive to insurrection, while undoubtedly influenced by the socialist and communist propaganda plentiful in Paris at the time, sprang chiefly from the events of the siege and the humiliations of the war. The program was primarily political and republican. In the minds of many, it is true, the Commune possessed a socialist significance, but before the 28th of March no content had been given to this symbol. It required the events of the next two months to give a meaning to the conception of the Commune.

THE FIRST INTERNATIONAL, PROUDHONISTS, BLANQUISTS, AND THE PARIS COMMUNE

Samuel Bernstein

Since the law of 1864 that had relaxed restraints on labor coalitions, French labor had grown into the best organized part of the republican opposition. By the end of 1869 trade union councils had arisen in Marseilles, Lyons, Rouen and Paris. In March 1870 they held a congress and set up a provisional committee with the high aim of calling into being a national federation. A summons for a national labor congress to be held in May went out from the labor federation of Rouen, led by Emile Aubry, a printer. Postponed to the

Samuel Bernstein, *Essays in Political and Intellectual History* (New York: Paine Whitman Publishers, 1955), pp. 135–140, 150, 165, 167–168. © Samuel Bernstein. Used by permission.

end of June, the congress was finally forbidden. The government had meanwhile arrested leading members of the First International in France and had already begun the third trial of its Paris bureau.

Evidence of labor's antagonism to the imperial system was the strike waves that passed over France, beginning in 1865. Most of the strikes seem to have been waged for higher wages. People were quick to lay them to the toleration given to trade unions by the law of 1864. Undoubtedly there was a connection between the law and labor's mounting unrest. With larger organizations workers were better prepared to defend their demands. But the deeper causes of the strikes must be looked for in the economic conditions with which the political situation was bound up. The cost of living had risen during the sixties in France, in fact in all of western Europe. The high cost of government in France, due to foreign adventure and preparations for war, had contributed to a reduced standard of living. But it also had its roots in the rebuilding of Paris in order to forestall street insurrections, in the rapid rise of modern industry, the wide employment of women and children, the beginnings of industrial concentration, and the larger world supply of precious metals after the discovery of gold in California. All these conditions were behind the many strikes in France during the sixties. In another respect, they were symptoms of opposition to the imperial system as a whole.

The story of French labor from 1865 to 1871 would be defective and jejune if it omitted the First International. Its history in France has been so overcast with vituperation, so coated in fustian and imbedded in ideological controversy, that a good account of it still awaits the historian. Within the space of a short essay can be given only its very general historical outline in France.

Many currents met to create the Association in London in 1864. The principal ones were: the renewed struggles for national liberation; the cotton famine in Europe, growing out of the American Civil War and painfully revealing labor's common interests, regardless of frontiers; the need of workers' mutual assistance against the menace of militarism; the bloody suppression of the gallant Poles in 1863; and finally the urgency on the part of labor, especially in England, of preventing the importation of scabs.

The first French bureau of the International was set up in Paris in 1865, in extremely modest headquarters and with an empty treasury. Its growth was very slow during the first two years. Inner friction between manual workers and intellectuals, Blanquist hostility to the Proudhonist program of the Paris branch, government suspicion and officially inspired rival organizations, charges of ties with the imperial palace leveled at its leaders, and emphasis in its program on credit and cooperation and on political neutrality, all of these factors together kept it from fanning out in its early period. Still in the first two years the bureau managed to distribute 20,000 copies of the rules and statutes of the International. A possible reason for the bureau's survival in its nascent period was its reliance from the start on the remaining cadres that had been formed around the Manifesto of the Sixty.

The changing political and economic climate steadily brought adherents to the International in France. Already in 1866, the General Council in London received news that sections were in existence in a number of French cities—in Rennes, Rouen, Lyons, Bordeaux, Vienne and in many smaller areas. They asked for more membership cards, announced large meetings organized by Internationalists and reported that employers were threatening to discharge workers if they joined the Association. In September 1866, its first congress in Geneva, attended by seventeen French delegates from four sections, officially adopted its statutes. Four of its resolutions called for the abolition of the wage system, the eight hour day, cooperation, and the united effort of workers in all countries to check the importation of strike-breakers. The congress had enough notice in the French press to bring upon it harassment by Napoleon's government.

From 1867 to the outbreak of the Franco-Prussian War in 1870 French Internationalists felt his heavy official hand. They inevitably became leaders of strikes, however incompatible that was with their Proudhonist convictions. They took part in politics by openly demonstrating against French reoccupation of Rome. And they countenanced the republican League of Peace and Freedom. This was too much for the imperial government. Two trials of the Paris bureau in 1868 ended in orders to dissolve and in penalties for its members.

The orders prevented the branch in the capital from functioning or solidifying its strength. But it apparently spread to the provinces. Of the eighteen French delegates at the third congress of the International in 1868, a number spoke for sections in new towns and cities, among them Caen and Marseilles, where a section had been in existence since October 1867. Twenty-seven French delegates at the congress of 1869 represented eight towns and cities. Sections in Amiens, Nantes and Avignon, for example, either could not afford the expenses of a delegate or were intimidated by the police.

The International in France went on growing, official pressure notwithstanding. Its strength derived principally from its close bonds with trade unions. Wherever important strikes went on, there Internationalists were in leading posts. This is not to suggest that they provoked strikes, for the policy was to avoid them whenever possible. But once workers laid down the tools or were locked out, Internationalists did what they could to achieve victory. They drew on strike funds and collected aid for the families. They appealed for help to local organizations and to the General Council in London; they organized meetings, assisted in the negotiations and dissuaded the strikers from acts of violence. Also, when a call for help came from other countries, French Internationalists asked workers for contributions. Actually that had become the practice in the entire organization.

Persecution naturally disorganized many sections of the International in France. They could not meet save secretly. The collection of dues was difficult, not to mention the recruiting of members. But the energy with which Internationalists built trade unions and defended strikers won workers' gratitude and enlistments. Entire unions allied themselves with the International. Inspired by Internationalists, they tended to unite in central labor councils. The first seems to have arisen in the fall of 1869 in Rouen, and the second in Marseilles, with twenty-two unions. Others followed in Lyons and Paris; and in March 1870, it has been pointed out, they held a special congress to project their federation. Further plans to unite nationally were cut short by an official order.

Seen superficially, the International in France gave the appearance of a powerful body that could marshal its millions of members. Government agents, whose secret reports indicate that they knew better, let it be known that the French branch alone had in its heyday from about 500,000 to 5,000,000 on its lists. But their estimates were fantastic. While an accurate count of French Internationalists has never been made, in view of the absence of reliable evidence, students of the organization in France have set the number of its followers much below that claimed by the authorities. And the students' estimates are at best very approximate. Louis Reybaud, a semi-official publicist, credited the entire organization in Europe with 1,000,000 members in 1867, even though it then had but small nuclei in Western Europe. In 1868, when it had barely begun to spread outside of the French capital, the government said it had 160,000 members in France. The figure for 1869 jumped to more than 357,000, and for 1870 to 433,485. More extravagant reckonings, on a par with Reybaud's, gave it millions of adherents. If we turn to comparatively sober accounts we are told that the organization had at most 250,000; and Benoît Malon, one of its leaders, set the figure at 200,000.

Even if we allow the inflated figures, the International was weak and badly knit. Reports of French sections to the General Council in London disclose a frightful lack of cohesion, a highly fluctuating membership, a perpetual struggle to keep alive, to hold meetings and collect dues. They were almost habitually poor. Sections usually inclined before the tenets of their leaders, and there were many different persuasions. Some shared Proudhon's faith in credit and cooperation, his political abstentionism and rejection of strikes, even his conservative views on women and education. Others, having started as his disciples but having found themselves at odds with the raw facts, scrapped his credo. Still others were drawn to Michael Bakunin's anarchism and talked of revolution as if it were a toy or an exciting escapade. Others still nourished their creed with memories of 1793 or were in sympathy with Louis Auguste Blanqui's teachings without enrolling in his party. Available evidence discloses that not a single leader of the International in France before 1870 subscribed to Marx's teachings. One explanation was that

Marx's name was practically unknown there before the Paris Commune, to say nothing of his principles. Léo Frankel, who adopted them after 1871, was a Proudhonist; and Varlin, perhaps the top Internationalist in France, came close to a syndicalist outlook. . . . A reading of the published and unpublished writings of French Internationalists prior to 1871 reveals a looseness of thought and a thoroughly meaningless, even reckless, use of concepts and terms commonly met with in labor theoretical literature. They were moved by some vague and ideal order that had not yet taken form in their minds. But political difficulties and the problems they encountered as leaders of trade unions saved many of them from violent fits of fancy, even held them knee-deep in reality.

Peripheral to the International were radical elements. The principal ones were the neo-Jacobin republicans and the small party headed by Louis Auguste Blanqui. The first, rejoicing in the expectations of yesterday, had their eyes fixed on the past rather than on new horizons. To them 1793 represented what had once and for all been settled and clarified. In enthusiasm for principles they had few equals. And though it was wedded to a cobwebbed cause, it was highly serviceable to the republican and democratic movements of the sixties. The second, the Blanquists, formed a compact group that took its orders from the small, austere, thin and ascetic looking, white haired Blanqui. He had had long practice in planning insurrections. His name inspired devotion and fear. He had the complete allegiance of disciples and of members of his party. Bonapartists, right republicans, even Proudhonists, however, trembled at the sound of his name. In economic thought he had not advanced beyond the Utopians of the third and fourth decades of the nineteenth century. His social theory was eclectic, an aggregate of many strands drawn from as many schools. But his political creed inspired apprehension. For his was the belief that a group of daring men of unquestioned obedience to the leader, could seize political power by a sudden, surprise attack. Such a group or party was necessarily clandestine, removed from the people, subject to a plan, worked out in advance in the highest echelons. Once the insurgents had taken up arms, the movement, it was expected, would assume a broad character and take in the workers.

The Blanquist party was pyramidal and closely united. Practically all its strength was in Paris, in the first place among students, and to a small degree among workers. In numbers it never exceeded 2,500 men; and its propaganda, at one time noisy and at another mysterious, was at best limited. Its press was ephemeral, designed more for the *déclassés*. Among workers it gained comparatively few recruits. Despite Blanqui's instructions "to pay more attention to the workers," the organization never succeeded in setting roots in labor groups. Actually its framework and tactics were utterly inadequate for agitation among workers, and all its efforts to compete with the Proudhonists for labor's following turned out to be fruitless.

For Proudhonists were trade union leaders whose programs promised either to secure the economic status of the craft worker through cheap credit or to restore his economic independence *via* cooperation. The failure of the cooperative bank in 1868 naturally shook confidence in the remedy and caused workers to rely more on political action. But many others continued to regard cooperation as the way to economic betterment, perhaps to salvation.

Blanquists made war on this persuasion, declaring it to be an illusion that enervated the labor movement. Partly because cooperation persisted as a fundamental tenet among French Internationalists, a breach existed between them and the Blanquists. Watching the proceedings of the Association from his exile in Belgium, Blanqui grew more mistrustful of it. All advances from London to reconcile Proudhonists and Blanquists were in vain. They remained apart, though a common enemy and critical situations should have united them. . . .

Six and a half months intervened between the proclamation of the republic on September 4, 1870 and the rise of the Commune on March 18, 1871. A fresco of the period would represent military disaster and invasion, irate patriotism, popular discontent and unsuccessful insurrections. . . . The Franco-Prussian War had disordered the trade unions that had grown up in the preceding decade. Their unifying force, the First International, had been no less damaged. Its ranks had thinned, in spots had melted; its press, never its greatest asset, had virtually ceased to exist. A breach in the Paris branch, lasting several months, divided old style Proudhonists and new, more active, Internationalists. The breach was closed in February 1871. But a move in March to reorganize and strengthen the branch had brought little improvement. Actually it was beyond repair. . . .

The most active defender of the Commune was the General Council of the International Workingmen's Association. The International had had no hand in starting the Paris Revolution, or as Engels wrote to Sorge, "the International did not lift a finger to produce it." But it "was without any doubt the child of the International intellectually." From the very beginning of the conflict the Council in London was in contact with Internationalists in Paris. After the middle of April, however, lines of communication were broken between the two cities, so that when information reached London it was usually old. During the first month of the Commune, the Council kept abreast of events and assessed them judiciously. When it learned in April of the first military reverses of the Commune, Engels, who was no tyro as a military analyst, ascribed them to want of resolution in the first days. He told the Council that "the time for action against Versailles had been when it was weak, but that opportunity had been lost; and now it seemed that Versailles was getting the upper hand and driving the Parisians back. People would not put up long with being led into defeat." The Communards, he continued, were losing ground, spending ammunition and consuming provisions. But "they could not be starved into submission as long as one side of Paris was open." The war, he was fairly certain, would not be terminated as rapidly as in June 1848, for the 200,000 Parisian workmen were "far better organized than at any former insurrection." An English delegate believed that the situation called for a public statement by the Council. . . .

The Council could justly be credited with an international agitation in behalf of the Commune. Mass meetings in Germany, Italy, Switzerland and the United States endorsed the principles of the International and made the cause of the Commune their own. In England the Council participated in public meetings that were induced to adopt resolutions in defense of the Communards. On March 28 it voted to issue an address to the Parisians, and Marx was asked to write it. But in view of the events in the French capital it was postponed. Further delays prevented its drafting. Finally, on May 30th, Marx read to the Council the *Address on the Civil War in France*. The General Council adopted it unanimously and ordered the printing of 1,000 copies.

The *Address* was completed while the Versailles troops were wreaking vengeance on their adversaries, making no exception of women and children. Writing as reports of mass slaughter were reaching him, Marx did not aim to produce a historical critique of the Commune, but a passionate defense of its combatants. The result was perhaps the greatest polemic he ever composed, and the one that caused more controversy than any other piece of writing on the Paris Commune. It is not the intention here to enumerate the particulars of Marx's brief. All that need be said within the given space is that he juxtaposed Versailles and Paris as the symbols of different social systems: the one, headed by an assembly of specimens of defunct regimes and bent on perpetuating the rule of the bourgeoisie; the other, "essentially a working class government," aiming at the emancipation of labor.

The *Address* won an immediate audience in several languages. Naturally, it had its critics and enthusiasts. Internationalists everywhere promoted its sale and defended its principles. Several English members of the General Council, finding it too radical, resigned. In the United States, it had a wider circulation than had been anticipated. Sections of the International issued special editions. *The Workingman's Advocate* in Chicago and *Woodhull & Claflin's Weekly* in New York republished the entire text; and the New York *World*, nearly all of it. Thereafter it received editorial comment throughout the nation.

It lifted to prominence its author and the organization it stemmed from. Journalists sought interviews with Marx; and the International was the subject of many articles, pamphlets and books. A whole new literature, international in scope, grew up around the Association, most of it as full of calumny and extravaganza as the accounts on the Commune.

Better than that, the police forces of several countries exchanged dossiers on the International and the great powers planned a new Holy Alliance against it. The Commune had been defeated, they argued, but its diabolical fomenter, the International, was there, with designs of other Communes. It had to be exorcized and crushed. Apparently men in power had fallen victim to an obsession. They believed in ghosts. The fact was the defeat of the Commune had drained the International or much of its vitality and closed an era in the history of labor.

THE ACTIVITY OF POPULAR ORGANIZATIONS DURING THE PARIS COMMUNE OF 1871

Eugene W. Schulkind

When on March 18, 1871, the more radical citizens of Paris obliged the Thiers government to flee to Versailles leaving themselves free to establish a "Commune de Paris," the popular organizations had already reached maturity. Throughout the five preceding months climaxed by the Prussian siege, the clubs had increasingly resounded with the call for government by a "Commune." Such a government was seen as the means of guaranteeing the existence of a republican form of government and of initiating a *levée en masse* against the invaders in the manner of the republican volunteers of 1792. A month of agitation around this slogan culminated in the demonstration of October 31 which in effect was the first armed attempt to establish the Commune.

As the population of the city began to feel the growing hardship of the Prussian siege, clubs served as tribunes for the expression of dissatisfaction with the provisional government. Economic distress, particularly among working people, was a favorite topic of discussion and contributed to the spread of egalitarian and socialist thinking. With growing conviction that the provisional government was betraying the nation went the belief that only a "Commune" could effectively reorganize defense around a policy of "war to the death." The famous "red poster" of January 6, issued by the Committee of the Twenty Arrondissements, reflected common sentiment in the following conclusion:

The policy, strategy, administration of the Government of September 4, a mere continuation of the Empire, are condemned.

Make way for the people! Make way for the Commune!

Eugene W. Schulkind, "The Activity of Popular Organizations During the Paris Commune of 1871," *French Historical Studies*, vol. I, no. 4 (Fall, 1960), 395–401, 403, 409, 411–415. © *French Historical Studies*. Used by permission.

This agitation exploded again in the insurrectional demonstration of January 21. The influential role that the clubs had played in it led the government to close their meeting halls and to suppress seventeen newspapers. Weakened by the defeat of this second armed attempt to install a Commune in Paris, the popular opposition was now even more incapable of preventing the conclusion of an armistice with the Prussians on January 28.

The class basis of the charge of "treason" raised against the provisional government is particularly significant for the study of subsequent popular activity under the Commune. The "betrayal" of the nation's defense was portrayed as a deliberate choice resulting from fear of the political and social ramifications of an armed popular mobilization under republican inspiration. Comparing the contemporary scene with that of the French Revolution, propagandists likened the bourgeoisie and landowners of 1870 to the aristocrats of the ancien régime and the working people to the revolutionaires.

After the signing of the armistice with the Germans emphasis rapidly shifted from the charge of "treason" to political and social grievances which form the basis for the popular activity that later accompanied the establishment of the Commune.

In this pre-Commune period a variety of socialist creeds spread in the predominantly working class neighborhoods. There was considerable support at a number of meetings for the program and list of candidates presented for the February 8 elections by the two major organizations of Parisian workers: the Paris sections of the International and the Federated Council of Trade Unions. This program, "in the name of a new world," stressed four points in the following manner:

The existence of the Republic not to be questioned under any circumstances;
Necessity of the advent of the workers to political power;
Liquidation of the governmental oligarchy and of industrial feudalism;
Organization of a Republic, which in giving to the workers their means of production, just as that of 1792 gave the land to the peasants, will achieve political and social equality.

Similarly, a general assembly of the neighborhood vigilance committees, originally concerned only with defense and the preservation of republican government, proclaimed in a *Déclaration de Principes* that:

Every member of a Vigilance Committee declares his adherence to the Revolutionary Socialist party. Consequently, it demands and seeks to obtain by all means possible, the elimination of the privileges of the Bourgeoisie, its downfall as a governing caste and the rise of the workers to political power. In a word, social equality . . . It recognizes labor as the sole base of the Social Constitution, labor, whose full product ought to belong to the Worker.

. . . It therefore will oppose by force, if necessary, the meeting of any Constituent or other alleged National Assembly, before the foundations of the present order of Society have been changed by social and political revolutionary liquidation. . . .

This declaration went on to envision a Communal government:

Until this definitive revolution shall have occurred, it recognizes as the government of the City, only the revolutionary Commune emanating from the delegation of the revolutionary socialist groups of this same city. It acknowledges no government of the country other than the government of political and social liquidation produced by delegates from the revolutionary Communes of the country and of the principal workers' centers. It undertakes to fight for these ideas and to propagate them by forming, where they do not exist, revolutionary socialist groups. It will federate these groups and place them in communication with the Central Delegation. Lastly, it is to place all means at its disposal in the service of propaganda for the International Association of Working men.

Although this may represent wishful thinking, it is nevertheless indicative of the growing image of a Commune as a workers' government.

That the Paris sections of the International aimed at installing a republican "workers" government committed to the ultimate attainment of some form of worker ownership of the means of production should not be surprising. But it is noteworthy that such thinking was also very prevalent in meetings of other organizations in working class neighborhoods during these months preceding the Commune. Its by-product was the transition that occurred in the meaning of "Commune." From a government which would preserve the republic and actively pursue the nation's military defense, it evolved into one which would bring about the social and economic "emancipation" of labor.

The common conclusion drawn from the February 8 elections to the Assemblée Nationale, namely that there was little or no socialist sentiment prior to March 18, is quite misleading. Indeed, the one-week period of preparation for these elections could produce only a potpourri of well-known republican political figures. The immediate issue of preserving the republican form of government in the face of monarchist sentiment in the rest of the country, automatically relegated social questions to a secondary position as an election issue.

The election of an overwhelmingly monarchist and conservative National Assembly, followed by the announcement of plans to cancel the moratorium on rents and maturities further aggravated social discontent. Intensifying economic difficulties for workers and shopkeepers, it increased popular opposition to the provisional government of September 4.

The assumption of governmental authority by the Central Committee of the National Guard on March 18 and the inauguration of the Commune on March 26, changed the popular organizations from an opposition force to a support of the new government. The majority of the clubs, largely working class in membership, grew in influence and attendance reflecting the growing conviction of working people that at last discussions of political and social change had become more timely than ever. One club which appears to have been among the most active during the Commune stated in a poster:

It is with the aid of public meetings that we have been able to recognize and defend our rights.

It is only at public meetings that we are able to enlighten ourselves regarding the stormy situation through which we are passing.

We thus ask your presence and participation in order that each citizen fully know what is occurring, how it is occurring and how it ought to occur.

Once having assembled, and everyone having been able to say what he thinks, it will be much simpler for us to reach decisions concerning events which may arise.

Strongly anti-clerical, clubs immediately set about taking over churches as meeting places or asking the Commune or local arrondissement mayors for the authority to do so at least in the evenings. The *Club communal du 3e arrondissement*, meeting in the Église Saint-Nicolas-des-Champs, eagerly urged other clubs to follow its example:

It is to you, citizens of all arrondissements that we address ourselves.

Follow our example; open communal clubs in all the churches; the priests will be able to officiate in the daytime; and you will conduct the political education of the people in the evening.

By May, clubs were meeting regularly in most of the larger churches of working class neighborhoods.

Corresponding to the new political situation, the clubs viewed themselves, in varying degrees, as intermediaries between the Commune and the citizenry. Their role may be summarized as follows:

1. Rally further support for the Commune by propagandizing its progressive political and social character.
2. Act as centers for the expression of grievances, suggestions and information of use to the Commune.
3. Participate in the drafting of measures to be presented to the Commune for deliberation and subsequent action.
4. Mobilize popular vigilance against the actions of pro-Versailles elements in the capital.
5. Aid in administration of arrondissements and application of Commune decisions.

On the other hand, the Commune generally failed to avail itself of the potential value of the popular organizations for purposes of propaganda and mobilization for defense. In spite of the failure to secure substantial material aid from the Commune, some organizations managed to publish newspapers, print posters and maintain headquarters. Still, lack of resources generally restricted their propaganda to club discussion and resolutions that were distributed to the Communard press and to other clubs. . . .

To the best of my knowledge, the Commune, with the possible exception of its Commission of Labor, Industry, and Trade, did not answer most of the numerous reports and letters which it received from clubs and individuals. It evidently missed the opportunity to utilize the popular potential effectively. Consequently, popular activity, like the policies of the Commune itself, remained largely unplanned and spontaneous. Amorphous and embryonic as political organizations, the clubs were incapable of forcing the adoption of concrete proposals. Nevertheless, while difficult to measure in any precise fashion, it would appear that a number of Communal actions were influenced by popular discussions and activity. Only two days before the final week of its existence, a member of the Commune made the following observation at a neighborhood public meeting:

The Commune has not drawn sufficient inspiration from the popular movement. It has not frequented the clubs enough. As I stated at Saint-Nicolas-des-Champs, when Robespierre or Saint-Just would arrive at the Convention, they were fortified because they came from the club of the Jacobins or of the Cordeliers, just as Marat was forceful because he wrote what he heard in the midst of the laboring population.

While this observation was more or less justified, minutes indicate that individual members of the Commune did occasionally participate at club meetings and in some cases may very well have been influenced in their thinking by this experience.

The nomination of candidates for the elections to the Commune, constitutes a particularly significant aspect of the latter's relationship to public meetings. In most of the predominantly working class arrondissements such meetings were called by various popular organizations including National Guard units, with the explicit purpose of selecting candidates. . . .

Once the Commune had become a reality, its military and political defense dominated discussion in the clubs. An extreme sense of vigilance combined with traditional anti-clericalism to see a major fifth-column threat to the Commune in the activity of the Church and clergy. For the Communards, inspired by ideals of rationalism and humanism, Church and clergy in the capital appeared as more tangible representatives of the enemy than the Versailles soldiers and the upper classes who had left. Since the clergy consequently was suspected of espionage and sabotage, proposals were made in clubs to limit their freedom, activity, and strength. These ranged from replacing nuns in hospitals with *mères de famille*, to the more significant confiscation of church property.

In addition to questions of restricting clerical activity and confiscation of church property, considerable attention was devoted to combatting religion as an ideology. "The pernicious influence of religions; means for destroying them," read the proposed agenda for a club meeting and indeed many clubs proceeded to wage just such a campaign.

The most important weapon in this direction appears to have been the campaign for the abolition of parochial schools and the establishment of a system of universal, free, laical instruction. . . .

There is seldom any mention of social questions by these moderate forces. Drawn largely from middle class strata, they were increasingly reserved in their support of the Commune as the civil war continued. The growth of radicalism during the months of April and May and the increasing awareness of inevitable military defeat undoubtedly hastened the disillusionment. Some of these groups, particularly several Masonic lodges, participated in futile attempts at conciliation between Versailles and the Commune.

The radical position appears to have been shared by the overwhelming majority of trade unions and clubs. In their vague formulations and debates can be distinguished outlines of a socialist society to which the transition would be initiated sooner or later by the Commune. Implicit in this view was the supposition that the Commune would be successful in its military defense. . . .

The generally vague solutions which were proposed for the *question sociale* varied in formulation. Some were more specifically socialist than others but all viewed the Commune's battle with Versailles as a struggle between the working class and the propertied classes (be they landowners or capitalists). . . .

The respect of popular organizations for the International was matched by a devotion to Blanqui, the famous revolutionary hero whom Versailles kept in a secret prison. Frequent mention was made at meetings of the need for retaliatory measures by the Commune in order to obtain his release.

In addition to the general views already cited concerning religion, public education and long range aims of the Commune, discussions also included related objectives such as the elimination of permanent armies, full equality for women, and abolition of capital punishment.

Interpreting the Commune as a government representing above all the working people, popular organizations looked to it for legislation to improve their immediate well-being within the limits imposed by the war with Versailles. In some cases their remarks probably contributed to whatever action the Commune did take. Among the measures which they discussed were: continued moratorium on rents, low coal prices subsidized by the Commune, tax reform, private employment offices to be replaced by public, non-profit ones, investigation into low wages paid by some employers, and financial aid to wounded Communard soldiers or the families of those who had died.

Of particular significance is the support of the trade unions for the work of the Commission of Labor, Industry and Trade. This was especially true with regard to the Communal decree calling for the confiscation of abandoned workshops. It is significant that the decree provided for participation of the trade unions in its execution. They were requested to form a committee in order to draw up an inventory of the workshops and to submit plans for their immediate conversion into cooperative enterprises operated by the workers employed there. The unions' response was prompt. Representatives were sent and resolutions were passed which in certain cases interpreted the decree as beginning the "emancipation of the workers." It is difficult to conjecture as to how far this relationship between the unions and the Commune might have developed since defeat was only a few weeks away. . . .

The Commune was criticized for forgetting that its "mandate is to save the nation, and consequently to act with energy, leaving aside for the moment, too great a respect for legality, a policy which only profits reaction." This view became more widespread as reports arrived of the Versailles army's cruelty to prisoners and as the military plight of the Commune worsened. The president of the *Club Saint-Séverin* perhaps spoke for other clubs when he wrote to a member of the Commune to "finish off the bourgeoisie in one blow. . . . For that I can see only one means: to take over the Banque de France. . . ."

In conclusion, the source material examined demonstrates the existence of vigorous Communard activity in the form of clubs, committees, unions, International sections and women's groups. In the main, such activity displayed a distinctly "proletarian" character. The radical view which before long became virtually the only view among the popular organizations interpreted the struggle between Versailles and the Commune as a battle between "exploiters" and "exploited"; the final aim became the achievement of some form of working class hegemony.

While it is difficult accurately to measure socialist sentiment, the common practice of evaluation based only on major newspapers, memoirs, and official Commune records is inadequate especially in describing the popular organizations. Nor would the quantity of explicit socialist declarations be a sufficient basis in itself although they certainly were not lacking. Clubs and unions generally seem to have recognized that no basic economic reforms could be effected without military security. Consequently, most discussions were concerned with improving the military defenses rather than with long-range social and economic planning. But the relegation of the latter to secondary importance as an immediate issue does not demonstrate lack of socialist thinking; the consciousness of ultimate socialist aims and immediate military defense were not exclusive of each other.

As was indicated earlier, a number of clubs, unions, and other groups had already expressed socialist aims when calling for a Commune during the period which incubated this revolution. The influence of the socialist-minded Communards continued to grow after March 18 while the disillusioned moderate supporters vacated the field. Nevertheless, serious elaboration of a socialist perspective could not develop because of the brevity of the Commune's life, the grave military situation, and the absence of a group intent on immediately developing one.

SUGGESTIONS FOR FURTHER READING

Bibliographical: JEAN GACON, "La Commune et ses historiens," La Pensée, 97 (1961), 102–107; J. ROUGERIE and G. HAUPT, "Bibliographie de la Commune de 1871," Mouvement social, no. 37 (1961), 70–92, and no. 38 (1962), 51–85; General: ROBERT BALDICK, The Siege of Paris (London, 1964); J. P. T. BURY, Gambetta and the National Defense (London and New York, 1936); HENRI GUILLEMIN, Les Origines de la Commune, 3 vol. (Paris, 1956); JEAN T. JOUGHIN, The Paris Commune in French Politics, 1871–1880; The History of the Amnesty of 1880 (Baltimore, 1955); MELVIN KRANZBERG, The Siege of Paris, 1870–71; a Political and Social History (Ithaca, N.Y., 1950); PROSPER OLIVIER LISSAGARAY, Histoire de la Commune de 1871 (latest edition, Paris, 1947); CHARLES RIHS, La Commune de Paris, sa structure et ses doctrines (Geneva, 1955); Special: (ideological) MAURICE DOMMANGET, Les Idées politiques et sociales d'Auguste Blanqui (Paris, 1957); JEAN-BAPTISTE DUROSELLE, Les Débuts du catholicisme social en France (1822–1870) (Paris, 1951); ROGER GARAUDY, Les Sources françaises du socialisme scientifique (Paris, 1948); LOUIS GIRARD, Etude comparée des mouvements révolutionnaires en France, en 1830, 1848 et 1870–71 (Paris, 1961); ELIE HALÉVY, Histoire du socialisme européen (Paris, 1948); GEORGE C. IGGERS, The Cult of Authority, Political Philosophy of the Saint-Simonians, a Chapter in the Intellectual History of Totalitarianism (The Hague, 1958); LEO A. LOUBÈRE, Louis Blanc (n.p., 1961); JOHN PLAMENATZ, The Revolutionary Movement in France, 1815–1871 (London, 1952); HENRIETTE PSICHARI, Renan et la guerre de 1870 (Paris, 1947); ALAN B. SPITZER, The Revolutionary Theories of Louis Auguste Blanqui (New York, 1957); PHILIP A. SPENCER, Politics of Belief in Nineteenth-Century France (London, 1954); (social) EDOUARD DOLLÉANS, Histoire du mouvement ouvrier, vol. I, 1830–1871 (Paris, 1948); GEORGES DUVEAU, La Vie ouvrière en France sous le Second Empire (Paris, 1946); EDWARD C. KATZENBACH, JR., "Liberals at War: The Economic Policies of the Government of National Defense, 1870–1871," American Historical Review, LVI (1951), 803–23; FERNAND L'HUILLIER, La Lutte ouvrière à la fin du Second Empire (Paris, 1958).

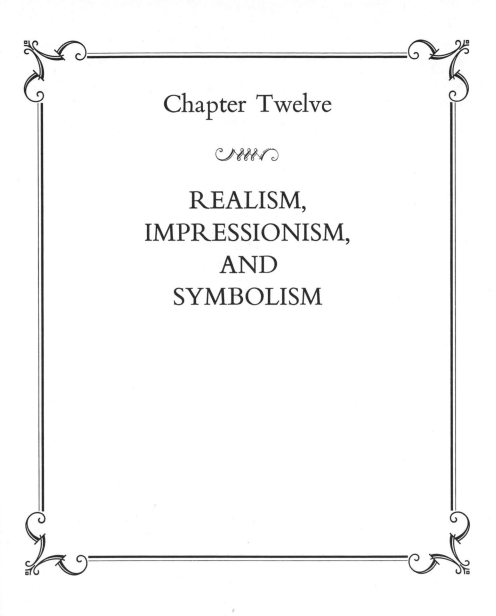

Chapter Twelve

REALISM, IMPRESSIONISM, AND SYMBOLISM

Howᴇvᴇʀ VARIED the thought and literature of the first half of the nineteenth century was, it could largely be subsumed under the title of romanticism. By contrast, the second half of the nineteenth century witnessed the proliferation of literary and artistic schools of thought. With the publication of Flaubert's *Madame Bovary* in 1856, the new school of literary realism was underway and the break with romanticism clear, as the French literary historian Pierre Martino relates below. Whereas romanticism had emphasized the exotic, the sublime, the infinite, and the momentary in attempting to transcend the limitations of reality, Flaubert attempted to represent reality as it existed. "To represent, we can only represent," and we must "feel things almost materially" was his literary creed. Meticulous observation of reality comparable to scientific observation was Flaubert's method, an indication of the influence scientism was exercising at the time. Parallel to literary realism was the philosophical positivism of Hippolyte Taine, the Biblical exegesis of Ernest Renan, and the social "science" of Tocqueville, Proudhon, and Marx. Scientism was infusing every field of thought.

In art, impressionist painting broke with the salon tradition of classicism (Ingres) and eventually with the realist school of landscapes (Courbet), as the late Italian art historian, Lionello Venturi, relates in the selection "Impressionism, a Break with Tradition." Beginning with Manet's *Olympia* in 1863, the sense impression of light and color which the artist received from nature became the new criterion in painting. The impressionists sought to capture the momentary illusion and vibrations of light practically to the point of dissolving substance. Hence the derisive term *impressionists*. Gone was the realists' compulsion to represent reality as it existed in nature. Freeing the artist from all standards except the representation of his own, momentary sense impressions, this art, Venturi maintains, focused on the essential act of the artist, the subjective, creative process, thus constituting the autonomy which has since characterized modern art.

Nurtured by the émigrés during the Revolution and passed on to the romantics, German idealism had long enjoyed an undercurrent of influence in nineteenth-century France. It also seems to have influenced the symbolist movement of the 1880's. Symbolism, like impressionism, represented a shift from positivist naturalism to a more subjective mode of thought. As the impressionist represented his perception with unconsciously selected fragments, so the symbolist saw the world as a representation of a more transcendental reality. More spiritualist and psychological in its orientation, symbolism marked a further withdrawal from realism and a more decisive step towards modern art than the optical subjectivity of impressionism. A. G. Lehmann, the British literary critic, traces the influence of German idealism on the symbolist poetry of Mallarmé, Rimbaud, and Verlaine. His essay concludes the description and analysis of the three important literary and artistic movements of *fin de siècle* France.

bar

FLAUBERT AND NATURALISM

Pierre Martino

To someone unaware of the change in the [French] intellectual atmosphere, the realistic novel and its successor, the naturalistic novel, might with some justification appear to have evolved quite naturally from the romantic novel. Indeed, there is no sharp break in the progression from the romantic to the realistic novel between 1830 and 1850; rather there is a bridge of intermediary forms. Writers and their readers passed unconsciously from the romantic novel favored in 1830 to the realistic novel of midcentury, and then, around 1875, to the naturalistic novel. The broad outline of this transformation can easily be traced.

Between 1850 and 1860 the various realistic schools, Flaubert's as well as Champfleury's, were obviously more than the "school of Balzac." But this was a purely theoretical opinion, since the influence of Balzac was only just beginning to be felt. Previously, the author of the *Human Comedy* had been either detested as the most typical representative of "industrial literature," or admired as the "most romantic writer who ever existed." His "naturalism" was discovered after his death. [Hippolyte] Taine, summing up this point of view, stated that his work was "the greatest store of documents we possess on human nature." Readers began to discover in Balzac's books not simply romantic complications, but universal examples of the most ordinary things in life—marriage, death, bankruptcy, concealed greed, shady enterprises, and even crime. The dominating factors in Balzac's work were the need and lust for money, a philosophy that pleased a generation tired of romantic idealism. At the same time, thanks to the recent spread of positivism, this generation better understood some of the suggestive ideas contained in the Preface to his *Human Comedy* (1842). There Balzac had presented a gigantic plan, buttressed with sociological concepts and broad analogies between society and nature. The novelist, he wrote, ought to describe "social types," to create characters who personified a given type. His books should, for example, study the structure of a nineteenth-century family of the upper bourgeoisie, or perhaps the life of a businessman. Balzac's plan, like that of his contemporary Comte, aspired to include everything—art, science, politics, and sociology. Zola was to remember the philosophy of the *Human Comedy* when he conceived the very idea of his Rougon-Macquart series.

The first realists sprang neither from Balzac nor from Champfleury nor Flaubert. Champfleury waged the first phase of the struggle for realism. Along with the painter Courbet and [the writer] Murger, he belonged to

Pierre Martino, *Le Naturalisme français (1870–1895)* (6th ed.; Paris, 1960), pp. 10–16. © Armand Colin. Used by permission. Translation by Louise Apfelbaum.

what was then called "bohemia." The romantic taste for the grotesque and unusual led him to depict bizarre characters and eccentric behavior. Originally he chose these characters and subjects because the poverty of his life kept him from contact with more conventional types. At first Champfleury hoped to embellish and dramatize his bohemian surroundings, but he quickly rejected this approach as false and vulgar. He realized, as well, that a segment of the public enjoyed these descriptions of the fringes of society, private worlds, and ordinary people. His approach became a style, the program of the "photographic" school, the "sincerity in art" school. Champfleury thus wrote some fifteen novels of lively documentary interest. The curious modern reader will discover in them a minutely detailed picture of the provincial life of the French lower middle class around 1830.

If realism triumphed by 1860, it was a different realism from that of the author of *The Bourgeois of Molinchart*. Moreover, Champfleury understood neither Flaubert nor the Goncourt brothers, and became frightened in the face of naturalism. [Louis-Edmond] Duranty, on the other hand, who had written *The Unhappy Life of Henriette Gérard*, a beautiful and intelligent novel of the Champfleury school, rallied to Zola's theories quite naturally. In these theories he recognized, with some satisfaction, some of the basic ideas he had defined twenty years earlier in his polemical journal, *Réalisme* (1856). Duranty compared himself to those soldiers of past wars who led the assault and were "thrown into the ditch" to serve as a bridge for those who followed. Zola and his friends were full of kindness for that veteran whose obscurity did not make him any the less acceptable. Duranty and Champfleury had clung to a narrow doctrine that forbade the writer to depict anything he had not seen with his own eyes, or to change it in any way. But like many men of letters and most men, their experience was quite limited. They quickly discovered that, despite great ambitions, they had nothing more to say.

Only the success of *Madame Bovary* assured the triumph of realism. Unanimous acclaim made Flaubert the head of the realist school. It is by now an article of literary faith that Flaubert is French naturalism incarnate. But today almost everyone realizes that this view gives a completely misleading picture of the whole of his work. Flaubert, too, was educated and formed in the midst of the romantic era. To the end, he followed the path of romantic lyricism, seeking grandiose images, exalted sentiments, and harmonious sounds. His first works are admirable specimens of the "romantic agony," and when he later created a new and more sober theory of art to calm his nerves and soothe a dream-wracked mind, he tried to retain as much of his true tastes as possible. "For me," he admitted, "a book has never been anything but a way of living in a given milieu, whatever it may be." The books that he most enjoyed writing were not *Madame Bovary* or the *Sentimental Education*, but rather *The Temptation of St. Anthony* and *Salammbô*; these allowed him to contemplate for whole years a marvelous and warlike scene, the fabulous ancient Orient of his dreams—savage, luxurious, and mystical. This vision consoled him for the ugliness of the modern world.

But romantic tendencies do not alter the fact that he wrote *Madame Bovary*. The most widely read and admired of all his works, it also possesses the greatest power of suggestion. The others, the antique dreams, are too personal. They translate a vision of art that is Flaubert's alone. *Madame Bovary* became the bible of realism and naturalism. Around 1860 the century found its most compelling literary aspirations magnificently realized in this novel. To call it the first great novel conceived in the spirit of positivism is no exaggeration. From the very beginning, Flaubert's concern for realism and the observation of reality strikes even the least initiated reader. Flaubert, moreover, used an actual news item as the basis for his book, and in shaping the plot, he confined himself to making the sequence of events clearer, simpler, and more logical. All the secondary episodes were taken from real life, or else reconstructed from genuine documents. He quickly discovered that he could not write on any subject whatsoever without first having assembled numerous notes on his work table.

Thus his doctrine of art, originally a purely esthetic one, gradually became tinged with a scientific philosophy. He considered literary work similar to scientific activity, in its methods if not in its laws. Each time he created a character or sketched a situation, Flaubert proceded as though it were a physiological experiment. He himself gathered or obtained much information on this or that mode of thought or behavior. Then, retaining only the most characteristic traits, he made a synthesis by describing a typical case. And he was full of confidence in his method. "Everything that one invents is true," he said. "Poetry is as precise as geometry, induction is as good as deduction. At a certain point, there can no longer be any doubt about what is in the soul. My poor Bovary is doubtlessly suffering and crying in twenty French villages at this very moment. . . . I maintain that the novel must be scientific—that is, it must remain within probable circumstances, etc."

If we examined the corpus of Flaubert's work, we would soon have to note the limits of his naturalism and positivism, showing how his concern for style and desire for beautiful artistic visions always conquered his preoccupation with technical detail. We would have to explain how, despite the education he gave his intellectual offspring, Maupassant, he could very reasonably state that he detested realism, calling Zola's theories sheer nonsense. It is enough, however, to have indicated . . . how positivist tendencies overtook and enveloped the entire work of Flaubert. Viewed with a certain bias—and it is difficult not to do so—*Madame Bovary* is one of the first "scientific novels" of the nineteenth century. This formula is fortunately incomplete and inadequate for defining the work itself. However, the prestige of [realist] art and its success had immediate impact. The formula was quickly enriched with the missing elements to become the formula of the naturalistic novel. This was the work of the succeeding decade from 1860 to 1870, the work first of the Goncourts, and then Zola and Taine.

IMPRESSIONISM, A BREAK WITH TRADITION

Lionello Venturi

A pictorial tradition is always varied and complex, sometimes even contradictory. It cannot be defined, but it can be described by explaining the characteristics of its greatest painters. This is true for the pictorial tradition preceding impressionism, which can be called romantic-realist, as well as for impressionism itself. These two traditions were complementary in certain respects, and contradictory in others. The break between them was not complete, but it did exist, and the importance of impressionism in modern artistic taste is due precisely to this break. It did not take place suddenly or under the influence of a single artist, but rather as a result of the collaboration of many painters, who can be placed roughly between Edouard Manet and Paul Cézanne.

Still, it is important to indicate one work which, in everyone's estimation, clearly marks the beginning of this break. The work is Manet's *Olympia*. The question then arises as to what exactly was the romantic-realist tradition in 1863 when Manet painted it.

The most typical representative of the neo-classical tradition in French painting was [Jacques] Louis David [1748–1825], and his doctrine was perpetuated, with some modifications, until the beginning of impressionism through the influence of Jean Dominique Ingres (1780–1867). . . . In 1855, Prince Napoleon declared that Ingres, "following the glorious traditions of the splendid ages of antiquity, devoted his entire life and all his talent to the genre which I personally regard as the eternal example of the beautiful." In 1867 at the death of Ingres, the [Imperial] Senate paid this tribute to its late member: "In Ingres there was a reflection of, and an inspiration from, Homer, and Homer is the father of the idea of perfection which the ages have enshrined and outside of which art is nothing more than a fashion and caprice." Thus official taste did not vary from Napoleon I to Napoleon III: statues from antiquity, Homer, absolute beauty, and the perfection of art were considered the artistic standards in 1867 as they had been in 1855, and apart from these standards, there was nothing but "fashion and caprice."

Lionello Venturi, "L'Impressionisme, rupture de la tradition," *Cahiers d'histoire mondiale*, vol. III, no. 2 (1956), 330–338, 340, 354–355. © New American Library. Used by permission. Translation by Ann New.

This attitude revealed a fierce hostility toward romanticism, which had been in existence for over half a century. . . .

Eugène Delacroix (1798–1863) was the incarnation of this romanticism which looked toward the future rather than the past. He liberated sensitivity from the supposed laws of reason and beauty, and asserted the power of color against that of line and plastic form. Delacroix substituted movement for the repose which plastic form demanded. And since actions of the mind are expressed in painting by movements of the body, the expression of emotions became the principal theme of his painting. He did not depict a sword on his canvas, but rather the glitter of light on a sword, a fact which even Victor Hugo found scandalous. Delacroix himself was forced to write that "the most beautiful works of art are those which express the pure imagination of the artist.". . . The official and literary worlds . . . criticized Delacroix for the deliberate inaccuracies of his drawing, without perceiving that it was nothing else but freedom of expression. . . .

Another tradition that contributed significantly to the rise of Impressionism was the genre of landscape painting. . . . Camille Corot (1796–1875) occupies a very special position because, by his personality he dominated the development of pre-impressionist landscapes. Despite his respect for tradition, he destroyed the panoramic character to which landscape painters had been attached and became the painter of small corners of nature. And he had such a consciousness of the part that light played in shaping the human form that his contemporaries perceived that his figures were treated in the same style as his landscapes. . . .

If Corot left the most outstanding examples of landscape painting, it was Gustave Courbet (1819–1877) who contributed most to creating the climate in which impressionism was to be born. Delacroix and Corot were scarcely appreciated by public opinion. . . . Courbet, for his part, openly rebelled against public opinion. In 1855, after the Salon had on several occasions refused his work admission, he himself organized an exhibition of forty of his canvases which he called "realism." He repeated his act of defiance in 1867 when he built a pavilion at the Universal Exposition to display his paintings. Edouard Manet's pavilion was located directly across from his. The political misadventures of Courbet [during the Paris Commune of 1871], which caused him to be condemned and to die in exile, created an unfavorable atmosphere for the impressionists when they exhibited together outside the Salon for the first time in 1874. They were viewed as dangerous revolutionaries. Some of the impressionists, notably Claude Monet and Camille Pissarro, most certainly shared the social convictions and democratic sentiments of Courbet, but they did not inject them into their paintings however.

The impressionists, on the other hand, were deeply influenced by the repugnance which Courbet felt toward religious and historical painting, as well as by his stoutly defended determination to paint only what could be seen. Angels and heroes from antiquity or the Middle Ages were, therefore, ruled out because no one had ever seen them. . . .

From his master [Thomas] Couture [1815–1879], Manet had learned techniques which were more academic than classic, romantic, or realist. As we know, he rebelled against them though he remained Couture's pupil for six years, while studying Velazquez, Goya, Raphael, and Franz Hals. He felt himself in a state of revolt, but he did not grasp the nature and purpose of his revolt. In reality he felt, just as Courbet had, that historical painting was not a true art form, and he would have preferred a form which, like that of Delacroix, was not overly finished. Yet at the same time, he felt a great dislike for Courbet, whom he considered vulgar. Nor did he care for Delacroix either, since romanticism was already outdated for the young men of 1860.

As Manet's friend, Antonin Proust, said: "With Manet the eye played such an important role that Paris had never known an idler who idled more profitably. . . . In his notebook he drew a nothing—a profile, a hat or any fleeting impression—and when a friend looking at it the next day told him 'You should finish this,' he was convulsed with laughter. 'Do you take me for an historical painter?'" For him, "historical painter" was the cruellest insult that could be hurled against an artist. "And what kind of hoax is it to reconstruct historical figures?" he added. "Do you paint a man from his hunting permit? The true way to do it is to paint what you see at first sight. When it's right, it's right. When it's not, then you start over. All the rest is sham."

The question of the unfinished look was of no importance after Constable and Corot, but skill of execution was still highly valued. In a Courbet canvas it is clear that the work of execution was more important than spiritual values. Insisting on the unfinished effect, Manet reaffirmed his desire to maintain spitirual values within the limits of the artistic medium. Neo-classicism, romanticism, realism—all these diverse ideals were imposed on art by intellectual or moral principles. But the ideal of the unfinished was born at the same time as the artistic creation itself, and it was the same as eliminating a certain illusionism in the imitation of nature. Manet replaced realistic finish with pictorial finish.

In contrast to Constable and Corot, Manet refused to bow before the taste of the Academy and public, and developed his new "unfinished" interpretation of reality. The public could not see the realism in his work and protested violently. Manet stuck firmly to his principles, was refused entrance to the Salon, and in 1867 opened a personal exhibition of his works. In the catalogue he wrote:

Monsieur Manet has never wanted to protest. On the contrary, he did not anticipate that it was against him that people would protest on the grounds that there were traditional rules governing the forms, methods and aspects of painting. It came about because those who were raised on such principles recognized no others. They displayed a naive intolerance. Nothing except their principles was of any value, and they became not only critics, but opponents and active opponents. Monsieur Manet has always recognized talent wherever it might be found, and has not intended either to overthrow traditional painting or to create a new one. He has simply wanted to be himself and not someone else. . . .

Despite his sincere desire to avoid sharp conflicts, he was considered the foremost enemy of the Academy, which could not forgive his independence toward the traditional principles of the illusory reproduction of reality.

The artist was liberating himself from a tradition in order to attain a new ideal. The traditional ideal was that of beauty. Delacroix invented a new kind of beauty, but Courbet denied beauty in order to devote himself to reality. Manet despised beauty as much as reality. What, then, was his ideal? To use his will and intelligence so as to isolate his sensitivity and then to allow it to create, free from any preconceived plan. Sensitivity is at the basis of all artistic creation, and for most artists it is also a point of departure for attaining reality or beauty. Can sensitivity alone become an ideal? Beyond any doubt, but under certain conditions. External reality is to the painter a form of chaos, from which certain elements must be chosen and others rejected in order to make a coherent whole. When this whole is created on the basis of physical objectivity, the realist is born. If it is created on the basis of the principle of beauty, the idealist painter emerges. But suppose that the painter is subjective; that is, he organizes only the impressions he receives from reality and forms an ensemble of impressions valid in themselves, without modifying or controlling them by reality or beauty. What would the result then be but the expression of our manner of seeing, of our pure vision, of a plastic and chromatic whole, of a form achieved as a result of pure, formal research. The romantics and realists had reformed the content of art. Manet was the first, however, to offer a new form system, without in the least suspecting that it was indeed new.

This was the novelty that Manet contributed to modern art. This was the point of rupture which enables us to say that modern art began with him.

The canvas in which this new system first appeared was the *Olympia*. That same year, 1863, Manet painted his *Picnic on the Grass*, which showed a nude young woman, Victorine Meurend, who was his favorite model. The pose revealed the artist's desire to reduce mass to allow relief. Yet the Parisian artist still paid tribute to the beauty of his model. But when he painted the *Olympia* several months later, Manet sacrificed the charm of beauty to the coherence of his vision. He transformed the woman into something of both an idol and a puppet. The mass of the body is light, but solid and firm, with dark contours to emphasize the energy of the form. The effect is that conspicuousness of the figure is greater than its relief. The same conspicuousness appears in the other objects represented—the pillow, the covers, the flowered scarf, the dress of the Negro maid. The general impression is that of several zones of light colors dispersed on a surface before a background of dark tones. There is no transition between light and dark, no chiaroscuro. Since chiaroscuro subdues the brilliance and purity of tones, its absence means that the colors become very important even when they are not intense. Each element is dependent on the general effect of the presentation of zones and color so intense and concentrated that their plastic value is emphasized despite the lowness of their relief.

The secret of the powerful effect produced is found in the presence, unexpectedness, rapidity, and magic of the vision. Beauty, truth, life—everything in fact—is absorbed into art, proclaimed [the writer] Théophile Gautier. But for him this was only a formula for praising the beauty of Ingres. For Manet, on the other hand, it was free creation, containing a principle the artist himself did not fully grasp, but one which opened the door for modern art—the principle of the autonomy of art.

This was a tremendous discovery, due to Manet's spirit of independence. His faith in the art which he was in the act of creating, rather than to what he saw in nature or in the works of the great artists of the past. . . .

Neither the Academy, nor the critics, nor the public of 1863 or 1865 had expected [the innovations that Manet presented]. Then, as now, they needed some base on which to stand . . . and from which they could approach the work of art. And they found this base in ideas that were foreign to art, even though they had points in common with it—for example, in nature, a historical or poetic subject, beauty, or in the attempt to create an illusion of reality.

The *Olympia* was neither a scene from nature nor a model of beauty; it inspired no real interest in the subject itself, and in fact, the title given the already completed canvas by a literary man intrigued the critics and made them suspicious. Nor was the painting a brilliant display of the skill of the artist. There was really nothing in it, it had no "merit," the term in use then, and yet it was impossible to remain indifferent to the *Olympia*. The young artists talked of nothing else and the public was fascinated. There was a charm in it that had to be exorcised, so as to avoid becoming the victim of a fraud. It was important to be indignant and to insult the man who was a threat to public order. . . .

Before 1870, Manet had achieved an art form autonomous from both nature and beauty. After 1870, thanks to impressionism, this autonomy became a synthesis of form, color, and light. It may be said of Manet and the impressionists that he gave them an esthetic and received a technique. Certainly Manet's name must be inscribed foremost among those who laid the foundation for the modern autonomy of art.

In 1883, the same year that Manet died, [the writer] Jules Laforgue explained that impressionism was not the same as fleeting reality, but the result of a visual sensitivity. The impressionist's eye had once more become primitive and saw "reality in the animated atmosphere of forms, decomposed, refracted, and reflected by both beings and things, in unending variations. ..." Subscribing to the esthetic of pure visibility of [the German writer] Konrad Fiedler [1841–95], Laforgue believed that the best painting was not one that exemplified the doctrines of some school, but that which showed an eye that had gone farther in the development of visibility "by the refinement of its subtleties or the complexities of its lines." He declared he was convinced of the esthetic legitimacy of impressionism. He contrasted its luminous vibrations to the absolute Beauty, absolute Taste, design, perspective and artificial light of the studio. He proclaimed the necessity of abolishing the Salon so as to leave modern painters free to exhibit their works in art dealers' shops in the same way that novelists issued their books through publishing houses.

It is impossible to explain the ideas of Laforgue without being familiar with the theories of Fiedler. Manet, on the other hand, ignored Fiedler as well as every other esthetic. But he invented an art which was more in harmony with Fiedler's theory than any other style of modern times.

The autonomy of modern art and its pure visibility were the meeting point of art and esthetic theory in the late nineteenth century. . . .

[Impressionism] represented a break with preceding tradition, as well as an ideal basis for the later development of modern art. The essential elements of this break were its rejection of the illusion of finish and its consideration that a canvas was finished when it expressed the natural ideal. If the finished quality of the unfinished work led to the creation of autonomy from nature, then the decreased importance of the subject, which was replaced by a motif, made painting independent of both literature and history. Moreover, the act of renouncing objective beauty concentrated the imagination on the purely *artistic* element; that is, on the value of the artist's imagination obeying his artistic needs and his own coherence (which in art corresponds to the logic of science), and free from all demands foreign to painting.

In renouncing the chiaroscuro which was so important in academic training, the impressionists stressed *relief*, that is, detachment of a figure by color. They thus achieved an immediate and striking effect, leaving the impression of magical power.

The intellectual necessity for the autonomy of art was proven in the years 1870–1890 by the theory of pure visibility of Konrad Fiedler, who did not know the impressionists and with whom the impressionists were unfamiliar. Jules Laforgue was the first to perceive the relationship between Fiedler's esthetic and the art of the impressionists.

The intuition of visual synthesis, or the principle of the division of colors, gave painting a more brilliant and lighter effect than it had achieved in all the preceding periods. And since this principle was extended to the depiction of any theme, it became the color integration of the autonomy of painting.

The division of colors was achieved first in landscapes, then in the human figure. In this way a unity of style was realized in which the figure and its setting were treated in the same fashion, precisely because they were no longer elements taken from nature, but rather pictorial elements.

Composition, too, was reduced to the simultaneous appearance of forms without any regular order. As a style, irregularity revealed, however, that the artist's sensitivity was freed from all intellectual principles. This freedom was expressed on the social level by a preference for cottages and cabbages instead of palaces and roses.

The importance of surface at the expense of the third dimension became general, and persisted even when a desire for the constructive enclosed sensation and imagination in an architectural setting. The awareness [Paul] Cézanne [1839–1906] had of the necessity of in-depth vision and his ideal of geometric form permitted him to set impressionism on a new formal foundation. For him the artistic universe existed alongside the reality of nature, without ever coming into contact with it. Any contingent detail was excluded from the canvas in order to obtain the perfect fusion of formal construction and perceptible vibration. Because of the vibration, the image was vital, and because of the construction, it assumed an external meaning. And it is precisely because of this double quality of the vital and the external that this art achieved its full autonomy, an autonomy which art had totally ignored before the nineteenth century.

GERMAN IDEALISM AND FRENCH SYMBOLISM

A. G. LEHMANN

Without there being ever so rigid an antithesis as a brief schematism would suggest, it is true to say, that to the curious but uninitiated literary world of after 1870 two 'systems' offered themselves, the first positivist, realist, naturalist, the second speculative, idealist, anti-naturalist. The first was in its origins largely French, its lineage including Auguste Comte, Littré, Taine, Renan, a host of physio-psychologists, the first students of evolutionary

A. G. Lehmann, *The Symbolist Aesthetic in France, 1885–1895* (Oxford: Blackwell, 1950), pp. 37–42, 47, 50–55. © Basil Blackwell. Used by permission. French passages in the original have been translated by the editors.

biology, and a wing of historians; the second was represented mainly by early nineteenth-century German philosophy enjoying an Indian summer in a tropical climate—Kant, Fichte, Schelling, Hegel, Schopenhauer. . . .

The first important entry of German transcendental philosophy into France dates from the popularizing work of Victor Cousin, notably the published lecture-courses of 1816–19 and the *Fragmens Philosophiques* of 1826; and the study of the great German classical philosophers from Kant to Hegel grew in volume, under the indulgent eclecticism of official philosophy after 1830. Having once made its appearance, German idealism was not easily dislodged. Powerfully entrenched in the academic hierarchy, the tradition was supported by frequent translation from the originals, which made the leading works of speculative idealism accessible not only to the student but to the general public as well. The result of this acquisition of a foreign tradition was to give the works translated a rather unusual force of authority, since in the earlier stages at least no attempt was made, except in specialist circles, to bring to view the great volume of controversy, and the bulk of rival and disintegrating development by disciples and critics in Germany and elsewhere, which clung round the central themes and problems treated in the works translated. To the writer of 1880, Kant or Schopenhauer (almost indifferently) were simply 'idealists': enormous figures, whose work, seen through a mist, appeared only in the vaguest outline. Less famous philosophers (i.e. those whose works, though perhaps important, remained untranslated) were figures entirely blotted out from sight, though doubtless inferred to stand at one point or other of the compass by relation to the Great Names; the rest of the German landscape was a void. It does not require a great deal of perspicacity to observe the results of such desultory "knowledge"; Barrès' novel *Les Déracinés* gives them in caricature; and we may do worse than turn to hear the moral pointed by another novelist at a slightly later date:

In fifth century Greece we see a harmonius development of Greek thought. It was admirable in its regularity, it was a perfect combination. This was the moment when education (as Plato put it) consisted of "introducing rhythm into the soul." We might speak of Greek rhythm, of Greek thought. But is there any in French thought? No, we are influenced by all the German philosophers, whether we have read them or not. Few have read Hegel, and yet almost no one has escaped his influence. . . . We pick up corners of thoughts like we pick up books in a library: we take fragments of the total ideology. There is a total, but this total is not a sum, because there is no harmonious or logical arrangement.

Nothing indeed can be more amazing than the obscurity in which, for the general public at least, Ravaisson, say, and Renouvier and Lachelier lived and taught, when compared with the lively interest professed for German Idealism. Modern French thought in this field hardly came into its own before the turn of the century.

With such a lack of solid familiarity and in the absence of any perspective view, it was inevitable that the writings of the German philosophers, like massive lumps of authority to be thrown about, should be simple playthings invoked in arguments in no way resembling those which they had been developed out of and designed to deal with, and a shining example of their abuse is provided by that branch of knowledge with which we are here concerned: aesthetic. Characteristic in their essential feebleness of hold upon French ground were the cases of Schopenhauer and Wagner, first-comers in a long sequence of "crazes." The reasons for Schopenhauer's popularity in the first years of the third republic have been frequently analysed, and with a fair measure of unanimity—in terms of a wave of national disillusion and frustration coinciding with a thorough-going pessimist creed. But there is more in the problem than that; and we shall not be digressing if we study in some detail a few examples of those general philosophic views which went with the literary generations of 1880 and 1890 by the name of "idealism."

A succinct version has been provided by Rémy de Gourmont, at a time when he himself would not have refused the label:

A new truth has recently entered literature and art: it is a thoroughly metaphysical, *a priori* (in appearance), and vital truth since it is only a century old and truly new, for it had not yet played a part in the aesthetic order. This evangelical, marvellous, liberating, and modernizing truth is the principle of the ideality of the world. In relation to man, a thinking object, the world, everything that is outside myself, exists only in the idea that I have of it.

We know only phenomena, we reason only about appearances; all truths in themselves escape us; the essence is unattainable. This is what Schopenhauer popularized through his simple and clear formula: the world is my idea. I do not see what is; what is, is what I see. There are as many different worlds as there are thinking men.

Here already, in a writer who was certainly one of the more intelligent exegetes of symbolism, is a reproduction of a view of Schopenhauer's which for adequacy leaves much to be desired. One might suppose from it that Schopenhauer's idealism was perilously near a vulgar solipsism; that outside a world of illusory images nothing may be held to exist at all. Rémy de Gourmont, in common with other popularizers of his time who aimed at a similar grounding for a symbolist aesthetic, says nothing of the panthelistic monism which, rather than his theory of knowledge, is the essential feature of Schopenhauer's philosophy, and provided the main problems for his German disciples and critics to face. We are, in fact, in the presence of our first example of what might be called selective misinterpretation; where the real aims of Rémy de Gourmont (briefly hinted at in the reference to "the aesthetic order") remain as it were "off the picture."

A slogan similar to Schopenhauer's "the world is my idea" was Ed. Dujardin's "only our soul lives," prefaced to his unusual novel *Les Hantises*

(1886) and quoted *ad nauseam* by an author and by Téodor de Wyzéwa in the *Revue Indépendante*. And yet, despite the lucidity of Ribot's study on Schopenhauer (1874) (expressly recommended by Wyzéwa to all prospective "idealists"), it cannot have been easy to form any other view of the philosophy of Schopenhauer in times when a presumably informed and certainly exalted reporter, writing in the *Revue des deux Mondes*, could give the following *glose* of the famous doctrine:

The world is my idea. If we imagine a differently constructed viewer—one, for example, endowed with another kind of cerebral makeup—the spectacle changes. Imagine it entirely gone, and the stage itself disappears into the night. If you think that something of it remains, it is because you find it difficult to erase the idea of a possible intelligence from your mind.

Here, if anywhere, is the solipsist myth; a solipsism which if it admits of no answer, certainly produces very little conviction on anyone considering it on its own merits. But this solipsism was not considered on its own merits by the writers with whom we have to do; it lingers on for several decades, owing its retention to the notion that it was essential as a presupposition to any aesthetic whatever that *allowed a place to the individual choice and style of the artist*. At a much later date, at the end of the symbolist vogue, in fact, we find in André Gide's *Journal* such traces of it as the following:

My mind had great difficulty in knowing whether it was first necessary to be before appearing, or first appear before being what appears.

and again

I never really succeed in convincing myself completely of the real existence of certain things. It always seems to me that they no longer exist when I no longer think of them. . . . To me the world is a mirror, and I am astonished when it reflects me badly. . . .

which position leads him more and more to conclude that a life of pure "introspection" is alone logically admissible, at any rate to the writer: and he quotes with enthusiasm from Lavater:

I tell it to all my adversaries; I think it every day of my life: to reflect about oneself is life within life. And we reflect so little about it! How rarely do we live our life for life (untranslatable: it reads: "wie selten machen wir unser Leben zum Leben!").

That these are no mere chance coincidences down the years is evidenced on all hands; for the case in point, that of Gide, it suffices to repeat his own testimony:

It seemed that in those days we were more or less consciously subject to some vague password, or rather that none of us listened to his own thoughts. . . . Supported by Schopenhauer. . . , I considered "contingent" (that was the word we used) everything that was not "absolute," the entire prismatic diversity of life.

It is not difficult to envisage this state of mind: the hero of Gide's novel *Paludes,* and Valéry's almost contemporary figure, Edmond Teste, are idealizations of this spirit of *disponibilité* which goes so closely with the literary "idealism" which seems, in 1880, to presuppose it by contrast with realistic and naturalistic literature's appeal to positivism. . . .

The typical symbolist knew roughly what he wanted of an aesthetic; and faced with the choice between a flourishing positivism seemingly committed to Zola and an alluring strange new field, chose the latter as better complying with the polemical requirements of the times. . . .

. . . The writer, in that complex of literary developments which we call symbolism, was seeking his liberty as a creator, and would pay any price for it; was seeking an unrestricted range of expression, free from the formal and emotional patterns imposed by a realistic art; and turning from a philosophy whose avowed aim was a reasoned account of the exact determining forces in every sphere of knowledge and experience, found for a time his haven in garbled versions of idealist epistemologies:

Chained within the cavern, the prisoner lamented and was afraid because fearful phantoms clashed on the wall before his eyes, [we read; but] once he recognized the true cause, he was free, and the prisoner in the cavern became the divine magus, the creative Magus.

The artist, the creative magus, can ignore the grim patterns of heredity and environment, the social problems of the day, since he is not obliged to report them. It is easy to see how such a liberation quickly turns into an attitude of refusal, of escapism, the selective preciosity of the ivory tower. . . .

From a different quarter symbolism received equal support in its antirealist drive; from mysticism. Hard as it is to define with precision the way in which young writers of the eighties embraced German idealism, our task becomes harder still when we try to assess the importance to them of so vague and indistinct an attitude as that implied by the term "mysticism." Nothing is easier than to profess to be a follower of Swedenborg or a student of oriental asceticism; nothing is more difficult to challenge; when all is said, however, the only sphere in which it is possible to define a mystic's ideas with any precision at all is when he comes to attack those intellectual standpoints from which his own position is invariably a revulsion. Of all men the mystic is the most eclectic: he will forage behind the enemy's lines regardless of the danger of being cut off; when such forays prove disastrous (as with the phenomena of electricity early in the nineteenth century), he will fall back on his strong point: his conviction and his inner voices; no rational army can ever hope to attack him there, and but for the fear of decay, he would never feel bound to issue forth again. Perhaps the defining feature which unites all mystics lies in that direction. The traditions of mysticism are at least as venerable as any others; and the mystic's freedom from obligations towards rational thinking and historical precision introduce into them a timelessness which to the adept is a source of strength. Since, essentially, mysticism is not only irrational but anti-rational, its periods of most vigorous growth coincide in modern times with the disappointment of excessive hopes and claims by the current representatives of the rational persuasion. So with Mme. Guyon, or Pierre Poiret, for whom a Cartesian account of the human mind did insufficient justice to the claims of the emotional life; so too in the nineteenth century, when the march of naturalism in its crude and uncompromising attacks on the problems of the human mind did violence to the experiences of a whole range of thinkers, among them dreamers and poets. Especially poets; for the weakest point in the whole naturalist front comes at the point where it attempts to give an account of the individual mind in the presence of art.

In the face of such relative failure, the appeal of mysticism in one or another of its forms was bound to be strong: any problem which threatened to prove insoluble, any factor which promised to escape analysis, was a hand pointing towards a system of *comprehensio incomprehensibilis*; where rational criteria give place to those of emotional sympathy, where opposed doctrines are not necessarily contradictory, and where the widest freedom of personal choice supplants the tight reins of a methodology.

The strength of literary mysticism in its various forms in the eighties has been variously estimated, according to the types of credo included in this generic title. Victor Chardonnel, writing in 1895, included in its sphere not only Melchior de Voguë, but also Paul Verlaine—evidently for him the anti-realist ticket was sufficient claim to inclusion. By those standards it would be hard to exempt any of the symbolists from it; but luckily it is possible to outline some of the more important groupings, such as Péladan's Rosi-crucianism. Orliac, among many others, finds in the whole course of French literature a subterranean thread of mysticism, making its appearance in Chateaubriand, Lamartine, in Balzac even; and (in the period under review) in the illuminism of de Guaïta, Papus, M. Barrès, Paul Adam, Dubus, Morice, Schuré, Vulliaud, Péladan, and others. Téodor de Wyzéwa, writing in the *Revue Indépendante* in 1887, gives a long list of recently published works of mystical tendency which certainly suggests a flourishing market for this literature; and in a rather witty article which follows this list Wyzéwa applies the beliefs of contemporary spiritualism to the task of rehabilitating an old Russian fairy tale, told him by his nurse; and succeeds in showing how te-lepathy, magnetism, and a whole gamut of occult forces can between them render credible each of the fantastic events that figure in it. But for the verve of Wyzéwa's restitution, we might be tempted to complain that it is wasted labour: the important point is that mysticism affects aesthetic theory not by enabling its adepts to "believe anything", but by giving them, or attempting to give them, an explanation of why they find art valuable at all. This explanation always takes the form of a variation upon one given theme: that in the aesthetic experience man is brought into more or less direct communication with his God. The classical account of this process belongs by right of precedence to Plotinus, virtually the first philosopher to advance a definitely "symbolic," as opposed to imitative outline of the metaphysic of art; and it is an account which, infinitely flexible, has lived through many centuries already. In a sense it is the essence of Schelling's theosophy, with which symbolism was quite as familiar as with the works of Kant and Hegel; it recurs over and over again in Carlyle, an author very much read by the generations with which we are dealing:

The Universe is but one vast symbol of God; nay, if thou wilt have it, what is man himself but a Symbol of God? . . .

Another matter is it, however, when your symbol has intrinsic meaning and is of itself *fit* that men should unite round it. Let but the Godlike manifest itself to sense; let but Eternity look, more or less visibly, through the Time-Figure (Zeitbild)! . . . Of this latter sort are all true works of art: in them (if thou wilt but know a Work of Art from a Daub of Artifice) wilt thou discern Eternity looking through Time; the Godlike rendered visible.

and it will be remembered that Baudelaire, himself one of the most direct formative influences on the symbolists, rested his theory of poetic symbols on an uncompromisingly mystical foundation. . . .

Virtually, then, the mystic's approach to literature differs in little but its terminology from that of the "idealist"; each sees in poetry, and by extension in every other form of art, the communication not of "information" but of some strong emotional experience. Moreover, so great is the reaction from the idea of imitative or didactic art, that there is a tendency, frequently observed in late nineteenth-century literature, to claim that the affective aspect of art can exist quite independently of the imitative—on occasion, that it must do so. The yogi pursues his dreams regardless of the existence or otherwise of a human world around him; nothing in his perfected state of inner harmony need ever cause him to yield to the essentially social claims of rational discourse. From there, it is but a single step to the kind of self-sufficiency which we find, much later, in *Dada*. There is, as we shall observe, a pronounced correlation in modern times between the growth of anti-intellectualism and the heritage of symbolism. For lack of a rational psychology, for lack of a systematic account of feeling, the nineteenth-century poet, whenever he stood out against a dry and repellent positivist aesthetic, capitulated in this side of his theory of art to the successors of Swedenborg. For a time, a very few years, around the turn of the century, literary opinion hovers over an intermediate position; we see a maturer Viélé-Griffin, for instance, or a Verhaeren, seeking an escape between the horns of the dilemma; but this escape was in the main never realized; and the dominant forces in aesthetic standpoints became more and more sharply divided between positive study of the *phenomena* of art, and irrationalist rhapsodies on the *experience* of art. The first course is naturally repugnant to the artist; the second wearies common sense. If quasi-scientific approaches in the late nineteenth century are responsible for the former diversion from rational inquiry, the symbolists have their share of responsibility for the latter. . . .

SUGGESTIONS FOR FURTHER READING

Literature: ANDRÉ BARRE, *Le Symbolisme. Essai historique sur le mouvement symboliste en France de 1885 à 1900* (Paris, 1911); ANGELO P. BERTOCCI, *From Symbolism to Baudelaire* (Carbondale, Ill., 1964); JACQUES-HENRI BORNECQUE and P. COGNY, *Réalisme et naturalisme* (Paris, 1958); A. E. CARTER, *The Idea of Decadence in French Literature, 1830–1900* (Toronto, 1958); PIERRE-GEORGES CASTEX, *Autour du symbolisme: Villiers, Mallarmé, Verlaine, Rimbaud* (Lille, 1955); JOSEPH CHIARI, *Symbolism from Poe to Mallarmé, The Growth of a Myth* (London, 1956); JEAN DUCROS, *Le Retour de la poésie française à l'antiquité grecque au milieu du XIXᵉ siècle* (Paris, 1918); ELLIOTT M. GRANT, *French Poetry and Modern Industry, 1830–70* (Cambridge, Mass., 1927); PIERRE JOURDA, *L'Exotisme dans la littérature française depuis Chateaubriand*, 2 vol. (Paris, 1938–56); HARRY LEVIN, *The Gates of Horn, a Study of Five French Realists* (New York, 1963); PIERRE MARTINO, *Parnasse et symbolisme (1850–1900)* (Paris, 1925); IRVING PUTTER, *Leconte de Lisle and his Contemporaries* (Berkeley, 1951); ERNEST RAYNAUD, *Baudelaire et la religion de dandyisme* (Paris, 1918); GEORGE R. RIDGE, *The Hero in French Decadent Literature* (Athens, Ga., 1961); JOHN SENIOR, *The Way Down and Out, The Occult in Symbolist Literature* (Ithaca, N.Y., 1959); KOENRAAD W. SWART, *The Sense of Decadence in Nineteenth-Century France* (The Hague, 1964); ARTHUR SYMONS, *The Symbolist Movement in Literature* (New York, 1919); ALBERT MARTIN TURNELL, *The Novel in France* (New York, 1958); (art): ALBERT CASSAGNE, *La Théorie de l'art pour l'art en France chez les derniers romantiques et les premiers réalistes* (Paris, 1906); LÉON GUICHARD, *La Musique et les lettres au temps du wagnerisme* (Paris, 1963); F. W. J. HEMMINGS, "Zola, Manet, and the Impressionists (1875–80)," *Publications of the Modern Language Association*, LXXIII, no. 4, pt. 1 (Sept., 1958), 407–417; PIERRE MORNAND, *Emile Bernard et ses amis Van Gogh, Gauguin, Toulouse-Lautrec, Cézanne, Odilon Redon* (Geneva, 1957); (philosophy): ROMEO ARBOUR, *Henri Bergson et les lettres françaises* (Paris, 1955); IAN W. ALEXANDER, "The Phenomenological Philosophy in France," in *Currents of Thought in French Literature; Essays in Memory of G. T. Clapton* (Oxford, 1965), and *Bergson, Philosopher of Reflection* (London, 1957); DONALD G. CHARLTON, *Positivist Thought in France During the Second Empire, 1852–1870* (Oxford, 1959).

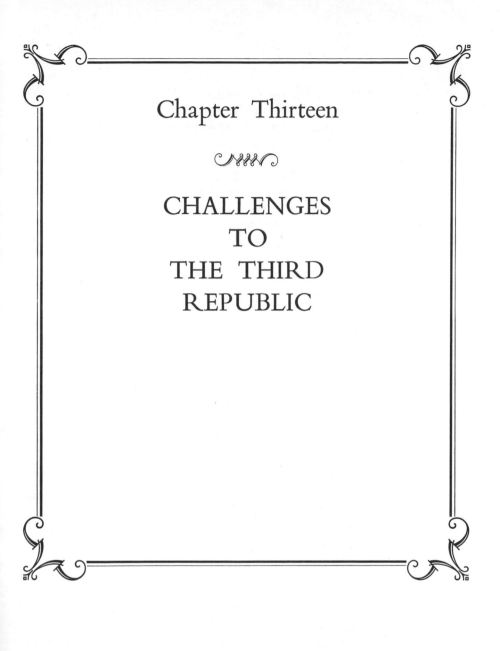

Chapter Thirteen

⟨⁂⟩

CHALLENGES
TO
THE THIRD
REPUBLIC

WITH THE DEFEAT of the Commune in 1871 and the departure of the last German occupation troops two years later, France was at last ready to begin her third republican experiment. The Republic was first only "provisional" and the direction it would take was uncertain. Attempting to shape its future were the Republicans, divided among a radical faction led by the brilliant young orator Léon Gambetta; a moderate center that included three Jules—Ferry, Simon, and Grévy; and a conservative wing headed by the shrewd old Adolphe Thiers, who had served as President of the Republic until 1873; and the monarchists, deeply split between supporters of the Orleanist Count of Paris and the Legitimist Count of Chambord. The latter pretender proved so uncompromising in his royalism that he unwittingly became the godfather of the Republic when he refused a monarchical restoration under any terms but his own—yet another example of the self-defeating quality of the Counterrevolution. In 1875 the interplay of these groups, frightened as they were by a Bonapartist resurgence, resulted in a compromise form of government. They produced not a real constitution, but a series of constitutional laws which provided for a bicamreal legislature, the Chamber of Deputies, elected by direct manhood suffrage; the Senate, elected by local deputies and councilors; and a President, elected by both houses for a seven-year term. Manhood suffrage, the legacy of the Second Republic and Empire, was preserved and the dangerous uses both Napoleons had made of the plebiscite were prevented. Similarly, the deadlock of 1851 between a legislature and an executive, both with popular mandates, was avoided by the indirect election of the President which remained a part of France's constitutions until the Fifth Republic. The laws of 1875 confirmed with only some modification the development of parliamentarism since Sedan, yet were not necessarily definitive. Monarchism was still compatible with this development and custom and adaptation to circumstances contributed equally to the future of the constitution. Although the national elections of 1876 favored Republicans, the latter would not take full control for several more years. To understand this process, one must look at the series of challenges which shaped the Third Republic.

The first of these challenges, the crisis of May 16, 1877, is discussed in the selection by the French historian Fresnette Pisani-Ferry. Attempting to thwart the growing Republican forces, the conservative President MacMahon dismissed Premier Jules Simon and replaced him with a monarchist. The ensuing confrontation between President and Chamber of Deputies raised serious questions of constitutional authority. But suffering from a conservative defeat at the polls and unwilling to resort to a *coup d'état*, MacMahon was compelled to resign in 1879, to be replaced by the Republican Jules Grévy. The crisis was surmounted, but it seriously weakened the French presidency by depriving it of the right of dissolution and installing the first of a succession of weak and shortlived presidents and unstable ministries. The undisciplined Chamber of Deputies emerged as the real victor of May 16.

A second threat, that of Boulangism, was to emerge in the late 1880's. Centering on the handsome, opportunistic General Georges Boulanger, Boulangism represented not the work of one man, but the coalescence of a national desire for revenge against Germany, the dissatisfaction with the ineptness and corruption of Republican politicians, and the effects of economic depression. The French scholar Adrien Dansette considers that its power sprang from its wide appeal to all classes and parties, but he emphasizes that its great weakness lay in Boulanger's personal frailty and unwillingness to move energetically when the right time came. For want of a real leader, Boulangism disintegrated but did not disappear. However, the flight of Boulanger in 1889 saved the regime at a critical moment and helped to give it another fifty years of life.

The durability of the Republic was, curiously, the source of a third challenge, the *Ralliement*, or attempted reconciliation of Catholics with the regime, fostered by the liberal Pope Leo XIII. This change of attitude, which Professor David Shapiro of the University of Essex, England, relates to the politics of the day, signaled a radical departure from tradition. Catholicism had usually been allied with monarchism, and the Republican Left had displayed its anticlericalism in the Ferry laws of the 1880's. Hence the toast raised by Cardinal Lavigerie to reconciliation challenged Catholics to accept the Republic; it also implicitly challenged Republicans to accept the continuation of the Church's position and influence. In the latter sense, the *Ralliement* attempted to deflect the Third Republic's course toward secularization. As Shapiro shows, the movement did serve to bring about an understanding between Catholic and Republican conservatives, especially during the Méline ministry of 1893–95. But the divisions between true supporters of the *Ralliement* and diehard Catholic conservatives, and then the development of the Dreyfus Affair, vitiated the hopes of Leo XIII.

The origins and significance of the Dreyfus Affair, the most famous challenge to the Third Republic, is recounted lucidly and dispassionately in the selection by Professor Douglas Johnson. Beginning in 1894 with the conviction of an obscure Jewish army captain charged with betraying military secrets, the Affair gradually became less concerned with the guilt or innocence of one man than with a renewed struggle between the two Frances. On one side stood the supporters of traditional French institutions; on the other, the defenders of the heritage of the Revolution of 1789, who, like Clemenceau, also used the case for their own purposes. The latter eventually triumphed when Dreyfus was pardoned and rehabilitated. Johnson concludes that the *cause célèbre* originated not in a conspiracy, but in a series of "logical mistakes." Yet he does not deny that it tapped the xenophobia, militarism, and anti-Semitism latent in France.

The Affair forged new solidarity among the Republican victors, who turned their fire against the Army and the Church. The latter, as during the Revolution, had rallied to the traditional and losing forces, but it never recouped its former position as it had under Napoleon I. The Affair increased anticlericalism and undid the work of the *Ralliement*. After provocative circumstances in 1905, the French government passed the Law of Separation of Church and State, thus revoking the century-old *Concordat*. The results of this act were initially the impoverishment of the Church, now deprived of government subsidization, and the movement known as "dechristianization." Eventually it may have contributed to the Church's dissociation from the Right, its independence, and what one author has called a "Second *Ralliement*" in the twentieth century.

The Dreyfus Affair also formed a new nationalistic Right which Professor EugenWeber of the University of California at Los Angeles describes in the final selection. He indicates that nationalist feeling, once largely leftist after the Commune of 1871, underwent a later metamorphosis beginning with Boulangism. Nationalism, he stresses, was a "vague, incoherent, tangible but indefinable" cluster of ideals—patriotism, order, discipline, moral values, anti-socialism—rather than a hard-and-fast doctrine. It might be added that the mounting international tension which made war with Germany increasingly likely was responsible for the hardening of nationalist sentiment in the years preceding 1914. The election in 1913 of Raymond Poincaré, the first really strong President since MacMahon, indicates the change in the tone of French political life.

By 1914 the Third Republic had survived repeated challenges from both Left and Right, and had endured longer than any other regime since 1789. The country, still predominantly agricultural, painfully slow to adapt its social institutions, troubled by religious animosities and industrial unrest, and characterized by ministerial instability, had now to confront the onslaught of a full-scale war. Never would national unity be so necessary as in the hour of this challenge from abroad.

⟡

THE ATTEMPTED *COUP D'ÉTAT* OF MAY 16, 1877

Fresnette Pisani-Ferry

May 16, 1877, is a date that has been remembered as a great event in French political and constitutional history, but its importance sometimes seems rather vague. It is recalled as the reason the right of dissolution of the Chamber of Deputies was brought into discredit. It is remembered as a *coup d'état* that failed and as a republican victory. May 16 is spoken of, just as August 10 and September 4 are, as one of those dates so familiar that we need not name the year. . . .

May 16 refers to that morning when Marshal MacMahon, President of the Republic, without any valid reason and without the cabinet's having been outvoted in Parliament, brought about the resignation of Jules Simon's ministry in order to replace it with one formed by Broglie. The Chamber of Deputies refused to approve Broglie; it was dismissed and then dissolved by the government. There were new elections over a poorly defined issue, but in which the fate of the nascent Republic, endangered by the conservatives, was at stake. Despite a violent campaign and strong administrative pressure, a republican majority was returned. But MacMahon, threatened by Gambetta

Fresnette Pisani-Ferry, *Le Coup d'état manqué du 16 mai, 1877* (Paris: Robert Laffont, 1965), pp. 23–28, 31–34. © Editions Robert Laffont. Used by permission. Editors' translation.

to "give in or get out," first refused to bend before the popular verdict and tried to form a hardline ministry under Rochbouët. It resulted in the defeat of the President, who was compelled to call the republican Dufaure to power and who, one year later, resigned his post and was replaced by [Jules] Grévy, another republican. It is the story of a *coup d'état* that failed.

France had been a republic for two years. Constitutional laws had been voted in 1875, though not without difficulties. The Assembly elected in 1871 after the disaster of the war was mostly conservative, and hoped to reestablish the monarchy. In 1873 it had attempted a restoration in favor of the Count of Chambord, heir of the elder branch of the Bourbons. It had failed due to the obstinacy of the Pretender who, clinging to the ideas of another era, demanded virtually absolute power and was attached to its symbol, the white flag.

Unable to restore a king to the throne, it wanted at least to keep the future open, and with the idea of establishing a seven-year presidential term, it approved the first republican law in 1873. In February and July, 1875, followed constitutional laws resulting from a bargain between the republicans and constitutional monarchists. Rarely in history has a constituent assembly lasted so long, only in the end to approve a constitution which everyone in his heart hoped would not last: the republicans desiring a republic permanently established by new institutions, the monarchists a revision that would enable the king to reclaim the throne of his fathers.

The principle of national sovereignty was nowhere mentioned in the text of the Constitution of 1875, and yet it must be considered its basis. The question was posed in the course of preparatory work, and the proposal by the Bonapartist Raoul Duval to approve the declaration that "sovereignty resides in the universality of French citizens," was rejected on a vote of 476 to 30. But it appears from the debate on this matter that the majority which had been against Duval's proposal was divided between those who, like Cottin, considered its affirmation to be dangerous, and those who, like Lepère, felt this principle to be so evident that there was no need to have it solemnly proclaimed.

Nor was the question of parliamentary rule formally mentioned in the laws of 1875. But all the features peculiar to this system are mentioned in the law of February 25, 1875: the lack of political responsibility of the President of the Republic, the political responsibility of the ministers, the right of dissolution of the Chamber of Deputies, responsibility of the President of the Republic only in case of high treason, and the untouchable and inviolable nature of his person. Broglie, moreover, attributed this last point to the influence of the Orleanists who were preparing the way for the Count of Paris. They were also responsible for the precautions taken to insure the President's independence of action in absolving him from responsibility by prolonging his legal existence beyond that of his electors, and by giving him the right of dissolution.

This constitution was no doubt only a "prelude to monarchy." But its laws were wise, so wise that, made to welcome and include a king, it was perfectly adapted to a republican regime which, whatever is occasionally said about it now, had its greatness and moments of glory.

"If a last battle is necessary, it might as well take place in 1877 as in 1880," wrote Emile de Girardin. This phrase sums up very accurately the reasons for the *coup d'état* of May 16.

The first elections after the constitutional laws were voted in 1875 and the dissolution of the National Assembly proved to be disastrous for the conservatives. The Chamber elected at the beginning of 1876 was composed of 340 republicans, 75 royalists, 75 Bonapartists, and 40 constitutional monarchists. In the Senate, elected by the delegates of the municipal councils of 1874, the conservative majority fell into two factions. A series of republican victories followed, and each by-election marked a victory for the Left: in February, 1877, at Saint-Malo, where Saint-Martin, a radical republican defeated Dumaine, a reactionary; in March at Bordeaux, where a radical republican defeated Caduc, a moderate republican; and in April, at Saint-Malo, where Durand, a republican, defeated Kerloguen, a candidate of the Count of Chambord.

These elections frightened the conservatives, all the more since they knew that the five tests to come would decide the political fate of the country. In November, 1877, the elections for half of the general councils and the local councils were to take place; in December, 1877, that of the municipal councils. These first two elections would determine the outcome of the Senatorial elections of January, 1879. Moreover, the next legislative elections were to take place in February, 1880, and the election of the President of the Republic in November of the same year. Thus, unless there was a sudden shift to the right, the regime would unquestionably slip towards the permanent and dynamic Republic.

The conservatives, frightened by the republican upsurge and terrified by the eventual Radical threat, were in no better position to effect the restoration than they had been four years earlier. But, as [the French political scientist] François Goguel has noted,

they wished to perpetuate conditions which, under more favorable circumstances, would allow them to achieve it without resistance. Most important, conservatives of all stripes deemed it necessary to check the progress of radicalism and anticlericalism so as to safeguard the traditional influence of the notables, and to put an end to the invasion of the administration by republicans. They intended, in short, to fight to keep a hold on what they considered to be the controlling levers over public opinion.

They sought neither conquest nor reconquest, but rather consolidation. . . .
A firm and definite conservative policy was the only solution possible,

and this is what some of the supporters of the May 16 affair themselves admitted. Thus the Vicomte de Meaux, a member of Broglie's cabinet of May 17, 1877, noted in his political memoirs that

it was not in fact a *coup d'état* that we wanted and should have attempted. We did not desire to change the legally established regime, but only intended to use all the means available to us to defend and maintain the threatened social order. . . . If this effort had succeeded, if they [the members of the government] had governed as they had already done, and not unsuccessfully, in this National Assembly, they would have safeguarded the religious, military, judicial, economic, and financial institutions which they had preserved and previously restored. . . . A truly conservative Republic—that would have been the first result of the May 16 episode if the conservative republicans had not caused its failure by allying themselves with the revolutionary republicans.

This in fact amounted to counting on the hope of a sudden shift in universal suffrage and "appealing from a misguided population to a better informed one."

To maintain the "status quo," to keep the way open for an eventual restoration of the monarchy—these were not very exalted aims to propose. In politics it is easier, unless fear enters the picture, to fight to conquer than to defend positions already won. And in 1877 the country was called to vote against the republicans who did not frighten the people. Fifteen months after the last elections held in February and March, 1876, the voters were asked to reverse their judgment for motives which they poorly understood, and when no dramatic event or any real crisis justified a radical change. A country filled with bloody memories of the war of 1870 and the Commune and which only asked to live and let live peacefully, was thrown into tumult. Neither economic crisis nor any political danger explained this sudden appeal. . . .

[May 16] seems essentially an absurd affair, one poorly begun and poorly conducted by individuals who did not really believe in it. The more clearsighted conservatives did indeed perceive the danger: the Chamber resulting from the new elections might be more radical than its predecessor. The desired shift to the right threatened to produce a coalition of republicans. Edmond de Goncourt wrote in his *Journal* on May 24:

This *coup d'état* has the weakness of things that are not carried out boldly, squarely, and decisively. It does not benefit from the touches of illegal brutality, and has against it all the opposition stirred by a violation of the law. I am greatly afraid that it will not succeed because of the honesty surrounding it.

There was, in fact, no way out except through a *coup* by force, and except for Fourtou, no member of the cabinet of May 17 had either the intention or the daring to resort to one. They wanted a legal *coup d'état*, without breaking the bounds of the constitution—an act of authority without violence. To succeed they used and abused all the resources of common law, even those provisions dredged up from the Empire, but they did not go so far as to put the army in their service. . . .

In any case, neither MacMahon nor Broglie was a man about to take the risk of plunging the country into fire and blood. MacMahon, who was perhaps unable to feel the popular pulse, who was ignorant of parliamentary diplomacy, who as a Legitimist had served the Orleanists and the Empire, who was a man devoted above all to conservative principles, and who was convinced of his rights in the affair of May 16, was nevertheless incapable of appealing to armed force to impose his political ideas since he was the protector of the constitution. "The idea of a *coup d'état* never entered his mind," said Jules Simon, head of the government dismissed on May 16. . . .

Legal violence was as far as the spirit of May 16 went. Violence sufficient to stir the ire of republicans yet violence insufficient to dare carry the action through, to employ every means possible to make it succeed. A prefect to whom Albert de Broglie revealed his scruples drew a moral from their conversation: "Monsieur le Duc, when you want a girl, you go at her with both hands."

Still, the campaign was not devoid of passion. For two political ideas confronted each other in a duel, symbolized by a conservative Senate and a Chamber in which a newly elected republican majority chafed with impatience. And the future was at stake.

Nothing, however, was more heterogeneous than the conservative coalition of May 16. It grouped Legitimists, the supporters of the Count of Chambord, his principles and his white flag; Orleanists, supporters of a constitutional and parliamentary monarchy; Bonapartists, conservative republicans, and Ultramontanes—all in agreement to fight against Radicalism and the rising Republic, and all opposed to each other. While the republican party temporarily stilled its internal dissensions and presented a united front in battle, the conservative faction could never impose a coherent discipline on its members.

Throughout the struggle the conservative faction refused to adopt a common program, and there was even a violent polemic among the various tendencies. The Vicomte de Meaux, a minister in Broglie's cabinet, recognized that "the conservative forces did not display either the same ardor, tenacity or discipline to hold on to power as the opposition forces did to conquer it." This attempt at union, this simple program of republicans, would bear fruit.

And this in spite of a terrible governmental pressure on the elections. The cabinet of May 17 would in fact use the entire barrage of repressive laws to oppose the republicans' campaign. Thus, between May and October, 1877, 1,385 civil servants were dismissed, 4,479 reassigned, 613 municipal councils dissolved, 1,743 mayors and 1,344 deputy mayors removed, 2,067 bars closed, and 344 clubs forbidden.

To be sure, the republicans replied with an active propaganda campaign, but one free of useless violence. Never was the person of the chief of state attacked, and correctness remained the rule. It was only after the elections, when the Marshal, first refusing to bow before the popular verdict, tried to substitute a Rochebouët ministry for that of Broglie, that the republicans' tone became aggressive and threats were made publicly. But once the President of the Republic "gave in," even before he "got out," the attitude of the victorious forces again became respectful both towards the office and the man. Likewise, it waited a few months, even a few years, to put the republican program into execution. And this moderation of the republicans is one of the most remarkable things about the crisis—they knew how not to abuse their victory.

Yet what a fine triumph it was, and May 16 founded the Republic better than the constitutional laws themselves did. It stamped the conservatives with the mark of opprobrium by giving them the reputation of being individuals who fought against the currents of popular will. "From then on," as [Jacques] Chastenet acknowledges, "their cause was lost, and France, after a moment's hesitation, would soon slowly reorient itself in a new direction and showed no desire to turn back."

The President of the Republic submitted in December, 1877, resigned in 1879, and was replaced by Grévy, who from the first, recognized the supremacy of the Chamber over the executive power. The great republican laws on schools and municipal government would soon follow, and soon Gambetta and Ferry would lead France along a firmly democratic path. Finally, in 1884 a constitutional revision fixed the republican form of the regime. The Republic was [firmly] established. . . .

THE SIGNIFICANCE OF
BOULANGISM

ADRIEN DANSETTE

It is difficult to determine which of the multitude of causes of Boulangism was the principal one: the will of a great, vanquished country to regain its faith in its destiny; the desire for a glorious revenge; weariness of a regime founded during the enthusiasm of a few years earlier and which, instead of accomplishing the reforms demanded by republican mystique, was trapped in ministerial instability; the sorrow of a believing population which considered its beliefs threatened by [Ferry's] education legislation; discontent created by the failure of important ventures and by the economic crisis;

Adrien Dansette, *Le Boulangisme* (Paris: Librairie Arthème Fayard, 1946), pp. 365–371, 374–377. © Librairie Arthème Fayard. Used by permission. Translated by Nancy Marcolla.

indignation provoked by the Wilson affair; and finally, the incapacity of the opposition parties to take advantage of the general unease resulting from the conjunction of so many diverse elements.

Boulangism already existed when Boulanger was still unknown. In the course of its continuous development, it expressed a profound disappointment with what existed, and a confused hope for something else. This disappointment was manifested in 1885 in the unpopularity of Ferry and the failure of the Opportunists in the legislative elections. How fair the Republic had been during the Empire! [Boulanger], the soldier, appeared on the scene, and thanks to him and the disappointment, hope was made flesh and was baptized with his name eighteen months after its birth.

What hope? The crowds of the Longchamps parade, of the departure for Clermont, of the Paris elections, the hundreds of thousands who voted for Boulanger, saw in him the man of a better France, one healthier and stronger. "You shout 'Down with the thieves!' but is your Boulangism honest?" Barrès was asked in 1889. Barrès replied: "It is not honest, but it will become so. . . . By that I mean," he added in his *Cahiers*, "the basis of Boulangism was a call to honesty." A call to honesty brought about by a disgust with parliamentarism, a burst of patriotic ardor in the sadness of defeat, as well as the hope of social renewal.

Born of Boulangism, Boulanger destroyed it. The appearance of the person differed from the reality, causing a tenacious popular illusion. Boulanger would die with it.

He was the superb soldier with commanding appearance, health, and courage—physical courage, at least. An excellent troop officer, he knew his profession and possessed the gift of command. As a result of brilliant campaigns, dash, and Radical political intrigues at a time when most generals were monarchists, he became a major-general at 48, and was installed in the Rue Saint-Dominique. This young Minister of War had a love of popularity and a genius for publicity: he inaugurated, presided, spoke, had his men eat off real plates, distributed new-model rifles, and threw down a challenge to Bismarck. "He's a fraud," said General de Miribel, recognizing the truth. All the same, Boulanger restored the pride of the army, humiliated in 1870.

After his rash action during the Schnaebelé affair, the minister was overturned. He expected politics to redo what it had just undone, but it was a decisive reversal. Success heightened his natural vanity, his superstitious self-confidence, and his lack of self-control. His luck faded because he abused it, and the general with a penchant for insubordination was expelled from the army when he chose the wrong way to return as its chief. And now he was astounded and furious, a politician and a candidate for dictator despite himself.

It was a great blunder! The country acclaimed a hero with ambitious aims, but Boulanger was nothing more than a civil servant out of work, given over to cheers on the streets, compliments in the salons, and the embraces of an elegant mistress. He had been somebody in the army; he achieved nothing in politics. Anything else would have been astonishing. Beneath the mask of a conceited actor vegetated a man of mediocre intellect, one without culture or character, lost in a world he knew nothing of, overwhelmed by too great a role. The hero France dreamt of, the master of tomorrow, was in reality no more than a poor wretch.

Boulangism, an antiparliamentary and authoritarian movement, had to overthrow Parliament and establish Boulanger as dictator. Such was its mission, and to fulfill it, the general would have had to strengthen the popular enthusiasm which supported him with some lofty ideal and address himself directly to the troops of all parties. But he let the Jacobin, Blanquist, Bonapartist, and royalist elements merge into Boulangism without attempting any effort to attain intellectual unity, being satisfied with negotiations with the political leaders that played one off against the other.

This doctrinal confusianism and the duplicity of this attitude could be explained if it were a tactic in preparation for a *coup* by force. But Boulanger was merely the "syndic of the malcontents." His equivocal maneuverings expressed his cunning less than they betrayed his incompetence as a thinker and his incapacity as a man of action. Imprudent without audacity, he wanted to conquer the Republic legally because he was afraid to destroy it. When the occasion for this presented itself, he retreated from danger, but danger pursued him, and his faith in his star was unable to resist the test. The soldier who would have risked the future of his country in an ill-prepared war, fled the threat of arrest. The illusion was dissipated and the mistake ended. Boulanger appeared as he really was—unequal to his destiny, a tin blade in a steel scabbard. Providence offered him many parts: Cromwell for the Republicans, Monk for the royalists, Saint-Arnaud for the Bonapartists, "General Revenge" for the patriots, a Caesar for his country; but to [his mistress] Marguerite he was only a neurotic Antony. Boulangism was morally stricken.

If we look at Boulanger, Boulangism was a farce that ended in melodrama. If we look at France, we see that the ephemeral vicissitudes of this farce veiled a political drama with lasting consequences.

At the birth of Boulangism, political parties corresponded to classes: the Radicals and the Socialists to the working classes; the Opportunists to the petite bourgeoisie and the peasantry; the conservatives to the upper bourgeoisie, supported in the towns and countryside by a clientele attached either to traditions or individuals. Briefly, the Left represented the popular classes, the Right represented the propertied classes.

Springing from all classes, Boulangism cut vertically across the parties. They were no longer grouped to defend social interests but rather on the basis of their support or opposition to the new movement. Whether right-wing or left-wing, peasant or aristocratic, the authoritarian parties—Prince

Victor's Imperialists, Prince Jerome's plebiscitarians, and the Blanquists —came to Boulanger; the liberal parties—Opportunists and Possiblists— fought him. Other parties, including both those of authoritarian and liberal bent, divided. This was the case of the Radicals and royalists. A minority of Radicals remained loyal to the general, while most leaders among the royalists who were of Orleanist (that is, liberal) origin became Boulangists only because they obeyed the instructions of the Pretender, while the troops, who were conservatives and had authoritarian inclinations, instinctively flocked to the man.

The true Boulangists, that is the authoritarian personalities with both national and social inclinations, were never more than a small minority, even within Boulangism, most of whose members were Bonapartists, Jacobins, Blanquists, and Conservatives. Contemporaries were most struck by the impassioned aspect of Boulangism and by its external signs. If they are to be believed, the people followed Boulanger because they loved him, which was all too obvious. But those who felt this love were inclined to be authoritarian and those who were not did not feel it. Consciously or not, each had a definite political temperament that a disturbance like Boulangism was likely to awaken. The Conservatives in particular, who were men of order, proved authoritarian when France suffered from any material or moral disorder. Boulangism did not transform temperaments, it merely revealed hidden temperaments. The others remained hostile. When it was said, "All France was Boulangist," this was a manner of speaking that explained the intensity of the phenomenon and its contagious power over irresolute natures, but neglected the silent and steadfast opponents. The indifferent proved ardent, and women, more personal and sentimental than men, and consequently more authoritarian even though they considered themselves liberals, were Boulangists. The impassioned phenomenon stemmed from the fact that the authoritarians who were not strictly Boulangists welcomed Boulanger—the French climate became tropical. However, we must not neglect the shadows because of the dazzling light: the congenital hostility of the fundamentally liberal fractions of public opinion and especially of the moderate republicans, the so-called Opportunists, who were firmly based in the provincial middle class.

The appeal to a man is characteristic of certain temperaments under certain conditions, such as those of the Year VIII [1799], 1852 and 1888. Boulangism was one of the manifestations of the authoritarian tradition recurrent in France since the Revolution. In French democracy there is always a latent Boulangism which, as circumstances demand, remains dormant or bursts forth.

. . . In the calm that followed the ordeal, the old parties wondered how they could regain [France's] heart. . . . For reasons of an historical nature, monarchist policy and religious policy had remained linked until now. After the downfall of Boulanger, [Pope] Leo XIII, considering the chances of a restoration diminished, advised Catholics to defend the moral and material interests of the Church within existing institutions. This was the Ralliement which for several years spared Catholics new defeats and accelerated the disintegration of the royalists to the point where it became the chief cause, having been first a consequence of it.

Dragging the right wing along in its rout and hastening its abandonment by the Church, Boulangism left it as compensation a legacy which it did not immediately take up—the cult of revenge.

As a result, while the advanced republicans now mistrusted the idea of revenge as they did everything that Boulanger had incarnated, the conservatives became increasingly susceptible to it, under the influence of the League of Patriots, which, beaten along with Boulangism, gradually ceased to be republican. Finally, whereas on the extreme left the Marxist propaganda of Jules Guesde began to wear down working-class patriotism, the Right hastened to approve the Russian alliance with all the more enthusiasm since the Empire of the Tsars was a reactionary country. These were the elements of a double trend which prepared long in advance the new position of the Dreyfus Affair—the Left abandoning the cult of revenge, the Right adopting it in its turn. The Left had derived it from Jacobin tradition; for the Right it was a child of Boulangism, Maurice Barrès, who furnished it with an intellectual justification as well as a nationalist doctrine.

Of the four great ideas defended by the royalists—the reestablishment of the throne, union with the Church, defense of peace abroad, maintenance of social order—the first three were severely crushed by the Boulangist crisis. Only the last remained intact, unfortunately too often confused with concern for personal interests. The position of the royalist party inspired Melchior de Vogüé to say (rather exaggeratedly), "It is a fashion, and no longer a political force."

Radicalism also emerged from the turmoil weakened. The father of Boulangism but unable to contain it, it recited a funeral oration and burned everything that the accursed son had adored. Boulangism had sacrificed to the cult of revenge; Radicalism forgot it. Boulangism had grown because of *scrutin de liste*;[1] Radicalism abandoned it. Boulangism had built its policy on revision of the constitution; Radicalism abandoned it. And this is one of the most important facts in the history of the regime. The Senate, ancient bastion of conservatism and then of Opportunism, appeared in the course of Boulangism as the defense system of the Republic against a possible aberration of universal suffrage. In their turn, following the Opportunists, the Radicals tacitly accepted the Senate, and consequently the Orleanist constitution. Beginning with the defeat of Boulangism, revision of the constitution, the

---

[1] Balloting by party lists in each Department. [Editors' note.]

elimination of the Senate, its modification or a decrease in its powers, remained in the Radical program merely out of habit. The resistance of the Bourgeois ministry, which for several weeks in 1896 refused to retire despite the opposition of the Senate, was the last manifestation of the Radicals' hostility toward the upper chamber. Taught by experience, almost all the Republicans were henceforth rallied to this parliamentary monarchy without a monarch which was the Republic of 1875.

But principles have their own lives, independent of those who profess or abandon them. The doctrine of political democracy, excluding the existence of the Senate, forsaken by the Opportunists, then by the Radicals, would be taken up by the Socialists, who added its logical complement, the doctrine of social democracy. And the workers, deceived by both the Radicals and Boulangists, turned to the Socialists. . . .

. . . Thanks to Boulangism, the parliamentary Republic decimated and dispersed its adversaries on the right, and wisened its loyal members on the left. It failed to show basic decency by not erecting statues of the "brave general" who, without wanting to, succeeded better than Gambetta or Ferry in perpetuating it.

THE RALLIEMENT IN THE POLITICS
OF THE 1890's

David Shapiro

. . . When the will of a people has been clearly declared, when the form of government has nothing in itself (as Leo XIII has recently declared) contrary to the sole principles by which Christian and civilized nations can live, since only a sincere adherence to the form of government can save the country from the horrors that threaten it, the time has come to . . . put an end to our division, to sacrifice all that conscience and honour allow. . . .

In these apparently innocuous terms the Archbishop of Algiers, Cardinal Lavigerie, addressed the company at a dinner given in honour of the French Mediterranean fleet. The response was icy; for the Cardinal was preaching acceptance of the Third Republic to a service notorious then as later for its lack of republican sentiment. The guest of honour, Vice-Admiral Duperré, an inveterate Bonapartist whose political convictions had only recently

David Shapiro, "The Ralliement in the Politics of the 1890's," *St. Antony's Papers*, no. XIII, *The Right in France, 1890–1919* (London: Chatto & Windus, 1962), pp. 13–19, 48. © David Shapiro. Used by permission of the author and Chatto & Windus Ltd.

caused a stir, had to be prompted to reply: "I drink to his Eminence the Cardinal and to the clergy of Algeria." On official instructions the telegraphed agency report added to his reply a sentence of thanks for the Cardinal's speech. The Ralliement had begun inauspiciously.

The Toast of Algiers of November 12, 1890, was made on the Vatican's initiative. In a survey of those whose attitudes, whether favourable or hostile, determined the outcome of the policy, it seems proper to begin by considering the motives of Leo XIII. Two of them were set forth in Lavigerie's speech, a desire that Catholics should accept the established form of government and should not at the end of the nineteenth century be opposing republican democracy as wrong in itself; secondly the wish to oppose socialism, "to save the world from the social peril," a need that inspired in politics the Ralliement, in social and economic thought the encyclical *Rerum Novarum*. The third motive, which remained unacknowledged, was the Roman Question: Leo XIII still cherished the hope of undoing the work of September 20, 1870. The more immediate objectives of the Vatican were in French internal politics. For twenty years the defence of the Catholic church had been linked with the dying cause of monarchism; for fourteen years, at five successive general elections, the partisans of ideological resistance to any republic had failed to arouse popular enthusiasm for a church gradually stripped of much of its power. Nothing worse could follow from attempting a policy of conciliation.

Yet the Vatican was not a monolithic, utterly consistent maker of policy. There were many forces at work in Rome. The Sacred College was dominated by Italians, some of whom were not unreasonably concerned to reach agreement with Italy, a policy that ran counter in certain respects to that of the Ralliement. Sympathies were confused: for example, Cardinals Capecelatro and Parocchi, concerned with the promotion of biblical studies, were on this issue allies of some of the French Social Catholic supporters of the Ralliement; about the Ralliement the Cardinals as Italians were lukewarm, since they desired accommodation with Italy to draw the Italian clergy out of stagnation. . . .

Equal disarray was to be found among the Catholic supporters of the Ralliement within France. They fell into three groups. First was a new, growing force, the Christian Democrats, turning eagerly to the working class, their most typical representatives being the abbés démocrates; they had inherited some of the Liberal Catholic tradition in politics, though not in economics. Then there were those politicians of the Right more concerned with social conservatism than with ideological monarchism. Thirdly, many devout Catholics both wished to obey the Pope and agreed that political conciliation would benefit the Church more than resistance to an established regime; this group included many adherents of the somewhat aristocratic Social Catholicism of La Tour du Pin and de Mun. This was an uneasy coalition. The conservative politicians were almost without exception liberals in their economic ideas; they looked askance, a laissez-faire economist like Leroy-Beaulieu even with trepidation, at the doctrines of *Rerum Novarum*. The Christian Democrats had considerable sympathy for those intransigent prelates who condemned the excesses of liberal economics; even Georges Goyau, the future academician, in 1892–3 a *normalien* studying in Rome and writing tracts on Social Catholicism, had a grudging admiration for Mgr. de Cabrières, Bishop of Montpellier, one of the most tenacious of the episcopal opponents of the Ralliement, who denounced laissez-faire doctrines. The devout Catholics who supported the Ralliement in pious obedience to the Pope found it difficult to work with the other two forces. Liberal Catholics did not altogether relish the co-operation of *l'Univers* even under the editorship of Eugène Veuillot, the less virulent of the two brothers. The Catholic groups that promoted the Ralliement seemed to offer each a different road to salvation. . . .

The forces working against the success of the Ralliement were at first sight more formidable. French politics had come to be dominated by the struggle of a Republican coalition against the monarchist-clerical threat. On the Republican side this left a strong sentiment of concentration against the traditionalist Right, a sentiment only temporarily and only tacitly allayed in 1887 by the transient threat of external war. Among the Catholics there was bitter resentment of the *lois scolaires*, proclaimed even by the most conciliatory republicans to be untouchable—not surprisingly since Ferry, their author, was among the heralds of the new course in French politics. The Catholics could hope only that existing legislation would be applied more leniently, although its very existence contravened their most cherished principles; the conservative republicans mistrusted the sincerity of inveterate monarchists proclaiming their acceptance of the Republic—de Mun and Mackau had been deeply implicated in the Boulangist adventure—and feared for the safety of the republican *lois scolaires*, about which the ralliés openly proclaimed their reservations.

This atmosphere of suspicion was not the only obstacle to the Ralliement. As so often in French politics the extreme Right and the extreme Left wished to destroy the possibility of a strong Centre coalition.

The extreme Right was formed largely of intransigent monarchists. But another group should not be forgotten, those who may be termed by a not outrageous anachronism "integral" Catholics. The tag that the ralliés were those who were catholics before monarchists, the *refractaires* those who were monarchists before catholics, breaks down at this point. The internal history of the Catholic church has been dominated from the beginning of the nineteenth century by the dialogue between those who wished to accommodate, as far as faith allowed, with the modern world and those who wished to refuse any adaptation. Under the pontificate of Leo XIII, the papal influence was in the main for accommodation. Some of his opponents, sincere Catholics and Catholics before all else, were ready to coalesce temporarily with intransigent monarchists such as Emile Ollivier and Paul de Cassagnac.

The coalition of these two elements supplied the big battalions on the Right, some fifty-odd deputies even after the electoral debacle of 1893, a tenth of the Chamber, thus grossly over-representing their real strength in the country; but in the Third Republic it was the individual deputy who mattered. That monarchism was dying they knew; only a handful dared to proclaim it in their electoral programmes. The rest were partisans of a more authoritarian state, some still sighed for the *juste milieu*. Emile Ollivier, the most respectable of their polemicists, was a republican converted to be a Premier of a Liberal Empire, who had become by ill-success a stubborn opponent of the Third Republic. Their opposition to the Ralliement was nourished by nationalist resentment of a Pope who canvassed support for Bismarck's Septennat and sought relief for Italian prisoners-of-war; it was encouraged by the successful and triumphant refusal of Leo XIII's political advice both by the Belgian Catholics and by the German Centre Party. But above all they were conservatives who wished for no compromise.

On the Left were the Radicals, the Radical-Socialists and the Socialists. The first two groups can be taken together; they represented as no other party the Frenchmen whose hearts were on the Left, but whose wallets. . . . The joke does not do sufficient credit to the honour of their political beliefs. They were convinced, and not without cause, that political freedom would not be secure in France until the influence of the Catholic church had been extirpated. There was justice in their claim that the church had shown itself to be profoundly anti-democratic in France; in 1890 French democratic Catholics could recall the golden dawn of 1848—and no more; incidents at elections in the West of France kept alive memories of past clerical pressure. But the Radicals were also uneasily aware that if the focus of politics shifted, they would have to take a definite stand on what was euphemistically termed "la question sociale." The dilemma was to be exposed during Clemenceau's government of 1906–9, it was put to them with eloquence in Jaurès' famous interpellation of Dupuy in November 1893. How much simpler for the Radicals would it be if the relations of church and state remained the centre of political controversy.

The Socialists might have followed the doctrine that the clerical issue was a bourgeois trap. Although Millerand sketched out such a line, that was intermittently followed by Jaurès, in time they came to adopt much the same attitudes as the Radicals. This for two reasons: anti-clericalism had taken too strong a hold on left-wing politics to be shaken off so quickly; secondly there is all the difference in the world between proclaiming the healthiness of a realignment of politics on social issues, between admitting, as a socialist, the need for a conservative party to encourage the formation of a socially left-wing party, and welcoming the success of a conservative government, such as Méline's, without trying to overthrow it. Yet the best means of defeating Méline seemed to be in the use of anticlericalism to revive the tradition of republican concentration.

The opposition to the new course in French politics came, at least initially, from the two extremes.

The Ralliement, opened with éclat by the Toast of Algiers, petered out with the fall of Méline's government. The hopes of a revival foundered in the Dreyfus affair with the suicide of Henry and the resignation of Cavaignac.

The first phase was from the Toast to the Papal encyclical of February 1892, *Au milieu des sollicitudes*, a time of uncertainty, more or less genuine, about papal intentions. Throughout the winter of 1890–1 the rival parties pleaded their cause at the Vatican, Freppel and Piou arriving within days of each other in February. By the end of 1891, in spite of the Gouthe-Soulard affair, played up by both the extreme Right and the Radicals, more and more Catholics were coming to accept the papal point of view. On February 17, 1892, *Le Petit Journal* published the interview of its editor, Judet, with Leo XIII; the first result was the overthrow of the Freycinet government by the two extremes in the Chamber.

From February 1892 until the general elections of August and September 1893 was a period of preparation and hope on the part of the ralliés. In the autumn of 1892 the dying Lavigerie could rejoice at the rallying of the episcopate to the new policy. The Union pour la France chrétienne had been dissolved in May, and de Mun had accepted Leo XIII's wishes ten days later. But although the monarchists were in disorder, it remained more difficult to organize the ralliés for the 1893 elections. Goyau's letters testify to Leo XIII's serious interest and to his impatience at the lack of progress. In general the monarchists maintained their candidatures in their fiefs, and left no pickings for the ralliés, many of whom were forced to appear as interlopers in their search for Catholic votes. The monarchists were reduced to some fifty, but on any definition the ralliés could muster barely thirty deputies.

The new Chamber reassembled with the ralliés' high hopes punctured. Yet it was in this period of political confusion, that lasted until the formation of the Méline government, that the successes of the two years 1896–8 were prepared. The electoral victory of the Socialists, who had gone out twelve and returned forty-eight, together with the mounting wave of anarchist outrages that culminated in the assassination of the President of the Republic, Sadi Carnot, in June 1894, demonstrated to all conservatives the need for unity. Spuller in a famous debate of March 1894 had called for "a new spirit" in the relations between Republicans and the Catholic Church, an end to mistrust and petty harassing measures. Two issues remained, however, to be cleared away in the relations between church and state: the public inspection of the accounts of the vestries and the taxation levied on the religious orders. The first was settled without great fuss; the second was made the occasion of a display of intransigence—as a royalist journalist, asked by Cardinal Bourret what he hoped to gain by the outcry, explained: "Nothing: we are playing an air beneath the ministers' balcony to please the gallery." By the winter of 1895–6 the agitation had died down, and the attention even of the extreme Right was devoted to the platonic efforts of the Bourgeois government, France's first all-Radical cabinet, to push the Chamber into voting for an income tax.

The formation of the Méline ministry in April 1896 marked the fourth and triumphant phase of the Ralliement, the justification of the whole policy. It was the first cabinet since 1877 to rely on the votes of the Right almost without disguise. The *lois scolaires* were applied with a generous laxity, the laïcizing of public primary education was quietly forgotten. Clemenceau, meeting Piou in the lobbies of the Chamber in 1892, had remarked, "You should have adopted this policy twenty years ago; it is too late now, we have had too much of a head start. But if you have a hope, it is in the Vatican's policy." For two years these hopes seemed justified. Then came the aftermath of the 1898 elections. . . .

It was the parliamentary Right . . . that had made possible the transitory achievements of 1893–1898. The Ralliement offered these deputies a chance to clothe their conservatism in a more modern garb. By doing so the traditional Right prolonged its life. If union with the conservative Republicans had proved impossible, at least for two years a new framework had been imposed on politics in the Chamber. The Ralliement had demonstrated that Republican concentration was no longer the only viable majority.

FRANCE AND THE DREYFUS AFFAIR

Douglas Johnson

The Dreyfus affair begins with the *bordereau*. This is the name which is usually given to the official form which lists the documents included in a file, and which was applied (with doubtful correctness) to a letter discovered in September 1894. This letter was supposed to have been addressed to the military attaché at the German Embassy in Paris, who was named Schwartzkoppen. He was suspected of gaining information on French military matters by all available means, including the use of spies and the purchase of information from Frenchmen. Therefore this letter, the *bordereau*, was particularly

Douglas Johnson, *France and the Dreyfus Affair* (London, 1967), pp. 13–14, 16–17, 28–31, 210, 46–48, 214–217, 219, 221–222. © Blandford Press. Used by permission.

interesting to that part of the French military establishment which was responsible both for the organisation of espionage outside France and for the supervision of foreign espionage within the country. This information or Intelligence service had the cover name of the Statistical Section and had offices in the rue Saint-Dominique. It was quite a small organisation and there were only five officers regularly serving there. It was one of these, Commandant Henry, a large, florid man from the Marne, who brought the *bordereau* to the office. All those who saw the *bordereau* that morning, on 27 September, were agreed that it was a most important find, which seemed to indicate that someone was supplying military secrets to the German attaché.

To be precise, this letter, which had been torn across, was undated and unsigned, written in ink on flimsy, semi-transparent paper and addressed simply "Monsieur." There was no envelope. The writer said that although he was without news, he was nevertheless sending some interesting bits of information. These bits of information were enumerated under five headings. First, a note on the hydraulic brake of the 120 and its behaviour (a reference to the 120 millimetre, 4.62 inch, field gun). Second, a note on the covering troops, modifications being necessary in the new plan (a reference to the troops who would protect the movement of men during a mobilisation). Third, a note on a change in artillery formations. Fourth, a note relative to Madagascar. Fifth, the project of a Firing Manual for Field Artillery (dated 14 March 1894). The last item was difficult to procure, and the writer said that he could only have it at his disposition for a few days. He wondered whether he should send it, or have it copied "in extenso." The letters concluded with the words, "I am just off on manoeuvres."

Within the Statistical Section it seemed that this letter revealed the presence of an audacious spy who was serving in the army, and who had knowledge of developments in the French army which were important and which ought to have been secret. The impression was strengthened by the fact that at the same time as the *bordereau* was discovered, there also came into the hands of the Statistical Section a list of questions which Schwartzkoppen had drawn up, indicating the subjects on which he desired information. Two, at least, of these requests seemed to have been answered, if the *bordereau* was to be believed. An agent therefore was supplying Schwartzkoppen with information in the subjects which interested him. . . .

By Monday, 8 October . . . suspicions . . . had fallen on Captain Dreyfus. Already a number of officers had known about the *bordereau* and about the fear that someone, possibly attached to the General Staff, was thought to be communicating secrets to the Germans. A certain malaise had existed. Those who knew about the matters referred to in the *bordereau* felt themselves suspect, or felt themselves obliged to look with mistrust on their colleagues. There must have been some relief among those who knew, on the Monday, that a particular officer had come under suspicion, and it would be surprising if there were not a noticeable change of atmosphere. The relief must have been all the greater because Captain Dreyfus was not at this time in any of the bureaux, but was attending a course of training in an infantry regiment stationed in Paris. Furthermore, and this is a point of some significance, he had no particular friends within the War Ministry, in spite of the time he had spent there. It seems likely then that officers, who were not normally renowned for their discretion, could have had the best of reasons for letting it be known, here and there, that the author of the *bordereau* might well have been found. . . .

It was from Tuesday, 9 October that [General] Mercier became really active in the affair. He was presented with three different categories of evidence. The reasoning . . . that the author of the *bordereau* could only be one of a small number of probationers. The belief that the *bordereau* was in Dreyfus's handwriting. And the reports, which were probably conveyed verbally to Mercier, that Dreyfus was not a popular officer and that several people were prepared to speak against him. Here must be pointed out one of the most important features of the case. Dreyfus was born in Mulhouse (in 1859) in Alsace, which had been annexed by Germany in 1871. His father (who was no longer alive) had been the owner of a textile factory, and while he had opted for French nationality, the eldest son, Jacques, had not made such an option. Therefore, although Captain Dreyfus had been French since 1872 and had been resident in Paris since 1874, an important part of his fortune existed outside France, and there were members of his family who were not French and who lived outside France. Furthermore, the Dreyfuses were not only Alsatian. They were also Jewish. Could a Jew, and an Alsatian Jew, be considered as wholly French ? . . .

On the morning of Wednesday, 19 December 1894, there was a large crowd outside the prison of the Cherche-Midi. The crowd had started to gather at dawn. But few people saw Dreyfus leave his prison when it was still dark. Those who attended the military Court, and who saw Dreyfus there, did not have long in which to observe him. Those who wrote about his appearance stressed the fact that he looked much older than his thirty-five years, and that his appearance was conspicuously unmilitary. But the prosecution asked that the hearing be in private, and that the court-room be cleared. In spite of the protests of Maître Demange, it was decided that if the case were held in public there would be a danger to public order. The public therefore had to leave, and only two spectators remained, the Prefect of Police, Lépine, and the representative of the War Minister, Commandant Picquart. . . .

The prosecuting council urged the judges simply to look at the document, convinced as he was . . . that the identity of the writings sprang to the eye. And apart from this there was the majority of experts who believed that Dreyfus was the writer. One of the experts who had declared that Dreyfus was not the author was Gobert of the Bank of France, who had behaved strangely. (Might he not have known Dreyfus?) Another of the experts, Bertillon, who had declared that Dreyfus certainly was the writer, brought a long and complicated theory, which was difficult to follow, but which gave the impression that in the eyes of science, Dreyfus had written the *bordereau* while trying to disguise his own handwriting. Secondly, there was the fact that having worked in different departments of the Ministry, Dreyfus was materially in a position to supply information on the subjects mentioned in the *bordereau*. The only subject on which he denied all knowledge at all was that of Madagascar. But it was established that a corporal had spent several days copying out a report on Madagascar in a room to which Dreyfus had had easy access. A number of witnesses testified to Dreyfus's curiosity. Thirdly, there was the intervention of Commandant Henry. Standing in for Sandherr, whom tradition forbade to appear in person, Henry gave assurances of Dreyfus's guilt in a dramatic manner. Pointing to Dreyfus he cried, "The traitor, there he is!" But even more impressive was his clear suggestion that, even in secret session, he could not say all that he knew. "There were," he said, "things within the head of an officer, which even his képi should not know." Coming indirectly from Colonel Sandherr, this was a weighty hint. Finally, on the last day of the trial, General Mercier decided to make Dreyfus's conviction a certainty by handing over [a] secret dossier. . . .

The judges, having heard the case, and having received secret evidence which had not been shown to Dreyfus or to his lawyer, came to the unanimous decision that Dreyfus was guilty. He was sentenced to life imprisonment on the penal settlement of Devil's Island. Dreyfus's defence took his case before an appeal court, but no reason why the decision of the Court should be annulled was given, since the secret communication to the judges remained secret. The sentence then was final. But before the case was closed one last ceremony was to be performed. It was decided that Captain Dreyfus should be publicly degraded.

On 5 January 1895, in the Place Fontenoy, in front of the École de Guerre, Dreyfus was marched on parade before a large assembly of troops and of the public. After the detail of his sentence had been read out, a carefully chosen giant from the Garde Républicaine tore from his uniform all the insignia of rank and unit. With one strong movement his sword was broken in two and thrown on the ground among the debris of the uniform. Dreyfus was then marched round the parade ground in front of the soldiers he had supposedly betrayed. As he marched he shouted in his toneless voice, "I am innocent. I swear by my wife and children that I am innocent. Vive la France!" And as he got near to the public who jeered and shouted at him, he shouted back, "You have not the right to insult someone who is innocent." To the end of the ceremony he maintained his bearing and his determination. Among the spectators there were some who wondered whether such courage and such resilience could not indicate his innocence. But in general, people were deeply moved because they felt that they were witnessing the ending of a man's life, the total humiliation and rejection of a human being. Dreyfus's protestations seemed almost irrelevant.

When everything was over, General Mercier gave orders that the secret dossier was to be dispersed. . . . He asked that all the officers concerned in the affair should give their word that they would not reveal what had happened. And Mercier and his colleagues must have hoped that the *Figaro* was right when it wrote, "and now that it is all finished . . . let us speak as little as possible about this sad affair." The Prime Minister saw the German Ambassador on 2 January and told him, "There is no longer any Dreyfus affair." . . .

The Dreyfus affair is not a single unit, the outcome of a single conspiracy. It is rather a series of logical mistakes, made by a number of people who were both over-credulous and over-suspicious and taking place in a community where such mistakes could not easily be recognised or rectified.

. . . There was no case against Dreyfus. There were only assumptions, rumours, coincidences and misinterpretations. But the belief that he was guilty was persistent and proofs were manufactured so that he would not escape. As the affair progressed and got under way, no one was prepared to admit that the basis of it all was an unscrupulous officer with a smooth pen. And the questions become even more insistent. How did this muddle become "l'affaire," the Great Dreyfus affair? . . .

To understand this it is necessary to understand the conditions within which the Dreyfus affair evolved. To follow the fortunes of Captain Dreyfus is to enter into the complexities of French history.

The defeats of the French army in 1870 and 1871 had come as a surprise to world opinion, but as a great shock to all France. The French had been assured, as is well known, that their army was ready to the last gaiter-button. They had been told that they had a weapon, the *chassepot* rifle, which was superior to anything possessed by the Prussians. They knew that their troops had proved themselves against the fierce fighters of Algeria and they were convinced that these soldiers were superior to any German units. Yet the French defeat had been total. And it could not be explained by the failure of the ordinary soldiers. Time and time again French troops had charged the enemy with unbelievable heroism, so that the legend existed of a Prussian officer calling on his men to present arms before so much courage. The explanation for the disaster lay elsewhere, with the General Staff, with the generals, with the politicians. The old revolutionary situation, whereby there was an enemy without and an enemy within, seemed to exist once again. But who was the enemy within? Perhaps it was the generals who had betrayed. Perhaps it was the officers who had had advancement thanks to the favour of the Emperor and the Empress. . . . Perhaps it was the politicians of Émile

Ollivier's so-called liberal empire (the government of 2 January 1870), or the populations which had risen to reject the Empire and proclaim the Republic (4 September 1870). Perhaps it was the revolutionary section of the French population, which had obliged the government to keep large forces in Lyons during the war, and which rose in the Paris Commune (March 1871). Perhaps there were elements within France which were indifferent to France, which preferred the triumph of their class, their ideology, or their interests, to the triumph and salvation of France. The diversity of France could be a source of strength; it was notoriously a weakness.

Thus the traditional divisions of France, made sharper by the economic progress of the century, were further complicated by the events of 1870 and 1871. Monarchists, aristocrats, Catholics, capitalists, financiers, bourgeois, intellectuals, militarists, Protestants, priests, Jesuits, corrupt politicians, Socialists, internationalists, Jews, anarchists, state schoolmasters: there was someone to point at every group and proclaim that there lay the enemy of France, the cause of French weakness. The Republic, it was said, was continually in danger. It was in danger from a General Boulanger, who might have seized power in 1887; from the activities of statesmen who launched the country on grandiose colonial schemes in Tunisia, Indo-China and tropical Africa, allegedly to satisfy commercial and financial interests; from the failure of the parliamentary system, which gave France a multiplicity of political parties and a confusion of unstable governments; from Jewish financiers who tried to corrupt the public men of France in the great Panama scandal of 1892–3, when they tried to prevent any revelation of the unsatisfactory progress being made on the Panama canal; from the violence of the anarchists who committed sensational crimes, including the assassination of the President of the Republic in June 1894. Abroad, the situation had grown more uncertain with the succession of the Emperor William II in Germany and with the death of Alexander III in Russia. (The appointment of Joseph Chamberlain to the Colonial Office in 1895 was, in French eyes, to add further to these uncertainties). Léon Blum has said that there is great significance in the Dreyfus affair coming immediately after a frustrated revolution, that of Boulanger. This is undoubtedly true, but it is truer to point out that it came at a period of general disillusionment. A former collaborator of Gambetta, the comte de Chaudordy, claimed in 1889 that the last ten years had been the most disastrous of French history, and the Panama scandal which followed his words can only have emphasised their apparent accuracy.

It was natural that in such a situation the position of the French army attracted a great deal of attention. Every newspaper had its military correspondent; there were many newspapers and reviews which specialised in military matters; every action of the War Minister, whoever he was, was watched with acute interest. Everyone wanted to know if the army was efficient, if its officers were capable, if it was loyal to the Republic, if it was becoming the embodiment of certain religious or political opinions, if it represented an independent power within the state. People had to decide whether the army was the enemy or the servant of the Republic, whether it would be the salvation of France or the destroyer of republican and democratic principles. Thus the nation as a whole was conscious of the army, and the army was self-conscious about its rôle within the country. . . .

[There was also] the strength of anti-Semitism in France and the apparent permanence of this force. Not only was it possible to write, as did Herzl in 1897, that all France was anti-Semite, but one has to recognise the long tradition of this anti-Semitism, under the July Monarchy, for example, and in our own time. François Mauriac has pointed out that the victory of the Dreyfusards did not mean that there was one anti-Semite less in France. . . . The explanation for this can only lie in French society and in French history. Anti-Semitism is often associated with social and national insecurity and the two have been constant in modern France. In particular, anti-Semitism has been associated with the bourgeoisie. Sartre speaks of anti-Semitism as a bourgeois phenomenon, and links it to a bourgeois tendency to interpret events in terms of individual initiatives, but it must also be associated with the prolonged uncertainties of the smaller bourgeoisie. The stagnation of the French economy left an important group somewhere between the proletariat and the more successful bourgeoisie. This group felt its economic instability and its social uncertainty as the proletariat seemed to become more powerful and as big business threatened to grow more enterprising. The capture of the political machine by some party which would allow the French consumer free access to the products of other countries would mean the ruin of the small enterprises, whether industrial, commercial or agricultural, on which this group depended. The failure of France to have an "industrial revolution" which would have resolved matters once and for all, the recurrence of social crises, the realisation of French insecurity (whether dating from 1815, 1840, 1870 or from some other date) all suggest an almost permanent insecurity for this group. And out of this insecurity comes anti-Semitism.

The Dreyfus case was able to crystallise this collection of resentments, fears and xenophobia because it dramatically presented the Jew in two of his traditional rôles, that of conspirator and that of traitor. It presented the Jew too as the enemy of the army, which was the symbol of security. . . .

It was clear that the Nationalists, allying insistence on the traditional values of France to popular enthusiasm and patriotism, were able to symbolise this unity in the French army. It has often been said that the aristocracy, which had sulked during the Second Empire, had flocked to join the army during the Third Republic, so that its officers were increasingly Catholic and aristocratic. No one would deny this, but the alliance of Catholicism, anti-parliamentarianism and militarism was also one of the themes of Nationalism. Catholicism was part of the tradition of France, and in those areas of France where Nationalism was not allied to Catholicism (in Paris, for example) then the Nationalists found it convenient to tone down their anti-clericalism in the interests of solidarity. Parliamentarianism increased the division of Frenchmen. The army symbolised France, and since the idea of France could only find expression in some grand enterprise, whether offensive or defensive, then the army was of overwhelming importance. . . .

More important than the . . . army was the fact that to the Nationalist and militarist conception of France was opposed another conception. Since periodically, in 1815, 1830, 1848 and 1870, for example, French history came to a stop, and another organisation had to be found for the country, there were those who saw France not as a reality in itself which had to be provided with a means of expression, but as a state which had to be created according to certain principles. It was believed that the state should be the embodiment of the ideals of justice, of individual rights, of society organised so that progress can take place, of freedom. Once again, the Dreyfus case was so positioned that it illustrated the conflict between these two conceptions. The Dreyfusards claimed that they represented the tradition of 1789, the principle that it is possible to discover what is wrong with a state and possible to remedy that wrong. Looked at in its most simple terms the Dreyfus case was about the rights of the smallest possible minority, the individual. A state ought to accept the duty of looking after each person, and this being so, it did not matter that the honour of the army was being impugned or that the force of the state system was being weakened by admitting an error. The principle of the state's existence could be contradicted if such injustice were committed. . . .

Finally, it must be said that so far as the mass of the French population was concerned, the Dreyfus affair touched upon a nerve which has always been sensitive. As Cavaignac put it, in a note destined for the Vatican, the Revolution and the Republic stood for independence from the various social influences which had governed France in earlier years. Frenchmen, and particularly the French peasantry, conserved a lively sense of this independence, and they were always ready to defend it, even against purely imaginary dangers. It may be that in 1894 the dangers were represented as the danger of the foreigner, the foreign agent, the Jew, the unscrupulous politician. But in time, with persuasion, the enemy was shown to be more traditional, it was the Church and the aristocracy. There was never any enthusiasm for Dreyfus, but France was seen to be Republican. Out of the Dreyfus conflict there emerged a Republican solidarity. . . .

THE NATIONALIST REVIVAL IN FRANCE

Eugen Weber

The Nationalist idea of the superiority and strength of France, an idea to which one could appeal in order to perfect national unity and self-consciousness, an idea which could be exploited for politically significant ends, was already a tradition to be remembered or revived. After 1871, Nationalism in France had been associated with the Left; chauvinism had been the preserve of the uncultured, of the masses. The Jacobin tradition of the Left was not dead. When the twentieth century opened, everyone still remembered its latest eruption in the Commune, and in the efforts and peregrinations of Gambetta.

Gambetta had been considered dangerous for fear that his *revanchard* intransigence would endanger the peace of France. But Gambetta's thought evolved as did his position, and increased power brought with it increased inclination to compromise. His political heirs, first Ferry then Méline, sought for peace without forgetting that much of their moderate Republican support lay in the patriotic and vengeful Eastern departments. Since the danger of war lay on the Rhine, they concentrated their efforts on reconciling colonial and financial expansion with a policy of *détente* towards Germany. This gave their supporters the satisfaction of French successes without the dangers of a German war. Ferry and Méline were moderate men, and a positive policy along such theoretical lines as the Nationalists advanced at the time could not be expected from them. This left the Nationalist and *revanchard* arguments, convenient weapons, in the hands of the opposition. Nationalism remained a Radical preserve for many years: Boulanger, for one, rose first to power, then to notoriety, with Radical support. Many of his followers were Jacobin and *revanchard*, lower- and lower-middle-class men of little or no property. His chief enemy was Jules Ferry. Boulangism is typical of such Nationalist movements as had to rely on a single leader, on the enthusiasms and prejudices of individuals rather than of groups, and on uneasy deals and alliances that might keep them going.

When faced with the opposition of established parties Boulanger collapsed, and his fragile structure collapsed with him. It was not Boulangism that survived, but ideas which had existed before it, and on which it had relied for its success. If Boulangism lived on, it was not through some strange virtue of its teaching, but because it was itself the transient, if convenient, expression of a tendency which took different forms and labels, sought different support, but remained fundamentally constant in character and

Eugen Weber, "Some Comments on the Nature of the Nationalist Revival in France before 1914," *International Review of Social History*, III (1958), 226–228, 230–238. © *International Review of Social History*. Used by permission.

aim. And it is worth noting that it was in the regions most inclined towards that tendency—in the North, in the East, and in Paris—that Boulangism reaped some of its most interesting successes with the General's triumphant elections in the North and in Paris, the electoral victory of young Barrès at Nancy, and the eventual defeat of Jules Ferry in his own Vosges constituency.

This spirit lived on. The Panama scandal of 1892 was the Boulangists' tit-for-tat with their victors of 1889. It has been said that the Dreyfus affair was the last effort of the Boulangist spirit. This attributes too much importance to one manifestation of a tendency that was much longer lived. We learn better if we look to *L'Appel au Soldat*, in which Barrès makes his young hero, Sturel, vow after the General's fall: "We will find some other Boulangism!" Sturel would not have been too old to take an active part in the nationalist activities of 1911–14, and many of Sturel's old companions did. His creator, Maurice Barrès, carried his ideas through the years, giving them first coherence, then a name. The name came when, in 1892, he first used the word "nationalism" in an article concerning the then-current debate between partisans of the classical French tradition, and "romantic" admirers of Tolstoy, Ibsen, and Maeterlinck. The transition from literary nationalism to political nationalism did not take too long.

The Dreyfus Affair offered the doctrine an opportunity both to spread and to affirm itself. It was then, in 1899, that Barrès defined his idea of a nationalist:

He is a man who relates everything to France, who judges everything, even the abstract truth, in terms of French interests. The assertion that a thing is good or true begs the question "In relation to what is this thing good or true?" Otherwise one might as well say nothing.

The Nationalism of Barrès was republican, traditionalistic, respectful of the established order even when he disapproved of it. Out of the Dreyfus Affair, however, inspired by Barrès but differing from him on many points, grew another Nationalism. A rebellious Nationalism, antirepublican, whose assertive traditionalism rejected a whole century of French tradition, revolutionary because Royalist, and chauvinistic by reaction against the foreign elements that it felt were swamping French life and culture. In the mood that prevailed in the prewar years the activities of these Nationalists had their clear share; their preaching heightened the defensive tone of France, and also the aggrievedly offensive tone of Germany. Effect and cause were so clearly interconnected that they are even now inseparable. Paris too must be granted its proper importance, for there the movement was in great measure concentrated. . . .

Here was a numerous public, relatively stagnant, relatively backward, opposed to changes which might threaten the established order and its own precarious social position, yet impatient of the established order which appeared weak, indecisive, inefficient, hardly a trustworthy champion of internal order or national prestige. "Respectable men" revolt against the corruption that would be the country's ruin and that could so easily be attributed to foreigners and foreign ideas. "Little men" revolt too, against the growing oppressiveness of state and money power, and become anti-semitic "because the Jews have all the money." It is all rather complex, hardly ever clear, but clearly good material for Nationalist agitation which offered a ground upon which persons moved by vague and contradictory aims and dissatisfactions could meet with profit. But, though numerous, such people do not contribute much to national opinion. "The best people" do. And the most influential of these were in Paris. . . .

. . . It would be difficult, also, to overestimate the significance and the influence of contemporary literary production—especially at its most accessible, most popular level, that of the novel and the play. . . .

. . . Even if we only mention the plays of Hervieu and Brieux, Emile Fabre and Jules Lavedan and Paul Bourget. Even if we remember only the novels of Barrès and of Ernest Psichari, of Romain Rolland and Paul Bourget, and the solitary but important work of Roger-Martin du Gard, which presents itself as an essential document for the student of the new atmosphere. Written in 1912, published in 1913, the changes of the time are emphasized in it because they appear emphatic to the author. And it was natural that Barois, the idealistic writer-politician formed in the Dreyfus period, should be struck by the change of temper among the young. Open *Jean Barois* anywhere and you will find a running chronicle of contemporary intellectual attitudes: open it at the chapter where Barois grown old inter-views the young representatives of the new Nationalist and Catholic middle class, and you will find the stuff of the times. The emphasis falls heavily on the catchwords of the period: "Discipline, Heroism, Renaissance, National Genius". . . . "New France, the France of the German menace, the France of Agadir." Order must replace anarchy. Positive knowledge must replace vague philosophizing. The reader is told that one of the young men is in *Normale-Sciences*, not *Normale-Lettres* and that the other studies Law and Political Science: more "positive," useful, subjects that the Philosophy which Barois' generation would have chosen. They are stern, firm, and positive, without the weaknesses of dreams, or humor, or self-doubt. Even their regard for tradition and religion, which they see almost as one, is of a positive sort: traditional (that is Catholic) morality must be restored because of its disciplinary virtues.

This last point is borne out by the evidence of Henri Massis who has presented the Catholic revival of the time as part of a trend towards authority, hierarchy and discipline, rather than of a search for ultimate truth. . . .

With Ernest Psichari we come to an ideal type of quite another sort; a patriot of good family, a grandson of Ernest Renan, a nationalist, an admirer of Maurras, a soldier by choice, a Catholic by conversion, the very image of the perfect youth of the Nationalist Revival. His evolution can be traced through his two novels: *L'Appel des Armes*, exalting the order, discipline and patriotic virtues of military service, and *Le Voyage du Centurion*, exalting the superior order, discipline and spiritual virtues of Christian service. In connection with Psichari, we might also notice Paul Acker whose novels are clearly vehicles for the discussion of militarism and anti-militarism, and of the new patriotic attitude that alone can save France from her present decadence.

With Acker, however, we touch the demarcation line between the writers who depict and those who propagand; and the most influential of these latter at this time was without any doubt Paul Bourget with his "campaign of national restoration." Anti-democratic attitudes played an important part in the Nationalist Revival, and so did the need felt by some to preserve or restore the social and moral order threatened or affected by the "prevalent anarchy." The work of Bourget affords an excellent illustration of these themes. The divisions and discords of the Dreyfus affair had inspired him to try his healing pen on the nation's wounds. The inspiration of his social and political concepts comes, like that of Maurras, from Comte, Bonald, Le Play and Taine; and his spokesmanlike characters, like Victor Ferrand in *L'Etape* (1902) are eager to cite their authority. *Un Divorce* (1905), *L'Emigré* (1907), continue to preach the virtues of "Work, Family, Country," social order and traditional values. The point is carried to a vaster public in the plays whose series begins in 1908 (some of them being novels adapted for the stage): *Un Divorce, L'Emigré, La Barricade, Un Cas de Conscience, Le Tribun*. The influence of the plays was the wider for being published also in the theatrical supplement of *L'Illustration* which would carry them automatically to the marble table-tops of many thousands right-thinking families. The influence of the literary figure was enhanced by that of the political columnist, co-author of the *Billet de Junius* in *L'Echo de Paris*. And there are others— Barrès, Bordeaux, Bazin, *revanchard*, patriotic, traditionalistic, *professeurs d'énergie*. Léon Daudet, better in his chronicles than in his novels; Charles Maurras—a poet, an essayist, a pamphleteer, but as a novelist only a novelist *manqué*. But Anatole France, whose *Histoire Contemporaine* so brilliantly reflected an earlier period (as did the *Roman de l'Energie Nationale* of Barrès), gives us nothing or only a few flashes for this later time in *La Révolte des Anges*, and nothing at all to compare with the adventures of M. Bergeret.

And if all these throw relatively little light on the activities of the Nationalist movement itself, they throw a great deal on the Nationalist mood, on the revival of patriotism, of national self-confidence and self-consciousness; on the new insistence on order, discipline, moral values, and the positive virtues; on the fashionable reaction against Free Thought, Socialism, empty values like Justice and Truth, internal divisions (those created by anybody else), and generally the pernicious anarchy that had been born in 1789 and that had triumphed in 1902. Words against words perhaps. But Carl Becker has taught us how to identify the climate of opinion of a time by the words it favors most. By this token, the weight of literary evidence for the years before 1914 confirms the contemporary impression of a national and patriotic revival. . . .

The new nationalism was different from the old; it overflowed the limits of the old parties, and looked beyond the anxieties of internal politics. . . .

Mr. F. Hertz has explained in his study of "Nationalism in History and Politics," that certain contemporary triumphs of extreme nationalism "were facilitated by the attitude of many statesmen and politicians who were not in sympathy with their aims, but either believed that it was too dangerous for their own position and that of their partners to take energetic measures against them, or even considered them as necessary evils." And this illuminates the tolerance, the sympathy, the support which old-style Nationalists received from the new, it indicates the real forces behind the Nationalist revival, and it helps to clarify the confusion between its various components. "The typical nationalist attitude," writes Mr. Hertz, ". . . is to assume that national power and prestige are the best keys to all the treasures of the world, and that a strong State alone can solve the social problems and secure the best possible conditions for the development of national civilizations. . . ." This helps to point out why conservative and nationalist programs cannot really be one: the conservatives aiming at the conservation of states, liberties, privileges, situations; the nationalists aiming rather at the creation of new ones, "with prestige and power as the supreme goals". But it also shows why the superficial observer at a time when moderates and nationalists emphasized the importance of strong government and national prestige, could not see much difference between their respective programs. Why, in fact, patriotic conservative *Poincarisme* should look very much like patriotic extremist *Nationalisme*—to all but a few who, like Poincaré or Maurras, were in a position to know better.

The apparent unity, then, of the Nationalist movement and of the nationalist mood in the years before 1914 is partly due to a confusion of catchwords, a concatenation of common slogans emphasizing patriotism, order, tradition, and discipline, a general tone whose coherence is more apparent than real. If we look closely we may distinguish an alliance of different tendencies, survivals, interests and tactics; and the sometimes-only-tacit collaboration of different men and groups leading to striking results, joining in striking policies, agreeing on striking measures, emphasizing first a latent then an elated patriotism. But the patriot tone which characterizes the period after 1905 was not new; it was, as we have seen, the same old thing carried to an extreme. Neither Barrès nor Bourget waited until the pre-war years to adopt it; Péguy was a rabid patriot even when leading the Dreyfusist bands of the Ecole Normale down the hill of Sainte-Geneviève; Brunetière's ardent nationalism never wavered; when Jules Lemaître joined the *Action française* in 1908 it was no new departure for the ex-pillar of the *Patrie française*. People like these did not need clowns like Jean Richepin to show them the way. The way had already been traced, and the men who followed it in 1914 had themselves laid some of its milestones in 1889 and 1899.

Thus, to many of the people they affected, old Monarchists, steadfast Catholics, unreconciled Boulangists, unrepentant anti-Dreyfusards, the slogans of the new Nationalism had long been familiar. Others had been shifting gradually to an appreciation of their use. Some were moved, as [Henri] Bazire has told us, by the revelation of foreign danger. And some, perhaps among the most politically-significant, merely saw them as handy slogans in a difficult political situation in which internal and external pressures were complicated by the demagogic demands of the current political system.

A movement, then, the nationalist revival? Only in the sense Professor Heberle tells us that we may sometimes use it, of "trend" or "tendency." A public opinion? Certainly as he defines it—"The prevailing publicly-expressed opinion on a matter of public concern, which can claim effective validity in a society." Effective? We can have little doubt of it when we survey the French political scene before 1914. But vague, incoherent, tangible but indefinable—and almost impossible to explain outside the detailed story of events. . . .

SUGGESTIONS FOR FURTHER READING

General: RUDOLPH BINION, *Defeated Leaders: The Political Fate of Caillaux, Jouvenel and Tardieu* (New York, 1960); D. W. BROGAN, *The Development of Modern France (1870–1939)* (London, 1940); JEAN-PAUL CHARNAY, *Société militaire et suffrage politique en France depuis 1789* (Paris, 1964); GUY CHAPMAN, *The Third Republic of France: The First Phase, 1871–1894* (New York, 1963); JACQUES CHASTENET, *La Belle Époque* (Paris, 1958); MICHAEL CURTIS, *Three Against the Third Republic: Sorel, Barrès and Maurras* (Princeton, 1959); ADRIEN DANSETTE, *Histoire des présidents de la République* (Paris, 1956); MAURICE DUVERGER, *Constitutions et documents politiques* (Paris, 1957); EDWARD M. EARLE (ed.), *Modern France: Problems of the Third and Fourth Republics* (Princeton, 1951); FRANÇOIS GOGUEL, *La Politique des partis sous la IIIᵉ République* (2nd ed.; Paris, 1958); MAURICE JALLUT, *Histoire constitutionnelle de la France*, 2 vol. (Paris, 1956–58); R. MANEVY, *La Presse de la IIIᵉ République* (Paris, 1955); PIERRE RENOUVIN, *Histoire des relations internationales*, vol. VI, *Le XIXᵉ siècle, de 1871 à 1914: l'apogée de l'Europe* (Paris, 1955); Special: (political) MALCOLM ANDERSON, "The Right and the Social Question in Parliament, 1905–1919," in *St. Antony's Papers*, no. XIII, *The Right in France, 1890–1919* (London, 1962), 85–134; MARVIN L. BROWN, JR., *The Comte de Chambord, The*

Third Republic's Uncompromising King (Durham, N.C., 1967); Guy Chapman, *The Dreyfus Case: A Reassessment* (London, 1955); G. D. H. Cole, *A History of Socialist Thought*, vol. II, *Socialist Thought, 1850–1890* (New York, 1957); Henri Contamine, *La Revanche, 1871–1914* (Paris, 1957); Harvey Goldberg, *The Life of Jean Jaurès, a Biography of the Great French Socialist and Intellectual* (Madison, Wis., 1962); Nicholas Halasz, *Captain Dreyfus: The Story of a Mass Hysteria* (New York, 1955); Daniel Halévy, *La Fin des notables* (Paris, 1930), and *La République des ducs* (Paris, 1937); James Joll, *The Anarchists* (London, 1964), and *Three Intellectuals in Politics* (London, 1960); Georges Lefranc, *Le Mouvement socialiste sous la Troisième République (1875–1940)* (Paris, 1963); Leo A. Loubère, "Left-wing Radicals, Strikes, and the Military, 1880–1907," *French Historical Studies*, III (1963), 93–105; Jean Maitron, *Histoire du mouvement anarchiste en France, 1880–1914* (Paris, 1951); Aaron Noland, *The Founding of the French Socialist Party, 1893–1905* (Cambridge, Mass., 1956); Samuel M. Osgood, *French Royalism under the Third and Fourth Republics* (The Hague, 1960); Richard H. Powers, *Edgar Quinet, a Study in French Patriotism* (Dallas, 1957); René Rémond, *The Right Wing in France: From 1815 to de Gaulle* (Philadelphia, 1966); David Shapiro, *The Right in France, 1890–1919* (London, 1962); Eugen Weber, *The Nationalist Revival in France, 1905–1914* (Berkeley, 1959); (religious) Emmanuel Beau de Loménie, *L'Eglise et l'Etat, un problème permanent* (Paris, 1957); Adrien Dansette, "The Rejuvenation of French Catholicism: Marc Sagnier's *Sillon*," *Review of Politics*, XV (1953), 34–52; Maurice J. M. Larkin, "The Vatican, French Catholics and the Associations Culturelles," *Journal of Modern History*, XXXVI (1964), 298–317, and "The Church and the French Concordat, 1891–1902," *English Historical Review*, LXXXI (1966), 717–39; Joseph N. Moody, "The Dechristianization of the French Working Class," *Review of Politics*, XX (1958), 46–49; Jean-Rémy Palanque, *Catholiques libéraux et gallicans en France face au concile du Vatican, 1867–70* (Gap, 1962); Alexander Sedgwick, *The Ralliement in French Politics, 1890–1898* (Cambridge, Mass., 1965).

Chapter Fourteen

IMPERIALISM,
TRIPLE ENTENTE,
AND
WORLD WAR I

IN THE DECADES that separated the Treaty of Frankfurt from the Treaty of Versailles, France transformed herself from a defeated and isolated nation possessing small, scattered colonial territories, into a victorious power, united with her allies, triumphant over her old enemy, and possessed of a vast colonial empire. These were the years of the growth of French imperialism, the creation of the Triple Entente with England and Russia, and the ultimate consequence of the two, a World War. The triumph of 1919 marks the high point of the Third Republic, which successfully resisted the onslaught of her foe for four years and avenged her humiliation at the hands of Bismarck.

The diplomatic situation of France in the early years of the Third Republic as well as the initial stages of her imperialist expansion are outlined by Fresnette Pisani-Ferry in the opening selection. She shows how France, humbled in the Franco-Prussian War and kept in diplomatic isolation by Bismarck, turned to imperial adventure under Jules Ferry in the 1880's. In his two terms as foreign minister, Ferry, without consulting the Chambers, acquired Tunisia and secured control over much of Indochina. Though the Chambers denounced Ferry's methods of obtaining appropriations for specific military purposes and then establishing a permanent French presence, they never repudiated his gains. More than anyone else, Ferry was responsible for France's participation in the scramble for colonies, especially in Africa, that was so general among Western European powers in the last quarter of the nineteenth century. As a result of his efforts France continued to expand into Africa and Madagascar, and acquired the world's second largest colonial empire by 1914.

But it should be noted that, with a few exceptions, the territories acquired were not great economic assets—little of France's overseas trade was carried on with them, they were expensive to administer, and never served as outlets for immigration—but they were sources of prestige, compensation for defeat and isolation, and diplomatic bargaining counters. Bismarck had encouraged France to enter the colonial race in hopes that she would take her eyes from the "blue line of the Vosges" as well as come into conflict with her competitors, especially Italy and Britain. His expectations were realized, as the Fashoda crisis with England in 1898, over penetration of the Nile Valley, demonstrated. But by 1904, as the English political scientist Sir Denis Brogan shows in the second selection, the two powers had reached an agreement with each other. By settling their outstanding colonial claims, they formed the basis of an Entente Cordiale that soon became a Triple Entente. (Russia, having seen her Reassurance Treaty with Germany lapse in 1890 following the fall of Bismarck, had sought out a new ally, and by 1894 had concluded a military convention with the French Republic, more out of necessity than liking.) Théophile Delcassé, French foreign minister from 1898 to 1905, was the man most responsible for strengthening the alliance with Russia and forging the entente with England. In this way, the German-dominated Triple Alliance was balanced by the Triple Entente, though the latter was not always free from internal stresses. The author also describes the Moroccan crisis of 1905, the first of a growing number of confrontations that were to heighten international tensions.

It was to be Russian ambitions in the Balkans rather than Morocco or French revanchism that involved France in a general war. Having backed down in the Bosnian Crisis of 1908–09, Russia did not do so again when the assassination of Austrian Archduke Franz Ferdinand in June, 1914, brought on a general European crisis. France, in honoring her commitment to Russia, mobilized against Germany on August 1, and almost immediately faced a powerful offensive through Belgium. Once this invasion was blunted in the Battle of the Marne in September, the war changed from one of movement to one of position and attrition. For four years France fought an enemy on her soil, suffering mounting casualties and straining to sustain a war effort when some of her most productive industrial and agricultural land was held by the Germans. How France formulated her war aims during this time is traced in the third selection, by the eminent French diplomatic historian Pierre Renouvin. By confining himself to France's war aims *vis-à-vis* Germany and by specifically excluding discussion of problems involving German colonies, Austria-Hungary, and the Ottoman Empire, Renouvin is able to present the picture of a country that endured much but that sought only justice in the form of the return of Alsace-Lorraine. Only late in 1916 did she begin to consider wider gains in Germany, but her hopes for these were soon dashed when revolution made Russia's continued participation in the war doubtful. The most extreme demands, he seeks to prove, were usually made by private groups and individuals, not by the French government itself, whereas the Socialists always sought to moderate any excessive government claims.

With American aid, the tide of battle was finally turned after a last German offensive, and the armistice of November 11, 1918, silenced the guns on the Western Front. The staggering cost of the war in men, money, and property is summarized in the final selection, by Jacques Chastenet, historian and member of the French Academy. From the figures he cites, it is easy to see why France desired a harsh peace settlement with Germany, and why in subsequent years France feared the consequences of another such catastrophe.

Deliberately signed in the same Hall of Mirrors at the palace of Versailles where the German Empire had been proclaimed in 1871, the peace treaty of 1919 returned Alsace-Lorraine to France without a plebiscite, demilitarized the Rhineland, placed the Saar under temporary French jurisdiction, required Germany to disarm and pay enormous reparations, and stripped her of her colonies. Georges Clemenceau, who had led France in the dark days of 1917–18 and who presided over the German humiliation, might be satisfied that a cycle of history had turned full circle. But Germany was not destroyed, and the wheel might yet again turn against France. This was to be France's anxiety in the two decades to come.

JULES FERRY AND THE GROWTH
OF FRENCH IMPERIALISM

Fresnette Pisani-Ferry

What was the situation of France when Jules Ferry became premier in 1881, when he returned to power in 1883 in one of the longest ministries of the Third Republic, and when he took over the Ministry of Foreign Affairs from Challemel-Lacour on November 21, 1883?

Europe dominated the world and Europe was dominated by Bismarck. Two successive wars had made Germany the foremost power, her Chancellor the undisputed master, and her people united and vigorous for the first time. China was still a nonentity, and while Russia with her 104 million inhabitants (compared with Germany's 47 million and France's 38 million) may have held a demographic advantage, she had little influence. Italy had just completed her unification, but she had not yet taken her place in the European alliance system. . . . All diplomacy revolved about Bismarck, the "prodigious Chancellor, who [as Ferry put it] was feared to the point of excess." He made foreign chancelleries tremble, and they carefully watched his mood and awaited his reactions.

France was isolated. Her collapse during the Franco-Prussian War of 1870–71 was astonishing, and the speed with which she recovered from the disaster disturbing. England was still her enemy. Germany feared that she would seek revenge, and Bismarck sought to keep her in isolation by all means possible. He preferred that France remain a republic rather than become a monarchy because he believed that the Republic would find less sympathy with other European chancelleries. Knowing that she would not forgive her defeat at Sedan, and that she considered the loss of Alsace-Lorraine an open wound, he feared his defeated enemy. His diplomacy would consist of denying her any alliances and pressing her into adventures outside Europe.

Seeking security against France, he would find it by constructing an extraordinary system of alliances, assurances, and reassurances against her until Berlin was the center of a web that covered all of Europe, while Paris, isolated, had understandings with no one. . . .

Most of Bismarck's agreements were secret, but they were suspected, and the Chancellor was not always adverse to "leaks" that gave his adversary a healthy feeling of insecurity. And in addition to the network of European agreements he had built up, he sought to create dissension and rivalry between France and any possible allies she might find. . . . But he did not want an

Fresnette Pisani-Ferry, *Jules Ferry et le partage du monde* (Paris: Bernard Grasset, 1962), pp. 9–13, 15, 21–24, 26–33, 42–45. Copyright Editions Bernard Grasset, 1962. Used by permission. Editors' translation.

armed conflict. Though he had not hesitated to provoke first one war with Austria, then one against France when he considered it necessary for the establishment of Prussian power, he now had no need for any. . . . He wanted peace. He stated this and we may believe him. But he wanted a Bismarckian peace, a Prussian peace. And as he himself admitted, he had nightmares about coalitions against Germany. In a speech on February 6, 1888, he declared: "Set in the center of Europe, we have at least three fronts open to attack. . . . Surely we are the nation most exposed to the danger of a coalition. God has placed us in a situation where our neighbors keep us from drifting into sloth or inertia."

. . . It is fair to say that after the Treaty of Frankfurt [1871], Bismarck never made a mistake. Until his fall he would maintain the peace, impose German hegemony, and impose his own will as well. With him would fall the astonishing diplomatic structure he had built, and in his retirement he would have the bitter experience of seeing his work destroyed in his own lifetime. . . .

When Jules Ferry arrived at the Ministry of Foreign Affairs he had no diplomatic training or preconceived plans. No alliances were possible, and he knew that Bismarck would seek to thwart a rapprochement with any other power. But there was an area in which Bismarck first displayed no interest, an adventure whose significance that great mind had not grasped— the partition of the world. Ferry had not realized it either, but when it confronted him, he understood. "A conquistador in a frock coat," he led France into colonial expansion and endowed her with a power overseas that Bismarck denied her in Europe. Germany would enter the contest too late, for England and France would have already taken the lion's share. Bismarck would dominate only Europe, and thus Ferry's work would, in the last analysis, prove more durable than that of the Iron Chancellor.

It was as Minister of Foreign Affairs that Jules Ferry began and directed France's colonial policy. This post alone enabled him to do so, since no acquisition of territory could take place without France colliding with the interests of other powers. Beginning in 1880, the struggle for colonies became the most important aspect of the rivalry among the great powers. Conquest was necessary, but so were negotiations, and the colonial adventure was coupled with a diplomatic one. . . .

. . . In France Ferry was neither followed nor understood. He was not popular, and he would become even more unpopular. He had been "hunger Ferry" [during the Franco-Prussian War] and would become the "Tonkinese," the "Prussian," and "Bismarck's lackey." . . . Ferry did not seek to influence public opinion over the head of Parliament, nor did he seek to win over the deputies themselves. This convinced republican, this deputy sprung from several generations of public servants, seems not to have attempted to convince the Chamber of Deputies and the Senate, not even to guide them.

Knowing the hostility the monarchists felt toward him, and having soon clashed over his colonial policy with the Radicals, who did not want to take their eyes from the "blue line of the Vosges," he appears to have knowingly deceived Parliament as to his true intentions. As long as he was in power, he never clearly set forth the real purpose of either his colonial or foreign policies. Each expedition, beginning with that to Tunisia, was carried out in "small installments." From the first, Ferry used the methods that would characterize his colonial ventures: request insufficient government appropriations and disguise the real purpose of an expedition so as to avoid alarming public opinion, send a few troops, begin military operations before informing Parliament, make expenditures before having secured appropriations for them, and commit the "honor of the flag" and the "prestige of France" to a point where the country felt obliged to pursue the adventure of final conquest.

From the start he never admitted the aims of his undertakings, and he never sought to make Parliament his ally. This process began with the Tunisian expedition, an expedition which he had earlier greeted with the exclamation, "You can't seriously be thinking of becoming involved in Tunisia in an election year!" Yet, given the diplomatic opportunities presented since the Congress of Berlin [in 1878], he made his decision but without informing Parliament. On April 4, 1881, General Farre, the Minister of War, announced that as a result of a new incursion by Tunisian Kroumirs into Algerian territory, "the government has taken measures to repress acts such as those which have taken place, and to prevent them in the future." On April 7, the government laid before the Chamber two bills granting the Ministry of the Marine special appropriations for 4 million and 1,695,276 francs. . . . On April 11, interpellations by Janvier de la Motte and Baudry d'Asson were discussed. To these questions demanding to know where the Tunisian affair might lead, Ferry replied ambiguously,

We are going into Tunisia to punish the crimes you are familiar with, and to take measures against their recurrence. . . . The government of the Republic does not seek conquests, it has no need to. . . . In the military repression that is beginning, it will go as far as it must to provide decisive and permanent protection for the security and future of French Africa. . . . The great majority of the Chamber of Deputies and the entire Senate have approved the Tunisian expedition. [At this point there were loud protests from the Right.] They have approved it because they voted the appropriations that we demanded for the purpose.

To this, Cuneo d'Ornano replied in the name of his right-wing colleagues that "in granting their approval, they intended to confine themselves solely and exclusively to approving the military repression of a tribal incursion into our territory, but they never intended to approve an expedition that went beyond this pure and simple repression.". . .

Still, the military operations continued, and on May 12, 1881, the Treaty of Bardo [with Tunis] was signed. Gambetta understood its significance full well when he wrote to Ferry: "My dear friend, I thank you for your letter and congratulate you from the bottom of my heart for this quick and splendid result. No doubt sour men will attack it almost everywhere, but France has regained her position as a great power. I send you my cordial regards."

On May 23, a bill ratifying the treaty was presented to the Chamber of Deputies. Clemenceau, who would be the most outspoken opponent of Ferry's entire colonial policy, opened his attacks with this first expedition. He remarked that the government had marched on Tunis without the approval of the Chambers "so that today we are confronted with a *fait accompli*." Still, the treaty was ratified by a vote of 430 to 1. . . . Clemenceau, the extreme Left, and part of the Right abstained. The Senate ratified the treaty unanimously on May 27. But there Gontaut-Biron also declared that

it would be difficult not to show some surprise if we compare the explanations which accompanied the text of the treaty itself with the circumstances that preceded and led to its conclusion. The treaty is only indirectly related to the repression of the Kroumirs, while it seriously modifies our relations with the Bey of Tunis himself, even though the government had continually assured us that we were not at war with him. . . . We are confronted with an accomplished fact.

The government almost immediately presented a new request for appropriations, this time for 14,226,000 francs, which the Chamber of Deputies granted it by a vote of 429 to 0.

When summer arrived, France was preoccupied with the elections to the new Chamber, while in Tunisia troubles had broken out and the government was forced to send reinforcements. When the Chamber interpellated him [on November 5], Ferry defended himself, but badly.

It has been said that we went to war without the approval of Parliament, and that we governed without controls. But we did not break diplomatic relations with the Bey of Tunis and we did not fight the troops of the Bey of Tunis. . . . It has been said, "The proof that you encroached on the rights of the legislative branch is that you made expenditures that were not authorized by the Chamber and you exceeded the appropriations allotted for the expedition." With a most anxious conscience I have examined this complaint, which would be serious if it were well-founded. I do not believe that it can bear a simple examination of the facts. The last Chamber had approved 17 million francs for the Tunisian war. I think I am sticking to the truth when I state that the appropriations were an advance and not a ceiling. These appropriations cannot be labeled restrictive because the outcome could not have been known at that moment. They could not and would not have been so since in a provision that is an integral part of the law granting the appropria- tion there is a sum of 2,300,000 francs for contingencies. We were not facing a limited expedition or an effort that the Chamber wanted to limit. No, the Chamber, faithful to the policy it followed in this affair, intended to give full authority, a blank check, until the Chambers reconvened.

But this line of argument did not convince the Chamber. Naquet replied cruelly . . . that

what we reproach you for is having lacked confidence in this Chamber which had shown you its complete and absolute confidence. What we reproach you for is having believed that the day when French interests were committed, the day when an accounting would be due on the task to be accomplished and the commensurate results to be obtained, this Chamber would not have granted you all the authority you might have requested. We would have granted it to you, and the French people, whose patriotism is still quite strong, would have approved the Chamber's vote. May I add that if you had acted in the way I suggest, the expedition would not have had the disastrous consequences we can point to, because you would have conducted it in another way. Your behavior in this Tunisian affair was decided by shabby preoccupations with domestic politics, by preoccupations with the elections. . . .

But completely at a loss, the Chamber rejected, one after the other, the most diverse motions from an outright tabling of the question to a demand for an inquiry offered by Clemenceau and one for impeachment presented by Baudry d'Asson. It was Gambetta who, having remained silent until now, proposed a motion that passed by a vote of 355 to 68—Clemenceau being among the "nays." It stated that "the Chamber, determined to carry out in full the treaty signed by the French nation on May 12, 1881, proceeds with the business of the day." As Gambetta would later write in a private letter, "Indignation drove me to the rostrum. I made them approve a policy of national pride." But Jules Ferry for his part alienated a considerable segment of Parliament by this first colonial expedition. Yet he would handle the Tonkinese affair in the same parliamentary way.

When Ferry returned to power for the second time on February 21, 1883, the Indochinese affair had already begun. Following Francis Garnier's reconnaissance expedition into the Red River, a Franco-Annamese treaty had been concluded on March 15, 1874, and under Freycinet's ministry, the Rivière expedition had penetrated Tonkin. On April 24, 1883, Ferry requested appropriations totaling 5,500,000 francs. Challemel-Lacour, the Minister of Foreign Affairs, told the Chamber of the Annamese violation of the 1874 agreement, and said that Annam had to be prevented from recruiting the "Black Flags" [bands of Chinese bandits and mercenaries], and France's protectorate made effective. But China considered that she herself had suzerainty over Annam and intervened. When the parliamentary session opened, the government distributed its version of the Tonkinese situation, in which China was represented as demanding the abrogation of the treaties of 1874 and 1883, as well as the evacuation of French troops.

Granet interpellated the government on October 30, 1883, and immediately launched his attack: "Why have you hidden the truth from the Chamber?" And Clemenceau went further: "Other methods were appropriate and you did not convene the Chambers. . . . Our troops and money have been committed without our approval. . . . We know that the appropriations are exhausted, but we still do not know what funds you have used to pay these expenses."

Ferry denied that he had launched a new adventure:

It is not I who first undertook an enterprise based on national traditions—traditions that are already almost a century old—glorious French military expeditions, two treaties, the exploits and amazing adventure of Francis Garnier, and finally the treaty of 1874, which was approved by the National Assembly. . . . It has been said, "You took Hué although you had promised not to do so without approval by the Chamber. . . ." There may have been good reasons for this, but these reasons evaporated the day that Emperor Tu Duc died, when the disorder and interregnum that followed provided us with an opportunity that would have put our policy to shame had we not seized it. We received a telegram from the General Commissioner that was supported by General Rouet and Admiral Courbet. The telegram stated that Tu Duc was dead and that it was time to act. This operation was absolutely necessary and we authorized it. And now Monsieur Clemenceau says that the Chambers should have been convened before replying to the telegram. In other words, that time should have been allowed to slip by until August when the monsoon makes the Hué River virtually unnavigable. . . . As for China, Gentlemen, there is at present no more a diplomatic break between China and France than there was last July. . . . We are not at war with China, and I scarcely think that we are about to see such a thing happen. . . .

But relations with China were strained. Her ambassador, Marquis Tseng, presented a note to the French government stating that China was occupying . . . the strong points that Ferry had set as the limits of France's advance and considered that any attack on them would be a cause for war.

Faced with a new request for appropriations, the Chamber witnessed a strenuous debate between Ferry and the opposition in December, 1883. Clemenceau noted that the original appropriations had been requested for the dispatch of troops against the Black Flags and irregular troops, but that now France was facing the Chinese government itself. Camille Pelletan demanded that this policy of sending expeditions to remote places "stop immediately." . . . Ferry's reply was marked by violent interruptions, but he did secure a majority of 373 to 139. The military operations were successful, and on May 11, 1884, China agreed to sign the Treaty of Tientsin delimiting the zones of influence. On May 20, 1884, Ferry presented the agreement to the Chamber and requested a special appropriation of 3,431,500 francs, as well as a supplementary credit of 30,483,000. "This was," he said, "a preliminary agreement, one to be completed by later negotiations, but valid in all its clauses, enforceable and presently being enforced." It was indeed being enforced, for on June 23, the column ordered to occupy Langson clashed with Chinese regulars. The French government accused China of poor faith and demanded reparations. China claimed that her text of the agreement was not identical with the French text, and that it was not enforceable. In any case, military operations had resumed when the discussion of the government's request for appropriations opened on August 14, 1884. . . .

Jules Ferry demonstrated the bad faith of China, and secured the appropriation by a vote of 218 to 47. Military operations continued, and by October he was compelled to request extra appropriations in the amounts of 16,147,318 and 43,422,000 francs. This request provoked a debate in the Chamber over Tonkinese affairs that opened on November 24 and lasted four days. The opposition became increasingly vehement and demanded clarification of the government's intentions. "This colonial policy," declared Edouard Lockroy, "has not been debated, either in the government's councils or in the Chambers. We have been led to conquer part of Tonkin by events that have taken place without the consent of the Chambers. . . . I remind you that we have been told twenty times that the adventure was over, and that the reinforcements were large and sufficient." "Does the government want to continue this way by the successive dispatch of small groups of soldiers or rather does it want to ask us for a considerable appropriation and finally send 30 or 40,000 men to deal with China?" inquired Anatole de la Forge. "Do you want to take all of Tonkin?" asked Granet. "Say so, but do not leave the Chamber in doubt about your plans." Once again Ferry recalled that the initiative for the Tonkinese affair did not begin with his government, but with those that had preceded it. He went over the history of Franco-Annamese and Franco-Chinese relations. He recalled the Treaty of Tientsin that French arms had secured the previous summer. He attacked Chinese duplicity and said that in the face of it, "we have adopted a policy of countermeasures in a spirit of moderation which I hope Europe has appreciated. It is this policy that we intend to pursue." The government intended to invade northern Formosa in order to bring China to negotiate.

"We are maintaining our rights. We want to see the Treaty of Tientsin executed. We desire no Chinese territory and have no more designs on China's honor than on her territory." He defended himself against the accusation that he dragged the reluctant Chambers along: "There was neither grand design nor preliminary discussions in the Tonkinese undertaking. And I ask you in what colonial history, in what great nation, do you find these programs thought out in advance. . . . The history of colonial enterprises is, more than any other, subject to the caprice of events.". . .

Military operations intensified and China, with doubts and hesitations, once again agreed to negotiate. She did so through an unusual channel, the Inspector General of Chinese customs, Sir Robert Hard, and his representative in London, Sir Duncan Campbell. But she demanded that the tightest security be placed around the negotiations. Ferry agreed, so that when Granet interpellated him on Tonkinese affairs on March 28, 1885, Ferry could not reveal that peace was imminent. Yet the attack was more violent than ever, and the majority, which had until now supported the cabinet, began to waver. Ferry defended himself with difficulty: "When China is ready to ratify and execute the treaty of May 11, 1884, we, for our part, will be ready to declare, with your consent and votes, that the French Republic has no aim other than the full, complete and faithful execution of the treaty. . . . Give me a solution and not useless criticism."

Things had reached this stage when, on the evening of March 29, a dispatch from Tonkin brought Paris the news of a French defeat at Langson. All things considered, this defeat seems a minor setback, but tempers had risen so high against Ferry that this incident was enough to cause a virtual panic, and a session of the Chamber filled with violence and injustice such as Parliament has rarely seen. The cabinet resigned and there were demonstrations in the streets. A motion for the impeachment of the ministers was defeated by only some 100 votes. The fear and hatred shown by the deputies was cruel and unfair. . . . The French legislature was not yet ready to grasp the importance of colonial conquests and did not realize that the era of the partition of the world had begun. . . .

It is perhaps wrong now to call Jules Ferry a "colonialist," with all the pejorative connotations that the term has to-day. If colonialization means white domination, then he was not a colonialist. His speeches in the Senate on Algeria [in 1891 and 1892] are proof of this. He had gone to North Africa on an inspection trip . . . and when he returned he drafted a report for the Senate . . . :

I dare say that French policy, to its credit, has always repudiated colonialization by extermination and renounced a policy of forced resettlement, so that it has and can have only one aim, assimilation. . . . To be sure, assimilation in the absolute is the work of centuries, but the civilizing mission which consists of uplifting the native, offering him a hand, and civilizing him, is the daily task of a great nation. . . .

Nonetheless, Jules Ferry remains the founder of France's colonial empire, the first man after the disaster of 1870 who dared to lead France on a great adventure which was then beginning for the peoples of Europe—the division of the world. And the impetus he provided continued. Despite the incident at Langson, no French government, not even a Radical one, would ever dare to renounce the territory acquired. Moreover, African expeditions would increase, and the idea of a colonial empire would take firm hold in the mind of the public until it became one of the fundamental bases of [French] political life. . . .

THE ENTENTE CORDIALE AND THE FIRST MOROCCAN CRISIS

D. W. Brogan

[In 1898] it had fallen to Delcassé, to a determined opponent of any fundamental agreement with Germany, to make, as gracefully as he could, the surrender of Fashoda. The Minister who began his career at the Quai d'Orsay under such a humiliating necessity, was to stay there for six years and, almost ignoring his successive colleagues as the necessities of politics changed them, he was to carry out a bold and dangerous reorientation of French policy. To forget Fashoda and come to terms with the triumphant English would take time, and for the moment there were other more urgent things to be done: to make the Dual Alliance stronger and the Triple Alliance weaker.

In the first place, Delcassé was worried, as he wrote to President Loubet, by the possible dissolution of the Austro-Hungarian Empire which might follow on the death of Francis-Joseph and which would, formally at least, make the military arrangements of the Dual Alliance void. It was to remedy this defect that, in the summer of 1899, Delcassé made his secret visit to Russia, secret in that its precise object was unknown. From Russia he brought back a substantial modification of the existing arrangements. The understanding between France and Russia was extended to cover not the mere *status quo*, but the "balance of power"; and the military convention was no longer to lapse on the dissolution of the Triple Alliance. Superficially, Delcassé had succeeded in his design. The policy of Russia, her diversion of interest in the Far East, the absorption of her resources in the building of the Trans-Siberian railway, the Tsar's action in calling the first Hague Peace Conference (whether it revealed economic strain or genuine pacifism) had all made it highly doubtful whether France could get much help, in any independent designs, from her ally. But by adding the "balance of power" to the objects of the Alliance, France was making it likely that, when and if the question of the Austrian Succession became urgent, the Alliance would bind her to follow Russia in her policy, for the balance of power *would* certainly

From pp. 391–403 of *France under the Republic: The Development of Modern France*, Vol. 2 (Torchbook edition) by D. W. Brogan. Copyright © 1966 by Harper & Row, Publishers, Incorporated. Reprinted by permission of the publishers. English edition, *The Development of Modern France (1870–1939)* (London: Hamish Hamilton, 1940), copyright by Hamish Hamilton, Ltd., and used by permission.

be in question if Austria dissolved. It was in vain to boast, as Delcassé did, of "the far-reaching plans" now made possible, unless he could be sure that these plans would be at least half-French. He was to learn, in a few years' time, how little regard for the interests and even for the dignity of her ally Russia could display.

More successful, if looked at from a realistic point of view, was the lessening of the tension between France and Italy. The ending of the tariff war in 1898 was mainly the work of Delcassé's predecessor, but it was Delcassé who reassured a nervous Italian Government that France had no designs on Tripoli. It took time for the economic peace to be followed by political consequences but, by 1902, the time was ripe for written assurances to Italy that her claims in Tripoli would be safeguarded and that Italy would remain neutral should France be attacked by one or more powers. . . .

Delcassé had, in his own mind, cleared the way for a more difficult achievement—a settlement with England.

At the beginning of the twentieth century, the existence of the independent Moroccan Empire, bordering on Algeria by land and only separated from Spain by the Straits of Gibraltar, was an anomaly. A vast area, reputed to be rich, occupying a most important strategic position on the Mediterranean and the Atlantic, was ruled, as far as it was ruled at all, by a curious bureaucracy, the *Makhzen*, which had some points of resemblance with the mandarinate of Annam and, like it, formally obeyed but usually controlled the monarch whose authority and prestige were increased by an alleged descent from the Prophet. The Sultans and the *Makhzen* had been fully conscious, ever since the conquest of Algiers, that their independence and authority were threatened by the infidel. . . .

France was not the only threat, for Spain, clinging to her garrison towns like Ceuta, waged war on the Sultan, and . . . forced concessions from him. Other powers followed suit, and it was in vain that the *Makhzen* tried to maintain a policy of economic and political isolation. . . . A more practicable policy was to assert the authority of the Sultan in the eastern frontier regions where the French colonists of Oran were covetously eyeing the rich lands of the neighbouring tribes. While the *Makhzen* was thus trying to make its authority effective, it was also trying to play off one power against another, especially Britain against France. . . .

From 1900 onwards, Morocco was plagued by wars started by pretenders to the throne, by bankruptcy, by tribal revolt, by rival concession hunters, by all the symptoms of the political and economic maladies which, in Tunis and Egypt, had made possible the imposition of European tutelage. The Moroccans were warlike; they detested the foreigner; they would resent the imposition, even under cover of imperial authority, of foreign rule; but if the European powers could agree, the independence of the Sheriffian empire was over.

M. Delcassé saw, or thought he saw, a way of making sure that the liquidation of that independence would be the task and the opportunity of France. She would step into the breach, restore and extend the authority of the Sultan and, in his name, open Morocco to development. This policy was a natural one; it made possible the rounding-off of France's North African empire, and it was certain that twentieth-century Europe would not indefinitely tolerate anarchy, barbarism, and the denial of opportunity for economic development in a large area at her very door. . . .

In 1903, anarchy in Morocco and incidents on the Algerian frontier made it evident that some method of pacification and modernization of the Moroccan territory had become necessary. . . .

Delcassé . . . had learned the lesson of Fashoda and was prepared to make a deal on a great scale with the main obstacle to French control of Morocco—Britain. Franco-British relations, embittered by Fashoda, had not been improved by the events of the Great Boer War. Within a few months of France's humiliation, British pride was being humbled in its turn by a series of ignominious defeats at the hands of well-armed farmers in tall hats. The press of the world took a cruel pleasure in rubbing it in, and the Paris press was, of course, more competently cruel than that of any other country. The sacred person of Queen Victoria was insulted and the anti-foreign passions bred by the Dreyfus case made matters worse. Nor did the attempt of the Right to use the hero of Fashoda as a stick to beat the Republican traitors with, conduce to good relations. Nothing could have seemed more remote, in 1900, than an "Entente Cordiale" between France and Britain.

There were other aspects of the situation. The Boer War had not merely irritated British pride, it had revealed her isolation, for German public opinion and the press had been as hostile as the French, and the clumsy overtures of Joseph Chamberlain to Berlin had been brutally rebuffed. The coming of Lord Lansdowne to the Foreign Office in succession to Lord Salisbury meant that British policy was now in the hands of a man who believed that the days of "splendid isolation" were over. Britain had had to draw close to the Triple Alliance ten years before; she now had to make friends somewhere. The official visit of the new King, Edward VII, to Paris was a bold stroke which turned out to be completely successful. The new British sovereign knew Paris well, and he was far better qualified to charm the Parisian population than was his nephew, the Tsar. It would be absurd, of course, to attribute too much or, indeed, very much, to the personal influence of the King, but a fondness for France and a dislike of his nephew, William II, made Edward VII a good symbol, if no more, of the willingness of both Governments to forget Fashoda. . . . A visit of President Loubet to London sealed the social side of the Entente. It only remained to complete the business deal. It was not easy. . . . But Britain was willing to pay a pretty high price to escape from the awkward position of having enemies on every side, ready to take advantage of her difficulties; and German rudeness, as well as the open German determination to build a navy big enough to threaten British naval supremacy, made it impossible to believe that much could be done in Berlin. As for France, the withdrawal of Britain from the German orbit was a great general diplomatic gain, and the settlement of all outstanding controversies would make the task of getting control of Morocco easy.

In 1904, the negotiations were completed by the signing of a general agreement. Most of the articles of the Franco-British agreements of 1904 were not important in their actual content. Long and tedious negotiations over the right of French fishermen to use Newfoundland beaches during the season, over the frontiers of Gambia or of Nigeria, over the *condominium* in the New Hebrides, or over the disputes between France and Siam, had little relevance to the main agreements except that they illustrated the willingness of both Governments to remove, as far as possible, *all* causes of dispute, even minor causes. Far more serious were the really important surrenders and exchanges, the abandonment by France of her long opposition to the British occupation of Egypt, her surrender of her powers of delay and wrecking, and the British recognition, in return, of a special French interest in Morocco, an interest which, if it was represented to the public as a bulwark of the *status quo*, was, in the minds of the negotiators and in the secret articles of the agreement, equivalent to the acceptance, in advance, by Britain of whatever action in Morocco should be determined on by France. If the condition of the rickety "empire" of Morocco called for active intervention by France (as it would), British rights were saved by the agreement of France not to fortify the coast opposite Gibraltar; and Spanish claims, by the reservation to Spain of a special zone of influence.

If Delcassé's calculations proved correct, if he had really bought off all opposition, he had made a good bargain, for he had exchanged the barren right of being a nuisance to Britain in Egypt for exclusive rights of political interference in the rich and weak Moroccan state. The rest of Europe would be presented with an agreement which it might not like, but would have to swallow. The Dual Alliance had won the long struggle for the hand of Britain, a conquest not only intrinsically important but making it more certain than ever that Italy's loyalty to the Triple Alliance would be very lukewarm. But at the very moment of triumph, Delcassé's plans were endangered by the threat of war between Japan and Russia, a threat that became a reality two months before the formal signing of the agreement with Britain. . . .

As an ally, Russia had never been satisfactory, always exercising a pressure approaching blackmail on her partner. In the conduct of her quarrel with Japan she displayed no regard for her own or French interests. For not only did the diversion of Russian strength to the Pacific mean that she was not an effective counter-weight to German military predominance in

Europe, but her rival in the Pacific was the ally of Britain. France was now in the ridiculous and dangerous position of close association with the ally of the enemy of *her* ally. When war finally came; when for, reasons that scandalized the French diplomats by their venal frivolity, the rulers of Russia refused all compromise, the situation grew worse. There were a few optimists who trusted in the Russian Army, but as defeat followed defeat, their numbers dwindled. The Paris bankers, whose clients had swallowed so many of the Russian loans in the past ten years, were alarmed at the need for financing the war. The press might be induced, by means involving considerable expense, to keep from the investing public the depressing truth that the Tsar's Government was faced with certain defeat and probably with revolution; but that truth would out. To persuade Russia to make peace while there was yet time was a tempting policy. Russia could not fulfil her part of the bargain while the flower of her army was in Manchuria, and France's financial support of her ally was coming to look like throwing good money after bad. But to advocate peace was to endanger the tepid loyalty of the Tsar to the Alliance. Nicholas was obstinate and was egged on by his cousin, the Kaiser, who had hopes of detaching the Tsar from his republican ally. The Tsar, it was decided, must be left to find out for himself that he could not win.

The same calculations lay behind a very risky policy that Delcassé felt himself bound to follow. The last Russian hope was the use of the Baltic fleet to take command of the sea. That involved a voyage half round the world for a squadron without any bases *en route* and whose port of destination, Vladivostok, could only be reached after defeating or evading the enemy fleet. It would have been a very serious undertaking for an efficient squadron; and the Russian squadron was very far from efficient. Unless French naval officers would help, the Baltic fleet would never reach Japanese waters. But how could help be given without discovery which would infuriate the Japanese and their English allies? . . .

There seemed for a moment to be no way to save both the Alliance and the Entente, for in crossing the North Sea, the nervous (and possibly drunken) Russians fired and sank some British fishing vessels which they took for lurking Japanese torpedo boats. There was panic in Paris. War between Britain and Russia would be the last straw, but Russia climbed down and an international investigation was agreed on. Meanwhile the doomed fleet moved on . . . , everywhere producing a bad impression on the French officers who had been chosen to help it to evade the rigours of neutrality. The Japanese were not deceived by the elaborate comedy and the ingenious French evasions of their obligations as neutrals. There was some ground to fear that the Japanese might attack the fleet as it lay in Indo-Chinese waters, but that danger passed and the Russians sailed on to be annihilated at Tsushima.

The game was now up, and the best that could be hoped for was a speedy peace which would enable the Tsardom to defeat the revolution that was obviously on the way. Although the Peace of Portsmouth came in time to do that, Russia was, as an ally, almost useless. If there was to be a showdown with Germany, France, from a military point of view, would have to depend almost entirely on herself.

The possibilities of the situation were not missed in Berlin. The Franco-British agreement showed up, as baseless, the great illusion of German policy, the belief that Britain would *have* to accept German terms for collaboration, as she could not successfully settle her disputes with France. The war in the East offered two possibilities of action. As the Russian defeats continued, the authority of the Tsardom was increasingly weakened; Russia was entering on a time of troubles and the Kaiser might hope to play on the fears of his cousin, the Tsar. Britain, after all, was the ally of Japan; Germany could make attractive offers of support to Russia, and the Tsar in turn, to save himself, could (it was hoped) force France to choose between the new Entente with Britain and the Alliance with Russia. On the other hand, if it was possible to show France in some conspicuous way that British support would be feeble, the French, in their disillusionment, might abandon the Delcassé policy and leave Britain once more in unsplendid isolation.

Which of these policies would be tried depended on the general situation. The French, by sending the Tallandier mission to Fez to impose "reforms" on the Sultan, and by making a bargain with Spain, obviously intended to dig themselves in in Morocco before any opposition could be organized. Bülow, against the wishes of the Kaiser, determined to strike a dramatic attitude. On March 31st, 1905, the Kaiser and the Chancellor landed at Tangier and in a speech that was heard round the world, William II insisted both on the interest of Germany in Morocco and on the full independence of the Sultan whom the French were obviously trying to reduce to the position of a client prince. It was an Ems telegram over again.

It was Delcassé's obstinate refusal to face the fact that France was running exactly the risk which had been the nightmare of the statesmen of the early years of the Republic, that alarmed his colleagues. However confident he might be that Germany was bluffing, he could not be certain. However plausible might be his formal replies to the German complaints that they had been kept in the dark over the Moroccan settlement, they did not affect the realities of the situation. He *had* stolen a march on Germany; he *had* greatly extended French power in one of the few important areas still open to colonial expansion. The greatest military power on the Continent saw no reason for submitting to such an exclusion. The British Navy and the tiny British Army could not save France—and the French Army under André, like the Navy under Pelletan, was not in the highest state of efficiency, while the state of the public mind was made plain by the political necessity of the reduction of the term of military service from three years to two.

The shrewd financier who had succeeded Combes as Prime Minister was fully aware of all these considerations. Rouvier, unlike the "Little Father," did not allow his Cabinet to disintegrate into a collection of departmental Ministers each doing what was right in his own eyes. The anarchy within the executive, which had arisen from the concentration of all the energies of Combes on the war with the Church and had allowed Delcassé to carry on, without any supervision, his own foreign policy, was now over.

The professional diplomats, who admired Delcassé's energy and firmness of purpose, yet saw clearly enough that he had kept his colleagues and his countrymen, as well as the Germans, too much in the dark. The France of 1905 and 1906 was not prepared to fight an almost hopeless war to exclude Germany from any share in the Moroccan settlement. If Germany was willing to go to the edge of war, France would withdraw. It was possible that Germany was bluffing, but it was certain that France was not in a position even to bluff.

Delcassé in vain tried to blind his colleagues to the realities of the situation by lavish promises of British help, promises that do little credit to his candour or, alternatively, to his judgment. The daring pilot was dropped, and Rouvier had to steer the ship away from the rocks and, after wriggling a little, accept the German demand for an international conference. It was a spectacular triumph for Germany which, at the same time, had managed to induce the panic-struck and isolated Tsar at Bjorkö to sign an alliance treaty with Germany, a treaty that Nicholas II had to renounce, but whose mere existence showed how broken a reed the Russian Alliance was.

As long as Germany had any hopes that the Tsar would keep his word and bring France over to the German side, she was willing to make handsome concessions to France in Morocco. But when the pressure of Russian and French Ministers had forced Nicholas II to withdraw his signature, when American intervention under the energetic direction of Theodore Roosevelt was securing the end of the Japanese War, Germany, if she was to reap any benefit from her activity, must do so in Morocco itself. In this last policy she was only in a minor degree successful. Only Austria gave her any real support at the Algeciras conference. Britain defended the French thesis with great tenacity; the Entente had stood the first strain put on it—and a secret but decisive event, the threat of war, had been followed by staff negotiations between Britain and France; begun by a Conservative Prime Minister they were continued by a Liberal. If any country was isolated it was Germany. . . .

France had been lucky. The Japanese War, followed by the first Russian revolution of 1905, the forcing on the Tsar of a parliament and the struggles between the Duma and the Autocracy, had made France's ally useless in the European balance of power. Germany had, in fact, lost a chance of easy military victory over France, a chance which grew less with every month that passed, for the Tsardom survived. Russia began, very slowly at first, to recover from the war—and, excluded from the Far East, to turn her attention to the Balkans where, of course, she ran across the interests of Austria. The German diplomatic difficulties which had plagued Bismarck plagued his successors. Vienna and St. Petersburg had to be kept, if possible, from irreparable hostility, but if a choice had to be made, it would have to be Vienna. Worse still, the Anglo-Russian agreements of 1907 meant that the old wedge that might be driven between Britain and France, the hostility of France's ally, Russia, to France's friend, Britain, had lost its dividing power. The Entente of 1907 might be a good deal less cordial than the Entente of 1904, but it marked unmistakably the decision of Britain, if she *had* to take sides, to take the anti-German side. From the French point of view, the diplomatic situation was rapidly improving. She had a powerful and, as Algeciras has shown, a dependable friend in Britain, and she had a convalescent and, as the aftermath of Bjorkö had shown, a moderately dependable ally in Russia. Italy, at Algeciras, had not even pretended to support her nominal ally, Germany, and France did not need to worry seriously any longer about the Italian front, even if the soldiers were not as fully aware of this as were the diplomats.

In Franco-Russian relations, the great power of a debtor was now fully revealed. France was committed to Russian financial stability; about a quarter of French foreign investments were in Russia, mainly in Government loans, and the number of French investors with Russian holdings was over a million and a half. In such circumstances, it was difficult to avoid throwing good money after bad. Despite the obvious shakiness of the Autocracy and the opposition of the Socialists—and of others—to the financial bolstering up of the tottering tyranny, Witte was able to finance his 1906 loans and thus defy the Duma. . . .

By 1914, the fifty-two Russian securities listed on the Paris market and totalling over 12,000,000,000 francs held France firmly to her imperial ally. She could make conditions, that loans should be spent on strategic railways for instance, but that was all.

In her relations with Germany, France might have used her financial power much more adroitly. The privilege of admission to the great source of cheap money, the Paris market, was worth a great deal to a rapidly expanding economy working on a rather narrow credit basis. To make Germany pay for financial privileges in return for concessions over Morocco was a plan attributed to M. Caillaux who, in any case, was not very enthusiastic about Russian loans, and Germany was, at times, ready to talk business. But sentiment and the widespread conviction that financing Germany was merely financing a future enemy were too strong. German firms were, of course, in close connection with French industry, especially in the steel industry, but the savings of the French peasant and bourgeois went, not to foster German war preparations, but to the diminution of the complete unpreparedness for war of Russia.

THE WAR AIMS OF THE FRENCH GOVERNMENT, 1914–1918

Pierre Renouvin

... There were three phases [in the formulation of France's war aims]:

Between August, 1914 and July, 1916 the government refrained from defining its "war aims." From July, 1916 to March, 1917, it thought it could take the risk, and in January, 1917, it laid down a wide program which the course of events soon destroyed. Beginning in March, 1917, until the final weeks of the conflict, its ambitions were limited.

The most striking feature of the first period was the contrast between the activity of certain currents of public opinion and the reservations shown by the government. Starting with the battle of the Marne and the last shots of the battle of the Yser, the conviction began to spread among the public that, despite the bargaining power she held because of her occupation of French territory, Germany would be at a disadvantage in a protracted war because she did not have human resources comparable to those of her adversaries and because she also suffered from the blockade. With Germans on French soil, any thought of a negotiated peace settlement had to be dismissed and the fight carried on until victory. Neither the Russian defeats in 1915 nor the darkest hours of the battle of Verdun seemed to shake this conviction. Except for a few leftist militants, those in the political world who had doubts kept quiet. The intellectuals and publicists who thought of themselves as shapers of public opinion did likewise.

What advantages would a victorious peace settlement bring? The primary objective of the war, the one which was supported by the great body of public opinion, from the extreme right to the extreme left—and even the partisans of a compromise settlement often expressed the conviction that it could be achieved by negotiation—was the return of Alsace-Lorraine. ...

Only one controversial question was raised in Socialist circles. The Entente powers had established themselves as defenders of the right of "self-determination." Should they not recognize then that the will of the people of Alsace-Lorraine would have to be expressed through a plebiscite? This argument was first expressed in February, 1915, at London, at the meeting of delegates of the Socialist parties of the various Entente powers. ... It led to some sharp debates in December, 1915, at the National-Socialist Congress, and in October, 1916, at a meeting of the [Socialist] parliamentary group. But it remained an insignificant factor in party thinking and never seemed to find any support among other parties or political groups. ...

Pierre Renouvin, "Les Buts de guerre du gouvernement français, 1914–1918," *Revue historique*, CCXXXV (1966), 2–14, 20–21, 33–35. Copyright by Presses Universitaires de France, 1966. Used by permission. Translation by Robert Pawlowski.

The demands which went beyond this essential war aim were quite remote from it in character. In October, 1915, the General Secretary of the *Comité des Forges* [the iron and steel manufacturers' association], Robert Pinot, introduced the Saar question. He did this first in a memorandum presented to the Senate Commission on Economic Expansion, and then in a December, 1915, report intended for the Bureau of Economic Studies. He advanced only economic self-interest in arguing that in 1913 France had been seriously deficient in coal (by some 20 million tons), and that if she recovered Alsace-Lorraine (with the same boundaries as in 1871), she would gain some important iron resources in Lorraine but very little coal. This would leave French metallurgy in an "excessively critical" situation. He was convinced, too, that the acquisition of the "Saar coal basin" was indispensable.

In a series of articles published in February, March and April, 1915, Maurice Barrès posed the question of the left bank of the Rhine. France must assure herself of a "defense zone against German infiltration" after the victory, he argued. "All German sovereignty" west of the Rhine therefore had to be eliminated. The inhabitants would have a choice between reintegration with France and an independent status with the stipulation of "perpetual neutrality." No doubt, said Barrès, the "affinities" between these people and "Latin civilization" would soon appear once Prussian domination was eliminated. A somewhat modified version of this idea was held by such historians as Ernest Lavisse, Alphonse Aulard, Philippe Sagnac, and Edouard Driault. And these men were certainly not members of right-wing political groups. The idea was supported in parliamentary circles by Antonin Dubost, the president of the Senate. . . .

What were the government's views? Until mid-August, 1914, before the first large-scale battles, the President of the Republic had (according to Barrès) disavowed all ideas of territorial expansion, except, of course, for the recovery of Alsace-Lorraine. Yet he was in favor of "breaking up" the German Empire. Then in 1915 and even more again in 1916, he tended to favor demands for the Saar and designs upon the Rhineland. He talked with certain officials about these questions. It was, however, the opinion of the Premier and Foreign Minister which mattered. Few pieces of information are available to help us understand their views.

On October 13, 1914, Isvolsky, the Russian ambassador to Paris, asked Delcassé, Foreign Minister in the Viviani Cabinet, how he viewed the war aims. Delcassé replied that it was too soon "to count the chickens" and that he had not yet discussed the subject with his colleagues. Nevertheless, he offered his own point of view. France, he maintained, wanted to shatter Prussian military power and destroy the German Empire. She claimed only Alsace-Lorraine. As the conversation proceded, he alluded to the German colonies, and to the rights of Denmark to Schleswig. Delcassé also mentioned

Hanover, whose independence Great Britain "perhaps" desired. But the question of the left bank of the Rhine was not raised.

The French ambassador to Russia, Maurice Paléologue, discussed these questions in a conversation with the Tsar on November 21, 1914. The conversation also touched upon the need to destroy Austria-Hungary, as well as upon Poland and Schleswig-Holstein. The Tsar also brought up the Hanover question. The ambassador indicated that the French would "perhaps" want some territorial acquisitions in the Rhineland in addition to Alsace-Lorraine. But these proposals were made on his own authority. Paléologue merely said that Delcassé "no doubt" would approve of them. Actually, when the Foreign Minister received a report of this conversation, he seems to have taken no further action on it.

On March 3, 1915, the Tsar reminded the ambassador of this conversation. He said that he subscribed in advance to "all that the French government might desire." "Take Mainz, take Coblenz, go further than that if it is necessary." But this declaration was quite obviously meant to make the seizure of the Turkish Straits, which the Russian government demanded, more readily acceptable. This time Delcassé took advantage of the Tsar's good intentions. On March 7 he proposed a meeting at which the French, English, and Russian Foreign Ministers would attempt to establish, through mutual understanding, the "essential bases of a peace treaty." But Sazonov replied that it was impossible for him to leave Russia, and Delcassé answered that he could not travel to Petrograd. Actually, the French government finally did give its assent to Russian claims on the Straits without asking some reciprocal concession.

The French Premier delivered a speech before the Chamber of Deputies when Parliament reconvened on December 22, 1914. In it he affirmed France's determination to fight until victory in order to restore "outraged rights" (an allusion to the violation of Belgian neutrality) and to return to the "French nation the provinces which had been taken from her by force." He also expressed the desire to shatter Prussian militarism. This program, noted Jacques Bainville in his diary, "can lead the Republic very far, but is one that nobody questions." In point of fact, the major preoccupation of the government appeared to be the containment of a current of public opinion favorable to a compromise settlement. General directives were given to the press on February 1 and April 28, 1915, which prohibited the publication of articles dealing with the anticipated settlement unless they were concerned with the assurance of the "triumph of Justice and Right.". . .

The government never alluded to territorial expansion at German expense, save for the return of Alsace-Lorraine, which it did not consider annexation. The government was convinced that this restitution could not be made conditional upon any preliminary conditions, and maintained that the protests of the deputies from Alsace-Lorraine in 1871 and the elections to the

Reichstag of 1874 were sufficient grounds for it to take place without consulting the inhabitants. When, in February, 1915, Marcel Sembat, once the minister who had taken part in the London conference of Belgian, Russian, and French Socialists, approved a resolution promoting "self-determination" for annexed peoples, the Council of Ministers refused to recognize it because it involved resorting to a plebiscite in Alsace-Lorraine. On February 18, the Premier reaffirmed the statement which he had made two months earlier, and added that the return of Alsace-Lorraine to France could not be considered a conquest since the population had shown "its attachment to its French homeland" since 1871.

After the serious Russian defeats and failures suffered in his Balkan policy in October, 1915, Viviani resigned and Aristide Briand became Premier. On November 3, in reply to a question put by the head of the Socialist parliamentary group, Pierre Renaudel, who wished to see the government disavow entirely any idea of annexation or conquest, Briand merely replied that France wished for the restitution of Alsace-Lorraine and a reassurance of Belgian independence. He thus made no mention of the intentions to shatter Prussian military power. Obviously, the new government did not want to discuss the issue further. On December 14 and 15, 1915, it gave the Board of Censorship strict instructions in this regard. The Board was to "prohibit all articles for or against the peace settlement so as to avoid untimely polemics on the question. Even articles which discuss or examine the problem without taking a position should be prohibited. Tolerate no exceptions to this order."

In this way the Premier avoided taking any initiative on the war aims question. On February 7, 1916, however, five days before the initial German offensive against Verdun, Colonel House's second European mission forced him to take a position. He simply told President Wilson's personal envoy that France wanted the restitution of Alsace-Lorraine and "would not consent to a settlement that did not meet this condition." Asked whether France would compensate for this restitution by allowing Germany hegemony over most of Asia Minor, Briand and Jules Cambon, general secretary to the Foreign Minister, replied that it was too soon to envisage a peace program. "Military and popular opinion argue that the situation does not allow such an initiative to be taken." ...

This reticence began to disappear in July, 1916. Although it was still headed by Aristide Briand, the government gradually committed itself to a new outlook. It began to study conditions for a settlement and soon adopted an extensive list of demands. The favorable changes in the military situation buoyed their optimism: the simultaneous offensives by the French, Russian, and Italian armies during the summer; Rumania's entry into the war; the increased effectiveness of the blockade; the crisis of military manpower in Germany revealed by the passage of a law establishing auxiliary patriotic service (December 2, 1916); the hope that the plan for a general offensive which was drafted at the Chantilly Conference would be executed as early as the end of February, 1917; and the success, in November, 1916, of the methods of attack advocated by General Nivelle, which raised hopes for cracking the enemy line—no doubt these developments explain the government's new frame of mind.

Yet these favorable developments were not the only factors which led the government to take steps in this direction. Maurice Paléologue, France's ambassador to Petrograd, was disturbed by the internal crisis in Russia. He was afraid that the Tsar's entourage might be promoting a separate peace settlement and sought to gain some pledge from the sovereign as a protection "against the weaknesses of his character.". . .

Finally, the evidence of public opinion encouraged the government to take an initiative. . . . Late in July, the Comité des Forges, despite the opposition of one of its members, adopted a resolution asking both the annexation of the Saar coal basin and adherence to demands for the Rhineland: "Any extension of our territory or economic domain beyond Alsace-Lorraine and the Saar can only simplify the solution to problems confronting our industry as a result of the return or annexation of these provinces, by making available new outlets, large coal supplies, or facilities for transport on the Rhine."

In September and October, 1916, the Parisian press frequently discussed the question of war aims and the Censorship Board virtually ceased to implement the orders it had received ten months earlier. The annexation of the Saar coal basin was sought by *L'Action Française, L'Echo de Paris, La Croix, L'Information*, and *Le Petit Journal*, while *La Victoire* was content to promote the French economic exploitation of the Saar territory. The Socialist newspapers did not join in this demand. Nor did the Congress of the League of the Rights of Man. The fate of the left bank of the Rhine was raised not only by a group of right-wing journalists which was influenced by Barrès's suggestions, but also by the *Journal des Débats*, which merely called for the "neutralization" of these territories, and by *La Croix*, which suggested their annexation to Belgium. . . . But the League of the Rights of Man refused to recognize "the dismemberment of states or territorial annexations" which might be carried out contrary to the will of their populations. Barrès resumed his campaign, and in October, 1916, addressed an open letter to the Premier. Finally, Charles Maurras suggested that the destruction of German unity would be the only sound basis for French security. Until the autumn of 1916, *L'Action Française* published a total of eleven articles on this subject, arguing that Germany must be "disassociated" and "divided" by reviving particularist sentiments, and by prohibiting federal and economic ties between states. Gabriel Hanotaux, in an article in the *Revue des Deux Mondes*, also encouraged the suppression of federal ties. . . .

During the winter public opinion was generally the same as it had been that autumn. The same newspapers promoted demands for the Saar or raised the issue of French rights to the left bank of the Rhine. In the "Demonstration of Large French Associations" held at the Sorbonne on March 8, 1917, at which the Socialists were not represented, the subjects were familiar. Topics included the refusal of all premature negotiations; the need to "punish" and "subdue" Germany; the desire to assure "the independence of oppressed nationalities," and, above all, the deliverance of Alsace-Lorraine from German domination. The only speaker who alluded to the issue of the left bank of the Rhine was Maurice Barrès. Again he simply argued that the drawing of new boundaries ought to enable "an invasion to be halted at the Rhine." He therefore adopted a formula which no longer involved annexation and which would be compatible with neutralization, provided that military occupation was involved. The new factor in this question of the left bank was the more obvious resistance of the Socialists. In the deliberations of their parliamentary group, Vincent Auriol and Mayéras openly disavowed any demands, but Renaudel, who acted like the party's leader, declared that he was ready to accept the "neutralization of the left bank of the Rhine." . . .

The government's actions must be placed in this context. What information do we have available about them?

The initiative was in the hands of the President of the Republic. On August 12, Raymond Poincaré asked Joffre to make a study of the military conditions for an *armistice*. And the study which the General Headquarters called for eventually produced the terms for a desirable *peace*. These terms were the annexation of the Saar coal basin; the formation of three of four states on the left bank of the Rhine "politically separate" from Germany, but united to France in a customs union; bridge-heads on the right bank of the Rhine opposite Strasbourg and Germersheim; and the redrawing of the political map of Germany so as to diminish Prussia and bring about a balance among the various German states.

On August 19, Poincaré asked the Premier to reply to Léon Bourgeois, who was openly hostile to the annexation of the left bank and would agree only to the "neutralization" of these territories. Briand undertook to convince Bourgeois that there should be at least a "prolonged occupation" in order to assure the payment of reparations.

Finally, on October 7, the Premier and the presidents of the two Chambers met for lunch at the Elysée Palace with Léon Bourgeois and Freycinet. The question of the left bank was the principal topic of conversation. Bourgeois argued for "the formation of a neutral country." Freycinet thought it was too soon to propose a solution, and that it would be enough to get the Allied governments to agree that this question depended on "the decision of France." It seems that Briand sided with Freycinet. He suggested that talks with Russia might be opened after an agreement was reached with England. In short, the Premier was at this time still avoiding the formulation of terms for a peace settlement. . . .

But the question of "war aims" was soon forced upon him after the Central Powers offered to negotiate and President Wilson sent a note to the belligerents on December 20. The Entente powers decided to address a common reply to the American President. Written on January 10, 1917, it was couched in very general, often very ambiguous terms, so that it might appear to constitute a veritable program for a settlement. When he was questioned about this in the Chamber of Deputies by a Socialist spokesman on January 19, Briand refused to debate since it would be "inopportune" inasmuch as he "would risk undermining the effectiveness of a document the sincerity and clarity of which, it may be said, had been acclaimed in all the free countries of the world." He obtained an adjournment *sine die* of the discussion by a vote of 437 to 57. The majority Socialists abstained, however.

At the same time that he refused to open a parliamentary debate on the war aims issue, the government decided to "exchange views" with her two great allies. Should it not be in a position to respond "to any possible proposal for an armistice made by a neutral power, notably the United States?"

The Premier, who was also Foreign Minister, sent instructions to the French ambassador in London on January 12. He included comments on the Polish and Balkan questions and also mentioned the possibility of forming a new organization for international relations. In regard to Franco-German relations, he clearly spelled out his demands. France, he said, wished to recover Alsace-Lorraine which was "our property" and thus not a "new acquisition." She wanted to obtain the Saar coal basin, "possession of which is essential to our industry," and therefore demanded a return to the "boundaries of 1790." As for the left bank of the Rhine, some Frenchmen demanded it, but this claim would be "considered a conquest" and presented "some complex problems." Better to be satisfied with securing a "protective shield . . . which would be as much a safeguard for Europe as for us." What would this safeguard be? "Germany must not have a foothold on the Rhine"; and the German territories on the left bank would be placed under a "temporary occupation" and have a "neutral status." Finally, France would have the authority to assert her "special and superior rights" in making good the settlement of war damages.

These instructions were a genuine act of *government*, having been discussed in the Council of Ministers. . . .

As far as we can tell from the information available, the exchange of views that the French government desired to have with its British counterpart did not take place. It was a few months later that the French ambassador read these instructions to the Secretary of State for Foreign Affairs. . . .

From the end of March, 1917, the question of French war aims was dominated by the consequences of the Russian Revolution. It was no longer possible to rely on the participation of Russian forces in the large-scale Allied offensive planned at the Chantilly Conference. The paralysis of the Russian army became obvious in May; by July Russia's Allies considered her defection probable; and with the seizure of power by the Bolsheviks in November, they considered it certain. By the beginning of March, 1918, a separate peace was an established fact. Germany was thus able to shift the offensive to the French front with an increasingly important number of troops who had seen action against Russia. The general staffs and governments of the Allies were fully aware of this danger, for they had precise estimates of the numerical superiority Germany would possess. To be sure, America's entry into the war, fifteen days after the first Russian Revolution, gave the Entente powers some moral "comfort," as well as an immediate reinforcement of the economic war and in the battle against German submarines. But most important, American intervention gave them the assurance that, as soon as all her resources were committed to the European battlefields, Germany's numerical advantage would not simply be neutralized, but overcome to the advantage of the Entente powers. This was a long-term prospect, however, because the United States had to put an army together first. American military participation began to be effective only in June or July, 1918. Most thought that it would not be decisive until 1919. In the spring of 1917 the urgent question, therefore, was whether Germany could take full advantage of the Russian collapse and gain a victory before the mobilization of American forces was complete. Victor Augagneur, a minister in the old Viviani cabinet, posed the same question on June 2, 1917, to the Chamber of Deputies meeting in Secret Committee. In the event of a Russian collapse "can we hope to carry on the war to victory, and how?" This was the central concern of the inter-Allied military conference of July 25, 1917, and it dominated all deliberations of the Superior War Council through the winter of 1917–18. The only answer appeared to be the conclusion of a separate peace with Austria-Hungary. But this was a vain hope. From that point on it was the outcome of the military conflict itself that was at stake. There was uncertainty about the outcome, so that the question of war aims became secondary. Only the demand for Alsace-Lorraine was still put forward. . . .

On January 11, 1918, in a session of the Chamber of Deputies, Foreign Minister Stephen Pichon affirmed the "common objectives" of France, the United States, and Great Britain. He insisted, of course, on the declarations concerning Alsace-Lorraine, and took pains to interpret them. The French claim, he said, was "superior to any form of plebiscitary deception." He made no allusion to "the boundaries of 1790" (that is, to the Saar), or to the left bank of the Rhine.

In fact, the entire effort of the French government was now directed at only one objective. This was to prevent a plebiscite in Alsace-Lorraine. The government was uneasy in this regard because Lloyd George's promise [to "stand by the French democracy to the death in the demand they make for a reconsideration of the great wrong of 1871"] was quite ambiguous, as commentaries in the British press clearly showed. The *Daily News* observed that the fate of Alsace-Lorraine should be decided "in accordance with the principle of the self-determination of peoples." . . . The weekly *Herald*, which was the organ of the left wing of the Labor Party, declared that the return of Alsace-Lorraine without a plebiscite "did not meet with the approval of the British nation." Finally, in an interview, [Arthur] Henderson, who had been a member of the War Cabinet until August, 1917, interpreted Lloyd George's phrase in this way: "The future of Alsace-Lorraine should be decided in accordance with the will of its inhabitants and of French democracy, and taking into account the attitudes of our French Socialist comrades." . . .

Finally, in another speech, given on January 18, 1918, Lloyd George went one step further. Alsace-Lorraine, he said, was "not a question of territory," but "a question of vital principle." France would not be able to live in peace until this question was settled once and for all. Thus it was the responsibility of the French people to decide.

The French government immediately prepared a report that it intended to submit to the Allies with the aim of establishing a common declaration on war aims. It proposed a formula—"reintegration of Alsace-Lorraine into the French homeland"—that ruled out a plebiscite. Its initiative was to no avail because Lloyd George declared it useless without some more precise qualifications.

Then, on February 15, 1918, speaking before the Senate Commission on Foreign Affairs, Stephen Pichon indicated the "necessity conditions for a lasting peace." He did not fail to restate the terms of his earlier report on Alsace-Lorraine, and added that this "reintegration" would repair what had happened in 1871. At no time, on this occasion as well as on the preceding ones, was any allusion made to the Saar, much less to German territories on the left bank of the Rhine.

In all the documents that I have been able to consult, I have discerned no change in the attitude of the French government over the following months. Beginning only in mid-August, when the prospect of imminent victory appeared—much sooner than had been anticipated—would Clemenceau no doubt think of evading the terms outlined by Wilson in his declarations. Yet, even when the political conditions of the armistice were fixed, he did not attempt to renew the demands that had been adopted in January, 1917, by the Briand ministry. It was only at the peace conference that these claims would be revived. . . .

THE COSTS OF WORLD WAR I

Jacques Chastenet

During the four years, three months, and eight days that the war lasted, 7,948,000 Frenchmen between the ages of 18 and 51, or 20 per cent of the population of France, were mobilized. Of these, 1,315,000, or 16.5 per cent, died—895,000 in battle, 245,000 of wounds, and 175,000 of disease. The heaviest losses were suffered in 1915 during the offensives in Artois and Champagne, as well as in "nibbling" attacks; and then, in decreasing order, during 1914 (in only five months of war), 1916, 1918 (in ten months and eighteen days of warfare), and finally 1917.

A full appreciation of the blow dealt France's population must also take into account the great decline in the number of births—most young men were at the front—and the mortality among the civilian population caused by shortages of all kinds. What seems especially pathetic is that it was the hope of liberating Alsace-Lorraine that constantly sustained the country throughout the war; yet, though France gained some 1,800,000 Alsace-Lorrainers, she had fewer inhabitants in the ninety Departments counted in the census of 1921 than she had in the eighty-seven Departments of 1913—39,210,000 as against 39,790,000, a decline of 580,000 persons.

Frightening in their quantity, these losses were even more appalling in their quality. Twenty-seven per cent of the men between eighteen and twenty-seven, the most vigorous part of the nation, fell in battle. Moreover, in terms of classes, it was the peasantry and the intelligentsia, the solid base and peak of the French social pyramid, who were hardest hit. . . . More than half the public school teachers called to the colors were killed. . . . Ten per cent of France's active population died, compared with 5.1 per cent for Great Britain and 0.2 per cent for the United States.

In addition, 2,800,000 Frenchmen were wounded, half of them at least twice; 500,000 suffered from the effects of illnesses contracted while in the army, and of the 490,000 prisoners of war, many would return from captivity with their health impaired. The number of those pensioned for permanent or temporary disability rose to almost 600,000, of whom 60,000 were amputees—so many men in the prime of life who had their ability to work reduced or even completely destroyed.

Nor was the overseas population free from the blood sacrifice. Before 1914 one of the major arguments of the colonial party had been that in case of war, overseas possessions would furnish the French army with troops whose support would be decisive. While it did not fulfill all these expectations, this aid was still extremely important. At the Battle of the Marne, it was the 19th

Jacques Chastenet, *Histoire de la Troisième République*, vol. IV, *Jours inquiets et jours sanglants* (Paris, 1955), pp. 340–344. © Librairie Hachette, Editeur, 1955. Editors' translation.

Army Corps, composed in part of native Algerians, that assured France of numerical superiority. After 1915, levies that were in principle voluntary (except in Algeria), but which were in fact often compulsory, were conducted on a very large scale, without meeting any grave difficulties. Altogether, the French overseas empire remained remarkably calm throughout the period of hostilities. Even in the darkest days, French prestige there remained intact. In all, 818,000 natives were recruited, of whom 636,000—449,000 soldiers and 187,000 workers—were sent to France. . . . And their losses were severe: some 70,000 died, more than half of them North Africans. . . .

To human losses were added the material destruction. The territory devastated to one degree or another represented about 7 per cent of France's total area, which in 1914 had constituted by far the most industrialized part, accounting for 66 per cent of her textile production, 60 per cent of her coal mining, and 55 per cent of her metal industry. It contained 10 per cent of her total population and 14 per cent of her industrial population.

In this region, 222,132 homes were totally destroyed and 342,197 partially so. The soil churned up included 2,125,087 hectares [4,891,090 acres] of farmland, 426,609 hectares [1,054,201 acres] of pastureland, 596,076 hectares [1,472,904 acres] of woodland and 111,792 hectares [276,248 acres] of building land. The nightmarish sight of scorched earth strewn with the skeletons of trees and blackened ruins stretched as far as the eye could see, where once there had been the thriving activity of one of the richest regions on earth. To cite only one example, the coal industry, we find that the eighteen flooded mines in the Nord and Pas-de-Calais Departments which had produced 18,662,000 tons of coal in 1913, produced only 2,433,000 tons when they resumed operations in 1920. Nor was livestock spared: 835,000 cattle, 377,000 horses and mules, 891,000 sheep, and 332,000 pigs were carted off by the enemy.

How much did these losses amount to in all? This question will long be debated and the most divergent figures proposed. After the war the French Minister of Finance estimated a sum as high as 134 billion gold francs, while the English economist John Maynard Keynes reduced it to 20 billion. All things considered, a figure of some 35 billion gold francs seems most plausible. But this destruction does not fully take into account the total material damage. Also to be considered is the evaporation of French investments in Russia (15 billion gold francs' worth, of which 11 billion had been lent before 1914, and 4 billion during the conflict), Austria-Hungary, the Balkan states, and Turkey. And to this should be added the gold exported and the foreign assets liquidated to help finance the war. In all the net worth of France, which was estimated at some 302 billion francs in 1914, fell to around 227 billion by the end of 1918, a loss of 25 per cent.

After the armistice all Frenchmen believed that Germany could be forced to bear the entire cost of reparations: "The Boche will pay." But, unfortunately, the history of the next few years would gradually show how great an illusion this was. . . .

SUGGESTIONS FOR FURTHER READING

General: GEORGES BONNEFOUS, *Histoire politique de la Troisième République*, vols. I–II (Paris, 1956–57); JACQUES CHASTENET, *Histoire de la Troisième République*, vols. I–IV (Paris, 1952–55); LESLIE DERFLER, *The Third French Republic, 1870–1940* (Princeton, 1966); GUY CHAPMAN, *The Third Republic of France: The First Phase, 1871–1894* (London, 1962); Special: PIERRE RENOUVIN, *Histoire des relations internationales*, vol. VI, *le XIXe siècle, de 1871 à 1914* (Paris, 1955); E. MALCOLM CARROLL, *French Public Opinion and Foreign Affairs, 1870–1914* (New York and London, 1931); STEPHEN H. ROBERTS, *History of French Colonial Policy (1870–1925)*, 2 vol. (London, 1929; reprinted, Hamden, Conn., 1963); HENRI BRUNSCHWIG, *French Colonialism, 1871–1914: Myths and Realities* (New York and London, 1964); AGNES MURPHY, *The Ideology of French Imperialism, 1871–1881* (Washington, D.C., 1948); THOMAS F. POWER, JR., *Jules Ferry and the Renaissance of French Imperialism* (New York, 1944); FREDERICK L. SCHUMAN, *War and Diplomacy in the French Republic* (New York and London, 1931); WILLIAM L. LANGER, *The Franco-Russian Alliance, 1890–1894* (Cambridge, Mass., 1929); BORIS NOLDE, *L'Alliance Franco-Russe* (Paris, 1936); IMA CHRISTINA BARLOW, *The Agadir Crisis* (Chapel Hill, N.C., 1940); PIERRE RENOUVIN, *Les Formes du gouvernement de guerre* (New Haven, Conn., 1925); ARTHUR FONTAINE, *French Industry During the War* (London, 1926); JERE C. KING, *Generals and Politicians* (Berkeley, Calif., 1951), and *Foch Versus Clemenceau* (Cambridge, Mass., 1960); Biographical: GEOFFREY BRUUN, *Clemenceau* (Cambridge, Mass., 1943); J. HAMPDEN JACKSON, *Clemenceau and the Third Republic* (London, 1946); KEITH EUBANK, *Paul Cambon, Master Diplomatist* (Norman, Okla., 1960); CHARLES W. PORTER, *The Career of Théophile Delcassé* (Philadelphia, 1936); JACQUES CHASTENET, *Raymond Poincaré* (Paris, 1948).

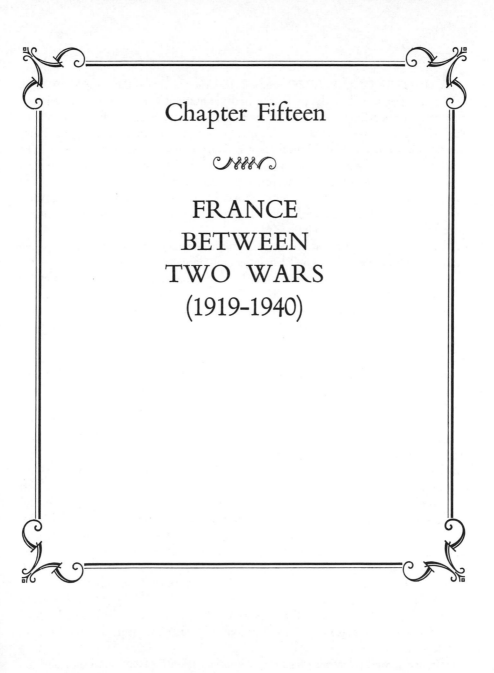

Chapter Fifteen

FRANCE
BETWEEN
TWO WARS
(1919-1940)

THE THIRD REPUBLIC seemed to emerge from the World War in triumph: after four bloody years, she had vanquished and disarmed her enemy, recovered Alsace-Lorraine, added to her colonial empire, and emerged as one of the arbiters of Europe's destiny. Yet little more than twenty years later, France would suffer a decisive and humiliating military defeat at Germany's hands. The reason for this reversal was that France's triumph in 1919 was more apparent than real. Her losses in manpower were staggering, and despite combat deaths and annexations, Germany's population remained far larger and more vigorous. Moreover, German industrial potential, virtually untouched by the fighting, remained superior to her neighbor's.

Once the Allies decided not to dismember Germany or even create a separate state in the Rhineland (as some French generals demanded), France had to face the distant but possible threat of a renewed German danger. For this reason, as the late Arnold Wolfers, longtime Professor of International Relations at Yale, demonstrates in the first selection, France became nervously preoccupied with "security," even in the moment of victory. He shows how difficult it would be for France to keep Germany in an inferior military and diplomatic situation for long without the help of willing allies. But of the allies she secured, Britain and the newly created Eastern states, the one would constantly urge her to make concession so as to conciliate Germany, and the small powers would provide more liabilities than assets.

To maintain her "security," France had the terms of the Versailles Treaty, which her military strength might enforce; the possibility of Allied assistance; and the authority of the fledgling League of Nations. Between 1919 and 1940, all these failed her, not only because her allies and the League proved weak reeds, but also because her domestic political situation oscillated so greatly. In the first years of her watch on the Rhine, from 1919 to 1924, France was energetic and vigilant in upholding the provisions of the peace treaty. Between 1924 and 1933, she gradually shifted to a policy of conciliation under Briand that enabled Germany to re-enter the family of nations and free herself of war reparations payments; in the third and final phase, beginning with Hitler's accession to power in 1933, France retreated into passivity, developing a "Maginot Line" psychology and forever haunted by a repeat of the slaughter of 1914–18. She watched as Germany destroyed the international safeguards of her "security" one by one. The final blow fell in 1940, when a divided and weakened France succumbed to the German blitzkrieg.

In the second selection, the French political scientist René Rémond outlines the reasons for the electoral triumph of the Right in the immediate postwar period. He shows that it was a continuation of the resurgence that had begun before the war, caused by the rise of nationalism in the face of the German peril, and was bolstered by fears raised by the Russian Revolution. It was the Right under Raymond Poincaré, President and then Premier, that sought to maintain a hardline policy toward Germany, as well as to preserve a balanced budget and stable currency, at the price of deflation.

But the "pendulum politics" of the interwar years, the alternation of Right and Left, saw the return to power of the latter in the *Cartel des Gauches* of 1924, following Poincaré's failure to enforce reparations payments in the Ruhr. Its disintegration, the triumph of the right-wing *Union Nationale* of 1928, followed in turn by a new victory for the Left in 1932, meant that internal politics was singularly confused, ministries frequently rotated, and passage of basic social and economic reforms made impossible. The shifting position of the Radicals in particular prevented the development of coherent programs.

Though the Depression that began in 1929 did not strike France hard at first, it had by 1932 created unemployment, falling national production, and increased political uncertainty. The traditional deflationary and protectionist measures failed to work, and the Republic, now more than sixty years old, seemed to show its age. Whereas much of the outside world underwent radical social and economic experiments France remained immobile, with the same aging leaders who reshuffled ministries but never exerted dynamic or imaginative leadership. A crisis of confidence developed that was to sap the regime and begin a process of political disintegration. The rise of the Rightist leagues, basically hostile to the Republic, and their role in the crisis of February 6, 1934, are analyzed in the third selection by the English historian Geoffrey Warner. He stresses the growing vulnerability of the Third Republic to charges of corruption and ineffectiveness, and sketches how the discontent of the Right exploded into mass demonstrations that threatened the life of the regime.

Yet this crisis was to have a beneficial effect: the threat from the Right united the Left—Communists, Socialists, Radicals—into the Popular Front of 1936, and presented France with what was perhaps her last chance to revitalize herself. The foreign menace had increased since the German remilitarization of the Rhineland in March, 1936, when France took no action to challenge this violation of the Versailles Treaty, and Germany had a free hand to move against the weak powers of Central Europe. But internal reform was still possible, and the appearance of the Socialist Léon Blum as premier seemed to open the way for it. But as the fourth selection by Georges Dupeux demonstrates, the hopes aroused for dynamic leadership and meaningful reform were dashed within a year. Blum claimed that he was unwilling to risk a confrontation with a hostile Senate for fear of splitting the Popular Front, provoking civil war, and risking dangers from abroad. Dupeux dismisses all these explanations and concludes that the Socialist premier resigned himself to failure when faced with opposition from management. In any case, by 1938 the Front had disintegrated and the pendulum had swung back to the Right, with little having been accomplished to prepare France for the impending struggle with Germany.

With his western frontier secure, Hitler proceeded to move against Austria, Czechoslovakia (to whose dismemberment France acquiesced in September, 1938), and a year later, Poland, for whom France could do nothing except declare war and wait behind the Maginot Line. France's own turn came in the spring of 1940, when the blitzkrieg overran her defenses and the Third Republic collapsed.

Who was to blame for this "strange defeat"? The Canadian historian John C. Cairns reviews the various charges leveled—conspiracy, fatality, divine will, intellectual incompetence, indifference—and concludes that none of these alone provides a reasonable explanation. He concludes that Frenchmen had decided that it was "impossible" to win. Perhaps the true explanation lies not only in superior German generalship—France was not the only country to fall in 1939–40— but in a lack of will to resist. The Right, pacifist since the rise of strongmen in Germany and Spain and alienated by the victory of the Left in 1936; and the Left— both the Communists, who were discredited by the Hitler-Stalin pact of 1939, and the pacific Socialists—showed little willingness to "die for Danzig," or even for the Third Republic. The prolonged "phony war" of 1939–40 gave the country a false sense of confidence in her ability to protect herself, and the memory of the losses of 1914–18 numbed it once the generals were outmaneuvered. The weaknesses of France in 1940 would more than be expiated by four years of trial and suffering under the German Occupation and the Vichy regime.

$$\mathcal{O}\!\mathcal{MMO}$$

FRANCE'S SEARCH FOR "SECURITY" AFTER 1919

Arnold Wolfers

Ever since the World War "security" [was] the keynote of French foreign policy. At least, this is what her statesmen . . . unanimously and consistently proclaimed. This term, taken by itself, does not throw much light on the particular character of French policy. After all, almost every government in the world professes to be seeking peace, safety, and security. The specific meaning of the term [became] more apparent when the French [spoke] of their desire for "guarantees of security against German aggression." France was obsessed by the fear of a new war with Germany. At Versailles, she was almost exclusively occupied with efforts to obtain protection from the menace of future German aggression. But the settlements reached at the Peace Conference did not allay her fears; she continued ever after to seek new guarantees. This psychological background has to be remembered in order to understand a policy of security such as France came to pursue. It was a policy directed not merely toward the defense and enforcement of the Treaty of Versailles (which was regarded as the minimum requirement for French security), but also toward the erection of still more safeguards against Germany.

At first sight it seems astonishing to find France already hypnotized by the "German menace," at a time when Germany was prostrate, exhausted, and internally disrupted. . . .

But the French were not concerned about the near future; they were convinced that the advantages France had gained, great although they might be at the time, were only temporary and precarious. "The present years are not really the dangerous years; they will come later," said Paul-Boncour in 1924. "Time, in passing," complained Poincaré in 1922, "has already worked against us." . . . Because the dangers that threatened the *status quo* were still remote, there was all the more reason to fear lest countries which were less vitally concerned and more prone to optimism, like Britain, fail to take the threats with proper seriousness and refuse to prepare in time the means with which to meet them.

Overshadowing all other considerations was the knowledge that Germany was potentially far stronger than France. A country of forty million inhabitants was facing one of seventy million. Add to this the French belief that the Germans were a particularly aggressive and military nation, which had been the cause of all previous encounters and which would seek revenge if given an opportunity, and the conclusions are obvious. On the basis of these assumptions, France could feel secure only if two conditions were fulfilled. She and the countries on whose assistance she could rely would have to be made capable of holding Germany permanently in a state of "artificial inferiority." In addition, France would have to possess sufficient military superiority of her own to ward off German invasion until her allies could come to her support. This was a program calling for a reversal of the natural order of power on the Rhine. It was a difficult, and in any event, a precarious undertaking.

It is only fair to add that the French insisted that they were seeking not superiority or hegemony, but merely trying to equalize Germany's natural advantages. But this is only a matter of terminology. What France wanted to equal was not Germany's actual power, but her potential strength. She justified her demand for relatively larger armaments for herself and for military control of German territory by contending that Germany would be able to make up for the difference by a superior "war potential." . . .

A policy such as France set out to pursue was in danger of becoming involved in a vicious circle. If Germany was regarded as so dangerous and potentially so powerful that the free development of her forces would have to be permanently crippled and parts of her territory taken away or put under military control, it was inevitable that her resentment would be aroused and her "aggressiveness" heightened. The British . . . never ceased to emphasize this fact. Was not the danger intensified by the very means which were designed to remove it? But the French believed that they had no alternative, since they could see no other way of eliminating the German menace. This accounts for the demands which they presented at Versailles and afterwards, the object of which was to defeat in advance even the most violent future German revolt.

The French Government did not propose the extreme program that some Frenchmen advocated. This would have consisted in breaking up Germany into small states and putting an end to the existence of an over-powering neighbor. Instead, France demanded that her strategic frontier be on the Rhine. . . . "Total security" for France, and, if the French were right, for the Anglo-Saxon democracies, required that the German territory on the left bank of the Rhine, as well as the Rhine bridges, be placed permanently under French or Allied military control. The Anglo-Saxon countries refused to accept this thesis. Instead, the treaty provided for the permanent de-militarization of the Rhineland and for its temporary military occupation by allied troops. To this, however, were added pacts of guarantee in which the United States and Great Britain promised to assist France in the case of unprovoked German aggression. These pacts and the provisions concerning the Rhineland were together considered by France's allies to be a satisfactory substitute for the establishment of the Rhine as a military frontier. The intention was to remove the danger of a sudden invasion of French soil by the demilitarization provisions and thus to give the Anglo-Saxon allies or guarantors time to come to France's assistance if Germany should neverthe-less try to attack her. The French, not without bitterness and disappointment, bowed to this compromise, rather than lose the friendship and future support of their great allies. What made them feel that they had "lost the peace" was the failure of these treaties to become effective, thereby destroying what France had even then regarded as only a second-best solution to her problem. Not only was the strategic superiority of France now brought far below her expectations, but the most effective promises of assistance for which France could hope had vanished. At the same time Germany's dissatisfaction was by no means removed.

At Versailles, France wavered between two methods by which Germany might be kept in check. Either she could try to rely largely on making herself superior in power and thus become less dependent on outside help, or she could put her faith primarily in the military assistance which she could obtain from others. At no stage of the negotiations, however, was the French Government ready to drop the demand for what she came to call "Allied solidarity." Even the strategic frontier on the Rhine was, Marshal Foch argued, to be a part of "the defensive organization of the Coalition." A coalition comprising all of the Great Powers with the exception of the two Central European Empires had been necessary to defeat Germany. The "inter-Allied nature of the victory," as Tardieu put it, was not forgotten by France. It convinced the French that Germany could be held in check only with the help of allies. . . .

In some form or other the grand coalition of the World War would have to be carried over into peace-time.

This accounts for the intense dismay of the French when, even before the adjournment of the Versailles Conference, they found themselves deserted by almost all of their great allies. Some of them were never to be recovered. Russia was struggling in the throes of the Bolshevist Revolution, and was for a long time considered as an enemy rather than as a friend. . . . Next, the United States turned her back on Europe and refused even to ratify the Versailles Treaty. Not only did the pact of guarantee which Wilson had negotiated with Clemenceau fail to materialize, but the pledges of assistance contained in the League Covenant did not become binding on the United States. . . . Britain was the only Great Power from which any semblance of "allied solidarity" could be expected.

Relations with Britain therefore became one of France's major preoccupations. But even there she had to cope not merely with resistance in minor matters, but with a complete lack of agreement on what was for France the crux of the whole matter, namely, the necessity of enforcing the treaties upon Germany and of supplementing the guarantees of security which they contained.

While it may not be hard to understand why French demands for security against a German attack from across the Rhine should have been so extensive, there is another and more perplexing aspect of her policy. . . . France, despite her fear, did not limit herself to preparation for the protection of her own soil, but left no doubt that she was determined to enforce the Peace Treaties in their entirety and to defend not merely as the "guardian of the Rhine"; her army was also to be the "guarantee of the political stability of Europe," the defender not only of her own frontiers, "but . . . of all frontiers, . . . of all peoples." It would seem that this was greatly multiplying the dangers by which she was threatened. Was she not entangling herself unnecessarily in Germany's quarrels in remote regions and drawing the wrath of the revisionist powers upon herself? If by nature she was as much weaker than Germany as she claimed, could she afford to take on responsibilities of a continental scale? There seems at first sight to be such incongruity in this attitude that some people have doubted the sincerity of French fears and have believed that her clamor for more security was but a façade hiding a desire to enjoy supremacy or hegemony on the Continent. More flattering to France, and more in line with many declarations by her statesmen, would be the supposition that, apart from considerations of her own security, she was genuinely and generously concerned in the fate of the new Slavic states in Central Europe which she, as a defender of the small powers, sought to protect from German aggression.

While we cannot hope to penetrate into the real and decisive motives behind French policy—and they probably varied from period to period and from statesman to statesman—it seems most likely that France was again involved in the same vicious circle. She had two obvious reasons for pledging assistance to countries like Poland or Czechoslovakia. She feared, for one thing, that Germany, if she were able to expand in the East, would become so powerful that she could turn around and attack France successfully. Also, she wished to assure herself of the assistance of those countries, whose military strength was by no means negligible as long as Germany was held to the provisions of the Versailles Treaty in regard to armaments. They were substitutes for France's pre-war ally, Czarist Russia.

But, while France was acquiring the support from them which she had not been able to obtain from the Great Powers, she was at the same time incurring grave new risks. The defenses in the East might prove to be not only inadequate but a source of German exasperation and a major cause of conflict. French entanglement, in that case, might be the surest means of bringing about the new war on the Rhine against which she was seeking to protect herself. Not until the French policy had met with serious setbacks did some Frenchmen, after 1936, come to express the opinion that the far-flung commitments were a mistake and that France should seek security by entrenching herself behind the Maginot Line.

By making the sanctity of treaties and the strict enforcement of the *status quo* the fundamental principle of her foreign policy, France became involved in the same contradictions which had afflicted her commitments in the East. She believed it necessary for her security not to allow any provisions of the Peace Treaties to be violated with impunity or changed in favor of Germany. A precedent . . . might otherwise be created. "Once the first piece of the structure falls," exclaimed Herriot, "the entire edifice will fall of itself." But in order to prevent any precedent from serving as a wedge by which Germany might start a general assault on the order of Versailles, France made herself the target for all revisionist attacks. If she was to adhere to her purpose consistently, she had to oppose changes of the post-war settlements, even though they might conceivably have satisfied the Germans and thus have removed the dangers which she was trying to avert.

The specific connotation of the term "security" as it was used by the French to explain their objective now becomes clearer. It referred to a state of things in which not only was the danger of a German invasion of French soil to be eliminated—security in the narrow sense of the word— but in which the entire new *status quo* as established in the Peace Treaties would be firmly protected by the superiority of the powers which were ready to defend it. "Security" came to play such an important role in post-war diplomacy that it is worth keeping this original French meaning in mind. Committees on "security" were established; pacts of "security" were negotiated; the relation of disarmament to "security" was debated at length. Later, interest came to center on "collective security." But even then something of the original

French connotation was attached to the term. It was still an attempt to lay the specter of a German revisionist "explosion" against the established order by assigning superior force to the defenders of the "law."

If it seems unworthy of a Great Power to be motivated so exclusively by fear, and to think of itself as "the only great people in the world whose life is threatened," it should be remembered that, while France may initially have acted only from fear of another German invasion, her policy of security had led her to become the champion of the *status quo* and of the entire order of Central as well as of Western Europe. Her anxiety was, therefore, that of a nation with responsibilities and ambitions truly continental in character and extent.

THE RESURGENCE OF THE RIGHT
AFTER WORLD WAR I

René Rémond

The War of 1870–1871, brief as it was, brought important and lasting changes to the equilibrium of political forces. The First World War, on the other hand, despite its length and its extent, affected only the surface of the French political situation. The years 1914–1918 do not mark a dividing line between two epochs. Once the tragic parenthesis of four years of war was closed, the postwar period smoothly resumed the prewar development. The only visible change was that which inevitably resulted from the natural aging of generations and the turnover, scarcely more rapid, of the political personnel and the electorate. Far from shaking institutions, the war confirmed their stability. Reinforced by forty years of routine, the regime was crowned with the prestige of a victory. The Republic had the right to claim credit for this victory in the exact measure as its enemies would have charged it with the responsibility for a defeat. For the moment at least, its critics abandoned trying to overthrow it, and the republican system was not at issue.

However, the general election of November 1919, the first after the armistice, marked the most important shift of opinion during the Third Republic, since it showed a complete reversal of the majority compared to the results of May 1914. The minority of yesterday became today's majority. The Right Wing, defeated once again in Spring 1914, came back in force and its numerical superiority was such that one must go back to the National

René Rémond, *The Right Wing in France from 1815 to de Gaulle* (Philadelphia: University of Pennsylvania Press, 1966), pp. 254–262. © 1966 by the Trustees of the University of Pennsylvania. Used by permission.

Assembly of 1871 to find its equal. . . . It seemed as if wars, whether they were disastrous or victorious, inevitably brought a reinforcement of the forces of order and conservation. The National Assembly of 1871 had numbered 400 to 500 Rightist Deputies out of some 750 representatives; the *Bloc National* won 437 out of 613 seats. Fortune had changed sides. The Right finally won the revenge it had so stubbornly coveted, and while between 1876 and 1919 it was almost constantly reduced to the pitiable state of permanent opposition, between 1919 and 1939 it controlled the government for fourteen years out of twenty. It was a radical change, to go from 150 representatives in the outgoing Chamber to 437 Deputies in the Blue Horizon Chamber.[1]

If inspected more closely, however, the change was clearly less profound than parliamentary arithmetic would suggest. . . . Far from contradicting the prewar evolution, the autumn elections of 1919 resumed the tendency which slowly moved the center of gravity of the political system toward the Right. Forget for a moment the results of 1914 and turn back a year earlier: the Progressists, temporary representatives of an older Rightist tradition, won three presidencies. The election of Raymond Poincaré as President of the Republic in January 1913 against the Leftist candidate Pams was greeted by the public as a victory for the Right. The same political majority carried Paul Deschanel to the Presidency of the Chamber and Louis Barthou to the premiership. The success of these men, all favorable to the three-year military service law, showed the strength of Rightist revival. But, and nothing demonstrates the continuity better, the same Deschanel, whose election in 1913 to succeed the Radical Henri Brisson had marked a victory of the Right-Center, was re-elected to the presidential chair of the new (1919) Chamber with 473 votes. A few days later the parliament chose him over Clemenceau to succeed Poincaré at the Elysée. Finally, an even more significant development: the outgoing President of the Republic, Poincaré, soon returned to office as head of the government, upheld by a Rightist majority to follow a Rightist policy.

Problems and slogans as well as personalities converged to weave a continuous thread between the prewar and postwar periods. However strange it may seem on the morrow of such an upheaval, political preoccupations and respective positions had hardly changed. . . . Right and Left continued to oppose each other on the same issues: military and financial. In 1914 the Right had conducted a campaign for three-year military service and against the income tax. After 1919 it fought for military security and a balanced budget. These two articles of its program corresponded point by point to two successive aspects of Poincaré's policy—the occupation of the Ruhr in 1923 and the defense of the franc in 1926.

---

[1] The Chamber elected in 1919 won this sobriquet because of the many blue-uniformed war veterans who sat in it.

The stability of personnel, permanence of problems, and identity of issues are all reasons which forbid us from opening a new chapter in the history of the Right with the elections of November 1919. But ten or fifteen years later these reasons are no longer so strong. Changes had occurred, subtle at first and scarcely noticeable to contemporaries, but soon they became so manifest that they were obvious to the least acute observer. . . . Where was the point at which the normal course of development was altered? February 1934 is too late; February 6 was already a consequence of the shift that we are seeking to date. Earlier, 1924 or 1926 still scarcely boded its approach. It was between these two points that the passage from one period to the following took place. We shall . . . set it in the year 1929. With the retirement of Poincaré in 1929 came the eclipse of one generation by another and a change in personnel; 1929 also was the beginning of the great economic depression which swept the world, even if France was not to feel its first blows for another two or three years. . . .

In 1919 as in 1873 it was a coalition . . . which opened the road to power for the Right Wing. Union was the necessary condition for their victory. It seems to have made short work of the old discords which had divided and weakened the Right Wing for so long. Renounced in the patriotic fervor of the Sacred Union, the old rancors melted before the rays of the victory whose prestige the *Bloc* expected to monopolize. The Right was even quite willing to cross out the fatal conflicts which in the past had opposed it to the Left. Only those shades of opinion incompatible with legitimate requirements of patriotism were excluded from a coalition which extended farther to the Left than at any other time. . . .

From this came that very revealing name of *Bloc National* in which the adjective had even more weight than the noun. It will be objected that this attitude was not new. Had not the Right for over twenty years gloried in its patriotism and opposed its nationalism to the internationalism of the Left? But in 1919 nationalism sacrificed its suffix, it soberly called itself national. From nationalist to national may seem a negligible nuance but it was of capital importance. At best nationalism was only one of several ways of understanding and serving the national interest; but when it was national, the *Bloc* was the nation. Everyone who was not with it was against the nation. The S.F.I.O. [French Socialist Party], for example, excluded from the *Bloc, ipso facto* found itself cut off from the national community. Henceforth the Right was to monopolize the word, the idea, and if possible, the reality behind them. . . .

The Right saw in the Left not only political adversaries, but bad citizens; the trench which ran between Right and Left no longer separated two blocs competing for power, it distinguished bad Frenchmen from good patriots. This conviction introduced into political struggles an additional measure of harshness and seriousness, for it involved national integrity.

Heir of prewar nationalism . . . , guardian of the "war veteran" spirit
. . . , the Right exalted patriotic sentiments and celebrated the national
glories. The *Bloc* made the feast day of Joan of Arc into a legal holiday and
authorized the movement to turn the memory of the Maid into an official
cult. At the canonization ceremony of this saint of the fatherland (May 16,
1920) by Benedict XV, 80 members of parliament from the Right and
Center attended in a body behind Gabriel Hanotaux. In return the Left
pretended to consider the festival of Joan of Arc as a clerical and reactionary
manifestation and refused to join in the annual solemnities.

Like all sincere sentiments, the patriotism of the Right was demanding
and intransigent. . . . It firmly meant to keep the fruits of victory for France,
and with the scrutiny of a pettifogging lawyer watched over the punctual
execution of the clauses of the Versailles Treaty. Wilsonian idealism always
seemed suspect to it, and the League of Nations, the principal edifice of this
sentiment, inspired only a limited confidence. . . .

However, the Right willingly accepted a League of Nations which
perpetuated France's privileged position and guaranteed the maintenance of
the *status quo*. But its realism ultimately preferred concrete guarantees to legal
assurances and utopian proposals. The trilogy *status quo*, armaments, alliance,
summarizes its entire foreign policy. The line followed by Poincaré: the
occupation of the Ruhr and the taking of guarantees, conformed in all points
to its views. . . .

In domestic policy the *Bloc National*'s position was expressed in another
aspect of Poincarism, strict financial orthodoxy, based on the postulates of
economic liberalism. The Right was opposed on principle, and perhaps also
for motives not foreign to the desires of its voters; to any increase in public
expenditures and to any rise in taxation. It thereby took up on its own account
the theme of cheap government exploited a hundred years earlier by the
liberal Left. By definition the budget was always too high. Then there was
the constant plaint that the government employees were too numerous. Onto
the major theme of budgetary prodigality was grafted the minor theme of
"budget-devouring" functionaries generously paid to do nothing. Many
Frenchmen wanted nothing better than to believe this but the consequent
rancor of the functionaries was expensive for the Right. In 1924 and 1936 the
success of the *Cartel des Gauches* and of the Popular Front was due in part to
their displeasure provoked by the Poincaré and Laval decrees.

The unity of the Right Wing was cemented by a third theme which
actually belonged to its arsenal of propaganda, namely anticommunism. In
this the national mystique and the attachment to the established order were
joined together. The poster showing the-man-with-the-knife-between-his-
teeth played a significant part in the victory of the *Bloc National*. . . .

THE STAVISKY AFFAIR AND THE
RIOTS OF FEBRUARY 6TH, 1934

Geoffrey Warner

In France the year 1934 began in an atmosphere of gloom. The shadow of the world economic depression hung over the country. Across her vulnerable eastern frontier, Adolf Hitler had just come into power; Nazi Germany had left the League of Nations and withdrawn from the Disarmament Conference. France had fought the first World War to obtain peace and security. In January 1934, it looked as if she might lose both.

The Republican form of government seemed ill adapted to cope with the problems ahead. There had been no fewer than seven Cabinets since January 1931, and Parliamentary ineptitude was infuriating public opinion. The danger was that normal criticism of a government, or a party in office, could easily turn into an attack upon the Parliamentary system, or even upon the Republic itself. Although most Frenchmen had come to accept the Republic, there was still an irreconcilable core of Right-wing extremists who did not. In the troubled climate of the early 'thirties, they were able to recruit many supporters from among the ordinary people of France.

Since the end of the first World War, Right-wing opposition to the Republic had assumed a new form. Hitherto centred mainly in the Church, the army and the higher grades of the Civil and colonial services, it now came down into the streets in the shape of the Leagues. The Leagues were extra-Parliamentary organizations, which tried to act as pressure-groups, attempting to display their strength in demonstrations and other forms of "direct action."

The oldest of the Leagues, the *Action Française*, was a Royalist body, founded in 1905 in the backwash of the Dreyfus affair. It owed much of its importance to the support it received from prominent intellectuals, such as Charles Maurras, Léon Daudet and Jacques Bainville. The other Leagues were founded during the late 'twenties and early 'thirties, often with support of big business. They obviously owed a great deal to the contemporary Fascist and Nazi movements, including in their vague programmes all the familiar Fascist stock-in-trade of authoritarianism, ex-servicemen's "mystique," corporatism, anti-Semitism and anti-Communism.

Besides the *Action Française*, the most important Leagues were: the *Croix de Feu*—originally an ex-servicemen's organization—the rowdy *Jeunesses Patriotes*, ... and the violently anti-Semitic *Solidarité Française*. No League had an active membership exceeding 100,000 and most members were Parisians, especially students. But their efficient, semi-military organization

Geoffrey Warner, "The Stavisky Affair and the Riots of February 6th 1934," *History Today*, vol. VIII, no. 6 (June, 1958), 377–85. Copyright by Geoffrey Warner, 1958. Used by permission of the author and *History Today*.

made the Leagues extremely dangerous, for Paris was the centre of government and the hub of economic and political life. The importance of Paris hid the fact that the Leagues enjoyed little support outside the capital.

At the beginning of 1934, the Leagues were given the opportunity to show their strength. For in January, a politico-financial scandal erupted that recalled the days of Panama. Its effects shook France to her foundations and almost brought the Third Republic to its knees.

The man responsible for the scandal was Serge-Alexandre Stavisky—a financial swindler. His favourite method of operation was the flotation of fraudulent companies. With the proceeds of one swindle he liquidated the debts of the previous one, thereby for years avoiding detection. At the end of 1933, one of his schemes collapsed, leaving him with 200 million francs' worth of bonds issued on the security of the municipal pawn-shop at Bayonne. When the affair came to light in January 1934, certain unsavoury aspects were revealed. A member of Parliament was up to his neck in it and a Cabinet minister had even written a letter recommending Bayonne bonds as a good investment. Worse still, Stavisky had been arrested in 1927 on a swindling charge, but had been provisionally released pending his trial. He was still on "provisional" release in 1934, having had his liberty extended nineteen times. It looked suspiciously as if he were being "protected" by someone in authority.

The Right-wing press exulted in the scandal and in the chance it offered to smear the Republic and Republican politicians. On January 9th, the Royalist daily, *Action Française*, effectively summed up public indignation when it said: "At a time when the Government and Parliament declare that they are incapable of balancing our finances . . . a scandal breaks, showing that . . . public savings, which the régime professed to guarantee, are available for the colossal swindles of an alien crook."

Parliament reassembled on January 11th after the Christmas recess, but not before the affair had taken another surprising turn. Stavisky had vanished after a warrant had been issued for his arrest, but on January 8th he was discovered at a villa in Chamonix—with a bullet through his head. The police said it was suicide, but *Action Française* thought otherwise. On January 10th, its headlines read: "Camille Chautemps—leader of a gang of thieves and murderers." . . .

Chautemps was the Prime Minister. He was a member of the Radical party, and it was Radical deputies who were involved in the scandal. His brother-in-law, Pressard, was head of the judicial department responsible for Stavisky's "provisional" releases. Both men were freemasons and, therefore, in the eyes of *Action Française*, members of an occult conspiracy bent on despoiling France. *Action Française* put two and two together and many of its readers agreed with its deduction, firmly believing that the politicians were capable of killing Stavisky to prevent him from "talking."

The situation was highly critical and Chautemps mishandled it. He refused a Committee of Enquiry, and this was construed as further proof of his complicity in the affair. The Leagues began to organize demonstrations against "Republican corruption" and after January 9th there was almost nightly rioting in Paris. By January 27th, Chautemps could stand it no longer and resigned. . . .

President Lebrun hastened to find a man who could form a new Government. After several refusals, his choice finally fell upon Edouard Daladier. . . . Alone of the Radical leaders, Daladier had emerged unscathed from the mud-slinging that arose from the Stavisky affair. He was an ex-serviceman, but not a freemason, and these assets might help to enhance his popularity with the public and, perhaps, even with the Leagues.

On Monday, January 29th, Daladier accepted President Lebrun's invitation and declared to the press: "I intend to form a Government of energetic and highly respectable men—men who will restore the authority of the state and an absolute confidence in the Republic." What Daladier had in mind was an above-party coalition, but none of the other parties would co-operate with him. In the end, he succeeded in obtaining only the services of two Centre deputies—Colonel Fabry at the Ministry of War and M. Piétri at the Ministry of Finance—and even Fabry's party disowned him.

Daladier's main difficulty was to obtain a majority; he was not popular with the Right, nor the Left, and even his own party, the Radicals, were annoyed with him for attempting to form a coalition. The ambitious ex-Socialist Minister of the Interior, Eugène Frot, provided him with a solution: if he dismissed Jean Chiappe, Prefect of the Paris police, he would be sure to obtain the Socialist votes in the Chamber of Deputies.

Chiappe was suspected by the Left of having Right-wing sympathies. Besides having many Right-wing political contacts, he had shown considerable leniency towards the Right-wing demonstrators throughout January, whereas he had always severely suppressed Left-wing demonstrations. He was also suspected of complicity in the Stavisky affair. . . .

Daladier was most reluctant to dismiss Chiappe. On January 30th, he had seen the Prefect personally and begged him to use all his influence to avert a big ex-service demonstration scheduled for February 4th. Chiappe had agreed and Daladier left him with the words: "You are not just *a* friend but *the* friend." Unfortunately, Daladier's attempts to obtain assurances of support from other parties failed, and he reluctantly gave in to Frot's pressure. . . .

At 9 A.M. on Saturday, February 3rd, Daladier telephoned Chiappe to inform him of his decision. He had decided to sweeten the pill by offering the Prefect the Residency of Morocco, but Chiappe refused to give up his post. A fierce row ensued and, according to Daladier, Chiappe terminated the conversation by threatening to start a riot. Chiappe, however, maintained that all he had said was that he would be penniless if he quit his job. . . . According to Daladier, Chiappe had said: "Je serai *dans* la rue"—that is, starting a riot; but Chiappe swore that he had really said: "Je serai *à* la rue"— that is, penniless. It would have taken a great deal of ingenuity on Daladier's part to have invented this story; yet at the same time, he could hardly have taken it seriously since he gave Chiappe time to think over his offer of the Moroccan Residency. It is hardly likely that he would have been so forbearing towards a man who he thought was going to lead a riot against his government.

Upon the news of Chiappe's dismissal, both Colonel Fabry and M. Piétri threatened to resign unless Daladier changed his mind. Both men went round to see Chiappe in an attempt to patch up the quarrel between him and Daladier. They might conceivably have succeeded, for Daladier was still upset and in two minds about the whole business. But Frot effectively destroyed any hopes of compromise by sending M. Bonnefoy-Sibour, Prefect of the department of Seine-et-Oise, to the Prefecture of Police to take over Chiappe's post. Fabry and Piétri promptly resigned and were replaced by Paul-Boncour and Marchandeau respectively. Both new ministers were Left-wingers, and thus all trace of above-party spirit was removed from Daladier's cabinet.

On Sunday the 4th and Monday the 5th, the press was full of the Chiappe affair. The Right-wing papers made no secret of their belief that Chiappe's dismissal was the result of a political deal between Daladier and the Socialists. . . .

There can be little doubt that it was Chiappe's dismissal that precipitated the great riot of February 6th. No mass demonstration had been planned for that date before the news of his dismissal became known. But, on the 5th and 6th all the Leagues issued appeals to their members and supporters to demonstrate in force on the night of the 6th, when Daladier was due to present his Government before the Chamber of Deputies. The Right-wing ex-service organization, the *Union Nationale des Combattants* (U.N.C.), also decided to join the demonstration. Not to be outdone, the Communist ex-service organization, the *Association Républicaine d'Anciens Combattants* (A.R.A.C.), joined in with the rest.

Not only the Leagues but all Paris was angered by Daladier's muddling over the Chiappe affair and the corruption revealed in the Stavisky scandal. The demonstration of February 6th promised to be a spectacular expression of public disgust with the whole Parliamentary system. . . .

The task of keeping order was entrusted . . . not to troops, but to the police. Unhappily, the recent sudden change in command hampered the latter in their operations. The Place de la Concorde, which lay just across the Seine from the Chamber of Deputies, was not cordoned off, although it was the obvious focal-point for a demonstration against the Chamber. Perhaps, as they later alleged, the police did not have enough men for the job, but there was no excuse for the pitifully inadequate force that guarded the newly-widened Concorde bridge and barred the way to the Chamber. At first there were only 70 policemen, 100 *gardes mobiles* and 25 mounted Republican Guards on the bridge. But between half-past six and eight o'clock, 620 men had to be rushed there as reinforcements.

The Leagues, paying scrupulous attention to their independence, had planned their assembly-points in different parts of Paris. By the time that they reached the Place de la Concorde the demonstration was already in full swing and beginning to turn into a riot. The crowd took offence at the police roadblock across the Concorde bridge and attempted to break through it, shouting "Down with Daladier!" and "Long live Chiappe!" Fierce fighting ensued. The mounted Republican Guards were bombarded with asphalt and iron railings, and their horses slashed with razor-blades attached to the end of walkingsticks. At half-past seven, the *Solidarité Française* column entered the Place de la Concorde from the Rue Royale and a concerted attack was made on the bridge. The police were nearly overwhelmed and, in their panic, opened fire on the crowd.

At 8:45, the U.N.C. column also passed through the Place de la Concorde on its way to the Elysée Palace to demonstrate before President Lebrun. They ran into a police roadblock and were turned back with violence. They returned to the Place de la Concorde to swell the ranks of the rioters. The fighting continued. The rioters erected counter-barricades to hinder police charges and the police suffered many casualties trying to smash them. Finally, at 11:30, the Leagues led another mass assault on the bridge, shouting, "Assassins! Assassins!" and, once again, the police panicked and opened fire. Just before midnight, the police counter-attacked in an attempt to clear the Place de la Concorde. It was late and the rioters had been discouraged by the shooting. The police were successful and although they kept guard over the bridge until two in the morning, there was no further trouble. . . .

In the Chamber itself, a vehement debate had been raging since three in the afternoon, when the session commenced. Daladier was shouted down during his ministerial declaration, despite the fact that it contained a promise to set up an Enquiry into the Stavisky scandal. Chiappe had now replaced Stavisky as the battle-cry of the Right. The President of the Chamber was forced to suspend the sitting twice and the uproar increased when the sound of firing was heard from across the Seine. Daladier eventually carried the day by 360 votes to 220. Many Deputies, fearing that the rioters would invade the Chamber, voted by proxy. The Socialists sided with the Government. But it was not a vote of confidence, explained their leader, Léon Blum, only "a fighting vote in face of the fascist danger."

Fourteen rioters were killed on the night of February 6th, 236 were seriously injured and 419 slightly injured. Of these, the Leagues had lost seven dead and 123 wounded, which proves conclusively that by no means all the rioters were affiliated to the Leagues. Police casualties were heavier, if account is taken of the smaller numbers involved. One was killed, 92 seriously injured and 688 slightly injured. . . .

Although the Government had survived the day, Daladier and his ministers were in a state of complete confusion. No one had a clear lead to give on what the Government's policy should be. The one exception was Eugène Frot, who seems to have totally eclipsed Daladier during the brief period that remained of his ministry. An emergency Cabinet meeting was held at the Ministry of the Interior at midnight on February 6th, at which Frot came forward with plans that showed he was prepared to crush another riot by all the means at the Government's disposal. He proposed in succession, to declare a state of siege, to arrest persons guilty of what he called "a plot against the security of the state" and to put police powers in the hands of the military authorities.

Daladier and the rest of the Cabinet were horrified at Frot's suggestions. It was discovered that Paris was technically an "open city" and that a joint meeting of both houses of the French Parliament would be needed to proclaim a state of siege. The Government's legal adviser, the Procureur-Général, expressed grave doubts about Frot's wish to arrest suspicious persons. . . .

But Frot had already decided to implement his plans—with or without Cabinet consent. Using a personal liaison officer, and thus bypassing the Prefecture of Police, he was sending orders to the Ministry of War, placing large numbers of troops on the alert for the 7th and ordering tanks to advance from the base at Satory. Even before the Cabinet meeting, Frot had decided that preventive arrests should be made. On his own initiative, he ordered the Prefecture of Police to detain prominent members of the Leagues, although Deputies, municipal councillors, journalists and war veterans were not to be arrested. These orders were illegal and Frot knew it, but he claimed later that the situation demanded them. A terrible slaughter would have occurred on February 7th had Frot kept his resolve, for the Leagues were already planning larger demonstrations if the Government did not resign.

The Minister of the Interior, however, did change his mind. By morning, Daladier had at last evolved a policy, which entailed proroguing the Chamber of Deputies. "It was obvious," Daladier later explained, "that if rioting recurred, the Prime Minister could not divide his time between the tribune of the Chamber . . . and the Place de la Concorde." . . . Several of Daladier's ministers, who feared more trouble in the streets, had already come to him, urging the resignation of the Government. Daladier decided to discuss his plans with the Presidents of the Senate and the Chamber of Deputies and with Léon Blum, and to obtain their views. In the middle of these consultations, an envoy from Frot rushed in, urging Daladier to resign immediately.

Why had Frot changed his mind? Perhaps the little sleep he had been able to snatch had restored his sense of reality. Perhaps his tour of the police hospital on the morning of the 7th had convinced him that the forces of order could not face another day's rioting. The bundle of police intelligence notes awaiting him at the Ministry of the Interior on his return from the hospital were certainly far from reassuring. One read: "In *Action Française* and *Crois de Feu* circles . . . it was decided to stage an energetic counter-stroke with revolver and bombs. It is confirmed that M. Frot, the Minister of the Interior, is condemned to death." Perhaps it was this last piece of information that made Frot change his mind. At any rate, at 1 P.M. Daladier, persuaded once more by his Minister of the Interior, tendered his Government's resignation to the President of the Republic. The preventive arrests ceased forthwith. . . .

Who was ultimately responsible for the riot of February 6th? The standard Left-wing theory, popularized by Daladier himself, is that the riot was part of a Fascist plot to overthrow the Republic. If so, it was very badly organized, for the Leagues concentrated all their forces in the Place de la Concorde, instead of trying to capture other key-points in Paris. It was rumoured that the army was sympathetic to the Leagues, and it is true, for example, that General Weygand disliked Daladier and detested his Minister of War, Paul-Boncour. But if the army had been a party to a plan for a *coup d'état* on February 6th, it would surely have taken action and not waited to see what would happen. . . .

. . . Whatever prompted the riot of February 6th, and we are never likely to know the whole truth, the events of that day were of tremendous significance. They intensified the increasingly bitter struggle between Left and Right in France, providing both sides with a highly-exploitable "myth." For the Left, February 6th was a "Fascist plot"; for the Right it was the first step in the regeneration of France. The conflict between these two ideals continued throughout the most tragic decade in France's recent history. The Popular Front of 1936 was originally a Left-wing alliance against the "Fascists" of February 6th. The Vichy régime, set up in 1940, was at least a partial heir of the Leagues of 1934. The triumph of the Resistance in 1944 meant the revenge of the Left as well as the expulsion of the invader. Thus it is false to study France during this period solely in terms of the struggle with Germany. The bitter internal conflict is just as important a part of the story, and for this reason, February 6th, 1934, is one of the most important dates in the annals of modern France.

LÉON BLUM AND THE FAILURE OF
THE POPULAR FRONT

Georges Dupeux

The Popular Front was not only a profitable electoral operation that sent 72 Communists and 147 Socialists to the Chamber of Deputies in 1936 (compared with 11 and 131, respectively, in 1932), while limiting the losses of the Radical-Socialists, who would most certainly have paid most dearly for their collaboration with right-wing governments if republican discipline had not prevailed. At the same time, it represented a great hope for all those who expected from its victory the end of the difficulties brought on by the economic crisis and the policy of deflation practiced with varying degrees of vigor by the governments of the preceding legislature, and, above all, an overhaul of social policies for the benefit of the most disadvantaged classes.

This hope was dashed, and much more rapidly than the parliamentary votes might indicate. Officially the Popular Front was dissolved at the end of 1938, when Edouard Daladier asked the Chamber for a vote of confidence in his "general policies" (December 9). The vote meant approving both the repression of the general strike of November 30 and the financial policy of Paul Reynaud. The Communists and Socialists voted against it, and were joined by about thirty Radical-Socialists. From then on the government relied on a majority comprising the center and right. But beginning with the vote of October 4, 1938, that approved the Munich agreements, the Communist Party, registered its hostility and broke with the former majority. In fact, the defeat of the second ministry of Léon Blum, which lasted less than three weeks, and the tolerance shown the two Chautemps ministries, the second of which enjoyed neither Socialist participation nor Communist support, had shown even earlier that if the term "Popular Front" had not yet been completely abandoned, its spirit had disappeared and illusions were dispelled.

The Popular Front was fatally stricken on June 21, 1937, when the first Blum ministry resigned after a year's exercise of power. On that day hopes for a durable government supported by a coherent majority and capable of realizing a policy of large-scale economic and social reforms had to be abandoned.

The conditions which led the Blum government to resign deserve a careful study, especially since they seem rather unusual. Indeed, the government retained the confidence of the Chamber to the very end. On June 15, by a vote of 346 to 247, it granted the government the "powers necessary to

Georges Dupeux, "L'Echec du premier gouvernement Léon Blum," © *Revue d'histoire moderne et contemporaine*, X (1963), 35–42, 44. Used by permission of the *Revue d'histoire moderne et contemporaine* and the author. Translation by Hans D. Kellner.

assure financial recovery." But the Senate did not follow the Chamber's example. The defection of the Radical senators . . . checked the government, which, after unsuccessfully requesting a vote of confidence, submitted its resignation to the President of the Republic. . . .

The opposition of the Senate could have been overcome in two ways. The first, which respected the constitution, would have put an end to the debate through universal suffrage. Now in a minority in the Senate, the government could return to the Chamber, request a new vote of confidence and, having revealed to all the deadlock between the two houses, could order the Senate either to bend and grant the financial powers it called for, or to pronounce the dissolution of the Chamber. New elections would have probably shown that the Popular Front retained the confidence of the voters, whose verdict would then be forcibly imposed on the recalcitrant senators. The second proposal was more dangerous: the government would refuse to bend before the Senate and would force it to change its attitude, through extra-political pressure, if necessary. Léon Blum himself entertained this plan, and considered it readily workable, if we are to believe [American] ambassador [William] Bullitt: "When he had to yield power under pressure from the Senate alone, he confided in me that he could have easily broken this opposition by giving free rein to the physical force of the people, without even openly calling for it."

The constitutional solution could not be applied because of the attitude of the Radical ministers. . . . The second alternative was rejected by Blum because of the critical foreign situation. . . .

Blum himself lucidly explained the reasons for his decision at the Socialist Party Congress held at Marseilles on July 10–13, 1937. He voiced this justification because certain speakers had, if not violently attacked, at least blamed him for having given way before the senatorial offensive. Blum replied that if battle had been joined with the Senate, he would have had to pursue it to its conclusion: "We would have had to fight to victory. Would the entire Popular Front have followed us into battle? Could we have carried on this battle without asking and obtaining the active support of the workers' organizations? Into what condition would we have thrown the country? Besides, you know full well . . . what the situation abroad was at that moment. . . . Considering the foreign danger, we said 'No, we have no right to do that. We have no right to do it to our party, we have no right to do it to our country.' So we withdrew."

Blum's argument rests on three points: the uncertain cohesion of the Popular Front, the danger of civil war, and the foreign threat.

That the cohesion of the Popular Front could be questioned will come as no surprise. We need only mention the difficulties of its formation, and especially the internal contradictions of this electoral alliance. But if this coalition was threatened with destruction in the long run, no one could have foreseen in June, 1937, that this danger was imminent. Certainly, the Communist Party had refused to participate in the government, and its "active" support could be considered only a clever form of extortion. It no doubt even wanted to capitalize on the discontent that the difficult exercise of power could not fail to arouse. In regard to the problem of nonintervention in the Spanish Civil War, the Communists had clearly shown their opposition to the government's policy. But even on this important issue, the party neither wished nor dared to split the Popular Front. At the time of the debate of December 5, 1936, in the Chamber, the party did not support the motion of confidence in the government, nor did it vote against it. It was content to abstain. In fact, it might be said that, at this time, the Communist Party had no long-term policy. Not wanting, for various reasons, to bring about a revolution that showed no sign of success, the party offered no viable alternative to the Popular Front. In the specific case of June, 1937, that is, when there was the possibility of a trial of strength between the government and the Senate, it would have been absurd to side with the Senate against the government. Nothing indicates that the Communist Party had the slightest intention of doing so. The danger sprang not from them but from the Radicals.

The problem facing the Radicals was this: would they or could they take the initiative in a split? The parliamentary debates proved that the Radicals did not dare to take this step—they let their colleagues in the Senate act. The hostility of the Radicals to a dissolution . . . shows that they gladly seized the chance to overthrow the Blum government. Was this done to destroy the Popular Front or, more simply, to replace a Socialist-dominated government with a Radical-dominated one supported by the same majority? No one knows. But if Léon Blum had decided to go through with a test of strength with the Senate, what would the attitude of the Radicals have been? Could they escape without eventually risking powerful reprisals if elections were held? What would their fate have been if they had had to face candidates of both Right and Left whom they could not persuade to stand down in the second electoral round? The Radical leaders knew the mood of the electorate too well to risk suicide.

As for the danger of civil war that Blum invoked as the second argument to justify the resignation of his government, it no longer seems very serious. The workers' organizations, whose "active cooperation" Blum considered indispensable, had been greatly strengthened since the victorious strikes of June, 1936, which had already demonstrated their power. A resolute government supported by them did not seem likely to meet any effective resistance. Moreover, his confidences to Ambassador Bullitt prove that Blum himself judged that the task would be "easy."

The third argument, the foreign situation, remains. It is certain that Blum was always very sensitive to the threat from abroad, and that the responsibilities he had assumed since June, 1936, had made him even more attentive to the German menace. But was it so definite and immediate in June, 1937? If so, it is hard to understand why, in a period of great danger, Blum should have become resigned to yielding power to a ministry headed by Chautemps, whose weaknesses he knew better than anyone else. It is difficult to see why he did not propose the formation of a government of "national union" in June, 1937, as he was to do nine months later.

Thus, taken separately, each of the reasons cited by Blum to justify his refusal to force a test of strength with the Senate hardly seems convincing. Taken together, they assume greater weight, but it is hard to believe that they could have made the head of government make the decision he did. More precisely, they seem decisive only if we concede that Blum considered that the dangers to which he would have exposed his party, his majority, and the nation itself, outweighed the benefits the country could expect had he kept office—in other words, unless we admit that Blum no longer had faith in the success of his "experiment." . . .

Following the elections of 1936, Blum outlined to the party faithful assembled at the National Congress the program he hoped to realize as head of government. After having pointed out that the Socialist Party was but one element in the Popular Front, he declared that "not only does the Socialist Party lack a majority, but all the proletarian parties together have none. There is no Socialist majority, there is no proletarian majority. There is the Popular Front majority, and that majority stands precisely on the program of the Popular Front. Our object, our mandate, our duty, is to attain and carry out this program. It follows . . . that we shall act within the present social order, within the same order whose contradictions and injustices we revealed during our election campaign. That is the object of our experiment. And the real problem that this experiment is going to pose is the problem of knowing whether . . . it is possible to draw from this society the degree of order, of well-being, of security, of justice, that are required for the mass of workers and producers. . . . The question is to know whether it is possible to insure a transition, a peaceful, amicable transformation from this society to the society whose final realization is and remains our goal."

Blum's government assumed power under very difficult conditions during the strikes of June, 1936, at a moment when the "transition" seemed anything but "peaceful." The solution, it is true, very quickly took the form of a surrender by management. The signing of the Matignon agreements had two happy results: it made it possible to avoid a test of strength between workers and employers, and it so strongly impressed the members of the Chambers, senators included, that a series of social laws was passed without difficulty, and in the shortest possible time. These included the laws of June 20, providing for collective bargaining and paid vacations, and those of June 21, providing for a forty-hour week and a higher compulsory school age.

It seems likely that at this time the head of government conceived the idea and nourished the hope of a reconciliation with management, or at least with one thinking, intelligent segment, as a means of realizing a plan of economic recovery and social reform that would make France better adapted to the needs of the moment. "The peaceful, amicable arrangement" that he had called for at the Paris Congress would doubtless have taken the form of a French New Deal.

Management still had to accept the faithful application of the Matignon agreements and the social legislation of June. We know that nothing of the kind happened. The leaders of the *Confédération Générale de la Production Française* [the organization representing management] which had signed the accords, had been disavowed by their membership; and the president, [René] Duchemin, had to resign in October. The *Confédération*, changing its name, became the *Confédération Général du Patronat Français*. The new C.G.P.F. did nothing to facilitate the application of the Matignon agreements, and on November 26, 1936, its president, [Claude] Gignoux, broke off negotiations with the *Confédération Générale du Travail* [the national workers' union] for a proposed general organization for conciliation and arbitration. He also addressed a letter to the Premier, requesting Blum to "denounce the damage done by the C.G.T. to the right to work."

The stiffening on the part of management had immediate political consequences. The Senate recovered its boldness and began a small war of skirmishes with the ministry. It refused to take quick action on the budget proposals for 1937 and dragged out into the last days of the year the debate on a bill which would create procedures for conciliation and compulsory arbitration, made necessary by the breakdown of the negotiations between the C.G.P.F. and the C.G.T.

What were Blum's reactions to this lack of understanding and the hardening resistance of the employers? First, an unhappy surprise, expressed in a speech at Narbonne on October 25, 1936. . . . Then, several weeks later, in a radio broadcast on December 31, he made an attempt at conciliation . . . : "Is the evidence not clear? Is it not obvious that we have pushed economic liberalism as far as any government in the past, perhaps even farther than any other government would have done in the present circumstances? . . . As a Popular Front government, loyal to its origin and its mandate, we claim to be a national government in the highest sense of the word. That is why we address ourselves today to all men and women of France. That is why we call for cooperation from whoever understands and is concerned for the national interest, from whoever is ready to accept his civic duty."

The conciliation offered to management was the "pause in the social and financial activity of the government," announced on February 13, 1937, and put into effect by decisions of the Council of Ministers on March 5. The government gave up its regulation of foreign exchange, new appropriations, and its policy of large-scale public works. With the decisions of the ministry made on April 26, the pause became outright capitulation: the creation of a national unemployment fund and the foundation of a home for elderly workers were "temporarily" set aside.

This policy failed. It failed first of all because management refused to grasp the hand offered to it. It continued to refuse any discussions with the unions. In the economic sphere it ruined the effects of the collective agreements by raising prices to such an extent that a wave of inflation was unleashed that endangered the economy of the entire country. The policy of conciliation also failed because it made the working class pay, in the form of decreased real wages, the price of abandoning objectives that were not specifically Socialist, but which were simply those of the program of the *Rassemblement Populaire* [the coalition of popular parties of 1936]. Above all, it failed because in doing this it destroyed the confidence that those who had voted for the Popular Front had placed in this government, and brought them discouragement.

It was probably because he was conscious of this failure that Blum so readily decided to bow before the Senate's opposition. Since a New Deal was not possible in the France of 1937, there was no deep reason to justify a test of strength and the risks, even minor ones, that it involved. Finally, there was no longer any reason to maintain the Popular Front as it had been conceived—as a means of securing from French society a certain "degree of order, well-being, security, and justice" which would have benefited "the mass of workers and producers." . . .

If Léon Blum resigned himself so easily to abandon powers which he could have retained without much trouble, it was because he did not confront a bourgeoisie capable of understanding and accepting what he offered it—a transformation without revolution of the economic and social structure of the France of 1937.

ALONG THE ROAD BACK TO
FRANCE 1940

John C. Cairns

Even now . . . the fall of France in the summer of 1940—by which is meant here both the military collapse and the surrender of the parliamentary Republic at Vichy—remains for some of us a vivid memory. It was indeed, as the then British Foreign Secretary so rightly recalled, "an event which at the time seemed something so unbelievable as to be almost surely unreal, and if not unreal then quite immeasurably catastrophic." . . .

To the man in the street . . . the fall of France did not require an inordinate amount of thought. Everyone who read the papers knew that old Marshal Henri Philippe Pétain had been faint hearted from the first, prepared to give up even during the difficult days of the war of 1914. Pierre Laval . . . , thought to be the Marshal's evil genius, had been marked out a quarter century before in the famous Carnet B, listing potentially dangerous pacifists and revolutionaries who might have to be arrested. Men like Georges Bonnet, so recently transferred from the Foreign Ministry to the Ministry of Justice in Edouard Daladier's last cabinet, who symbolized an even more suspect variety of appeasement than that associated with Neville Chamberlain, were thought to have exerted a disastrous influence behind the battle and in the parliamentary corridors. . . . Plainly the fall of France was the result of conspiracy, subversion, and a distasteful bargain, as that disillusioned champion of the mortally smitten League of Nations, Lord Robert Cecil, put it, "by which a sordid adventurer induced a Marshal of France to sell the honour of his country for the satisfaction of his servile ambition." . . .

It was true that the Germans had Pétain marked down as a pacifist, as an enemy of the existing regime and of the war, at least as early as the fall of 1939. "France's greatest mistake," he was reported in Berlin to have told close associates the following spring, "had been to enter the war. In the present state of the country, when peace was concluded the internal disintegration of France which would then clearly emerge would exclude her from European politics for decades to come." But there was no evidence that he was privy to any conspiracy, although his pessimism evidently hardened to the point of his believing in the imminence of defeat and of foreseeing for himself a role in possible army *défaillances à la* 1917. He had even, it is true, discussed the question of forming a new government (although in September he had refused to associate himself in a ministerial capacity with the colleagues of Daladier). He had gone so far as secretly to summon his friend Senator

John C. Cairns, "Along the Road Back to France 1940," *American Historical Review*, vol. LXIV, no. 3 (April, 1959), 583–600, 602–603. Copyright by John C. Cairns and used by permission.

Henry Lémery to San Sebastien to pursue the matter. But all that was hardly incriminating. . . . The idea of conspiracy, however, was fixed. . . .

It was not hard to believe, then, that the fall of France was at least partly the result of conspiracy and general political skulduggery; the famous Stavisky scandal of 1934 stood as a kind of permanent reminder of this continuing element in French public life. At the same time, the events of 1940 came to be interpreted as having been marked out by the very nature of things: inevitable. This grand fatality was proclaimed while the war raced across the fields of France in the fierce heat of splendid summer days. General Maxime Weygand, recalled at seventy-two years of age to succeed General Maurice Gamelin, remarked the very day the Battle of France opened on the Somme, "What we are paying for is twenty years of blunders and neglect. It is out of the question to punish the generals and not the teachers who have refused to develop in the children the sense of patriotism and sacrifice." The school system alone had brought about the crumbling of the nation; and those reserve officers who had abandoned their units, the Marshal was to inform Ambassador William C. Bullitt afterward, were the products of "teachers who were Socialists and not patriots." The country had been "rotted" by politics, he told Major General E. L. Spears. "We must pay now, and pay dearly, for the anarchy we have indulged in for so long." Weygand even put such dark thoughts down formally on paper. "The old order of things," ran a memorandum he drew up shortly after the battle had been lost, "a political regime made up of masonic, capitalist and international deals, has brought us where we stand. France has had enough of that." In defeat the soldiers assuaged their pain and humiliation by appeals to the utter hopelessness of the situation they had inherited from the politicians. . . .

Even the civilian great of the Third Republic who had played the game of politics down to the very end did not hesitate to damn themselves in condemning the regime. "The simple people of the country are as fine as they have ever been," Camille Chautemps, one of the *chefs* of that Radical Socialism on which the political life of France had balanced for decades, remarked somewhat vaguely after the Armistice. "The upper classes have failed completely." Or as Adrien Marquet, Pétain's second Minister of the Interior, explained to the press on June 28, "It is not France that has been conquered. It is a complaisant regime of opportunism and weakness that has collapsed." . . .

Other patterns of interpretation emerged. Conspiracy and ineluctability . . . were joined by yet a third and supernatural agent. In the immediate aftermath, amid the wreckage of the Republic and all its military glory, the old gods lived again. And . . . the Marshal's attentive ear caught the sound of Jehovah's thunder directed against an erring people. It was not news to him, this Old Testament wrath. Heaven knew he had warned against it for years, begging his fellow countrymen not to forsake their spiritual role, pleading with them to abandon that "very wantonness which is the cause of our divisions. In the midst of magnificent post-war achievements," he told ex-servicemen in 1938, "it was the country's soul that suffered most—because the ideals that bound us together had been lost sight of." For all this the army of France was not to blame; it alone had remained pure, faithful to the religion of France. Sure of this before the outbreak of war, Pétain was unshaken by the conduct of the battle. "Our defeat," he explained as the Armistice went into effect, "is punishment for our moral failures. The mood of sensual pleasure destroyed what the spirit of sacrifice had built up." God and family and country, they had all been sacrificed. It was so obvious that all right-thinking people must agree. . . .

With changing times and the reversal of fortunes . . . fashions in history also change. And in the aftermath of 1945 what one might call the providential approach to the fall of France seemed less than congenial. . . .

It was hardly surprising, then, that from the ranks of the army . . . should come a fourth explanation, summed up in the haunting phrase "the war of lost opportunities." Taking this for his title and theme, an old soldier from the First World War, a regimental commander in the Second, and a sometime assistant professor of history at Saint-Cyr, Colonel Adolphe Goutard, proceeded to show that France had been defeated through a succession of command mistakes, ignorance, failure of nerve, lack of foresight, and, above all, one abandoned opportunity after another. Naturally this thesis was no more novel than the phrase itself. It had appeared at the curious and confused Riom trial in 1942, when the government at Vichy had sought to establish the criminality of the Popular Front and the culpability of General Maurice Gamelin. The rather anarchic proceedings, however, had tended to make such uncomfortable reading for everyone, French and German alike, that Berlin submitted its complaints and displeasure, and the trial was adjourned sine die. But now Goutard, better armed than the defense counsel of Daladier, Blum, et al., and drawing on the enemy's revelations and the findings of the postwar Parliamentary Commission investigating . . . events in France between 1933 and 1945 . . . demolished the army's former charges of matériel deficiencies, at least to his own satisfaction. The ultimate conclusion was simply that "our defeat may be attributed essentially to an intellectual deficiency expressing itself in conservatism, conformity, preconceived ideas and unreal speculations; in short, to a colossal command mistake, made irremediable by a current lack of resilience, much more than to basic impotence of the Army and the country from which it issued." . . .

Thus to the leitmotifs of conspiracy, fatality, and providential retribution was added in the military sphere the theme of intellectual incompetence: the unnecessary defeat. From this it was not much of a step to the grand idea of the absurd defeat. This fifth . . . explanation was announced by a common soldier of the army of 1940 after just thinking about it for the better part of two decades. Whatever other values it might possess, his book had the immense advantage of being by far the most hilarious account of the fall of France. Novelist and satirist, Jean Dutourd seemed in his *The Taxis of the Marne* to be making good Henri Peyre's estimate of him as "one of the rare entertaining writers of an age that prefers to wallow in its anguish rather than to laugh at it." . . . Looking back, he decided that the debacle had been not only unnecessary but disgraceful and absurd. Without quite saying so, he suggested that it had been entirely senseless. . . . The strong point of his account, however, was neither logic nor method, but rather a wild kind of splenetic anger that resulted in a good many hits on target—it could scarcely have been otherwise since the target was France—and a lot of broad misses. The scene was set as attractively as possible and the players were costumed with sufficient realism to be recognizable as historical characters. But they were manipulated so madly as to reduce the whole event to fantasy. Across the years the sun still shone down on the fair land of France. "The weather," Dutourd recalled, "was as beautiful as it was in August 1914. I see again the nut trees standing motionless along the unpaved roads. . . . The leaves seemed polished by the light. . . ." Every prospect was pleasing, and only man was foul. For across this idyllic landscape trooped such an unlovely collection of patriots and warriors that the gods must have rocked in mirth and anger: peace-loving generals whose highest ambition was to die quietly at home with their boots off; officers not yet so far advanced in the hierarchy fleeing westward in well-laden cars, abandoning an undisciplined soldiery whose special concern was to bury its arms, escape the enemy, and loot the local populace; a government that was the very symbol of decay, crowned by a president who "trotted behind the Government like an usher"—all of them evidently watched by a stolid, solid peasantry who on occasion summoned up courage enough to cry, "Get out. If you had fought, you'd be fed now instead of having to beg." Exceptions to this general panorama Dutourd admitted. But the prevailing mood, he insisted, had been a lighthearted abandonment. From start to finish the war had been absurd. Nothing could be more absurd, then, than this defeat. . . .

. . . This thesis of the absurd defeat rested on an unwarranted assumption. "Without realising it," wrote Dutourd, "the *Canard Enchaîné* discovered the motto of slavery. By repeating and repeating, 'What do we care?' we ended up not caring about losing the war, being occupied, dishonored, and trampled on." . . .

. . . But surely the conclusion of mass indifference was . . . unjustified. . . . It was no exaggeration to say that the war had found France in "a certain disarray, as regards our state of mind," as Daladier so delicately and elliptically put it during a secret session debate. As no observer could doubt, energies and aggressions were directed against Frenchmen that might better have been harnessed to the war effort. The unanimous applause in the

Chamber greeting the Premier's famous remark in December, 1939, about the determination of the government to be "sparing of French blood" might have been as unrealistic as the promise was politically expedient and eventually worthless. The one thing it did not indicate was indifference. . . .

. . . Like the fallacy of national indifference, Dutourd's assumption of two generations, 1914 and 1939, one brave, one spineless, seems less than convincing. Evidence of shockingly bad morale existed, of course. That General Maurice Gamelin had spent part of his last days on active service drawing up an indictment of the common soldier is true. "Disposed to criticize ceaselessly all those having the least authority," ran his report which the government had requested on the eve of his dismissal from the supreme army command, "encouraged in the name of civilization to enjoy a soft daily life, today's serviceman did not receive in the years between the wars the moral and patriotic education which would have prepared him for the drama in which the country's destiny is going to be played out." The allies of France were equally critical, and Lieutenant General Sir Alan Brooke, commanding the Second Corps, British Expeditionary Force, stood appalled beside General André G. Corap as a slovenly winter parade passed in review. Brooke recalled, "I can still see those troops now. . . . What shook me most . . . was the look in the men's faces, disgruntled and insubordinate looks." . . . But the French Army was nothing if not diverse. Not every division belonged to the reservist, undertrained, and underequipped Series B formations, or to the "apartment-house janitors" of the Maginot Line, as described by Dutourd, "trailing about the corridors in slippers, playing innumerable games of cards under the silent guns, yawning from morning to night." The whole French Army had not simply waited to be captured or bolted before the enemy, as Adolf Hitler was soon informed. "Very marked differences become apparent in the French when their military ability is evaluated," he wrote to the Duce on May 25. "There are very bad units side by side with excellent ones. On the whole difference in quality between the active and nonactive divisions is extraordinarily noticeable. Many of the active units have fought desperately, the reserve units are for the most part obviously not equal to the impact of battle on morale." The reality and the record then were more complicated than many critics suggested. If it had not been so there would have been no evacuation at Dunkirk—and not even a six weeks' war. . . .

All in all, without wishing in any way to contribute to what Dutourd called the myth of the glorious defeat in French history, one might still feel that comparisons between 1914 and 1940 were difficult, even impossible, and that whatever purpose they served, it was not that of demonstrating that the generation of 1940 was unworthy of its fathers. An army in defeat is unlikely to look very well at any time. . . .

. . . Clever and telling though a social critic like Dutourd may be, he does not in this instance prove much more illuminating than an old Marshal of France who before the event had diagnosed the malady, predicted the demise of the patient, and arranged a program for his resurrection—all in the certainty that almighty providence had delegated powers and that the result was sure. "It's an accepted fact," Pétain told war veterans in 1938, "that defeat always brings Frenchmen to life." The thesis of the absurd defeat, like the thesis of defeat by conspiracy or by incredible bungling (the unnecessary defeat), has the attractiveness and the conviction of simplicity. Moreover, as it requires little thought and apparently eliminates every technical difficulty as irrelevant, it has a certain therapeutic value ... in a disintegrating domestic situation where the national psyche has been the object of a thousand prescriptions. But anyone who tried to wrestle with the question of the French Army alone, as being the principal problem of 1940 would have to do more than blacken the generals and ridicule the men. ("For in the last analysis," Daladier insisted before the Parliamentary Commission, "this French defeat was a military defeat. Its causes were profoundly military.") The careful studies already made of this army, its leaders, its doctrines, and its struggles with the civilians show the complications involved in trying to estimate the state of the French war machine and the responsibilities for its condition and employment. It would not do simply to repeat ... after Daladier the very evident half-truth that legislature and people never refused the army anything it wanted. It would not do simply to fix on the Marshal's notorious preface to General Louis Chauvineau's unhappily titled and timed book *Une invasion, est-elle encore possible?* (it appeared in March, 1939), because one would at once be confronted by Pétain's article in the *Revue des deux mondes* for 1935, warning against a blitzkrieg and the menace of aircraft which were, he said, becoming "more and more formidable." For the fact was that if one combed the pages of the military journals he could find pretty much whatever he sought. The notion that French military thought between the wars was entirely sterile would certainly not stand. The great problem was rather to discover who fixed the pattern, when and why. For, as was pointed out years ago, generals like Pétain and Weygand had "haphazardly talked about everything, merely increasing the confusion."

And naturally not only French military doctrine was in question. What about the vast and vague subject of morale? What about the human material the nation provided, the indictment of their fellow countrymen by the great commanders? What had happened, for instance, to the complaints about the poor quality of officers being turned out? What truth was there in that unforgettable and shattering portrait Lucien Rebatet sketched of his army comrades—an undisciplined armed horde, broken down, utterly out of condition, potbellied and humpbacked, with the doctors taking almost anyone capable of simple locomotion? Such statements might be shown to be mere literary exaggerations, or matters of fact; they could hardly be ignored. ...

What of the unending social wars of the Republic, of the effects achieved by the outlawed Communist party in its increasingly defeatist publications and activities during the long, wretched winter of 1939–1940? What of the provocative—though in wartime veiled—diatribes of *Gringoire, Candide,* and *Je suis partout* among Frenchmen of another social milieu? What of that deep-seated tradition of pacifism which in the 1930's gained ground with the intelligentsia of the Right (where earlier it had been the preserve chiefly of the Left) and was to lead everywhere to a militant neutralism opposed to the policy of external commitments east or west, expressing itself in literary, political, business, and labor circles, feeding upon the social struggle, driven temporarily underground by the outbreak of war, until it emerged in the dark days as a full-fledged and insistent defeatism? So many considerations converged on that ultimate question involved in explaining the fall of France. . . .

All this, then, merely suggests that the fall of France poses a problem not only in internal matters, military and civil, political and social . . . but in diplomacy and allied warfare also. . . . It becomes evident that simple formulas explaining defeat or lost opportunities for victory will not suffice. More seriously, perhaps, they are misleading. Possibly at this point the haunting title of Marc Bloch's little study may be recalled, the best title anyone has yet chosen: *Strange Defeat.* And there comes to mind also those evocative opening words of that other, very different book, Antoine de Saint Exupéry's *Pilote de guerre,* "Surely I must be dreaming. . . ."

The war ended, however, not because it was absurd . . . but because for a whole concatenation of reasons it had become impossible. "We did not go on fighting," De Saint Exupéry remarked later, "because the whole army understood instinctively that it was no use." However vague and partial such a formula as defeat by bewilderment might be, it would at the very least seem superior to defeat by conspiracy, defeat through fatality, defeat at the hands of outraged providence, or merely the unnecessary defeat. As for the absurd defeat and the golden memory of Galliéni's taxicabs in that other war which for twenty years was the cause of pride, fear, and sorrow, comparison of the two seems unprofitable—the product of nostalgia for a lost and comfortable past: a remembrance of happier things past. . . .

SUGGESTIONS FOR FURTHER READING

General: JACQUES CHASTENET, *Histoire de la Troisième République,* vols. V–VII (Paris, 1960–63); DAVID THOMSON, *Democracy in France since 1870* (4th ed.; New York and London, 1964); FRANÇOIS GOGUEL, *La Politique des partis sous la IIIᵉ République* (2nd ed.; Paris, 1958); CHARLES BETTELHEIM, *Bilan de l'économie française, 1919–1946* (Paris, 1947); ALEXANDER WERTH, *The Twilight of France, 1933–40* (New York and London, 1942); JAMES JOLL (ed.), *The Decline of the Third Republic*

(London, 1955); Special: EUGEN WEBER, *Action Française: Royalism and Reaction in Twentieth Century France* (Stanford, Calif., 1962); GORDON A. CRAIG and FELIX GILBERT (eds.), *The Diplomats* (Princeton, 1953); PETER LARMOUR, *The French Radical Party in the 1930's* (Stanford, Calif., 1964); CHARLES A. MICAUD, *The French Right and Nazi Germany, 1933–1939* (Durham, N.C., 1943; reprinted, New York, 1964); JEAN-BAPTISTE DUROSELLE, "France and the Crisis of March 1936," in EVELYN M. ACOMB and MARVIN L. BROWN, JR. (eds.), *French Society and Culture since the Old Regime* (New York, 1966), pp. 244–265; WILLIAM E. SCOTT, *Alliance Against Hitler: The Origins of the Franco-Soviet Pact* (Durham, N.C., 1962); JOHN T. MARCUS, *French Socialism in the Crisis Years, 1933–1936* (New York, 1958); GEORGES DUPEUX, *Le Front Populaire et les élections de 1936* (Paris, 1959); HENRY W. EHRMANN, *The French Labor Movement from Popular Front to Liberation* (New York, 1947); ARTHUR MITZMAN, "The French Working Class and the Blum Government, 1936–37," *International Review of Social History*, IX (1964), 363–390; RAOUL GIRARDET, "Notes sur l'esprit d'un fascisme français, 1934–1939," *Revue française de science politique*, V (1955), 529–546; PHILIP C. F. BANKWITZ, "Maxime Weygand and the Fall of France: A Study in Civil-Military Relations," *Journal of Modern History*, XXXI (1959), 225–242; MARC BLOCH, *Strange Defeat* (London, 1949); DONALD C. MCKAY, "The Third Republic in Retrospect," *Virginia Quarterly Review*, XXXIII (1957), 46–60; Biographical: JOEL COLTON, *Léon Blum, Humanist in Politics* (New York, 1966); RUDOLPH BINION, *Defeated Leaders: The Political Fate of Caillaux, Jouvenel and Tardieu* (New York, 1960).

Chapter Sixteen

"FRANCE
AGAINST HERSELF":
VICHY
AND THE
RESISTANCE

PROBABLY NO PERIOD in modern French history was as anguished and fratricidal as 1940–44, the years of defeat and occupation, Vichy and collaboration, Free France and the Resistance. France was split in two, both by the armistice line laid down by the Germans in June, 1940, and by the choice millions of Frenchmen eventually had to make between either obeying a regime subservient to the occupier or joining what long appeared to be a hopeless struggle against him, whether under de Gaulle or in the Maquis. Frenchmen fought Frenchmen in a war within a war, and the latent struggle between the "two Frances" created by the Revolution was waged with bullets as well as words.

By terms of the armistice agreement, some three fifths of the country was occupied by Germany, all French prisoners of war remained in her hands, occupation costs were charged to the French, and the free zone was virtually disarmed. France did retain her fleet and Empire. The government of Marshal Pétain, who had been brought to power to arrange an armistice, established itself at the spa of Vichy. There on July 10, the guilt-ridden and confused Parliament abdicated its authority to the elderly Marshal, conferring all powers on him and giving him the authority to "promulgate by one or more acts, the new constitution of the French State." The Third Republic died unmourned, and Pétain wasted no time in putting his "National Revolution" into effect.

The nature of this "National Revolution" is outlined by the French historian Robert Aron in the first selection. Pétain assumed almost dictatorial powers, ruled by decree, and aimed at nothing less than the total regeneration of France to cure her of what he considered the accumulated evils in her political, economic, social, and cultural life. His aim was to strengthen the state, the family, the church, and tradition against the pernicious influences of secularism, individualism, republicanism, capitalism, and industrialism. Symbolically, the Revolutionary triad, "Liberty, Equality, Fraternity" was replaced by "Work, Family, Country." Although some of these changes were overdue and even necessary, many (especially measures against democratic institutions, foreigners, and Jews) were alien to the best of France's heritage.

But it was one thing to attempt to revitalize France from within; it was another to deal with the concrete realities of German power and the continuing war. In the occupied zone, Germany annexed Alsace-Lorraine in violation of the armistice, attached the Nord and Pas-de-Calais Departments to the German military command in Belgium, surveyed and interfered with the French administration, and exploited the region for her own purposes. In the second selection, by Henri Michel, a French specialist on the 1940–44 period, the nature of the relations between Germany and Vichy are described, and the increasingly harsh demands made by the occupier discussed. Under Pierre Laval, the Vichy regime, which had sought to retain its independence of action and avoid the worst, gradually moved from a policy of collaboration to subservience, especially after the German invasion of the free zone in November, 1942. The Germans held the whip hand and exerted great pressures on Laval, who desperately attempted to deflect them, until Vichy had little left to bargain with. The increasingly feeble Marshal Pétain became a figurehead with scant authority by the time of the Allied invasion of June, 1944.

The strength of Vichy waned as that of Free France and the internal Resistance grew. A lonely exile who fled his country in June, 1940, to carry on the fight against Germany, Charles de Gaulle, became the focus and voice of the Free French movement. This little-known brigadier general with unquenchable faith in the honor of France and his own destiny was forced to depend on British help. But he gradually gathered around him the nucleus of a second, free France. By the end of 1940 he had rallied several thousand Frenchmen and won over colonies in Africa, Asia, and the Pacific. The next year a French National Committee was established in London, and by 1942 it had become a virtual government in exile. Despite Allied suspicion and hostility, de Gaulle managed to gain the upper hand in liberated Algeria by outmaneuvering General Giraud, and began to make plans for the reorganization of postwar France.

The program of Free France is traced in the third selection, also by Henri Michel. He emphasizes both its reformist and traditionalist aspects—national regeneration and national grandeur—which de Gaulle hoped would supplant the discredited Third Republic and authoritarian Vichy regime with a socially responsible and politically viable government, one that would unite all Frenchmen and insure a key role for France in world affairs. But for all their antipathy, it must be noted, the programs of Vichy and Free France shared common ideas about what France ought to become.

The increased tempo of the Resistance within France and then the Allied invasion in 1944 brought the war to a close: Germany was driven out, the Vichy regime dissolved, and a Provisional Government headed by General de Gaulle installed itself in liberated Paris. But the months of fighting that began with the Normandy landings of June, the Maquis attacks, militia reprisals, German atrocities, and localized vengeances, tore France apart, so that the physical agony of Liberation was worse than the spiritual agony of defeat.

In the final selection, Stanley Hoffmann, Professor of Government at Harvard, weighs the impact that the war had on French society and politics. Unlike the 1914–18 conflict, which did not substantially modify the structure of French life, that of 1940–44 broke what Hoffman calls the "stalemate society" so characteristic of the Third Republic. This society esteemed stability and security above innovation and dynamism, and cultivated an appropriate political style that produced much discussion but little forward motion. Weakened by the crisis of the late 1930's, it came under full attack by both Vichy and the Resistance for different reasons. The end result was to shake France from her prewar lethargy and make her reshape her institutions. But, as he points out, if French society and economy have been transformed as a consequence, no new political synthesis has emerged from the war.

Although the human and physical cost of the war was great and the task of reconstruction enormous, the shock of defeat, the consciousness of the need to undertake drastic changes in French life, and the national energy released by victory gave the country hopes of a brighter future under the Fourth Republic to come.

VICHY'S "NATIONAL REVOLUTION"

ROBERT ARON

"We, Marshal of France, Head of the French State . . . the Council of Ministers being in agreement, DECREE . . ." These words, drawn up by the Government of a defeated country, which was three-fifths occupied by the enemy, preceded, from the 11th July, 1940, all Pétain's legislative decisions: after seventy years of a Parliamentary Republic they strike one as somewhat surprising.

The three first constitutional acts . . . promulgated in the *Journal Officiel* of the 12th July, implied indeed a radical change of regime.

Drawn up secretly by [Pierre] Laval and [Raphael] Alibert even before the sitting of the Assembly, safe from all German interference, according to plans conceived long before by Pétain's "preceptor," these documents form one of the shortest and most brutal pieces of constitutional machinery of which French history can furnish an example.

By Constitutional Act No. 1, which consisted of five lines, Pétain abrogated the Presidency of the Republic and declared that he "assumed the functions of the Head of the French State."

By Constitutional Act No. 2, the rights and prerogatives of the Head of the State were defined in ten paragraphs. He acquired "full governmental powers," and the power of appointing and dismissing "Ministers and Secretaries of State who are responsible only to him." "He exercises legislative power in the Council of Ministers" until the formation of new Assemblies and, after their formation, "in case of external tension or serious internal crisis." "He promulgates the laws and assures their being put into execution." "He has the right of appointment to all civil and military posts, for which the law has not laid down some other method of nomination." "He is invested with control of the armed forces," "with the right of reprieve and amnesty," "the right to negotiate and ratify treaties," "and may declare a state of siege."

There was only one reservation, which corresponded to the pledges given on the 10th July: "He cannot declare war without previous assent from the Legislative Assemblies."

This constitutional law gave Pétain greater powers than those of the ancient Kings of France.

Constitutional Act No. 3 dealt with the future of Parliament. In conformity with the promise given by Laval on the 10th July in Pétain's name, Clause 1 left the Senate and the Chamber of Deputies in being, "until

Robert Aron, *The Vichy Regime, 1940–44* (London: Putnam & Co., Ltd., 1958), pp. 161–164, 173–180. Copyright, 1958, by Putnam & Company, of London. Reprinted by permission of McIntosh, McKee and Dodds, Inc.

the formation of the Assemblies laid down by the Constitutional Law of the 10th July, 1940," but Clause 2 circumvented the promise made to the National Assembly by placing Parliament in recess:

"The Senate and the Chamber of Deputies are adjourned until further orders.

"In future they may only meet on being convoked by the Head of the State."

Constitutional Act No. 4, signed immediately after the 12th July, and promulgated in the *Journal Officiel* on the 23rd July, dealt with the provisional structure of the new French State. It dealt with the questions of the deputy and successor to the Head of the State; it re-established the *"delphinat,"* a dignity abolished in France since the Ancien Régime, and whose first incumbent was to be Pierre Laval. . . .

A fortnight later, there was a fifth Constitutional Act, signed on 30th July and promulgated on the 31st July in the *Journal Officiel*, inaugurating an institution which was to allow the new Head of the State to bring his Republican predecessors to trial:

"A Supreme Court of Justice is created whose organisation, competence and procedure will be laid down by law."

This was an explicit document which made political repression subject to the Marshal's pleasure. Justice was also subject to his authority.

Constitutional Act No. 6, of the 1st December, 1940, published in the *Journal Officiel* of the 4th December, 1940, authorised the Marshal to pronounce the disqualification of members of Parliament. . . .

Long before the promulgation of this last Act, the Republic was already dead. In most public buildings, the democratic formula "Liberty, Equality, Fraternity" had been replaced by "Work, Family, Country." . . .

Seven days after the vote of the National Assembly there began a series of discriminatory measures which in fact resulted in the abolition of the Rights of Man as defined by the Declaration of 1789.

This new legislation re-introduced two offences which had long been off the statute book, the offence of subversive opinion and the offence of belonging to subversive organisations, the latter permitting an innocent man, if he belonged to some organisation which was considered detrimental, to be prosecuted; it also made these laws retroactive.

These discriminatory measures, which upset the traditional idea of the law, followed quickly upon each other during the first months.

In July, they made it possible that, by simple ministerial decree, all magistrates, functionaries, civil or military personnel could be relieved of their posts; they closed all public employment to people born of a foreign father; they enjoined the revision of all naturalisations granted since 1927; they announced that all persons who had left French Metropolitan territory for abroad between 10th May and 30th June, 1940, were disqualified from holding French nationality; and they created a Supreme Court of Justice to try the Ministers and ex-Ministers of the Third Republic who were "accused of having committed crimes or misdemeanours in the exercise or on the occasion of their functions or who had betrayed their responsibilities."

In August, all secret associations were forbidden; all civil servants had to take an oath that they did not belong to any forbidden organisation.

This law of the 13th August was aimed in particular at Freemasonry.

In September there was a law which allowed, on a mere prefectorial decision, the arrest of all persons deemed "dangerous" to National Defence or Public Security. The law also set up a Court-Martial for the purpose of trying, as a matter of urgency, the followers of de Gaulle.

In October there was a law concerning the status of Jews, which prohibited them from holding most public posts and positions of control in the Press and in industry; there were also laws authorising the internment of foreign Jews and withdrawing the status of French citizenship from Algerian Jews. There was also a law suspending General Councils and Councils of Arrondissements.

In November, a new law authorised the Ministry of the Interior to announce the dismissal from office of General Councillors, Councillors of Arrondissements and Municipal Councillors.

These discriminatory measures formed one of the most completely repressive series of laws that France had ever known: from then on, there was no single person in France, whatever his associations or his personal status, who might not become subject to administrative sanctions. There were certain categories of Frenchmen who, *a priori*, were excluded from the protection of the laws. There was now no longer any elected political assembly which was not subject to the decisions of the Government. The Republican regime was dead. . . .

The National Revolution had not for sole ambition the creation of a new political structure or of the reformation of institutions: it also wished, and perhaps principally wished, to affect morals and transform man himself.

The idea of a sterling Frenchman, of a new man arising by Government decree and by the will of the prince, was a somewhat idyllic and paternalistic conception: nevertheless, the National Revolution neglected nothing that might conduce to his appearance by formulating a comprehensive system of measures which were to accompany him, stage by stage, through life from the cradle to his coming legally of age.

The school teachers, whose duty it was to form this *homo nationalis*, were to mould him, not only with their knowledge, but also with their loyalty and their morality. There would no longer be teachers such as the Right and the Marshal himself had denounced for their subversive outlook and for their responsibility for the defeat. They knew that, if they did not keep loyal to the regime and the virtues it encouraged, nothing could protect them from the appropriate sanctions.

The school must be right-thinking: it must also think correctly, its intellectual tone must be on a level with its moral tone. Teachers from now on must have passed through secondary education and have taken the first part of the *baccalauréat*. The standard of their teaching would be improved: the fledgling *homo nationalis* would profit by it from the start.

He would also benefit, if he profited by secondary education, from being obliged to learn Greek and Latin. He would be taught civics: "His duty towards the State and the general interest, respect for the law, the meaning and dignity of the idea of service, his duty towards his country and national and patriotic pride."

Finally, he would be told about God, which would do no harm: God whom the Republican school had made into the "Great Absent" would thus return to the curriculum.

"*Mens sana*," or "*sacra*," "*in corpore sano*," physical education would give the child as much bodily strength as mental strength: "Ten hours a week in primary education, nine hours in secondary education shall be devoted to activities in the open air: games and physical education, outings, excursions, singing, manual labour . . ."

As soon as the child left the primary school, another school received him and perfected the moulding of his character, the youth camps, in which he spent eight months.

And thus, when the child was grown up, he would be in the bosom of the new Order, a conscientious and organised citizen.

The Guardian State would protect his family and professional life.

Pétain's first object was to keep the woman in the home and this led him to propose Government measures benefiting the girl who became engaged, the mother and the father of a family. . . .

The *virgo nationalis* would receive a grant from the State if she promised not to take any paid job. The *mater nationalis*, after her third child, would have the advantage of a *carte de priorité*, while her husband would have the right of working overtime at his trade and, if he inherited money, to financial allowances which might amount to an exemption from tax.

He was also protected against the vice of alcoholism which ruins so many homes. The privilege of distilling was suppressed and certain detrimental beverages, such as absinthe, were forbidden.

Finally, if the individual wished to divorce, he would find more difficulty in doing so, and then only in grave and limited circumstances.

Moral health, physical health, family health . . . these were the personal benefits that, whether he liked it or not, the new man was to acquire under the National Revolution. And now he had to earn his living.

If he were a peasant, he was lucky! He benefited by all the measures which encouraged the return to, or the remaining on, the land: a re-organisation of the conditions of labour, re-distribution of abandoned land, and the repairing of his house. His trade was organised by an autonomist agricultural corporation in which big finance was no longer the dominant influence, and in which the State intervened only for purposes of control and co-ordination . . . in principle, of course.

If he were a labourer . . . he would have the advantage of a theoretically similar organisation, that of the Comités d'Organisation, which only the misfortunes of the times obliged to adopt a certain authoritarian appearance and to employ despotic methods.

If by any chance he were a doctor, he registered with the Conseil de l'Ordre, which maintained discipline in the profession and represented it with the Government.

If his natural eloquence had made of him a lawyer, he was rejoiced to see his profession re-organised by two measures, one of which implied a prohibition of all political action and the other of which altered the necessary professional qualifications. . . .

Preached at as an adolescent, honoured as the father of a family, organised as a worker, the new man might also be an ex-Serviceman, disciplined and respected, who could join the French Legion of Combatants, by taking an oath which was in conformity with the ideals of the regime:

"I swear to continue serving France honourably in peace as I have served her under arms.

"I swear to devote all my strength to the country, the family, and to work. I promise to give friendly and mutual aid to my comrades of both wars, and to remain faithful to the memory of those who fell on the field of honour. I freely accept the discipline of the Legion in everything that I may be ordered to do for the realisation of this ideal."

And with all this, what was to become of his political life? It appeared to be extremely reduced. The new order was hierarchical. Elections were abandoned, except in very limited cases.

No more voting, clearly. As far as local assemblies were concerned, the General Council and District Councils were suppressed and their functions handed over to the Prefects.

As for the Municipal Councils, if he lived in a township of at least 2,000 inhabitants, he still voted for the election of the Mayor and his Councillors. But in other cases, he had to leave to the Préfecture or the Government the duty of appointing his aediles.

At this birth of a new order, there were four important institutions, whose geneses are worth recounting in detail, in order to establish the political circumstances in which the National Revolution took place.

These are the Legion of Combatants, the Youth Camps, the Comités d'Organisation and the Agricultural Corporation. . . .

The problem of youth came to the fore at the armistice: in the first place it was a question of re-grouping the recruits of the 1940 class, who had been mobilised in the month of June and whose military life had consisted only of disaster.

For their benefit, the Law of the 30th July, 1940, created the Youth Camps, in which they were grouped for six months under the command of General de la Porte du Theil; on the 18th January, 1941, when this first stage was over, a new Law determined that all young Frenchmen of the age of twenty years in the free zone would be called up to these camps for eight months.

The avowed object of the Camps was to take in hand demoralised youth and prepare it for the tasks of the immediate future. But General de la Porte du Theil had another object; in complete agreement with the general staff of the army, he wished to maintain recruiting in the southern zone and camouflage reservists in a post-Youth Camp Association; thus, if the day came when hostilities were resumed, the Army Command would have at its disposal, over and above the army permitted by the armistice, a mass of disciplined and organised men, provided with transport, rations and arms hidden in secret depots.

But the material conditions in the Youth Camps became more and more harsh. General de la Porte du Theil was eventually to deplore that some of them gave the impression of being concentration camps.

In professional and economic matters, the new order was to be *co-ordinated and controlled.*

In practice, a distinction must be made between industry and commerce on the one hand, and agriculture on the other.

Contrary to its principles, the National Revolution inaugurated State direction over industry.

The Law of the 16th August, 1940, which created provisional Comités d'Organisation, completely subjected industry and commerce to the Government.

It established a Comité d'Organisation for every branch, giving it powers over every business within that branch whether it formed part of a Trust or was independent. Its composition and its activities were subject to the State; its directors could not be appointed without the agreement of the Minister of Production and Labour. Its decisions had to be ratified by him. Its competence extended over all professional matters: the census of businesses, production programmes, raw materials, salaries, hours and conditions of work, the price of products, etc.

Later . . . the State went even further towards direction and itself took decisions without consulting the Comités.

This inconsistency with the doctrine of the National Revolution is explained by the necessity to withstand the pressure of the occupying power.

The Law of the 16th August was . . . "a law required by the circumstances." . . . Considered and drawn up in forty-eight hours, 9th–10th August, 1940, by a committee of five people sitting almost continuously in the Minister's office, promulgated seven days after work on it had begun, its essential aim was to protect the industry of the northern zone against the pressure of the occupying power by interposing between the managers of isolated businesses and the German demands the screen of the French State.

The Law of the 18th September, 1940, concerning joint stock companies . . . took a "workman's pick" to one of the essential arrangements of modern capitalism: the personal irresponsibility of the directors of joint stock companies.

From then on the president of a board of administration was in the same position as a merchant, personally responsible for the management of the business before the law and his shareholders.

Furthermore, in order to prevent certain private interests dominating too large a proportion of the economic life of the country, pluralism was limited: no one could hold more than two presidencies of boards of administration. No one might be a member of more than eight such boards of businesses registered in France. This number was reduced to two for persons over seventy years old.

Finally, on the 9th November, 1940, three decrees, made under the Law of the 16th August, simultaneously dissolved centralised organisations whether of employers or Trades Unions. . . .

In fact, the directors of the Trusts preserved in most cases their influence. Was it not laid down that the State would choose the heads of the Comités d'Organisation among those "who were experienced in industry . . . owing to their previous positions and by their experience in management"?

On the other hand, agriculture was subject to a professional reorganisation which conformed to the doctrines of Vichy, that is to say, corporative and not centralised in the State.

The Law of the 2nd December, 1940, concerning the corporative organisation of agriculture inaugurated the Agricultural Corporation, the first proposal for which had been put forward by [Pierre] Caziot long before the advent of the totalitarian regimes.

Contrary to what had been done in industry, where the central organisations of Trades Unions and employers had been dissolved for political reasons, none of the organisations which had already been set up by the peasants to protect their interests was suppressed. Co-operative associations, mutual benefit associations, specialised organisations representing one or another form of production, all preserved their powers, some on a local level, others on a national scale. They merely took their place in a unifying structure which respected their autonomy.

The Assembly of Regional Delegates created a National Corporative Council and elected a permanent committee of ten members who were to administer the Corporation.

These diverse organisations no longer limited themselves, as had the agricultural associations before 1940, to representing and protecting their interests. They now had legal powers to "promote and administer the common interests of peasant families in the moral, social and economic spheres."

In principle, there was no control over the local committee: it chose its own chairman as it pleased. The nominations of the regional delegate and of the standing committee were submitted for ratification to the Minister of Agriculture, though he took no part in the elections. The Government Commissioners, who were allowed to attend local regional or national meetings, were limited to transmitting to the Minister for endorsement the regulations or decisions formulated by the meeting; they did not intervene in discussions. In all these cases, the State did not direct: it co-ordinated and controlled.

Thus, as opposed to the Fascist or National Socialist corporation, the French corporation was, in theory at least, an autonomist institution.

THE VICHY REGIME AND COLLABORATION

Henri Michel

. . . The Germans had considered it a clever idea to permit the existence in the southern zone of a French government that was seemingly free and which, for the time being, assured them that French forces would cease fighting and England would remain alone in the struggle. It ultimately would guarantee the application of an armistice agreement very advantageous to the victors. They considered that these temporary terms would not prevent them from imposing a peace treaty to their own liking on France at the right time.

As the war continued, however, the Reich felt an increasing need to possess powers which it had left in French hands. The Vichy government was useful to it in administering the territories which it could not directly control and was convenient for obtaining raw materials, supplies, and men, which it

Henri Michel, "Aspects politiques de l'Occupation de la France par les Allemands (juin, 1940–décembre, 1944), *Revue d'histoire de la Deuxième Guerre Mondiale*, quatorzième année, no. 54 (avril, 1964), 23–29, 36–39. Copyright by Presses Universitaires de France, 1964. Used by permission. Editors' translation.

consumed in great quantities. Cooperation within the framework of the armistice agreement thus had to be established and maintained, but with modifications in its terms at the Germans behest as circumstances required.

For its part, the Vichy government was recognized as the government of France by all foreign powers, including the United States and the Soviet Union. It possessed the remnant of an army, it ruled over an inviolate empire—one, however, that did not remain deaf to the siren call of rebellion —and even though partially disarmed, it did retain an important fleet at its disposal. But on several occasions the empire and fleet seemed threatened by the British, and thus the Germans were offered the possibility of enlisting the forces they had left France in their war against England. As for the Vichy government, it believed it could exploit the hopes and fears of the Germans in regard to the forces which France still had, in exchange for a reduction in the burdens of the armistice, promises by the Reich concerning the fate of France, and an increase in the very forces which would improve France's position at the signing of the peace treaty. From the temporary cooperation written into the armistice, one which the course of events tended to prolong, both sides gradually accepted the idea of political collaboration.

But if some Frenchmen occasionally placed great hopes, indeed their only hope, in this collaboration, the Vichy government had to take into account recalcitrant public opinion, the risks which accompanied a break with the Anglo-Saxons, and the real chances of a final German victory. For the Germans, engaged in a world war, the added factor of Vichy, minimal in itself, had significance only in a certain situation. Of course, the views of the two parties did not coincide, or at any rate, the relationship was most unequal because of the pressure which the occupier could exert on Vichy.

To what degree did the leaders of the Reich desire lasting collaboration with France, one capable of being continued after the war ended, one allotting France a choice position in a Europe dominated by Germany? The man whose policy this was appears to have been [Otto] Abetz, and he was virtually the only one. Founder of the Franco-German Committee before the war and married to a Frenchwoman, Abetz was first an adviser at the German embassy in Paris. On November 20, 1940, he became the German ambassador to Paris, responsible for all political questions in both zones. His titles and responsibilities thus apparently increased, but his audience remained limited.

In his memoirs, Abetz complains that he was neither heeded nor followed. There were, he writes, as few proponents of collaboration on the German as on the French side. Specifically, he reproaches Goering and Sauckel for having thought only of pillaging France. Indeed, Goering expressed his "ideas" on the question with cynical brutality: "The French, Belgian, and Dutch peoples are all our enemies and you will gain nothing for your cause through humanitarian measures. . . . The day [the English] invade, the Frenchman who dines with you today will quickly prove to you that he is and will remain the enemy of the Germans." . . .

The guidelines of German policy toward France seem to have been drawn by Goering, who, speaking to Laval on November 9, 1940, said: "The war against England is the beginning and the end of German policy. All decisions are dictated by military necessity." England today, the U.S.S.R. tomorrow—the enemy changed, but military necessity remained. The Reich possessed too many ways of imposing its wishes on the Vichy government to feel required to negotiate. Brought on stage as a lure, Abetz returned to the wings when force seemed preferable to diplomacy.

In order to bring the Vichy government around to their way of thinking, the Germans had three main weapons at their disposal in addition to the permanent threat to occupy the southern zone: sealing the demarcation line, exchanging war prisoners, and encouraging collaborationists in the occupied zone.

The object of the demarcation line was to separate the occupied zone from the free zone militarily, but the occupying authority made it an administrative, economic, and even political limit, using it on the French government like "the bit in a horse's mouth."

In the beginning, its operation was extremely harsh: postal communication between the two zones was suspended, identification cards (*auswies*) for crossing the line were handed out sparingly, each minister at Vichy could telephone only three or four minutes a day to Paris, and official letters had to be shown and opened at the German check point at Moulins. Some concessions were gradually obtained, such as the restoration of certain telephone and telegraph lines; limited deliveries of funds, administrative and commercial correspondence, and private correspondence on cards of standard format printed in advance, etc. But while persons under German jurisdiction or foreigners protected by the occupying authority entered the unoccupied zone freely, the line was tightly sealed like a frontier against passage in the other direction. Departments were cut in two, the authority of the Vichy government was considerably reduced in the northern zone, and products in oversupply in one zone were lacking in the other. The French were also faced with innumerable and painful family problems.

In a normal armistice an exchange of prisoners of war is arranged. According to Articles 19 and 20 of the German armistice agreement, all German prisoners of war were to be returned without delay, but all French prisoners remained captive "until the conclusion of peace." Thus, some 1,500,000 men became virtual hostages, a guarantee of the docility of the Vichy government. Marshal Pétain wanted to secure their freedom from the Reich—this was a principle of his policy—so these prisoners became the objects of bargaining in all negotiations of the "collaboration." All liberated prisoners pledged on their honor not to resume the fight aagainst the Reich, and were placed "on leave from captivity." A rupture of the armistice agreement risked causing the return to Germany of all freed prisoners of war, who numbered about 600,000 by 1944. . . .

In November, 1940, the Vichy government came to play the role of protector nation for its own prisoners, and [Georges] Scapini was charged with this mission, being given the rank of ambassador. Thus the prisoners were largely left to their own devices and had the discouraging feeling of having been abandoned. But the cost of these concessions was passive acceptance of their fate—Vichy counseled them to be resigned and discouraged escapes.

Every action which provoked the displeasure of the occupying authority was taken out in sanctions that caused the prisoners to suffer: a halt to the distribution of gift packages, a delay in forwarding mail, and an interruption in releases. The escape of General Giraud brought about brutalities forbidden by the Hague Conventions—there was no repatriation of prisoners, even the sick, and all, or nearly all, generals were placed in fortresses. In certain camps the commandants created additional hardships. Because of the great number of prisoners, the majority of French families was sadly affected by these actions. . . .

To these hostages, who were victims of the defeat, were added others, who were victims of the Compulsory Labor Service, or S.T.O. (*Service du Travail Obligatoire*), instituted by the Germans. In 1942, 100,000 French workers labored in Germany. This figure rose to 300,000 at the beginning of 1943 and reached 600,000 by the end of the same year. Of these, half were young men between eighteen and twenty-four. No international convention protected them, and the minute they crossed the border, these workers were subject to German laws and regulations. . . .

The true French collaborationists were . . . few but active. To be sure, the Vichy government had established a regime styled the "National Revolution," which might in many respects appear to have been inspired by fascist ideologies. . . . [But] the "National Revolution" differed profoundly from National Socialism. The latter was pagan and profoundly anti-Christian because Christianity was basically Jewish and because it infected nations with the germs of weakness, while Catholicism was constantly honored at Vichy. Moreover, Nazism was statist, whereas the "National Revolution," inspired by Maurras and the thinkers who attributed all the evils of the age to the propagation of the "principles of 1789," leaned toward regionalism and corporatism.

Thus it was in the northern zone that the collaborationists prospered. After having founded several movements that were harmless because they were so ridiculous, the Germans subsidized virtual political parties with experienced leaders: the Popular French Party (*Parti Populaire Français*) of [Jacques] Doriot, the Popular National Rally (*Rassemblement National*

Populaire) of [Marcel] Déat, and the Francism (*Francisme*) of [Marcel] Bucard. On July 15, 1940, [German ambassador] Abetz, in a report to General Streccius, concluded that "the agreements with politicians of every stripe, the creation of new newspapers and their success, and the number and strength of collaborationist organizations gave him reason to believe it was possible to influence political developments not only in the occupied zone, but also in the free zone," given the disarray of the population since the defeat and the hostility of the French toward every attempt by former members of Parliament to return.

The process was simple. Every German measure affecting France was magnified and extolled by the Paris press. The least reservation shown by the Vichy government unleashed this press against it. To avoid being bypassed, the Vichy government was compelled to give pledges. To be better heard and obeyed, it demanded on several occasions that it be allowed to move to Paris as the armistice agreement had provided. Under various pretexts . . . the Germans refused. In the northern zone the members of the collaborationist parties served as auxiliaries to the German forces. Over Vichy hung the constant threat that the Germans would unify all the collaborationist groups into a single party and that they would institute another French government entirely at its bidding at Paris. But they found it simpler to bring into the Vichy government itself some of the extreme collaborationists in their pay.

The way in which the occupier behaved toward the Vichy government is clearly illustrated by an oft-repeated but particularly dramatic example. In order to repress attempts on the lives of their soldiers, the Germans exacted the creation of a special French court, and the law establishing it was given retroactive authority. To force Vichy to yield, the Germans threatened to shoot 150 hostages without trial. The method, which became the rule, worked this way: the occupier put pressure and threats on the Vichy government to make it obey; the Vichy government surrendered to German demands after receiving a few concessions; Vichy placed some of the authority and forces left her at the disposal of the occupier in exchange for the abandonment of pressure and the withdrawal of threats, until new circumstances made new pressures and threats necessary.

The frontier which cut France in two, the hostages in prison camps, and the Parisian puppets brandished by the occupier were only the most visible signs of the great weakness of the Vichy regime. In these conditions, a collaboration between equals, between victor and vanquished, was possible only in an exceptional situation when the victor requested a favor. In general, the situation could be merely that of a dominant power and its satellite. . . .

After an Allied strategic initiative, the American invasion of North Africa, one of the most important clauses of the armistice agreement, the existence of an unoccupied zone with a theoretically free government, was finally annulled. On November 11, 1942, the German army entered the southern zone and occupied it in several hours. Two generals, one German, one Italian, were installed at Vichy. The Gestapo proceeded immediately to make arrests on its own authority, beginning with that of General Weygand. At the same time, Italian and German troops invaded Tunisia.

On November 13, Abetz put pressure on Vichy to make France declare war on the Allies. On November 14, [the General Delegate of the French Government] de Brinon arrived at Vichy bearing an ultimatum demanding a declaration of war within twenty-four hours. Up to a certain point the Reich again needed Vichy: it was important that in North Africa the Americans encounter resistance as strong and as lengthy as possible.

But events moved swiftly. Darlan's surrender made a declaration of war against England and the United States ineffectual. Actually, the Vichy government no longer held a single attribute of real sovereignty: all French territory was occupied by a foreign army, the armistice army was disbanded, the fleet lay at the sea bottom, and the empire seethed with rebellion. . . .

. . . France became a satellite state in the orbit of the Reich. Hitler considered the Vichy government subject to his orders, and wrote Pétain on April 28, 1943, that "in order for me to form a clear opinion of the political situation in France, I have summoned M. Laval, head of the government, to my general headquarters tomorrow." Abetz, the man who had sought mutual collaboration, was henceforth in disgrace.

Directly or by creating parallel organizations, the Germans took for their own use such forces as the Vichy government still had. On January 4, 1943, by a telephone call, Sauckel demanded 250,000 workers for the S.T.O.— they were to leave before March. A circular was sent to prison wardens ordering them to turn over to the Germans all prisoners they might claim. After an attempted assassination, Hitler exacted the destruction of an entire section of Marseilles, on January 30, 1943. The Militia (*Milice*), composed of "volunteers to assist in the maintenance of internal order," was imposed on the regular police. . . .

In exchange for so many services, Laval tried to secure a German promise concerning the future of France and her place in the "New Order." He wrote Hitler to this effect and met with him on April 29. Hitler refused to agree to any declaration whatsoever; all that counted was the needs of war, which necessitated all possible aid from occupied countries. Taking this point of view, Sauckel expressed his satisfaction concerning France, which, alone, "had carried out the program of supplying manpower 100 per cent."

German concessions affected only the usual points of detail such as the attachment of the Nord and Pas-de-Calais Departments to the German administration at Paris, abolition of the demarcation line (which no longer had a reason for being), and transformation of prisoners of war into "free workers." These actions served the occupying power, but they did not alter the occupation terms and in no way decided the future.

Meanwhile, beginning in the summer of 1943, France once more became a battlefield, due to the growth of the Resistance, the increased number of acts of sabotage and assassinations which it perpetrated, and the birth of the Maquis. With the Allied invasion of Normandy on June 6, 1944, completed by the invasion of the Mediterranean coast on August 15, France was again a major theater of operations. Henceforth the occupation authorities had a double concern—to check growing opposition and to bring those forces still at the disposal of the French under their command.

[In the fight] against the Maquis, the Germans and the mercenaries in their service relieved the "free corps" of gendarmes . . . instituted by Vichy and who appeared increasingly less reliable to them. . . .

But their favorite weapon quickly became brutal, ugly repression. The Germans refused to consider those in the Resistance as regular soldiers, proclaimed that "international law does not accord the protection that regular soldiers can claim to individuals participating in an insurrectionary movement against an occupying power." They also invoked the armistice agreement, which provided that French nationals who took up arms against the Reich could be treated as snipers, that is, liable to the death penalty.

To combat the Resistance, the Germans tempted the population with promises of rewards—the freeing of prisoners of war, for example—in exchange for information leading to the arrest of "terrorists." But it also employed terror. Patrols fired at uncovered windows; those who refused to reveal a cache of weapons were condemned to forced labor; property which sheltered members of the Resistance was destroyed, etc. . . . Arrests and searches multiplied.

French authority was rendered helpless by these events. It confined itself to publishing the German decisions and urging the population to obey them, "in order to avoid useless tears and grief." It thus presented no obstacle to repressive acts, even if it sometimes endeavored to mitigate them.

Meanwhile, the Germans gradually supplanted it. In the military zones, the Wehrmacht took charge of distributing passes. In December, 1943, [Joseph] Darnand, head of the Militia, was named Secretary General for the Maintenance of Order, after S.S. General Oberg threatened to assume control of the French police. The penal administration was removed from the Minister of Justice and attached to the Secretariat, and prisoners were thus subject to the Militia, whose orders of March 12, 1944, indicated clearly that its authority stemmed exclusively from the German commander in the region. Since January 10, Darnand had had the power to create courts martial, where all the judicial guarantees of common law were suspended.

Besides taking charge of all French forces of repression, the Germans demanded that all changes in laws planned by the Vichy government be first approved by them. Finally, the old threat became a reality, when the leaders of the collaborationist parties of Paris were introduced into the Vichy government itself.

And still the fiction continued. While pretending to see Pétain as the head of state recognized by the armistice agreement, but henceforth treating him like Schussnigg or Hacha, the Germans dragged him from chateau to chateau before carting him off to Germany in their baggage and installing him at Sigmaringen. But by this time, the occupation of France was entering its last moments.

FREE FRANCE AND ITS PLANS FOR THE FUTURE OF FRANCE

Henri Michel

General de Gaulle defined Free France ... as "the great current, bond, and heart of national revival." To be sure, this revival was first and foremost that of the French fighting force, but it was also that of the nation in all its forms. In May, 1942, just after securing the allegiance of the Resistance Movement, de Gaulle had demanded that Fighting France "not be confined to a purely military organization." In October, 1942, he wrote President Roosevelt that he would not recoil from using the word "political" "if it rallied the French nation in the war," because "only the French can be the judge of French interests."

The dispute with General Giraud hastened this development. Beyond the immediate problem of uniting French forces in the struggle, there was also that of ... French institutions after the Liberation, and beyond that the broader problem of the "great regeneration" which victory would necessarily bring with it. Winning the war was the primary objective, of course, but the conduct of the war had already become a political question of the highest order—a fact which de Gaulle emphatically made clear to Giraud on several occasions. In any case, how could the war be waged without the post-war period being considered? The authority and prestige of the Third Republic were destroyed, and the government which had emerged from defeat, Vichy, was discredited. How could the void be filled other than by the new forces that helped to revitalize the country? It fell to Free France— which increasingly identified itself with France herself—to be ready for the tasks which the fulfillment of its mission certainly required during the Liberation and perhaps even after it.

Henri Michel, *Histoire de la France Libre* (Paris: Presses Universitaires de France, 1963). © 1963 Presses Universitaires de France. Used by permission. Translation by Charles L. Noyes.

THE DEVELOPMENT OF GENERAL DE GAULLE'S IDEAS

The Free French, including those who formed its original nucleus, belonged to all schools of French thought. Although they rightly denied that they were émigrés, they could not escape the fact that they were exiles, cut off from their country and involved in an enterprise which they sometimes felt was hopeless. They were thus forced to define their self-image more precisely. Accused of being in the pay of the British, they proved inflexibly uncompromising towards their Allies, on whom they were dependent. Assailing the French State for abandoning the colonial empire, they became the protectors of its smallest pieces and displayed . . . imperialist tendencies. Some, who feared being labeled sympathizers of the Third Republic, hurled the very taunts and slanders against it which had been the monopoly of the extreme right before the war. They resorted to a violent Germanophobia in order to combat the movement towards collaboration under way in France. In short, their very reason for being, a haughty and exalted patriotism, bordered on traditional nationalism, which was not vitiated by a certain admiration for and imitation of totalitarian regimes. At first there was a touch of xenophobia, even anti-semitism added to the permanent traits of Free France—anti-parliamentarism, the mystique of the leader, and an attraction to one-party rule.

But events gradually altered the face of the movement, and its leader showed the way. A man of tradition and duty, General de Gaulle had been greatly disillusioned by the "betrayal of the notables." After his initial failure to make their most important representatives take the lead, he had expected that the government officials, great military leaders, high figures in the administration, members of parliament, and captains of business and industry would rally to him. Most of them had not only failed to do so, but even approved of the Vichy regime's submission to, if not actual collaboration with, the enemy. On the other hand, the ranks of ordinary Frenchmen—teachers, civil servants, railway workers, labor union members—provided the supporters of Free France and the founders of the Resistance. The fact that worth and ability were inversely proportional to social standing came as a bitter revelation.

The heroic and merciless struggle waged by the Soviet people may have provided useful examples of the inexhaustible reserves of strength and true power of the popular masses. There were indeed Frenchmen in London known for their "left-wing leanings" . . . and the dispute with Giraud reinforced this tendency as the demands of propaganda required. It had already been confirmed even earlier by the arrival of Resistance fighters from the "Left" like Christian Pineau, André Phillip, and Philippe Brossolette. But long before, a change had apparently already taken place in de Gaulle's own thinking. For example, he wrote René Pleven that he had chosen a union leader, Adrien Tixier, over a diplomat as the Free French delegate to the United States because, as he said, "the great question of tomorrow will be the social question."

THE EMPIRE

To keep the Empire in the war—or to force its re-entry—to preserve it intact against the cupidity of other powers and even to expand it as circumstances might allow . . . and to exalt the "civilizing mission" of France in her overseas possessions—such were the primary, if not the permanent, concerns of the Free French, many of whom had once served in the colonial administration and army, as well as belonged to colonial business circles.

Equatorial Africa provided the starting point for the movement, which was due to the work of its Governor General, [Félix] Eboué. The isolation of the territory he administered enabled him to fulfill his cherished ideals. Eboué . . . believed that colonialism had to serve the natives, who were not "a means, but an end in themselves." Rejecting assimilation, the golden rule of French colonialism, he considered the native no "isolated and adaptable individual," even though his mind might seem primitive by European standards, but rather "a human being possessing his own traditions and bound to his family, village and tribe, capable of progress in his own environment and probably doomed if taken from it." . . .

The role of the colonist had to change entirely: he must no longer exploit the land only for his own profit. He should establish model farms that would serve as examples for the progressive improvement of native holdings.

General de Gaulle immediately supported Eboué's policy. "Thanks to you," he wrote in satisfaction, "the war will not have delayed the progress and development of the status of the subject and dependent peoples of France."

In protectorates such as Syria and Lebanon, the native elites were also heard from and put forward their own demands. Even before the return of the Free French forces there, Generals de Gaulle and Catroux were convinced that the mandated territories must be granted independence and, despite some difficulties, they made and kept this promise. But what were the implications for the rest of the Empire, especially North Africa?

Even before leaving London, de Gaulle had in a message to the Moslems proclaimed "the union of all Frenchmen, without racial or religious discrimination." After his Constantine speech [of 1943] several tens of thousands of Algerian Moslems were granted French citizenship and allowed a greater voice in the administration of their country.

The Brazzaville Conference of January, 1944, marked the logical outcome of this new policy. Composed exclusively of administrators, it explicitly rejected autonomy for the African territories and any development outside the French community. But the Conference did endorse the continuation of traditional political institutions, administrative decentralization which "encouraged political identity," and the substitution of the idea of a French federation for that of the Empire. A step had been taken which would permit no return to the past.

THE REPUBLIC

Out of principle, the Free French recognized republican legality and solemnly reestablished it in those territories seized from the Vichy government, notably Réunion. But there was hardly a speech dealing with the prewar period in which General de Gaulle did not sharply criticize the Third Republic for it slack of authority, its "shadow governments," its "political impotence," its scandals and intrigues, the moral weakness and mediocrity of its leaders, its social inequalities and timidity in the initiative and use of political power, and the subordination of national to private interests.

In his declaration to the Resistance Movements in the spring of 1942, de Gaulle showered equal abuse on the prewar and wartime governments: "The former had abdicated in defeat after decadence had paralyzed it."

Parliament in particular had a bad press among the Free French. It was generally felt that France would be condemned to perpetual impotence if the old parties re-emerged. The rivalry with Giraud and the hostility of the United States forced General de Gaulle along a path which he probably followed only with great reluctance. Alongside the secretly reorganized Communist and Socialist parties, the old parties . . . were also represented in the National Council of the Resistance organized by Jean Moulin. But now virtually lifeless for want of men and organization, their participation was necessary to show that the entire French political spectrum was behind de Gaulle. At the same time, this implicitly gave them a right to re-emerge after the war.

On several occasions, however, General de Gaulle expressed his views on the "Fourth Republic." They allowed little room for parliamentary intrigues. He did not formally propose a constitution because of his promise to let the French people decide their own destiny. Nevertheless, he did commit himself to "a real democracy, without the machinations of politicians and morass of intrigues." He argued that a firmly based authority was necessary, and before the Consultative Assembly in Algiers, he outlined the separation of power between "an elected body holding strictly to a political and social role quite different from that of the Third Republic, and an executive whose power and stability embodied the authority of the state and the international greatness of France."

Moreover, his London and Algiers experiences caused de Gaulle to reiterate his belief that whatever their constitutional forms, great national enterprises were realized only by a close harmony between a leader and his people, the one guiding and relying on the other.

ECONOMIC AND SOCIAL REFORMS

The prewar divisions among Frenchmen, one of the causes of defeat, resulted from a chronic social malaise, for which patriotism must find a cure. Led to the conclusion that "France had been betrayed by her ruling and privileged elites," de Gaulle condemned "the decrepit ruling class, worn-out politicians, somnolent academicians, generals exhausted by their rank ..., the old facade of pomp and show, crumbling hierarchies, and sordid intrigues." The old elites, whose worthlessness the war had proven, thus would have to give way to the new, who had been revealed by the same ordeal.

If there was a desire for revolution, it aimed primarily at a change in personnel and a moral transformation. "The new spirit," Eboué declared, "the spirit of national community, must, with all the sacrifices it demands, profoundly alter habits and replace selfish calculation. Unselfishness alone will restore vitality and nobility to our country."

But experience had shown that it was the common people who had answered the call of their country in its distress, and whose patriotism deserved to be rewarded. It was only right, de Gaulle argued, that "the country give its children, workers, artisans, and peasants their due in the attainment of the great common good." It was necessary, General de Larminat insisted at Algiers, "to resolve the social question in such a way as to achieve the unity of Frenchmen as well as the greatness of France," so that morality might triumph and injustices no longer compromise French national unity.

The many men of tradition among the volunteers of the Free French thus came to the conclusion that patriotism would achieve the necessary social and economic revolution. General de Gaulle defined his objectives in this way: "No monopoly, no faction must be allowed to dominate the state or to determine the fate of individuals. ... The nation must recover what belongs to it. ... The nation desires that national resources, labor and technology no longer be exploited for the profit of a few."

General de Gaulle himself was no economist, and he had never discussed economic problems in his prewar writings. He made no mention of socialism, quoted no theoretical works, and did not attack the foundations of capitalism, only its abuses. But he did condemn trusts, and envisaged an improvement in the condition of the working class through a managed economy, on the assumption, of course, that the great transformation needed would be accomplished in an orderly fashion from above. ...

FOREIGN POLICY

The Free French had been inspired by the traditional Germanophobia of French nationalism, even before the defeat and establishment of the Vichy regime cut it into two separate halves on either side of the Channel. Germany was the hereditary enemy. "We know full well," de Gaulle stated, "that

Germany is Germany. We have no illusions about her hate and ferocity. At the first sign of fear or anger, this unbalanced people will resort to crimes." . . .

This deadly threat to France had to be ended once and for all. Of course, Nazi war criminals would be punished, the spoils taken by the plundering occupier recovered, and the German economy controlled so that it could never again serve pan-German imperialism. But the Free French saw effective safeguards in the political and territorial demands traditional in French diplomacy. After the proclamation of the Atlantic Charter in August, 1941, de Gaulle, in a telegram from Brazzaville, declared that France reserved the right to make annexations in the Rhineland. In February, 1944, he specifically proposed an independent Rhineland astride the Rhine, one independent of the Reich and allied with the West.

De Gaulle never doubted that France would emerge from the conflict as strong as, if not stronger than, she had been before the war. . . . [But] he observed that "the course of events has continually restricted the independence of nations in terms of their security, economic activity, and communications," so that "it has become inconccivable for any state to act alone, no matter how large or strong it might be."

France, therefore, had to join an international organization. But which one? Some of the Free French . . . naturally favored a revitalized League of Nations. De Gaulle apparently agreed with them when he advocated to the Resistance a "world organization which would permanently establish international solidarity and cooperation in all realms," one capable of "the rational exploitation of the world's resources," and "making possible and guaranteeing the security, dignity, and development of each nation by all the others."

But France must play an important part in this organization and prevent the new great powers from running the peacetime world without considering her as they had done in waging the war. Consequently, she would spread "her humanitarian influence" throughout the world, and through her Empire extend her influence beyond Europe to Africa and the Arab states. To achieve this, de Gaulle saw France leading a "Western federation whose economic foundation was as broad as possible and whose arteries would include the English Channel, Rhine, and Mediterranean." His vision was broad, but its form unclear. France's influence did in fact extend beyond the Mediterranean, but it could not expand beyond the Channel. Apparently, England would have to exclude herself or be excluded from this vast scheme, whereas the defeated nations—Germany and Italy—would be integrated into it once they had accepted France's leadership.

GAULLISM

The ideas de Gaulle suggested and the plans he outlined during the war concerning foreign and domestic policy could be realized only in the postwar period. The question of the need or possibility of continuing the movement that had rallied around him during the war therefore arose.

The question would not arise during the period of political vacuum and of intense emotions and hatreds which characterized the Liberation period, when there was hope for the best and fears for the worst, when all Frenchmen, and later the Allies, accepted General de Gaulle as head of the Provisional Government. Within the limits of the Allied coalition, these extraordinary circumstances granted the government dictatorial powers, legalized by the consent of the nation. General de Gaulle presided over events during this equally disturbing and exhilarating period. The most pressing problem was to restore "republican stability under the authority of the state." True, collaborationists and the Vichyite leaders had to be punished for their crimes and errors, but since purges were necessary for moral reasons, they were "the state's responsibility, not a matter of personal grudges and local grievances."

Therefore, "only a politically responsible public authority was recognized. All artificial power blocs outside the government were intolerable and automatically condemned." The tactics of the Communists, despite the obscurity of their real intentions, were thus anticipated, but they enjoyed the support of the internal Resistance. His refusal to proclaim the Republic from the balcony of the Hôtel de Ville once Paris was liberated marked the logical outcome of de Gaulle's repeated contention that the Republic had never ceased to exist—the Free French had preserved both its continuity and that of France.

After the Liberation no one wanted the Third Republic restored. As a result, who other than those whose foresight and courage had achieved their country's deliverance and the restoration of her prestige could play a part in France's institutional and moral regeneration? This was the opinion of the rank-and-file member of the Free French: "Because we were not afraid to risk our lives for France, only we should have the right to rebuild her." United behind their leader, linked together by their difficult struggle, and elated by their miraculous success, the Free French, despite their quite diverse backgrounds, became a relatively homogeneous group with its own emblem (the Cross of Lorraine), ceremony (June 18), and knighthood (the Order of the Liberation). Henceforth, every level of French life contained "companions" of General de Gaulle, ready to answer his call and bound to him by personal loyalty. . . .

THE SIGNIFICANCE OF FREE FRANCE

. . . The Free French succeeded primarily because General de Gaulle's gamble of June 18, 1940, had placed him in the victors' camp. Had the legitimate government not abdicated in June, 1940, but transferred its operations to French North Africa, France might, like the Dutch, have experienced a victorious return to the homeland by the very leaders who headed the government during the disaster of 1940.

When this solution was made impossible by the failure of the *Massilia* adventure, three other possibilities remained open. The example of Prussia after 1806 might have inspired the new regime to become the center of opposition to the occupiers. But Marshal Pétain was not satisfied to act as a provisional executive to administer French interests as best he could. He refused to rejoin the Allies and he wanted to bring about a "National Revolution" on the ruins of defeat. Worse yet was his government's gradual decision to collaborate, first through Darlan, then through Laval after his return to power in the spring of 1942.

In view of this, a popular movement might, as in Yugoslavia, have been able to establish a powerful resistance movement which formed the basis of a new government. But this movement would probably have been led by the Communists, would have only caused increasing distrust among the Western Allies, and would have resulted in a military occupation.

The Free French had three advantages: they kept French forces alive throughout the war, they retained a certain independence towards the Allies in their defense of French interests, and they succeeded in unifying anti-German forces, thereby creating the basis of a power that installed itself after the Liberation without great difficulty.

Thus it saved France from more than civil war. De Gaulle not only helped to restore the prestige of the liberated nation, but also gave it the blue-print for its economic regeneration, the transformation of its colonial empire, great international ambitions, a plan for a presidential republic, and the foundation of a political doctrine based on the close harmony between the executive and his people.

THE EFFECTS OF WORLD WAR II ON FRENCH SOCIETY AND POLITICS

Stanley Hoffmann

. . . It is the theme of this article that in the period 1934–1944 a political and social system which had gradually emerged during the nineteenth century and which had flourished in the period 1878–1934, was actually liquidated; that from 1934 to 1940, this system, which I call the Republican synthesis,

Stanley Hoffmann, "The Effects of World War II on French Society and Politics," *French Historical Studies*, vol. II, no. 1 (Spring, 1961), 28–29, 31–33, 35–52, 60–62. Copyright by the Society for French Historical Studies, 1961. Used by permission of *French Historical Studies* and the author.

suffered severe shocks; that the events of 1940–1944 turned these shocks into death-blows, for a return to the previous equilibrium has been made impossible; and that many of the political, economic, and social forces which have carried post-war France increasingly farther from the pre-war pattern have their origins in the war years. What the next equilibrium will be like is hard to say, and France still seems far away from any. But it is in 1934 that movement began in earnest, and by 1946, when a political "restoration" did in fact take place, the departures from the previous equilibrium were already considerable. . . .

The equilibrium which France had painfully attained before 1934, can be analyzed as follows: The basis was a certain kind of social and economic balance, which will be referred to here as the "stalemate society" . . . not a *static* society . . . but a society in which social mobility and economic evolution toward a more industrialized order were accepted only within sharp limits and along well-defined channels. Economic change was welcome only if new factors (such as industrial techniques) were fitted into pre-existing frameworks, so that the traditional way of life was affected only slowly. Social mobility presented some very special features . . . class barriers could be crossed but not destroyed; when one jumped over such a barrier, one had to leave one's previous way of thinking and living behind, and accept (for oneself and one's family) the values and attitudes one found on the other side of the fence. . . .

The genius of the Third Republic had been to devise an institutional set-up most effectively adapted to such a society. In conformity with the desire of the "consensus groups" the role of the state was strictly limited. Economic intervention was justified only when it served to preserve the economic equilibrium described, either through legislation or through piecemeal administrative interventions. Otherwise the state's function was an ideological one: it was a state wedded to the social status quo; it was neither industrial . . . nor reformist, but politically doctrinaire and economically beleaguered.

Its organization was such that an effective executive, clear-cut economic or social alternatives and a strong party system simply could not emerge. Parliament was supreme but immobile: its supremacy, under the French doctrine of delegated national sovereignty, freed it from any mass pressures from below; its role was deliberative rather than representative. Law was the product of a compromise between opinions, rather than the result of a weighing of forces. Parties, thanks largely to the electoral system, were primarily parliamentary collections of "fief-holders," their function was to occupy power rather than to govern. Political life was close to the model of a pure game of parliamentary politics, i.e., the government of the nation by a Parliament which dictated policy-making, put the life of cabinets constantly at stake, and knew no effective institutional restraints on its powers. This game, which was being played in isolation from the nation-at-large by a self-perpetuating political class, saw to it that the fundamental equilibrium of society would not be changed by the state.

This system rested in turn on the rosy hypothesis of an outside world distant enough to allow the French to care primarily about their private affairs. Pride in the universality of French values combined with a pleasant sense of superiority or distance to keep the number of people concerned with France's demographic decline or economic retardation small. After World War I victory plus new alliances plastered the cracks opened by the shock of invasion. Indeed, World War I—the one war which has not led to a change of regime—froze French society in many ways. . . .

The challenge of the 1930's, by contrast with previous challenges such as World War I, the Dreyfus case, or Boulangism, undermined all the foundations of the Republican synthesis.

First, the equilibrium of society was shattered by the depression and by the financial policies of the Conservative governments of 1932–36 (the policy of deflation, with its "mystique" of the sanctity of contracts and its stubborn faith in tax cuts and balanced budgets symbolized beautifully the nature and beliefs of the stalemate society). . . .

Secondly, the institutions proved of course too weak to weather such a storm. At a time when executive action was needed, the deep divisions within Parliament condemned cabinets to shorter lives than ever before, and to immobility or incoherence during their brief existence. The impotence of Parliament itself was underlined by the abdication of its legislative powers through decree-laws. The ordinary weaknesses of a multi-party system were aggravated by the splits which appeared within some of the major parties.

Finally, the outside world, whose pressures had been strong, though ignored, ever since Versailles, simply could not be explained away anymore. In a world of motion, indeed revolution . . . , France and England began to appear . . . like big logs of dead wood. . . .

I want to turn now to the process of destruction of the Republican synthesis. . . .

The participants in the revolt against, or dissent from, the Republican system belonged to many categories. . . . On the one hand, there were dissidents from existing political parties, such as the three men, who, ironically enough, were the first to speak of a Popular Front, only to be kept away or to turn away from it later: Doriot (ex-Communist), Déat (neo-Socialist) and Bergery (ex-Radical); Tardieu switched also from being one of the main statesmen of the regime to being one of the chief publicists against it. Those dissidents rubbed elbows with various political figures which had turned anti-parliamentary before 1934: the Maurrassiens, the Jeunesses Patriotes of Taittinger. One can put into the same category . . . the newspapers which came more and more to support the themes of anti-Republicanism and played such a crucial role in bringing to France the climate of Vichy before Vichy.

On the other hand, the 1930's were marked by the "politization" of various groups of men who, in happier days, would not have dreamed of singing the "bawdy song" of politics: large quantities of intellectuals, after a period in which intellectuals had been singularly non-political ... surprising numbers of engineers, especially from the École Polytechnique students, who built up impressive-sounding youth movements (at a time when the parties also reactivated or created youth sections); veterans' associations, who substituted the jargon of national overhaul for the vocabulary of special financial complaints (the Croix de Feu are of course the biggest example); union leaders and businessmen who turned from their previous attitudes of non-cooperation or of no-comment on politics, to studies of general reform and examples from other countries. ...

Coming from so many different milieux, counting so many people whose sudden discovery of public affairs had gone to their heads like extra-fine champagne, these groups amounted more to a maelstrom of confused anger than to a coherent onslaught on the Republican synthesis. ...

Nevertheless they had common grievances against [it]. ...

The most superficial common theme was the critique of French parliamentarism. ... Practically all the dissenters from the Republic argued in favor of a stronger State, one less dependent on the whims of the representatives and less submissive to the individual pressures of the voters on the parliamentarians.

A deeper theme is an attack, not so much on the stalemate society as such, but on its individualistic form. This meant two things:

1. An attack on the neglect of groups in French "official" thought and public law. ...
2. An attack on French capitalism. ...

... All ... agreed ... that present disorganized (i.e. neither state—nor self-regulated) capitalism was rotten; for it wasted national resources through the excesses of competition (Doriot), it demoralized the nation through its materialism (La Rocque), it encouraged uprooted adventurers and nomadic speculators (Bardoux), ... it crushed "les petits" and benefited only "les gros" (*Frontisme*), it built new "feudal orders" in France (veterans' movements). There is marvelous irony in the spectacle of so many people denouncing in the fiasco of French 1934–5 capitalism the discomfiture of "l'économie libérale," if one remembers how little free competition and indeed how much self-regulation there was in this most restrictive economy. ...

The ways in which all these groups participated in the demise of the Republican synthesis and pushed France out of the drydock in which it had been waiting for permanently postponed repairs are far too complicated to be described in detail, but two points are of major interest.

First, the confusing mass of dissenters ultimately split into two blocs. . . . On the one hand, all the people who ended on the side of Vichy . . . the Maurrassiens—hermetically sealed counter-revolutionaries; the Fascists of occupied Paris (literary types, like Drieu, or gangsters, like Doriot's pals) and of Vichy France (muddleheaded activists like Darnand or schemers like Benoist-Méchin), the much bigger groups of disgruntled conservatives . . . like La Rocque, Pétain's Légionnaires and so many of his civil servants, business or peasant leaders; pacifists whose left-wing origins had been erased by their prolonged fight against communism and for appeasement, like Belin and many of Déat's friends. On the other hand, all those dissenters from the Third Republic who nevertheless hated defeat and Nazism more than a French form of democracy and who became the leaven in the more political Resistance organizations, where they met thousands of intellectuals, journalists, doctors, lawyers, military men, etc., . . . many of whom had had no previous political activity. Those future "Résistants" dissenters belonged largely to two groups: a relatively tight one, the Christian Democrats, whose "personnalisme" was politically liberal, not authoritarian, and whose pluralism was democratic, not élitist; a much more loose group, the former "planistes" from business or from the unions. It was only later in the Resistance that the members of the parties of the Third Republic (and, of course, not all of them) joined those former dissenters, gradually submerged them, and turned the Resistance into a second coming of the Popular Front.

Secondly, if one looks at the direction taken by France after 1934 . . . , one can distinguish . . . two phases. First there was, under Vichy, a movement of contraction: the triumph for a few years of a reactionaries' delirium, which broke with the "individualistic" society of the Third Republic in order to establish a "société communautaire" whose organized and self-regulating groups were even more Malthusian in economic practice, and more dominated by the anti-industrial, anti-urban ideal than the Republic had ever been. Then, after 1944, movement went into the opposite direction: economic expansion, a loosening up of society instead of the tight and petrified moral order of Vichy.

. . . The participants in the two revolutions of Vichy and the Resistance had some common (if often negative) ideas, and since many of Vichy's dreams were beyond realization . . . many of Vichy's reforms inevitably turned into directions Vichy neither expected nor desired, or even produced effects contrary to those which the authors of these reforms had hoped to obtain.

If we look at changes in society at the end of the war, we see both major innovations and a few sharp limits. As for the innovations, the most significant is largely due to Vichy's impact. A number of groups in society emerged from pre-war chaos or confusion with the kind of organization which made of them possible levers for economic and social change. . . . Vichy's motives in setting up these bodies were mixed: corporatist ideology (the "restitution" to organized groups in society of powers which the Republican state had supposedly usurped) was strengthened by the need to set up bodies which could administer the restrictions forced upon the French economy by defeat and occupation. Furthermore, some of Vichy's authorities wanted to prevent the Germans from controlling the French economy, as they could otherwise have done, either by benefiting from its lack of organization or by setting up a German-directed organization. . . .

Continuity here has been most striking. In spite of their revulsion against Vichy corporatism, the Resistance movements did not propose a return to pre-war "individualism." The shortages of the Liberation made a continuation of the Vichy-created bodies inevitable anyhow (under different names). But, more significantly, the programs of the main Resistance movements and parties contained, in addition to ritual attacks on "féodalités économiques" and "corporative dictatorship" a plea for a new economic system in which the economy would be directed by the state after consultation with the representatives of economic interests. The pluralism advocated by the MRP in particular contributed to remove any tinge of illegitimacy from the organized groups which had survived the Vichy period. Vichy certainly did not create these bodies for purposes of industrialization, economic modernization, or education toward a less fragmented society. But after having been the transmission belts for Vichy's philistine propaganda or for the German war machine, such institutions could serve as the relays of the Monnet plan. Indeed, the sense of shame or embarrassment which many of the leaders of business felt after the Liberation, at a time when the business community was widely accused of having collaborated wholesale with the Germans, probably contributed to making these men almost eager to prove their patriotism by cooperating with the new regime for economic reconstruction and expansion.

A second phenomenon was also initiated by Vichy. The business and peasant organizations set up in these years were put under the direction of men far less reluctant to break away from economic Malthusianism than the spokesmen for "organized" business and farmers before the war. . . .

In the business committees, delegates of big business, not of small enterprises, were put in charge; furthermore, these men were managers rather than owners. Indeed, spokesmen for small business and representatives of certain traditional, patriarchal family enterprises expressed considerable hostility toward the Committees; they realized that in these bodies men with bolder ideas, who were far from scared by the thought of planning and of economic cooperation with the government, were entrusted with more means of action than the leading businessmen had ever had in France's predominantly non-organized economy before the war. The solidarity between small and large business . . . was severely tried by the circumstances of

1940–1944; under German pressure, but with less resistance from some of the Committee's leaders than from some of Vichy's officials, measures of concentration of enterprises were put into effect. . . .

Thus the more dynamic elements of the economy were given effective positions, instead of remaining dispersed or submerged. . . . The "new men" had a less parochial and less compartmentalized view of the economic problems of their profession and of the nation than their predecessors. Here as in other areas, one of the paradoxical results of a period which saw France divided into more administrative zones and separate realms than at any time since the Revolution—in part because of the restrictions on, and later the breakdown of, communications—was to inject a greater awareness of the nation-wide scope of economic problems. Consequently, the need for attacking these problems at least from within the framework of a whole profession, rather than through reliance on individual and local pressures, also became understood. The physical fragmentation of 1940–44 dealt a heavy blow to the economic and social fragmentation of pre-war France.

This became apparent in another way as well. Because of the defeat and later in reaction against Vichy there occurred a kind of rediscovery of France and of the French by the French. Common sufferings did a great deal to submerge, if not to close, some of the fissures which the social fabric of France had suffered before the war. . . .

When Vichy became a shrunken, isolated and Fascist-dominated little clique, common opposition to the occupants and the collaborators brought together people and groups who had remained separated both in pre-war France and in the period of Vichy which preceded Laval's return to power. The collaborators played in 1944–5 the sad but useful role of scapegoats, and the shrillest of their enemies were often men who had first put their faith in Pétain and shared in Vichy's integral nationalism of 1940–1. The myth which the Resistance men gladly endorsed—that almost all of France was "résistante" in 1944—contributed to healing some of the wounds which the clash between Vichy's forces and the Resistance had opened. . . . The extraordinary nationalist fervor of the Communists in the Resistance and Liberation days was far more than a tactical shift. It constituted in many cases a genuine emotional wave of relief after (or should I say expiation for) the somber period 1939–1941, when Communist opposition to the war had pushed the Party's members and sympathizers outside of the national community—or out of the Party. . . .

The revival of community was obviously far from complete or final, and it is impossible to measure the degree of community in a nation. But . . . it has been much higher after 1944 than in the 1930's, despite the return of the Communists into their ghetto, and such phenomena as Poujadism. . . . France as a *political* community may have been almost as pathetic after 1946 as before 1939. But there are other levels or forms of community as well, and those, which had been badly damaged in the 1930's, were in much better shape after the Liberation. . . .

Relations between workers and other social groups were not permanently improved. Indeed, they did not improve at all under Vichy, where the policy practiced both by the state and by business organizations was one of reaction and repression. The legislation which the Popular Front had made in order to bring classes closer together had failed almost completely. The bitter denunciations of business attitudes toward Labor in most Resistance platforms indicate how deep this fissure had become. The bad memories left, on the workers' side, by the Labor Charter and the rump unions sponsored by Vichy or by Paris collaborators, and, on the management side, by the reforms of the Liberation, were going to doom legislative attempts such as the Comités d'Entreprises (needless to say, Communist domination of the labor movement contributed to the failure). Nationalization has not noticeably contributed to the "reintegration of the proletariat into the nation" which the Resistance wanted to achieve and which Socialists saw as one of the main advantages of public ownership. . . .

The changes on the political front have been more contradictory than those in society. . . .

Power fell into the hands of the previous "minorities"—of those groups of men who, for one reason or another, did not belong to, or had become separated from, "la République des Camarades." The fall of France was the "divine surprise" of many of the dissenters or enemies whom we have mentioned before; metropolitan France became the battlefield between the factions into which those groups split—corporatists against "belinistes," pro-Pétain Christian-Democrats against Maurrassiens, and of course Fascists against conservatives or technocrats—or against other Fascists. Those dissenters who either refused to support Vichy or abandoned Vichy after a few months of hesitation . . . became . . . the backbone of the early Resistance. One of the paradoxes of the restoration of 1945–6 is that although it brought back many of the parties discredited in 1940, and political institutions close to those which had collapsed on July 10, the political personnel of the Third Republic never succeeded in coming back in toto. . . .

A second and major change was the acceptance of an interventionist state—at last. Vichy's philosophy was, to start with, diametrically opposed to it; Vichy's dream was the "absolute but limited" state, so dear to counter-revolutionaries ever since Bonald. But despite its theory of decentralization and of corporations running the economy under a distant and discreet check from the state, Pétain's regime was unable to practice what it preached. In the business organizations Vichy set up, civil servants, and managers learned to run the show together. . . .

On the other side of the political fence, the need for a more active state had become one of the main planks of Resistance platforms: planning by the state, nationalization, big public investments, "economic and social democracy," state control over cartels, prices or capital movements, all these suggestions showed that the revulsion against the lopsided "economic liberalism" of pre-war times had become irresistible. The measures taken in 1944–6 in order to put these proposals into effect are well known. None of the "conquests of the Liberation" has been seriously threatened since; the attacks against "dirigisme" by Radicals and Conservatives were successful only when they were aimed at price controls and at those measures of intervention into the affairs of rural France which the peasant organizations had not requested themselves.

A change in public issues resulted. Already before 1939, a subtle shift had occurred. On the one hand the key ideological issue of the Third Republic had begun to fade away, for official hostility to the Church had weakened ever since the Popular Front. Except for the years 1945–1951, private schools have received help from the state since 1941. . . .

On the other hand, the state began to promote measures of income redistribution which went far beyond what the theory of the stalemate society allowed, or showed concern for social welfare on a scale unknown before. The "politique de la famille" has been followed by every regime since Daladier's decrees of July 1939. Vichy gave tremendous publicity to its main contribution to social insurances: the old age pensions for retired workers. Resistance platforms emphasized the need for extending protection against social risks, and the social security system of the Liberation was built by a man who had been one of the main drafters of the law of August 1940 setting up Vichy's business committees. The participation of workers' delegates in at least some of the activities of the firm became the subject of various laws, from the Popular Front's shop stewards to Vichy's comités sociaux and the Liberations' comités d'entreprises. Thus, economic and social issues tended to replace the old ideological ones, and this shift contributed to the "nationalization" of opinion and issues which proportional representation accelerated. The fragmentation of the political scene into "fiefs" and local issues began to fade just as economic fragmentation did.

The bulk of the conservatives which had followed La Rocque, read more and more the anti-Republican press of the 1930's and joined Pétain's Legion, discovered in the last, tragic months of Vichy that Thiers had been right after all: it is still the Republic which protects those forces best against disorder. In a country where the majority is composed of members of the middle classes or of peasants who have no interest in social subversion, it is majority rule which has the best chances of defending the status quo against the revolutionaries of the far left and the nihilists of the far right. These conservatives came to realize that they were far closer to the political system of pre-war France than to the totalitarian delirium of the Laval-Darnand period. . . . Hence a new Ralliement to the Republic in 1944; it is from those groups that the MRP received much of its unexpected support in 1945–46.

Ever since, conservatives, having understood the lesson of 1934–44, have concentrated on organizing their parties and pressure groups more effectively than before the war, so as to gain better access to power. When the challenge of communism seemed too strong for the Fourth Republic, only some of those elements deserted to the RPF, and many of these men either deserted the RPF in turn when the danger seemed over, or simply used the RPF as an elevator which would carry them back up to the floor of Power from which they had been pushed down by the politicians of "tripartisme." Indeed, anti-parliamentary movements since 1944 have found more recruits among the groups which had provided the social basis of the "Republicans" of the Third Republic (peasants and shopkeepers) or among the "new" middle classes of engineers, modern businessmen and white-collar workers, than among the former Pétainistes. . . .

By way of a summary and instead of a conclusion, here are a few paradoxes for our meditation.

First, the Resistance and Vichy, which fought one another so bloodily, cooperated in many ways without wanting or knowing it, and thus carried the nation to the threshold of a new social order. . . . Vichy brought into existence social institutions which could become the channels for state action, and gave a considerable boost to the descendants of the Saint-Simonians, men who were willing to serve as agents of the Count's old dream—organization, production, industrialism. The Resistance brought to power teams of engineers, civil servants and politicians determined to use these agents and these channels for economic and consequently for social change. Had those teams not arrived, it is quite possible that the social institutions erected by Vichy would have withered away. . . . But without readily available trans-mission belts and without the shock of discovery produced on French economic elites by sudden and brutal contact with foreign economies, post-war planning might have failed. The transformation of the French economy and society since 1952 is due to the combination of the wills of a statist De Gaulle—and a Saint-Simonian Monnet—who used instruments prepared by Vichy and strengthened them by adding quite a few of their own (nationaliza-tions, Planning Commission, a reform of the civil service, etc.). The meekness of the *patronat*, unwilling to oppose the government of the Liberation, and the big production drive of the Communists in 1944–7 which contrasted with labor's prewar attitude, both contributed to the initial success of the move-ment. The process is far from completed, and no transformation of French political life has resulted from it so far. But World War II had on French society effects opposite from those of World War I.

Secondly, the continuity between Vichy and its successor, which we have noted when we mentioned the economy, family protection, the "rediscovery" of youth and the revival of Catholicism, appears also, in more ironic fashion, in a number of failures. The hope of reconciling the workers and the employers has not been fulfilled. Neither the paternalistic solutions of the Vichy Labor Charter nor the social measures of the Liberation have succeeded in overcoming a long tradition of mutual suspicion. . . . Both Vichy and the Resistance movements emphasized the need to preserve, in agriculture, the traditional family units; their post-war decline has been spectacular, and no amount of protection from the state has been able to suspend it. Indeed, mechanization of the farms has often contributed to this process, for it increases the financial difficulties of farmers whose products sell at prices which remain at a lower level than the cost of the machines, as well as the plight of peasants whose land is too small for efficient production. Both regimes have failed to preserve the morale, the unity and the strength of the army. Finally, both have failed to stabilize the French political system. The new society of France still awaits a political synthesis comparable to the early Third Republic; all it presently has is a respite.

Thirdly, both regimes provide us with choice examples of serendipity. Vichy, which wanted to coax the French back to the land and back to rule by traditional notables, consolidated instead the business community and demonstrated conclusively that the elites of "static" France could not provide leadership any more. Vichy also wanted to restore old provincial customs and dialects and peculiarities—instead of which it put into motion powerful forces of further economic and social unification. The Resistance, which wanted to purify French political life and was prone to proclaim the death of the bourgeoisie, ended as a political fiasco, but was the lever of an economic modernization which has certainly not meant the demise of the bourgeoisie. Indeed, those of the dissenters from the Third Republic who turned against it because they wanted to save the stalemate society which the Republic seemed unable to defend, an order based on the preponderance of the middle classes, could remark today that French society is still dominated by these classes. The proportion of industrial workers has barely increased.

However, French society is no longer the same. The division between proletarians and "indépendants" has been largely replaced by a less original hierarchy of functional groups in which many of the workers partake of middle class characteristics and in which managers, "cadres" and employees are increasingly numerous. The village is less important as an economic unit; the family is a less tightly closed one; the attitude toward savings and credit has been reversed; there is less distance between ranks and statuses in society; businessmen, peasants and shopkeepers alike are more dependent on the national economy than on a mere segment of it; the economy is far more planned . . . and the market is at last seen as growing instead of frozen. In other words, a more dynamic society has replaced the tight stalemate society of the past. . . .

SUGGESTIONS FOR FURTHER READING

Documentary: A. J. LIEBLING (ed.), *The Republic of Silence* (New York, 1947); *France During the German Occupation, 1940–1944,* 3 vols. (Stanford, Calif., 1958–59); General: PAUL REYNAUD, *In the Thick of the Fight, 1930–1945* (New York, 1955); PAUL FARMER, *Vichy, Political Dilemma* (New York, 1955); GORDON WRIGHT, "Vichy Revisited," *Virginia Quarterly Review,* XXXIV (1958), 501–14; STANLEY HOFFMANN, "Aspects du régime de Vichy," *Revue française de science politique,* VI (1956), 44–69; HENRI AMOUROUX, *La vie des français sous l'occupation* (Paris, 1961); P. ARNOULT et al., *La France sous l'occupation* (Paris, 1959); HENRI MICHEL, *Histoire de la Résistance (1940–1944)* (Paris, 1950), and *Les Courants de pensée de la Résistance* (Paris, 1962); ROBERT ARON, *France Reborn: The History of the Liberation, June, 1944–May, 1945* (New York, 1964); CRANE BRINTON, "Letters from Liberated France," *French Historical Studies,* II (1961–62), 1–27, 133–156; Special: ADRIENNE HYTIER, *Two Years of French Foreign Policy: Vichy, 1940–1942* (Geneva, 1958); ROBERT O. PAXTON, *Parades and Politics at Vichy: The French Officer Corps under Marshal Pétain* (Princeton, 1966); ROBERT MENGIN, *No Laurels for de Gaulle* (New York, 1966); ARTHUR L. FUNK, *Charles de Gaulle: The Crucial Years, 1943–1944* (Norman, Okla., 1959); Biographical: CHARLES DE GAULLE, *War Memoirs,* vol. I, *The Call to Honour, 1940–42* (New York, 1955), vol. II, *Unity, 1942–44* (New York, 1959); DAVID THOMSON, *Two Frenchmen: Pierre Laval and Charles de Gaulle* (London, 1951); JEAN-RAYMOND TOURNOUX, *Sons of France: Pétain and de Gaulle* (New York, 1966); HUBERT COLE, *Laval, A Biography* (London, 1963); ALFRED MALLET, *Pierre Laval,* 2 vol. (Paris, 1955).

Chapter Seventeen

THE
"UNLOVED"
FOURTH REPUBLIC

THE FOURTH REPUBLIC has been called *la mal-aimée*—the "unloved"—because it disappointed the bright hopes for a responsible and stable regime raised during the Occupation and Resistance. Its failures in political affairs alienated most Frenchmen, few of whom regretted its sudden death (or suicide) in 1958.

Politically, the Fourth Republic was never intended to be what it in fact became—a close copy of the thoroughly discredited Third Republic. Both Vichy and the Resistance had denounced the party fragmentation and perennially unstable governments which had denied France the leadership she required in an age of international crisis. Not surprisingly, then, the French electorate (including newly enfranchised women) voted overwhelmingly against returning to the Third Republic in the referendum held in October, 1945. But it was easier to condemn the past than to build the future, and the Constituent Assembly, divided as it was among Communists, Socialists, and Christian Democrats, eventually adopted a new constitution that satisfied no one. Though minor changes eliminated some abuses of the prewar constitutional system, the Fourth Republic still operated through a weak President (the first being the socialist Vincent Auriol) and a two-house legislature dominated by the popularly elected National Assembly. The new constitution also made provisions for a "French Union" including France's colonial possessions, but the scheme never matured.

In the second selection, the French political scientist and sociologist Raymond Aron examines the political "system" of the Fourth Republic to discover why and how it operated. The spectrum of parties in the National Assembly, he concludes, was traditional and "natural," representing in microcosm the profound divisions within French society itself, arising from class, religious, or historical antagonisms. The divided Assembly evolved its own style of politics in which responsibility was avoided, ministerial portfolios rotated with regularity (though among a small group of deputies), and political crisis became a way of life. Tolerable perhaps during normal times, this "system" proved inadequate in the postwar years of economic dislocation, colonial revolt, and Cold War. Worse yet, to the three large existing parties and the enfeebled radicals were added new groups to the right, formed about first an embittered General de Gaulle and then the demogogic Pierre Poujade, who were basically hostile to the very existence of the Fourth Republic. These and the isolated yet powerful Communist Party on the left squeezed the center parties so that they were unable to govern effectively. Guy Mollet lasted longest of any premier—sixteen months.

The result of political instability was the failure of any reasonable solution to the war in Indochina, which had erupted in 1946 when the French attempted to restore their sovereignty there. Despite a growing awareness of its futility and attempts to win over the Vietnamese by belated political concessions, France continued to fight until her troops suffered a severe defeat at Dien Bien Phu in 1954. The vigorous Pierre Mendès-France, who was named premier to salvage the situation, secured a peace settlement at Geneva that led to French withdrawal from all of Indochina. But his attempts to loosen French control in Tunisia and Morocco, combined with his plans for economic and social reform at home, aroused personal and political animosities that helped to bring him down early in 1955.

Ironically, it was during his premiership that the second major colonial conflict began, this time in Algeria. In the third selection, the English political scientist Dorothy Pickles analyzes the reasons why France was unable to resolve the rebellion that discredited France in the eyes of the world, drained her energies, divided her people, and helped topple the Republic itself. The Fourth Republic did not realize fully that the "winds of change" were blowing in Africa and failed to satisfy legitimate demands of the native Algerians until it was too late. Moreover, the officials on the scene, who were reluctant to make any concessions, always blocked or delayed long-needed reforms. Defeated and humiliated in Indochina, the army wanted to win a military victory over the Algerian rebels and mistrusted the "soft" civilians at home. Finally, the political divisions in Paris, especially the existence of a large Communist Party, prevented any real continuity or firmness of policy. It might also be noted that Algeria, a French possession for over a century and heavily populated by Europeans, was not considered a colony by France, but rather an integral part of the country. Hence the idea of independence was for a long time unthinkable.

How the Algerian situation led to the overthrow of the Fourth Republic in May, 1958, is set forth in detail in the fourth selection, by Philip Williams, Fellow in European Politics at Nuffield College, Oxford. He describes the rise of dissatisfaction among the various European groups in Algeria, and shows how, with the collusion of the army, which had no love for Paris, they engineered a revolt in Algiers that posed the threat of a military invasion of France itself. Divided and fearful of civil war, the political leaders of the Fourth Republic reluctantly relinquished power to Charles de Gaulle, who had spent his years out of office writing his memoirs and awaiting just such a moment. Stepping in to assume the premiership, de Gaulle restored control over the insurrectionists of Algiers and set about creating a new regime that would erase the mistakes made in 1945–46.

The overwhelming vote approving the constitution of the Fifth Republic in September, 1958, showed how little support the regime had left. But though it was generally discredited for its ineffectiveness and instability, the Fourth Republic has, with the passage of time, come to be regarded in a more favorable light. The years 1944–58 must now be considered the period when France's society and economy underwent a profound transformation, when the "stalemate society" was at last replaced with a more vital one. France at the Liberation faced an enormous task of reconstruction, and despite inflation, repeated devaluation of the franc, and the drain of colonial wars, she managed to repair the ravages of the war and end the economic stagnation of the 1930's. As Jean Lecerf shows in the first selection, this was made possible with the help of Marshall Plan aid, the international coordination of the Organization for European Economic Cooperation, the stimulation of the Monnet Plan, and far-reaching "structural" reforms, including nationalization of key industries and resources. Though Lecerf does not mention it, the Common Market, instituted in 1957 and climaxing numerous other attempts at European economic cooperation, departed from France's traditional protectionism and compelled France to compete and modernize. Along with economic recovery and encouraging it came an increase in the birth rate and a rise in France's long-stagnant population that would give the nation a new demographic vigor. It is therefore in the realm of economic and social progress that the Fourth Republic deserves to be remembered. Without it, the general prosperity of the Fifth Republic would never have been achieved.

❦

THE TRANSFORMATION OF THE FRENCH ECONOMY AFTER WORLD WAR II

Jean Lecerf

In a gallant uprising, Paris surprised the world by driving out the [German] enemy before the Allies could arrive. The war went on, but a page had been turned. Yet how could three such days wipe away the ruins left by the blitzkrieg of 1940, four years of Occupation, aerial bombardment, the work of the Resistance and Liberation, the landing and fighting in Normandy, and the combat which was now taking place in the Vosges and Alsace? It was a ravaged France that emerged from her prison. Some 115 major railway stations, including twenty-four marshalling yards, were either destroyed or damaged. Of 12,000 locomotives, 2,800 remained, and no trains ran between Paris, Lyons, Marseilles, Toulouse, Bordeaux, Nantes, Lille, and Nancy. Her canals, rivers, and seaports were unusable, and her electric power lines were cut. In August, 1944, France produced 600 million kilowatt hours, less than half of her 1938 output. Three thousand harbors had been destroyed. Of every ten cars, nine needed repairs and the other had no gasoline. No airplanes flew and airports were pocked with bomb craters. Telegraph and telephone lines functioned poorly, as did radio transmission.

In his *Memoirs*, General de Gaulle noted these accumulated disasters with alarm, so uncertain did they make his government. He described the misery of men reduced to 1,200 calories by government rationing; the ruinous and demoralizing black market; the shortages of wool, cotton, and leather; the threadbare clothing and wooden-soled shoes; the towns without heat during one of the coldest winters ever; and the lack of coal, most of

Jean Lecerf, *La Percée de l'économie française* (Paris: B. Arthaud, 1963), pp. 11–16, 19–21, 25–30, 35–37. © B. Arthaud, Paris, 1963. Used by permission. Editors' translation.

which was reserved for the armies, power plants, essential industries, and hospitals. There was virtually no gas or electricity. Four million of France's young men had been mobilized, deported, or taken as forced laborers to Germany, and a quarter of the population was homeless or refugee. Added to this was the existing housing shortage, which became tragic due to bombardments, the influx of refugees, and the need to house government employees. . . .

The situation was heart-rending, but it was also a challenge, for something "new and viable" now had to be constructed. The man who would be responsible for this had been the insubordinate officer of London, the dissident leader of Algiers, the touchy junior partner of Churchill and Roosevelt, a distant voice whose phrases were engraved in people's memories: Charles de Gaulle wanted to lead France not only to greatness, but also to prosperity. . . . He had no economic training other than the desire for factual information acquired in his years on the General Staff. But the pages devoted to this problem in his *Memoirs* are nonetheless clear, lucid, and well stated. Self-justification it may have been, but it was also a heightened awareness of his responsibilities.

He had not yet learned what money really was or what role it played in a nation's greatness. He needed money for France and of what use was classical economics? Ideas about such matters were being totally rethought. He was open-minded and had no set program. And while the country was much preoccupied with shortages of bread, wine and tobacco . . . General de Gaulle was launching a series of profound reforms in the structure of France's economy. . . .

NATIONALIZATION

On October 4, 1944, the Renault Company, whose factories had, like so many others, worked for the German occupier, was seized; on November 15 the enterprise was confiscated; and on January 16, 1945, it was nationalized under the name of the National Renault Works. In May, 1945, the government expropriated the Gnome and Rhône airplane factory, which became the National Board for the Study and Construction of Airplane Motors (S.N.E.C.M.A.). . . .

But these were only the prelude to a long series of nationalizations. They had been envisaged in the midst of the war, when plans for the reconstruction of France were being laid down in London, Algiers, and France itself. The program of the National Council of the Resistance adopted on March 15, 1944, provided for the

creation of a true economic and social democracy through the elimination of the economic and financial feudalism that has controlled the economy . . . the intensification of national production along lines of a state-drawn plan . . . the return to the nation of the principal means of production which have been monopolized and which are the fruits of common labor: sources of energy, underground wealth, insurance companies, and great banking houses. . . .

In his *Memoirs*, General de Gaulle described these first nationalizations as having been thought out during his travels. Speaking at the Palais de Chaillot on September 12, 1944, he announced that he wanted to "make sure that private interests are always subordinated to the general welfare, that the great sources of common wealth will be exploited and regulated not for the profit of a few, but for the good of all." He became more specific in October, 1944, after he visited the Nord and Pas-de-Calais Departments. There in the faces of the miners he saw the absolute necessity for deep reductions in the privileges of money and for a great transformation in the condition of the workers' lives.

On December 4, 1944, an order appeared in the *Journal Officiel* creating the "National Coal Industry of the Nord and Pas-de-Calais," which was placed under the authority and control of a Minister of Mines. Their owners, concession-holders, lease-holders, and developers were indemnified. . . .

On June 26, 1945, an order made retroactive to September 1, 1944, transferred to the state the ownership of shares in the airline companies Air France and Air Bleu. . . . The law of April 8, 1946, nationalized the electric and gas industries. . . . The Bank of France and the four major deposit banks—*Crédit Lyonnais*, B.N.C.I., the *Société Générale*, and the *Comptoir d'Escompte de Paris*—were nationalized in turn. Shortly afterward, a "National Council on Credit" in which professional men, civil servants, union members and consumers participated, was charged with organizing and regulating the profession. . . . A vast sector of the economy came under state control. . . .

SOCIAL REFORMS

The daring social program that both de Gaulle and the Resistance had dreamt of soon became a concrete reality in the form of workers' committees in industry, labor representation, and reforms in social security and family allotments. On September 29, 1941, the Council of Ministers had approved the principle of the creation by ordinance of mixed committees in large-scale enterprises that would be required to serve as the link between management and labor. The ordinance itself organizing these workers' committees appeared on February 22, 1942. But their role was not to present demands—this was left to the workers' delegates. . . .

This was a useful reform, but experience has not shown conclusively that it met its objectives. These, as General de Gaulle would later write, were

to offer the workers in the national economy some responsibilities that would greatly enhance their role as instruments of production, to which they had been limited until now. They would participate in the operation of the business, their labor would have the same rights as capital, and their salaries, like stockholders' dividends, would be linked to profits growing out of production. That is what I hope to accomplish.

But due to insufficient understanding and the absence of any dialogue, these workers' committees were generally restricted to the drafting of a considerable and useful social budget. But they allowed business leaders to teach their labor representatives something about business operations and encouraged some workingmen to assert their authority. This was progress even if limited.

The law of April 16, 1946, gave new status to the workers' representatives created by the law of June 24, 1936, which had virtually ceased to operate since the war. The ordinance of October 4, 1945, increased the scope of social security, and greatly overhauled it. The measure was hotly debated because it did away with mutual insurance and organized a single insurance fund. But the communist Minister of Labor, Ambroise Croizat, stoutly defended his plan, and the new system went into operation on September 1, 1946.

"There is no progress," General de Gaulle would write,

if those who make it with their hands receive no reward for it. The Government of the Liberation believes not only that there should be wage increases, but also that they be won by institutions that make a basic change in the condition of the working class. The law of 1945 must completely modernize and expand the social security system into new areas. Every wage-earner will have compulsory coverage. In this way will disappear an anxiety as old as the human race, one caused by sickness, accident, old age and unemployment, which have burdened the working man. There will always be poor among us, but they need not be wretched.

In addition, we must mention the statute dealing with agriculture, which sought to slow the flight from the farm, and especially to establish a full system of family allowances, which has remained the most generous in the world. . . .

These social reforms, especially those dealing with the role of workers' representatives in industry, did not have the full impact that their supporters expected, but they were valuable and remain in effect. They were steps on the road to progress. . . .

THE MONNET PLAN FOR INDUSTRIAL MODERNIZATION

If France launched a daring social program through basic structural reforms, how could it also recover its economic strength? This problem failed to stir the masses, but it became one of the most crucial following the Liberation. We must go back to 1945 and examine this Plan for Modernization and Equipment, generally known as the Monnet Plan.

Jean Monnet was then fifty-seven. His extraordinary career had begun before World War I when he represented the family cognac business in North America. During the war he was the French member on the Allied resource allotment boards. After 1919 he found work in an American bank, the League of Nations, the cognac trade, the reorganization of Chinese railways, and financial advice in the development of Poland and Rumania. In 1943 he became a member of General de Gaulle's National Committee as commissioner for armaments, food supply and reconstruction. After the Liberation he served as France's delegate general to the United States. . . .

It was Monnet who conceived a program to rejuvenate France and won de Gaulle over to it. Named Commissioner General for the Plan for Modernization and Equipment, Monnet found an office . . . in a small hotel near the Invalides where he set to work. . . . The method and aims of the Plan had to be formulated quickly, for they were needed as arguments in the many conversations at this time for securing, not foreign exchange, but credits. Monnet's assistant was a young man also from the Charente Department, the future premier, Félix Gaillard. In an interview given in May, 1946, he discussed the idea of the Plan:

QUESTION: What is your aim?
ANSWER: First, to increase production in metropolitan France and its overseas territories and their world trade, especially in those areas where they are in a favorable position to do so. At the same time, we must raise labor productivity to the level of those countries where it is highest, assure full employment, and improve living conditions and the quality of life. These are the very words used in the decree of January 3, 1946, which created the Council of the Plan.

To achieve these ends, we first had to gather precise information on the extent of the damage suffered by France, on her needs and on her resources. This was the first task of the Commissioner General of the Plan, Jean Monnet, and his twenty aides.

At the first session of the Council of the Plan, the conclusion was reached that such an effort would be possible only if our production and exports greatly surpassed the figures reached in the years immediately preceding the war, and even those of our best year, 1929.

Q.: What is the role of the Council of the Plan?
A.: The Council is an important body with thirteen Ministers, representatives of management and labor, and technicians. It is responsible for drafting the Plan. At its first meeting it adopted, after a long discussion, the entire set of proposals presented by the Commissioner General and set the production figures which were to be reached in 1950 in the principal branches of French production.

Q.: Doesn't such a scheme risk becoming a dead letter? Has the Council of the Plan indicated the means to fulfill it?
A.: Not yet. The Council can set the means to be used only when its decisions are worked out by the technicians of the fourteen commissions for Modernization and Equipment. Each of these commissions knows what level of activity its branch

must reach during the four coming years. Its role is to decide what resources will be necessary, which bodies must be created, what laws must be changed, etc.

Q.: Who are the members of these commissions?

A.: Some are officials drawn from the Council of State or various ministries. There they meet with representatives of unions, industry, the trade press and such diverse individuals as former colonial governors, farmers, stockraisers, and scientists. The reports that are studied and put into final form will permit the drafting of a working plan that will be presented to the Cabinet.

Q.: Have measures already been drawn up that will serve to direct and stimulate the French economy, such as control over credit, allocation of raw materials, and price controls?

A.: Some direct controls are inevitable, but the important role allotted to representatives of private enterprise in the commissions allows the adoption of solutions permitting as much liberalism as possible. Our Plan will not be worked out within a closed circle like those of Russia or Germany. On the contrary, we want to open our frontiers, as our cooperation with America proves. . . .

The order of priorities chosen by the Plan quickly came under fire. If its efforts had first been concentrated on housing and those goods most in demand by the French people, it might have brought out perceptible improvements, but would have run the risk of exhausting itself. Monnet felt that it was necessary to turn out steel and cement before building housing, and to produce electricity and coal before making automobiles. This was logical, but the Germans who, without any preconceived plan, adopted the reverse order did not find themselves too badly off. . . .

In 1946, eighteen commissions on modernization were at work, and their reports allowed the first Plan to be completed and executed over a period of five years.

It made a strong appeal to the good will of business. This was easy since the programs had generally been prepared with the aid of professionals in each field—entrepreneurs, technicians, and union members. An effort was made to publicize its significance, but it was never really successful.

Legislation had been passed giving the government wide powers to deal with the private sector of the economy. It could conclude contracts with businessmen who pledged to install equipment, produce a certain quantity of goods at a certain price at a certain date. From then on, their plants, their personnel, their supplies and capital would all have to be put to work in order to honor their agreement. If the commitment were not kept, the state had the right to requisition the business, a right it never used.

On the other hand, the Ministers promised to provide the factory that worked for them and its suppliers as well with the necessary raw materials. If a free contract was not enough, the responsible Minister might, on the advice of the consulting committee and the interested unions, simply give orders for production. But this was never done.

Today these provisions seem rather authoritarian, although the advocates of "democratic planning" hope they will be dusted off and used. It was not necessary to use them to make the French Plan a great success, however. . . .

THE MARSHALL PLAN AND THE O.E.E.C.

The United States was quick to realize that a devastated Europe would take a long while to recover. With the world cut in two by the Iron Curtain, the nations of Europe would put up only feeble resistance to a Communist takeover if an economically depressed zone existed too long beside the "people's democracies." The political reasons behind American action were numerous.

This did not prevent President Truman's Secretary of State, George C. Marshall, from deciding that the United States would offer aid to assist Great Britain and the rest of Europe to recover. The steps he took were as generous as they were daring, and assumed a size never before seen in the history of the world.

Marshall Plan aid hastened France's recovery, first through its money, but primarily by compelling her to consider her problems in a European framework. It helped modernize the French industrial plant and assisted her in becoming a great economic power once again. Marshall Plan aid operated by offering credits in dollars to countries whose trade balance was unfavorable. Virtually all had a dollar shortage that was considered to be as fundamental and permanent as it was general. Thus the United States opened the way for France to import coal and other raw materials indispensable to industry free of charge.

What France bought was resold to her own citizens, and the francs that accumulated were set aside for the Treasury—these became known as "counterpart funds." Governments might use them as they chose, after consulting with American authorities. The Germans made good use of them to finance their conversion to peacetime industries, which in turn quickly helped to finance their sales abroad. The French, on the other hand, used them for long-term investments in heavy industry, those that the Plan considered to be of first priority. They felt that it was easier to finance the others from available funds.

For several years Marshall Plan funds played an important role in balancing the French budget. They also gave weight to the advice the Americans gave France. The fear of drying up a source of foreign exchange and of seeing unemployment mount because of a lack of raw materials, was certainly the beginning of wisdom for members of France's legislature.

But one of the most constructive aspects of American aid was its demand that European nations agree as to how they would share it. Sixteen countries, including Great Britain, met at Paris . . . in 1948 and agreed to form the Organization for European Economic Cooperation (O.E.E.C.). Its first secretary was ... Robert Marjolin, an aide to Jean Monnet on the French Plan, who had played an important part in its creation.

The new body had no pretensions of becoming a "superstate." Its decisions were made by unanimous vote, meaning that policies that were too revolutionary would not be adopted. Still, there was not only agreement on the division of Marshall Plan aid, but also on the question of gradually freeing international trade from the import quota system.

Normally, entry of goods into a foreign country is free on payment of customs duties. But since the Depression days of 1930, prohibitions on imports of various goods except by agreement with the government in the form of an import license became the rule in most countries. This tactic facilitated controls over foreign exchange which were then in operation everywhere, but which paralyzed trade. It allowed virtually only barter between two countries, a strictly equal trade regulated by treaty. ... More complex arrangements were needed to increase commerce.

A working method was at length devised by the O.E.E.C. Each state would gradually free from licenses those products whose importation represented a certain percentage of the volume of purchases elsewhere abroad during the base year 1948. Along with the Monnet Plan, this cooperation ... was one of the most important legacies of the immediate post-war period. Now more than fifteen years later, when the United States is no longer the nation with inexhaustible credit it once was, at a time when Europe is reasserting itself and setting conditions, it would be unfair to forget that America provided France with the financial assistance she needed to recover, and that France was shown the road to prosperity through European cooperation. ...

THE POLITICAL "SYSTEM" OF THE FOURTH REPUBLIC

Raymond Aron

The way in which French parliamentary procedure operates has always been an object of astonishment for observers, and for specialists, deputies, and journalists a source of "poisons and delights."

The seemingly distinctive feature of French parliamentary government was, according to almost unanimous opinion, ministerial instability, more

Reprinted by permission of the publishers from Raymond Aron, *France, Steadfast and Changing: The Fourth to the Fifth Republic.* Cambridge, Mass.: Harvard University Press. Copyright, 1960, by the President and Fellows of Harvard College.

or less combined with the weakness of the executive power, and government by the legislature. Ministerial instability does not date from the Fourth Republic; it was already known and deplored under the Third, when the Chamber of Deputies included only a few members who were hostile to the regime. Consequently a distinction is called for: the French legislature, even when made up exclusively of "constitutional" deputies, did not avoid ministerial crises; and the latter, despite their frequency, did not endanger the survival of the constitutional system.

What is the reason for this ministerial instability which none of the French Republics has been able to curb? Perhaps the answer will be easier if we first try to find out how this instability has been prevented in different times and places.

In modern democracies all groups organize freely to express their opinions and defend their interests. The deputies are elected by all the citizens; the government, finally, must win the support of legislators sensitive to the complaints of their constituents and the claims of producers, consumers, and taxpayers. In such circumstances, administrations are compelled to listen to the dissonant, more or less passionate voices of these idio-collective interests. But the very existence of the government is not thereby endangered. The President of the United States is elected for four years, and nothing except death, illness, or voluntary resignation can put an end to his term of office. The British Prime Minister, since the number of parties has been reduced to two, has the constant support of a parliamentary majority subject to a strict discipline. Except in the case of a revolt within his party or of public opinion ... the Prime Minister alone chooses the time for the dissolution of Parliament and new elections.

In the absence of a two-party system and of a presidential government, stability may be assured either when one of the several parties holds an absolute majority, either alone ... or with the assistance of a secondary party ... or when several parties form an alliance on a specific program for one term of a legislature. ... When none of these conditions is met, when the government depends on temporary and revocable agreements between numerous parties, no one of which is subject to discipline when it comes to the vote, a certain ministerial instability is unavoidable. ... For instability to become understandable, it is enough to recall that the Palais-Bourbon never knew any organized, disciplined parties capable of making long-term agreements.

If there had been no parties at all the parliamentary game would have been dominated by the rivalry of a few leaders around whom groups of followers formed. If all parties had been of the same sort, with or without disciplined voting, a definite type of coalition would have emerged. But the French Assembly has always been composed not only of numerous parties but of heterogeneous parties as well. ... Parties were based, some on a more or less imaginary class concept (the Socialist Party), others on a religious ideal (the Popular Republican Party), some on temperament or on historical memories (the Radical Party), still others on an ill-defined conservatism (the Independents). How can we be surprised that none of them was united when it came to settling a real issue or choosing a head of government?

The structure of the French Assemblies has been the constant, necessary if not sufficient, cause of ministerial instability. It has given the functioning of the government its peculiar characteristic: an all-but-permanent state of strife. Everything took place as though the opposition were undertaking to upset the Cabinet a few days, a few weeks, or at most a few months after it had been formed. When the Assembly contained but a single majority, the government changed within the same majority. If there were several possible majorities, the orientation of the government would change without the voters having given the slightest indication of a change of mind. Democracy in France under the Third and Fourth Republics was a form of government in which the people delegated their sovereignty every four or five years to six hundred elected deputies, who disposed of it as they saw fit. . . .

The permanent nature of the struggle for power bred uncertainty concerning both men and action. Who would be premier tomorrow? What would the next government do in Morocco, or in Algeria? To make a prediction, it was necessary to haunt the corridors of the Palais-Bourbon and chat with the different groups. The deputies participated in secret rites, played an esoteric game: they belonged to a sect both secret and open. They were representatives of the people, of course, but they were following also a unique trade, the parliamentary profession. . . .

. . . The special psychology of the French deputy seems to me to have been not so much the cause as the result of the system. Among Western legislators, only the French deputy took part in an execution (the overthrowing of a Cabinet), in a festivity (ministerial crisis), and in a prize-giving ceremony (the formation of a Cabinet), every three, six, or twelve months. In the interval between these ceremonies he was recovering from the last one, and getting ready for the next.

Not that the "ceremony"—ministerial crisis or election of the President of the Republic—is peculiar to French parliamentary government. [A] study . . . devoted to the election of René Coty,[1] gives one the feeling less of something unique than of the perfecting of a genre or the stylizing of practices which are in themselves normal. A parallel automatically suggests itself: the choice by the American parties of candidates for President of the United States.

The similarities are many and immediately discernible. In both instances, elected delegates or deputies have to choose by election one man from among

---

[1] C. Melnik and N. Leites, *The House Without Windows* (New York, 1958).

several candidates. Some candidates have made public announcements, others are in reserve, biding their time. Among the delegates, some obey strictly the directives of the group to which they belong, while others retain their freedom of choice. The groups are heterogeneous, some large and compact, others small, and always on the verge of break-up. In cases where the principal groups are evenly balanced and no candidate can obtain an absolute majority, small groups can tip the scales one way or the other and play a part out of proportion to their proper weight. A dark horse may triumph, expressing less the real preference than the resignation of the majority.

Aside from the language and style of the participants, the development of the presidential election of 1953 with its successive stages . . . hardly offers anything strikingly original. The groups are too numerous to agree in advance, they are not united enough to foresee the outcome of a trial of strength, they are forced to . . . show that a certain individual cannot win the necessary number of votes. These polls take time and slowly change the atmosphere until general impatience and the weariness of those whose hopes have been deceived force a solution.

Some . . . expressions . . . apply to the search for a premier as well as for a President of the Republic . . . : "once around the track" (one individual who knows he has no chance spends several days in conversations devoid of significance), "lift the mortgages" (an individual whose chances are few but not inexistent tries an experiment so that the number of possible solutions will be gradually narrowed down to the conclusion). These rites had originally a reasonably intelligible function: the lack of discipline in the groups did not allow the leaders to come to an understanding because none of them knew the exact number of votes he could count on. Gradually the function was forgotten and the ceremonial aspect became dominant. And yet, the ceremony retained a psychological function: since the new Cabinet would inevitably resemble the former one, men had to forget previous quarrels so as to prepare for the morrow's understanding.

It is easy to see that both French public opinion and foreign observers would gradually become exasperated by the repetition of crises each of which required several weeks of settling. But it would be too easy to blame the "politician's deformity" alone. The major fact is that the deputies, because of the structure of the system, were waging a perennial battle for power. This battle . . . was renewed under the French system every time there was a ministerial crisis.

There were times under the Third Republic (1928–1932), or even under the Fourth Republic (1948–1951), when governments might have lasted, since a single parliamentary majority was possible. . . . But since 1932 France has usually been faced with issues whose gravity would have tested any regime: how was the economic depression to be alleviated? What policy was to be adopted toward the Third Reich? After the Liberation the questions were neither less numerous nor less pressing: what was to be the attitude toward the Communist Party? toward European unity? How was France to preserve, transform, or abandon the French Union? In twenty-five years neither the country at large nor the politicians ever gave a unanimous answer to these fateful questions. France, herself, was as deeply divided as her governing classes. Our form of government, because of its structure, tended to enlarge real disagreements, multiplying them by the quarrels among the professional politicians.

For twenty-five years every party, except the Communist Party . . . has split each time a vital issue has come up. . . . Consequently, disagreement on immediate problems was added to the traditional dissensions. Public opinion continued to rail against parties which had ceased to exist as units.

In such circumstances the parliamentary game developed a complexity which discouraged all but the expert. There was no longer any need to change the majority in order to change the policy. The representatives of two opposing policies . . . might have occupied the same Moderate bench, had they belonged to the same Assembly. . . . In order to form a Cabinet the consent of the central committees of certain parties and also the votes of enough deputies voting independently were necessary. The choice of each cabinet member took on significance. Not only did the representatives of each of the traditional groups have to be in balance (right, left, Socialist, Radical, moderate), but also those of the nonofficial groups ("Europeans" and "non-Europeans," "Ultras" and liberals). The difficulty of getting a majority in order to form a Cabinet or to approve a decision became such that the concern over parliamentary consent finally obscured the basic issues. . . .

This discussion brings us automatically to further questions: why so many weak and heterogeneous parties? Why so many extremists of both right and left?

Let us begin with a common-sense statement: a plurality of parties, not the two-party system, is natural. If nothing obliges them, or at least incites them, voters and their representatives will not organize themselves into two blocs, but will instead scatter into many different parties. Now, the two chief factors in this organization are the electoral law and the functioning of the legislature. Since 1789, and even since 1871, we have tested many electoral systems, but never the only two which could have eliminated splinter parties or brought about a synthesis: the English method of election by simple majority in single-member constituencies whose direct simplicity pitilessly eliminates "marginal" individuals or groups, and proportional representation with the clause adopted by the German Federal Republic, by which parties not winning 5 per cent of the votes throughout the whole country have no right to a seat. Proportional representation biased in favor of the big parties one time, another time favoring the little ones, election by double ballot in single-member constituencies, election by double ballot of lists on a *département* basis—none of these laws (not even the last one, which applied only once) obliged the candidates to follow the party policies, or the voters to confine their votes to the candidate of one party. The mixed system, in which some candidates owed their election to their personal position in the district or *département*, others to the success of a party, was never overcome. This mixed system at the electoral level corresponds exactly to the mixed system at the parliamentary level. In electoral districts as at the Palais-Bourbon, the political struggle was sometimes one of individuals, sometimes one of parties. In both cases it appeared as a conflict of ideas, and usually it brought to grips both parties and men—parties divided in everything but traditional preferences and men whose quarrels did not always express the clash of ideas. . . .

Neither the electoral laws nor parliamentary rules have set up any barrier to the proliferation of parties in France; they have merely reflected it. The statement is debatable: the electoral and legislative practices may be considered the cause and the multiplicity of parties the effect. It is a question of two complementary aspects of the same phenomenon. . . . The greater the tendency in a free society for factions to multiply, the more legislation must favor the organization of but a few strong parties.

Admitting this weakness on the part of the legislators, are the French more heterogeneous, more susceptible to division, than other European countries? All the Catholic or predominantly Catholic countries . . . find it hard to adapt parliamentary institutions of British origin. There seems to be some sort of relation between religious pluralism and the two-party system in politics, and between the more or less exclusive domination of one church and political pluralism. This relationship could not be considered a scientific law, but the reasons for it and its origin are vaguely apparent. The opposition between right and left in France coincides to a certain extent with that between the adherents of the Church and the laity (not to say believers and rationalists). The importance of the religious question (for or against clericalism, the Church, parochial schools) prevents, on the right, the organization of a large moderate party which would include Voltairists and Catholics, and on the left it creates a solidarity, traditional but today illusory, among liberals, Socialists and Communists. Moreover, those who stand opposed to a Universal Church with a dogmatic theology accept the Communist counter-religion more readily than do Anglo-Saxon nonconformists. The French party system is different from both that in Italy and the system which existed in Republican Spain. A few common traits may be nonetheless found: a left divided into at least three branches, Communists, Socialists, and rationalists (liberal or radical), and a right which, in not being unified into a single party of Catholic inspiration . . . , is also composed of three sections: the anticlerical conservatives, those imbued with the Catholic or Christian spirit, and those opposed to the democratic or republican order. These six groups make up what may be called the spontaneous expression of political attitudes in a predominantly Catholic country, with the left-wing rationalists and the anti-clerical conservatives likely either to merge, or, on the contrary, to form more than two splinter parties. . . .

In 1945–46, just after the Liberation, a combination of circumstances, General de Gaulle's prestige, proportional representation, and fear of Communism, led to the appearance of the Popular Republican Movement, the large moderate party the experts had long hoped for. First the R.P.F., and then traditional conservatism drew their strength from the circumstantially inflated forces of the Popular Republicans. The latter after a few years were back to their traditional constituencies in a few well-defined regions (Brittany, the Département du Nord, Alsace, and a few *départements* in the west). Supporters of the M.R.P., some conservative, others more liberal, are almost all recruited in the provinces where Catholic sentiment is still deeply rooted.

The development of a Christian Democratic party incapable of taking the place occupied by its sister parties in Germany and Italy could only add to the pluralism and the confusion. A deplorable phenomenon certainly, but one hard to avert, since nothing, either in the electoral law or in the parliamentary regulations, tended to prevent this proliferation. In all countries organized parties have arisen on the left rather than on the right. The right has answered a threat, responded to a challenge. . . .

Economically and socially, France is more heterogeneous than Great Britain, though less so than Italy. The difference between the regions north and south of the Loire is less marked than that between the Po basin and the provinces of the defunct kingdom of Naples. Nevertheless, French industry is still concentrated in a few areas (Paris and its gradually spreading environs, the north and east around the two coal basins, the regions of Lyon-Saint-Etienne, Marseilles, and Grenoble). Aside from these complexes we hardly find anything but secondary centers . . . and light industries scattered among mainly agricultural provinces. Whole regions in the west, southwest, and southeast have kept the old ways of life. Why should politics have changed its style and be subject to the dictates of the masses and of organizations? The socio-economic diversity of the country, which has not prevented the development of movements on a national scale, has had two main consequences: it has been reflected among supporters of each of the great parties (the Communists recruit votes among the farmers and tenant farmers in poor agricultural *départements* as well as among workers in *départements* in full industrial expansion), and it has crystallized the multiple expressions of center and right, assuring the solidity of a party such as the M.R.P., which became regional. . . .

Neither the electoral statutes, the multiplicity of ideologies, or the socio-economic diversity raised any insurmountable barrier to a system of a few well-organized parties. No one could maintain that it would be enough to eliminate one of these factors (and how eliminate the multiplicity of ideologies?) for the political scene to be simplified and for the functioning of the regime to become more efficient. The fact remains that the nature of these elements is in harmony with the multiparty system. That system is the product of a Catholic country whose varied regions have evolved differently, whose individuals cling to contradictory politico-metaphysical convictions— a country where the vote is dominated by traditions or by ideas as much as it is by clearly recognized interests, either private or collective. Whatever one may say, if democracy requires the representatives to express the wishes of the electors, then the composition of the Assemblies was in singular conformity with the ideal.

And yet in France more than in any country in Europe people speak of the disparity between "legal" France and the real country. During the last years of the Fourth Republic people were always denouncing the "alienation" of the professional politicians, lost amid oversubtle schemings which the ordinary citizen failed to grasp and which he watched with growing irritation. That the crisis, which had become an almost permanent condition in 1957–58, was severely criticized by Frenchmen is certain. Most certainly, it was not what they wanted. This does not mean that the Assembly, as constituted, reflected a distorted image of the nation.

Either knowingly or through a misunderstanding, the voters sent to the Palais-Bourbon more than 150 Communist deputies and about 50 Poujadists. More than five million Frenchmen voted for the Communist Party, more than two million for candidates representing Pierre Poujade, whose mode of speech would make Hitler's sound cultivated by comparison. In January 1956, the French got the Assembly they earned on election day. . . . The party openly obeying orders from Moscow and the candidates offered by a rabble-rouser together obtained 40 per cent of the votes. . . .

There was little to be feared from Poujadism itself. Its leader's mediocrity, the emptiness of its program, the ineffectiveness of the policy it adopted, kept it from increasing the number of its supporters, as the Fascist or National-Socialist parties had done a generation earlier. Warm feeling, noble ideals, both altogether necessary to a rightist revolution in industrial societies where materialism rules during time of peace, were lacking in this almost burlesque movement whose leaders resembled the mass and which, united from top to bottom more in hatred of taxation than in love of greatness, resolved to "kick the rascals out" . . . rather than to sacrifice themselves for the recovery of the empire.

Poujadism had both meaning and consequences nonetheless. It provoked the moderate right to demagogy and exaggeration. By preventing the working of the political alliances (*apparentements*) it increased the parliamentary strength of the Communists and was partly responsible for the composition of an ungovernable Assembly. Finally—and this is perhaps the main thing—it brought into the open an often-misunderstood social mechanism: economic progress creates as many demands as it satisfies. . . .

. . . At the beginning of 1956, France had just experienced three years of exceptional prosperity, of increasing stability in prices, with her foreign exchange in balance. Real wages had increased from 15 to 20 per cent in three years—an abnormally rapid increase. Yet in the 1956 elections nearly 40 per cent of the vote was against the system. Expansion had not appeased wage earners but had irritated thousands of independent workers, businessmen, craftsmen, tenant farmers, and land-owning peasants.

There is always the danger that economic growth will involve hardship, especially in a country where the working population is not increasing. In these circumstances it operates by transfer—of labor toward more productive activities, and of population to areas where development is favored by geographic or economic factors. Stagnant regions as a result undergo a relative, at times absolute, decline. Those remaining in the less favored zones are embittered, especially those engaged in tertiary services, particularly merchants, who are doomed by the slackening of activity. . . .

But the movement spread to the rest of the country and won, in certain *départements* undertaking rapid industrial expansion, a percentage of votes equal to or above its national average. Studies suggest an explanation of the same sort, but different in detail: some groups feel that they are victims of fate and of the State in a period of prosperity. The number of such victims, or those who so consider themselves, is especially great because France contains many "marginals," independent persons who struggle to maintain a traditional way of work and life. It is also likely that the protests against excessive taxation were often more justified than was believed in the cities. French taxes are heavy when strictly paid. They are insupportable when they strike areas or professions on the decline. Even if they are equitable in the abstract and represent a normal share of over-all national expenditures, they are resented as unjust if they force reconversion of out-of-date enterprises in accordance with the wishes of economists but contrary to the desires—and they too are legitimate—of the interested parties. Elsewhere these protests would have been expressed through party or professional organizations. In France the double tradition of peasant resistance to taxation and of hostility to the regime favored the Poujadist expression of discontent.

The vote of more than five million Frenchmen for the Communists poses a similar problem in collective psychology. . . .

Analysis of election returns combined with polls of public opinion make it possible to describe in detail the social make-up of Communist support. About half of it comes from industrial workers, and the other half is recruited from all social strata—peasants, merchants, craftsmen, civil servants, and so on. Geographically the party's strongholds are in the industrial zones (around

Paris and the Département du Nord), but also in predominantly agricultural areas which may be likened to underdeveloped areas (the Creuse district, for instance), and, finally, in localities of the southeast, where it apparently owes its success as much to leftist tradition as to proletarian spirit, or a revolt against stagnation. . . . But nowhere does the strength fall below 10 per cent, nor does it anywhere noticeably exceed a third of the votes. The most characteristic feature of this electorate is neither professional nor geographic: by far the great majority of Communist voters are recruited among those having low or mediocre incomes. Tocqueville saw in the French Revolution a vast protest against social inequality, the inequality expressed in the estates. Perhaps he would see Communism today as a vast protest against economic inequality. . . .

Inquiry as to the consequences of governmental instability under the Fourth Republic leads to a series of questions which have no answers: would stronger governments have averted the war in Indochina? would they have entered sooner into negotiations with the Viet Minh? The provisional government of General de Gaulle had sent an expeditionary force, and although General Leclerc was in favor of an accord with Ho Chi Minh, another Gaullist, Admiral Thierry d'Argenlieu, bears a great responsibility for the onset of the war. In retrospect, we reproach the succession of governments from 1947 to 1954 with the steadiness of purpose worthy of a better fate in so far, at least, as Indochina is concerned. Are we to conclude that this steadfastness was the result of a lack of authority and tenure on the part of those at the helm? Doubt persists.

As for French public opinion, by 1958 it was no longer in doubt. It was to the system—that is, the Parliament and the members of Parliament—that responsibility for the national failure and, above all, the loss of empire, was attributed. Whereas world opinion was convinced that France's mistake had been to wage war in Indochina, or, at least, to persist in it after the Communist victory in China, the French themselves, victims of propaganda and their collective vanity, blamed their disappointments in Asia and Africa on those who had been in power since 1945. The fall of the Fourth Republic and the advent of de Gaulle to power led, in November and December of 1958, to the election of an Assembly as coherent as the one in 1956 was ungovernable. But the nation had changed less than its government, and in the very act of re-electing its legislature gave evidence of its enduring character. . . .

WHY THE FOURTH REPUBLIC FAILED
TO SOLVE THE ALGERIAN PROBLEM

DOROTHY PICKLES

It is obvious ... that the causes of failure ... of the Fourth Republic's efforts to deal with the Algerian problem ... were multiple and that what really led to the inextricable tangle that it presented by 1958 was the kind of chain reaction, or series of vicious circles, which different obstacles created, sometimes in turn and sometimes simultaneously. The French were themselves divided about what they ought to try to do, partly because of the inherent difficulties of the problem, partly because they were divided on almost everything else. Algeria, therefore, became part of the internal political struggle, and Communist opposition made the achievement of any positive majority difficult and often impossible. Under the Fourth Republic, the presence of right-wing, as well as left-wing, extremists in the National Assembly meant that a positive majority required the agreement of almost everyone else, and there were few issues simple enough or clear enough to permit that. Fragile majorities thus constituted a major political problem in themselves, and so the clamor of French voices helped to drown the voices of those Algerians with whom they ought to have been discussing the problem of Algeria's future.

It had always been difficult to identify the voices of authentic Moslem spokesmen, and when war made it impossible, that problem, too, became part of the quarrel. The progress of the war convinced Moslem leaders that intransigence paid, and the French record confirmed their suspicions that the French were not to be trusted. Yet they had no alternative to discussion with the French, sooner or later. Both sides were well aware that Algerian independence was impossible without French help, and it ought to have become clear to both much sooner than it did that neither side could impose its will militarily on the other. By waiting too long, both sides increased their own as well as the other's difficulties and may well have rendered the kind of settlement that both wanted, and eventually reached on paper, impossible to carry out in practice. Both sides were, in fact, the prisoners of their own myths, and each failed to realize the essentially similar predicament of the other. "It was insane," said Raymond Aron in 1958, "for one side to say 'Now' and for the other to say 'Never.' " ...

... It is possible to discern, over and above party quarrels and the inherent difficulties of the Franco-Algerian relationship as it had been built up over the years, at least three general factors that contributed to the Fourth Republic's failure.

Dorothy Pickles, *Algeria and France: From Colonialism to Cooperation* (New York: Frederick A. Praeger, 1963), pp. 49–59. © Frederick A. Praeger, Inc. Used by permission.

The first was attributable to bad luck rather than bad judgment, at least for a time. The French experiment in assimilation in Algeria had its fictions, as has been seen. But it also had concrete achievements to its credit, among which was the extent of real educational and cultural assimilation. If Algerian *pieds noirs* developed many of the white-settler reflexes, the Moslem student or politician in France found a lack of race consciousness and of race superiority that compared very favorably with the situation encountered by colored students elsewhere. In the fields of social and economic policy and of administration, France's record could easily stand comparison with that of any other colonial power.

Where Algeria was concerned, however, French methods proved to be less adapted to the spirit of twentieth-century anticolonialism than those of other colonial powers (with the exception of Belgium and Portugal), or even than her methods in her own colonies. It was comprehensible that, after the four war years during which she had been cut off from some overseas territories and, in any case, had only a provisional government-in-exile, France should have failed to realize, as she did at Brazzaville in 1944, how rapid would be the development of nationalism in dependent territories. All colonial powers made this mistake. At least the evolution in the French colonies was slow enough to enable the Fourth Republic to begin to make up for lost time and for General de Gaulle to be able to finish the job. In Algeria, the problem of reversing engines was both politically and administratively difficult. It was politically difficult because the most progressive minds, those who in America or Great Britain would have been described as "anticolonialist," were not anti-assimilationist. The difference between "colonialist" and "anticolonialist" was the difference between those who clung to the fictions of assimilation and those who wanted to make it a reality. The mistake of too many French politicians and administrators was that they did not recognize quickly enough that assimilation had ceased to be a possible road for even moderate nationalist opinion, and that the movement of opinion was irrevocably in the direction of self-government. Politicians like M. Mendès-France, M. Mollet, a number of MRP leaders—even M. Soustelle at one time—were neither colonialist nor dishonest. They were progressive in a traditional way, in a revolutionary situation. They tried sincerely to improve Franco-Algerian relations, but always in ways that were two or three stages behind what was required in the circumstances. All but one of the five Prime Ministers who wrestled with the problem from 1954 to 1958 ended by becoming convinced that some form of independence was inevitable. But their conviction came far too late.

Even if it had come earlier, however, it is improbable that they could have persuaded enough of their parliamentary colleagues and electors to follow them rapidly enough along this unfamiliar road. The myth had by then, particularly for many army officers, become a compensation for military defeat—defeat in Europe in 1940 and in Indochina in 1954—and for the loss of Tunisia and Morocco. All that can be said is that they did not try. Instead, they refused to face the facts and too often deceived themselves as well as the public with words. Verbal escapism is a characteristic of French politics that more than one of the presidents of newly independent states has resented in the course of negotiations with France. M. Bourguiba, for instance, has complained:

You French have a peculiar genius for using words in inappropriate senses. What you called a "protectorate" was "colonization." ... What you called "internal autonomy" was, as I soon grasped, a kind of protectorate—a genuine one—and what you call "independence" is really no more than "internal autonomy." I don't know how to make the French understand that we are truly independent.

French critics, too, have complained about the use by politicians of the Fourth Republic of "verbal magic" in default of a policy. After the 1956 elections, one commentator wrote:

Recourse to verbal solutions is a national habit. Once we have found a word, we feel that we have answered the question and resolved the problem. This is doubtless what foreigners call French logic. ... Since the liberation, we have had an orgy of formulas. The word "colony" has been banned; we condemn "native," though we tolerate "indigenous." ... Assimilation, integration, internal autonomy, *départementalisation*, independence within the French Union, independence within interdependence, cosovereignty, joint management, association. ... In reality, the words always lag behind the facts. We can no longer catch up with facts by inventing new words. ... Time is irrevocably against us. ...

The second factor that contributed to the Fourth Republic's failure was that, even if its politicians had been more successful in bringing their ideas into line with the facts and in converting their electors as well, they would have found the application of any new and radical policy in Algeria administratively difficult, and probably impossible in the short run. Indeed, they found even minor changes impossible to introduce in the face of opposition from high officials as well as European residents. Throughout the Fourth Republic, Algeria's chief administrators were overwhelmingly either Frenchmen from France or European Algerians, and this had important consequences. First, as Lyautey put it, French administrators "have direct administration in the blood," and in Algeria direct administration remained possible long after it should have given way to preparation for some real degree of "internal autonomy" (the French term for self-administration), even if not for self-government. The centralized administrative machine could easily find recruits in France, owing to the geographical proximity of Algeria and the favorable economic conditions (Algerian taxes, for instance, were appreciably lower than French taxes). There was, moreover, no language barrier, owing to the generalized use of the French language, which remained the official language of Algeria and was taught in all Algerian schools. There was also a plentiful supply of European administrators on the spot, as well as a small French-speaking and French-thinking Moslem elite, often as sentimentally attached to France and to French ways as were the Europeans.

There was, therefore, no incentive to train Moslems to run the country, and little or no pressure to do so from the bulk of the Moslems, who remained both politically and economically backward, primarily interested in finding work either in Algerian cities or in France. . . .

In 1956, nearly two years after the outbreak of the Algerian rebellion, the Minister residing in Algeria, M. Lacoste, stated that, of 864 high administrative posts in Algeria, only 8 were held by Moslems. The first Moslem member of the *Conseil d'Etat* was not appointed until October, 1958. In the French Army, which included upward of 60,000 Moslems, there was, in 1958, only 1 Moslem general; and he had been appointed only that year, and there were only 400 Moslem officers out of a total of some 30,000 officers. The Arabization of Algerian administration had hardly begun, and the European population was determined that it should remain the virtual European monopoly that it had always been.

It was also an administration that had acquired a high degree of autonomy. Tightly controlled by Paris in theory, it succeeded in practice in evading central control. Successions of weak governments and constant governmental interregnums in Paris meant that Ministers were often not in office long enough to learn their job properly or to carry out any concerted policy, even if the government had had one. The fragility of government majorities meant that the Minister, even when relatively secure in office, often had his mind more on the problem of how to keep himself and his colleagues there than on his departmental functions, and his colleagues in the Cabinet were too preoccupied by their own problems to worry about his. In 1955, M. Soustelle, assimilationist then as later, but at that time in his progressive period, complained that he was not backed up by Paris and that his reports and requests were consistently ignored. Yet he was doing little more than trying, belatedly, to apply a Statute voted eight years earlier. A *de facto* community of outlook between large sections of the administration and the *colon* interests too often combined with these political factors to prevent any changes in the *status quo*. Even M. Schuman, who did hold office through a number of governments, admitted that the control of the Quai d'Orsay over Residents-General in Tunisia and Morocco under the Fourth Republic had been something of a fiction. *Mutatis mutandis*, his description of the relationship between Paris and the Residents-General was no less true of that between Paris and the Governor-General of Algeria:

The two Residents-General are on the spot. They receive and furnish all the information; they have a vast and varied scope for initiative, which they are always tempted to extend, particularly when their views and those of the French population coincide; they interpret instructions from Paris and decide how they are to be carried out. Their resistance to the constant temptation to use the *fait accompli* is praiseworthy—that is to say, when they *do* resist it. In relation to some of their departments (police, information, and so on...), their own position is similar to that of the Minister in relation to them.

If this had not been, generally speaking, the state of affairs in Algeria, it would not have been necessary for M. Mollet, in 1956, to accept responsibility after the event for the arrest by Algiers officials of M. Ben Bella and his four companions—an arrest that he had not only not ordered, but had not even known anything about until it had happened.

Given a situation like this, it is easy to see how, starting out with the best of intentions, a Governor-General could end by becoming the agent instead of the head of this vast semiautonomous bureaucratic machine. Two things encouraged this tendency: his constant subjection to pressure from powerful *colon* interests, and the special atmosphere of Algiers, with its mixture of pomp and ceremony—"honors and military parades are more splendid in Africa"—and the exuberant and heady enthusiasm of the Algiers crowds. . . .

The third factor that contributed to the failure of the Fourth Republic was the political evolution of the army and the alliance of some of its leaders with the Europeans in Algeria. However autonomous the Algerian administration was (and however close its relations with the *colons*), a successful revolt of Algeria against France would have been inconceivable without the support of considerable sections of the army, and without the anxiety of French governments (including that of General de Gaulle) not to add army disunity and civil war to the war against the Moslem rebels. The "politicization" of the army, which Raymond Aron had warned his compatriots against in 1958, had by then already gone too far, and it is probable that both the Fourth Republic's leaders and General de Gaulle underestimated the hold that the army's version of the *Algérie française* myth had obtained over regular officers.

This was all too easy to do. Many regular officers had, by 1958, spent some eighteen to twenty years away from metropolitan France, either in North Africa, in French overseas territories in Saharan Africa, or in Indochina. The Indochinese war had lasted for almost eight years, and its outcome had created a deep sense of bitterness and humiliation. The sense of betrayal by civilian leaders, which lay behind a good deal of this politicization, really dates from these years, as does the myth of the insurgent colonels who were to sympathize with or lead the OAS—the myth that France's colonial wars are part of the defense of the West against Communism and that the West must fight as the Communists do with ideological and political as well as with military weapons.

But however the army's alienation from the state came about, its consequences were to be disastrous. What remained of the authority of weak and divided governments was dissipated. Algeria was able to defy France. The Algerian problem divided France as well as Algeria to the point at which the mythmongers' dream of a French Algeria was accompanied by the real danger of the Algerianization of France.

For many Frenchmen, there was a fourth factor, whose contribution to the Fourth Republic's failure was more important than all the others. It was the existence of a solid bloc of Communist voters—for most of the time, one-fifth of the electors and one-fourth of the voters—which ensured that, during one of the most difficult periods of French history, successive governments could never find a stable majority for any policy. This permanent opposition, sometimes in conjunction with the extreme Right, gave pressure groups far more influence than they would otherwise have had. Where Algeria was concerned, it strengthened the "Algeria lobby." In a National Assembly, in which, in the last decade of the Fourth Republic, two-fifths of the members were in permanent opposition to the regime, the government, and each other, "to detach thirty deputies from the governmental majority was enough to paralyze the executive. L'Algérie française had her loyal servants in several center parties. . . . It was not enough to decide on a policy in Paris. It still had to cross the Mediterranean."

It was not so much the size of the Communist problem in itself that helped to defeat the Fourth Republic, but its size in relation to other problems of the time. In his study of the foreign policy of the Fourth Republic, Alfred Grosser attributes the Fourth Republic's failure in that sphere essentially to two factors: the inability of French politicians to face facts (which has already been mentioned), and the conjunction in France of two "antagonisms" at one and the same time, that between the old and the new world—the colonialist and the anticolonialist—and that between Communism and anti-Communism. It might have been possible, he says, to handle either of these two antagonisms singly, but the two together were too much for France. . . .

It is difficult to decide whether or not Communism in postwar France was a cause or a symptom of the failure of the Fourth Republic. The Fifth, which at least for the first four years had virtually no Communist problem to deal with, found the Algerian problem almost, if not quite, as intractable as had the governments of the previous regime. But the Fifth Republic inherited, along with the basic problem, those that the Fourth had created in trying to solve it, just as the Fourth Republic had had to try to make up belatedly for the errors of the Third. It is arguable that one of the main reasons for the failure of successive governments and regimes to deal satisfactorily with the problem of Algeria is precisely this kind of continuity —the extent to which the evil that successive regimes did lived after them.

In 1958, then, the Fourth Republic handed over to General de Gaulle the whole insoluble problem of Algeria, with all the contradictions that its divisions had created. . . .

HOW THE FOURTH REPUBLIC DIED: THE REVOLUTION OF MAY, 1958

PHILIP WILLIAMS

In May, 1958, France went through a cold revolution. In form it was commonplace. Not only the law but the constitutional conventions were observed; the National Assembly merely elected a new prime minister by an unusually comfortable majority, and conferred on him emergency powers of exceptional scope. Yet a bare month earlier the deputies would not have dreamed of accepting either the man or the powers. They gave way because they feared the intervention of the army, and knew that no effective force—official or popular—would defend the legal government. Georges Bidault said that De Gaulle needed only ten words for his speech to the Assembly: "*Messieurs, entre la Seine et vous, il y a—moi.*" ["Gentlemen, between the Seine and you, there is—me."]. . . .

Algiers has always been a conspirational city. On 6 February 1956 the extremists organized a riotous European mob to greet the new Socialist premier, Guy Mollet, and alarmed him into changing his policy and his Minister for Algeria. In subsequent weeks they built up "counter-terrorist" societies to fight the FLN's nationalist terrorists with bombs and kidnappings. In December 1956 a general, Jacques Faure, was arrested for conspiring to seize power in the city. A month later a bazooka shell was fired into the office of the Commander-in-Chief, General Salan, whose aide-de-camp was killed.

One extremist group was associated with the Poujadists; their chief was the intellectual of the movement, Dr. Bernard Lefèvre. Another was the "Christian Fascist" *Union française nord-africaine* (UFNA), whose leader Robert Martel was interned for a time by Lacoste. Both were involved, along with the Gaullist adventurer Biaggi, in organising the riots of 6 February 1956. Both supplied recruits to the counter-terrorists, whose chief organisations were the CRF (*Comités de la Renaissance française*, dissidents from UFNA) and the ORAF (*Organisation de Résistance de l'Algérie française*, linked with the Poujadists). ORAF's leader was a doctor and champion swimmer of Hungarian origin, René Kovacs; he was associated with General Faure's plot

Philip Williams, "How the Fourth Republic Died: Sources for the Revolution of May 1958," *French Historical Studies*, vol. III, no. 1 (Spring, 1963), 1, 4–18, 20–24. Copyright by the Society for French Historical Studies, 1963. Used by permission of *French Historical Studies* and the author.

and responsible for the bazooka attempt against General Salan. Arrested, he tried to escape punishment by boasting of his powerful political and military protectors; brought to trial soon after De Gaulle came to power, he conveniently escaped abroad.

Both UFNA and the Poujadists dreamed of using a revolt in Algiers to destroy democracy in Paris. Martel of UFNA was in touch with a counter-revolutionary secret society in the capital, the "Grand O." . . . Its leaders were a former commander-in-chief in Algeria, General Cherrières (who had left in 1955 after quarrelling with Governor-General Soustelle) and a former air force commander in Indo-China, General Chassin, who was now President of the *Anciens d'Indochine*, a turbulent body of ex-servicemen under violently anti-democratic leadership.

More respectable settlers' leaders, like Sérigny, had less ambitious aims. They wanted a "Government of Public Safety" dominated by their "quartet" of parliamentary allies, Jacques Soustelle, Georges Bidault, André Morice, and Roger Duchet. Although Sérigny had been an ardent Pétainist in the war, he had recently financed and organized an Algerian section of Soustelle's largely Gaullist *Union pour le Salut et le Renouveau de l'Algérie française* (USRAF). And he was in constant touch with the Resident Minister, Robert Lacoste (appointed after the riots of 6 February 1956). Lacoste had long been warning Paris that a change of policy would mean an outbreak in Algeria; by May 1958 this prospect no longer wholly displeased him, for his fellow-Socialists had thrown him over and accepted a change. Finally, a tiny handful of Gaullists were resolved to use the expected rising to bring the General back to power.

There were very few Gaullists among the Europeans of Algeria. In the army there were rather more; and without the army (which now enjoyed wide powers of civil administration as well as decisive force) there could be no hope of success. Because part of the officer corps rallied to them, the Gaullists seized the leadership of the movement in Algeria from their locally stronger rivals. Because of their wide military, police, and administrative contacts in the French governmental machine, they were able to enforce a revolutionary transfer of power. And because of De Gaulle's personal prestige they were able to achieve their objectives without bloodshed in France, and with unexpected Moslem goodwill in Algeria.

The political crisis opened in September 1957. The Radical Prime Minister Bourgès-Maunoury introduced a mild Algerian reform bill, the "loi-cadre," which set up a single electoral college and so deprived the Europeans of their privileged political position. A hostile demonstration was called for 16 September; General Massu stopped it. Sérigny then called on his parliamentary friends, who overthrew the government; Massu called this "a crime . . . which will probably lose us Algeria." The ministerial crisis lasted the record time of 37 days. From it emerged another Radical premier,

Gaillard, who put through a still milder bill. The ex-servicemen and the Students' Union (AGEA) called another demonstration, which was a failure, and Lacoste retaliated by deporting some of the leaders and drafting the president of AGEA—who was succeeded by a more extreme character: Pierre Lagaillarde.

In February 1958 the crisis became acute. Exasperated by Tunisian aid to the FLN,[1] army leaders—without governmental authorization—bombed the frontier village of Sakiet. Ministers feared to offend the army by disciplinary sanctions, but they bowed to international opinion by accepting the "good offices" of British and American mediators. Civilians and soldiers in Algeria feared this would entail a humiliating capitulation to the FLN. In Algiers the temperature mounted, and in Paris the Right overthrew another cabinet, their third in twelve months.

Both the Right and the army had miscalculated. Instead of stiffening the government's Tunisian policy, the Sakiet raid had weakened it. Now Gaillard's fall further undermined the influence of the friends of Algiers— even in their own parties. President Coty's first nominee for the premiership was Georges Bidault of MRP[2]; the party president, Pflimlin, demurred. The Radicals would not join a Pleven cabinet which was to include the right-wing Radical leader André Morice. The Socialists would enter no government at all; this ensured the eviction of Lacoste from the Ministry for Algeria. The crisis, provoked by the settlers, was used to eliminate the men the settlers wanted. Finally Coty put forward Pierre Pflimlin, the man who had vetoed Bidault and had even talked of negotiating with the FLN.

The Assembly was to vote on Tuesday 13 May. That same afternoon in Algiers, military chiefs and civilian crowds were to assemble at the War Memorial to commemorate three French soldiers executed by the FLN in Tunisia. On previous occasions, army and populace had clashed; this time it was different. The change was due mainly to the Gaullists, and in particular to Léon Delbecque.

Many Gaullists believed that the General could be brought back to power only through a tremendous psychological shock, which could come only from Algiers. In November 1957, at the suggestion of Soustelle, Delbecque—an old Gaullist who had served in Algeria as a reserve officer— was taken on the staff of the new Gaullist Minister of Defence, Jacques Chaban-Delmas. By April he had made 27 trips to Algeria. There he fostered contacts between soldiers and civilians and forged an instrument intended to turn to De Gaulle's account the explosion which he saw as inevitable. After Gaillard's fall, he founded a Vigilance Committee (embracing 22 parties, student groups, and ex-servicemen's leagues) to canalize the popular discontent.

---

[1] FLN = *Front de Libération Nationale*, the Algerian independence organization.
[2] MRP = *Mouvement Républicain Populaire*, the Christian Democratic Party.

Only at the last minute did Lacoste learn of these activities. . . . Promptly he demanded that Gaillard have the conspirator withdrawn; otherwise he would appeal to President Coty. But Delbecque managed to return . . . and organized a large orderly demonstration on 26 April which showed he had his following well in hand. . . .

As Pleven gave up his attempt to form a government on 8 May, the tension in Algiers mounted. Fanning the flames, Lacoste was proclaiming everywhere the imminence of a "diplomatic Dien Bien Phu." Sérigny and Delbecque were now working together; they saw him (separately) on 9 May and, at Soustelle's suggestion, pressed him to put himself at the head of the movement for a Government of Public Safety, assuring him that De Gaulle would come out in their favor. Delbecque organized Vigilance Committee delegations to reinforce their plea. Lacoste hesitated; he favored an *Algérie française* demonstration but not a revolt against the Republic. Finally he refused, and on the 10th he left for Paris. . . . Disappointed, Sérigny now turned to De Gaulle (of whose integrationist opinions he had been assured by Soustelle). In an editorial on Sunday 11 May he appealed to the General to speak out.

Originally Delbecque had intended to act in August. But he seized the opportunity Lacoste had created. From the 9th, USRAF was distributing tracts demanding a Government of Public Safety. Over the weekend, preparations were hardly concealed. For the 13th, Delbecque in Algiers and Biaggi in Paris decided to organize simultaneous demonstrations culminating in the setting up of CSPs, Committees of Public Safety. . . . The Algiers CSP, composed of Vigilance Committee members and led by Soustelle, would take over Lacoste's office in the Ministry of Algeria (better known as the Gouvernement-Général, "GG") and launch an appeal to De Gaulle. However, a rival plot was being hatched under Delbecque's nose. For the Fascist "ultras" had formed a Committee of Seven including Lagaillarde, Martel and Dr. Lefèvre, which meant to steal the Gaullists' revolution as Delbecque was stealing Lacoste's riot. The ultras would attack the GG first, at 6 P.M. on the 13th; the army would have to join them or shoot them. They had no doubt of its choice, especially as their candidate for power was the army itself.

For the army was no longer willing to obey the government unconditionally. Salan and Massu were not themselves plotting, and indeed the Gaullists meant to arrest them. But several of their subordinates were involved with the Gaullists or with the ultras (Colonel Thomazo with both). And the whole army opposed negotiations with the FLN. Lacoste stiffened their hostility, bitterly upbraiding the generals on 8 May for their "cowardly" silence. Thus encouraged, Salan warned President Coty next evening that the election of a "sell-out government" would produce incalculable results among his forces. General Ely, chief of staff in Paris, supported his protest.

And when Lacoste finally decided to ban the 13 May demonstration, Salan once again refused to enforce the order.

On the morning of the 13th the activists distributed their leaflets. USRAF charged that Pflimlin meant to hold peace talks during the summer holidays; Algiers must stop his election and demand a Government of Public Safety under the "quartet." At 1 P.M. a general strike began; it was complete. . . . At 5 P.M. the Vigilance Committee loudspeaker began spreading incendiary slogans: treacherous politicians and intellectuals in Paris were the real murderers of the three executed soldiers, show them not your scorn but your anger, we will accept no government of the System, no sell-out government, only a Government of Public Safety. After the ceremony at 6 o'clock, the army leaders returned to their headquarters and the crowd began to disperse. Neither realized that a revolution was in progress not far away.

This revolution was not very well organized, since the operation Lagaillarde and Martel had planned for the end of the ceremony was anticipated by their rivals. It was not wholly serious, since these rivals were the schoolboys of AGELCA (*Association générale des élèves des lycées et collèges d'Algérie*). And it was not too risky, since the paratroop colonels were sympathetic or privy to the plot. . . .

Even before the ceremony began, the *lycéens* were climbing the broad stairway from the War Memorial up to the Forum, the open square in front of the GG. The top was held by riot police (CRS), who threw tear-gas grenades which infuriated the crowd. AGELCA loudspeakers denounced the CRS provocation; and the under-20's charged the steps. As schoolboys toured the city on their scooters spreading the word, the crowd swelled. Suddenly the CRS withdrew into the building. Maisonneuve (Lacoste's assistant) protested to the prefect Baret, and was told paratroops would replace them. None had come. He ordered the CRS to make a sortie; they cleared the Forum, and he phoned Lacoste in Paris that it was all over. But at the War Memorial, as the generals left at 6:05 P.M., Lagaillarde was shouting "Everyone to the GG against the rotten regime." Now, half an hour late, a few paratroops arrived and took their place on the stairway; they allowed the crowd to break through to the square.

At 6:15 the attack began; fewer than five hundred took part. The CRS were stoned and drew back behind the gates of the GG. . . . By 6:30 more intrepid *lycéens* had broken into the library at the corner of the building. Senior officers appealed for calm; without loudspeakers they were quite inaudible. . . . The parachutists stood by as one of their own trucks was used as a battering ram against the gates; about 6:45 these gave way. More tear-gas grenades were thrown from the windows, and a few shots fired; most of the crowd retreated, but a few broke through into the building, including Lagaillarde who, protected by his parachutists' uniform, climbed to an upper floor and vigorously (but inaudibly) urged his followers on. The CRS had disappeared, and the crowd began sacking the offices and flinging the files from the windows. . . . The Committee of Vigilance were still sitting not far away, unaware that they were being robbed of their revolution. Massu arrived at 7:30, followed by Salan, who came by the subway from military HQ through which the senior officials (and apparently also the CRS) later escaped from the building. Massu was furious. . . . Before long Paris telephoned, and Lacoste warned Massu against promoting sedition; the story persists that Massu asked whether to fire on the crowd. Lagaillarde and the riot leaders were urging him to become president of a Committee of Public Safety (CSP); he told a press conference next day that he agreed in order to keep them under control (Salan said nothing; the crowd had howled him down when he tried to speak). The committee, formed about 8:45, was very unlike that envisaged by Delbecque and the Vigilance Committee. The seven unknown individuals occupying Maisonneuve's office were all members; they proved to be Fascist sympathisers. Three parachutist colonels were added, and (at the army's suggestion) four Moslems; Delbecque, who arrived soon afterwards, was—as Soustelle's representative—made vice-president and, amid violent scenes, several Vigilance Committee members were brought in. . . .

In Paris the news produced a sensation. The deputies, absorbed in the ministerial crisis, had shown little concern for Algerian reactions to their decisions. . . . Returning one by one from dinner, members were plunged at once into feverish agitation. But Algiers had again miscalculated. The demonstration to stop Pflimlin converted a very doubtful vote into a certainty; the Communists decided to abstain, and probably a few defiant members swung to his side. He was elected by 274 to 129. . . . Coty as commander-in-chief ordered the army by radio proclamation to obey the legal government. And at dawn, when the crowd had left the Forum and one foreign observer thought the government might have recovered control of Algiers, the prime minister went to bed.

The cabinet's policy was fatally contradictory; it alarmed the army leaders by threats, while soothing public opinion by professions of confidence in the generals. Yet without regaining their allegiance there was no hope of recovering control of Algeria. The premier was encouraged to try by a long telephone call from Salan on the morning of the 14th, and a mild press conference by Massu that afternoon, in which he insisted that his aim was to keep the civilians from getting out of hand, that the army was still in control, and even that the CSP would remain only until a new Minister for Algeria arrived. "Including Pflimlin's Minister?" he was asked. "My reply was quite clear. Until a new Minister for Algeria takes over the GG." Delbecque's press conference just afterwards was less reassuring; he claimed that the CSP did not recognize the Pflimlin ministry, and would sit till France had a Government of Public Safety under General de Gaulle. Later that evening Massu declared he had been "misunderstood"; the CSP would remain till a new Minister could take over with the consent of the people. . . .

Meanwhile in Algiers events had taken a decisive turn. On the morning of Thursday 15th Salan spoke to the crowd in the Forum. His position was most disagreeable. The mob suspected him of republicanism, and on Tuesday night they had howled him down. . . . He knew that as Pflimlin's official representative, still in touch with Paris, he was suspected by the whole CSP of playing a double game; yet his trust in the government was as fragile as its confidence in him. On the 15th he took his first step towards open revolt. Ending a skilful and successful speech in traditional style, "Vive l'Algérie française, vive la France!," he stepped back amid cheers to face Léon Delbecque. After a moment's visible hesitation he came forward again. "Et vive De Gaulle!" Hitherto, the Liberator's name had aroused little enthusiasm. Henceforth it dominated the crisis.

Six hours later De Gaulle replied with his first public statement, concluding, "I am ready to assume the powers of the Republic." Algiers was delighted. . . .

The cards had been distributed; it remained only to play them. Suppose Salan had not appealed to De Gaulle, or he had not responded? Conceivably the movement in Algiers would have collapsed. But its driving force came from junior officers who were quite out of touch with opinion in France: far more likely the civilian and military extremists would have arrested Salan and Massu and launched an attack on the mainland. The successful appeal to De Gaulle ensured that the movement would neither crumble nor fall under Fascist control. It attracted support from Moslems, whose wholly unexpected demonstrations in Algiers on the 16th, and later elsewhere, seemed at last to offer a hope of reconciliation. It won maximum sympathy in the metropolitan army and administration. And it neutralized republicans who would not believe that De Gaulle aimed at dictatorship. . . .

Now the joker was slipped into the pack; Soustelle escaped from his police guard. Friends chartered a Swiss plane, and at 1:30 P.M. on the 17th he arrived unheralded at Algiers. The surprise was total. . . . Salan feared both that Soustelle's arrival would deter Pflimlin from resigning, and that so popular and powerful an ally would challenge his own authority. . . . The civilians, however, insisted that Salan telephone Pflimlin and discover his intentions; Soustelle agreed to leave at once if the premier meant to resign. At 3:45 P.M. Salan learned that Pflimlin was determined to stay. A dramatic and emotional meeting of the two leaders was then staged before a crowd quite unaware that they had been thinking of arresting one another a couple of hours before. . . .

In Paris the second week of the crisis opened with a cabinet meeting on Sunday 18th. Some ministers were anxious to act strongly against the generals and Soustelle, and even against De Gaulle; their proposals were vetoed by the prime minister. Next day, at 3 P.M., the General held his tensely awaited press conference at the Palais d'Orsay. He indignantly denied that he would ever infringe the fundamental liberties he had himself restored fourteen years before; he recalled the socialistic achievements of his government in 1944–6; he referred by name only to two persons, "my friend" Lacoste and Mollet "whom I esteem;" and he recalled with emotion an unforgettable (though unfortunately quite imaginary) meeting with the latter in 1945. But he adroitly avoided condemning the Algiers leaders; he praised the action of the army; and while saying in answer to Mollet that he would take power only from the Assembly, he demanded an exceptional procedure. The balancing act was so skilful that both sides were dissatisfied; the Algiers extremists felt De Gaulle had betrayed them and was compromising with "the System," and their confidence returned only when the Socialists denounced him for flouting the constitution. . . .

In public the cabinet's only reaction was to press on with constitutional reform proposals to take the wind out of the General's sails. But behind the scenes a race now began between the preparations for insurrection developing in the country, and negotiations being set on foot between Paris and Colombey. On Wednesday 21st the prime minister and President Coty both saw Pinay, an old anti-Gaullist; next day the CNI[3] leader visited the General's home and returned enthusiastic. Piette, Socialist deputy and close friend of Mollet, followed on Friday. . . .

But at the weekend the apparent lull ended abruptly. . . . On Saturday 24th came . . . the seizure of Corsica. Soustelle has claimed that the operation was intended to shatter the government's resistance quickly without an airborne attack on Paris. The island was garrisoned by parachutists who were stationed alternately at Calvi and in Algeria. More Corsicans live in North Africa than at home, and the insurgents could count on local sympathy. Henri Maillot, a distant cousin of De Gaulle and Resistance leader in the island, had made contact with Algiers, where Massu was already seeking reliable Corsicans. On the 19th Pascal Arrighi reached Algiers; two days later he broadcast to his compatriots. On Thursday 22nd there was a demonstration in favour of the police superintendent, removed for permitting a previous rally. Maillot's friends met at 9 P.M. on Friday night and resolved to seize the Ajaccio prefecture next evening; Algiers may not have expected such quick action. At 5:15 A.M. on Saturday, Arrighi, with three companions chosen by Massu and an order from Salan, landed in a military plane at Calvi and won over the police and army. The Ajaccio demonstrators met at 6 P.M., the paratroops arrived from Calvi at 6:35, and ten minutes later they held the prefecture. Delbecque and Sérigny flew over next day with a CSP delegation. . . . At Bastia there were three distinct CSP's, a determined Socialist acting mayor . . . , and a pro-government municipal council; but only a hundred

---

[3] CNI = *Centre National des Indépendants*, independent conservatives.

people came out to demonstrate. No one would die, or even march, for the fourth Republic. . . .

Corsica showed that the government was no longer obeyed. The prefect indeed stayed loyal, the sub-prefect of Sartène did not meet the new authorities till Pflimlin had resigned, and the military commander Colonel Prigent, finding Arrighi had misled him, returned in disgust to the mainland. But the other five sub-prefects, the police and the gendarmerie all went over. The Bastia sub-prefect said pathetically . . . "I don't know which side will fire me," and the Colonel, "I don't know which side will shoot me." . . .

Encouraged by reports from Bastia, the cabinet met at 9:30 on Saturday night and decided to retake the town before dawn on Monday. CRS were sent to the south coast, and orders given to the fleet. But at 5:30 on Sunday afternoon Admiral Nomy saw the prime minister and President Coty, and the cabinet meeting half an hour later overruled Moch and cancelled the operation. Ministers feared to deplete their few reliable forces; the army would not undertake to hold Bastia against airborne reinforcements from Algeria; the navy, though not mutinous, was clearly reluctant. . . . Communications with Corsica (where supplies were low) soon had to be reopened because the Marseilles prefect feared trouble among the many Corsicans in the city. The government's total inability to react to the loss of the island displayed their impotence before the world—and above all to themselves. Asked in his press conference what Algiers would do if the government used force in Corsica, Salan's spokesman replied, "What force?"

The Corsican collapse completed the withering away of the French state. For years disastrous policies had repeatedly been imposed on Paris by colonial administrations (supported by Gaullist and Conservative politicians who simultaneously deplored the weakness of government). Then the army acquired a taste for local policy-making. Now all governmental authority disappeared, even in metropolitan France. Certainly ministers encouraged confusion by pretending that Salan was their loyal agent. But this alone cannot explain the passive disobedience and active sabotage which confronted them everywhere.

The Navy, once a bulwark of Vichy, was non-committal. The air force was Gaullist; it showed its sympathies symbolically by flying its planes in Cross of Lorraine formation. . . . The army was in "moral rebellion." . . .

Pleven summed up: "We are the legal government, but what do we govern? The Minister for Algeria cannot enter Algeria. The Minister for the Sahara cannot go to the Sahara. The Minister of Information can only censor the press. The Minister of the Interior has no control over the police. The Minister of Defense is not obeyed by the army." Said a left-wing Gaullist in the Assembly, "You are not abandoning power—it has abandoned you."

Resistance was absurd without the Communists, impossible with them; for that alliance would have alienated most of the nation and broken up the cabinet itself. As the third week of the crisis opened, therefore, some determined Ministers were seeking, not to keep De Gaulle out at all costs, but to obtain from him an honourable alternative to bloodshed, military rule, and an ultimate pro-Communist reaction. Always avoid civil war, said Moch wryly, especially when you are sure to lose. . . .

These Ministers proposed to test De Gaulle's purposes by demanding first (in vain) a disavowal of the Corsican coup, later (successfully) an acceptance of the customary parliamentary procedure for coming to power. In France, where symbols are taken seriously, this latter concession both assured legal continuity and formally affirmed De Gaulle's loyalty to the Republic. On the afternoon of Sunday the 25th, Mollet gave to Guichard a six-page letter for the General stating the Socialist doubts and scruples, which he showed the premier next morning. Pflimlin then asked his party colleague Maurice Schumann (former Free French radio spokesman in London) to visit Colombey on his behalf. But De Gaulle had already answered Mollet and, by the local prefect, asked both Pflimlin and Mollet to meet him that night— this invitation to be published if they refused.

The two leaders agreed at once, though Mollet was later persuaded by Moch not to go unless De Gaulle repudiated the Corsican coup. The General and the prime minister both shook off the journalists, and met about midnight at the house of an old Gaullist, the curator of the château of St. Cloud. Thinking of Parliament, Pflimlin asked De Gaulle for a disavowal of Corsica; thinking of the army, the General replied while he would never take power illegally, to disavow as a private citizen would merely destroy for nothing his usefulness as an arbiter. As president of MRP, Pflimlin offered to arrange a meeting with the party leaders, which De Gaulle welcomed; but as nominee of the Assembly, the premier would not abandon the post entrusted to him. De Gaulle was unwilling to announce a disagreement. They parted at 2 A.M., Pflimlin now convinced of the General's bona fides. So at midday, he was thunderstruck to read De Gaulle's third public statement, "I have begun the regular process of forming a republican government," with its appeal to all, particularly the armed forces, to maintain order. The premier dared not deny the untruth, and therefore seemed to have betrayed his colleagues and supporters.

What had happened? De Gaulle had learned that Algiers' planned Operation Resurrection was to go into effect that night. Four days earlier General Miquel had approved a 32-page timetable for a paratroop descent on the 27th. The aerodromes of Le Bourget and Villacoublay were to be occupied by tank units of the Paris garrison. From the south-west, 2,500 men were to fly in from 2:30 A.M., reinforced from 5:30 by another 1,500 from Algiers. Most of the few fighting troops in France were involved in the plan, and in controlling the capital they were to be supported by recalled paratroop reservists and Indo-China veterans—and by the police and CRS with whom the government hoped to oppose them. . . .

In eighty provincial towns there were CSP's ready, based on Gaullists, Pétainists, or Poujadists, paratroop and Indo-China reservists, or expatriates from North Africa. As they took over the southern prefectures at 5:30 P.M., the army would stand by benevolently to "preserve order." . . .

At 10 A.M. on the decisive Tuesday, Moch learned from a friendly diplomatic source that the strike was for that night, and took precautionary measures. Moreover, General Beaufort—who was to command the revolt in Paris—kept President Coty informed of his own plans and deadlines. The army leaders all hoped that the threat alone would suffice; it does not follow that they—let alone their subordinates—were merely bluffing. Ministers did not think so, and Moch, on reading the General's communiqué, at once concluded that De Gaulle had acted to keep open the legal road to power, which an invasion would close forever. He was right: the communiqué led Algiers to postpone the operation. . . .

In political circles De Gaulle's announcement stiffened the opposition. At a joint meeting that afternoon the Socialist parliamentarians and executive were violently critical of Mollet (who was in cabinet) and voted by 112 to 3 never to accept De Gaulle. MRP too came out against the resignation of the government, and many Radicals were strongly anti-Gaullist. For once a parliamentary majority was struggling desperately to keep a reluctant cabinet in office. It was expected that Pflimlin would make the vote on the constitutional reform bill a pretext for resignation; so more than two-thirds of the deputies (408 to 165) voted the bill. But the CNI, against Pinay's advice, instructed their Ministers to resign. . . . On this excuse, despite Socialist protests, the premier resigned at 4:13 A.M. on the 28th.

The crucial role now fell to President René Coty. . . . Coty summoned Pinay, Mollet, and Teitgen of MRP and told them that he would send for De Gaulle rather than risk a Popular Front. He chose three men to see the General on his behalf: his predecessor Vincent Auriol, André Le Troquer the Socialist President of the Assembly, and Gaston Monnerville, [President of the Senate]. . . . As Auriol declined, Monnerville and a reluctant Le Troquer went alone to a stormy midnight meeting at St. Cloud. The General, who had sworn twelve years before never to set foot in the Assembly again, demurred at appearing for the investiture debate as Le Troquer insisted, and demanded not only prolonged exceptional powers but also the right to draft a new constitution. Le Troquer was indignant, De Gaulle exasperated, Monnerville conciliatory but firm. They separated in anger, and at 1 A.M. the two Presidents reported back to Coty.

Next morning, Le Troquer spoke almost gloomily to a Socialist meeting; and in Algiers the invasion plans were resumed for that night. At 2:30

P.M. Moch (unknown to Pflimlin) ordered the prefects to take to the maquis if attacked. Half an hour later the deputies met, standing to hear their President read the first and last special message from a President of the Fourth Republic. Coty warned that only a De Gaulle government could prevent civil war. If his nominee were rejected, he would resign and transfer his powers, under Article 41 of the Constitution, to Le Troquer as President of the Assembly. . . .

Oppressed by the knowledge that invasion was only ten hours away, Coty had gone far beyond the President's normal role. But he had alienated instead of persuading the Socialists—without whom there could be no parliamentary majority for De Gaulle.

Two developments later in the afternoon changed their minds. First, it became known that Monnerville's interpretation of De Gaulle's position differed sharply from that put about by President Coty's putative successor. Secondly Vincent Auriol obtained from the General (and the censor) permission to publish De Gaulle's very conciliatory reply to his letter of three days before. It changed the climate at once. By 62 to 29 the Socialists accepted Auriol's letter as a basis for negotiation. At 7:30 P.M. De Gaulle entered the Elysée and agreed to form a government. He asked to see a Socialist delegation, and next day (Friday 30th) first Auriol, then Mollet and Deixonne—president of the Socialist deputies—flew to Colombey. Deixonne went an opponent and returned a supporter. . . .

On Saturday afternoon the General met twenty-six party leaders at the Hotel Lapérouse; the Communists refused to attend. The Socialists (and Coty) persuaded him to appear before the Assembly, though not to submit to the normal barrage of questions . . . by which prospective premiers were always assailed and sometimes entrapped. He outlined his constitutional proposals; the politicians showed anxiety about ministerial responsibility to Parliament and over his attitude to the CSP. At 6 P.M., the Socialists resolved by 77 to 74 to support De Gaulle (but not impose party discipline). Deputies and executives were still hostile, but the senators—who knew and trusted their President—swayed the decision. On Sunday, June 1, at 11 A.M., Guichard telephoned to Salan to be ready to invade if necessary. Four hours later De Gaulle entered the Assembly to read the shortest investiture speech of the Fourth Republic. During the brief debate the candidate withdrew. In the vote, at 7:35 P.M., he was elected by 329 to 224; 42 Socialists voted for, 49 against. Three weeks earlier, he would not have had a hundred votes.

SUGGESTIONS FOR FURTHER READING

Documentary: *L'Année politique* (Paris, 1946–59); General: JACQUES FAUVET, *La IVe République* (Paris, 1959); JOSEPH BARSALOU, *La Mal-aimée, histoire de la IVe République* (Paris, 1964); ALEXANDER WERTH, *France, 1940–1955* (London, 1956);

Herbert Luethy, *France Against Herself* (New York, 1955); David Schoenbrun, *As France Goes* (New York, 1957); Special: Philip M. Williams, *Crisis and Compromise: Politics in the Fourth Republic* (3rd. ed.; London, 1964); Nathan Leites, *On the Game of Politics in France* (Stanford, Calif., 1959); Dorothy Pickles, *French Politics: The First Years of the Fourth Republic* (London and New York, 1953); B. D. Graham, *The French Socialists and Tripartism, 1944–1947* (Toronto and Canberra, 1965); Stanley Hoffmann, *Le Mouvement Poujade* (Paris, 1956); Frederick F. Ritsch, *The French Left and the European Idea, 1947–1949* (New York, 1966); Russell B. Capelle, *The MRP and French Foreign Policy* (New York, 1963); Alfred Grosser, *La IVe République et sa politique extérieure* (Paris, 1961); Ellen J. Hammer, *The Struggle for Indochina, 1940–1955* (Stanford, Calif., 1966); Bernard B. Fall, *Street without Joy* (Harrisburg, Pa., 1964), and *Hell in a Very Small Place; the Siege of Dien Bien Phu* (New York, 1967); Josselyn Hennessy et al., *Economic "Miracles": Studies in the Resurgence of the French, German and Italian Economies since the Second World War* (London, 1964); Warren C. Baum, *The French Economy and the State* (Princeton, 1958); John Sheahan, *Promotion and Control of Industry in Postwar France* (Cambridge, Mass., 1963); Laurence Wylie, *Village in the Vaucluse* (2nd ed.; Cambridge, Mass., 1964); Gordon Wright, *Rural Revolution in France* (Stanford, Calif., 1964); Stanley Hoffmann et al., *In Search of France* (Cambridge, Mass., 1963); Julian Park (ed)., *The Culture of France in Our Time* (Ithaca, N.Y., 1954); James Meisel, *The Fall of the Republic: Military Revolt in France* (Ann Arbor, Mich., 1962); J.-R. Tournoux, *Secrets d'état* (Paris, 1960); Merry and Serge Bromberger, *Les 13 complots du 13 mai* (Paris, 1959); André Siegfried, *De la IVe à la Ve République* (Paris, 1958); Biographical; Charles de Gaulle, *War Memoirs*, vol. III, *Salvation, 1944–1946* (New York, 1960); Alexander Werth, *The Strange History of Pierre Mendès-France and the Great Conflict over French North Africa* (London, 1957).

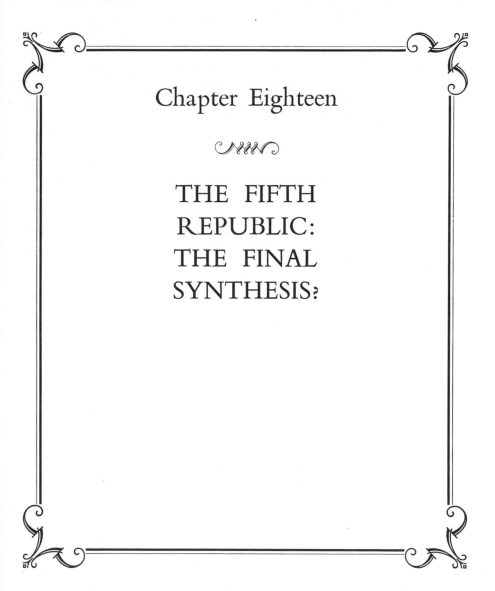

Chapter Eighteen

THE FIFTH
REPUBLIC:
THE FINAL
SYNTHESIS?

I T IS OBVIOUSLY impossible to make any definitive judgment about the present regime in France, the Fifth Republic of Charles de Gaulle. But its tone has been set, and the nature of its policies has been so clearly laid down that the only major question is really whether they can be continued without him. Brought to power after twelve years of political exile by the uprising in Algiers, de Gaulle considered his return to be only natural and inevitable. Addressing the country in January, 1960, he spoke of the "national legitimacy" that he had "embodied for twenty years," that is, since his call to resistance in the summer of 1940. In this way he wrote off the Fourth Republic as if it had never existed. And in 1958 he proceeded to reorganize the government along the lines he had laid down during the war and which he had amplified in a speech at Bayeux in June, 1946. The Fifth Republic, therefore, is de Gaulle's Republic and to understand it his ideas must be understood.

In the first selection, Douglas Johnson discusses the political principles of de Gaulle—his belief in the nation state, the need for strong leadership (without interference from a legislative assembly), the need to strengthen (hence to modernize) the state, and the need for the leader to maintain an implicit understanding with his people through direct contact. Though Johnson does deny it, de Gaulle's government is indeed in the tradition of the "savior" regimes of the two Napoleons and even Pétain, all of which replaced faltering republics with strong personal rulers. The true difference between de Gaulle and these others is that he has disavowed dictatorship and permitted the existence of democratic institutions and political opposition.

Besides drafting a new constitution that would give the President of the Republic greater power than the Assembly, especially the authority to designate the premier and to initiate national policies, de Gaulle undertook the difficult task of liquidating the endless war in Algeria. Although the Fourth Republic had taken steps to liberalize relations with the colonial empire and had granted Morocco and Tunisia independence, it was de Gaulle who moved decisively in this area. In the second selection W. W. Kulski describes how de Gaulle was able to remove the colonialist stigma from France by granting independence to her African possessions and, after continued bloodshed and extended negotiations, how he allowed Algeria to become a separate state in 1962. The ambiguities of his first two years were finally resolved in favor of separation, even though this meant the uprooting of many thousands of die-hard European settlers. As Kulski indicates, this permitted France to woo the "Third World" as well as to assume a more independent foreign policy vis-à-vis the United States. (It is not difficult to argue that France's nuclear policy, the force de frappe, is to a large extent compensation for her loss in colonies.)

But decolonization is but one aspect of a wider foreign policy, the outlines of which are sketched by Alfred Grosser, the French political scientist, in the third selection. Like Johnson, Grosser stresses the importance of the nation state in de Gaulle's conception of foreign policy and emphasizes the need for national power, and the necessity for independent action by each nation, especially France. To these basic conceptions, de Gaulle has added his personal touches, notably his rapprochement with both Soviet Russia and Communist China, and his desire to assume leadership of a Europe in which France plays the key role—all of which has proved annoying to the United States and to other European powers which do not recognize France's predominance.

In the final selection, the American political scientist Louis J. Halle offers a cool appraisal of de Gaulle's policies in Europe, especially the "grand design" for French hegemony from the Atlantic to the Urals. The general, he feels, is advocating a French nationalism outmoded in the twentieth century. Despite a personal admiration for the man's abilities, Halle believes that the French president's efforts to reshape Europe to his own liking will have less enduring value than the work of men such as Jean Monnet, who advance international cooperation.

Most Frenchmen seemed to accept the general's program of a strong presidency, nationalism, decolonization, and an independent foreign policy. But they grew increasingly unhappy with his authoritarian style and the failure of the nation's workers and peasants to receive a fair share of France's growing prosperity. This dissatisfaction was made clear by the resurgence of the Left in the presidential election of 1965—the first by popular vote since 1848—which forced de Gaulle into an embarrassing if successful second round of balloting, and the legislative elections of 1967, which left the Gaullist parties with only a bare majority in the Chamber of Deputies. Far more serious were the violent outburst of student protest and general strike of May–June, 1968. These paralyzed the country and threatened the foundations of the regime itself. But the threat of anarchy reawakened the national sense of conservatism, giving de Gaulle a solid victory in the parliamentary elections called in June. How he used this new mandate to strengthen the Fifth Republic would help determine whether he would be able to pass it on intact to his eventual successor. But only when the general himself departs will the viability of the institutions he has created really be tested. The uncertainties of the post-de Gaulle era will provide new problems for France, which has seen so many rulers and regimes since the death of the Sun King. If de Gaulle has built well, then the Fifth Republic may indeed prove to be the final synthesis.

THE POLITICAL PRINCIPLES OF GENERAL DE GAULLE

DOUGLAS JOHNSON

The career of General de Gaulle should be the preoccupation of the historian as well as of the student of international affairs. Too often the historian is tempted to dismiss the General as one of the ghosts of French history,

Douglas Johnson, "The Political Principles of General de Gaulle," *International Affairs*, vol. XLI, no. 4 (October, 1965), 650–662. Copyright by Douglas Johnson, 1965. Used by permission of the author and *International Affairs*.

illustrating the tradition whereby authoritarian régimes, such as those of Napoleon, Napoleon III or Pétain, temporarily succeed the more liberal assembly-type régimes. To recall history in this way is to assume that the Fifth Republic is simply a stage in a recurrent process and is to avoid understanding its significance. Too often the historian abandons any attempt to understand the phenomenon of General de Gaulle, by accepting the viewpoint of those who represent the policies and evolution of the Fifth Republic as arising entirely from the character and personality of its creator. Too often articles on, and assessments of, the General concentrate entirely on him, and lack any sense of historical perspective, apart from ironic references to Joan of Arc or to Louis XIV. . . . They do not attempt to understand General de Gaulle as an historical phenomenon; they do not try to discern the principles which he has evolved over a long life, a great part of which has been devoted to the study of history and to the study of ideas. . . .

Many Gaullists have maintained that Gaullism is not a doctrine, just as it is not a party. Some have said that there is no such thing as "Gaullisme," there is only de Gaulle. Other observers, less committed to polemics, prefer to see as the significant feature of de Gaulle's rule, not a movement of ideas or principles, but a movement of personnel, the arrival of a class of capable technicians at positions of authority. De Gaulle's opponents, while considering the cult of reality and "intuition" as inappropriate terms for political unscrupulousness and ambition, are no less categorical in their rejection of the General as a man of thought. . . .

It is natural too that the General's methods should have attracted most attention since they have been conspicuously successful, and since they have a particularly dramatic quality. It is noticeable that they also have a certain unity. In the summer of 1940, for example, when the French armies had been defeated on the continent, General de Gaulle insisted on removing the emphasis away from this disadvantageous position, and by insisting that the war was a world-wide war, making the position of France and of the French empire more advantageous *vis-à-vis* the whole world. With the Liberation, preoccupied by the power of the Communists within France, he transformed the question into one of Franco-Soviet friendship; in 1958, faced with the crowds of the Algiers forum, he removed the subject from the uncertain and controversial future of Algeria, and insisted on the renovation of France. Perhaps it is the same tactic which, since the Evian agreements ended the Algerian war, has led the General to emphasise his hostility to the United States. At all events, on each major occasion, General de Gaulle has always elevated the subject at issue away from a position where he is at a disadvantage, and towards an aspect which is more favourable to him. Such a method is also linked to a highly contrived ambiguity in many pronouncements, together with the frankly experimental nature of many of his policies. One saw this most clearly in his Algerian policy, which was more hesitant, less far-seeing and less deceitful than has often been suggested. . . . Sometïmes it is even suggested that the method is everything, that de Gaulle is presenting a spectacle which is pure illusion, that the realities of power have eluded him, and he compensates for this by being a sort of Walter Mitty amongst world statesmen.

Thus, when one wants to examine *"Gaullisme"* in terms of principles, one not only finds all the usual difficulties which normally beset such an enterprise . . ., but many particular obstacles are put in the way. Yet it would be strange if Gaullism did not imply a coherent doctrine. Before the war, in 1940, and again from 1958, Gaullism has essentially depended upon words. The written word, the lecture, the discussion group, and the microphone— for a long time these were the only available weapons. Now, better equipped, it is the televised press conference which has been called the absolute weapon of the Fifth Republic. The de Gaulle who emerged from obscurity in 1940 had prepared himself for his task by study and meditation. He had made a theoretical analysis of the sort of leader he was to become long before he had any experience of leadership or power. It is clear, too, that de Gaulle stands in complete contrast to the only two other statesmen who, as leaders of governments in the Fourth Republic, succeeded in attracting some form of popular support. In M. Pinay some Frenchmen were pleased to identify themselves, admiring the respectable head of a family business. In M. Mendès-France some saw the dynamic, technical leader whom they thought necessary for a modern state. But de Gaulle is neither of these. He has always impressed rather than attracted. And one of the ways in which he has impressed is by placing his utterances within a large, theoretical framework, by enunciating general principles to which he remains faithful and which hold the attention of the audience to which he appeals. . . .

It is impossible to begin any consideration of de Gaulle's thought without "a certain idea of France." But this is often misunderstood and is elevated into something mystical, even unreal. It is true that de Gaulle speaks of France as a person, but this is within a long tradition. It is true that he assumes the necessity for the individual to have some sort of patriotism, but this is often found amongst French moralists. . . .

It is true, too, that de Gaulle makes the assumption that France is important, indispensable, to the rest of the world, but this is also a common assumption; as pacific a statesman as Guizot maintained that France had only to stay still, "with folded arms," to fill her place in the world. But de Gaulle associates this importance of France specifically to the role of France in Europe and to the importance of European civilisation in the world. His conception of France is dramatically explicit . . . , but it is hardly mystical. . . .

. . . Essentially de Gaulle allies a certain contempt for political ideology along with his confidence in national realities. Ideologies such as Communism will pass, or can be accommodated. The nation-state will remain. National leaders, such as Roosevelt or Churchill, may cloak their policies with idealistic phraseology, but essentially they will try to advance the interests and the power of their countries. In a similar way de Gaulle himself will always endeavour to strengthen the international position of France within the hierarchy of power, whether by attempting to change the frontier, or by a particular defence policy. . . .

From this there are certain conclusions which can be drawn. If the nation-state is the basis of policy, then there are certain political organisations which are not likely to develop, whilst there are new nation-states which can come into being. This would explain de Gaulle's attitude towards colonialism, which many have found puzzling. In the first place de Gaulle does not seem to have been a convinced believer in the realities of colonial rule. After six months in the Levant, during 1929, he wrote to Lucien Nachin his impression that Europe had not penetrated a civilisation which was essentially different, and that a great distance separated the European from the native populations. . . . In the same line of thought one can understand his readiness to accept the emergence of new nation-states . . . and his reluctance to envisage French settlers as a permanent force in Algeria. One can perhaps understand something, not only of his scorn for international bodies such as the United Nations . . . , but even perhaps for the United States of America, and it might not only have been a *boutade* when he . . . recalled the American Civil War and claimed that it was still continuing. . . . His belief in the nation-state also helps one to understand the episode of his unsuccessful political party, the RPF, since the period of its greatest success coincided with the period of possible war with the Soviet Union (or Russia, as de Gaulle prefers to say). The RPF opposed the French Communists, essentially because they would have introduced alien influence into the country.

Other consequences are of particular interest for France. The French are traditionally divided amongst themselves. In this they contrast strikingly to other countries, such as Great Britain. . . . There is conflict between the internal demons which divide the French, and the greatness and permanence of France. Therefore the idea of France not only corresponds to a profound but sometimes obscure reality, it is also a device whereby Frenchmen can be made to forget the elements of discord amongst them. Sometimes it is necessary to do this in some great enterprise, undertaken in the name of France. Sometimes it is necessary for France only to appear to have made the effort. . . .

Those who have found the essence of Gaullism as being a preoccupation with effect and with show should remember that, whether in reality or in appearance, the principle is that the state should remedy the internal conflicts of the country, and that this principle is traditional in France. . . .

The question of sovereignty is less familiar outside France, but it has been constantly an issue in France since 1789. . . .

In 1940 the question was posed anew when France was defeated and lost her independence. Up to this moment de Gaulle, as he has been frank (or foolish) enough to admit, had felt himself called upon to fulfil some great destiny, but his career had languished, and up to a late moment in the summer of 1940 his main effort was to convince the élites of France to take certain particular actions. But once he realised that these élites had failed him, it was then that he decided that the sovereignty of France had fallen on him. He has reproached Pétain, not so much with capitulating, but precisely with signing the armistice and thus giving up "the treasure of French sovereignty." Those who regarded Pétain as a legitimate ruler failed to realise that the sovereignty of France had gone to the part of France which was independent. Those who found de Gaulle difficult and touchy during the years after June 1940 failed to realise his need to preserve the reality and the appearance of independence, and thus "the treasure of French sovereignty." From this preoccupation came the quarrels with Giraud, who thought that there could be no French government until the end of the war, and the quarrels with Roosevelt and Churchill, who thought that they were dealing with an awkward leader, whose slender means made him dependent upon their support. From this came all the storms and furies whenever someone seemed to dispose of or to disregard France. Therefore, too, all the sneers and references to "megalomania," to "inferiority complexes," Joan of Arc and so on. But therefore, too, the success of General de Gaulle. According to his own account, General de Gaulle asked Churchill, if he were not the representative of France, then why was Churchill dealing with him? Churchill (it is said) did not reply. "I was France," recalled the General, "I was the independence and the sovereignty of France, and it was for this reason that everyone obeyed me." . . .

When Georges Bidault, at the Hôtel de Ville, asked de Gaulle to proclaim the Republic, de Gaulle replied that there was no need. The Republic had never ceased to exist, since June 18, 1940 when de Gaulle had made his statement in London. Since then and recently, de Gaulle has spoken of incarnating the sovereignty of France since 1940, discounting the period of his resignation, and embroidering the crown of Lorraine on the tricolour as a permanency. This assertion of sovereignty, derived from the principle of the nation-state as the basis of political reality, is within the framework of discussion which has been important in France for many years.

Everywhere, in de Gaulle's writings and statements, one finds underlined the need for a strong state. . . . The symptom of the decline of France between the two world wars was the weakness of the French State, unable to take effective action when danger threatened. De Gaulle's political experience of these years brought him into contact with the ineffectiveness of French institutions. When the Germans were defeated in the Second World War, this did not mean that danger had disappeared. The whole of modern existence represents danger, the whole trend of contemporary developments is to increase that danger. Both supporters and opponents of General de Gaulle associate him with crisis and with disaster. He himself saw his legitimacy as being latent in a period without anxiety, but it would be invoked "as soon as a new laceration threatened the nation." . . . Opposed to the country returning to what he calls "the easy ways," de Gaulle has always emphasised "the brutal fact," that France is in perpetual danger of sudden death and therefore must have some permanent authority which can take the necessary decisions (January 14, 1963). "Politics is action, an ensemble of decisions which are made, things which are done, risks which are taken" (July 23, 1964).

This being so, the government of a country cannot be entrusted to an assembly. An assembly cannot ensure a strong state. It exists for debate and deliberation, it does not exist in order to take decisions. Assemblies, despite their fine speeches, are, according to de Gaulle, governed by fear of action. And although de Gaulle (like other critics of the French parliamentary system) was personally attracted by the Assembly, as he recalls in his *Memoirs*, and as was noticed by observers during his appearances before the Chamber in the 1958 crisis, he has never varied in his opposition to the Assembly as the source of government. He has recognised that his insistence upon a Head of State is in direct opposition to the fundamental principle of the French parliamentary régime, which de Gaulle has characterised as "let no head show above the trenches of democracy," indicative of a timorous, anonymous, ineffective system.

In order to make France a strong state, in order to promote change, one man must lead the country, must make decisions and give direction. . . .

. . . The task of the Head of State is to find means of effecting change and reform, and governmental methods have to be examined in the light of this principle rather than that of ideologies. "Like everyone else," as he puts it, he realised that in our time technology dominated the universe, and the great debate of the century was whether the working classes would be the victims or the beneficiaries of this technical progress. Hence the need for profound and rapid social change. Hence the need for technicians and administrators who would answer the aspirations and fears of the masses and, by implication, remove the need for the various political banners . . . which floated over the battlefields. Such a policy as nationalisation does not exist because it is inherently just or desirable, but because through nationalisation economic change can be promoted. Much of the insistence on military and defence projects can be interpreted as ways of promoting economic change. . . .

Yet the task of the leader is not merely that of providing the decision-making machinery whereby the state will be strengthened. His function exists in relation to the principle of the nation-state. As has recently been remarked, nationalism is nothing else but the desire to bring together the juridical reality which is the state and the sociological reality which is the national group. De Gaulle sees the leader as effecting this coincidence. There is the people, the people is sovereign. The source of power lies with the people, and although he writes of the occasional value of a temporary period of dictatorship, and of the temptations of dictatorship, yet his conclusion is simple, "no man can substitute himself for a people." His practice followed his theory. As he boasted, on May 19, 1958, he could have imposed his dictatorship with the Liberation; instead he restored the Republic. His resignation in January 1946 may have been a miscalculation, but he never attempted to organise a *coup d'état* against the Fourth Republic. During the crisis of 1958 all the initiatives which he took were based upon the assumption that he could assume power legally. "I cannot consent to receive power from any other source than the people, or at least its representatives."

And this contact with the people has to take place directly, and without intermediaries. The intermediaries pervert and corrupt the relations between the leader and the people. Intermediaries tend to mean élites and de Gaulle has always been suspicious of these. He believed, even before the war, that the old élites in France were losing their value, and that whilst men could not dispense with being governed and directed, the respect which had formerly been shown to birth and position was now being accorded to those who showed ability. . . . His experience in 1940 confirmed his impression. The élites failed to support him, and none of the "guiding lights" of France condemned the armistice. With the Liberation came the realisation that the élites had betrayed France, and de Gaulle's realisation, at a meeting at the Palais de Chaillot, that his dealings with the professional politicians would be complicated, and that he must seek his support from the people.

The constitutional change of 1962, whereby the President of the Republic is to be elected by the whole population, and not by an electoral college of 70,000 notables, has also to be seen in the same theoretical framework. Amongst the élites which were to be mistrusted are, above all, the political parties. De Gaulle's contempt for their limitations is well known . . . ; his mistrust for their sectarianism, for their tendency to represent particular rather than national interests, is allied to the conviction that in modern times there is bound to be a decadence of political parties and of their ideologies. Nothing in de Gaulle is more striking than his alliance of theory and practice, his confidence in the people, his realisation of the value of modern techniques. . . .

The General has two fundamental and contradictory beliefs. That France is united, that there is a fundamental unity; that France is diverse and multiple, with many spiritual families. . . . The contradiction is resolved in great moments of crisis and drama. It disappears when de Gaulle, at the Liberation, stands at the Arc de Triomphe and sees the population massed around him. It reappears when the tension slackens. De Gaulle might well have been thinking of his own position when he wrote of Winston Churchill, "His countenance, etched by the fires and the frosts of great events, had become inappropriate in the era of mediocrity." It is necessary therefore to maintain the tension and the drama. . . . De Gaulle believes that man needs something more than material things, that one must take risks, that one must hope. In 1940 he took the side of adventure against what seemed to be the course of history. In 1958 . . . he again chose adventure.

Any attempt to analyse de Gaulle's principles must necessarily be incomplete. He must have written many letters which would reveal more about him than his public countenance allows one to divine. One knows little about his religion. Doubtless since the leader must identify himself with the whole of the nation rather than with a section, de Gaulle has been careful not to emphasise his Catholicism. It is noticeable that he always claimed that the RPF was not a political party, but a Rally, and when it was first formed membership of the RPF did not involve immediate resignation from other political parties. When the RPF got caught up in the political system, then the General abandoned it. He has deliberately chosen to escape from the current French political theorist's insistence on classifying politicians either on the Right or the Left. He unites the traditional values of the Right with the traditional energies and Jacobinism of the Left. Like Cromwell he stands as both the revolutionary and the conservative leader of his epoch. Gaullism as a political phenomenon . . . is more than the thought of the General. Gaullism as a form of political action has developed and changed since 1940, since the days of the RPF, or since 1958. But the preoccupation with unity through diversity remains in Gaullism as it remains essential to French history. And the conviction that history forms a French nature which transcends French division, a conviction represented symbolically by the Fifth Republic's achievement in cleaning the monuments of Paris, emphasises the unity of de Gaulle's thought and brings me back to "a certain idea of France." These principles suggest that de Gaulle is not an isolated phenomenon or an anachronism, but a phenomenon relevant to France.

DE GAULLE AND THE DECOLONIZATION OF AFRICA

W. W. KULSKI

De Gaulle's policy of decolonization must be examined under two separate headings: sub-Saharan Africa and Algeria. In 1958 the two problems seemed to him and all Frenchmen to be two different questions, although he ultimately conceded the same unrestricted independence to both areas. In 1958, or probably earlier, he conceived the concept of transforming the colonial empire into a French Community which would include autonomous countries closely associated with France. Algeria was to find an ill-defined place within that Community.

He did not expect to encounter any difficulty in carrying out this plan insofar as sub-Saharan Africa was concerned. The Framework Statute of 1956 prepared the ground. He was sure that French public opinion would not oppose the widening of the scope of self-government, and that the French-speaking Africans would not ask for more than domestic autonomy. His Grand Design was faithfully reflected in the Constitution of the Fifth Republic. Part XII (now a dead letter) of the Constitution changed the name of the former French Union (which had been the old colonial empire in disguise except for the reform contained in the Framework Statute, but not in the Constitution of the Fourth Republic) to the French Community. This French translation of the British Commonwealth marked the Fifth Republic's intention to inaugurate a new policy. Article 77 conceded to the colonial possessions the name of states and the autonomy in their domestic affairs. However, Article 78 reserved for the Community, in fact for France, jurisdiction over several matters: foreign affairs, defense, currency, economic and financial policies, strategic raw materials, justice, higher education, means of external transportation and telecommunications. . . . The French Community was to be a federation. The President of the French Republic was to be *ipso iure* the President of the Community. An Executive Council was to be composed of the President of the Community, the French Prime Minister, the heads of overseas governments, and the French Ministers in charge of matters reserved for the jurisdiction of the Community (in fact, for French jurisdiction). A Senate was to be formed of delegates designated by the French and African parliaments. Finally, a Court of Arbitration was to settle disputes between the member states. All in all, this was progress, but rather limited in scope. However, the most important provision was contained in Article 86, which conceded to each overseas possession the right to secede and

W. W. Kulski, *De Gaulle and the World: The Foreign Policy of the Fifth French Republic* (Syracuse, N.Y.: Syracuse University Press, 1966), pp. 334–347. Copyright © 1966 by Syracuse University Press. Used by permission.

proclaim its independence, if such were the wish of its legislative assembly confirmed in the local popular referendum.

In September 1958 France and her overseas possessions were asked to approve the new Constitution in a referendum. The rejection of the Constitution by any overseas possession was to be interpreted as a vote for an immediate independence. De Gaulle made it crystal clear that he expected all African possessions to accept the limited self-government the Constitution offered, but that he would reluctantly agree to an immediate independence if a territory rejected the Constitution. . . .

The referendum held in September 1958 brought a massive yes in all the African possessions, except for Guinea, which rejected the Constitution and opted for complete independence. Sékou Touré did not want to cut off all ties; rather he preferred to associate his country in some form with France. But de Gaulle remained true to his threat. He stopped all aid to Guinea and recalled the French personnel. Guinea was left to her own meager resources. De Gaulle's ultimatum misfired this time. Guinea turned toward the Soviet Union and immediately received its assistance. Later the United States came to the rescue.

The Guinean example proved to be contagious. During the following two years other African states asked for independence. The French President was wiser after the disappointing experience with Guinea; he readily acquiesced to their demands. Chapter XII of the Constitution of the Fifth Republic was discarded, and the French Community became a true Commonwealth of independent states that continued to cooperate with France. . . .

De Gaulle did not want to see the French influence disappear altogether, but he hoped that it would take a new form palatable to the independent states. France was to stay in Africa, but only because of her cooperation with the former colonies. His new philosophy is well formulated by a French specialist on colonial problems: "While relinquishing the external signs of our political sovereignty, we have tried to preserve in our former colonies an economic presence and a cultural influence which are, in the modern world, the only true realities."

De Gaulle is not a man who would waste his time and effort on trying to ignore the changing realities of international life. He does not immediately yield if his policy encounters difficulties, but if his arguments and threats are to no avail, he adjusts his policy to the facts which he has not been able to change. His rather easy abandonment of the concept of French Community and his grant of independence to the former African possessions should be borne in mind by all his future adversaries. He concedes defeat if nothing else can be done and readjusts his world view in consequence. Then he immediately looks toward new successes along the road which he formerly refused to enter. . . .

The grant of independence to thirteen African republics and to the Malagasy Republic was accompanied in 1960–61 by the signature of bilateral agreements on mutual cooperation. The main points of these agreements were as follows:

1. France assumed the diplomatic representation of those states in foreign capitals and international organizations, if they themselves did not intend to open their own embassies.
2. France and they promised to consult each other on matters of foreign policy, but they retained complete freedom in formulating policies and in concluding international treaties.
3. They remained within the French monetary zone.
4. France and they conceded a preferential tariff treatment to each other. The French market was to remain open to their tropical products at prices higher than those prevailing on the international market. The commercial policies of African states were to be co-ordinated with French policy toward third states.
5. France promised to supply instructors and military matériel to the armed forces of African states. She and these states were to cooperate in matters of defense, while France was to retain her garrisons and military bases in some of them. The African governments were empowered to ask for French military assistance to maintain internal order and defend themselves against an external aggression. . . .
6. French was recognized as the official language of the African states, while France promised to offer her assistance in developing the African school system by sending teachers and receiving African students at the French schools and universities. France also undertook the obligation to help found African universities.
7. Finally, France was given priority in buying strategic raw materials.

These agreements are not a heavy mortgage on the African independence. They may be denounced; if anything is sure, it is that de Gaulle would not try to reimpose them by force. Gabon excepted, France has never tried to maintain a pro-French government overthrown by domestic revolt. The French guaranty against external aggression might be useful in view of the ambitions of other African states, which would not mind enlarging their territory by encroachments on others, including those where French is spoken. . . .

He has strong assets in his hands: preferential treatment for the African tropical products, financial assistance, and help in raising the cultural standards of French Africa. The colonial rule left a precious inheritance to both Britain and France: African elites educated at the British or French universities; and the English or French language as the only *lingua franca* for the

Africans, who speak several different native tongues in each country. The French cultural influence, like the British, is there to remain. De Gaulle knows all this and has consistently done his best to strengthen further these economic and cultural ties, which, he hopes, will assure the permanence of French political influence. There is truth in this confident French statement: "France is today the power which awakes the least distrust among Africans." . . .

General de Gaulle liquidated the colonial regime in sub-Saharan Africa without encountering any resistance in French public opinion. The Algerian problem confronted him with the threat that his Fifth Republic would perish, like the Fourth Republic, at the hand of a rebellious Army. He surmounted the dangers owing to his sense of reality, the force of his will, his undaunted courage, and popular prestige. None of the Prime Ministers of the Fourth Republic had all these assets and qualities.

It is not easy to reconstruct the successive stages of his mental evolution, because initially he was unable to disclose his true thought. The Army officers who had brought him to the Elysée Palace did not trust him. The Algerian Europeans, whose revolt against the Fourth Republic also helped him return to power, hoped they could compel him to follow their wishes as they had done with the Prime Ministers of the Fourth Republic. He could count only on himself and on his popularity in France. It was impossible to be frank in that precarious situation.

On June 4, 1958, he went to Algeria. He immediately faced the Algerian Europeans with the logic of their own propaganda slogan that Arabs were patriotic Frenchmen. If this slogan were true, he told them, then "France believes that there is in all of Algeria only one category of inhabitants: full-fledged Frenchmen, all of them with the same rights and obligations." Hence, he concluded, "All the privileges must disappear." This was the last thing the Europeans wanted.

On his return to France he disclosed a bit of his real thought by beginning to talk about "the ten million Algerians," not "Frenchmen." If they were Algerians, their country was not simply another French province. The theory of assimilation of the Moslems was repudiated. De Gaulle replaced it by his concept of a "fraternal association" between France and Algeria. On his second visit to Algeria, in October 1958, he revealed his intention. He said: "In any event, the future of Algeria will be built up, this being in the nature of things, on a twofold foundation: its own personality and its solidarity with metropolitan France."

In May 1959 he frankly acknowledged: "There is no one who ignores the fact that nothing will be accomplished by the struggle and that a reconciliation is the only solution. . . . Daddy's Algeria is dead." The French tutelage and the privileges of French settlers were dead; the continuation of the war could not bring victory. He realistically conceded that even a military victory would not solve the Algerian problem. . . .

From these premises he deduced the conclusion: "I do not prejudge the nature of the political status of the future Algeria. . . . We shall not have Algerians with us if they themselves do not want this." This amounted to saying that the only solution was an agreement between France and the Algerians on the future political regime of Algeria. On September 16, 1959, he felt secure enough to proclaim the right of Algerians to "self-determination," the very word he used in his broadcast allocution. The self-determination was to be "the free choice of the future the Algerians wish to make."

At this stage, he rejected the assimilation of Algerian Arabs as a sterile and naive slogan, but he did not hide his lack of sympathy for the secession. He threatened that, if the Algerians were to choose complete independence, he would not only cut off all French financial aid but would partition Algeria and move Europeans and loyal Moslems to a portion of the territory that would remain under French administration. Moreover, he did not intend in any event to abandon French sovereignty over the Sahara with its newly discovered oil and natural gas wealth.

He denied that the rebel organization was the only legitimate representation of Moslem Algerians. . . .

Who could have predicted in September 1959 that a proud de Gaulle, who hated to bow to the will of others, would less than three years later conclude an agreement with the rebels which was to concede complete independence to their country?

On January 24, 1960, barricades were erected in the city of Algiers. The Europeans intended to overthrow the Fifth Republic as they had destroyed the Fourth less than two years before. The Army and the local authorities tolerated the rebellion, as they did in 1958. They ignored the orders coming from Paris. The President was in no mood to be blackmailed; on January 29 he renewed his pledge to grant self-determination to the Algerians. Finally, his will triumphed. The Army did not join the Europeans as it had done in May 1958; having to choose between mutiny and obedience to de Gaulle's orders, it opted for obedience after a week of uncertainty. On February 1 the Europeans were gently told to dismantle their barricades and to go home, which they did. The President won the first round in the undeclared war of will with the Army officers.

In March 1960 de Gaulle still thought that his will would compel the Arabs to accept his plan for a domestic autonomy in close association with France. He reiterated the threat of partition in case the Algerians were to choose complete independence, this time adding another, more serious, threat—that of expelling the Algerian workers from France. Those 400,000 Algerian workers were supporting their relatives in Algeria, approximately two million destitute Arabs. . . . The rebel organization was not frightened.

In June 1960 the first contacts took place between the French government and the rebels, unsuccessful because the two positions were too far apart.

But de Gaulle was gradually approaching the time when he would understand that the rebel organization was the true voice of the Arabs. On
September 5, 1960, he admitted that: "I am neither blind nor unjust enough
to ignore the importance of the movement of wounded souls and of awakened hopes which has led so many Algerians to insurrection. I know very
well what resonance the insurrection has found in a section of the population."
But he refused to negotiate solely with the rebel organization. The rebels
were not yet in his eyes "the only representatives of the whole of Algeria."
He still hoped that negotiation would be conducted with several Arab
organizations, the rebels being only one of them. The other Arabs, he thought,
would be less demanding, and the rebels would be finally persuaded to
accept a domestic autonomy in close association with France. He was to find
out later that there was no serious substitute for the Algerian Provisional
Government in exile as a valid interlocutor. When he exclaimed: "This I
shall never do!" he forgot that "never" is a word missing from the political
dictionary.

In the meantime, the President was doing his best to convince the Army
officers, the only opposition he feared, that Algeria was not, as he said,
another Lorraine or Provence. He soon learned that he had found no
sympathy for his thesis. Then he decided to confront the officers with the
will of the people. A popular referendum was to be held in France in January
1961. . . .

The referendum held on January 8, 1961, proved that the French people
supported de Gaulle's policy. Over seventy-six per cent of registered voters
took part in the referendum. Over 15 million votes were cast for the Algerian
self-determination as against less than 5 million. The Algerian Europeans
and a number of officers answered by forming a terroristic organization
called the Organization of the Secret Army (O.A.S.).

On April 11, 1961, de Gaulle finally recognized the inevitable:

. . . It is difficult to pretend that the Algerian population as a whole desires to be
a part of the French people. . . . France does not raise any objection or intend
to erect any obstacles if the Algerian population decides to create a state which
would undertake the mission of governing their country. . . . Insofar as I am concerned, I am convinced that this state will be sovereign at home and abroad.

The die was cast. De Gaulle at last conceded complete independence. The
will of the rebels had won a victory over him, but the test of wills with the
Army was not yet over.

The Army officers in Algeria, led by the well-known generals, rose in
revolt on April 22, 1961. De Gaulle, sure of popular support, was not
frightened. After a few days the mutiny collapsed for lack of support among
the military units in France and because the young conscripted soldiers
threatened to disobey the officers' orders. The second round was won. Now
the road was cleared for final negotiations with the representatives of the

Algerian government in exile. In May the negotiations were opened. In vain, the O.A.S. tried to wreck the negotiations by its terrorist action in Algeria and in France. Neither their plastic bombs exploding in Paris nor their attempt at de Gaulle's life on September 8, 1961, could stop him once he had made his decision. He wanted to put an end to the war at almost any price; he conceded to the rebels that they would be invited to participate in the provisional administration which would supervise the referendum in Algeria, and that the Sahara would not be detached from an independent Algeria. No serious obstacles remained for a final settlement. On October 2, 1961, he publicly told the rebels that France was ready to reach an agreement for the restoration of peace, the definition of conditions of self-determination, and the determination of terms for future French-Algerian cooperation. In fact, he capitulated before a stronger will than his own.

In the meantime, the year 1961–62 looked like one of civil war in France with the continuous terrorist activity by the O.A.S. Many Frenchmen doubted that the Fifth Republic would be luckier than the Fourth and survive. They were wrong, because a true civil war would need the support of at least a large section of the French population; the immense majority of Frenchmen were with de Gaulle, including his most resolute domestic opponents. His Algerian policy was the policy of France. In November 1961 he conceded what he had not believed in earlier years, namely that the rebels had the support of "almost all Algerian Moslems." The negotiations with the Provisional Algerian Government dragged on, but were finally ended by the Evian agreements on March 19, 1962. Their main points were as follows:

1. A cease-fire.
2. Full independence for Algeria, if confirmed by the referenda held in Algeria and in France.
3. The Algerian guaranty of respect for the rights of the European minority and for the economic interests of France, including the acquired interests of French corporations in the exploitation of Saharan oil and gas resources. This was a major item for de Gaulle who wanted to ensure France a certain independence of the foreign (in fact, mainly "Anglo-Saxon") supplies of oil.
4. France pledged herself to give Algeria financial and technical aid in proportion to its justification by the existence of French interests in Algeria.
5. A preferential treatment in the mutual trade.
6. Algeria would remain within the French monetary system.
7. The French obligation to indemnify French citizens who would be expropriated in consequence of the Algerian agrarian reform.
8. Algerian workers in France would enjoy the same benefits of the French social legislation as French workers.

9. French troops in Algeria would be reduced to 80,000 men and would be garrisoned at places fixed by common agreement. France would retain her naval base at Mers-el-Kabir for fifteen years, and would have the use of seven airfields.
10. France would have the nuclear testing grounds in the Sahara at her disposal for five years.

This was a total victory for the rebels. It was even greater than they believed possible in March 1962. Their cooperation with France could have been endangered by the existence of the French minority of one million people. This problem was "solved" by the unbelievable stupidity of the Europeans. Their answer to the Evian agreements was an indiscriminate reign of terror against all the Moslems—men, women, and children—and a scorched-earth policy. They were murdering defenseless Arabs in the streets of Algerian cities, the same Arabs whom they claimed in 1958 to be loyal Frenchmen. They wantonly destroyed public buildings, schools, and public utilities. When the time had come for the French troops' evacuation, the Europeans knew that they had to depart. The European minority was quickly reduced from one million to less than 80,000. . . .

The French referendum for the approval of the Evian agreements was held on April 8, 1962. De Gaulle's main argument in the appeal to his countrymen was: the restoration of peace after the intermittent hostilities which France had to wage since 1939 in Europe, in Indochina, and in Algeria. The French approval was overwhelming: 17,866,423 positive votes against only 1,809,074 nays. . . .

The Algerian chapter was closed, except for the small minority represented by the O.A.S. who almost succeeded in murdering de Gaulle in August 1962 and have never renounced their intention to get revenge on the man who liquidated the colonial empire.

The Algerian story not only shows de Gaulle at one of his greatest moments, but especially proves that he is not a statesman who never retreats. He may be compelled to accept the point of view of others, if the other party demonstrates clearly to have an equal will and adequate means for overcoming his resistance.

The colonial career of France was terminated in 1962. Free of that burden which had been absorbing the French energies and had been paralyzing her foreign policy in the world, the French vessel could take any course its bold captain selected. The ocean of the Third World was at last open to its navigation. The colonialist stigma was effaced from the French forehead. . . .

THE FOREIGN POLICY CONCEPTIONS
OF GENERAL DE GAULLE

Alfred Grosser

Why does this subject merit consideration? It is not merely because the fundamental decisions of the Fourth Republic have allegedly been modified under the Fifth. We shall have occasion later to consider whether or not the major choices that have been discussed have in fact been modified under the Fifth Republic. The thesis that I shall expound . . . is that none of the fundamental decisions of the Fourth Republic—although they were often counter to General de Gaulle's position at the time—has been really called into question under the Fifth Republic. But, there has been a change in tone, a change in style, a change in the ideological inspiration of foreign policy. And finally, there has been a change in the mechanisms of decision making. There is no doubt that it is General de Gaulle himself who makes the decisions on foreign policy issues.

Theoretically, his decisions are based on Article 52 of the Constitution: "the President of the Republic negotiates and ratifies treaties" . . . ; "he is informed of any negotiation tending to the conclusion of an international accord not submitted to ratification. . . ." Since he makes the major decisions concerning foreign policy, one might conclude that the President of the Republic overshadows the Prime Minister in this domain. Is this also true of the Minister of Foreign Affairs?

In a number of books and commentaries . . . Couve de Murville's role is minimized to the point of labeling him "His Master's Voice." I believe that the description in *Time* magazine, dedicated largely to Monsieur Couve de Murville, is much closer to the truth. "In fact," writes *Time*, "Couve plays a much larger role than would appear at first sight." During the negotiations in Brussels in December, 1964, notably, the French Minister of Foreign Affairs enjoyed much wider power of acceptance or rejection than his foreign colleagues. The President of the Republic establishes the major directions within which the Minister of Foreign Affairs enjoys an appreciable latitude of action.

Moreover, it is a fact that General de Gaulle's interest in a given problem is intermittent—this is one of his techniques of governing. At times, he takes up a question; at other times, he takes no part at all. In any case, General de Gaulle certainly exhibits a distrust of diplomatic personnel, which he expressed in the second volume of his *Mémoires* . . . apropos the year 1945. But the expression seems to me as valid for the period of the Fifth Republic as well: "First of all, the personnel of our diplomatic corps concurred only

From *French Foreign Policy Under De Gaulle* by Alfred Grosser, translated by Lois Ames Pattison. © 1965, Editions du Seuil; English translation copyright © 1967, by Little, Brown and Company (Inc.). Reprinted by permission of Little, Brown and Company.

remotely with the attitude I had adopted. For many of the men in charge of our foreign relations, concord with England was a kind of principle. But between the impulse I was trying to transmit and the behavior of those who actually wrote the notes, maintained the contacts and established the communications, the discrepancy was too apparent to escape our associates, thereby weakening the effect of my own determination." (Whence the necessity of keeping in line and maintaining close surveillance over French negotiators.)

The style, the inspiration, the monopoly over decisions, all contribute to the importance of studying the political thought and attitudes of General de Gaulle.

THE NATION AND NATIONAL AMBITION

... *The State and the Primacy of Power.* What is the state? "I regarded the state," wrote General de Gaulle, "not as it was yesterday and as the parties wished it to become once more, a juxtaposition of private interests which could never produce anything but weak compromise, but instead an instrument of decision, action and ambition, expressing and serving the national interest alone. In order to make decisions and determine measures, it must have a qualified arbitrator at its head." In other words, the goal of the state is external ambition, and this is what justifies very broadly the presence at the helm of a person in possession of the power of the state, and capable of acting toward the world outside.

This is why the various ministerial departments are conceived as a function of foreign policy. In refusing to allot one of the three major ministries to the communists in 1945 . . . , General de Gaulle explained himself as follows: "I did not feel it would be justifiable to entrust them with any of the three key foreign policy posts—Foreign Affairs, which express the policy, the War Office, which upholds it, or the Police, which protects it." The Ministry of the Interior is seen less as an organ of administration than as an organ of public order making it possible to conduct foreign policy. Accordingly, almost all, if not all internal undertakings have a purpose in foreign policy. General de Gaulle recalls in his *Mémoires*, with a satisfaction that seems justified to me, the social works undertaken by the Provisional Government from 1944–46: legislation on tenant farming, social security, etc. But what led him to make this kind of decision? "Once again I remarked that if the goal was perhaps the same for them as for myself, the motives guiding them were not identical with my own. Though they adjusted their attitudes to accord with the prejudices of their respective tendencies, such considerations did not affect me. On the other hand, I perceived that they were scarcely aware of the motive inspiring me, which was the power of France." The ultimate purpose of social security and legislation on tenant farming is the power of France.

The same inspiration underlies nearly all the texts of the Fifth Republic. Two examples will suffice. First, the New Year's message for 1963: "Our prosperity has reached a level that we have never known before, and we have realized unprecedented social progress. In proportion as expansion and reason lead us to power, France regains its status, its allure, its means." And again, in the message to the National Assembly on December 11, 1962: "To pursue the development of our country in such a manner as to enhance at the same time the condition of the individual, national prosperity, and the power of France."

The French People and "France."   The economy is a means. The prosperity of the French people is a means, especially in that they are not the objective of policy. The objective of policy is "France," which is very distinct from the sum of the French people, who are all engaged in its service. This explains a political attitude which scorns the various divisions between Frenchmen, or at least, which considers them inconsequential. In terminating his message to the Constituent Assembly on March 2, 1945, General de Gaulle exclaimed: "A single party or a new one? Certainly not! Not more so tomorrow than yesterday! They are good Frenchmen, of all opinions, origins and inclinations, who wherever they are, set the example of enthusiasm and act in such a manner that, in each of the political, social or professional sectors, they make their interests and passions subservient to the superior interests of France."

This means, in other words, that all ideological and political divisions among Frenchmen are subordinate, of little moment, in relation to the national interest, which in turn is oriented toward foreign policy. It also implies that this national interest exists—in other words, that at any given moment, one can always define the interest of the national community in a plain, clear, and evident fashion. Finally, it also means that there can be no debate among citizens on what the national interest *is* at a given moment. The result or the consequence of this conception . . . is to deprive politics of its highest substance—to permit citizens to choose among different conceptions of the national interest. It also leads politically to what I shall overstate in speaking of the "double nature" of each Frenchman. Each Frenchman has two souls. The one leads him to membership in social, economic, and political groups; through it, he belongs to a family, a religion, a profession, to everything that divides the French people. By virtue of the other soul he is a member of a united community and is represented by the President of the Republic, who defines what the national interest is by expressing what the French people, unconsciously, should conceive as being that interest.

A Vision of International Affairs.   Out of this notion of national interest, of the nation, and of the nation having ambitions in the outside world, there emerges a whole conception of international affairs. What is important and enduring in international affairs are nation-states, and not regimes and ideologies. Nation-states are not whatever is legally defined as such. It is clear that for General de Gaulle the African countries have not yet arrived at the nation-state stage. Some antiquity is required. Certain countries, like China, are "older than history" and are more specially nation-states. A certain age is required in order for a country to constitute a bona fide nation-state. In his press conference of January 31, 1964, General de Gaulle spoke of "the regime that *presently* dominates China." The regime is what is transitory. This in turn accounts for de Gaulle's conception of international relations based primarily on bilateral relationships. In December, 1944, when General de Gaulle was in Moscow negotiating the Franco-Soviet treaty with Stalin, he received a telegram from Churchill asking, "May I be a third party?," which would have made a tripartite pact. General de Gaulle became indignant and said to Stalin, according to the minutes of the meeting, "Between France and the Soviet Union, there is no object of direct contestation. With Great Britain, we always have had and always will have differences." Slightly less than twenty years later, in a newspaper interview—seemingly prompted by the Élysée—Edgar Faure declared: "The fact that the tensions which could exist between France and China no longer exist today . . ." etc. This is the very same formula as with Stalin in 1944. . . .

The greatest difficulty for General de Gaulle, with his concept of the nation-state, is not to conceive of regimes and ideologies, but rather to conceive of a political entity distinct from and superior to the nation-state. In any case, he has a deep horror of all so-called supranational organisms, whether it be the general secretariat of the United Nations, or the general secretariat of NATO, or the Common Market Commission. His preference runs to a Directory of the major powers: five in the UN, three in NATO, two in Europe, and one alone in France. . . .

However, the problem of Europe is the most vexing. Can there be a "Europe" without a certain transcendence of the notion of nation-state, as it exists in the thinking of General de Gaulle? What sort of unity can be achieved in a mere conglomeration of nation-states? And at present, the principal difficulty in the dialogue between France and countries like Germany or Italy is that General de Gaulle tells his European partners: "You are bad Europeans because you want Europe without in the least knowing what you would do with it. What interest is there in building Europe if it is only to contribute to an Atlantic community dominated by the United States? Why bother passing through a European stage?" And they respond: "But in order to achieve a Europe such as you desire, which would be a political entity, we must pass the stage of the nation-states France, Germany, Italy, that stand at the heart of your opposition to any notion of supranationality." We shall have occasion to return to this issue.

"REALPOLITIK"?

. . . Force and Its Diplomatic Use. It is a fact that General de Gaulle not only believes in power, but in addition, being a general, he attributes a special importance to military power. But, to begin with, he holds to a sort of cynical conception of international confrontations. It is the sort of "deal" or "tit-for-tat" approach commonly and wrongly labeled "Machiavellianism." Thus, for instance, when de Gaulle negotiated with Stalin in 1944 and the question of the boundaries of Germany came up, the decisive argument advanced by de Gaulle in favor of the Oder-Neisse line was that this boundary would forever prevent an agreement between Germany and Poland. This represents what one might call at least a very realistic conception of international relations. . . . Force is indispensable. Good will is not enough. We are faced with a very general conception of the role of force in political affairs. . . .

Consequently, there is a preoccupation with realism, a preoccupation with playing the role of a power in international relations. Out of this emerges a consequence that has been decisive in European politics during the last two years: the difficulty of conceiving of a style in international relations different from the traditional style of *Realpolitik*, the politics of power. The press conference of January 14, 1963, rejecting the British entry into the Common Market, was considered an offense by France's European partners much less because of the substance than because of the diplomatic procedure utilized. Members of a community do not behave in such a fashion. . . .

It must be noted, however, that *Realpolitik* has a limit. It applies to everyone except France. In describing his interview with President Truman, whom he finds to be a very mediocre man, de Gaulle explains that his welcome in the United States was very warm, not so much because he was General de Gaulle, but because of the ". . . extent of the city's extraordinary love of France." I believe this is very important. All states are cold-blooded monsters, but *France is loved*. This is what justifies her receiving a special status, not entirely independent of her power, but despite her lack of power. It is better that she should be powerful. More powerful, she will be more typically France. But even though not powerful, she benefits from a capital of affection in the world that no other country possesses, because no other country is France.

The Intrusion of History. It is at this point that *Realpolitik* becomes tempered by what one might call the intrusion of history into the political conceptions of General de Gaulle. We encounter this phenomenon on several levels: to begin with the most evident, the history experienced by General de Gaulle himself. His anti-American attitudes are in large part attributable to the relations between de Gaulle and Roosevelt between 1940 and 1944. The determination not to see the French army integrated within an Atlantic army, it seems to me, can be amply explained by the Strasbourg episode of January,

1945. During the German offensive in the Ardennes, the population of Strasbourg would have experienced great suffering if the evacuation orders of General Eisenhower had been respected, if the integrated command, insensitive to such a detail, had not been blocked by de Gaulle's order to General de Lattre to refuse to follow Eisenhower's orders. The attitude toward the French population in Algeria—cold, to say the least—can be explained, at least in part, by the attitude of the French Algerians toward General de Gaulle from 1942 until the Liberation.

In the second place, there is the very traditional concept of struggles and wars. This is well expressed in a phrase from de Gaulle's *Mémoires*: when Germany was invaded by French troops in 1944–45, de Gaulle commissioned General de Lattre ". . . to conquer cities, land and trophies. . . ." The concept of trophies, of the flags that one captures, is really the most traditional in military history. At the same time, one notes the will to see geography frozen in its historic forms. In speaking of Germany beyond the Elbe, General de Gaulle speaks more willingly of Prussia or Saxony. To say the very least, Prussia and Saxony hardly exist any more. I add, nonetheless, that insofar as General de Gaulle is a master of the equivocal statement, it is perfectly possible that he employs this terminology because it obviates the need to speak of the "German Democratic Republic," "East Germany," or the "Soviet Occupation Zone." I nonetheless favor the first interpretation, since the expression "Prussia and Saxony" is found recurrently, from the meetings with Stalin to the press conferences of 1959–61.

The third aspect of the contribution of history is that it provides the ideological sources of his nationalism. Those sources are two-fold, and I should like to emphasize this point.

General de Gaulle is at once heir to the Jacobin patriotism characteristic of the Left since the Revolution, and to the nationalism that has swept across a part of the French Right for a century. De Gaulle is the heir both of the Jacobins and Maurice Barrès and of the "Action Française" historian, Jacques Bainville. Hence, we see plainly that for General de Gaulle, the trip through Germany in 1962 marked the culmination of . . . a millennium of conflict. But in ending his press conference of January 31, 1964 by an allusion to the liberty, equality, and fraternity that France gave the universe 175 years ago, he was expressing the ideological expansionism of the French Revolution. One of the foundations of Gaullism consists precisely in its assuming the double heritage of Jacobin patriotism and the nationalism of the Right.

Another intrusion of history—the fourth aspect—lies in the conception of neighboring countries. . . . Whether in reference to Germany, England, or Russia, no analysis of a situation is ever presented independently of what Great Britain, Germany, or Russia has represented forever, across the centuries. But at the same time, over against this intrusion of past history, there is a sort of *vision of future history*. It appears that during one of the rare interviews that General de Gaulle accorded to Marshal Juin after he became President of the Republic, the latter reproached him with seeing only what was in the distant past or what is in the distant future—and not what was before his eyes.

On the one hand, we find a man full of nostalgia for the past glory of France, with a very traditional conception of diplomacy and of power relationships, On the other hand, we see an outstanding capacity to look into the future; to see, even in 1959, what was later to happen in Sino-Soviet relations; to conceive . . . of cooperation with the independent African state as a new form of an old French vocation.

THE MAN AND HIS STYLE

General de Gaulle is himself perfectly aware of being an exceptional personage. This explains the well-known formula in his radio message during the putsch of 1960 in Algiers: "In the name of the legitimacy that I have incarnated for twenty years. . . ." But there is a great deal of deliberateness in this will to be an exception—an attitude described earlier in *The Edge of the Sword*. . . . Concerning character, de Gaulle noted: "A leader of this sort is distant, for there is never authority without prestige, nor prestige without distance." . . .

. . . It is impossible to distinguish in General de Gaulle's behavior, sincerity—that is, deep conviction of what one says, as well as the reality of an emotion—from the calculated game—that is, consciously utilizing an emotion one feels as a conviction in order to obtain a political result. Sincerity and calculation are inextricably intertwined.

De Gaulle the actor, but also de Gaulle the exceptional man—the leader who is conscious of living his own biography. Ordinary men live their own lives. *General de Gaulle lives his biography.* This is extremely important; for to live one's biography means to behave according to what history will say. I am convinced, rightly or wrongly, that General de Gaulle does not know today when he will leave power. He would never accept being a physically declining President, for that would tarnish the image that history would hold of him, even if he were to remain in power until the end of his life. Better at that point to add a final prestige to the supreme prestige, that of Cincinnatus withdrawing when the *patrie* has been saved—Cincinnatus who would then write an additional volume of his *Mémoires*.

There is another aspect to General de Gaulle's personality that must not be underestimated. Like many Frenchmen, he is a man of letters, with all the good points and bad points that that entails. . . . In the *Who's Who* listing on General de Gaulle, there is a heading entitled "Works," beginning with *Une mauvaise rencontre*, a play in verse, 1906—written at the age of sixteen. This appears important to me as an element of explanation because General de Gaulle has a love of language—and he handles it admirably—

and it also explains another characteristic of the man of letters—the inability to resist the pleasure of the *bon mot*. . . . The taste for the *bon mot*, the love of the well-turned phrase takes on such proportions, moreover, that General de Gaulle has coined many new expressions, both in domestic and international politics—as proven by the number of words he has brought into fashion or returned to fashion.

The sense of biography and the sense of one's posture also carry with them a great source of justified popularity—the refusal of pettiness, the refusal of petty satisfactions. In *Le Maître de Santiago*, Montherlant has one of his characters say something like this: "In other times, people loved gold which led to power, which made it possible to undertake great things. Today, men love the power which leads to gold, which makes it possible to do little things."

In this sense, General de Gaulle is truly ambitious; and there are few ambitious men in French politics, if we define "ambition" as the will to act, and not merely the desire to profit from the advantages of power. . . .

Finally, whatever General de Gaulle's conception of politics, whatever his means of proceeding, whether we criticize him or not, he has replied in advance. In a chapter of his *Mémoires* entitled "Departure," after analyzing the situation in 1945 following the election of the Constituent Assembly, he wrote: "After the Assembly had elected Félix Gouin, as its president its next task was to elect the President of the Government. Naturally I abstained from submitting my candidacy or making any reference to my eventual platform. They would take me as I was or not take me at all."

DE GAULLE AND THE FUTURE OF EUROPE

Louis J. Halle

. . . It is common to say of any man who rises to the summit of state power that he is a complex and enigmatic character; and it is often said of de Gaulle. I can hardly believe, however, that it is said of him by those who have made themselves familiar with his writings as well as his career. For de Gaulle, among his other prodigious attributes, is a master of language who will surely occupy a place in the history of French literature equivalent to the

Louis J. Halle, "De Gaulle and the Future of Europe," *The Virginia Quarterly Review*, vol. XLIII, no. 1 (Winter, 1967), 4–19. Copyright by *The Virginia Quarterly Review*. Reprinted in abridged form by permission of *The Virginia Quarterly Review* and the author.

notable place that Churchill will surely occupy in the history of English literature. It is hard to see how one could read *The Edge of the Sword*, first published in 1932 and the three-volume *War Memoirs*, without being impressed by the monolithic simplicity of the man, and without concluding that there is nothing particularly enigmatic about his thinking, his motives, his policy, or his purpose.

Stalin, who was not always wrong, told Roosevelt at Yalta ... "that he had found de Gaulle to be an uncomplicated individual and also unrealistic in his estimates of France's contribution to the winning of the war." De Gaulle's unrealistic estimates of France's contribution to the winning of the War show the consistency of his mind, which in turn represents its lack of complication. The references to the First World War in *The Edge of the Sword* leave the impression that France fought and won it all alone. . . .

The Edge of the Sword exemplifies de Gaulle's consistency in other ways as well. The epigraph that he chose for it is a loose translation from "Hamlet": "Être grand, c'est soutenir une grande querelle" (to be great is to sustain a great quarrel). He has been faithful to this concept throughout his career. When, in 1943, the British Foreign Minister, Mr. Anthony Eden, said to him: "Do you know that you have caused us more trouble than all of our European allies?" it apparently gave him a moment of notable satisfaction. "I don't doubt it," he replied. "France is a great power." . . .

When one seeks to understand the political motivation of any individual's mind, the first question to ask is what represents, for it, the normal world. All thinking, to the extent that it is not chaotic, is normative. The mind is shaped to the vision of a normal order that represents propriety, and whatever departs from that order seems to it, in one sense or another, improper—whether as a temporary necessity imposed by abnormal circumstances, or as the product of human failure. In de Gaulle's mind, for example, the world supremacy of France represents the normal order, an order that was temporarily subverted in the period from the middle of the last century to the middle of our present century by a combination of unfortunate circumstances and the inadequacy of those who directed French affairs. In a broadcast of April 27, 1965, he referred to the international rôle that France had played up to a hundred years ago—that is, up to the time of Germany's rise under Bismarck and France's concurrent decline under Louis Napoleon—and he said: "We are coming back a long way to play our international rôle anew." His mission is to restore normality after a series of disasters has come to its end. . . .

What does de Gaulle's mission to restore normality represent in larger terms?

For many men, the normative order is that to which they were brought up in childhood. . . . De Gaulle . . . was born in 1890, midway in that period between the Franco-Prussian War and the First World War when a defeated

France was mourning its lost provinces, eating its heart out in bitterness at its humiliation, and dreaming of revenge. Throughout this period the statue of Strasbourg in the Place de la Concorde, representing the Alsace-Lorraine for which France mourned, was veiled in black. The mourning and bitterness, which continued unappeasable until 1914–1918, is movingly represented in Alphonse Daudet's short story, "La dernière classe," which ends with the son of eternal France bowing his head to the conqueror, but crying out at the same time: "Vive la France!" Read this to understand de Gaulle.

And read, then, just the first two pages of his *War Memoirs*. The fallen greatness of France, and the absolute necessity of restoring it, was the passion of his childhood, of his young manhood, of his entire career. It came to him from the environment in which he was born, from a father who taught him the history of France in terms of it, and from a mother who had "an intransigent passion for the fatherland equal to her religious piety." . . . Like Joan of Arc, he never doubted that he was to have the occasion of rendering some signal service to a France about to undergo "gigantic trials." The narrowness as well as the intensity of this conception is represented by one sentence in which he refers to a crippled France that was able, nevertheless, to draw out of her own self the incredible effort that enabled her to terminate the trial of World War I by victory—as if no contribution to that victory had come from outside. He does not hesitate to say, in the opening sentences of his *Memoirs*, that his idea of France is inspired as much by sentiment as by reason. Ten thousand expressions of that idea in his writings show that there is little room in it for magnanimity toward the non-French world, and his bitterness toward the Anglo-Saxon world is especially marked. . . . (There is evidence, however, that de Gaulle finds it easier to be forgiving toward the enemies of France than toward the allies on whom France's dependence has been so humiliatingly great.)

The nationalism of de Gaulle today is the narrow European nationalism of the second half of the nineteenth century. His normative thinking is that of Bismarck, though it comes a century later.

Metternich, in the generation before Bismarck, had written: "Since . . . an isolated State no longer exists, . . . we must always view the *Society* of States as the essential condition of the modern world." To most of us, this conception is the only workable conception in the nuclear age. What characterized the second half of the nineteenth century, however, was an exclusively self-regarding nationalism that taught its votaries to set their own nation-states in opposition to all other states, or to any society of states. This represented, in nationalistic terms, Hobbes's view of the international anarchy as he set it forth in the "Leviathan," where he wrote that "in all times, kings and persons of sovereign authority, because of their independency, are in continual jealousies, and in the state and posture of gladiators; having their weapons pointing, and their eyes fixed on one another; that is, their forts, garrisons, and guns upon the frontiers of their kingdoms; and continual spies upon their neighbours; which is a posture of war."

In de Gaulle's childhood this Hobbesian conception had its most distinguished representative in the aged Bismarck, of whom G. P. Gooch wrote: "Vast and splendid as was his intellect, he could see nothing and imagine nothing beyond the sovereign state pursuing exclusively its own supposed interests. Europe was only a geographical expression. The vision of an organized world was beyond his ken."

In our own day, this narrow and exclusive nationalism, which dominated the Europe of the second half of the nineteenth century, has gone out of date, even though one finds its manifestations still in the provincial backwaters of our civilization. It has been discredited by its consequences, for it led to the two world wars with all their destruction. . . . In de Gaulle's mind, however, the opposed conception, the Bismarckian conception that dominated the world of his childhood and youth, still represents the norm to which the world must, under the leadership of a great man, return. All that has been added to it is the peculiarly embittered nationalism (which belongs to the same period) of the defeated France in which he grew up. . . .

. . . I have the impression that the concepts for which de Gaulle stands do not arouse anything like the emotional support among the French people that they did before the First World War. The French of today seem inclined to be cynical about nationalism, and much as they resent foreigners they seem unenthusiastic about going it alone. De Gaulle has taken France out of NATO in accordance with his personal will, but I rather think that a plebiscite among the French people would not show a majority in support of this deed. I feel quite sure it would not have the support of a majority among French staff officers.

De Gaulle has said that a great nation must have its own self-contained defense, and that France intends to have such a defense. I think there are few military officers around him who believe that this is remotely possible in the nuclear age, but they can express themselves only in private. . . .

He has repeatedly talked about returning to a Europe "from the Atlantic to the Urals," and I wonder whether the Russians do not have some misgivings about this application to the future of the significance attached to the Urals in the geography school books of his childhood.

He has also referred, on occasion, to America being another world, far apart from Europe, with its own separate destiny, but I doubt that there are many educated Frenchmen who are as ready to overlook alike the experience of half a century and the technological developments that today place New York as near to Paris as Bordeaux was in his childhood—indeed, that place it nearer than Versailles if one takes account of missiles.

Since 1945, France has been the theater of a conflict between two opposed concepts, with their corresponding political movements. One is represented by Jean Monnet, by the Schuman Plan, and by the Pleven Plan that failed of realization in 1954. This concept has its basis in the lesson of the disasters that France has suffered from the narrow and exclusive nationalism of the past. In a Hobbesian or Bismarckian Europe, the demographic and industrial superiority of the Germans is bound to prevail. France will not have the strength to avoid falling under the domination of Germany. Messrs. Monnet, Schuman, *et al.* proposed as the solution of this problem a supranational organization of Europe to be achieved in successive steps. As part of a United States of Europe, the strength of Germany would have no separate existence and could not be exercised independently. A brilliant beginning was made in the realization of this concept by the foundation of the Coal and Steel Community and the subsequent organization of the Common Market. In Monnet's conception the united Europe of his vision would be associated with the United States as a partner in every respect equal to it, no longer under what de Gaulle refers to as American hegemony.

What was bound to strike a man of de Gaulle's mind, however, was that Monnet's proposed Europe, while it would contain and absorb Germany, would also contain and absorb France. Hence his opposed concept of an "Europe des Etats," to which he also applies the adjective "united," but in a different sense. In this concept . . . Germany would be contained and absorbed, but France would not, for the "Europe des Etats" would have its capital in Paris and would be, in some sense, a French empire.

Because political propriety is associated in de Gaulle's mind with the past, he has repeatedly ridiculed what he refers to as "a so-called integrated Europe which [as he puts it] . . . would automatically be subordinate to the protector from overseas. . . ."

De Gaulle is moved . . . only by the exclusive French nationalism that he has himself said is the obsessive passion of his life. He is no more concerned with the greatness of Europe in itself than Bismarck was. He is concerned only with the greatness of France. According to his grand design, the unification of Europe under the leadership of Paris is to be accomplished in the first instance by the device of a Franco-German axis in which West Germany lends its weight to a France that is undertaking such a unification.

During the War, the allied leaders had to resist and oppose de Gaulle at every turn because, while their whole objective was to win the War, his own exclusive objective was the greatness of France—its greatness, in the circumstances of the day, relative to its allies. We see time and again, even in his own memoirs, how his claims for France, if accepted, might well have jeopardized the objective of military victory in North Africa, in Italy, across the Channel. The same problem arises now with his grand design for Europe, since its sole objective, to which the rest of Europe is expected to contribute by some form of subordination, is the greatness of France. . . .

This grand design has already failed, however. . . . One asks oneself how it could have been otherwise, since the nationalism of no country is for export. There is among the peoples of Europe a general desire to unite under a European flag, but outside France there is no desire to unite under a French flag. The grand design reflects the one point on which, as Stalin observed, de Gaulle's lack of realism is notable.

The grand design was dramatically inaugurated in January, 1963 . . . under circumstances that, as we can now see, were poignant. For de Gaulle, the event represented the culmination of a plan that he had held in his head for at least fifteen years. As early as October, 1948, he had objected to the new European defense organization called Western Union because it was centered in London when it ought, he said, to be centered in France. In 1951, when he was still out of office, he had declared that a European federation was to be formed only on the basis of (1) a strong France, (2) the firm incorporation of Germany in European institutions in order to abolish the danger of German hegemony, and (3) a Franco-German understanding brought about by direct negotiations between the heads of the two states. . . .

In the contemplated confrontation between the heads of the French and German states de Gaulle would have expected to emerge on top, by force of will and inflexibility of purpose, despite Germany's greater strength. After that it would have been a relatively simple matter to draw the lesser states of Europe into his orbit. . . .

I say that the grand design was launched under poignant circumstances because by that time, while de Gaulle had achieved the power to assure France's participation, Adenauer had no like power over the German state whose Government he headed, and he was rapidly losing such power as he had had. A grand statesman who had presided over Germany's recovery from defeat and humiliation, at the age of eighty-seven he had at last been compelled to announce his forthcoming retirement and the termination of his long career. The powerful leader who for fifteen years had spoken for Germany was no longer able to speak for Germany in January, 1963, because he was leaving office. His career was closing just short of the point where he would otherwise have been able, as it seemed, to realize the dream he had long cherished of a Franco-German reconciliation and association. Still, he did his best and, on January 20, with so little time to spare now, he arrived in Paris to conclude with de Gaulle the treaty that was to be the cornerstone of the new Europe. By its terms, the two states would henceforth march together side by side for the reconstitution of Europe, of the North Atlantic association, of the world itself. Henceforth they would consult each other "before taking any decision, on all major questions of foreign policy," and on "all matters dealt with in the North Atlantic Treaty Organization and the various international organizations in which the two Governments take a part, . . ." et cetera.

No one who knew de Gaulle's repeatedly stated principles and policy could believe that the obligations of the treaty, in so far as they were limiting on the conduct of France's foreign affairs, would be taken literally by him. What he had in mind was that Germany should consult France in order to keep German policy in line with French policy, and the nominal reciprocity of the obligation was merely for the sake of appearances. Only one week earlier, without previously consulting or even informing Adenauer's Government, or any of the other governments that were supposed to be concerting their wills in the European Economic Community (the Common Market), he had publicly rejected Britain's application for membership, which the other five members had been getting ready to accept. . . . Six months later, in spite of the treaty's provision for prior consultation on precisely such matters, the German Government had no advance information of the French decision, announced on June 21, to withdraw all the French naval units from NATO Atlantic and Channel Commands. In de Gaulle's eyes, actually to consult Germany on French policy would have been in derogation of French greatness. On this point his principles were not unknown or in doubt. . . .

Three years and more have passed. De Gaulle has, in those years, asserted Europe's essential independence of the United States, an assertion that should, in principle at least, be welcome to Americans. . . . The time is long past when the defense of Europe was properly more an American than a European responsibility. De Gaulle has usefully put in question the whole concept of NATO that, however relevant it may have been in the circumstances of 1950, had become outdated by the middle of the 1960's. These, however, are negative achievements that were to have their positive corollary, and their justification, in the construction of a united Europe around a Franco-German axis. Since the creation of the axis has failed, however, the grand design has not gone forward. De Gaulle has been able to erect nothing on the ground that he has cleared.

Surprisingly enough, the alternative to the grand design, associated with Monnet, is in better shape. The Common Market of Monnet's conception has shown unexpected strength in resisting de Gaulle's intransigent opposition to the line of development that it represents, and the economic bonds that it has formed over the few years of its existence have at last become indissoluble. There it is still, for a time impeded and almost brought to a stop in its development, but untouched in its essential vitality. It is a base to build on after de Gaulle goes. . . .

What remains of his grand design, after the failure to move forward in the construction of the united Europe it projected, is only the Hobbesian concept of independent and rival sovereignties. But the failure to enclose Germany within a European system under French hegemony makes the continued advocacy of a return to Bismarckian nationalism dangerous in its implications for France. Under the circumstances no Frenchman, especially, should wish for the restoration of conditions that led to the decimation of France by German arms in the First World War, and to its defeat in the Second. If every great nation is again to enjoy untrammeled sovereignty, independence, and its own means of defense, then what is to save France from again falling victim to the superior strength of Germany? One may wonder whether Moscow, itself, may not be worried by the implications of de Gaulle's advocacy. . . .

A generation has passed, now, since de Gaulle saved France in the greatest catastrophe of its history. His title to fame and honor is secure. In the second half of the twentieth century, however, his ideas are no longer relevant to the needs of France, to the needs of Europe, or to the needs of the world at large.

Referring to Marshal Pétain in his declining years, de Gaulle wrote: "Old age is a shipwreck. So that nothing should be spared us, the old age of Marshal Pétain was to be identified with the shipwreck of France." If the old age of General de Gaulle is not, in turn, to be identified with the shipwreck of France, that may be because history will have proved too strong even for him.

SUGGESTIONS FOR FURTHER READING

Documentary: *L'Année politique* (Paris, 1959–   ); General: Pierre Avril, *Le Régime politique de la Vᵉ République* (Paris, 1964); Roy C. Macridis and Bernard E. Brown, *The de Gaulle Republic: Quest for Unity* (Homewood, Ill., 1960), and *Supplement* (Homewood, Ill., 1963); Dorothy Pickles, *The Fifth French Republic* (3rd ed.; New York, 1966); Nicholas Wahl, *The Fifth Republic: France's New Political System* (New York, 1959); Alexander Werth, *The de Gaulle Revolution* (London, 1960); Philip M. Williams and Martin Harrison, *De Gaulle's Republic* (2nd ed.; New York and London, 1961); Special: P.-M. de la Gorce, *De Gaulle entre deux mondes* (Paris, 1964); Stanley Hoffmann, "The French Constitution of 1958," *American Political Science Review*, LIII (1959), 332–357; Edgar S. Furness, Jr., *De Gaulle and the French Army, A Crisis in Civil-Military Relations* (New York, 1964); George A. Kelly, "Algeria, the Army, and the Fifth Republic (1959–1961): A Scenario of Civil-Military Conflict," *Political Science Quarterly*, LXXIX (1964), 335–59; John and Ann-Marie Hackett, *Economic Planning in France* (London, 1963); W. Randolph Burgess, "The Economic and Political Consequences of General de Gaulle," *Political Science Quarterly*, LXXVIII (1963), 537–47; Nora Beloff, *The General Says No* (Baltimore, 1963); Edward R. Tannenbaum, *The New France* (Chicago, 1961); Pierre Viansson-Ponté, *The King and His Court* (Boston, 1965); Biographical: Robert Aron, *An Explanation of de Gaulle* (New York, 1966); Jean Lacouture, *De Gaulle* (New York, 1966); François Mauriac, *De Gaulle* (Garden City, N.Y., 1966); Alexander Werth, *De Gaulle, A Political Biography* (New York, 1966).

Chapter Nineteen

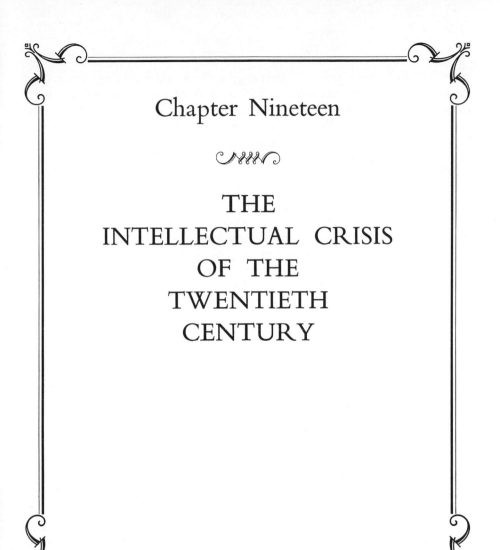

THE
INTELLECTUAL CRISIS
OF THE
TWENTIETH
CENTURY

$\mathbf{I}$N FRENCH ART, literature, and thought, the twentieth century has witnessed the continuation of the late nineteenth-century trend toward subjectivity, but a subjectivity enormously influenced by the world wars and their aftermath. The First World War has often been considered the watershed between the two centuries, between the crumbling world of accepted and objective norms and values, and a world in which all criteria were decidedly shattered. The Dada experience, described by the French literary historian, Georges Lemaitre in the opening selection, was the earliest and most expressive reaction to the war. The Dadaists believed that the war had destroyed more than simply a million lives, but the meaning of life itself. Dadaism, unlike impressionism and cubism, represented not just a change in the instrumentality or technique of conceiving reality nor yet another shift of emphasis from nature to the mind of the artist. It was an assault on the world, paralleling that of the war. Thus while Dadaism widened the split between nature and art, it also registered a closer correspondence between art, life, and society.

A similar paradox is elucidated by the English author John Cruickshank in the next selection. If twentieth-century French fiction has evinced the fragmentation of belief and the chaos of values, the French novel has become the principal medium of philosophical expression. While thoroughly marking the post-Christian world and the end of the Western tradition of *mimesis* in literature, the novel has carved out an almost medieval role for itself. The literature of *engagement*, the tightening relationship between the novel and life is the work of the novelist-philosopher. Its involvement with life is not in the meticulous imitation of the ordinary and seamy sides of life, as with Flaubert, but with the "big questions"—the meaning of life, death, hope, anguish, happiness, despair, the relationship of one man with another, and of man with the external world. Thus François Mauriac could write, "I am a metaphysician who works in the concrete."

The separation between the metaphysician and the novelist is bridged in part by the trend of French philosophy itself. With Bergson at the beginning of the century, metaphysics was no longer conceived as the Cartesian abstraction of static essences, but as a study of fluid motion and concrete individuality which could only be grasped by intuition, not analysis. The influence which Henri Bergson exercised, particularly in French letters, was enormous and the distance between pure philosophy and literature was consequently diminished. The novelist could be a philosopher partly because the philosopher had approximated the novelist in his conception of reality.

The disintegration of external values, the emphasis on time, change, and evanescence as in the novels of Proust, the increased attention given to psychological analysis led to one underlying presentiment—evil, nothingness, and despair, and hence the pervasive pessimism of much twentieth-century thought. This pessimism led to a new urge to define one's relations with the outside world in the writings of Sartre, Camus, and the novelists of the Resistance. Sartre clearly states this in his essay "Existentialism." For Sartre man is nothing except what he makes himself—hence the need for action. This need is also evident in the novels of

Saint-Exupéry and André Malraux. In the former, action becomes a cult and a defiance of softer feelings; action is the end of life. With Malraux, it becomes the means by which one continues to exist in spite of the awareness of the death of a Christian world.

Since 1955 the "new novel" has constituted a complete break with the *engagé* literature of Sartre, Camus, Saint-Exupéry, and others. The geometrical descriptions of external objects in the writings of Robbe-Grillet marked a reaction against the earlier literature and fostered a renewal of "Art for Art's sake." It opposed emphasis on change for a new way of looking at reality *sub specie aeternitatis*.

Although not all novelists and writers reached the same conclusion on the absurdity and ultimate banality of existence, the Christian reaffirmation, visible in the plays of Paul Claudel and the novels of Georges Bernanos and François Mauriac, all start from the presupposition that if all is not banal, evil is all pervasive. Their pessimism, however, was the backdrop and justification for the need for God, hope, grace, and salvation—tenuous and tortured as their attainment might be.

In a sense, one characteristic of the twentieth century in France has been a dialogue between belief and unbelief, which the two essays on existentialism by Sartre and Gabriel Marcel exemplify. For Sartre the starting point is atheism, and his essay is an attempt to draw *all* the consequences of being an atheist. He defends his position against its opponents and aptly demonstrates that for the atheistic existentialist, the death of God does not mean the loss of all values and meaning. There is a reaffirmation but one which is established on different foundations. For Marcel, a Catholic existentialist, the dilemma of atheistic existentialism is to find a philosophic justification for the denial of God's existence as well as for the ethical commitments subsequent to the denial of God.

The last selection, by Professor H. Stuart Hughes of Harvard, describes the transformation which has taken place in French thought in the 1960's. The end of the Resistance, the "thawing" of the Cold War, and France's new relations with Russia and China were paralleled by a general relaxation of the crisis mentality of the 1940's and 1950's. Professor Hughes sees in the fact that Teilhard de Chardin, Albert Camus, and Lévi-Strauss all found their inspiration outside of France, a significant sign of the decline of French nationalism of which Gaullism is only a survival. Similarly, the sacrifice of content to structure in the thinking of this anthropologist shows a drift to questions of method which the wave of positivism in Britain and America brought several decades earlier. The critique of material progress, resulting from Lévi-Strauss' discovery of the affinity between primitive tribes and modern society—the difference being one of *content* only, not of *form*— returns the focus to man and undermines the industrial and nuclear progressivism of postwar Europe. The natural savage reappeared not to mock the *Christian* religion, but the religion of progress. Structuralism seemed to be answering the same "big questions" but more indirectly. It began as linguistic analysis and has since pervaded all disciplines. Michel Foucault in philosophy and the history of ideas, Jacques Lacan in psychoanalysis, and Louis Althusser in Marxist ideology have broken away definitively from existentialism and dialectical Marxism.

⤳⤳⤳

DADAISM

Georges Lemaitre

The short-lived but notorious movement known as Dadaism, which interrupted the regular evolution of modernistic literature, was a direct consequence of the first World War. For the men who reached their twentieth year between 1914 and 1918, the war was more than a tragic experience; it definitely warped their entire outlook upon life. Arriving at the age when every young man takes stock of what existence has offered him so far, tries to find his bearings and to map his course into the future, the war generation discovered only ruin and despair. With the uncompromising spirit of generalization natural to youth, these victims of circumstance systematized their distress and in all sincerity pictured the world as an abode of unmitigated gloom.

Actually, there was at that time no dearth of moral and physiological causes to substantiate this attitude. The lack of adequate nourishment for young growing organisms, the nervous strain due to long-distance bombardments and to frequent air raids, above all the tension prevailing in a country threatened with total destruction, tended to create in all sensitive minds a grave and permanent neurotic state. What with the wave of war profiteering, with the plight of French and Belgian refugees, and with gross immorality now rampant everywhere, French society presented a sorry spectacle indeed. Those who were at the front could find in their own sacrifice or in the comradeship of the trenches an element of uplifting idealism. But for those still too young to take part in the struggle and for those who, being disabled, had to spend endless months in the hospitals behind the lines, demoralization seemed universal and complete. Thus a feeling of profound disgust and a haunting obsession with death preyed upon these unfortunates, leading in the years to come, as in the generation which followed the Napoleonic wars, to a long trail of suicides.

Indeed, almost everything that gives life its meaning and purpose had fallen suddenly into the utmost disrepute. Religion had become subservient to nationalism; practically everywhere the churches were heard to preach both hatred and slaughter; science was obviously responsible for the most horrible features of contemporary warfare; art and literature had also been

Reprinted by permission of the publishers from Georges Lemaitre, *From Cubism to Surrealism in French Literature*, Cambridge, Mass., Harvard University Press, Copyright, 1941, by the President and Fellows of Harvard College. Pp. 155–158, 169–172, 175–177.

enlisted in the conflict and had been turned into instruments of propaganda. This was the outcome of centuries of efforts towards civilization! The prospects for the future were still more bleak and discouraging. . . . Amidst the general bankruptcy of all respected values, nothing seemed deserving of salvage. Before such an accumulation of moral ruin men felt the irresistible urge to clear the ground of all the dismal wreckage that remained and to sweep all the spiritual and intellectual refuse into final oblivion. This destructive impulse was not prompted by the conscious hope of building anew on a better plan: nobody dreamt of reconstruction at that stage. The mad desire prevalent among young men of the war and post-war period to get rid of everything indiscriminately was only a spontaneous reaction to the state of our civilization, prompted by anger, disgust, and despair.

Yet, even if suicide was the logical conclusion of these mental shambles, very few, on the whole, cared to pursue their ideas to such an extremity. In order to remain alive, men had to adapt themselves somehow to an unprecedented moral and material confusion. The spectacle offered by the modern world was too atrocious to be accepted with equanimity and calm. It was bearable only when regarded as a vain and empty phantasmagoria. Swayed by the instinct of self-protection and self-defense—and not at all by frivolity, which was inconceivable in the midst of the cruel circumstances of that day—they came to consider the whole of life as a jest. There was, of course, nothing gay and diverting in their conception of this "jest," but they found in ironical and contemptuous bravado a measure of courage with which to face their disastrous destiny. . . .

. . . The World War was not alone responsible for the growth of the bewildering notions which flourished with such abundance during that period. Many wars had been fought by France before without bringing about any comparable disruption of human mental categories. In the particular case of the 1914–18 conflict, the younger men found in the doctrines put forward by the generation that had immediately preceded them a nucleus around which they crystallized their own disastrous experiences. Even though they rejected practically all the Cubist and Futurist constructive principles, they were, for the negative part of their views, the direct successors and heirs of Cubism. The Cubists had for many years deliberately discounted the importance of external reality; they had used humor as an instrument of methodical destruction. The existence of such a school enabled dissatisfied individuals to turn their bitterness into a coherent system. Without the precedent of Cubism, the woes and sufferings of the World War period undoubtedly would have found some confused modality of expression, probably without general bearing; but encouraged by the audacities of its predecessors, the war generation dared to launch into a furious destructive movement which was soon to acquire a cyclonic force and leave nothing in its wake but devastation and ruin. . . .

Dada must not be considered as a philosophical movement or as an artistic theory; it is merely an expression of collective despair and anger. This mood was felt by many young men of the post-war period who were burning with a mad desire to insult everything that was still respected and honored by the sheep-like masses. They yearned to slap the face of an inept, sanguinary world and to drag through the mud the idols of a complacent, self-satisfied society. They found in their own outrageous behavior a measure of relief for their distress, and in their blasphemies a strange, almost sadistic delight.

The only "idea" which could be discovered behind this outburst of deep-rooted rage was one of ruthless and frantic destruction. As Tristan Tzara had said, "A furious wind, we are tearing apart the fabric of clouds and prayers, and preparing the great spectacle of disaster, fire, and decay." Yet the Dadaists never attacked social institutions or intellectual standards as though they were dangerous obstacles whose resistance was to be broken by force. The very nature of their sarcasm implied that, in their view, our civilization was already in a state of total disintegration and decay. Their negations were intended to show the lack of real value, the lack of existence, as it were, of all qualities and all personalities—including our own—to which we assign a fictitious, illusory importance. That is what Georges Ribemont-Dessaignes wanted to express when he said: "What is beautiful? What is ugly? What is great, strong, weak? What is Carpentier, Renan, Foch? Don't know! What is 'I'? Don't know! Don't know, don't know, don't know!"

In their negative frenzy the Dadaists spared no one, not even their own spiritual forerunners. The Symbolists and Cubists had, to various degrees and with different objectives, denied practically all intrinsic value to external reality; with that part of their doctrines the Dadaists were in thorough agreement. But both Symbolists and Cubists had retained a mystic belief in a higher essence beyond the visible terrestrial shapes. The new generation refused to go that far. Said Jacques Vaché: "We ignore Mallarmé, without hatred, because he is dead. We don't know Apollinaire any more because we suspect him of indulging in art too consciously . . ."; and also: ". . . Max Jacob . . . but then, you know, he has ended by taking himself seriously—grave intoxication, indeed!"

The Dadaists refused to take anybody or anything seriously. According to them, even to criticize a fact in earnest would confer upon it an importance which nothing on earth can possibly deserve. The best way to denounce the absurdity of the world is to paint it, to write about it, or to describe it as a blatant absurdity. The systematic stupidity of the Dadaist productions had an intention, if not a meaning: its aim was to convey the feeling that absolutely everything is idiotic and senseless. To those who asked for explanations, the Dadaists were unable to give an intelligible response without defeating their own purpose. As a rule, they replied with obscene or sacrilegious ejaculations, adding that, if people failed to understand, they were really grasping the very spirit of Dadaism, which was, by definition, meaningless. At a public meeting organized by the Dadaists on February 5, 1920, in the Salon des Indépendants, Francis Picabia read the following typical statement: "You do not understand, of course, what we are doing! Well, my dear friends, we understand it still less. How wonderful, isn't it, that you are right! . . . You don't understand? Neither do I; how sad!"

Indeed, such lucubrations were profoundly sad, not only on account of their very silliness but because one could perceive in their expression the throb of a genuine pain. That a large number of young men, many of them well gifted and sincere, should have indulged in similar nonsense, conclusively shows how tragic their distress was. With all principles, all directions, and all bearings irretrievably lost, the new generation, forlorn and wretched, could at first do nothing but proclaim its agony; and its clamor, however incoherent and inarticulate, was at bottom infinitely less ridiculous than pathetic and even moving.

Moreover, there was in the very violence of their attitude a proof of insuperable vitality. If they had been really overwhelmed and crushed by their hostile environment, they would have submitted resignedly to their fate. Their vehement protestations proved that their spirit, at least, had not been destroyed. They refused categorically to accept life and the world as they were. But was there not in this refusal the implicit postulate that life and the world could be improved? They themselves offered no plan whatever for improvement, but their very revolt indicated potential hopes for a possible general transformation. For the time being, it is true, blinded by their own fury, they were not even conscious of their secret yearnings. But when the flood of their anger ebbed away, the old hopes emerged again. These aspirations showed little change since the time of Cubism and Futurism, but they were now rising in the midst of an entirely transformed moral landscape. Dadaism, like a short but furious storm, had wrecked everything in its path. Of the ancient traditional conventions, nothing had been left standing. The emancipated spirits found themselves with a perfectly clean slate—a consummation of their long-cherished desire. . . .

The Dadaist movement had been essentially the result of temporary circumstances. The sufferings brought about by the first World War and the consequent period of morbid despair had linked together men who had no really deep affinities. The violence of their feelings of disgust had stifled for a while individual antagonisms in temperament and outlook. An overwhelming spiritual revolt, general and sincere, had brought the movement into being. But, as the conditions which had started the movement came to an end, the wave of anger subsided. Soon the different characters and personalities reappeared in their normal guise, all the more sharply defined now that they had been cleared of all the intellectual sediment formerly deposited by convention and culture.

Moreover, Dadaism had carried within itself from the very beginning the germs of its own dissolution. Dada was admittedly the negation of all possible moral or artistic doctrine. But was not such a stand the very negation of Dada itself, as a doctrine? Sooner or later the absolute nihilism of the Dadaists was bound to turn against them. Those whom they had exhorted to consider everything as a jest profited so well by the lesson that they refused to take seriously even their exhorters. Some of the most rabid Dadaists were ready to accept the consequences of that vicious circle of hopeless absurdity. But for a few of them—for the best and for the most sincere—the situation had become positively unbearable.

Above all, there was in many, after the tremendous, wanton destruction caused by the war, a secret desire to rebuild. This normal aspiration, which had been obscured during times of anguish and stress, began to make itself felt again. Art had been ridiculed, along with the rest, unmercifully; but even though joining in the derisive chorus for a while, true artists could not but suffer inwardly from such a challenge to their deeper nature. They must have realized, of course, that Dada meant for them complete emancipation from the shackles of the past. Yet their productive faculties craved expression; at the end of 1920 a marked dissatisfaction with Dada and its principle became evident almost simultaneously everywhere. . . .

THE NOVELIST AS PHILOSOPHER

JOHN CRUICKSHANK

It has become a commonplace to say that general agreement exists less today than ever before concerning the validity of many traditional moral beliefs and practices. In the past, almost universal assent was given to the theory that virtue should be rewarded and vice punished. Even more important is the fact, emphasized some years ago by David Daiches, that near-unanimity existed about what actually constituted virtue and vice. This is obviously no longer the case. Absolutes and abstractions command little intellectual loyalty. Political and social events during the last twenty-five years, together with the accelerating pace of scientific discovery, have destroyed or seriously undermined belief in most of the traditional humanist assumptions. A whole conception of man, accepted in much the same form over a long period of time, has now been called in question. Even in the nineteen-twenties Duhamel, in his *Vie et aventures de Salavin*, presented us with a typical modern hero whom he described as being "a man deprived of any metaphysics."

What is now the extreme fragmentation of belief, and often the destruction of belief, has been reflected in much modern writing. The literature of this century has registered, above all, the breakdown of a settled, established intellectual and moral order. In providing the age with a nihilistic rhetoric it has also explored, on occasions, the possibility of a new coherence. . . .

Because agreed standards and shared assumptions are largely absent, recent fiction disturbs many ordinary readers, and is meant to disturb them. The desire to entertain and reassure has gone. Novels of disquiet reflect an age of anxiety. Bernanos, for example, attacked many intellectual assumptions and the pharisaism of much public morality. In his *Journal d'un curé de campagne* (1936), quite apart from his non-fictional works, he exposed materialism, boredom, lack of spiritual awareness, particularly in their more deceptively innocent forms. All this is regarded by Bernanos as evidence of what he considered to be the dominant contemporary phenomenon: "the fermentation of a Christianity in decay." In the same novel, the village priest's comment on his parishioners: "their serene security appalls me," sums up Bernanos's view of his potential readers and indicates the general nature of his attack on them. The novels of Malraux, lacking the religious affirmations of Bernanos, are perhaps even more disturbing with their insistence on the individual's loneliness (a loneliness that is metaphysical in essence) and their preoccupation with death. This view of "the human condition"—an expression that gained very wide currency after the publication of Malraux's novel, *La Condition humaine*, in 1933—is repeatedly examined by Queneau, Sartre, Beckett, Blanchot, Simone de Beauvoir, Cayrol, and Camus. Sartre reacts with "nausea" to the superfluity and arbitrariness of the physical world and man's relation to it; Beckett's tramps and Cayrol's outcasts dramatize aspects of the human dilemma; Camus, insisting on the incoherence of experience and the tragic conflict of life and death, described alienated man in his first novel, *L'Étranger* (1942). Whether they accept the fact or not, Sartre is attacking most of his potential readers in his onslaught on bourgeois standards and traditional humanist values in *La Nausée* (1938). A broader and more radical attack, in so far as it is both literary and moral, is present in the novels of Robbe-Grillet. . . .

It is a characteristic of many novelists in the twentieth century to make sweeping claims on behalf of their work. . . . Naturally, seriousness of purpose and ambitious claims take widely differing forms. In the case of Bernanos, for example, they arise from the close connexion he himself established between his role as a novelist and his deep religious feeling. In a letter of 1945 he stated: "The profession of writing is no longer a profession but an adventure—and primarily a spiritual adventure." Two years earlier he had given striking expression to his own conception of his function as a novelist by writing to another correspondent: "As I grow older I understand with increasing clarity that my humble vocation really is a vocation—*vocatus*." For what may seem more precise, if also more narrow, reasons, Sartre has emphasized the potential power of the novelist and asserted the supremacy, from a certain point of view, of prose over poetry. He argues in *Situations II* (especially pp. 63–64) that the novelist uses words as signs and as instruments, that his concern is with the things to which words point, whereas the poet treats words much more as objects and is primarily interested in them for themselves. This is one of the explanations offered by those who claim, no doubt rightly, that the novel is the most important and influential literary vehicle of modern society. It also lies at the basis of Sartre's theory of a "committed" literature and prompts him to regard writing as a form of political and moral action. This view has been taken by a number of other novelists; for example, Blaise Cendrars in *Rhum* (1930) and Michel Leiris in *L'Age d'homme* (1939). Cendrars even claims that his *reportage romancé* was written "to prove . . . that a novel can also be an act."

A rather different view, asserting that the novel must attempt to encompass the whole metaphysical status of man, has been held by a number of French writers in recent years. Malraux and Blanchot are particularly explicit on this point. In one of the numerous comments which he added to the text of Gaëtan Picon's *Malraux par lui-même* (1953) Malraux says: "In my view the modern novel is a privileged means of expressing the tragic element in man; it is not an elucidation of the individual" (p. 66). Malraux also describes the novel as "an instrument of metaphysical consciousness." Blanchot expressed a similar view, in an article published in *L'Arche* for September 1945, when he claimed that any novel of importance being written today "offers us an image of our condition in its entirety and is an attempt to show its meaning or its lack of meaning." This kind of statement, although based on very narrow aesthetic assumptions about what now constitutes an "important" novel, has led to even broader assertions on behalf of fiction. A number of writers, including Malraux and Camus, see the novel—and indeed all art—as a way of rejecting the created universe by means of rebellion and replacement. In *L'Homme révolté* (1951) Camus argued that the novel can present us with "an imaginary world created by 'correcting' the real world" (p. 325). He adds that man can endow himself, in fiction, with the very qualities and conditions he vainly seeks in daily life, so that the novel "rivals creation and wins a provisional triumph over death" (p. 327). . . .

. . . The separation implied by most definitions of fiction and of philosophy has long proved irksome to certain novelists and philosophers alike. Apart from the metaphysical ambitions of various novelists, it is already clear in the nineteenth century that some philosophers, such as Kierkegaard and Nietzsche, were drawn to the creation of a literary vehicle in order to express their ideas adequately. There is increasing agreement now that to discuss Kierkegaard and Nietzsche as less serious philosophers than their contemporaries, or as *littérateurs manqués*, is to miss the point. It seems clear that they wrote as they did because of the nature of their philosophical outlook, because of what they had to say, and because of their discovery that it was impossible to work within the abstract, formalist limits of a thought which showed itself content to observe the laws governing its own exercise, with little or no reference to action or experience.

It is this broad movement away from formalism and abstraction, favoured in particular by certain continental philosophers, which has done much to encourage the steady convergence of literature and philosophy in France in recent years. The ambiguity of experience, and the alien nature of the world in its resistance to rational systematization, were ideas which forced themselves with growing insistence on the attention of writers who thought about the raw material of their novels. At the same time, although academic philosophy often clung to abstraction and seemed indifferent to actual human experience, phenomenology was preaching a return to more concrete thinking with Husserl's slogan: "We want to get back to things-in-themselves." One should add, however, that the phenomenologists eventually developed an idealist philosophy out of their realist ambitions, whereas writers such as Sartre, who was deeply influenced by his contact with the German phenomenologists, have done much to emphasize and preserve the original philosophical aim of a return to things as they are. . . .

The invasion of the novel by metaphysics is no doubt the most striking single feature of French fiction during the last quarter-century. At the same time, however, this invasion has taken a variety of forms and had a number of subsidiary effects. In the case of Sartre and Simone de Beauvoir it has produced the kind of synthesis described above, but in writers such as Cayrol, Beckett, Blanchot, and Robbe-Grillet it has led to very different results. The novels of these four writers are dissimilar on many counts, but they have one characteristic in common. All of them are the novels of writers who, in different ways and to varying degrees, have turned their backs on the traditional procedures of character analysis. All are novels in which the human element is subject to severe pressures and at times almost totally absent. This tendency, already strongly marked in the strange world of the improbable charted by Blanchot, reaches a culminating point in the novels of Robbe-Grillet where a painstaking description of material things has largely ousted characters altogether. It is also a tendency, incidentally, which has its counterpart in much French poetry of the same period. In short, fiction in France since 1935 has turned steadily away from character analysis and turned increasingly towards the scrutiny of inanimate objects. There has been a progressive dehumanization of fiction which has often had complex links with the metaphysical ambitions of certain novelists. This trend has been so vigorous in itself and so varied in its effects that it must rank as a second major feature of French fiction during the period in question.

The rejection of the traditional forms of character analysis, a rejection which gradually encouraged the surge of objects into fiction, is something that was already being occasionally discussed immediately after World War I. The feeling grew that the omniscient analysis of their heroes and heroines was a weakness in Balzac and Dickens, in Flaubert and Tolstoy. The great nineteenth-century novelists, with a few exceptions such as Dostoievsky, offered the reader a series of remarkably precise answers to the questions he was likely to ask about their characters. But the objection was increasingly made that we do not experience other people in this way. In daily life we lack an omniscient analyst. In fact, the "realists" of the nineteenth-century novel were strikingly unrealistic in their assumption that human behaviour is clear-cut in a way that allows of systematic and predominantly rational explanation. About the time that such objections were being made to neatly motivated fictional characters further confirmation became available in the disturbing picture of human behaviour arrived at by analytical psychology. The emphasis was on disintegration and confusion—an emphasis reflected in the pioneering fiction of Joyce and more aggressively expressed in the theory and practice of Surrealism. In the beginning, the result for the novel was not the disappearance of character studies. But a note of uncertainty had entered in. Various aspects of the fictional characters of some writers tended more readily to dissolve into imprecision, or to collapse into unresolved contradictions. It is significant that within ten years of the completed publication of *A la recherche du temps perdu* critics were pointing out this new feature in Proust's characters as he presented them, after revision, in the later volumes of his novel.

Apart from certain psychological theories the widespread weakening of religious conviction, in France as elsewhere, made difficult any easy differentiation between good and evil and, ultimately, any satisfactory definition of human nature in general. This mood was doubtless intensified by the experiences of war and occupation. Shame and fear, heroism and collaboration, deportation and the moral ambiguities of resistance—all these experiences, together with the spectacle of a war spelt out in terms of Rotterdam, Warsaw, Auschwitz, Hiroshima, seemed to bring about a final exposure of traditional humanism. Severe blows were dealt to the French *moraliste* tradition and to assumptions about human perfectibility, the rational nature of man, the inevitability of progress. A new generation was growing up which had little patience with the ageing spokesmen of this tradition: Gide, Duhamel, Martin du Gard, Maurois. Attention turned inevitably to Malraux's query: "Is there a human nature?" and to Sartre's assertion: "Man is a useless passion" (however much this latter statement may have been misunderstood). Such a mood, especially among people with literary interests who reached maturity from the mid-'thirties onwards, was bound to prompt dissatisfaction with the assumptions lying behind character portrayal in most novels written before World War II. The attitudes of Bernanos and Malraux to these assumptions, attitudes that were exceptional among novelists already writing in the late 1920s and early 1930s, are among the features which most clearly make them founding fathers of post-Liberation French fiction. . . .

It would be foolish to try to demonstrate more common ground than actually exists between such different writers as Sartre, Camus, Baalchot, Queneau, Arnaud, and Merle. Yet all are, in their way, representatives of what Nathalie Sarraute has called "the age of suspicion." That is to say all of them suspect many elements in the traditional picture of human nature and hence they suspect the kind of hero who dominated the prose literature of the nineteenth century. . . .

Since the last war especially, the tradition of literary character analysis has been widely discredited in France. At first this tradition was replaced by the violent, anti-intellectual and consciously non-literary heroes of novels claiming American fiction as their model. These mindless, pragmatic heroes, in their turn, made easier both discussion and acceptance by the reading public of other characters lacking psychological depth but created for much more subtle intellectual purposes. (I am bound to add, in parenthesis, that French writers and critics—characteristically enough—have usually taken their anti-intellectualism very intellectually just as they have often been highly intelligent in their presentation of mindlessness.) In both the "tough" and the "metaphysical" novels, however, material objects seem to have occupied the scene more and more as the portrayal of character has become increasingly abstract and non-psychological. The hard, laconic heroes of Arnaud, for example, fulfil themselves by the conquest of material things. These become transformed from obstacles to achievement into objects of achievement. On the other hand, in the case of such writers as Sartre, Camus, Cayrol, and Beckett, the alien, self-sufficient nature of objects is stressed in order to emphasize man's metaphysical predicament in the modern world. In this case material things prevent human fulfilment and act rather as the catalysts of mental anguish or spiritual tragedy.

EXISTENTIALISM

Jean-Paul Sartre

I should like on this occasion to defend existentialism against some charges which have been brought against it.

First, it has been charged with inviting people to remain in a kind of desperate quietism because, since no solutions are possible, we should have to consider action in this world as quite impossible. We should then end up in a philosophy of contemplation; and since contemplation is a luxury, we come in the end to a bourgeois philosophy. The communists in particular have made these charges.

On the other hand, we have been charged with dwelling on human degradation, with pointing up everywhere the sordid, shady, and slimy, and neglecting the gracious and beautiful, the bright side of human nature; for example, according to Mlle Mercier, a Catholic critic, with forgetting the smile of the child. Both sides charge us with having ignored human solidarity, with considering man as an isolated being. The communists say that the main reason for this is that we take pure subjectivity, the *Cartesian I think*, as our starting point; in other words, the moment in which man becomes fully aware of what it means to him to be an isolated being; as a result, we are unable to return to a state of solidarity with the men who are not ourselves, a state which we can never reach in the *cogito*.

From the Christian standpoint, we are charged with denying the reality and seriousness of human undertakings, since, if we reject God's commandments and the eternal verities, there no longer remains anything but pure caprice, with everyone permitted to do as he pleases and incapable, from his own point of view, of condemning the points of view and acts of others. . . .

As is generally known, the basic charge against us is that we put the emphasis on the dark side of human life. Someone recently told me of a lady who, when she let slip a vulgar word in a moment of irritation, excused herself by saying, "I guess I'm becoming an existentialist." Consequently, existentialism is regarded as something ugly. . . .

Actually, it is the least scandalous, the most austere of doctrines. It is intended strictly for specialists and philosophers. Yet it can be defined easily. What complicates matters is that there are two kinds of existentialist; first, those who are Christian, among whom I would include Jaspers and Gabriel Marcel, both Catholic; and on the other hand the atheistic existentialists, among whom I class Heidegger, and then the French existentialists and myself. What they have in common is that they think that existence precedes essence, or, if you prefer, that subjectivity must be the starting point. . . .

J.-P. Sartre, *Existentialism* (Translation by Bernard Frechtman, N.Y., 1947), pp. 11–13, 15, 17–18, 25–27, 34–39, 42–44, 53, 59–61. © The Philosophical Library. Used by permission.

In the eighteenth century, the atheism of the *philosophes* discarded the idea of God, but not so much for the notion that essence precedes existence. To a certain extent, this idea is found everywhere; we find it in Diderot, in Voltaire, and even in Kant. Man has a human nature; this human nature, which is the concept of the human, is found in all men, which means that each man is a particular example of a universal concept, man. In Kant, the result of this universality is that the wild-man, the natural man, as well as the bourgeois, are circumscribed by the same definition and have the same basic qualities. Thus, here too the essence of man precedes the historical existence that we find in nature.

Atheistic existentialism, which I represent, is more coherent. It states that if God does not exist, there is at least one being in whom existence precedes essence, a being who exists before he can be defined by any concept, and that this being is man, or, as Heidegger says, human reality. What is meant here by saying that existence precedes essence? It means that, first of all, man exists, turns up, appears on the scene, and, only afterwards, defines himself. If man, as the existentialist conceives him, is indefinable, it is because at first he is nothing. Only afterward will he be something, and he himself will have made what he will be. Thus, there is no human nature, since there is no God to conceive it. Not only is man what he conceives himself to be, but he is also only what he wills himself to be after his thrust toward existence. . . .

This helps us understand what the actual content is of such rather grandiloquent words as anguish, forlornness, despair. As you will see, it's all quite simple.

First, what is meant by anguish? The existentialists say at once that man is anguish. What that means is this: the man who involves himself and who realizes that he is not only the person he chooses to be, but also a law-maker who is, at the same time, choosing all mankind as well as himself, can not help escape the feeling of his total and deep responsibility. . . .

When we speak of forlornness, a term Heidegger was fond of, we mean only that God does not exist and that we have to face all the consequences of this. The existentialist is strongly opposed to a certain kind of secular ethics which would like to abolish God with the least possible expense. About 1880, some French teachers tried to set up a secular ethics which went something like this: God is a useless and costly hypothesis; we are discarding it; but, meanwhile, in order for there to be an ethics, a society, a civilization, it is essential that certain values be taken seriously and that they be considered as having an *a priori* existence. It must be obligatory, *a priori*, to be honest, not to lie, not to beat your wife, to have children, etc., etc. So we're going to try a little device which will make it possible to show that values exist all the same, inscribed in a heaven of ideas, though otherwise God does not exist. In other words—and this, I believe, is the tendency of everything called reformism in France—nothing will be changed if God does not exist. We shall find ourselves with the same norms of honesty, progress, and humanism, and we shall have made of God an outdated hypothesis which will peacefully die off by itself.

The existentialist, on the contrary, thinks it very distressing that God does not exist, because all possibility of finding values in a heaven of ideas disappears along with Him; there can no longer be an *a priori* Good, since there is no infinite and perfect consciousness to think it. Nowhere is it written that the Good exists, that we must be honest, that we must not lie; because the fact is we are on a plane where there are only men. Dostoievsky said, "If God didn't exist, everything would be possible." That is the very starting point of existentialism. Indeed, everything is permissible if God does not exist, and as a result man is forlorn, because neither within him nor without does he find anything to cling to. He can't start making excuses for himself.

If existence really does precede essence, there is no explaining things away by reference to a fixed and given human nature. In other words, there is no determinism, man is free, man is freedom. On the other hand, if God does not exist, we find no values or commands to turn to which legitimize our conduct. So, in the bright realm of values, we have no excuse behind us, nor justification before us. We are alone, with no excuses.

That is the idea I shall try to convey when I say that man is condemned to be free. Condemned, because he did not create himself, yet, in other respects is free, because, once thrown into the world, he is responsible for everything he does. . . .

As for despair, the term has a very simple meaning. It means that we shall confine ourselves to reckoning only with what depends upon our will, or on the ensemble of probabilities which make our action possible. When we want something, we always have to reckon with probabilities. I may be counting on the arrival of a friend. The friend is coming by rail or street-car; this supposes that the train will arrive on schedule, or that the street-car will not jump the track. I am left in the realm of possibility; but possibilities are to be reckoned with only to the point where my action comports with the ensemble of these possibilities, and no further. The moment the possibilities I am considering are not rigorously involved by my action, I ought to disengage myself from them, because no God, no scheme, can adapt the world and its possibilities to my will. . . .

Given that men are free and that tomorrow they will freely decide what man will be, I can not be sure that, after my death, fellow-fighters will carry on my work to bring it to its maximum perfection. Tomorrow, after my death, some men may decide to set up Fascism, and the others may be cowardly and muddled enough to let them do it. Fascism will then be the human reality, so much the worse for us.

Actually, things will be as man will have decided they are to be. Does that mean that I should abandon myself to quietism? No. First, I should involve myself; then, act on the old saw, "Nothing ventured, nothing gained." Nor does it mean that I shouldn't belong to a party, but rather that I shall have no illusions and shall do what I can. For example, suppose I ask myself, "Will socialization, as such, ever come about?" I know nothing about it. All I know is that I'm going to do everything in my power to bring it about. Beyond that, I can't count on anything. Quietism is the attitude of people who say, "Let others do what I can't do." The doctrine I am presenting is the very opposite of quietism, since it declares, "There is no reality except in action." Moreover, it goes further, since it adds, "Man is nothing else than his plan; he exists only to the extent that he fulfills himself; he is therefore nothing else than the ensemble of his acts, nothing else than his life."

According to this, we can understand why our doctrine horrifies certain people. Because often the only way they can bear their wretchedness is to think, "Circumstances have been against me. What I've been and done doesn't show my true worth. To be sure, I've had no great love, no great friendship, but that's because I haven't met a man or woman who was worthy. The books I've written haven't been very good because I haven't had the proper leisure. I haven't had children to devote myself to because I didn't find a man with whom I could have spent my life. So there remains within me, unused and quite viable, a host of propensities, inclinations, possibilities, that one wouldn't guess from the mere series of things I've done." . . .

A man is involved in life, leaves his impress on it, and outside of that there is nothing. To be sure, this may seem a harsh thought to someone whose life hasn't been a success. But, on the other hand, it prompts people to understand that reality alone is what counts, that dreams, expectations, and hopes warrant no more than to define a man as a disappointed dream, as miscarried hopes, as vain expectations. In other words, to define him negatively and not positively. However, when we say, "You are nothing else than your life," that does not imply that the artist will be judged solely on the basis of his works of art; a thousand other things will contribute toward summing him up. What we mean is that a man is nothing else than a series of undertakings, he is the sum, the organization, the ensemble of the relationships which make up these undertakings. . . .

Thus, I think we have answered a number of the charges concerning existentialism. You see that it can not be taken for a philosophy of quietism, since it defines man in terms of action; nor for a pessimistic description of man—there is no doctrine more optimistic, since man's destiny is within himself; nor for an attempt to discourage man from acting, since it tells him that the only hope is in his acting and that action is the only thing that enables a man to live. Consequently, we are dealing here with an ethics of action and involvement.

Nevertheless, on the basis of a few notions like these, we are still charged with immuring man in his private subjectivity. There again we're very much misunderstood. Subjectivity of the individual is indeed our point of departure, and this for strictly philosophic reasons. Not because we are bourgeois, but because we want a doctrine based on truth and not a lot of fine theories, full of hope but with no real basis. There can be no other truth to take off from than this: *I think; therefore, I exist.* There we have the absolute truth of consciousness becoming aware of itself. Every theory which takes man out of the moment in which he becomes aware of himself is, at its very beginning, a theory which confounds truth, for outside the Cartesian *cogito*, all views are only probable, and a doctrine of probability which is not bound to a truth dissolves into thin air. In order to describe the probable, you must have a firm hold on the true. Therefore, before there can be any truth whatsoever, there must be an absolute truth; and this one is simple and easily arrived at; it's on everyone's doorstep; it's a matter of grasping it directly.

Secondly, this theory is the only one which gives man dignity, the only one which does not reduce him to an object. The effect of all materialism is to treat all men, including the one philosophizing, as objects, that is, as an ensemble of determined reactions in no way distinguished from the ensemble of qualities and phenomena which constitute a table or a chair or a stone. We definitely wish to establish the human realm as an ensemble of values distinct from the material realm. But the subjectivity that we have thus arrived at, and which we have claimed to be truth, is not a strictly individual subjectivity, for we have demonstrated that one discovers in the *cogito* not only himself, but others as well.

The philosophies of Descartes and Kant to the contrary, through the *I think* we reach our own self in the presence of others, and the others are just as real to us as our own self. Thus, the man who becomes aware of himself through the *cogito* also perceives all others, and he perceives them as the condition of his own existence. He realizes that he can not be anything (in the sense that we say that someone is witty or nasty or jealous) unless others recognize it as such. In order to get any truth about myself, I must have contact with another person. The other is indispensable to my own existence, as well as to my knowledge about myself. This being so, in discovering my inner being I discover the other person at the same time, like a freedom placed in front of me which thinks and wills only for or against me. Hence, let us at once announce the discovery of a world which we shall call inter-subjectivity; this is the world in which man decides what he is and what others are.

Besides, if it is impossible to find in every man some universal essence which would be human nature, yet there does exist a universal human condition. It's not by chance that today's thinkers speak more readily of man's condition than of his nature. By condition they mean, more or less definitely, the *a priori* limits which outline man's fundamental situation in the universe. Historical situations vary; a man may be born a slave in a pagan society or a feudal lord or a proletarian. What does not vary is the necessity for him to exist in the world, to be at work there, to be there in the midst of other people, and to be mortal there. The limits are neither subjective nor objective, or, rather, they have an objective and a subjective side. Objective because they are to be found everywhere and are recognizable everywhere; subjective because they are *lived* and are nothing if man does not live them, that is, freely determine his existence with reference to them. And though the configurations may differ, at least none of them are completely strange to me, because they all appear as attempts either to pass beyond these limits or recede from them or deny them or adapt to them. Consequently, every configuration, however individual it may be, has a universal value. . . .

In this sense we may say that there is a universality of man; but it is not given, it is perpetually being made. I build the universal in choosing myself; I build it in understanding the configuration of every other man, whatever age he might have lived in. This absoluteness of choice does not do away with the relativeness of each epoch. At heart, what existentialism shows is the connection between the absolute character of free involvement, by virtue of which every man realizes himself in realizing a type of mankind, an involvement always comprehensible in any age whatsoever and by any person whosoever, and the relativeness of the cultural ensemble which may result from such a choice; it must be stressed that the relativity of Cartesianism and the absolute character of Cartesian involvement go together. . . .

This does not entirely settle the objection to subjectivism. In fact, the objection still takes several forms. First, there is the following: we are told, "So you're able to do anything, no matter what!" This is expressed in various ways. First we are accused of anarchy; they say, "You're unable to pass judgment on others, because there's no reason to prefer one configuration to another"; finally they tell us, "Everything is arbitrary in this choosing of yours. You take something from one pocket and pretend you're putting it into the other."

These three objections aren't very serious. Take the first objection. "You're able to do anything, no matter what" is not the point. In one sense choice is possible, but what is not possible is not to choose. I can always choose, but I ought to know that if I do not choose, I am still choosing. Though this may seem purely formal, it is highly important for keeping fantasy and caprice within bounds. If it is true that in facing a situation, for example, one in which, as a person capable of having sexual relations, of having children, I am obliged to choose an attitude, and if I in any way assume responsibility for a choice which, in involving myself, also involves all mankind, this has nothing to do with caprice, even if no *a priori* value determines my choice. . . .

Man makes himself. He isn't ready-made at the start. In choosing his ethics, he makes himself, and force of circumstances is such that he can not abstain from choosing one. We define man only in relationship to involvement. It is therefore absurd to charge us with arbitrariness of choice.

In the second place, it is said that we are unable to pass judgment on others. In a way this is true, and in another way, false. It is true in this sense, that, whenever a man sanely and sincerely involves himself and chooses his configuration, it is impossible for him to prefer another configuration, regardless of what his own may be in other respects. It is true in this sense that we do not believe in progress. Progress is betterment. Man is always the same. The situation confronting him varies. Choice always remains a choice in a situation. The problem has not changed since the time one could choose between those for and those against slavery, for example, at the time of the Civil War, and the present time, when one can side with the Maquis Resistance Party, or with the Communists.

But, nevertheless, one can still pass judgment, for, as I have said, one makes a choice in relationship to others. First, one can judge (and this is perhaps not a judgment of value, but a logical judgment) that certain choices are based on error and others on truth. If we have defined man's situation as a free choice, with no excuses and no recourse, every man who takes refuge behind the excuse of his passions, every man who sets up a determinism, is a dishonest man. . . .

I've been reproached for asking whether existentialism is humanistic. It's been said, "But you said in *Nausea* that the humanists were all wrong. You made fun of a certain kind of humanist. Why come back to it now?" Actually, the word humanism has two very different meanings. By humanism one can mean a theory which takes man as an end and as a higher value. Humanism in this sense can be found in Cocteau's tale *Around the World in Eighty Hours* when a character, because he is flying over some mountains in an airplane, declares, "Man is simply amazing." That means that I, who did not build the airplanes, shall personally benefit from these particular inventions, and that I, as man, shall personally consider myself responsible for, and honored by, acts of a few particular men. This would imply that we ascribe a value to man on the basis of the highest deeds of certain men. This humanism is absurd, because only the dog or the horse would be able to make such an over-all judgment about man, which they are careful not to do, at least to my knowledge.

But it can not be granted that a man may make a judgment about man. Existentialism spares him from any such judgment. The existentialist will never consider man as an end because he is always in the making. Nor should we believe that there is a mankind to which we might set up a cult in the manner of Auguste Comte. The cult of mankind ends in the self-enclosed humanism of Comte, and, let it be said, of fascism. This kind of humanism we can do without.

But there is another meaning of humanism. Fundamentally it is this: man is constantly outside of himself; in projecting himself, in losing himself outside of himself, he makes for man's existing; and, on the other hand, it is by pursuing transcendent goals that he is able to exist; man, being this state of passing-beyond, and seizing upon things only as they bear upon this passing-beyond, is at the heart, at the center of this passing-beyond. There is no universe other than a human universe. The universe of human subjectivity. This connection between transcendency, as a constituent element of man—not in the sense that God is transcendent, but in the sense of passing beyond—and subjectivity, in the sense that man is not closed in on himself but is always present in a human universe, is what we call existentialist humanism. Humanism, because we remind man that there is no law-maker other than himself, and that in his forlornness he will decide by himself; because we point out that man will fulfill himself as man, not in turning toward himself, but in seeking outside of himself a goal which is just this liberation, just this particular fulfillment.

From these few reflections it is evident that nothing is more unjust than the objections that have been raised against us. Existentialism is nothing else than an attempt to draw all the consequences of a coherent atheistic position. It isn't trying to plunge man into despair at all. But if one calls every attitude of unbelief despair, like the Christians, then the word is not being used in its original sense. Existentialism isn't so atheistic that it wears itself out showing that God doesn't exist. Rather, it declares that even if God did exist, that would change nothing. There you've got our point of view. Not that we believe that God exists, but we think that the problem of His existence is not the issue. In this sense existentialism is optimistic, a doctrine of action, and it is plain dishonesty for Christians to make no distinction between their own despair and ours and then to call us despairing.

THE PHILOSOPHY OF EXISTENTIALISM

GABRIEL MARCEL

We must . . . turn our attention to that "freedom" of which Sartre constantly speaks and ask ourselves in what it consists. Sartre claims in conversation that he is the only man who today can speak of the absolute because for

Gabriel Marcel, *The Philosophy of Existentialism* (Translation by Manya Harari, New York, 1956), pp. 76–79, 82–83, 85–89. © The Philosophical Library. Used by permission.

him freedom has the value of an absolute; I can think of nothing more preposterous. What then is this freedom? His definitions of it are obscure. We must not be put off by such formulæ as that freedom is man's faculty to secrete his own non-being, or that it is man's capacity to be the foundation of himself; as in the case of existence, we must refer to his actual experience of freedom as he describes it, particularly in *Le Sursis*. . . .

Now along the warm stones there was nothing but a little acrid and familiar taste, ant-like and quite negligible. My hands—the inappreciable distance which reveals these things to me and for ever separates them from myself. I am nothing, I have nothing. I am as inseparable from the world as light, and I am as exiled as light, gliding over the surface of the stones or of the water, never gripped nor held. Outside, outside the world; outside the world, outside the past, outside myself: freedom is exile and I am condemned to freedom.

These words "I am condemned to freedom" should be underlined. What would they have sounded like, say, to a Descartes or to a Biran or to any other genuine philosopher of the past? Surely as a most regrettable *flatus voci*. To what indeed can I be condemned? Surely it must be to a loss, to a deprivation—whether of life, of wealth, of honour or of freedom. I cannot be "condemned" to freedom unless freedom is a deprivation, a loss. And indeed, for Sartre freedom is, like consciousness, a deprivation, a defect; it is only by a kind of paralogism that he later represents this defect as the positive condition of the emergence of a world and thus bestows upon it a creative value. . . .

Freedom coincides at its roots with the non-being which is at the heart of man. For a human being, to *be* is to choose himself; nothing comes to him either from without or from within himself that he can receive or accept. [Note this sentence, which is so heavy with meaning and with consequences.] He is wholly and helplessly at the mercy of the unendurable necessity to make himself be, even in the smallest details of his existence. Thus freedom is not a being, it is the being of man, that is to say his non-being. If we begin by conceiving of man as a fulness it becomes absurd to look in him for psychic moments or regions of freedom; we might as well look for an empty space in a vessel which we have filled to the brim. Man cannot be at times free and at other times a slave: either he is always and entirely free or he is not free at all.

This passage from *L'Etre et le Néant* [*Being and Nothingness*] seems to me one of the most significant and explicit in all Sartre's work. I do not believe that in the whole history of human thought, grace, even in its most secularized forms, has ever been denied with such audacity or such impudence. . . .

For Sartre, to receive is incompatible with being free; indeed, a being who is free is bound to deny to himself that he has received anything. But I wonder if here the author of *La Nausée* does not fall into one of the worst errors which can be attributed to Idealism. Granted the many qualifications to which any statement on the history of philosophy must be subject, it is true to say that because Kant and some of his followers conceived the spirit in terms of constructive activity, they tended to make a confusion between receiving and suffering and to ascribe receptivity exclusively to matter. This is another illustration of the misleading role played by material images. As soon as the one who receives is conceived as a "recipient," the true character of receptivity is ignored. As soon as receptivity in a spiritual, or even in a living, being is confused with suffering in a material sense (in the sense in which wax suffers the imprint of a seal) it becomes impossible to conceive the concrete and organic relationship between the individual and the world. There remain only two terms of reference: an actuality which is, so to speak, inert, and a freedom which denies it only to assume it in an incomprehensible way at a later stage.

What is, at any rate, certain is that, in such a philosophy, the notion of freedom, be it even as non-being, or to use a concrete image, as an air-pocket in the midst of being-in-itself, is just as inexplicable and much more deeply unintelligible than the notion of creation which Sartre rejects and for which he has nothing but contempt. The truth is that Sartre unites the idealism of which I have spoken with a materialism which derives from the eighteenth-century tradition of French thought. . . .

But perhaps we should recall at this point the assertion made by Sartre himself of the existence in each of us of an initial pattern which existential psychoanalysis should be able to reveal. Should we not ask what is the pattern at the origin of Sartre's atheism? The answer can be only one of two things. Either he must admit that his atheism derives from an attitude of the will or from an initial resentment (as would be the case of a man who, from the very depth of his being, willed that God should not exist); such an answer would be in keeping with his doctrine, but it would destroy much of its metaphysical bearing. Or else he must take up his stand on the traditional ground of objective thought and declare that *there is no God*, as one might say that there are no people on Mars; but in that case he must give up the plane of existentialism and fall back on the most obsolete positions of traditional rationalism.

This metaphysical aspect of the problem raised by Sartre's philosophy is not, however, the one with which this paper is intended to deal. The essential question is, to my mind, whether this philosophy is not heading for the abyss into which the forces of self-destruction threaten to drive our unfortunate race. For my part, I am convinced of it and this is the crucial point on which I must insist in conclusion.

I have recently surprised and even scandalized some of Sartre's followers by classifying his philosophy among the "techniques of vilification," by which I mean techniques which result, whether deliberately or not, in the systematic vilification of man. I admit that, superficially, this would seem to be a paradox, for does not Sartre ceaselessly exalt man and his freedom in the face of the radical absurdity of the universe? But it must not be forgotten that the Fascist dictatorships, whether in Germany, Italy or elsewhere, similarly exalted "the people" and offered it a ceaseless and cheap adulation; yet what contempt did not this adulation conceal, and to what abject depth did they not reduce their citizens. I greatly fear that the relationship between Sartre and his disciples on the one hand and between them and the humanity they claim to exalt on the other may follow an analogous pattern. Etymologically, to vilify a thing is to take away its value, its price. This can be done in the case of merchandise by flooding the market, and this is just what Sartre does to freedom: he debases it by putting it on every stall. "If freedom were easy, everything would fall to pieces at once," says Pierre Bost in his remarkable recent short story, *Monsieur l'Amiral va bientôt mourir*. No doubt, Sartre would indignantly protest against the suggestion that, in his philosophy, freedom is easy. But in that case he can surely not maintain the statement which he makes in *L'Etre et le Néant* and again in *Les Chemins de la Liberté*, that "we are condemned to be free." If we are condemned to be free, then freedom must be easy. It is true that a distinction can be made between freedom and the use of freedom, but this is out of keeping with the doctrine; for we must not forget that Sartre does not regard it as an instrument which is at the disposal of man and of which he can consequently make a good or a bad use; he regards it as man's very being—or his lack of being.

So that it is only by a kind of slieght of hand that this freedom which man is and which he cannot help being, can be later converted into a freedom which he owns and of which he can make a wrong use.

This raises the whole question of values as they are conceived by Sartre. From his standpoint, values cannot be anything but the result of the initial choice made by each human being; in other words, they can never be "recognized" or "discovered." "My freedom," he states expressly, "is the unique foundation of values. And since I am the being by virtue of whom values exist, nothing—absolutely nothing—can justify me in adopting this or that value or scale of values. As the unique basis of the existence of values, I am totally unjustifiable. And my freedom is in anguish at finding that it is the baseless basis of values." Nothing could be more explicit; but the question is whether Sartre does not here go counter to the exigencies of that human reality which he claims, after all, not to invent but to reveal.

Not to deal exclusively in abstractions, let us take a concrete case. Sartre has announced that the third volume of his *Les Chemins de la Liberté* is to be devoted to the praise of the heroes of Resistance. Now I ask you in the name of what principle, having first denied the existence of values or at least of their objective basis, can he establish any appreciable difference between those utterly misguided but undoubtedly courageous men who joined voluntarily the Anti-Bolshevik Legion, on the one hand, and the heroes of the Resistance movement, on the other? I can see no way of establishing this difference without admitting that causes have their intrinsic value and, consequently, that values are real. I have no doubt that Sartre's ingenuity will find a way out of this dilemma; in fact, he quite often uses the words "good" and "bad," but what can these words possibly mean in the context of his philosophy? . . .

I would suggest in conclusion that existentialism stands to-day at a parting of the ways: it is, in the last analysis, obliged either to deny or to transcend itself. It denies itself quite simply when it falls to the level of infra-dialectical materialism. It transcends itself, or it tends to transcend itself, when it opens itself out to the experience of the suprahuman, an experience which can hardly be ours in a genuine and lasting way this side of death, but of which the reality is attested by mystics, and of which the possibility is warranted by any philosophy which refuses to be immured in the postulate of absolute immanence or to subscribe in advance to the denial of the beyond and of the unique and veritable transcendence. Not that there is anything in this which, in our itinerant condition, we can invest like a capital; this absolute life can be apprehended by us only in flashes and by virtue of a hidden initiative which can be nothing other than grace. I am, of course, thinking of the extravagantly dogmatic negativism which is common to Sartre, to Heidegger and even to Jaspers. It is true that Sartre has criticized with some force the notion of being-for-death which dominates the thought of Heidegger; but it is all too clear that there is little to choose between that view and his own, which is equally opaque. I cannot help stating once more in this connection the dilemma to which I referred earlier on: either this assertion of man's total mortality is the expression of an existential wish—and in that case it cannot be other than contingent—or else it presupposes an objective, pseudo-scientific realism in regard to death, and implies a crass materialism which belongs to the infra-existential levels of philosophy.

Sartre verbally admits this materialism: "What will you," he says, "matter is the only reality I am able to grasp." Yet I am persuaded that this negative realism, this way of cramping the spirit to the experience of the senses, while relating this experience whenever possible to behaviourist illustrations, cannot go without a corresponding devaluation of the truly human modes of existence. . . .

CLAUDE LÉVI-STRAUSS AND THE CHANGING TEMPER OF THE 1960's

H. Stuart Hughes

Whatever date one selects—the mid-1950's and the beginnings of prosperity, 1958 and the advent of De Gaulle, or 1962 and the end of the Algerian War— it is apparent that sometime around 1960 French society underwent a profound change. In his last published work [Maurice] Merleau-Ponty, with his customary sensitivity for psychological nuances, began to ruminate on the altered ideological climate he found about him. It was an emotional atmosphere, he surmised, in which the old appeals to "history" had lost their force —in which conservatives could concede the innocence of Captain Dreyfus as a "commonplace" and remain conservatives just the same. The verities of the postwar Left, the passionate belief in "revolutionary heroism and humanism," had "fallen into ruin." Merleau-Ponty's own generation was filled with remorse for speaking about such matters "too dispassionately." . . .

Once again, then—and at least as acutely as at any previous point in the century—a conflict of generations separated those who thought of themselves as the young from those who in fact were not so many years their seniors. Just as the men coming to maturity in the 1930's had been impatient with the refinements of the "last generation of French classicism," so those who grew up in the 1950's failed to understand their elders' absorption with ideology and revolutionary rhetoric. In this situation of mutual incomprehension, a mediator was required; and it was fortunate that the man who emerged as Sartre's rival and successor as France's intellectual laureate was ideally equipped to perform the role.

Claude Lévi-Strauss was only three years younger than Sartre; but his fame had come more than a decade later than that of the author of *Being and Nothingness* and in an atmosphere in which the attractions of both existentialism and Marxism were already on the wane. In his personal style, Lévi-Strauss combined the rationality and humanism of a philosophe in the great tradition with a thorough grasp of the latest techniques in social science. He was close enough to the familiar pattern of French thought to be able to lead along with him the more adventurous of those who still dwelt in that intellectual universe. Yet in recasting the pattern of thought in a new terminology, he in effect exploded it. And in so doing he accomplished the feat of reuniting his countrymen with the world of social speculation beyond France's borders and of epitomizing in his own person the fact that France had finally produced a social theorist who was universally acknowledged as a master. . . .

With the publication of his *Structural Anthropology* in 1958, the theoretical outlines of Lévi-Strauss' position had been established; the following year he received a newly-created chair at the Collège de France. It now remained for him to make fully explicit what he had earlier sketched out and to reply to the impatient critics who stood ready to trip him up. This process he began with a small book entitled *Totemism*, the prologue to the most important of his theoretical writings, *The Savage Mind*, published in 1962.

If *Tristes tropiques* [1955] had made Lévi-Strauss famous, *The Savage Mind* made him controversial. As the sharpest expression of his views he had yet set forth, it aroused passionate discussion among social scientists, philosophers, and men of letters. For its combination of ultra-relativism and the new dogmatism of the structural method had something in it to upset or displease almost every French school of social speculation.

The mind of the savage, Lévi-Strauss argued, was neither so simple nor so wayward as it was ordinarily supposed to be. In point of fact primitive man thought in an exceedingly complicated fashion; his logic was merely of a different order from the logic of abstract science to which Western man had become accustomed. Still more, the savage thirsted for objective knowledge and was adept at observing the concrete; the systems by which he classified plants, animals, and natural phenomena were detailed and sometimes even intellectually elegant. The results of his speculations were preserved in a "science of the concrete"—the "memory bank" of techniques in agriculture, pottery, and the domestication of animals which had made possible the beginnings of settled habitation in neolithic times. After that enormous cultural revolution, mankind had stopped in its tracks—and most cultures had remained there. Even in the West, thousands of years had gone by before the advent of modern science: the scientific speculation of classical antiquity and the Middle Ages was still neolithic in temper. The only way to explain this "level plain" of "stagnation" was to postulate "two distinct modes of scientific thought"—"one roughly adapted to that of perception and the imagination: the other at a remove from it." The former—the "primitive" science of the concrete—had to its credit the achievements secured ten thousand years ago which still remained "at the basis of our own civilization."

Having thus established the credentials of the savage way of thought, Lévi-Strauss went on to point out the vestiges of such thinking in contemporary Europe and America. These vestiges were of the sort that the Freudian school of therapy condemned as magical—that is, the conviction of hidden affinities and sympathies between human actions and the world of nature. But the word "magic"—like everything else in the mental universe of primitive man—held no terrors for Lévi-Strauss. Magic too had its logic: it would be better, he maintained, "instead of contrasting magic and science, to compare them as two parallel modes of acquiring knowledge"; the former, unlike abstract scientific thought, postulated a "complete and all-embracing determinism." And once the principles of such determinism had been fully understood, they were found to work rather like a kaleidoscope: they re-shuffled bits and pieces of traditional lore into endless variations of basically similar structural patterns; they displayed both "internal coherence" and a "practically unlimited capacity for extension."

The magical—or totemic—way of thinking was by its nature anti-historical. But it did not deny the category of time: the savage mind simply could not bring itself to believe that anything really changed. Nor did the lack of a sense for history denote some ineradicable inferiority of feeling: an "obstinate fidelity to a past conceived as a timeless model," Lévi-Strauss argued, "betrayed no moral or intellectual deficiency whatsoever." As opposed to the usual "clumsy distinction" between "peoples without history" and those who thought of themselves in historical terms, he pre-ferred to speak of "cold" societies that tried to stay in equilibrium and "hot" ones that were forever on the move. Thus a thorough-going ethical relativism lay at the end of Lévi-Strauss' search for the principles of primitive thought: in their acute understanding of the plant and animal world, in their sense of an overarching cosmic harmony, those who dwelt in the "cold" cultures displayed a nobility of temper that the super-heated West had long ago forgotten.

Finally, the structures the mind of primitive man revealed could be presumed to be universal. Under the lofty scaffolding of modern science, the mental patterns of the contemporary city dweller in the West were much like those of his neolithic ancestor. The task of the anthropologist was to find those patterns—proceeding on the principle that "either everything, or nothing, makes sense." And when they had been sufficiently understood, Lévi-Strauss concluded, "the entire process of human knowledge" would assume "the character of a closed system."

The completion of *The Savage Mind*, by Lévi-Strauss' own account, marked a pause in his thought. But the task he had set himself was far from accomplished. He had affirmed the existence of basic mental structures: now he had to prove it. He had declared that myths were capable of structural analysis: to date he had given only a few scattered examples. The purpose of the four-volume series entitled *Mythologiques* which he launched in 1964 was to show the structural method in action—to derive from an exhaustive "coding" of mythic material a "picture of the world already inscribed in the architecture" of the human mind.

Drawing his data from the Indians of South America whom he knew at first hand, Lévi-Strauss focused his attention on myths dealing with food, tobacco, and the transformations raw meat and plants underwent in being prepared for human use. The first volume analyzed how the practice of cooking had altered man's relations with nature; the second traced the more complex symbolic significance of smoking and eating honey. In the remote past, the mythic material suggested, men had simply laid out their food on stones to be warmed by the heat of the sun: the sun's rays had united heaven and earth in a harmony in which mankind felt itself to be in no way separate from the world of nature. With the change to cooked food, these relations were profoundly altered: the introduction of cooking was the decisive step in the passage from nature to culture; man was cut off both from the gods and from the animals who ate their food raw. In consequence his world became problematic and threatening. Only through the mediation of friendly and helpful animals—the tapirs or jaguars or opossums who were the protagonists of the major myths—could a precarious cosmic order be restored. . . .

[Lévi-Strauss] who ostensibly made no claim to being a literary figure in fact very consciously contrived his work for its effect as literature. And the stance he adopted toward his subject matter was equally ambivalent— stoicism and disengagement alternating with warm human sympathy. If on the one hand he ruthlessly saw through all meanings and directed his attention alone, he was not ashamed to give voice to his own values when his emotions were stirred: he could write with transparent anger of the ravages of a Western technology that converted South Sea islands into "stationary aircraft-carriers" and threw its "filth . . . in the face of humanity"; he could bemoan the irony of his profession that condemned him to hasten "in search of a vanished reality." He loved his métier; yet it brought him to near-despair as he watched how contact with "advanced" societies dissolved his subject matter before his very eyes. To the young French of the 1960's such reflections carried the ring of truth: in France too the achievement of technical modernity was being purchased at a painful psychic cost. In sum, the secret of Lévi-Strauss' immense influence lay in his talent for "carrying out a rigorous and strictly scientific work, while at the same time reflecting on this work, examining its method, extracting the philosophic elements from it, and remaining through it all a kind of Rousseau, both misanthropic and a friend of mankind, who sometimes dreams of reconciling East and West by completing the economic liberation inherent in Marxism with a spiritual liberation of Buddhist origin."[1] . . .

Lévi-Strauss . . . believed that content in itself had no meaning; it was only the way in which the different elements of the content were combined that gave a meaning. But once meaning had been drained of content, what was left? This was the ultimate question historians and philosophers and social scientists proposed: was there in fact any meaning to Lévi-Strauss' infinitely ingenious constructions?

The basic trouble with his method—quite aside from the closed conceptual universe it presupposed—was that it made no value distinctions

---

[1] Jean Lacroix, *Panorama de la philosophie française contemporaine* (Paris, 1966), p. 222.

among the coded relationships it established. Nor could it even lay claim to an exhaustive process of coding: the elements that went into it, as in the performance of a computer, were limited to the small number that were capable of unambiguous manipulation. The result was perhaps no more than a glorious cerebral game. Or, in terms of formal philosophy, it amounted to a "discourse" at once "fascinating" and "disquieting"—an "admirable syntactical arrangement" that said nothing.[2]

Thus in one guise Lévi-Strauss could be considered the most extreme and consistent of the students of society who in the 1940's and 1950's— throughout the Western world—were inaugurating a new and more sophisticated positivist method. He was convinced that he had fulfilled—or was about to fulfill—the social scientist's eternal dream of integrating method and reality. He had re-established the structure of the mind as basically rational; he accepted the word "determinism"; he was unafraid of materialist explanations. In so doing, Lévi-Strauss accomplished the extraordinary feat of carrying out a universally-applicable and intellectualist program in the dominant French tradition while at the same time linking up with the work of other neo-positivists outside France who were attracted by the rigor and elegance of his method: he broke out of his countrymen's cultural confinement while remaining authentically and recognizably French.

But there was also Lévi-Strauss' second guise as moraliste and philosophe, the heir of Montaigne, Montesquieu, and Rousseau. If his first incarnation was of greater interest to the world of science, the second was the source of his prestige among the general public. For it was here that in true eighteenth-century manner he held up the cultural universe of the "primitives" among whom he had dwelt as a mirror in which the French (and Westerners as a whole) could find a critique of their own society. He grieved over the defenseless savages whose way of life stood condemned by material "progress." . . .

We who dwell in "hot" societies, he constantly implied, could well take lessons from those who have no truck with change. And in an interview he gave after the publication of the second volume of his *Mythologiques*, he made this injunction, and with it his own attitude, explicit at last:

I have little taste for the century in which we live. What seems to me the present tendency is on the one hand man's total mastery over nature and on the other hand the mastery of certain forms of humanity over others. My temperament and my tastes lead me far more toward periods which were less ambitious and perhaps more timid but in which a certain balance could be maintained between man and nature, among the various and multiple forms of life, whether animal or vegetable, and among the different types of culture, of belief, of customs, or of institutions. I do not strive to perpetuate this diversity but rather to preserve its memory.

---

[2] Paul Ricoeur in "Réponses à quelques questions," *Esprit*, XXXI (November, 1963), p. 653.

Thus—despite the contradictions he recognized in such an attitude—Lévi-Strauss found that an anthropologist like himself almost inevitably became a "critic at home" and a "conformist elsewhere." Abroad he resented the inroads of "civilization" on his "primitives." In his own country he saw more starkly than his fellow-citizens what was out of the human scale in modern industrial society. The same range of sympathy came into play in both cases. In this perspective it was perfectly consistent for Lévi-Strauss to preserve an attachment to the ideological Left; it was thoroughly understandable that he should have joined Sartre and the other members of the celebrated "121" in their opposition to the Algerian War.

Yet with Lévi-Strauss—whether in his mood of conservation or with his voice of protest—there was a difference of "register," as he would put it, from other intellectuals of his generation. There was a tone of acceptance, of cosmic resignation in the face of nature reminiscent of Buddhism. "The world began without the human race," he declared in one of his most quoted utterances, "and it will end without it." Lévi-Strauss was anything but a doctrinaire opponent of progress; his outlook necessarily made him favor the kind of change that would reduce human want and suffering. But he was far more aware than the run of his contemporaries of the enormous price in ugliness and cultural dislocation which progress entailed. His conception of freedom, alternately elegiac and utopian, was authentically of the late twentieth century in that it looked beyond the liberal or radical or Marxist ideology to a time which Saint-Simon had glimpsed in his prediction that humanity would finally pass "from the government of men to the administration of things." Lévi-Strauss yearned for that distant era when the imperative of progress would have ceased to operate—or better, when machines would have taken over the task of social improvement—and when the characteristics of the hot and the cold cultures would be gradually fused, until humanity was liberated at last from the "age-old curse which forced it to enslave men in order to make progress possible." . . .

In French intellectual life of the 1960's Lévi-Strauss found no lack of counterparts or imitators. By the middle of the decade "structuralism" had become the mode—the word was discussed everywhere, whether or not those who spoke of it had any precise idea of its meaning. Most of them probably did not: the writings of the leading "structuralists" were austere, hermetic, and difficult to follow. Such was notably true of the work of Louis Althusser on Marxism and of Jacques Lacan on psychoanalysis. Both of these emptied the original teaching of its humanist content and recast it in the form of a rigorous logic; in both cases the structural interpretation relentlessly emphasized a single aspect of the theory in question. In an ironic sense, psychoanalysis might finally be said to have become acclimatized in France since it had produced in Lacan its own indigenous heretic.

Most broadly, the philosophical turning-point of the 1960's could be defined as a concerted attempt at the liquidation of traditional humanism. Lévi-Strauss' successors let drop the moraliste content in his work and devoted their exclusive attention to his structural method. In this new perspective, the three decades 1930–1960 began to look like a transition era in which a succession of thinkers—often against their announced intention—had tried to salvage whatever items in the classical humanist baggage could still serve the needs of heroism or despair. The structuralists of the 1960's banned both humanism and the starker attitudes that had issued from it: all smacked of a subjectivity that was no longer tolerable. Whether Catholic or Marxist, existential or Weberian, the thought of the previous generation stood condemned as irremediably subjectivist and amateurish. The new stress was on the formal aspects of syntax and of thinking itself. It was symptomatic that the most influential of the younger structuralists, Michel Foucault, composed an "archaeology of the human sciences" delineating the successive abstract categories in which man's reflection on his own works had expressed itself since the sixteenth century.

Language, logic, and coding having become ends in themselves, French thought was undergoing, "with thirty years delay, its crisis of logical positivism."[3] It was experiencing the sort of change that had occurred in Anglo-American philosophy a generation earlier. From this standpoint, structuralism might have been expected to provide a bridge to the world of speculation abroad. But it came too late to perform such a role: by the time the structuralist onslaught hit France, the British and Americans were having second thoughts about logical positivism and linguistic analysis and were becoming more tolerant of other types of philosophical discourse. Furthermore, it came encumbered with characteristically French accretions that made it difficult to export. The writing of the structuralists lacked the literary leanness and colloquial manner of the best English work in analytic philosophy. It was over-argued and over-sophisticated, affected, pretentious, and given to esoteric word-games—"mandarin" in the most unfavorable meaning of the term. In respect to the rhetoric of social thought, the structuralist revolution had had the melancholy effect of reintroducing, under the guise of philosophical rigor, the age-old vices of the Gallic mind. And these weaknesses obscured the richness and originality of what someone like Foucault had to offer.

As the century reached the two-thirds mark, the self-confidence of the French, whether in international affairs or in the realm of the intellect, had quite apparently been regained. But it had been restored at a heavy cost. Although the elections of 1967 seemed to announce the twilight of De

---

[3] Lecture by Mikel Dufrenne at the annual congress of the review *Esprit* at Melun, December 4, 1966. For a fuller statement see his "La philosophie du neo-positivisme," *Esprit*, XXXV (May, 1967), 784.

Gaulle's regime, the experience of Gaullist rule was likely to leave its mark for a long time to come. In the intellectual sphere the counterpart to the pride —the orgueil—that the General-President had taught his countrymen was the resurgence of a cultural nationalism against which writers as diverse as Camus and Teilhard and Lévi-Strauss had warned in vain.

With the twentieth century two-thirds past, of fourteen leading thinkers of the contemporary era eight were dead. Three more—Marcel, Malraux, and De Gaulle—for a number of years had published little major writing. Of the three remaining, Lévi-Strauss alone—with half his *Mythologiques* still to go—seemed to be in full course. . . .

SUGGESTIONS FOR FURTHER READING

Literature: GERMAINE BRÉE, *The French Novel from Gide to Camus* (New York, 1962), and GERMAINE BRÉE (ed.), *Camus; A Collection of Critical Essays* (Englewood Cliffs, N.J., 1962); VICTOR H. BROMBERT, *The Intellectual Hero; Studies in the French Novel, 1880–1955* (Philadelphia, 1961); PIERRE-GEORGES CASTEX, *Albert Camus et l'Etranger* (Paris, 1965); KENNETH CORNELL, *The Post-Symbolist Period; French Poetic Currents, 1900–1920* (New Haven, 1958); HENRI PEYRE, *French Novelists of Today* (New York, 1967); EDITH G. KERN, *Sartre; a collection of Critical Essays* (Englewood Cliffs, N.J., 1962); Art: GEORGES HUGNET, *L'Aventure Dada, 1916–1922* (Paris, 1957); ROGERT SHATTUCK, *The Banquet Years, The Origins of the Avant-Garde in France, 1885 to World War I* (New York, 1959); EDITH WEBER (ed.), *Débussy et l'évolution de la musique au XXᵉ siècle* (Paris, 1965); Philosophy: GEORGE BOAS, "Bergson (1859–1941) and his Predecessors," *Journal of the History of Ideas*, XX (1959), 503–514; HENRI BOUILLARD, "The Thought of Maurice Blondel: A Synoptic Vision," *International Philosophical Quarterly*, III, no. 3 (Sept., 1963), 392–402; EDOUARD KUNNEN, "Bergson et nous," *Revue internationale de la philosophie*, XVII (1963), 68–91; *Le Centenaire de Maurice Blondel, 1861–1961, en sa Faculté des lettres d'Aix-Marseille* (Gap, 1963); JEAN LACROIX, *The Meaning of Contemporary Atheism* (New York, 1965), *Marxisme, existentialisme, personalisme. . .* (Paris, 1949), and *Panorama de la philosophie française contemporaine* (Paris, 1966); JACQUES MARITAIN, *Bergsonian Philosophy and Thomism* (New York, 1955), and *The Degrees of Knowledge* (2nd ed., New York, 1959); MADELEINE MADAULE-BARTHÉLEMY, *Bergson et Teilhard de Chardin* (Paris, 1963); Catholicism: ADRIEN DANSETTE, *Destin du catholicisme français, 1926–1956* (Paris, 1957), and *Religious History of Modern France*, 2 vol. (Freibourg, 1961); JEAN-PAUL GÉLIMAS, *La Restauration du thomisme sous Léon XIII et les philosophies nouvelles. Etude de la pensée de Maurice Blondel* (Washington, D.C., 1959); JACQUES MARTEAUX, *L'Eglise de France devant la Révolution marxiste* (Paris, 1958); RENÉ RÉMOND (ed.), *Forces religieuses et attitudes politiques dans la France contemporaine* (Paris, 1965); Structuralism: LOUIS ALTHUSSER, *Pour Marx* (2nd ed.; Paris, 1966), and *Lire le Capital*, 2 vol. (Paris, 1966); GEORGES CHARBONNIER, *Entretiens avec Claude Lévi-Strauss* (Paris, 1961); MICHEL FOUCAULT, *Les Mots et les choses; une archéologie des sciences humaines* (Paris, 1966), and *Madness and Civilization, a History of Insanity in the Age of Reason* (New York, 1965).

Index

Africa: French colonization in, 404, 416, 420–421, 425, 444
  invasion of, 495–496, 586
  decolonization, 500, 519, 541, 567–574, 581
Algeria: under France in Fourth Republic, 519, 529, 537–543
  rebellion of, 543–554, 616, 621
  independence of, 560, 567, 570–574
Alsace-Lorraine: recovery of, 417–418, 434–443, 448, 584
American Civil War: effect on France, 273, 301, 311, 313, 347, 562
American Revolution: French
  financing of, 15, 70, 78–82, 93, 94, 104, 106
  influence on France, 38, 41, 63, 65–67, 105–107
Ancien Régime, 13, social classes under, 6–33, decline of, 70–97, 100–101
  see also Old Regime
Anti-Semitism, 383, 405
Antraigues, Comte d', 135, 153–156, 162
Armistice (World War I), 473, 474
Artois, Count of, 134, 137–141, 156
  see also Charles X
Assembly of Notables, 15, 20, 30, 94, 312
Assignats, 122–124
Atlantic Charter, 503
Austrian Succession, War of the, 75, 84

Babeuf, Gracchus, 335, 336, 338

Balzac, Honoré de, 210, 211, 246, 247, 259, 363, 377, 602
Bank of France, 266, 269, 402, 522
Barrès, Maurice, 59, 373, 377, 390, 393, 408–411, 435, 438, 439, 580
Bismarck, Otto von, 300, 301, 318, 322, 324–330, 416, 418, 419, 583–586, 588
Blanc, Louis, 251, 334, 337–340
Blanqui, Louis Auguste, 334, 342, 349, 350, 358
Blum, Léon, 449, 463, 465–471, 474
Bonald, Louis, Vicomte de, 59, 141, 161, 162, 163, 410, 512
Bonaparte: see under Napoleon
Bonapartists, 197, 215, 282, 291, 293, 307, 350, 382, 386, 388, 391, 394
Boulanger, General Georges, 382, 383, 390–393, 404, 407
Boulangism, 382–384, 389–394, 407–408, 412, 507
Bourbons, 6, 100, 154, 196–198, 226, 229, 231–232, 239, 243, 244, 282, 302, 306, 312
Briand, Aristide, 437, 439, 440, 442
Brienne, Loménie de, 86, 102, 107, 108, 142, 172, 173
Broglie, Albert, Duc de, 236, 384, 387–389
Brumaire, coup d'état of, 120, 121, 129, 130, 171

Calonne, Abbé de, 14, 15, 86, 90, 102, 106, 107, 138–139, 161–162, 164

Camus, Albert, 592, 593, 599, 600, 603, 623

Catholicism, 2, 30–33, 36, 43, 47–52, 72, 105, 141–146, 179, 258, 290, 291, 300, 302–309, 311, 313, 324, 383, 393, 394–399, 404–406, 409, 410, 412, 494, 515, 532–534, 566, 593, 622

Chamber of Deputies, 196, 232, 235, 236, 285, 327, 330, 337, 342, 382, 384–386, 389, 399, 419–422, 424, 436, 440, 441, 461, 465–468, 476, 484–485, 528, 559, 564

Chamber of Peers, 196, 208, 229, 230
see also under Senate

Chambord, Comte de, 282, 385, 386, 388

Charles X, 202, 204, 205, 212–217, 219, 226, 228–230, 259, 289, 302, 336
see also under Artois, Comte de,

Charter: of 1814, 196, 197, 201, 202, 208, 210, 213, 215–217, 336
of 1830, 232, 239, 240

Christianity, 36, 37, 40, 43, 44, 46, 240, 338, 394, 410, 494, 532, 592, 593, 599, 604

Christian Democrats, 395, 396, 509, 512, 532

Civil Constitution of the Clergy, 134, 136, 141–143, 144

Clemenceau, Georges, 383, 397, 399, 417, 421–423, 442, 453, 456

Combes, Emile, 431–432

Committee of Public Safety, 101, 121, 156, 546, 548

Common Market, 519, 578–579, 586, 588

Commune of 1871, 334–335, 338, 341–346, 350–360, 382, 384, 407

Communism, 345, 449, 450, 466, 468, 478, 501, 504, 505, 511, 514, 518, 519, 531–537, 541, 542, 548, 552, 560, 561, 562

Concordat of 1801–1802, 2, 168, 179, 383

Congress of Vienna, 196–200, 282

Constituent Assembly: of 1789–1791, 124, 134, 142, 143, 145, 153, 244
of 1848, 227, 251, 256, 339
of 1945, 577, 582

Constitution: of year III, 170
of years VIII, X, XII, 283
of 1852, 283

Constitutional Laws: of 1875, 382
of 1940, 484–485

Consulate, 19, 124, 129, 168, 171, 180, 283, 287

Continental Blockade, 179–182, 186, 187, 243

Coty, René, 529, 545, 546, 548, 550, 553, 554

Council of State, 177, 185, 237, 267, 279, 283–285, 525

Dadaism, 592–598

Daladier, Edouard, 461–466, 472, 474, 475, 477, 513

Darlan, Admiral Jean François, 496

Declaration of the Rights of Man, 100, 118, 135, 143, 338, 485

Delacroix, Eugène, 127, 367–369

Delbecque, L., 545–550

Delcassé, Théophile, 416, 426–430, 431–432, 435–436

Diderot, Denis, 37, 39, 42–44, 52, 62, 605

Dien Bien Phu, 518, 546

Directory, 19, 101, 120–122, 125–130, 135, 168, 171, 304

Dreyfus Affair, 383, 384, 393, 398, 399–406, 408, 410, 411, 428, 459, 507, 616

Dutourd, Jean, 475–476

Egypt: campaign of Napoleon I in, 101, 128

Elysée, the, 282, 439, 456, 463, 554, 578

Empire: First, 168–193, 208, 209, 226, 237, 243, 257, 264, 340, 405

Second, 264–331, 382, 388, 390, 397, 404

Enlightenment, 1, 36–67, 104, 193, 335

Entente Cordiale, 416, 426–433
Triple Entente, 434, 440, 441

Estates General, 15, 30, 40, 55, 71, 93, 100, 107–110, 163, 208

Existentialism, 592, 604–615

Fascism, 491, 509, 511, 512, 534, 606

Fashoda crisis, 416, 426, 428

Ferry, Jules, 382–383, 389, 394, 407, 408, 416, 418–422, 424, 425

First Estate, 6, 8, 11, 30–33, 109

First World War, 125, 309, 434–445, 455, 459, 474, 507, 514, 524, 583–585, 589, 592, 594, 597, 602

Flaubert, Gustave, 251, 362–365, 592, 602

Fouché, Joseph, Duc d'Otrante, 121, 177, 178, 184

Fourier, Charles, 334, 338, 339

Franco-Prussian War, 340, 348, 351, 416, 418, 583

Franklin, Benjamin, 78, 79, 81

Free France, 482–483, 498–505

Freycinet government, 398, 439

Fructidor, *coup d'état* of, 126–129, 170, 171

Gallicanism, 9, 10, 13, 93, 105, 141, 142, 145

Gambetta, Léon, 291, 329, 382, 384, 389, 394, 407, 421, 422

Garnier-Pagès, Etienne-Joseph, 257, 259, 329, 337

de Gaulle, General Charles, 3, 310, 482, 483, 486, 498–505, 514, 518–524, 536, 538, 541–589, 616, 623

Gaullism, 543–546, 566, 580, 593, 623

Germanophobia, 399–412, 499, 502

Germany: war with in 1870–71, 323–330, 455 (*see also* Franco-Prussian War)

Entente against, 416–417, 426–433
war with in 1914–1918, 434–445, 450
security from after 1919, 448–455, 459, 465, 469
collaboration with in World War II, 491–498
liberation from occupation of, 498,

Giraud, General, 483, 494, 498, 501, 563

Girondins, 100, 134, 136, 157, 207, 282

Gramont, Antoine, Duc de, 325–330

Grévy, Jules, 382, 385, 389

Guesde, Jules, 338, 393

Guizot, François, 216, 226, 227, 232, 235–242, 337, 561

Helvétius, Claude Adrien, 39, 53–58

Henry, Commandant, 398, 400, 402

Hitler, Adolf, 448–450, 459, 476, 496, 534

Hohenzollern Candidature, 323–330

Holbach, Baron d', 39, 53–57, 62

Holy Alliance, 162, 352

Hôtel de Ville, 228, 341, 342, 504

Hugo, Victor, 226, 245, 246, 258, 259, 264, 341, 367

Hundred Days of 1815, 196, 237, 292

Idealism, 372–379, 613

Imperialism, 418–426
(*see also under specific countries*)

Impressionism, 362, 366–372

Indo China: French imperialism in, 300, 404, 416, 422–425, 518, 536, 544, 553

Industrial Revolution, 1, 227, 243, 244, 246, 247, 273

Ingres, Jean Auguste Dominique, 362, 366

International, First Workers', 281, 335, 340, 344, 346–353, 354

Italy:
Napoleonic imperialism in, 128, 180, 184, 185, 187–189, 192

Italy (*cont.*)
  campaign of Napoleon III in, 300–
    309, 311, 315, 316, 320

Jacobins, 43, 122, 130, 139, 145, 160,
    168, 170, 171, 197, 338, 339, 344,
    357, 391, 393, 407, 566, 580
Jansenism, 72, 83, 84, 105
Jaurès, Jean, 93, 111, 397
Jena, battle of, 200, 329
Jesuits, 9, 37, 47–52, 83, 84, 91, 105, 178,
    196, 219, 220, 404
Jews, 268, 399–406, 409, 486, 494
Joan of Arc, 255, 458, 560, 563, 584
Journal de Trévoux, 47–52
July Monarchy, 183, 226–261, 267, 270,
    405
July Ordinances, 230, 232

Kant, Immanuel, 373, 378, 605, 608, 613
Keynes, John Maynard, 444

Lacoste, Robert, 540, 544–548, 550
Lafayette, Marquis de, 41, 66, 78, 107,
    109, 207
Laffitte, Jacques, 204, 216, 228, 231
Lamartine, Alphonse de, 245–247, 339,
    377
Lamennais, Félicité de, 247, 337
Laval, Pierre, 482, 484, 485, 493, 496,
    505, 511
Lavigerie, Cardinal, 383, 394–395, 398
Law of Separation of Church and State,
    383
League of Nations, 448, 453, 458–460,
    472, 503, 524
Lebrun, President Albert, 461, 463
Left Wing, 101, 130, 232–234, 271, 329,
    383, 384, 386, 391, 393, 397, 407,
    449, 450, 456, 457, 462, 465, 468,
    499, 559, 566, 580, 621
Legislative Assembly of 1791–1792, 100,
    129, 146

Legislative Body under Napoleon III,
    279, 280, 283–286, 288, 289, 308,
    326
Legitimists, 229, 260, 306, 382, 388
Liberals, 197, 202–205, 310
Liberation of France (World War II),
    498, 504, 505, 510–513, 519, 520,
    523, 530, 533, 549, 565, 580, 603
Leo XIII, Pope, 383, 393, 394–398
Lévi-Strauss, Claude, 593, 616–623
Loubet, President, 426
Louis XIV, 9, 10, 47, 58, 70–72, 74, 75,
    168, 293, 560
Louis XV, 6, 9, 10, 11, 44, 65, 70–74, 76,
    83, 85, 102
Louis XVI, 12, 13, 70, 78, 80, 82, 95,
    102, 137–139, 141, 142, 164, 176,
    177, 296
Louis XVII, 154, 155, 159, 160
Louis XVIII, 156, 164, 197–202, 205,
    229, 239
Louis-Philippe, 215, 216, 226–232,
    234–236, 245, 247, 256, 258–260,
    266, 282, 288, 302
  see also Orléans, Duc d'

MacMahon, Marshal, Duc de Magenta,
    282, 341, 382, 388
Maginot Line, 448, 449, 454, 476
Maistre, Joseph, Comte de, 161–163
Malraux, André, 593, 599, 600, 603, 623
Manet, Edouard, 362, 366–371
Marcel, Gabriel, 593, 604, 623
Marshall Plan, 519, 526, 527
Marxism, 11, 12, 251, 252, 335–338,
    340, 349, 350, 352, 362, 393, 593,
    616, 619, 621, 622
Maupeou, Chancellor René Nicolas,
    12, 17, 59, 73, 85, 86, 102
Maurras, Charles, 410, 411, 438, 459,
    494, 507, 509, 512
Méline, Jules, 398, 399, 407
Mendès-France, Pierre, 518, 538
Mexican expedition of Napoleon III,

300, 309–314
Mirabeau, Comte de, 87, 109
Mollet, Guy, 518, 538, 541, 543, 550, 552, 553
Monnet, Jean, 510, 523, 524, 527, 559, 586, 588
Montagnards, 101, 170
Montesquieu, Baron de, 10, 11, 43, 44, 59, 60, 62, 65, 71, 104, 163, 620

Napoleon I, 2, 3, 85, 101, 120, 127, 128, 130, 164, 168–193, 196, 198, 200, 208, 209, 220, 226, 240, 243, 255–260, 277–278, 282, 287, 292, 293, 300, 305, 306, 366, 382, 383, 558, 560
Napoleon III, 3, 227, 261, 263–331, 341, 348, 366, 382, 558, 560, 583
Napoleonic Code, 168, 180, 184, 185, 207, 209, 303
Napoleonic Legend, 255–260, 282
National Assembly: of 1789–91, 93, 141–146; see also Constituent Assembly
  of 1849–52, 227, 282, 287
  of 1870-75, 343, 355, 385–387, 423, 455
  of 1940, 485
  of the Fourth Republic, 518, 529, 531, 537, 542, 543
  of the Fifth Republic, 577
National Defense, Government of the, 334, 342–344
National Guard, the, 145, 148, 228, 234, 251, 252, 344, 345, 346, 357
N.A.T.O., 578, 585, 587, 588
Necker, Jacques, 20, 86, 91, 96, 102, 106, 109, 164

O.A.S., 573, 574
Old Regime, 6, 27, 36–38, 70, 71, 82, 100, 101, 104, 137, 147, 168, 169, 170, 175, 189, 196, 197, 207, 208,

210, 255, 300, 306
  see also Ancien Régime
Ollivier, Emile, 285, 288, 290, 296, 323, 325, 326, 329, 301, 327, 330, 397, 404
Opportunists, 390, 391, 394
Orléans, Duc d', 9, 73, 107, 108, 228
Orléanism, 226, 267, 275, 290, 382, 385, 388, 392, 393

Parlements, 14, 15, 17, 18, 19, 30, 72, 73, 82–87, 102, 103, 105, 106, 108–110
Périer, Casimir, 216, 231, 232, 294
Pétain, Marshall Henri Philippe, 3, 472–474, 477, 482, 484, 487, 493, 498, 505, 512, 558, 560, 563, 589
Pflimlin, Pierre, 545, 547–549, 552, 553
Pius IX, Pope, 303–308
Poincaré, Raymond, 384, 411, 439, 448, 449, 451, 456–458
Polignac, Armand de, 140, 212–215, 230
Popular Front, 449, 458, 466–471, 507, 512, 513, 553
Poujadism, 511, 518, 534, 535, 543, 544
Protestantism, 36, 72, 77, 108, 235–237, 268, 310, 404
Proudhon, Pierre Joseph, 60, 261, 334–336, 339, 340, 347, 348, 349–351, 362

Quai d'Orsay, 426, 540

Radicals, 386, 388, 390–394, 397–399, 407, 420, 425, 449, 461, 466–468, 473, 513, 529, 531
Ralliement, 393, 395, 396, 398, 399, 513
Renan, Ernest, 59, 362, 372, 409
Republic: First, 110–130, 134, 171, 176, 181, 217, 220, 260
  Second: 227, 228, 248, 249, 252, 253, 255, 256, 257, 282, 288, 291, 382

Republic (*cont.*)
    Third, 40, 242, 281, 291, 301, 309,
        342, 345, 354, 382–478, 482, 483,
        485, 486, 498, 499, 501, 504, 506,
        508, 509, 512–515, 528–530, 542
    Fourth, 483, 501, 514, 518–554, 558,
        561, 563, 565, 567, 570, 575
    Fifth, 382, 519, 520, 542, 558–589
Republicans, 226, 330, 341, 350, 382,
    383, 391, 394, 396, 398, 399, 406,
    428, 459, 460, 461, 485, 486, 487,
    505, 507, 508, 510, 514
Resistance Movement, 465, 482, 483,
    497–499, 501, 503, 504, 509–515,
    520–522, 550, 592, 593, 614, 615
Restoration, 149, 159, 164, 178, 183,
    196–222, 232, 233, 237, 244, 258,
    260, 282
Reubell, Jean François, 120–122, 127–
    129
Revolution: of 1789, 6, 37, 38, 40, 58–61,
    81, 82, 93, 94, 100–130, 134–138,
    142, 144, 146–152, 155–157, 162,
    169, 170, 171, 174, 175, 181, 182,
    189–191, 196, 197, 201, 214, 217,
    230, 240, 243, 248, 251, 253, 254,
    287, 334–336, 354, 362, 383, 392,
    511, 536, 580
    of July, 1830, 201, 212–222, 226, 228,
        282
    of February, 1848, 226, 227, 234, 235,
        248–255, 256, 260, 265, 287, 340
    of Vichy ("National Revolution,"
        1940–1944), 482–515
Rhineland, 127, 128, 146, 187, 199, 200,
    266, 315, 318, 319, 326, 329, 407,
    417, 435, 436, 438–440, 448, 451–
    454, 503
Right Wing, 101, 130, 161–163, 232,
    234, 261, 329, 383, 384, 393, 395–
    398, 420–421, 449, 450, 456–460,
    463, 465, 468, 478, 486, 542, 545,
    566, 580

Robespierre, Maxmilien, 37, 101, 111,
    118, 119, 135, 136, 157, 158, 168,
    204, 339, 357
Romanticism, 242–248
Rouher, Eugène, 271, 279, 281, 308,
    309, 317, 321, 322
Rousseau, Jean Jacques, 37, 39, 40, 43,
    53, 59, 62, 74, 85, 104, 105, 111,
    121, 190, 339, 620
Royalists, 197, 206, 408, 459, 460

Saint-Simon, Henri, Comte de, 267,
    269, 309, 337, 338, 340, 621
Salan, General, 543, 544, 546–549, 551,
    554
Sans-culottes, 110–120
Sartre, Jean Paul, 592, 593, 599–601,
    603, 611–616, 621
Second Estate, 6–18
Sedan, 104, 301, 341, 342
Senate, 177, 178, 188, 284–286, 305,
    329, 382, 393, 394, 419, 467, 468,
    469, 484, 485
Seven Year's War, 70, 74–77, 78, 163
Sieyes, Abbé, 42, 73, 129, 130, 170, 171,
    283
Simon, Jules, 271, 382, 388
Socialism, 335–340, 354, 391, 394, 397,
    417, 433, 434, 437–440, 442, 449,
    450, 463, 471, 512, 531, 532, 543,
    545, 550, 553, 554
Socialist Party, 354, 457, 467, 469, 501,
    529
Sorel, Julien, 125, 208, 247
Soustelle, Jacques, 538, 540, 544–546,
    548–550
Spain: 137
    Napoleonic Imperialism in, 180, 189,
        192
Stavisky Affair, 459–465
Stendhal (Henri Beyle), 19, 191, 230,
    246, 247
Symbolism, 372–379, 596

Taine, Hippolyte, 59, 362, 363, 366, 372, 410

Talleyrand, 126, 128, 142, 170, 176, 177, 196–198, 200, 325

Terror of 1793–1794, 2, 101, 135, 146, 149, 157, 160, 201, 338

Thermidor, 101, 121, 136, 157–160, 170, 173

Thiers, Adolphe, 216, 227, 228, 241, 282, 291, 316, 317, 329, 330, 337, 346, 513

Third Estate, 6, 8, 13, 14, 23–25, 87, 105, 109, 163

Toast of Algiers, 395, 398

Tocqueville, Alexis de, 7, 59, 103, 104, 105, 362, 536

Treaty of Frankfurt, 301, 416, 419

Treaty of Versailles, 416, 450

Turgot, A. R. J., 70, 86–92, 102, 106, 257

Ultras, 202, 203, 229, 259, 531

United Nations, 562, 578

Utrecht, treaties of, 74, 88

Varennes, flight to, 100, 134

Vichy Régime, 450, 465, 472, 474, 482–515, 551

Vendée insurrection, 135, 143, 146–152, 155, 156

Vergennes, Comte de, 67, 79, 81, 82

Verlaine, Paul, 362, 377

Vigny, Alfred de, 245, 247

Villèle, Comte de, 207, 237

Viviani Cabinet, 435, 437, 441

Vogué, Melchior de, 377, 393

Voltaire (François-Marie Arouet), 37, 39, 42–44, 47, 50, 53, 57, 59, 62, 64, 65, 72, 104, 105, 532, 605

Waterloo, Battle of, 169, 265, 296, 330

Weygand, General, 465, 473, 477, 496

White Terror, 135, 136, 157–160, 197, 260

Wickham, William, 156, 159

Wilson Affair, 390

World War II, 482–515, 563, 589, 603

Wyzéwa, Téodor de, 375, 377, 378

Yalta Conference, 583

Young, Arthur, 110

Zola, Emile, 363–367